T0320819

Labour in Global Value Chains in Asia

This book brings together a set of studies on labour conditions in GVCs in a variety of sectors—ranging from labour-intensive sectors like garments, fresh fruits, and tourism, to medium- and high-technology sectors like automobiles, electronics and telecom, and knowledge-intensive sectors (IT software services). The studies span a number of countries across Asia—Bangladesh, Cambodia, China, India, Indonesia, Sri Lanka and Vietnam.

While pointing out that participation in GVCs has provided many benefits to Asia—which include employment, poverty reduction and women's employment, the book notes that there is a high incidence of precarious employment in low-knowledge sectors, along with new forms of Taylorism. The book also documents the uneven distribution of benefits along the value chain, the uneven patterns of the knowledge flows associated with out-sourcing and the contested nature of the impact of lead-firm business practices on wages and employment and work conditions in supplier countries, alongside the benefits of upgrading and job enlargement that have accompanied these same processes.

In trying to identify spaces for progressive action and policies in the current GVC-linked global work environment, the book goes against the grain in searching for an alternative to laissez faire forms of globalization.

Dev Nathan is Visiting Professor at the Institute for Human Development, New Delhi, and Visiting Research Fellow at the Center on Globalization, Governance and Competitiveness at Duke University, USA. He is an economist, and his main research interests are global value chains, labour conditions, rural and indigenous peoples' development, and gender issues.

Meenu Tewari is Associate Professor of Economic and International Development at the University of North Carolina, Chapel Hill. Her research focuses on the political economy of development, industrialization, and on institutional reform in the public and urban sectors. She is particularly interested in the changing nature of work in rapidly urbanizing low-income economies, and in the challenge of skill formation and upgrading within regional and global production networks.

Sandip Sarkar is Professor at the Institute for Human Development, New Delhi. He has previous working experience with research institutes like Institute of Economic Growth and Institute for Studies in Industrial Development. His areas of research interest are industry, poverty, labour and employment, on which he has experience of more than two decades.

Development Trajectories in Global Value Chains

A feature of the current phase of globalization is the outsourcing of production tasks and services across borders, and increasing organization of production and trade through global value chains (GVCs), global commodity chains (GCCs), and global production networks (GPNs). With a large and growing literature on GVCs, GCCs, and GPNs, this series is distinguished by its focus on the implications of these new production systems for economic, social and regional development.

This series publishes a wide range of theoretical, methodological and empirical works, both research monographs and edited volumes, dealing with crucial issues of transformation in the global economy. How do GVCs change the ways in which lead and supplier firms shape regional and international economies? How do they affect local and regional development trajectories, and what implications do they have for workers and their communities? How is the organization of value chains changing and how are these emerging forms contested as more traditional structures of North-South trade are complemented and transformed by emerging South-South lead firms, investments, and trading links? How does the large-scale entry of women into value chain production impact on gender relations? What opportunities and limits do GVCs create for economic and social upgrading and innovation? In what ways are GVCs changing the nature of work and the role of labour in the global economy? And how might the increasing focus on logistics management, financialization, or social standards and compliance portend important developments in the structure of regional economies?

The series includes contributions from many disciplines and interdisciplinary fields and approaches related to GVC analysis, including GCCs and GPNs, and is particularly focused on theoretically innovative and informed works that are grounded in the empirics of development related to these approaches. Through their focus on the changing organizational forms, governance systems, and production relations, volumes in this series contribute to on-going conversations about theories of development and development policy in the contemporary era of globalization.

Series editors

Stephanie Barrientos is Professor of Global Development at the Global Development Institute, University of Manchester.

Gary Gereffi is Professor of Sociology and Director of the Center on Globalization, Governance and Competitiveness, Duke University.

Dev Nathan is Visiting Professor at the Institute for Human Development, New Delhi, and Visiting Research Fellow at the Center on Globalization, Governance and Competitiveness, Duke University.

John Pickles is Earl N. Phillips Distinguished Professor of International Studies at the University of North Carolina, Chapel Hill.

Endorsements

"...an impressive number of case studies from several Asian countries to show how their specialized location in GVCs as 'supplier countries', different distribution of surplus along those chains and varying governance types structure...wages, employment relations and working conditions...This link between an increasingly important type of participation in international trade and conditions in the labor market and thus the process of development in general throws much-needed light on a topical subject of great concern in Asia and elsewhere."

Pranab Bardhan, Professor of Economics, University of California, Berkeley

"...a conceptually coherent and empirically rich assessment of the complex and shifting position of labour in GVCs in Asia...very effectively uses different GVC governance types as an organising frame, but also gives full weight to the place-specific or 'horizontal' factors that powerfully shape the outcomes and opportunities for labour in GVCs ... an exciting contribution which deserves a wide readership across the field of GVC/global production network research and beyond."

Neil Coe, Professor of Geography, National University of Singapore

"This important book demonstrates...that GVCs are not delivering a fair share of the economic benefits to workers and that private compliance approaches have failed. It contributes to a better understanding of the underlying causes, which should help governments, companies and others interested in positively influencing working conditions in GVCs to distinguish worker-centered strategies that can lead to genuine change from mere window-dressing."

Jenny Holdcroft, Policy Director, IndustriALL Global Union

"...a major contribution to knowledge of how GVCs work, the wage and skill patterns that they create, the conditions under which gains for labour can be maximized and the ways in which the actors concerned are responding. It is required reading for anyone who wants to get behind the rhetoric of the global economy to understand the realities on the ground."

Gerry Rodgers, Former Director,
International Institute of Labour Studies, Geneva

Labour in Global Value Chains in Asia

Edited by

Dev Nathan

Meenu Tewari

Sandip Sarkar

INSTITUTE FOR
HUMAN DEVELOPMENT

CAMBRIDGE
UNIVERSITY PRESS

CAMBRIDGE
UNIVERSITY PRESS

University Printing House, Cambridge CB2 8BS, United Kingdom
One Liberty Plaza, 20th Floor, New York, NY 10006, USA
477 Williamstown Road, Port Melbourne, vic 3207, Australia
4843/24, 2nd Floor, Ansari Road, Daryaganj, Delhi – 110002, India
79 Anson Road, #06–04/06, Singapore 079906

Cambridge University Press is part of the University of Cambridge.

It furthers the University's mission by disseminating knowledge in the pursuit of
education, learning and research at the highest international levels of excellence.

www.cambridge.org
Information on this title: www.cambridge.org/9781107103740

© Institute for Human Development 2016

First published 2016

Printed in India by Shree Maitrey Printech Pvt. Ltd., Noida

A catalogue record for this publication is available from the British Library

Library of Congress Cataloguing in Publication Data
Names: Nathan, Dev, editor. | Tewari, Meenu, editor. | Sarkar, Sandip, 1961-
    editor.
Title: Labour in global value chains in Asia / edited by Dev Nathan, Meenu
    Tewari, Sandip Sarkar.
Description: Cambridge, UK; New York: Cambridge University Press, 2016. |
    Includes bibliographical references and index.
Identifiers: LCCN 2016002557 | ISBN 9781107103740 (hardback)
Subjects: LCSH: Labor market--Asia. | Labor--Asia. | Industries--Asia. |
    Economic development--Asia. | Asia--Commerce.
Classification: LCC HD5811.85.A6.L324 2016 | DDC 331.1095--dc23 LC record available at
http://lccn.loc.gov/2016002557

ISBN 978-1-107-10374-0 Hardback

Contents

Modular Governance

Relational Governance

Conclusions

Figures

Tables

Tables

Foreword

Global Value Chains (GVCs) have emerged as an extremely important form of organization of production and value creation, thanks to technological change and the process of globalization. India is rather a late comer in this system, and even now it comparatively accounts for a smaller proportion of value creation under GVCs as compared to most of middle and high income countries.

The Institute for Human Development (IHD) has been one of the few institutions in India which pioneered in creating interest in this increasingly important issue. IHD with support from ILO and Indian Council of Social Science Research (ICSSR) had organized an international conference way back in 1998 on this subject in Bangalore, selected papers of which were brought out as an edited volume. The present volume, largely an outcome of the Capturing the Gains (CtG) research programme, supported by DFID and implemented by the University of Manchester, has been coordinated by the IHD where many of the Asian case studies included in this book were conducted.

The papers in this volume bring together studies of labour and working conditions in many GVCs across Asia. Participation in GVCs has provided many benefits to Asia—increased employment in increasing return activities, such as manufacturing and services; reduction in poverty; and the enhanced participation of women in these modern sectors. This book, however, also points to the continued weaknesses and negativities in these developments such as the continuation of sweatshop conditions, even child labour, in many parts of GVC manufacture; the appearance of new forms of Taylorism in Call Centres; and so on.

There are other books and papers too dealing with issues of workers in global production networks. This book is different in its approach, it has tried to identify the positive factors that can work to improve the conditions of labour. It emphasizes the role of workers' organizations in the new areas of worker concentration. It stresses women's entry into the modern sectors of the economy as a factor that enables them to challenge and change existing restrictive gender norms. With an increasing sphere of GVCs creating new forms of institutions, including labour market institutions is very important. This book fills an important gap on the subject, although more such analyses will be needed in future, which it will facilitate.

Alakh N. Sharma
Professor and Director
Institute for Human Development
New Delhi

Preface

The editors and many of the authors have spent much of the last decade researching various dimensions of Global Value Chains (GVCs). This is also the decade in which GVCs have grown in importance as the manner in which global production and trade is organized today. There are many aspects of the rise of GVCs and its implications for labour that demand closer analysis and examination as we move from trade in goods to trade in tasks. This book concentrates on the two-way interaction of GVCs with labour in supplier firms in late industrializing economies. This dialectic between employers, suppliers and labour within GVCs plays out in terms of both the volume and quality of employment that GVCs generate in supplier economies; and the recursive impacts of labour on the re-formation of GVCs. Both of these relations of labour within GVCs are relatively under-researched and under-theorized. An attempt to fill these gaps at the empirical and theoretical levels provides the *raison d'etre* of this book.

The splintering of production implies a deeper and finer division of labour in the organization of work. As the foundations of production and technology shift in the new 'knowledge economy', researchers have begun to read this new division of labour as a division of tasks and indeed, a division of knowledge. Splintered tasks, and the differentiated knowledge and skills associated with them, have also to be coordinated or governed. This book is organized on the basis of the manner in which tasks are divided and governed. The case studies in the book shed light on the knowledge intensity and complexity of these tasks and of the often contested organizational arrangements that govern them. The organizational arrangements that the book focuses on lie at the intersection of global value chains and the vast array of institutions that lead firms and their suppliers interact with in places where they originate, and where they touch down. These institutions range from market mediated ties, to links with state and civic actors as well as workers' own agency. At their most basic these varied relationships and governance systems result in what the literature calls captive, modular or relational governance structures. Each assigns differing distributions of knowledge and degrees of power to the actors involved— lead firms, suppliers, states, and workers, and lead to varied distributions of the capture of value in the GVCs.

These vertical relations of power, governance, and distribution of value, however, intersect with deeply varied contexts – or place-based conditions in which particular supplier firms and workers enter into particular GVCs. These lateral or horizontal relations influence the nature of productive relations in particular places, and mediate variable conditions of labour supply and demand, gender relations, technology absorption and working conditions in particular places. These place-based or horizontal forces and processes, over which local actors have some control, intersect with vertical relations to provide different outcomes for work and labour even in the same industry.

These variations in labour market outcomes transcend wages and employment within GVCs. With technical change, and labour supply shifts, such as the addition of tens of millions of women involved in GVC production in late developing economies, new practices of earning independent incomes and traversing public spaces including those outside the workplace, have challenged standard narratives of how GVCs impact work and workers in supplier countries. In dealing with the development impacts of GVCs and the employment and conditions of work they help create, the case studies in this book therefore go beyond the narrow confines of employment relations to examine the spatial and social conditions associated with the political economy of work.

The chapters in this book consistently elaborate both the opportunities and the challenges provided by GVC-based production in Asian economies. The outcomes are conflictual, contradictory and Janus-faced: There are sweatshops as well as successful struggles to end sweatshops. There are better quality employment systems alongside dead-end, deskilled work even in high tech sectors. There is value capture by some lead firms, as well as instances of those at the bottom of the chain carving out niches from where they fight back.

Rather than seeing the spread of globalized production as the elimination of worker agency, this book shows the possibilities for, and importance of, workers themselves in the transformation of GVCs as we know them. There are also growing possibilities for a Polanyian double transformation of the conditions of globalized production, one that would improve the manner in which labour is incorporated in globalized production.

Volume Editors

Acknowledgements

This book draws together many of the studies conducted under the Capturing the Gains (CtG) research initiative supported by DFID and coordinated by the Brooks World Poverty Institute of the University of Manchester and the Center for Globalization, Governance and Competitiveness (CGGC) of Duke University. Our thanks to Stephanie Barrientos and Gary Gereffi for their leadership in shaping this research programme.

We thank the other members of the CtG Research Coordination Committee, Shane Godfrey, Frederick Mayer, William Milberg, John Pickles, Ann Posthuma, Joonkoo Lee and Michelle Christian, who also contributed to shaping the wider research of which the case studies reported in this book are a part. We are grateful to numerous colleagues who contributed valuable comments, provided important feedback and offered discussion at various stages of the research and writing that strengthened our work. We particularly thank Jennifer Bair, Stephanie Barrientos, Gary Gereffi, Raphael Kaplinsky, Douglas Miller, Nicola Phillips, John Pickles, and Cornelia Staritz for their excellent comments on written drafts of these chapters and at conferences where versions of them were presented. We thank the three anonymous reviewers of Cambridge University Press who offered very helpful advice and critical comments that have strengthened the book and many of the individual chapters in it.

Many of the papers were presented at workshops on GVCs organized by the University of Manchester, the Institute for Human Development (IHD), New Delhi, the Indira Gandhi Institute for Development Research (IGIDR), Mumbai, the Centre for Policy Dialogue (CPD), Dhaka, and CARE, Dhaka. We thank the organizing institutions for their support and workshop participants for their feedback. We also thank several students of the University of North Carolina at Chapel Hill's Department of City and Regional Planning for excellent research assistance to the editors, and the Indian Council for Research on International Economic Relations (ICRIER) for hosting Meenu Tewari for part of the research process.

Our thanks also go out to the International Labour Organization (ILO) for funding support for some of the research on which a subset of the chapters are based.

IHD was the host organization for conducting and coordinating many of the case studies reported here and for the production of the book. We thank Alakh Sharma for his support for the project. We also thank Lindsey Block, then of DFID in India, who was instrumental in getting additional support from DFID India for the workshops at IHD and the production of the book.

We are especially grateful to Priyanka Tyagi, Communications Officer of IHD, for overseeing the production process and ensuring that the work was in order and kept moving along. Ashwitha Jaykumar did a great job in editing many of the chapters through several drafts.

At Cambridge University Press, we thank former and present staff at Delhi, Dhiraj Pandey, Qudsiya Ahmed, Debjani Mazumder, along with Sohini Ghosh and Suvadip Bhattacharjee, and Chris Harrison in Cambridge for their wonderful support, encouragement and partnership throughout the editorial process and for putting up with all the delays that inevitably came up along the way. We are especially grateful to Chris Harrison who saw the wider potential in this work and turned what was initially a single book into a series.

Our special thanks to all our colleagues and co-workers who at our various stages of the process helped with their support, encouragement, comments, feedback, and advice that collectively improved our work and kept our spirits up.

Dev would like to thank Govind and Pallavi for not only putting up with all the pressures and tensions of coming out with this book but also often being the first on whom he tried out various ideas. Meenu Tewari is grateful to Roberto Quercia, then Chair of the Department of City and Regional Planning at UNC Chapel Hill, for his support throughout the project.

Volume Editors

Introduction

1

Introduction[1]

Dev Nathan, Meenu Tewari and Sandip Sarkar

Since the 1970s and 1980s, Asia, and especially China, has become the factory of the world. To a lesser extent, India has become the back office of the world. These momentous shifts in the location of global economic activity have fuelled economic growth in the emerging economies of Asia: between 1995 and 2009 income from global value chains (GVCs)-related trade increased 6-fold for China and 5-fold for India (OECD, WTO, UNCTAD, 2011). The GVC trade accounts for about 30 per cent of GDP of developing countries (UNCTAD, 2011). Many of the new employees in GVCs, whether engaged in electronics, garments or IT services, include large numbers of women, which evokes notions of transformation in Asian labour markets. Poverty in developing Asia has also decreased: it is in single digit figures in East and Southeast Asia, though most of South Asia still lags behind, with poverty levels at three times or more than those found in East and Southeast Asia (World Bank, 2014).

In the midst of this unparalleled growth and transformation, there are all-too-frequent stories of disasters—whether of suicides by workers in China in electronic assembly factories or of fires and factory collapses in Bangladesh—that kill hundreds of workers. In the midst of unprecedented advances, there are also serious problems and the benefits of GVC-led growth are deeply uneven. It is thus necessary to ask how and to what extent labour has benefited from the advances of firms and economies in both manufacturing and service production in the developing countries of Asia. Who benefits and why, who does not and why not? What are the reasons that limit these benefits? And, going forward, how can labour in Asia benefit more substantially from economic growth in the region?

These are some of the questions that motivate this book. The book is itself a product of a larger research collaboration on the study of economic and social

---

[1] We thank Jennifer Bair, Stephanie Barrientos, Raphie Kaplinsky, Govind Kelkar and John Pickles for helpful comments at various stages of writing this Introduction.

upgrading in GVCs as part of the Capturing the Gains (CtG)[2] initiative. The CtG project brought together a large network of scholars who carried out research on these themes in a number of countries and sectors. In this book, however, we also include some studies that were not part of the CtG Project but became part of the larger collaboration it fostered.

The book brings together studies on labour in GVCs across several Asian countries: Bangladesh, Cambodia, China, India, Indonesia, and Sri Lanka. The studies cover a number of sectors spanning the agrarian economy (agro-foods), manufacturing (garments, electronics, automobiles), and services (information technology [IT], software services, and tourism). Given the wide country and sectoral coverage of the case studies reported in the book, this volume may be considered reasonably representative of labour trends in developing Asia as a whole, in the context of the growing incorporation of Asian economies as supplier nations in GVCs across a range of sectors.

In the rest of this introductory chapter, we set forth the conceptual framing of the relationship between lead firms, supplier firms and labour in GVCs,[3] and the geographies in which these relationships are embedded as the analytical context for the case studies that follow. This conceptual framing discusses both the distributional issues and business practices that shape GVCs and their governance structures. We then examine how these governance structures in turn interact with a variety of sector- and country-specific institutional factors that influence employment conditions within GVCs, particularly in Asia. Specifically, we focus on the interaction between profits, rents, and conditions of value capture as forces that shape 'vertical' relationships between lead firms and supplier firms within GVCs. Similarly, the interaction between wages, knowledge, skills, and 'governance' rules (control and flexibility) shape the horizontal relationships between supplier firms and labour. Together, they produce the wide variation in employment conditions and bargaining power that we see in various places and cases on the ground.

---

[2] The CtG research program was led by Stephanie Barrientos of Manchester University and Gary Gereffi of Duke University.

[3] There is a considerable literature using the term global production networks (GPNs)—see for example, Dicken (2007) and Coe et al. (2008). We do not go into the debate about which metaphor, chain or network, more correctly represents the nature of splintered production, but use both terms GVC and GPN interchangeably. Some of the authors in this book use the term GVC while others use GPN.

1.1 Buyer and supplier relations: Locating labour within GVCs

We begin with the evolving relationships between buyers and sellers in various institutional contexts, including GVCs. At the economic level, one can distinguish three types of stylized relations between buyers and sellers.

The first is that of *arms-length purchase*, i.e., the kind of transaction that characterizes the vast majority of commodity trades. Sellers and buyers get together, bids are made, and money and goods are exchanged. In these atomistic, purely market-based transactions, there need not be any relationship between the buyer and seller either before or after the sale. Through history, much of international trade has been of the arms-length variety. It is also a trade of product for product, cloth for wine in Ricardo's famous example of comparative advantage in trade between England and Portugal.

The second type of trading relationship is that of the *hierarchical intra-firm* exchange. The advent of transnational corporations (TNCs) led to trade between various units of the same TNC that were set up in different countries. This exchange is not free trade on the market, but a hierarchically decided trade, where price (transfer price) is often determined by the firm itself. TNCs could, for instance, under-price inputs supplied from one country in order to increase margins earned in another country. Such pricing decisions could be dictated by differential tax regimes or TNC strategies. Intra-firm trade within units of the same TNC reflects the disintegration of production across national boundaries, e.g., crude oil may be produced in one country and refined in another. But such intra-firm international transactions do not necessarily represent a disintegration of ownership. While they are not of the classic market variety, they are carried out at the behest of the conglomerate or TNC.

The third type of trading relationship that has evolved in the past 40 years, and the one that we are concerned with in this book is that of contracted sales within a GVC. Unlike the standard TNC, in a GVC, production is vertically disintegrated both geographically and in terms of ownership. The different production units that make up a product's value chain are independent firms, but with highly uneven power relations. 'Supplier firms' lower down the chain and located mostly in low-cost developing countries do not sell their product on the market; rather they undertake contracted production for the 'lead firm,' which is most often located in high wage industrial markets.

In a GVC, the different component and assembly firms are independent firms that are linked by their role as contracted producers who are managed or governed by the lead firm. The lead firm or buyer manages the supply chain, integrates the production segments, and takes the resulting product to the market.

The disintegration of production segments across firms and even across countries is an extension of the notion of the division of labour which Adam Smith identified within an individual factory, extended across the world. Various tasks are carried out in different GVC segments, e.g., design in one firm, detailed engineering design in another, the manufacture of components in other firms, assembly or final production in another firm, with the highest value tasks such as design, branding and marketing controlled by the lead firm. Different production tasks are thus carried out in different firms located in many different countries, and which together form a GVC.

This splitting up or splintering of manufacture from design, branding and marketing, or even of one part of manufacture (e.g., assembly) from other parts (e.g., component manufacture) is what was characterized (Dicken, 2007) as the specific feature of *globalization* of production, as against the pre-GVC spread of production, which he termed *internationalization*. The WTO video on the manufacture of the Nokia smartphone calls this process that of being 'Made in the World'.[4]

Where these tasks are carried out, and by what kinds of firms has implications for the kinds of employment relations and capabilities that are fostered in those locations (Grossman and Rossi-Hansberg, 2006). At the level of international trade, what this means is that trade ceases to be trade in products, e.g., cloth for wine, but instead becomes trade in tasks, e.g., cut-make-trim (CMT) for design and marketing. Given that tasks are not whole products in themselves, and have value only when integrated into the production of a final good or service, how these differentially valued tasks are split within a GVC and dispersed across countries has a bearing on how these firms and the countries they are located in are positioned to find ways to move up the value chain—or not.

In this volume, we are concerned with the implications for labour, working conditions and economic development in 'supplier countries'–places where most GVC-linked firms are suppliers, or non-lead firms. A fair majority of GVC-linked Asian firms, whether in the manufacturing or service industries, generally do not produce and market whole products in the global marketplace. These firms are part of global production networks (GPNs) or GVCs and carry out various tasks for lead firms at the head of these networks as contracted producers. The lead could be major brands, such as Nike or Levi Strauss, big-box retailers, such as Wal-Mart or Tesco, automobile assemblers, such as Toyota or Suzuki (Maruti), or consumer electronics producers, such as Apple and Samsung. The lead firms could also be one that contracts out IT services, or firms that provide tourism services through tour agencies. What is significant is that most of the Asian firms we focus on do not produce and sell directly on the market, but rather do so indirectly as contracted producers.

---

[4] See the WTO video 'Made in the World' on YouTube.

What are the implications of this GVC structure for labour, employment relations and working conditions in developing countries, such as those in Asia where most supplier firms are concentrated? To unpack this question we explore more deeply the nature of outsourcing relationships and their implications for labour.

1.2 Vertical and horizontal relations

Two issues about the organization of the buyer–supplier relationship within GVCs are likely to have an important bearing on the structure of labour relations within the chain: (i) the distribution of the surplus along the chain and (ii) the business practices of lead firms. The distribution of the surplus is significant because it ultimately makes possible or inhibits certain wage policies and benefits reforms. For instance, if a firm that is part of a GVC earns only a competitive profit, it is unlikely to be able to pay more than a competitive or market wage to its workers; on the other hand, a firm that earns some rent (net revenue above competitive profit) could potentially share a portion of that rent with its workers. Similarly, a lead firm whose business strategy is based on 'fast fashion' will have very tight delivery schedules with closely peaked orders, which could push manufacturing firms to manage periods of increased demand not with additional fixed investment, but with mandatory overtime and additional temporary labour.

Thus, both surplus distribution and the business practices of lead firms can affect the labour employment relations of developing country suppliers (Locke, 2013; Anner et al., 2013). Together, these two factors constitute what are called the vertical relations in a GVC.[5] In the next section, we develop these ideas in greater depth.

1.2.1 Profits and rents or vertical relations

In order to make the analysis simpler, we will assume a stylized GVC model with two segments, one focused on high value activities such as design, branding and marketing, and the other focused on production and manufacturing. The lead firm, the buyer, carries out the design-branding-marketing tasks, while the developing country supplier firm is the manufacturer. Surplus is produced in the GVC, but how is it distributed between the two segments? The distribution of GVC surplus is the result of outcomes in the firms' respective product markets, i.e., the final product market of the lead firm and the task or GVC segment market of the supplier firm.

The final product is owned and marketed by the lead firm. Therefore, any excess profits or rents that are gained through the sale of the product will accrue to the

---

[5] The terms vertical and horizontal relations in GVCs were used in Neilson and Pritchard (2009).

lead firm. The net gain from trade for the lead firm is the reduction in costs due to outsourcing or contracting out manufacturing tasks to lower cost producers. What the supplier firm receives will depend on the contractual relations and agreements between it and the lead buyer, instead of market relations such as of the consumer-facing lead firm. In an approximate manner, we can assume the cost reduction referred to above as the wage difference between the two countries—the country in which the buyer is based and the supplier country. Questions therefore arise about how the gains due to cost differential are negotiated over and shared between the developed country lead firm and the developing country supplier firms? What factors shape the bargaining power of the supplier?

One factor that can shape a supplier's bargaining power is the complexity of the capability required to perform the outsourced task. The more complex the capability required, the more likely it is that the firm embodying this capability will be able to negotiate a higher share of the gain from trade. But if the capability required is routine and very widely available, then the supplying firm is likely to get less, or even none, of the gain. A very widely available capability or a task, whose performance has low entry barriers, is not likely to get more than the prevailing market price for that service. For instance, there are many countries that can carry out cut-make-trim (CMT) or basic assembly operations in garment manufacture, and so garment manufacturing firms are not likely to get more than the prevailing market price for CMT tasks. However, when there are relatively few firms with the capability to produce IT software, for example, and the high cost of fostering this capability results in high entry barriers, then IT software-producing firms are likely to get a higher price for performing outsourced tasks. Thus, garment and IT processing firms in the same supplier country can exhibit differential bargaining power with respect to their contracts with lead buyers.

The availability of alternative suppliers, itself related to the ease or difficulty of entry, is thus a key factor in bargaining power within a GVC: '... if a firm's bargaining power is an inverse function of the availability of alternatives, then transport equipment producers [who are less numerous] should have more power than garment producers [who are more numerous], and vice versa for buyers', (Mahutga, 2014, p. 163).

It is not only the number of possible substitute producers that counts, however. It is also the number of possible buyers that matter. For example, if there is only one buyer for a particular task, i.e., a monopsony situation, then the seller would be in a weak bargaining position irrespective of complexity of capability. There could also be an oligopsony situation, i.e., only a few possible buyers, such as in the case of a maker of sports shoes, which could curtain suppliers' bargaining power. But, if there are many possible buyers, then the supplier could end up strengthening its bargaining position. In a contractual relationship, it is therefore the relative numbers of buyers and sellers in a segment market that shape relative bargaining power.[6]

Thus, the factors that influence GVC bargaining power are (1) the difficulty or ease of producing or acquiring the capability required; (2) the number of possible producers of the task; and (3) the number of alternate buyers for the task. Combining the possibility of monopoly and oligopoly positions as buyers and sellers, we distinguish four different combinations of market positions: (1) many lead firms (buyers) and many sellers; (2) few buyers and many sellers; (3) many buyers and few sellers; and (4) few buyers and few sellers.

In the case (1) where there are many lead firms and many suppliers, the suppliers are not likely to get any excess profits or rent from the cost savings from outsourcing. For the buyers, who then have to sell the product to consumers, competition among lead firms is likely to reduce final product prices to their competitive minimum. In this case, there is no rent within the GVC, since cost savings are all transferred or dissipated as consumer surplus. Such a case does actually exist; it is not just a logical possibility. In the Chinese tourism value chain, discussed in this book (Chapter 6 by Yang Fuquan, Yu Yin and Dev Nathan) where there are both large numbers of tour agencies (lead firms) and tourism destination service providers, intense competition for customers has led to the 'zero-fee' tour, where all surplus is dissipated as consumer surplus.

In the case (2), where there are a few lead firms (buyers) and many suppliers, we have monopsony or oligopsony outcomes. The many suppliers will compete among themselves and bring margins down to the competitive minimum of normal profits. All the cost savings accrue as rent to the lead firms. This is the textbook example of a garment GVC, with the brands or retailers taking all the rents, while the CMT producers in, say, Bangladesh or Cambodia, getting only normal profits.

In the case (3), where there are many buyers and few suppliers, the suppliers are likely to be in a stronger bargaining position. The few sellers would be able to capture some, or most, of the benefit of lower costs. But if the number of providers of this service were to increase, then the suppliers' margins would decline. This is seen in the case of software service providers, where Indian IT firms initially had strong bargaining positions. These bargaining positions have become weaker as more firms, including those from developed and other developing countries, have entered the market, with a resultant erosion of margins.

In the case (4), where there are few buyers and few suppliers, both sides could be quite evenly poised in their negotiating positions and bargaining power. The rents would likely then be shared. The supply of IT services to telecom companies is one

---

[6] We thank Jennifer Bair for this formulation.

example of this case, with rents being shared between the telecom companies and the IT service providers. Again, competition among telecom companies could result in rents being passed on as consumer surplus through lower prices.

The discussion of the distribution of the surplus produced in the chain as rents (excess profits) of buyers and competitive profits of suppliers in a GVC and their relative bargaining power has direct relevance for how wage and benefits regimes are shaped among suppliers. We develop this idea more fully next.

1.2.2 Wages or horizontal relations

The distribution of surplus is a key aspect of vertical relations between lead firms and supplier firms in GVCs. (The other aspects of vertical relations are business practices and governance relations which we discuss in subsequent sections). These vertical relations have a key bearing on the horizontal relations between supplier firms and labour in developing (or supplier) countries. In our view, the wage and working condition outcomes constitute horizontal relations in a GVC. They embody the capital–labour relationship that prevails at each node of a GVC. These horizontal relations are not independent of the outcomes of vertical relations in a GVC.

For example, the distribution of surpluses, in the form of competitive profits or rents, does not determine, but does influence wages. Historically, Kalecki (1971) and others have argued that the rent earned by a firm is likely to shape the wage relationship within the firm. Whether the worker is a cleaner, works in marketing or in the design segment, the rent a firm earns is likely to have a skill-differentiated impact on wages down the line. In his theory of wage determination, Kalecki hypothesizes that wages depend on the degree of monopoly or the rent earned by the firm: 'High mark-ups in existence will encourage strong trade unions to bargain for higher wages since they know that firms can "afford" to pay them' (Kalecki, 1971, p. 161).

A number of studies support the Kalecki proposition that workers' wages are positively connected to rents earned by the firms. Mishel (1986) showed that wages in the US are influenced significantly by an employer's 'ability to pay' (Mishel, 1986, p. 91). Unions, he argued, were able to bargain for higher wages in industries that were concentrated and had entry barriers. In a study of Belgian firms, Dobbelaere (2005) argued that workers' bargaining power and firms' mark-ups are positively associated. A recent study of Indian wages (Pal and Rathore, 2014) argued that both workers' power and firms' mark-ups had declined since liberalization. Therefore, while the presence of unions and labour advocacy institutions is an important source of realizing the link between rents and wages, and unions, at least initially, were in decline after liberalization across Asia, there is empirical support for the link between high mark-ups and higher wage outcomes.

The connection between the firm's power to earn a high mark-up and demands for higher wages is fairly straightforward. Firms that can procure mark-ups can potentially cover an increase in costs due to higher wages. With mark-up power, they operate in a cost-plus product market. In such a situation, union demands for higher wages are likely to be conceded, since the increase in costs can be passed on to buyers. However, where, firms have to take prices as given, as in a competitive market, covering increases in costs with a price mark-up is less likely. Where industry-level bargaining does not take place, firms in a competitive market would resist increases in wages. Thus, the degree of competition in the GVC suppliers' market would affect wages in supplier firms within a GVC chain.

There are other factors besides the strength of trade unions that influence wage levels. But the product market outcomes, or vertical GVC relations, set limits to the margins within which local capital–labour relations and other social factors can influence wage outcomes. This is a key point in the analysis in this volume and we will return to it later, particularly in the concluding chapter.

We now turn to the connection between product markets and factor markets and wage outcomes.

1.3 Linking vertical and horizontal relations

The connection between surplus and wages (or, between product and labour markets) can be represented by a 2×2 matrix (Table 1.1). Product market outcomes can result in competitive profits [P1] or rents (excess profits) [P2]; and labour market outcomes can include competitive wages [W1] or wages that include a

Table 1.1 GVCs and the distribution of profits and wages

		Profits (Product market)	
		P1	**P2**
Wages (Labour Market)	W1	A	B
		P1, W1	P2, W1
		Low profits, low wages	*High Profits/Rents, low wages*
	W2	C	D
		P1, W2	P2, W2
		Low profits, high wages	*High Profits/Rents, high wages*

share of rents [W2]. In what follows we use the two terms rents and high profits interchangeably. The important distinction is between rents as high profits of lead firms and competitive profits of suppliers.

There are four quadrants in the matrix above. The first quadrant, A is characterized by competitive (low) profits and market-rate (low) wages. This could be the situation faced by CMT apparel manufacturers, where there are many competing suppliers, even excess capacity (Milberg and Winkler, 2013), resulting in low or competitive profits. Wages are also low at the prevailing competitive level and may even be below legal minimum wage with a fair degree of outsourcing to informal segments of the value chain.

In quadrant B, the firm(s) can earn some rent or high profits, P2, but wages are competitive, W1. This, one could say, is a situation in which low wages in the face of high rents could trigger the possibility of a strong workers' struggle developing and even being successful in securing a share of rents in the form of a higher wage. This is the type of situation predicted by Kalecki's analysis above. A workers' movement, or even government intervention for that matter, would then shift the firm(s) into quadrant D, where there is some rent for the firm, P2, and some part of this rent is shared with labour, leading to higher than competitive wages, or W2.

Quadrants A and D could together form a GVC. The lead firm would be in D, earning rents and sharing some of that with its workers. The supplier would be in A, with both the firm and its workers earning just competitive profits and wages, respectively.

Finally, we come to quadrant C, where firms earn competitive profits, P1, but wages, W2, are above-market wages. This could be either because legacy wages are high, W2, or the capabilities demanded are complex. With the increasing entry of suppliers into this segment, margins could come down from P2 to P1. It could also be a public sector unit, functioning in a loss-making situation, but able to continue in business by accessing the public exchequer through what Janos Kornai (1986) called the 'soft budget constraint'.

The situations represented in all four quadrants are unstable, in that the firms and workers in these situations all have their own agendas and strategies. Firms have upgrading strategies, such that they might try to move from earning just competitive profits, P1, to earning some rents, P2. Garment manufacturers might try to move from being CMT operators to becoming full-package or FOB suppliers. This, as is argued in Chapter 3 on Bangladesh, is what garment manufacturers in that country did in order to increase their margins. This kind of economic upgrading by garment manufacturers was not in any immediate or automatic sense followed by higher wages, but a series of strikes by Bangladeshi garment workers, along with safety scandals involving factory collapses and fires forced improvements in wage and working conditions over time.

The key point of the above analysis is that the market structure of oligopsonistic lead firms as buyers and competition among manufacturers as suppliers results in rents being captured by the lead firms. With suppliers earning only competitive profits, there is little scope for an improvement in wages in the absence of redistribution of rents within the GVC. As Kaplinsky puts it, suppliers are caught between a rock and a hard place, with no room to manoeuvre (Kaplinsky, 2005). The need for the redistribution of surpluses between buyer and supplier as a way to improve working conditions and labour market outcomes in a sustained way is also argued by others (Nathan and Sarkar, 2011; Locke, 2013; Milberg and Winkler, 2013; Anner et al., 2013).

A good example of the manner in which rents are concentrated in the lead firm is that of Apple. Apple designs, brands and markets the iPhone and other iGadgets, but Apple had only 60,000 employees in the US in 2012, while its contract manufacturers in China and other countries employed around 1.2 million workers (who also worked to assemble or manufacture other electronic devices). Apple's oligopolistic position in the market for consumer electronics, combined with its oligopsonistic position as a buyer of manufacturing services, resulted in a combination of annual profits of $400,000 per employee, while many workers in the Foxconn assembly plant in China earned less than $400 per month (Milberg and Winkler, 2013, based on Duhigg and Bradsher, 2012) because there was no distribution of rents earned by Apple down the value chain.

This oligopoly in the product market, combined with oligopsony in the contract manufacturing market, and a surplus labour situation, itself an outcome of competitive, low-wage labour in labour-abundant developing economies, results in a concentration of rents in GVC such as those of Apple, with the USA-end of the value chain retaining the largest share. Is this concentration of rent due to control over high value activities such as design, branding and marketing activities by Apple, USA? Neo-classical theory attributes shares of value or distribution of income to the marginal productivity of each input. But classical theory would argue that in a product with more than one input, it is really not possible to attribute any share of value created to just one input; the product is jointly produced by many inputs. What branding and other forms of intellectual property rights and other institutional protections do is enable the rent of the product to be captured in the GVC segment that includes the design, branding and marketing functions.

Thus, we see that although value is jointly produced all along a value chain, the rent is captured by certain segments, because of their capability and positional power (Mahutga, 2014) in the GVC. Prices are paid for manufacturing services depending on the bargaining strengths of the contract manufacturers. With many organizations that can carry out contract manufacturing and many possible locations for these tasks, contract manufacturers are unlikely to get much more than competitive profit. Even Foxconn, the world's largest contract electronics manufacturer, gets margins of just 3–5 per cent (Chapter 15).

The capture of rent by lead firms is one aspect of vertical relations in a GVC that has an impact on labour conditions at the competitive manufacturing end, where only competitive profits are received. This is a tendency that could be modified by various factors, such as moving up the value chain to take on more complex tasks, or instituting other more transparent measures of accountability between buyer and supplier.

Besides restricting profits at the lower end of the value chain, there are two other aspects of vertical relations that impact labour systems: business practices and governance systems within GVCs. With regard to the business practices that lead firms follow and diffuse down the chain to suppliers, quick lead times, fast fashion and the volatility of orders are widely discussed in the GVC literature in relation to current production systems. Similarly, the manner in which outsourcing is carried out, variations in the kind of knowledge and skill levels required for the tasks, or in other words, the manner in which GVC contracting relations are governed is another important aspect of GVC relations that shape wage and employment relations down the chain.

In the next two sections, we discuss how the various business practices that are part of vertical GVC relations influence labour relations and then sum up governance systems that affect employment practices in supplier firms.

1.4   Order systems and flexibility

The way in which lead firms place orders to their suppliers is an important part of GVC relations. These order systems specify delivery schedules. With the rapid obsolescence in electronics products and the rise of quick turn-around 'fast fashion' in garments and other consumer products, the volatility of orders has increased. Lead times are shorter in order to meet changing market demands and quality requirements have been ratcheted up. These shifting order systems and business practices have a direct impact on labour and employment relations within GVCs. We therefore explore in this section how flexibility in production is linked to and produces flexibility in employment relations.

A feature of the consumer electronics industry is the rapid obsolescence of products, which leads to shorter and shorter product life cycles. This clock speed increases dramatically as we move from '... the technology source to the consumer application' (Fine, 1998, p. 97). While chip-making factories tend towards obsolescence over a decade or so, downstream mobile phones, computers and other consumer products become obsolescent much faster, with production cycles often lasting less than a year.

Short product life cycles lead to rapid price erosion as retailers are forced to sell off older stock at massive discounts. Rapid price erosion makes buyers reluctant to stock inventory finished goods at their own cost (Minnich and Maier, 2007). This changes the meaning of 'just-in-time' production—it is not just that parts arrive in time for assembly into the final product, but that the assembly of the final product is itself postponed till point-of-sale information arrives. A study of electronics manufacturing in Europe shows that there could be a variation of 89 per cent or more in weekly orders placed by the buyer (Kapia et al., 2006). HP inkjet printer assembly varied by 250 per cent between low and high production periods, while mobile phone production in 2006 spiked over an 8-week period, rather than the previous 8-month period.

In other words, supply risk of obsolescence is passed on to the supplier/ manufacturer and, as a consequence, suppliers are reluctant to hire a full staff of permanent workers, resorting instead to using contract labour whom they can easily hire and fire as the volume of orders increases or decreases. The growing precariousness of work, the rise of temporary, part time and contract labour is deeply correlated to the search for flexibility by buyers and suppliers as a way to hedge risk in rapidly shifting and volatile markets. Several of our chapters in the volume explore ways in which this plays out in different sectors as well as innovations—both institutional and organizational—to prevent the risk of volatility from being passed on to vulnerable workers (Chapters 7, 11–13).

We now turn to the role of knowledge or skill requirements in influencing employment relations within GVCs.

1.5 Knowledge and skill requirements of outsourced tasks

One of the key points of GVC analysis is to look not just at products or services, but at the inter-firm and international distribution of tasks involved in production. The production of low-tech and broadly labour-intensive products, like garments, could involve some tasks that are either knowledge-intensive and creative (design) or even high-tech (requiring the use of CAD, i.e., computer-aided design or virtual trials). Similarly, the production of overall high-tech or knowledge-intensive products, like IT services, could include tasks that are relatively low-skill tasks, such as programme testing, or cleaning and security.

Tasks have characteristics that would affect the employment relations of workers performing these tasks. Some tasks, such as assembly of electronic products or garments, require skills that are relatively easy to acquire. This would mean that the entry barriers to become a performer of these tasks are relatively low. Other tasks, such as the designing of garments, require higher levels of knowledge and skill on the part of those who perform them. Entering such segments would be more difficult and thus, those performing these tasks are likely to command higher incomes. The complexity of knowledge required to perform tasks is a factor that influences employment conditions.

The knowledge needed to perform a task can be of two types: formal, explicit or generic knowledge that can be codified, or tacit, often firm-specific knowledge, or situated knowledge that is not codified. Formal, generic knowledge is easily acquired, while tacit knowledge is less readily diffused. Whether the knowledge in question is more or less codified becomes a way to represent the manner in which this aspect of knowledge affects the organization of work. Codified knowledge is easily acquired and transmitted and hierarchically controlled; while tacit knowledge is harder to acquire and requires more interaction in its use and diffusion.

As already noted, a GVC entails the breaking up of production into tasks, where the tasks are carried out by separate firms that also cross national boundaries. Broadly speaking, tasks are split up within a GVC, and their location is decided across countries depending on supplier capabilities available in each country and the costs of those capabilities. More knowledge-intensive tasks or those requiring less routine skills may be concentrated in the lead firms in their home country environments, while more routine tasks or those requiring less complex knowledge or more readily available skills are more easily outsourced to suppliers in developing countries. This, in a sense, is the traditional picture of a GVC, but in reality the process of off-shoring is increasingly more complex as more and more complex, knowledge-intensive task are also outsourced. In garment manufacturing, for example, some developing countries and intermediaries, such as Li and Fung, have moved from full package supply to the joint development of products, including design. Activities such as R&D of high-tech products are being located in centres in emerging economies, such as China and India. These are emerging trends, but most GVCs still resemble the traditional division of tasks on the basis of knowledge, skill, codifiability of knowledge, and the complexity of capabilities.

In the next section, we overlay this analysis of vertical relations between buyers and suppliers and horizontal relations between suppliers and labour with an exploration of how GVCs are governed and how they interact with national institutions.

1.6   National institutional factors

National institutional factors in both lead-firm and supplier countries affect employment relations in supplier firms and influence the nature of local capital–labour relations. National institutional factors usually include governmental labour regulatory systems that are responsible for monitoring and ensuring compliance on labour standards. However, with the rise of GVC-based production relations between firms that extend beyond national boundaries, much of the governance and monitoring of agreements between units at different nodes of the chain is implemented through a system of 'privatization of compliance' (Locke, 2013). Corporate responsibility is not merely about compliance with the rule of law in a national context, but mediated by contractual agreements between units situated in different national geographies. These agreements, in turn, are influenced by the prevailing business climate in buyer countries, and to a lesser extent in supplier countries. More recently though, as with the California Transparency in Supply Chains Act (2012) legislation is beginning to require firms to take note of labour conditions or conduct due diligence all along their supply chain irrespective of cross-national location (Pickles and Zhu, 2013; Phillips, 2015).

In the first phase of GVC-related development, lead firms utilized the weaknesses of developing country labour institutions and the Washington Consensus doctrine of market fundamentalist labour systems. Not only were wages kept down to or even below national minimum wages, but existing institutional systems, such as child labour and forced labour, were allowed to be part of the accepted workings of supply chains. Over time, however, the exposure of child labour and forced labour, or even of forced overtime abuses, led to pressure from civil society organizations and consumer groups in buyer countries to compel reform in GVC labour practices. The non-use of child labour, for instance, became a necessary condition for supplier firms to participate in GVC production systems. Along with setting up such standards, lead firms also contracted organizations to conduct third party audits to monitor compliance, which became part of the 'privatization' of labour standards referred to above (Locke, 2013).

National institutional factors in supplying countries are not the creation of GVC-lead firms, but have often been exploited by lead firms, or, have at least remained unopposed by them till recently. Child labour, for instance, existed before the initiation of GVC-based production and continues to exist in the production of non-tradables, such as roadside eateries or auto repair workshops in India (see IPEC studies of child labour). Similarly, systems of forced or bonded labour are older than GVC-related production and also exist quite independently of GVCs. But GVC-related demand has supported the adverse inclusion (Philips and Mieres, 2014) of workers as bonded labour, in the production of raw materials (e.g., coltan in the Congo, Nathan and Sarkar, 2012) or in household-based segments of production (Bhaskaran et al., 2010). These are either geographically hard to reach or dispersed locations such as fields and households. As Ford Motor pointed out, there was forced labour in its value chains in the production of charcoal which was 'far outside Ford's direct control' (quoted in Phillips and Mieres, 2012, p. 9). But as Tewari (Chapter 13) in this volume points out public shaming of large lead firms has led to new alliances with corporations partnering with local governments and place-based civic actors to create area-based compliance within labour markets, rather than merely firm-based compliance.

Another institutional factor in developing countries that has an impact on wages and employment conditions is that of local laws and the quality of their enforcement. Where laws allow precarious employment, as of workers indirectly employed through labour brokers, then such labour could be used even without or beyond any requirement for flexible employment relations. Data on India, for instance, show that the proportion of indirectly hired labour, working on a regular basis, is much higher than that of directly hired labour, working on a casual basis (Nathan, 2015).

The state of the labour market is clearly of importance in matters like wage determination. The deepening structural transformation from agriculture to manufacturing, that is taking place in many Asian economies, can at times create shortages of labour leading to an upward pressure on wages, as is occurring in China (Mei and Wang, Chapter 9). Labour shortages can also have mixed outcomes. For instance, India is facing a shortage of both English speakers and trained software engineers, which has led both to higher wages and high rates of attrition in call centres and IT software service sectors (Sarkar and Mehta, Chapter 19). While in other segments where 'surplus' labour still exists, manufacturing or GVC-related manufacturing is less likely to face labour market's pressure for upward revision of wages. These pressures and how effectively they are leveraged in favour of labour, however, requires agency and concerted action. Bhattacharjee and Roy (Chapter 4) cautions us though that in the context of GVC production where supplier countries with differing labour market structures and different degrees of structural transformation are often woven together in the same GVC one might need to go beyond 'national' labour market dynamics to push for an Asian Floor Wage that can help dampen price wars between nations to obtain GVC orders and investment.

1.7 Structure and agency in re-working employment relations in GVCs

So far, we have examined the manner in which surpluses within a GVC are distributed between lead and supplier firms, the business practices of lead firms and their effects on supplier firms, and the manner in which GVCs are governed. All this sets out, in a sense, the structural underpinning of GVCs. But the identification of these structures leads to additional questions: do workers have any agency in the formation or re-formation of employment relations within GVCs? Is there any role for other non-GVC-linked societal factors in the formation and re-formation of employment relations in GVCs?

In an attempt to answer these questions, we now focus on employment relations in GVC-supplier firms and on factors that influence agency, from both within and outside the GVC, including national rule of law and institutional structures of national labour markets. Supplier firms in developing countries respond to labour and labour movements. For instance, the proliferation of low levels of literacy among women workers in Bangladesh is a key factor in the Bangladesh garment manufacturing industry's emphasis on low value production, whereas the availability of substantially better educated women workers in Sri Lanka has enabled that country to emerge as a key manufacturing centre for better paying middle- to high-value garments. But when hundreds of thousands of women (in Sri Lanka) and millions (in Bangladesh) work regularly in garment manufacturing, things do not remain static. As is discussed in some of the papers in this book (Chapters 3, 11 and 12) women who may start out as (or presumed to be) docile workers could eventually become a force for improving work conditions and generally a force for improving gender relations in their respective countries.

What are the components of workers' power and how are they affected by the development of GVCs? The first aspect of workers' power, one that Marx emphasized, is that of the concentration of workers, enabling the development of workers' associations or trade unions, which can provide workers with some degree of associational power.[7]

Similarly, gender relations intersect with worker power—or the lack of it—in significant ways. In Bangladesh and Sri Lanka, the garment workforce is dominated

---

[7] Wright (2000) distinguished this associational power from workers' structural power, which arises from their place in the economic system. Later, structural power was sub-divided into two parts by Silver (2003), who distinguished between marketplace power and workplace power.

by women, who make up around 70–80 per cent of the total work force in this industry. This shift of women from domestic to industrial work, or rather the addition of industrial work to women's already existing engagement with domestic work, is a structural transformation in its own right that is often neglected in GVC analyses. For example, despite their strength in numbers, women workers still struggle to enlarge the sphere of their bargaining power in the labour market. But, in part their continuing domestic work burden in addition to industrial work remains an important reason behind women's poor bargaining power in the marketplace. The manner in which unpaid care work is distributed within a family and society is, in turn, a result of the prevailing structure of gender relations (Folbre, 1994; Antonopoulos and Hirway, 2009). The effects of the burden of unpaid care work on women's work point to the need to include gender relations as a factor affecting women workers' bargaining power in GVCs.

1.8 Governance types

The manner in which production is coordinated despite being splintered across countries is often studied under the rubric of *governance* of value chains in the GVC literature. Governance goes beyond mere technical coordination to also relate to the use of power in contractual relations, the distribution of rents across segments of the chain, and the setting of labour and related standards in production. These are all matters of governance. In this section, we relate our discussion about the vertical (buyer–supplier relations, distribution of surplus, and business practices) and horizontal relations (wages and national institutions) within GVCs to the discussion of governance relationships between firms in different segments of GVCs. Governance relations, then, are a way of capturing the variation between different kinds of vertical relations, leading to a stylized typology for relations between lead and supplier firms. Variation in horizontal relations, in turn, complicate and/or provide more nuanced contextual character to how governance relations can differentially influence labour relations within GVCs.

Relations between lead and supplier firms in GVCs were initially conceptualized in the two-fold distinction between producer-driven and buyer-driven supply chains (Gereffi, 1994). This was modified to elaborate different forms of governance or coordination of relations between the nodal firms and their suppliers (Gereffi et al., 2005). Suppliers could be of different kinds—with varying degrees of bargaining power. Five types of governance relations followed from this analytical scheme, ranging from markets to hierarchy. These were markets, modular value chains, relational value chains, captive value chains, and hierarchy (2005, p. 83–84).

To briefly characterize these analytical categories, paraphrasing and slightly modifying Gereffi et al. (2005, p. 83–84) we can say that:

1. Chains government mostly by *market linkages* are those where the exchange relationship is characterized by standard hands-off purchase and sale on the market, which is the form of exchange staple to standard theories of trade.
2. *Captive value chains* are those where suppliers make products or services to lead firm specifications, but generally supply most of their output to a single or few lead firms, and thus are captive to these powerful lead firms.
3. *Modular value chains* are those where suppliers have some bargaining power. While lead firms still determine specifications, the need for rapid innovation and hedging of risks in the cost of innovation, as well as technical advances lead to modularity in the interface between different segments of the chain. As long as the modular interface is met, suppliers can innovate and gain power or economies of scale. This has led to the rise of large intermediaries in the middle of the chain—between lead firms and suppliers lower down the chain.
4. *Relational value chains* are those where complex and recursive interactions between suppliers and lead firms often result in mutual dependence and interlocking asset specificity.
5. *Hierarchical linkages* are those where lead firms set up their own FDI units in the manner of vertical integration, leading to intra-firm exchange and governance relationships.

What are the implications of this GVC structure for labour, particularly labour in developing countries, where most supplier firms are concentrated?[8] What are the prospects for upward mobility, learning, skill formation, adaptation of skills to progressively higher value tasks, and the institutionalization of good working

---

[8] Differences in factor costs are clearly important determinants of the location of tasks in different geographies, but costs, wages, and factor prices are not all that drive these decisions. The location of tasks also depends on a country having the broad *capability* for performing that task in relation to its cost of production. In order for, say, software programming to be located in a country, that country must have the capability—if not for software programming, then for something of a related nature. For instance, space engineers in Bulgaria were able to adapt their skills to software design (Pickles, personal communication). In addition, the cost of production and employment of relevant personnel must be lower than the cost of the same in competing locations. Trade, then, is based not on the competitive production of a product, but on the competitive production of the capability to carry out a task, or manage a segment of GVC activity. This approach to trade at the intersection of costs and capabilities has important implications for development theory and policy, which is the subject of a separate, forthcoming companion volume.

conditions? What are the relative roles of structure and agency in influencing workers' conditions in GVC-related production? How does participation in GVCs enable workers, women in this case, to redefine the gender relations that operate in society? How do the different governance types play out with regard to employment relations in supplier firms? These are the key questions that have motivated the case studies and the book as a whole.

1.9 Contents of the book

In our analytical framework outlined in this introductory chapter, we have made efforts to unpack some of the key factors that influence labour relations within supplier firms of the kind that are concentrated in Asia. Through a stylized analysis of the nature and structure of GVCs, we argued that a cluster of factors that can be classified under vertical relations within GVCs (i.e., between segments—such as the distribution of surplus and profits, business practices) and horizontal relations within GVCs (i.e., within segments, such as wages, institutional norms around labour, and wages) influence the nature of labour relations and working conditions within supplier firms in GVCs. We then linked this schematic classification to the kinds of governance relations that characterize GVCs in the literature. Our goal of doing so was to point out the room to manoeuvre for action and policy associated with different kinds of GVC relationships that we find on the ground.

If governance types are broadly related to employment relations in supplier firms, and present insight into the kinds of policy action that might be possible within them to improve labour outcomes, then it makes sense for the case study chapters to be arranged on the basis of the dominant governance relation highlighted by each of the cases, i.e., captive, modular, or relational governance. Some of the cases, e.g., electronics (mobile phone) manufacture in China and India (Chapter 14) deal with more than one governance type—both modular and hierarchical governance—but the main analysis in those chapters is of modular governance, and hence are placed there. It is also telling that across our research the fewest cases were of relational governance—presumably the category where buyer and supplier relationships within GVCs are the least contested. In contemporary Asia, there are few such examples, at least at the present time.

The first set of case studies in agro-foods, garments, and tourism, deal with supplier firms in *Captive Governance* systems. In these value chains, knowledge requirements are low, though they may be on the rise, as in the case of fresh grapes. The suppliers produce to lead firm specifications; in addition, they depend on large buyers. Many suppliers deal with relatively fewer buyers and get no more than competitive profits, while workers also get low wages that are around the minimum in their countries. Our chapters in this section lay out not only the narrow room to manoeuvre for suppliers in this kind of GVC relationship, but several chapters explore reforms and collaborative efforts to improve the conditions of work under low margins and low wages.

The garments value chain, which is the staple of GVC analysis, is the subject of a number of chapters in the book. Chapter 2 discusses the ILO-IFC Better Work Asia Programme, which started in Cambodia, and traces how the benefits have accrued to workers over time. Chapter 3 deals with the garment industry or ready-made garments (RMGs) industry in Bangladesh. They outline the manner in which wages have increased even in low wage settings in a country like Bangladesh where workers' low educational attainment and price pressures have long kept wages low. Ashim Roy and Anannya Choudhury (Chapter 4) discuss another innovation—the Asian Floor Wage initiative, which aims to create conditions that will prevent a race to the bottom in the Asian garment sector by moving wage setting from the national minimum wages to living wages as the standard for the garment industry in Asia.

Sukhpal Singh in Chapter 5 deals with labour conditions in the newly-developed export value chain in table grapes in a district of India. He contrasts labour conditions in GVCs against production conditions in the supply chain for domestic production or less-regulated regional export markets.

Tourism is also a relatively low-knowledge service and thus has few barriers to entry. The tourism GVC is organized with many service providers and few buyers, since tourists, particularly foreign tourists, tend to rely on tour operators and organizers when travelling in Asia. The 'zero fee' study of the Chinese domestic tourism value chain in the chapter by Yang Fuqian, Yu Yin and Dev Nathan (Chapter 6), deals with an interesting case of an oversupply of the service, leading to high competition among both buyers and sellers and its perverse consequences for the firm and labour. Chapter 7 deals with one regional innovation to deal with the problems of the zero-fee tour. The chapter documents the different ways in which the over-supply of tour operators and suppliers of services was controlled in Lijiang, with tourism in this region having a substantial impact on reducing poverty in the region.

The study of Bali by Girish Nanda and Keith Hargreaves (Chapter 8) examines the effects of recession on tourism and analyses the consequences of terrorist bombings and later the financial crises, on the organization of the tourism value chain, and the manner in which the burden of the crisis came to be distributed along the value chain.

High volumes of employment in labour-intensive activities may lead to a shortage of labour, both nationally and locally. Lixia Mei and Xici Wang (Chapter 9) argue that such a shortage in the labour-intensive clusters along the East coast of

China has set off a dynamic of shifting labour-intensive tasks to interior parts of China, where both labour and land are cheaper.

As activities are split among enterprises, the low value-capturing segments of value chains, such as harvesting of fish, which are also low-paid and associated with arduous conditions of work, are the preserve of migrant workers from poorer countries. Chapter 10 by Yuko Hamada discusses the role of migrant workers in upstream segments of sea-food value chains in Asia.

In *Modular Governance*, the knowledge requirements are moderate, leading to entry not being as easy as in captive governance value chains. The number of suppliers is not so large in relation to the buyers. Profit margins may still be low, as in contract manufacturing in electronics, but the skill requirements from workers are somewhat higher, leading to higher wages.

Lingerie is part of the garment value chain but represents a product category that is distinguished by the somewhat higher level of knowledge complexity in its production and the relatively few centres, mainly Sri Lanka and Turkey, where they are produced. Lingerie is represented by two studies of workers in Sri Lanka.

In Chapter 11, Annelies Goger extends the analysis to the changes in social and gender relations related to women's work in the Sri Lankan garment industry, known for its prominence in the high value niche of lingerie manufacture. Rather than merely looking at the way in which gender relations frame women's participation in GVC labour, this paper also investigates whether women's participation re-frames gender and social relations.

Working conditions include not just wages and overtime, but also relate to occupational health and safety (OHS) matters. Chapter 12 by Kanchana Ruwanpura deals with the way in which OHS issues are scripted in Sri Lanka's garment industry, which is known for its participation in high-value lingerie manufacture.

Meenu Tewari in Chapter 13 examines the rise of informal spaces within formalized garment value chains where new vulnerabilities such as child labour and trafficked labour become inserted in GVCs. The chapter examines new forms of relational regulation that are helping craft new alliances between lead firms, national governments, and civil society institutions to experiment with novel place-based initiatives to monitor informal segments of GVCs. The chapter discusses the contours of an attempt in Mewat, India to eliminate child labour while preserving the ability of women to work close to their homes.

Modular governance is also represented by mobile phones as consumer electronics, with studies that focus on labour conditions in the production of mobile phones in China and India. Chapter 14 by Joonkoo Lee, Gary Gereffi and

Sang-hoon Lee compares wage and employment conditions in Nokia plants and contracted producers in China and India.

Jenny Chang, Pun Ngai and Mark Selden (Chapter 15) deals with a topic often neglected in GVC studies—worker resistance to conditions in GVC supplier factories, in this case in the well-known Foxconn electronics factory in China, which is notorious for numerous cases of worker suicides.

Sumanagala Damodaran (Chapter 16) discusses the important outsourcing model developed by the Indian telecom service provider, Bharti Airtel. In terms of its outsourcing model, the suppliers fall into two different governance types, depending on the levels of knowledge required for the supply of services. The supply of IT software services is an area with high profits and high wages, while that of tower construction falls into low profits and low wages.

Chapter 17 on the automobile value chain in India by Praveen Jha and Amit Chakrabarty also focuses on the complexity of the auto industry's value chain structure. It examines labour processes across different value chain segments of automobile production and focuses particularly on the shifting role of contract workers in the automotive chain in one plant in India.

The case studies of labour in *Relational Governance* systems are of IT software services in Chapter 18 by Ernesto Noronha and Premilla D'Cruz and Chapter 19 by Sandip Sarkar and Balwant Mehta. The knowledge requirements in these are high and the products are developed through complex interactions between the supplier and buyer. Knowledge requirements from employees, however, are not uniformly high—for example, low wage, low value call centres are also included in the IT chain as are customer service firms that might fall into the modular governance system.

The book has two concluding chapters. Chapter 20 by Dev Nathan analyses the structure of employment systems as they vary between the different governance systems. Chapter 21 draws on the findings from the various case studies and focuses on whether and, if so, to what extent there have been changes in labour conditions in GVCs, as also the likely changes in gender relations. Drawing on Polanyi's double movement of labour under capitalism, the chapter invokes a 'second movement' of labour that is visible and emergent in Asian GVCs and wage movements. The pushback by contract workers and the contestation of gender relations by women workers in GVCs have destabilized established relations of power and created new openings for labour reform, however, incomplete it might be at the moment. These shifts in employment relations within many segments of GVC-related work in Asia portend the importance of workers' agency and the manner in which it helps restructure and re-form GVCs.

Going against the grain of all the pessimistic analyses, e.g. Castells (2000), Burawoy (2010), of the destruction of workers' agency through globalization, the case studies in the book show that the agency of workers—both women and men—has been recreated within the interstices of globalization.

References

Anner, M., J. Bair, and J. Blasi. 2013. 'Towards Joint Liability in Global Supply Chains: Addressing the Root Causes of Labor Violations in International Subcontracting Networks.' *J Comp Labor Law Policy* 35 (1): 1–43.

Antonopoulos, Rania, and Indira Hirway. 2009. *Unpaid Work and the Economy: Gender, Time-Use and Poverty in Developing Countries*. London: Palgrave-Macmillan.

Burawoy, Michael. 2010. 'From Polanyi to Pollyanna: The False Optimism of Global Labor Studies.' *Global Labour J* 1 (2): 301–13.

Castells, Manuel. 2000. *The Rise of the Network Society*, London: Wiley.

Coe, Neil, Peter Dicken, and Martin Hess. 2008. 'Global Production Networks: Realizing the Potential.' *J Econ Geogr* 8 (3): 468–84.

Dicken, Peter, 2007. *Global Shift: Mapping the Changing Contours of the World Economy*. London: Sage Publications.

Dobbelaere, S. 2005. 'Joint Estimation for Price Cost Margins and Union Bargaining Power for Belgian Manufacturing.' IZA Discussion Paper 1466.

Duhigg, C., and K. Bradsher. 2012. 'How the US Lost Out on iPhone Work.' *The New York Times*, January 21.

Fine, Charles, 1998. *Clockspeed: Winning Industry Control in the Age of Temporary Advantage*, New York: Perseus Books.

Folbre, Nancy, 1994. *Who Pays for the Kids? Gender and the Structures of Constraint*. London: Routledge.

Gereffi, Gary. 1994. 'The Organization of Buyer-Driven Global Commodity Chains.' In *Commodity Chains and Global Capitalism*, edited by G. Gereffi and M. Korzeniewicz. Westport: Praeger.

Gereffi, Gary, John Humphrey, and Timothy Sturgeon. 2005. 'The Governance of Global Value Chains.' *Rev Int Polit Econ* 12 (1): 78–104.

Grossman, Gene, and Esteban Rossi-Hansberg. 2008. 'Trading Tasks: A Simple Theory of Offshoring.' *Am Econ Rev* 98 (5): 1978–97.

Kalecki, Michal. 1971. 'Class Struggle and the Distribution of National Income.' In *Selected Essays in the Dynamics of the Capitalist Economy, 1933–1970*. Cambridge: Cambridge University Press.

Kapia, R., H. Korhonen, and H. Hartiala, 2006. 'Planning Nervousness in a Demand Supply Network: An Empirical Study.' *International Journal of Logistics Management* 17 (1): 48–65.

Kaplinsky, R. 2005. *Globalization, Poverty and Inequality: Between a Rock and a Hard Place*. Cambridge: Polity Press.

Kornai, Janos. 1986. 'The Soft Budget Constraint.' *Kyklos* 39 (1): 3–30.

Locke, Richard. 2013. *The Promise and Limits of Private Power: Promoting Labor Standards in a Global Economy*. Cambridge: Cambridge University Press.

Mahutga, Matthew. 2014. 'Global Models of Networked Organization, the Positional Power of Nations and Economic Development.' *Rev Int Polit Econ* 21 (1): 157–94.

Milberg, William, and Deborah Winkler. 2013. *Outsourcing Economics: Global Value Chains in Capitalist Development*. Cambridge: Cambridge University Press.

Minnich, Dennis, and Frank Maier. 2007. 'Responsiveness and Efficiency of Pull-Based and Push-Based Planning Systems in the High-Tech Electronics Industry,' available at, http://www.systemdynamics.org/conferences/2007/proceed/papers/MINNI334.pdf. Accessed December 9, 2014.

Mishel, L. 1986. 'The Structural Determinants of Union Bargaining Power.' *Industrial Labour Relations Review* 40 (1): 90–104.

Nathan, Dev. 2013. 'Industrial Relations in a Global Production Network: What Can Be Done.' *Econ Polit Weekly* 38 (30): 29–33.

———. 2015. *Impact of GVCs on Employment Relations*. Geneva: ILO; Mimeo.

Nathan, Dev, and Sandip Sarkar. 2011. 'Profits, Rents and Wages in Global Production Networks.' *Econ Polit Weekly* 46 (36): 53–7.

Neilson, J., and B. Pritchard. 2009. *Value Chain Struggles: Institutions and Governance in the Plantation Districts of South India*. London: Wiley Blackwell.

OECD, WTO, and UNCTAD. 2013. *Implications of GVCs for Trade, Investment, Development and Jobs*, Note prepared for the G-20 Summit. Available at, http://unctad.org/en/PublicationsLibrary/unctad_oecd_wto_2013d1_en.pdf, accessed on March 26, 2015.

Pal, Rupayan, and Udayan Rathore. 2014. 'Estimating Workers' Bargaining Power and Firms' Mark-up in India,' paper presented at ISLE Conference, Ranchi, 18–20 December, mimeo.

Phillips, Nicola, 2015. 'Human Trafficking, Slavery and the Governance of Global Production,' mimeo.

Phillips, Nicola, and Fabiola Mieres, 2014. 'The Governance of Forced Labour in the Global Economy,' *Globalizations*. doi: 10.1080/14747731.2014.932507.

Pickles, John, and Shengun Zhu. 2013. 'The California Transparency in Supply Chains Act.' *Capturing the Gains Working Paper* 2013/15.

Silver, Beverly. 2003. *Forces of Labor: Workers' Movement and Globalization since 1870*. Cambridge: Cambridge University Press.

UNCTAD. 2011. *World Investment Report*. Geneva: UNCTAD.

World Bank. 2014. *World Development Indicators*. Available at, http://data.worldbank.org/sites/default/files/wdi-2014-book.pdf.

Wright, Erik Olin. 2000. 'Working-Class Power, Capitalist-Class Interests and Class Compromise.' *Am J Sociol* 105 (4): 957–1002.

Captive Governance

2

Achieving Better Work for Apparel Workers in Asia[1]

Arianna Rossi

2.1 Introduction

In the last few decades, one of the key foci of policymaking at the national and international levels has been to understand how global production networks (GPNs) operate and function in the global marketplace, and their significance to employment and working conditions. Analysing the outcomes of participation in GPNs for workers, especially those operating in supplier firms in developing countries, means assessing how workers' rights, working conditions, voice, empowerment, and the opportunities afforded to them within and outside the workplace, have changed as a result of their employment in firms that are part of GPNs. This is particularly relevant for apparel workers in Asia, where the industry has grown dramatically in the last few decades and provides new employment opportunities for young, mostly female workers. However, these jobs have been largely characterized by exploitative and unsafe working conditions; a visible and striking example of this was the collapse of the Rana Plaza building in Bangladesh in 2013. The imperative to improve working conditions in the apparel industry in Asia has been a centrepiece of public policy interventions by a variety of stakeholders, ranging from international brands, civil society organizations, international trade unions, and the United Nations' International Labour Organization (ILO). The ILO's partnership with the International Finance Corporation (IFC) led to the establishment of the Better Work programme in 2007,[2] with the objective of improving working conditions and promoting competitiveness in global apparel supply chains.

---

[1] The views expressed in this chapter are those of the author and are not attributable to Better Work, the International Labour Organization or the International Finance Corporation.

[2] For more detailed information on the Better Work programme, see http://betterwork.org.

This chapter builds on evidence from Cambodia, Indonesia, and Vietnam to analyse the experiences and recent developments of the Better Work programme's operations in Asia. It focuses on the programme's efforts to harness the potential of GPNs to simultaneously achieve social and economic upgrading. Aimed at improving working conditions and promoting competitiveness in the global apparel production network, the Better Work programme uses GPN analysis from an applied perspective, through identifying the key actors who shape the social and institutional contexts within which garment production is situated and interacting with global, regional, and local stakeholders in its operations. The chapter argues that Better Work is a policy instrument that is increasingly building evidence to demonstrate that compliance with labour standards and respect for workers' rights are not only moral obligations, but also contribute to achieving economic upgrading and increased competitiveness in GPNs.

After a brief literature review of the different intervention models aimed at improving working conditions in GPNs, I discuss the history of Better Work, underlining the aspects that make the programme's projects unique in the governance landscape of the apparel GPN, and highlighting the steps that led to its establishment in Cambodia, Vietnam, Indonesia, and Bangladesh. Subsequently, the impact of the programme on working conditions, worker well-being, and firm competitiveness is discussed. Finally, I illustrate Better Work's policy influencing agenda and my concluding remarks point to future research in the area of working conditions in the global apparel industry.

2.2 Labour in GPNs: Corporate social responsibility and beyond

Despite a wealth of empirical work concerning labour in GPNs, the evidence is mixed regarding the implications of participation in GPNs for firms and workers in developing countries, particularly those engaged in apparel production. On the one hand, globalized production in developing countries is often associated with employment growth and an increase in labour force participation rates in worker categories that did not previously have access to waged employment, such as women workers (Bernhardt, 2014). Moreover, there is evidence that wages in export processing zones are higher than those in sectors oriented to the domestic market (Harrison and Scorse, 2010). On the other hand, there is also robust evidence that the globalization of production has often been associated with an increase in flexible and vulnerable labour arrangements, such as temporary, contract, and migrant labour. For these categories of workers, participation in GPNs may have led to increased vulnerability and insecurity (Barrientos et al., 2011; Locke, 2013; Oxfam International, 2004; Raworth and Kidder, 2009; Rossi et al., 2014).

The global apparel industry has long been under scrutiny for its poor working conditions and violations of labour standards (Collins, 2003; Hale and Willis, 2005). Since the early 1990s, the media and civil society have exposed well-known brands for manufacturing their products in sweatshops in developing countries, sometimes involving child labour (Locke, 2003, 2013). These exposes created the first momentum for apparel brands to take action, paving the way for the rise of Corporate Social Responsibility (CSR) as a unilateral response, with virtually all brands developing codes of conduct outlining the basic labour requirements to be followed in their supply chains.

From a scholarly perspective, buyer codes of conduct, their content, and their impact on working conditions and labour rights also took centre stage (Blowfield, 1999; Jenkins et al., 2002; Lund-Thomsen, 2008; Merk, 2009; O'Rourke, 2003; Pearson and Seyfang, 2001; Utting and Marques, 2010). Codes of conduct and auditing infrastructure that lie at the core of buyers' CSR activities have had an observable impact on specific issues. Barrientos and Smith (2007) show in detail that codes do succeed in changing occupational safety and health practices, especially in terms of raising awareness on the importance of emergency preparedness and the negative implications of hazardous chemical use. Codes of conduct also seem to effect improvements in terms of good housekeeping, i.e., better management of contracts and payslips. However, CSR initiatives have been plagued by criticism. First, many codes of conduct do not directly acknowledge the ILO core labour standards (Mamic, 2003). Secondly, the audit process through which codes of conduct are monitored in factories, whether carried out internally by the buyer or by a third-party auditor, is often flawed (Frank, 2008; Locke and Romis, 2006, O'Rourke, 2002). Problems range from basic inaccuracy and lack of attention to detail, to the failure to consult workers, cultural differences and translation problems, and corruption. Furthermore, due to the urgency with which buyers reacted and their desire to differentiate themselves as particularly socially responsible, buyers developed their codes of conduct and associated implementation guidelines individually, with little coordination. This has created two significant problems that further limit the success of codes of conduct in improving conditions for workers in low-income countries. First, the content of codes and associated guidelines are not homogeneous, which creates confusion and even cynicism among supplier factories. Second, each buyer typically conducts or arranges for its own labour audit of supplier factories. For most supplier factories that are producing for many buyers, this can lead to scores of audits every year, constituting a considerable waste of resources in direct costs and lost productivity.

Another important dimension that hinders private CSR initiatives from having a sustainable long-term impact on workers' well-being is the fact that they are unilaterally developed and implemented by buyers, often without prior consultation of the other actors in the GPN. As a result, these initiatives might prevent worker organizations from taking a lead role in the improvement process and could weaken state regulation (Seidman, 2009), as well as potentially creating parallel regulatory systems (Posthuma, 2010). For this reason, the new millennium has seen the emergence of a variety of multi-stakeholder initiatives, especially in the apparel sector, bringing together different mixes of brands, trade unions, NGOs, and employers' associations in supplier countries. Having explicit commitments from brands, suppliers and worker organizations have contributed to advancing the impact of labour compliance initiatives (Barrientos and Smith, 2007). However, these initiatives often engage mainly with the commercial and social actors of the GPN, without directly encompassing government or institutional actors. This lack of engagement with public authorities and local institutions undermines the efforts for sustainable change, since public labour administration and inspection services, as well as the local industry associations and trade unions, are the institutions responsible for enforcement of national labour law, collective bargaining, dispute resolution, and social dialogue.

The ability to convene governments, workers' organizations and employers' organizations as well as brands is one of the key factors differentiating the Better Work programme from multi-stakeholder initiatives. The fact that Better Work is a partnership involving firms, inter-governmental agencies, such as the ILO and the IFC, and national governments in the governance of labour standards, has been noted as a unique policy case to explore (Wetterberg, 2011). The programme is further discussed in the Section 2.3.

2.3 Better Factories Cambodia and Better Work

The ILO's direct involvement in monitoring working conditions in apparel factories dates back to the establishment of the Better Factories Cambodia (BFC) project in 2001, which was intended to monitor working conditions in apparel factories in Cambodia. The programme was designed to provide neutral and reliable information on labour standards compliance to further the implementation of the US-Cambodia Bilateral Textile Trade Agreement of 1999. This granted increased quotas for Cambodian garment exports under the Multi-Fibre Arrangement (MFA) in exchange for improvements in compliance with labour standards. Better Factories Cambodia marked the first time in which the ILO became directly involved in factory-level monitoring, something that Polaski (2006, p. 922) identifies as a '[...] a critical element of continued relevance for the ILO, as global production chains increasingly elude the control of national labour ministries and labour inspectorates'.

Better Factories Cambodia is based on a model of positive incentives. Initially, the mechanism rewarded improved compliance with labour standards with preferential access to the US market. As the Ministry of Trade linked export licenses to participation in BFC, all Cambodian garment-exporting factories joined the project, making it effectively industry-wide[3]. The programme was therefore the expression of policy coordination between different institutional actors at the global and national levels, aiming to improve the competitiveness of the Cambodian garment industry alongside compliance with international and national labour legislation. With the MFA being phased out in 2005, there was concern that the Better Factories Cambodia programme would end in the absence of a trade policy incentive. Policymakers and advisors in Cambodia were even more concerned that a purely competitive global garment market would endanger the entire Cambodian garment industry, which was expected to lose out to competition from other low-cost and more logistically efficient suppliers in Asia. However, the fact that all BFC stakeholders[4] committed to standing by the project, including the buyers, who continued to source from Cambodia after the MFA phase-out because of its adherence to labour standards (FIAS, 2005), guaranteed the survival of the industry and the consolidation of its competitiveness on the basis of ethical working conditions (Berik and van der Meulen Rodgers, 2010). The positive incentives at the core of BFC therefore evolved from being trade-based to market (buyer)-based.

Stemming from the scenario in Cambodia, the Better Work Programme was founded in 2007 as a partnership between the ILO and the IFC, with the objective of improving working conditions and promoting competitiveness in global supply chains. As of June 2014, Better Work is operational in Haiti, Indonesia, Jordan, Lesotho, Nicaragua, and Vietnam, covering nearly 1 million workers, and has recently launched a programme in Bangladesh, see Table 2.1.[5]

---

[3] Since 2012, BFC covers also second-tier suppliers.

[4] BFC is advised by a project advisory committee, composed of the Royal Government of Cambodia, the Garment Manufacturers Association in Cambodia (GMAC) and the country's trade unions. For a detailed account of the negotiations among different stakeholders and how the project design was finalized, Kolben (2004).

[5] At the time of writing, factory operations have yet to commence in Bangladesh.

Table 2.1 Overview of Better Work programmes (as of June 2014)

	Year of establishment	Number of factories	Apparel industry coverage
Cambodia	2001	527	Industry-wide
Jordan	2008	63	Industry-wide (since 2011)
Vietnam	2009	251	Opt-in
Haiti	2009	25	Industry-wide
Lesotho	2010	16	Opt-in
Nicaragua	2011	21	Opt-in
Indonesia	2011	93	Opt-in
Bangladesh	2013	–	Opt-in

2.3.1 At the factory level

Building upon the experience in Cambodia, where the programme primarily conducted factory monitoring, and recognizing the limitations of a monitoring-only approach, Better Work significantly expanded service delivery by providing a range of advisory and training services aimed at building the capacities of workers and managers to foster improvement. While BFC offers a training curriculum and is piloting advisory services, remediation efforts have been at the core of the design of the Better Work programme from the outset. Better Work recruits and trains local staff to perform factory assessments aimed at identifying non-compliance with the ILO core labour standards (child labour, discrimination, forced labour and freedom of association, and collective bargaining) and national and international legislation regulating compensation, contracts, occupational safety and health, and working time. Assessments are unannounced, take an average of four person-days per factory and are carried out approximately once a year by a team of two Better Work Enterprise Advisors. After each assessment is completed, a report is shared with the factory management and with the current or prospective buyers who have subscribed to Better Work.

Unlike most buyer-driven models, the compliance assessment marks just the first step in engagement with the factory on labour issues. At the foundation of the Better Work model is a process of improvement built on factory-level social dialogue, following one of the ILO's guiding principles under the decent work agenda. Once the areas of non-compliance are identified, Better Work staff members launch advisory services. This involves a series of factory-level meetings aimed initially at establishing a Performance Improvement Consultative Committee (PICC) that is composed of equal numbers of factory management and worker representatives. Once the PICC is formed, a list of priority actions to remediate the areas of non-compliance identified during the assessment is established and monthly meetings are scheduled. Identified needs for capacity building are addressed through tailored training courses on subjects such as occupational safety and health, supervisory skills, workers' rights and responsibilities, and human resource management. Members of Better Work staff accompany the PICC through the process of establishing priorities and implementing changes, facilitating the discussions and emphasizing the value of social dialogue between workers and management.

2.3.2   At the industry and GPN levels

Besides the factory-level activities of assessments, advisory services, and training, Better Work also works at the industry level in an attempt to address endemic issues and promote a culture of compliance. Polaski (2006) identified regular consultations among BFC stakeholders and clarity on the goals and objectives of the project as critical components to its sustainability and to its potential to be replicated as a model elsewhere. Building on that, each Better Work country programme is advised by a project advisory committee composed of members of the government (often from the ministries of both labour and trade) and employers' and workers' organizations. The goals of such committees are to establish a dialogue at the national level to discuss the non-compliance challenges assessed by Better Work staff and to address national-level policy decisions that directly impact supplier factories' ability to comply with international labour standards.

Better Work also aims to stimulate policy dialogue on labour issues of importance through the publication of compliance synthesis reports in every country programme. An aggregate overview of non-compliance findings across factories participating in each country programme is regularly published on the public website. In Cambodia, synthesis reports originally included the names of factories found non-compliant with each topic. This degree of transparency has been identified as a contributor to ensuring continued improvement in compliance, particularly for factories not selling to reputation-sensitive buyers (Polaski, 2009; Robertson et al., 2011). In 2006, due to limitations in the information system being used, as well as to stakeholder pressure, this policy was discontinued, and BFC started to publish only aggregate compliance findings in its synthesis reports. This move was subject to criticism especially from civil society, because it took away the opportunity for labour activists to use empirical compliance findings as leverage for campaigns to stimulate policy changes, and it decreased the overall transparency of the programme (Sonnenberg and Hensler, 2013). Due to these pressures and to the desire of spurring compliance improvements in factories with consistently low rates of compliance. BFC resumed its transparency policy in 2014[6]. Through this step, the BFC model now fulfils again the three dimensions identified by Sabel et al. (2001) in their Ratcheting Labour Standards model as the key ingredients needed to foster better working conditions: industry-wide participation, independent monitoring of labour standards compliance, public disclosure, and pressures from consumers and investors. While other country programmes are taking steps to increase transparency in reporting at the factory level, at time of writing BFC remains the only country programme in Asia to publicly report on non-compliance by disclosing factory names.

Understanding the dynamics of GPNs is crucial to identifying the effective leverage points in the chain and stimulating improvements, taking into consideration that there is a shared responsibility among all actors involved in ensuring that compliance with labour standards is upheld. BFC and Better Work put significant emphasis on the role of global brands in sustaining change at the factory level. For this purpose, the programmes have created a partnership model with global brands, which entails close communications and policy coordination, and hold regular global and regional Buyers' Fora that bring together global brands, vendors, and suppliers to discuss labour challenges along the GPN.

2.3.3 Expansion of Better Work in Asia

The vast majority of garment workers in the world reside in Asia (UNIDO, 2013). As the objective of Better Work is to improve working conditions and promote competitiveness in the global garment industry, it follows that specific attention has been devoted to replicating the BFC model in other Asian countries that are emerging as key sourcing locations. Better Work Vietnam was launched in 2009, targeting apparel producers in and around Ho Chi Minh City. Unlike BFC, Better Work Vietnam does not have industry-wide coverage and is not linked to trade incentives nor mandated by the government. It is therefore an opt-in programme, to which factories most frequently subscribe as a result of their buyers' demands. Better Work Vietnam was, together with Better Work Jordan, the first testing ground for the programme's strategy involving workplace dialogue through bipartite committees. The success of the establishment and implementation of Better Work Vietnam (which currently covers more than 250 factories and has recently started operations also in the north of the country) led to further expansion in Asia to

---

[6] Transparency reporting is available on a quarterly basis at http://www.betterfactories.org/transparency

Indonesia in 2011. Better Work Indonesia follows a similar model, also operating in specific geographical clusters (Greater Jakarta Area and Central Java) and with voluntary subscription to the programme.

The years of operations in Vietnam and Indonesia were critical in informing Better Work's strategy to establish a programme in Bangladesh, for which preparatory work has been underway since 2012. The Tazreen factory fire at the end of 2012 and the collapse of Rana Plaza in April 2013 underscored in the most tragic way the need for effective factory-level interventions in Bangladesh aimed at improving worker safety and respect for workers' rights. Better Work Bangladesh was officially launched in November 2013 as part of a broader ILO intervention in the ready-made garment industry in Bangladesh.[7] Factory operations are expected to start in Gazipur in the second half of 2014.

2.4 The impact of Better Factories Cambodia and Better Work

Understanding the potential for Better Work to be an effective policy instrument that strengthens labour protection in GPNs requires an assessment of its impact on social and economic upgrading, i.e., on improving working conditions, contributing to workers' well-being and that of their households, while simultaneously promoting competitiveness at the factory and sectoral levels. This section presents findings based on two sets of primary data: the compliance data collected in each Better Work factory on an annual basis, and the worker and manager surveys independently administered to measure the effectiveness and long-term impact of the programme.[8]

2.4.1 Impact on working conditions

The most immediate measurable impact of Better Work is on compliance with labour standards on the factory floor. The programme's Enterprise Advisors collect data on compliance with the ILOs core labour standards (child labour, discrimination, forced labour, and freedom of association and collective bargaining) and with four clusters regulated by national law (compensation, contracts, occupational safety and health, and working time). Compliance is determined based on factory observations, document review, and interviews with workers, managers and trade

---

[7] For more details on the ILOs strategy in the ready-made garment sector in Bangladesh, please see http://www.ilo.org/global/about-the-ilo/activities/all/safer-garment-industry-in-bangladesh/lang--en/index.htm

[8] For more information on the impact assessment methodology, Brown et al. (2011a).

union representatives. Analysing compliance rates over time provides an initial snapshot of the changes brought about by Better Work.

Publicly available data from BFC show that overall compliance, as well as compliance within nearly every individual category of working conditions, has improved over time and consistently in the period 2001–2008. By the fourth assessment visit, average compliance rates range from a low of 52 per cent to a high of 95 per cent, with the mass of the distribution lying between 75 and 95 per cent compliance. However, the strain brought about by the 2008–2009 financial crisis is a likely explanation for the average plateauing and worsening of certain indicators of compliance in the period 2008–2011 (Better Factories Cambodia, 2014a). This trend contributed to the return to a policy of full transparency in 2014, as discussed above. Preliminary analysis (Better Factories Cambodia, 2014b) suggests that the renewed commitment to publicly disclosing non-compliance findings, both for 'critical issues' and for factories that are significantly and consistently below average in terms of non-compliance rates, is creating new momentum for factories to come into compliance.

However, the recent labour unrest in the garment sector reveals that many challenges remain in Cambodia. Studies (Arnold and Shih, 2010; Miller, 2008) have argued that while BFC has shown sustained improvements in terms of measurable standards over the years, worker representation is still flawed and that the proliferation of unions in the garment sector is an indication of still immature industrial relations. The BFC transparency database also includes information about unions, including strikes and their compliance with legal requirements.

In Vietnam, despite the limitations of national labour legislation in terms of protecting workers' right to freedom of association and collective bargaining, the programme observed an 18 per cent improvement in compliance, in terms of workers being allowed to meet without management present. In addition, an increasing number of factories are coming into compliance in terms of consulting with unions where legally required, with 28 per cent of factories still in non-compliance after three visits by Better Work Vietnam. Measurable improvements in compliance since the programme's establishment have been recorded in the areas of contracting procedures, grievance systems, handling of hazardous chemicals, emergency preparedness (including fire safety) and in management systems related to occupational safety and health (including the establishment of factory bipartite committees for this purpose).

Since the establishment of Better Work Indonesia in 2011, factories' compliance has improved, particularly in terms of removing recruitment materials leading to gender discrimination, improving welfare facilities such as water and sanitation, and working environment indicators related to noise, heat, and ventilation. In both Vietnam and Indonesia, there has been no progress or even a worsening in compliance in terms of working time, and of excessive overtime in particular. This issue is endemic within the global garment industry and requires an approach along the GPN, ensuring that business practices are in line with the requirements on overtime established by national legislation in each country. This is further discussed in Section 2.5.

There is evidence showing that these compliance trends are directly associated to the assessments, advisory, and training services provided by the Better Work programme in factories. Brown et al. (2014a) analyse the exposure to Better Work Vietnam services by looking at the number of months since a factory's assessment and since the bipartite PICC was established. They demonstrate that the establishment of the PICC leads to higher wages, and that the months since the first Better Work assessment are associated with lower verbal abuse, lower perception of supervisors being obstacles to promotion, and an increased perception of supervisors being fair and respectful (*ibid.*, 200).

2.4.2 Impact on workers' well-being and livelihoods

Improved compliance with international labour standards and national law is the most tangible outcome of Better Work. However, it is critical to understand what improved compliance means for workers' well-being, and for their families and livelihoods. This requires looking at short- and long-term changes within and beyond the factory floor. Using data from Better Work Vietnam, Domat et al. (2013) demonstrate that greater compliance with core labour standards improves the life satisfaction and well-being of workers, who report greater levels of life satisfaction and well-being in factories with greater compliance with laws regarding child labour, workplace discrimination, and forced labour. Similarly, worker well-being is higher in factories where workers report better working conditions, especially in terms of having a safe work environment, being satisfied with wage levels and having access to health facilities.

In Cambodia, the expansion of the apparel sector that took place in concomitance with the establishment of the BFC programme has created new opportunities for waged employment and potential prospects for escaping poverty, especially for previously marginalized workers. Evidence (Robertson et al., 2009) shows that Cambodian households that include one garment worker earn 36.3 per cent more than the national average income for similar households with no garment worker(s). Moreover, this premium for Cambodian households is significantly more than the difference between garment and non-garment household income in other garment-exporting countries without a Better Work programme at the time

(El Salvador, Honduras, Indonesia, and Madagascar). In addition, the gender wage gap in the Cambodian apparel sector has considerably reduced, from 39 per cent in 1996 to 14 per cent in 2007 (Robertson, 2011).

An important dimension of the potential for the garment sector to be an engine of growth for developing countries lies in migrant workers' ability to remit wages to their home communities. Better Work surveys show that approximately 80 per cent of workers are supporting family members by sending money home from their jobs either 'regularly' or 'occasionally' remitting significant amounts of money (in Vietnam, this amounts to approximately 20 per cent of GNI per capita in 2010) (Better Work, 2012). In Vietnam, the top three reported uses for remittances among family members were for basic needs like food and clothing, and debt repayment. Brown et al. (2014a) show that workers in factories where the PICC is established tend to remit larger sums of money, suggesting a higher developmental impact.

2.4.3 Impact on business competitiveness

In order to be effectively bought into by factories as a useful model, the sustainability of improvements facilitated by Better Work relies to some extent on the presence of business logic for improved working conditions. There is a significant and growing body of evidence from BFC and Better Work that supports the hypothesis that good working conditions can create business opportunities and sustain productivity and efficiency, both at the factory and industry levels.

At the industry level, in parallel to the establishment and development of BFC, Cambodian garment firms on average grew since the early 2000s, with output, value added, profits, employment, and labour productivity all growing continuously (Asuyama and Neou, 2014). Total factor productivity also increased between 2002 and 2008 (Fukunishi, 2014). The financial crisis of 2008–2009, which had a dramatic impact on Cambodian garment exports and employment, offers an opportunity for a natural experiment on the role of labour compliance in business resilience. Exports to the United States, which is Cambodia's main market, declined by almost 25 per cent between August 2008 and August 2009. Brown et al. (2011b) analyse the relationship between factory survival and compliance with labour standards and show that compliance with a number of labour standards is statistically correlated to a higher probability of surviving the financial crisis. More in detail, they find that paying wages as promised is always correlated to a higher probability of survival, and that compliance with communication and workplace systems (including shop stewards, liaison officers, and workplace operations), modern human resource practices (including discipline and termination, information about wages, and regular working hours), and compensation (including payment of wages, contracts, social security, leave payments) all are significantly correlated to factory survival. Across all areas of compliance-related factors studied, only those firms that had just made significant investments in occupational safety and health infrastructure (such as a new ventilation system or a new emergency exit) see a negative correlation with survival. Other factors that are correlated with firm survival are size (large firms are less likely to close) and having a reputation-sensitive buyer. This finding is in line with what was observed in the aftermath of the MFA phase-out. Buyers that value the ethical sourcing reputation of Cambodian garments continued to source from their established supplier base in the country.

Longitudinal studies of the relationship between various types of buyers and the compliance levels of the factories they select to manufacture their products find further evidence that better compliance records can contribute to better business outcomes. Supplier factories with higher compliance on core labour standards were 56 per cent more likely to retain their buyers. Furthermore, suppliers with higher compliance rates had typically longer-term relationships (at least 4 years) with their buyers (Oka, 2012), a factor that is considered key for business success.

There is growing evidence from Better Work Vietnam data that higher compliance with labour standards and improved working conditions, particularly on issues related to communication and problem solving such as worker committees and collective bargaining, are associated with higher profits (Brown et al., 2014b). Furthermore, factories in which workers do not have concerns about whether their wages were paid correctly and do not express concerns about verbal and physical harassment are also likely to have higher profits (*ibid.*). In particular, the authors find that in those factories where workers perceive improvements in their sense of physical security and assurance in wage payments there was a 5.9 per cent increase in profitability. Similarly, firms do better when they go beyond merely avoiding conditions associated with sweatshops and instead create a comfortable and trusting workplace environment: profitability increased 7.6 per cent in those sampled factories where workers are comfortable in raising workplace concerns, where workers express greater satisfaction with water and air quality, and where there is greater satisfaction with restrooms, canteens, and health services provided within the factory. Evidence from Better Work Vietnam also shows that factory profits decrease as worker concern with verbal abuse increases (Rourke, 2014).

In terms of labour productivity, Rourke (2014) shows that in Vietnam, workers concerned with verbal abuse require almost one additional hour per day to reach their production target, relative to workers who are not concerned with verbal abuse. Basic training also increases worker productivity: Better Work Vietnam factory workers who report receiving basic skills training need less time to reach their production targets. This evidence suggests that modern human resource management systems that respect workers' rights are correlated to higher profits and to improved business performance.

2.5   Changing policies in GPNs: The role for Better Work

As discussed in Section 2.3, the Better Work programme is distinguished from other past and present initiatives aimed at improving working conditions in global apparel GPNs by the involvement of national governments and institutions, such as worker and employer organizations, in the governance of the programme. In addition to building support for the programme's core services, this tripartite engagement also opens up the opportunity for a deeper influence on the policy dialogue and overall labour market governance in each country where the Better Work programme operates. This is key, especially in light of systemic non-compliance issues that must be addressed at the national or GPN levels. These include, for example, excessive overtime, which is often influenced by lead firms' highly flexible production requirements and last minute changes in orders or limitations in freedom of association due to discrepancies between national legislation and ILO conventions. Examples of this agenda of influencing policy are discussed below.

The Better Work programme's buyer partnership model provides an entry point for addressing systemic non-compliance issues along the GPN, such as excessive overtime caused by intense production schedules and rushed orders. The partnership foresees a commitment by brands to promote decent work, rely on Better Work audits and avoid duplication, work together on remediation, and proactively engage in policy issues at the national and industry levels. Buyers' Fora provide an opportunity for the Better Work programme to highlight non-compliance findings that are found across industries and require a concerted approach from all actors in the GPN.

Sustainable change can only be achieved by building the capacity of national institutions to assert greater control over labour market governance. Better Work programmes attempt to do so by complementing the factory-level interventions with activities to build the capacities of government and social partners, for example, in the form of training for labour inspectors and coaching for divided trade union movements to develop a unified approach to representing themselves to employers in sector-level bargaining.

In addition to the direct engagement of Better Work in capacity building activities, the programme has been branching out to facilitate broader ILO interventions to more influence policy changes related to weaknesses in labour market governance that are often the root cause of non-compliance in individual enterprises. For example, since its establishment in 2009 in Vietnam, Better Work identified systemic non-compliances in freedom of association. Within the socialist system in Vietnam, workers are clearly not allowed to join or form independent trade unions, but there was scope to improve the extent to which factory-level unions operated independently of management and were held accountable by worker members. In 2012, Better Work Vietnam developed pilot projects with the Vietnam General Confederation of Labour (VGCL) to establish methodologies for more effective worker representation. Currently, implementation decrees for the new Labour Code and Trade Union Law are being drafted. Among these, the implementation decree on 'democratic regulation and dialogue at workplace level' introduces a new institution, the 'Dialogue Group', to undertake regular bipartite dialogue at the workplace level, requiring regular meetings and elected workers' delegates at all enterprises. This mechanism was inspired by the experience of the PICCs in Better Work Vietnam factories and may instil a dramatic change in workers' voice and representation in the country.

In Indonesia, Better Work is supporting four trade union federations in a training programme to better represent and organize their members and negotiate with employers. Furthermore, the programme has developed protocols to engage labour and occupational safety and health inspectors at the provincial level. These include close communication on non-compliance issues arising from factory assessments and the development of viable solutions in order to contribute to stronger regional evidence-based policymaking regarding wage setting and other working conditions.

2.6 Conclusions

This chapter has looked at the Better Work programme as an example of a policy intervention in the Asian apparel industry that supports the assumption that GPNs can be harnessed to simultaneously achieve social and economic upgrading. Despite operating in contested political and institutional environments that pose particular challenges to social upgrading, in particular in terms of workers' freedom of association, a critical factor of the programme is the involvement of all stakeholders concerned with the functioning of the apparel GPN. In each country of operation, the programme started by identifying the key actors who shape the social and institutional context in which garment production is situated and operates through continuous interaction with global, regional, and local stakeholders. In this context, two main sets of dynamics should be highlighted. First, the uniqueness of the programme lies in the opportunities it creates for social dialogue at the factory, national and international levels, between governments, employers and workers' organizations and driven by its mandate within the ILO. In particular, it is the direct engagement with national governments that differentiates Better Work from multi-stakeholder initiatives aimed at improving labour standards, because their involvement is critical to ensure systemic change in labour legislation and administration. Secondly, strong relationships with global buyers and their commitment to the programme have had a demonstrated impact on Better Work's objectives of fostering economic and social upgrading.

The leverage that Better Work can exert on participating factories is two-fold: on one side, as shown in Section 2.4, there is evidence of considerable improvement in compliance with international labour standards. These changes, especially in measurable standards, such as occupational safety and health and modern human resources management (including compensation and contracts), are often spurred by their 'business case', i.e., their economic rationale. In this context, there is growing evidence that compliance with these standards and regulations can facilitate business competitiveness and respect for labour standards and workers' rights is not only a necessary floor but a ladder fostering economic upgrading in GPNs. On the other side, there are more systemic issues in the GPN, related, for example, to incompatibility between international labour standards and national labour law, or to tensions between labour compliance requirements and buyers' purchasing practices, that cannot be addressed solely by factory-level interventions. These policy changes often go beyond the direct scope of the programme's interventions, and require the involvement of national and international actors, ranging from state actors to trade unions to employers' representatives and global buyers. In this context, through its existing governance structures and through engagement with its stakeholders in each country, the Better Work programme may facilitate the establishment of effective social dialogue, thereby ensuring sustainable change.

References

Arnold, Dennis, and Toh Han Shih. 2010. 'A Fair Model of Globalisation? Labour and Global Production in Cambodia.' *J Contemp Asia* 40 (3): 401–24.

Asuyama, Yoko, and Seiha Neou. 2014. 'Cambodia: Growth with Better Working Conditions.' In *The Garment Industry in Low-Income Countries*, edited by Takahiro Fukunishi and Tatsufumi Yamagata, 38–76. Palgrave Macmillan.

Barrientos, Stephanie, Gary Gereffi, and Arianna Rossi. 2011. 'Economic and Social Upgrading in Global Production Networks: A New Paradigm for a Changing World.' *Int Lab Rev* 150 (3–4): 319–40.

Barrientos, Stephanie, and Sally Smith. 2007. 'Do Workers Benefit from Ethical Trade? Assessing Codes of Labour Practice in Global Production Systems.' *Third World Q* 28 (4): 713–29.

Berik, Günseli, and Yana van der Meulen Rodgers. 2010. 'Options for Enforcing Labour Standards: Lessons from Bangladesh and Cambodia.' *J Int Develop* 22 (1): 56–85.

Bernhardt, Thomas. 2014. 'Economic and Social Upgrading of Developing Countries in the Global Apparel Sector.' In *Towards Better Work: Understanding Labour in Apparel Global Value Chains*, edited by Arianna Rossi, Amy Luinstra, and John Pickles, 40–67. Palgrave Macmillan.

Better Factories Cambodia. 2014a. Thirty-First Synthesis Report on Working Conditions in Cambodia's Garment Sector. Accessed October 8, 2015. http://betterfactories.org/?p=8587

———. 2014b. Better Factories Cambodia Transparency Database Report, 2nd Cycle. Accessed October 8, 2015. http://betterfactories.org/transparency/uploads/26ba7-better-factories-cambodia-transparency-database-report,-2nd-cycle.pdf

Better Work. 2012. Vietnam Baseline Report: Worker Perspectives from the Factory and Beyond. Accessed October 8, 2015. http://betterwork.org/global/?p=197

Blowfield, Mick E. 1999. 'Ethical Trade: A Review of Developments and Issues.' *Third World Q* 20 (4): 753–70.

Brown, D., R. Dehejia, F. Jacobs, S. Mukand, A. Rappaport, R. Robertson, B. Rosenberg, and Rosenthal, T. 2011a. 'Measuring the impact of Better Work.' Paper presented at the conference 'Workers, Firms and Government: Understanding Labour Compliance in Global Supply Chains,' IFC, Washington, D.C., October 26–28.

Brown, Drusilla, Rajeev Dehejia, and Raymond Robertson. 2011b. 'Working Conditions and Factory Survival: Evidence from Better Factories Cambodia.' *Better Work Discussion Paper Series No. 4*. Geneva: ILO and IFC.

Brown, Drusilla, Rajeev Dehejia, and Raymond Robertson. 2014a. 'Regulations, Monitoring and Working Conditions: Evidence from Better Factories Cambodia and Better Work Vietnam.' In *Creative Labour Regulation*, edited by D. McCann, S. Lee, P. Belser, C. Fenwick, J. Howe and M. Luebker, 185–203. ILO and Palgrave Macmillan.

Brown, Drusilla, George Domat, Rajeev Dehejia, Selven Veeraragoo, and Raymond Robertson. 2014b. 'Are Sweatshops Profit-Maximizing? Evidence from Better Work Vietnam.' *Better Work Discussion Paper Series No. 16*. Geneva: ILO and IFC.

Collins, Jane. L. 2003. *Threads: Gender, Labour and Power in the Global Apparel Industry*. Chicago and London: Chicago University Press.

Domat, George, Paris Adler, Rajeev Dehejia, Drusilla Brown, and Raymond Robertson. 2013. 'Do Factory Managers Know What Workers Want? Manager-Worker Information Asymmetries and Pareto Optimal Working Conditions.' *Better Work Discussion Paper No. 10*. Geneva: ILO and IFC.

FIAS. 2005. 'Cambodia: Corporate Social Responsibility in the Apparel Sector and Potential Implications for Other Industry Sectors.' Foreign Investment Advisory Service, IFC/World Bank.

Frank, T. A. 2008. 'Confessions of a Sweatshop Inspector.' *The Washington Monthly*, 40 (4): 34–37.

Fukunishi, Takahiro. 2014. 'Cross-country Comparison of Firm Performance: Bangladesh, Cambodia, and Madagascar.' In *The Garment Industry in Low-Income Countries*, edited by Takahiro Fukunishi and Tatsufumi Yamagata, 283–307. Palgrave Macmillan.

Hale, Angela, and Jane Willis, eds. 2005. *Threads of Labour: Garment Industry Supply Chains from the Workers' Perspective*. Blackwell Publishing.

Harrison, Ann, and Jason Scorse. 2010. 'Multinationals and Anti-Sweatshop Activism.' *Am Econ Rev* 100 (1): 247–73.

Jenkins, Rhys, Ruth Pearson, and Gill Seyfang, eds. 2002. *Corporate Responsibility and Labour Rights: Codes of Conduct in the Global Economy*. London: Earthscan.

Kolben, Kevin. 2004. 'Trade, Monitoring and the ILO: Working to Improve Conditions in Cambodia's Garment Factories.' *Yale Hum Rights Develop Law J* 7 (1): 79–107.

Locke, Richard M. 2003. 'The Promise and Perils of Globalization: The Case of Nike.' In *Management: Inventing and Delivering its Future*, edited by Richard Schmalensee and Thomas A. Kochan, 35–70. Cambridge, MA: MIT Press.

Locke, Richard M., and Monica Romis. 2006. 'Beyond Corporate Codes of Conduct: Work Organization and Labour Standards in Two Mexican Garment Factories.' *MIT Sloan Working Paper 4617-06*. Cambridge, MA: Massachusetts Institute of Technology, Sloan School of Management. Available at, https://mitsloan.mit.edu/newsroom/pdf/conduct.pdf. Accessed on October 8, 2015.

Locke, Richard M. 2013. *The Promise and Limits of Private Power*. New York: Cambridge University Press.

Lund-Thomsen, Peter. 2008. 'The Global Sourcing and Codes of Conduct Debate: Five Myths and Five Recommendations.' *Development and Change* 39 (6): 1005–18.

Mamic, Ivanka. 2003. *Business and Code of Conduct Implementation*. Geneva: ILO.

Merk, Jeroen. 2009. 'Jumping Scale and Bridging Space in the Era of Corporate Social Responsibility: Cross-border Labour Struggles in the Global Garment Industry.' *Third World Quarterly*, 30 (3): 599–615.

Miller, Doug. 2008. *Business—As Usual? Governing the Supply Chain in Clothing Post MFA Phase Out. The Case of Cambodia*. Geneva: ILO.

Oka, Chikako. 2012. 'Does Better Labour Standard Compliance Pay? Linking Labour Standard Compliance and Supplier Competitiveness.' *Better Work Discussion Paper Series No. 5*. Geneva: ILO and IFC.

O'Rourke, Dara. 2002. 'Monitoring the Monitors: A Critique of Corporate Third-party Labour Monitoring.' In *Corporate Responsibility & Labour Rights: Codes of Conduct in the Global Economy*, edited by Rhys Jenkins, Ruth Pearson, and Gill Seyfang, 196–208. London: Earthscan.

———. 2003. 'Outsourcing Regulation: Analyzing Nongovernmental Systems of Labour Standards and Monitoring.' *Pol Stud J* 31 (1): 1–29.

Oxfam International. 2004. *Trading Away Our Rights: Women Working in Global Supply Chains*. Oxford: Oxfam International.

Pearson, Ruth, and Gill Seyfang. 2001. 'New Hope or False Dawn? Voluntary Codes of Conduct, Labour Regulation and Social Policy in a Globalizing World.' *Global Soc Pol* 1 (1): 49–78.

Polaski, Sandra. 2006. 'Combining Global and Local Forces: The Case of Labour Rights in Cambodia.' *World Development* 34 (5): 919–32.

———. 2009. *Harnessing Global Forces to Create Decent Work in Cambodia*. Geneva: IILS.

Posthuma, Anne. 2010. 'Beyond Regulatory Enclaves: Challenges and Opportunities to Promote Decent Work in Global Production Networks.' In *Labour in Global Production Networks in India*, edited by Anne Posthuma and Dev Nathan, 57–80. New York: Oxford University Press.

Raworth, Kate, and Thalia Kidder. 2009. 'Mimicking "Lean" in Global Value Chains: It's the Workers Who Get Leaned On.' In *Frontiers of Commodity Chain Research*, edited by Jennifer Bair, 165–189. Stanford: Stanford University Press.

Robertson, Raymond. 2011. 'Apparel Wages Before and After Better Factories Cambodia.' *Better Work Discussion Paper Series No. 3*. Geneva: ILO and IFC.

Robertson, Raymond, Drusilla Brown, Gaëlle Pierre, and María Laura Sanchez-Puerta, eds. 2009. *Globalization, Wages, and the Quality of Jobs*. Washington, D.C.: World Bank.

Robertson, Raymond, Rajeev Dehejia, Drusilla Brown, and Debra Ang. 2011. 'Labour Law Compliance and Human Resource Management Innovation: Better Factories Cambodia.' *Better Work Discussion Paper Series No. 1*. Geneva: ILO and IFC.

Rossi, Arianna, Amy Luinstra, and John Pickles, eds. 2014. *Towards Better Work: Understanding Labour in Apparel Global Value Chains*. ILO and Palgrave Macmillan.

Rourke, Emily L. 2014. 'The Business Case Against Verbal Abuse.' *Better Work Discussion Paper Series No. 15*. Geneva: ILO and IFC.

Sabel, Charles, Dara O'Rourke, and Archon Fung. 2001. *Can We Put an End to Sweatshops? A New Democracy Forum on Raising Global Labour Standards*. Boston: Beacon Press.

Seidman, Gay W. 2009. *Beyond the Boycott: Labour Rights, Human Rights and Transnational Activism*. New York: Russell Sage Foundation.

Sonnenberg, Stephan, and Benjamin Hensler. 2013. *Monitoring in the Dark*. Stanford, California: International Human Rights and Conflict Resolution Clinic, Stanford Law School; Worker Rights Consortium.

United Nations Industrial Development Organization (UNIDO). 2013. *International Yearbook of Industrial Statistics*. Vienna, UNIDO.

Utting, Peter & Marques, José Carlos, eds. 2010. *Corporate Social Responsibility and Regulatory Governance: Towards Inclusive Development*. New York: UNRISD/Palgrave.

Wetterberg, Anna. 2011. 'Public-Private Partnership in Labour Standards Governance: Better Factories Cambodia.' *Public Admin Develop* 31 (1): 64–73.

3

Improving Wages and Working Conditions in the Bangladesh Garment Sector

The Role of Horizontal and Vertical Relations

Nazneen Ahmed and Dev Nathan

3.1   Introduction

In 2011, Bangladesh became the second largest garment exporter in the world, second only to China. Between 2006 and 2010, the minimum wage in the garment sector had increased by 33 per cent, which was considered as a major positive economic phenomenon. However, in 2012 and 2013, horrific incidents of fire and building collapse took the lives of thousands of workers. Accounting for these contradictory developments is the central purpose of this paper.

During the post-MFA (Multi-Fiber Arrangement) period, from 2005 onwards, the Bangladesh ready-made garment (RMG) industry grew at a rate of more than 25 per cent per year. However, since the arrival on the scene of garment exports from Bangladesh in the late 1970s, and even now, Bangladesh has often been held up as an example of the 'race to the bottom' in the global competition for contracts and jobs (as an example, Muhammad, 2011). In the 1990s, the prevalence of child labour in the garment factories of Bangladesh was the centre of European and US campaigns against 'sweatshops'. Even after the elimination of child labour, the country's garment factories were still held up as examples of poor wages and working conditions. Several incidences of fire and building collapse have served only to confirm the unsafe working conditions of garment workers.

After a brief background section on the organizational structure of the Bangladeshi garment industry, this paper discusses changes in wages and working conditions over time. This discussion is based on a combination of primary field data collected through interviews with workers in factories and secondary data. Interviews were conducted with workers in factories both within export promotion zones (EPZs) and outside these.

The changes in wages and working conditions are then placed within the context of upgrading of Bangladeshi firms, moving from just cut-make-trim (CMT) to free-on-board (FOB) production. This is followed by a discussion of the links between the economic upgrading of firms and the social upgrading of workers. The various buyer initiatives for better compliance and their impacts are discussed next. Social upgrading, however, is not only a matter of buyer pressure but also, possibly more importantly, a result of workers' struggles. After considering the role of workers' associational power in improving wages and other working conditions, we look at the limits that vertical relations in global production networks (GPNs) place on social upgrading and argue for the necessity of modifying vertical relations in order to extend the extent of social upgrading of workers' conditions. This is illustrated with a historical discussion of the role of remaking vertical relations in dealing with sweatshops in the US garment industry in the twentieth century. The paper's concluding section brings together the analysis of workers' associational power and firm agency in upgrading in GPNs.

3.2 Bangladesh garment industry: Organization and structure

The garment industry in Bangladesh has two main sections—knitted garments (sweaters, T-shirts) and woven garments (shirts, trousers, etc.). The industry started with woven garments, carrying out the characteristic CMT segments of work. Over time, however, knitwear has become more important in the product mix, going up from just above a 15 per cent share of exports in 1992/1993 to a share of nearly 50 per cent of exports in 2011/2012 (calculated from BGMEA, 2013). In recent years, then, the knitwear segment has grown rapidly.

This growth could be the result of the 'China effect', as higher wages in China have led to the shift of some labour-intensive production segments to other countries (Chandra et al., 2013 for a comprehensive analysis of this phenomenon; also Frederick and Staritz, 2012 for an analysis vis-à-vis garments). An important factor in the changing composition is the higher local value added in knitwear compared to woven-wear. With yarn now produced locally, the value added is 75 per cent in the case of knitwear as against 25 per cent in the case of woven-wear (BKMEA and IART, 2010–2011, p. 4). The overall growth of the garment industry in Bangladesh occurred due to a combination of three factors: early government initiatives to support the industry, trade preferences and the China effect.

Garment factories operate in two kinds of locations, those within EPZs and those outside. Initially, foreign direct investment (FDI) was allowed only within EPZs.

This restriction was withdrawn after 2005, but even after that there was not much FDI outside the EPZs (Frederick and Staritz, 2012). Besides generally being larger in size, EPZ units monitor work conditions more strictly; this is undertaken by a system combining the Bangladesh Export Processing Zone Authority (BEPZA) and a system of 'councillors', who carry out regular factory checks.

EPZ factories, however, comprise a relatively small proportion of the total factories and employment in the garment industry. In 2012, there were 403 garment units in the EPZs, with about 0.33 million workers. These account for less than 10 per cent of the total number of garment factories or employment in the industry.

In terms of the production network, RMG firms can be divided into three tiers. Tier 1 firms are those that secure orders from buyers or intermediaries. They are generally the larger units, usually employing two thousand or more workers. There are about one thousand Tier 1 firms, accounting for some 20 per cent of the total number of garment firms (Birnbaum, 2013).

Tier 2 firms are medium-size units with a few hundred workers. They are sub-contracted by Tier 1 firms and are often used to fill capacity gaps or to produce specific lines. The important characteristic of these firms, however, is that most of them do not get orders directly from buyers. They are also outside the 'compliance net' of buyers, whose compliance audits are confined to those to whom they give direct orders. Some medium-size units do get direct orders, when the buyers are not able to complete their buying requirements from the larger units. The Tazreen garment factory, where a fire in November 2012 killed more than a hundred workers, was one such medium-size factory that had obtained direct orders from a large buyer.

Tier 3 firms are those supplying inputs, various items of trim or accessories. With the growth of Bangladesh's garment industry, suppliers of various accessories, such as zips, set up factories within the country using the FDI route.

What is important about the structure of the garment industry in Bangladesh, particularly when compared with that in neighbouring India, is that there is not that large a layer of informal enterprises, either unregistered workshops or home-based work. There is, of course, a large unregistered, informal manufacturing sector, but it is not in the garment industry (ILO, 2013). However, there is some informal garment work in Bangladesh (ICF International, 2012), even if it is not as large as in India. Why does Bangladesh not have much of a small-scale and informal sector in RMG export manufacture?

There used to be small manufacturing units in the garment sector. But, as Bangladesh has specialized in large-volume supply, these small units have not been able to continue in the business. They have not grown into medium units, but have just vanished from the scene. In addition, Bangladesh manufactures very little in terms of hand-embroidered garments. Such hand embroidery, as seen in the case of New Delhi (Bhaskaran et al., 2010), tends to be carried out at home by women and often involves child labour. Bangladesh has some hand embroidery, for example, of *nakshi katha*, for export. But this work comes under non-governmental organizations (NGOs) such as BRAC and is a small part of Bangladeshi exports. In any case, it does not come under the supply-to-order RMG sector.

The garment industry is largely within the three tiers as noted above. But 'largely' does not mean entirely. There is an informal sector, taking single-task orders through a sub-contracting route. And it is in this informal sector that child labour still exists, most often working along with parents and other family members, on jobs taken on contract. These contracts are used when Tier 1 suppliers are stressed on having to service large and quick orders (ICF International, 2012).

In India, the substantial existence of child labour at the household level, where it is both legal and difficult to monitor, has not allowed for an elimination of child labour in the garment industry (Bhaskaran et al., 2010). In Bangladesh, on the other hand, once child labour was eliminated at the easily monitored factory-level, the main issue became one of handling rehabilitation. However, the continued existence of some child labour in the informal sector, linked to the formal sector by sub-contracting chains, needs to be noted.

3.3 Wages

The competitiveness of the RMG industry of Bangladesh rests largely on the availability of low-cost workers. The government has increased the minimum wages of RMG workers three times during the past 18 years, in 1994, 2006, and 2010 (Table 3.1).[1] A minimum wage for unskilled workers was first introduced in 1994 and was set at Tk 930 ($23.25 at that time) per month. In 2006, responding to a large episode of labour unrest, which often halted production in many apparel factories, the government's Minimum Wage Board increased the entry-level wage to Tk 1,662 (around $24.80), as against Tk 930 in 1994. The salary levels of upper-grade workers were also adjusted. In 2010, workers again started an agitation for higher pay, following which the Minimum Wage Board again increased the minimum wage of RMG workers, this time to Tk 3,000 ($43.40 at the then prevailing exchange rate) at the entry level, coming into effect from November 2010. But, while increasing the base or entry-level wage, the wage

---

[1] Another increase in the minimum wage took place in December 2013, analysis of which was out of the scope of this paper as the field survey was performed before this wage increase. This wage increase took place after the numerous post-Rana Plaza worker struggles.

Table 3.1 Inflation-adjusted minimum wage

Year	Actual minimum wage rate per month (Tk)	Inflation-adjusted wage rate that would keep the real wage at the previous level	Increase in real wages (%)
(1)	(2)	(3)	(4)
1994	930		
2006	1,662.5	1,526.9	8.8
2010	3,000	2,242.6	38.3

Source: Own calculations for columns 3 and 4 based on minimum wage rate.
Note: Inflation-adjusted wage rates have been calculated by adding each year's average inflation rate with the previous year's value.

structure was changed to reduce the gap between workers working at different levels. This reduction of the gap between junior and senior workers, and between low-skilled and skilled workers, in turn led to another round of industrial unrest.

The horrific incidents of factory fire (December 2012) and building collapse (March 2013) have led to further demands for not just improvements in safety and working conditions but also wage increases. The government responded to wage demands by agreeing to ask the Minimum Wage Board to revise the minimum wage and according to its suggestion increased the wage by 77 per cent compared to that of 2010. It should be noted that there was a 38 per cent increase in the minimum real wage of RMG workers in the earlier 4-year period between 2006 and 2010; this was much higher than the increase of just 8.8 per cent in the previous 12-year period (between 1994 and 2006).

In order to assess the extent of the wage increase and its impact, a survey of workers and management personnel in both EPZ and non-EPZ factories was conducted using semi-structured questionnaires. In the case of EPZ factories, 36 workers of various levels and two management personnel of two RMG factories in the Dhaka EPZ were interviewed. In the case of outside-EPZ factories, 75 workers engaged at various levels in different RMG factories were interviewed. The managers of 16 RMG enterprises were also interviewed, in order to understand their attempts to cope with the wage increase.[2] Both male and female workers were interviewed. The sample is admittedly small, but the purpose of the sample study was to understand some details of the changes in wages. The main argument of this paper is based on the increase of minimum wages, where the data are unambiguous.

---

[2] Whereas workers were chosen randomly from factories in Gazipur and Dhaka districts, factory managers were chosen randomly from factories in Dhaka and Tangail.

The two EPZ factories surveyed are woven RMG factories with an annual turnover of $23.6 million and $10 million (in 2010), respectively; each employs more than 2,000 workers. The non-EPZ factories surveyed are smaller than the EPZ factories. Out of the 16 surveyed non-EPZ factories, 7 are woven product factories and 9 are knitwear factories. Of these, 15 are individually owned; the remaining factory has more than one owner. The average yearly turnover of these factories in 2011 was Tk 100 million (around $1.25 million). The main products of these factories are T-shirts, followed by pants and different woven products. On average, these factories have 1,200 workers, with 61 per cent of them women. The participation of women workers in the sample factories was lower than the widely accepted national average of 70–80 per cent women in the industry. In the current case, the reason for a lower proportion of women workers may be the dominance of knitted RMG products in the sample, which are predominantly manufactured by men.

In terms of implementation of the increase in minimum wages, no significant difference was found between the EPZ and non-EPZ factories.[3] All surveyed workers said they had received higher salaries since November 2010, but the increase was not given all at once. The wage was gradually increased over a period of 2–3 months. Table 3.2 presents details of the actual salaries workers of various grades received. It is interesting to note that, although workers received higher salaries, many of them

Table 3.2 Breakdown of the monthly salary received by workers

Grade	Basic pay	House rent allowance	Transport allowance	Medical allowance	Other regular benefits	Total salary (without overtime)
1	7,862.50	3,595.00	500.00	200.00	1,742.00	15,024.50
2	6,170.00	2,448.00	500.00	200.00	1,236.00	10,574.00
3	4,150.42	1,576.83	500.00	200.00	1,185.17	7,695.75
4	2,780.00	1,112.00	500.00	200.00	1,156.00	5,748.00
5	2,362.50	945.00	500.00	200.00	1,095.83	5,103.33
6	2,270.83	908.33	500.00	200.00	1,151.67	5,030.83
7	2,018.18	807.27	500.00	200.00	928.18	4,430.91

Source: Fieldwork.

---

[3] Moreover, many comparisons could not be made between EPZ and non-EPZ factories as the survey of EPZ factories was conducted during the preliminary phase of this study by administering a limited questionnaire.

were not aware that this was spurred by government intervention. For instance, half of the Grade 7 workers—beginning workers, most likely to be fresh migrants from rural areas—were not aware of the government's intervention.

In addition to their regular salaries, workers also receive overtime payment, the details of which are presented in Table 3.3.

Total wages (regular wage plus mean overtime payments) range from $70 for entry-level workers to $250 at the highest worker level. This should be compared with Bangladesh's 2008–2012 gross national income (GNI) of $65 per month (calculated from World Development Indicators 2013). The lowest rung of garment workers earn just above the average per capita income for the country. With a purchasing power parity (PPP) conversion factor of 0.4 (World Bank, 2013), this gives a monthly income at the entry level of $175 PPP per month, or $5.80 per day.

A large survey of 1,200 workers conducted by Awaj, a workers' organization, from March to April 2013, estimated a total wage, including overtime, of Tk 6,300 for female sewing machine operators with 2–5 years of experience (Awaj et al., 2013, p. 40). This would place the worker in Grade 6 or 5, for which our survey gave a wage, including overtime, between Tk 6,163 and 6,284. There is thus a correspondence between the findings of the two surveys.

The workers were initially happy with the new wage but there was dissatisfaction among them as regards the annual increment. Previously, workers used to enjoy an annual increment of 10 per cent over the total wage (excluding only overtime). After the new wages were fixed, however, the annual increment was tied to basic pay

Table 3.3 Monthly overtime and total income of workers of different grades

Grade	Maximum	Minimum	Mean	Regular wage	Total wages (Tk)	Total wages ($)
1	5,000	3,600	4,494	15,024.50	19,528.50	250
2	3,200	1,550	2,930	10,574.00	13,504.00	173
3	2,350	1,500	2,058	7,695.75	9,753.75	125
4	1,425	1,350	1,390	5,748.00	7,138.00	92
5	1,250	1,100	1,181	5,103.33	6,284.33	81
6	1,150	1,100	1,133	5,030.83	6,163.83	79
7	1,100	1,000	1,009	4,430.91	5,439.91	70

Source: Fieldwork.
Note: Takas have been converted to US dollars at the current (May 2013) rate of Tk 78 = $1.

only (excluding medical and other allowances which are a part of the total wage). Some workers feel that if they were to get an annual increment in accordance with the previous rule, then they would have benefited even without an increase in their basic wage.

All surveyed workers agreed that the increased wage had helped them improve their lifestyle, especially in terms of providing them with better food and better clothing, as well as facilitating repayment of loans for those who were in debt. Some were also able to send more money to their family members back in their villages. However, they noted that the increase in wages was still not enough to allow them to save regularly for the future. In general, they felt the change in wages was not very substantial.

3.4 Working conditions

Working conditions include a number of aspects. These include the space provided for workers, whether adequate or cramped; lighting; provision of toilets; and safety equipment and materials, such as availability of first aid boxes. The poor working conditions of workers have been underscored by the March 2013 building collapse (Rana Plaza) and outbreaks of fire, including at the Tazreen garment factory in December 2012 (Miller, 2012). The various buyer compliance norms that have been instituted basically include working conditions on the shop floor and do not go into the observance or otherwise of building codes. There is, in general, however, large-scale violation of building norms in Bangladesh, and garment factories are no exception. Meanwhile, the high density of workers in RMG factories means violations of building regulations are likely to have very high fatality rates, with the Rana Plaza collapse ranking as one of the largest industrial disasters in the world in terms of deaths.

A number of agencies monitor observance of compliance norms. In the EPZs, there is a system of 'councillors' who report on compliance with norms. Outside the EPZs, where the bulk of the factories are located, NGOs are often engaged in carrying out audits on behalf of buyers on the issue of compliance.

In the EPZs, three consecutive monthly reports of non-compliance can lead to the cancellation of the import–export licenses of a factory. Obviously, factories in the EPZs are keen that they should not lose their license, as that would put them out of business. But others who get direct orders are also under pressure to be compliant. One of the suppliers, in fact, openly stated, 'Things are changing and if I do not comply, I cannot get the orders' (McKinsey & Company, 2011, p. 13).

Can compliance reports be bought? There is no reason to believe this cannot happen. But, both experts on corporate social responsibility (CSR) and buyers generally report an improvement in compliance. More than 90 per cent of the chief purchasing officers (CPOs) of international buyers whom McKinsey interviewed reported an improvement in compliance standards, with 26 per cent of them stating that the level of compliance had improved significantly during the 5-year period before 2011 (McKinsey & Company, 2011, p. 12). The CPOs also pointed out that there was a high degree of variance in the compliance standards among suppliers. Out of 5,000 suppliers, just about 50–100 are thought to have attained very high standards of compliance (*ibid.*, p.13).

For those who have been studying or observing garment factories in Bangladesh over the past two decades, however, there is little doubt about the noticeable and general improvement in standards, although serious issues of violations of building and safety laws do still remain to be addressed.

But there is a critical lacuna in the monitoring of working conditions: the difference between Tier 1 and Tier 2 firms. The former type of firms who get direct orders from buyers generally tend to belong to the group of compliant firms. The Tier 2 firms, however, secure sub-contracted orders from Tier 1 firms and obviously get a smaller margin than that offered by buyers' purchase prices. The Tier 2 firms are also smaller in size, employing a few hundred to about a thousand workers. They are usually not subject to compliance audits and are generally understood to have poorer working conditions. They are often located in residential areas and workers carry on their work in very cramped spaces.

Other studies have reported a difference between directly contracted and sub-contracted firms. In a survey in 2008, 16.7 per cent of workers in sub-contracting firms reported accidents resulting from poor electrical systems, and also that all sub-contracting firms locked emergency exits (Khatun et al., 2008, p. 43); EPZ factory workers reported no such accidents and 4.5 per cent of workers in non-EPZ, directly contracting firms reported such accidents.

Another study, this one of 10 garment factories in Bangladesh, 5 compliant and 5 non-compliant, found that the compliant factories were those with direct orders from international buyers, whereas the non-compliant factories worked on sub-contracts. Compliant factories received 'direct orders from reputed buyer and also better product price from the buyer' (Baral, 2010, p. 129). In addition, the compliant factories were about three times as large as the non-compliant factories. The former had a turnover of just below $1 million, whereas the latter had only around $300,000.

Two tentative statements can be made about Tier 2 firms. First, they make up the bulk of the non-compliant firms; second, they are the ones that have been involved in the recent fire and building collapse incidents. The Rana Plaza building had a few thousand workers in it, but they were divided among a number of firms with a few hundred to a thousand workers each. These fall in the category of medium-size firms. This statement needs further investigation—whether the killer violations of building safety norms are concentrated in the Tier 2, non-compliant factories.

Of course, since the Tier 2 firms act as sub-contractors to Tier 1 firms, particularly taking up the slack when there is a seasonal rush, there is a responsibility that extends down from the buyers through to Tier 2 firms. In mentioning such responsibility one should not omit the government, which has the main responsibility in terms of ensuring that building norms are not violated.

3.5   Economic upgrading

Supplier firms in developing countries do not merely take and stick to orders from lead firms. Even in the initial MFA quota-hopping investments by South Korean firms, such as in the Desh–Daewoo investment, there was substantial capability development through both capital import and training (Rhee, 1990). As the title of Rhee's paper suggests, those trained by Daewoo acted as catalysts for developing local capabilities.

The issue that needs to be analysed post-1990 is whether capability building ended with these first investments, and whether CMT firms in Bangladesh remained within the bounds of CMT activities. In the terms being used by Capturing the Gains (CtG) programme, the question that needs to be considered is: what happened to economic upgrading within the garment GPN? This is the vertical dimension of the GPN relationship (Coe and Hess, 2012; Neilson and Pritchard, 2009). Here, it is important to move beyond a static division of labour analysis to a dynamic analysis of the economic upgrading strategies of firms in developing countries within a GPN framework.

While moving beyond a static and fixed division of labour analysis, it is also necessary to take into account buyer strategies and the manner in which they change. For instance, do buyers tend to develop longer-term relationships with suppliers? Or, are they entirely footloose in awarding annual or even seasonal contracts?

An increase in wages and improvements in working conditions both require some financial commitment. If profit rates are to be maintained, there must be some increase in revenues per employee. Economic upgrading resulting in an increase in revenue per employee is a favourable condition for social upgrading in the form of an increase in workers' wages. In the 12 non-EPZ factories covered by the survey, revenues per employee increased by 33 per cent in 2010 before the minimum wage increase. The managers of firms reported that revenues increased because of not

Table 3.4 Unit prices of selected products produced in the surveyed factories

Product	Average $ price per unit			% increase
	2009	**2010**	**2011**	**2011 over 2009**
Baby wear	2.50	2.40	2.67	6.8
Full shirt	9.50	10.00	10.50	10.5
Half shirt	8.00	8.50	9.50	18.8
Jogging top	10.00	11.00	12.50	25.0
Jogging pants	2.45	2.75	2.33	−5.0
Sweater	4.00	4.50	5.00	25.0
T-shirt	4.50	5.40	5.86	30.2

Source: Survey findings.

only higher volumes but also higher prices for the products supplied, as shown in Table 3.4.

With garments such as shirts, T-shirts, and sweaters dominating the product mix of the 12 surveyed factories, the price increase over the 3 years ranged from 10.5 per cent in 2009 to 30.2 per cent in 2011. The increase in unit value, however, did not occur only in the surveyed factories. In case of garment exports from Bangladesh as a whole too, there was an increase in the unit value, both during the two-decade period of 1990–2009 and even over the more contemporary period of 2000–2009. The increase in unit value over the period 1990–2009 at 16.86 per cent (Bernhardt and Milberg, 2011, Table 5, p. 23) was not very large. However, to put it in a comparative international perspective, the increase in the unit value of garment exports for Bangladesh (16.86 per cent) was higher than for either India (10.96 per cent) or China (13.25 per cent); the unit export value of Vietnam almost stagnated, with a minimal 1.35 per cent growth (*ibid.*).

This increase in the unit value of exports in Bangladesh took place in conjunction with a change in the composition of garment exports—away from woven garments towards knitted garments. These figures are clear indicators of economic upgrading of the garment industry in Bangladesh.

Another indicator of economic upgrading is the increase in garment export earnings per worker, which is a rough measure of productivity. Productivity per worker is important in that it indicates the possibility of increasing wages. If export earnings are taken as a measure of industry revenue, then per worker export earnings increased by 75.5 per cent, from $2,718.38 in 1999/2000 to $4,772.42 in 2011/2012 (Table 3.5).

Table 3.5 Garment export earnings per worker

Year	No. of Workers (millions)	Export earnings ($ million)	Export earnings per worker ($)	Increase in export earnings per worker (%)
1999/2000	1.6	4349.41	2718.38	
2009/2010	3.6	16204.65	4501.29	65.5
2011/2012	4.0	19,089.69	4772.42	6.0
Increase 1999/2000–2011/2012				75.5

Source: Calculated from BGMEA (2012/2013).

There are, thus, clear indications of economic upgrading in the Bangladeshi RMG industry. The increase in export earnings per worker does not itself tell us what brought about this change. It could have been the result of either higher price realization or higher productivity per worker with a stagnant or even lower price realization. However, the increase in export earnings per worker means there has been a reduction in costs, which could have been brought about by economizing on logistics and related non-manufacturing costs (functional upgrading) or a reduction in the manufacturing costs themselves (process upgrading). Further research is needed to identify the factors that led to economic upgrading.

Bangladeshi factories operate largely in the CMT segment. On the whole, this segment does not require very skilled labour. Management requirements are also not very complex. There are capital costs, but the capability requirements to operate in the CMT segment are not very substantial. Consequently, the pure CMT segment of garment manufacture would not get a price above the competitive market price. For that, it would be necessary to take up functional upgrading and move into work segments that require more skills to perform.

Quite early on, suppliers in Bangladesh had acquired sample preparation and re-engineering skills. There is also clearly enhanced capability in supply chain management, seen in the increase of direct orders versus orders through intermediaries. During earlier decades, a large portion of the orders used to be sourced through intermediaries, who undertook overall supply chain management. Now, however, the prevalent trend is mainly that of direct sourcing by buyers, which means suppliers undertake the acquisition of the necessary fabric and overall supply chain management. The McKinsey & Company (2011) report estimates that 72 per cent of the European and US buyers in Bangladesh source their products directly; this fact is endorsed by the 66 per cent of suppliers who stated that they focused on working directly with international buyers. Khatun et al. (2008) reported that direct sales had increased between 2001 and 2005—from 45 per cent to 76.7 per cent in EPZ firms and from 24.3 per cent to 56.8 per cent in non-EPZ firms. At the same time, average stock of machinery in surveyed units increased by 100 per cent in EPZ firms and about 50 per cent in non-EPZ firms over the same period (*ibid.*, pp. 37–38). The rise in the proportion of direct sales and the increase in average stock of machinery are both indicative of upgrading by RMG firms.

The high degree of direct sourcing is an indicator of improved supply chain management capabilities, advancing from CMT functions to what has been called FOB functions (Frederick and Staritz, 2012). Direct sale is likely to result in higher prices and returns than sales through intermediaries, wherein the intermediaries would keep their own profit on the supply price.

Two other factors have enabled some suppliers to improve their bargaining position: the development of 'preferred supplier' arrangements and of new markets other than the US and European Union (EU). Bangladesh has acquired a reputation for supplying good-quality and large orders for lower- to middle-end markets. Over time, a number of buyers have entered into 'preferred supplier' arrangements, wherein they work with suppliers to improve quality, productivity, and compliance with labour standards. These developments indicate that relations between suppliers and buyers are not so footloose. Somewhat sticky buyer–supplier relations are prompted by the transaction cost involved in setting up new suppliers. Thus, provided a supplier is of reasonable quality, a buyer might prefer to work over a period of time with 'preferred suppliers'. In fact, 84 per cent of CPOs interviewed by McKinsey described their supplier relationships as 'long-term' (McKinsey & Company, 2011, p. 13).

A long-term relationship with buyers is likely to yield somewhat higher returns for suppliers than a short-term relationship. In turn, gaining confidence from continuing orders, suppliers could invest in machinery and equipment that would further increase their productivity and improve quality. This point is reinforced by the fact that 85 per cent of CPOs interviewed in the McKinsey survey expected suppliers to upgrade their outputs into more sophisticated products, which would be possible only if acquiring orders fostered increasing confidence among them.

In addition to the confidence emanating from long-term relationships with buyers, another factor that has helped improve the bargaining positions of Bangladeshi suppliers is the growth of new markets, that is, markets other than the traditional North Atlantic markets. Exports to the Japanese market from Bangladesh have been rising very fast during the past few years.

This indicates that RMG manufacturers in the latter country have succeeded in producing high-end and high-quality products. The interest of Japanese buyers in the RMG products of Bangladesh has immense implications for economic and social upgrading in supplying factories. In order to ensure quality, Japanese buyers usually bring a total package, specifying not only design and materials but also the technologies to be used, to their sourcing countries. Thus, Japanese buyers have set up local offices to monitor quality at the production stage and to ensure the use of the right technology. They also invest in the skills development of workers.

In addition, discussions with suppliers revealed that sweater makers deliberately sought out markets in the southern hemisphere, such as Brazil and South Africa. Their different winters would help sweater makers spread the process of sweater-making over the year, thereby reducing the pressure to seasonally lay off workers or reduce wages, which has often been an occasion for worker protests.

The growth of new markets is accounted for not only from the southern hemisphere but also from other emerging economies such as China and India. For instance, the Indian denim maker, Arvind, announced that it would set up a large-scale garment factory in Bangladesh, in collaboration with a Bangladeshi company. Overall, garment exports to the emerging markets had a compound annual growth rate (CAGR) of 56 per cent during 2008–2010 (McKinsey & Company, 2011, p. 9).

The growth of these alternate markets has strengthened the bargaining position of sellers. The McKinsey report went so far as to talk of a transition from a buyers' to a suppliers' market. It pointed out, 'The most developed suppliers have even begun choosing their customers very carefully—at times, even breaking off ties with long-established buying partners in order to upgrade their customer base' (McKinsey & Company, 2011, p. 19). The growth of supplier capabilities, of long-term relationships with buyers and of new markets all point to the strengthening of the bargaining position of Bangladeshi suppliers *vis-à-vis* buyers.

3.6 From economic to social upgrading

Contrary to the usual prognostications of local capitalists or the owners of CMT firms, an increase in wages and an improvement in working conditions need not result in the much-feared loss of international competitiveness. To put it in another way, there is scope for reworking wage and working conditions even within the bottom-of-the-ladder CMT factories. As seen in this paper, there has been a substantial increase in the wages of garment workers and an improvement in their working conditions. These still do not amount to what the International

Labour Organization (ILO) terms 'decent work'[4], and the minimum wage in Bangladesh is not yet a living, family wage, but there can be no doubt that these are 'better work' conditions. Further, this has been done without any seeming loss of competitiveness, as the Bangladesh CMT industry keeps growing. Even after the increases, the Bangladesh minimum wage is less than half of that in competing countries—$39 per month against $80 in Cambodia, $71 in India, $79 in Pakistan, and $78 in Vietnam (ILO, 2013).

Before proceeding, we should discuss what better work and its dimensions mean. Better work relates to two types of movements. First is the movement from being unpaid, and usually unacknowledged in the case of women, family labour to being waged income earners. There is also the intermediate category of the self-employed, such as those who take microcredit loans and run tiny businesses. In either case, there is a big difference between the minimum wage earned by a starting garment worker and what she could get in the village. In the case of self-employed, microcredit-based work, the difference could be at least 100 per cent higher income (Rehman and Islam, 2012). In addition to the wage earned, substantial benefits in terms of self-esteem and social respect come from being a garment worker, as discussed in a considerable literature on women garment workers in Bangladesh (Dannecker, 2000; Kabeer, 2000). The creation of more than 4 million jobs in the industry has been an important factor in the decline in the incidence of poverty in Bangladesh from just below 50 per cent in 2000 to around 31.5 per cent in 2010 (ILO, 2013).

The above type of social upgrading, particularly for young women migrating from rural areas, owes to the very creation of garment jobs in the country. The second type of better work movement relates to the wage increase and improvement in working conditions for those who are already waged employees in the industry. This is the social upgrading that we connect with the possibilities created by economic upgrading and thus higher net revenues of garment firms in the country.

What are the factors that have translated economic into social upgrading? An increase in wages and an improvement in working conditions are not things that come about automatically, as CtG research took as its very starting premise. It requires certain conditions of worker agency, possibly both local and international, and government intervention, coupled with GPN-style corporate governance, to bring about such improvements. These are, in a sense, the locally embedded conditions or

---

[4] Decent work includes the following: employment opportunities; adequate earnings and productive work; decent working time; combining work, family and personal life; work that should be abolished; stability and security of work; equal opportunity and treatment in employment; safe work environment; social security; and social dialogue between employers' and workers' representation (ILO, 2012, p. 15).

horizontal relations (Nielson and Pritchard, 2009) that come into play during the course of the transformation of economic upgrading by developing country firms into the social upgrading of workers' conditions.

Of additional interest here is the implication of the observed transformations of wage and working conditions for female workers, who are employed for their supposed docility (Dannecker, 2000). But workers have undergone a transformation during the course of their over two-decade long involvement in production for global markets. As one observer wrote, 'the women workers became a new social force in the labour movement [...] though RMG workers do not have trade union rights, they have created the strongest workers' mobilisation in recent years in Bangladesh' (Muhammad, 2011, p. 26). As noted even in 1999, the 'concentration on the actual exploitation has left hardly any room for the analysis of the modes of resistance and networking as strategies of women workers to cope with and reshape the ongoing changes' (Dannecker, 1999, p. 2).

3.7 Worker struggles

An important factor in a key part of social upgrading, that is, an increase in minimum wages, has been the growth of worker struggles in the garment industry. Such struggles not only create problems of public order but also could adversely affect the country's main export earner. For these reasons, the struggles of garment workers prompt political responses by the government. As noted by the ILO, wage increases in the garment industry have usually followed 'mass protests and strikes that disrupt the industry' (ILO, 2013, p. 9).

More than 4 million workers in garment factories are mainly situated around two centres, Dhaka and Chittagong. Such large geographic concentrations of workers also have consequences for worker organizing and struggle. In the 1980s or early 1990s, the condition of being a garment worker was a novelty. In addition, given the fact that this was the one sector of modern industrial work that women could enter as independent income earners, garment work was, for some, a prized job, despite the low wages and poor working conditions. However, over a period of more than two decades, such jobs for women have become routine on the Bangladesh labour scene.

Further, the rapid growth of the industry has meant it is relatively easy for a worker to quit a job she does not like and shift to a job in another factory. The exit possibility is revealed by the attrition rate of workers in RMG factories. McKinsey & Company (2011, p. 15) estimates the attrition rate of workers at more than 5 per cent; Impactt (2012) puts it at around 12 per cent. The ability to switch jobs reduces the pressure to remain quiet about the negative aspects in any job, or, to put it in a positive manner—in Hirschmannian terms—the possibility of exit gives more scope for voice. This indicates a difference from the earlier situation, characterized as one wherein there was no possibility of workers having a voice (Ahmed, 2004).

The growing voice of garment workers, including women, is now seen in the numerous instances of worker struggle against low wages and poor working conditions. The past decade has seen numerous instances of 'wildcat' or unannounced strikes. Starting as flashpoints for airing grievances in a particular factory, these strikes often spill over into many factories in the area. For instance, on 23 September, 2007, a strike in the Tejgaon region involved many factories and about 25,000 workers.[5] In September 2013, there was another round of strikes around Dhaka. These strikes by women workers have led to a change in the characterization of women garment workers, as seen in statements such as 'sudden outburst of mostly docile garment workers for higher wages' (The News Today, 2012).

Although there are trade unions, many strikes are not led by these. Again, while women do not dominate the leadership of these unions, there are also separate organizations of women garment workers. Many advocacy groups propagating women's rights are active among garment workers. Overall, there is a multiplicity of organizations in the RMG sector. But many strikes and related struggles are of the unorganized variety.

In addition, the struggle by Bangladesh garment workers to improve their working and wage conditions has gained considerable international support. The International Garment and Leather Workers' Federation (now part of IndustriALL) was prominent in securing international support for the struggles of Bangladeshi garment workers.

The importance of garment workers in terms of their numbers and their presence on the social landscape of Bangladesh has made them a force to reckon with, and government is compelled to respond to their needs and demands. These struggles and the response of various governments have been key factors in the social upgrading that has followed economic upgrading in the Bangladesh garment industry.

But their success has been limited. Workers' voices are scarcely heard. For instance, in the Rana Plaza collapse, workers had reported cracks but were forced to come back to work the next day, when the building collapsed. It is instructive to note that in the same building there was a bank branch, which was closed on the day

---

[5] See https://libcom.org/news/garment-workers-struggles-escalate-again-bangladesh-23092007 (accessed 15 April 2013).

of the crash because of the cracks seen the day before: the bank staff could get their branch closed, but garment factory workers could not.

In the wake of the Rana disaster, the government announced it would make registration of unions easier. Lists of workers wishing to form a union will no longer be submitted to the management for 'checking', which used to lead to intimidation. While workers' councils could in some manner function at the factory level, wide unionization is necessary to carry forward the movement to establish workers' voices. This could also see a shift from the persistent pattern of wildcat strikes to more orderly protests and negotiations, or mature industrial relations (Miller, 2013).

Workers' struggles, however, have not been the only type of pressure for social upgrading. Buyers, under pressure from civil society organizations and trade unions in their own countries, have also put pressure on suppliers to improve labour standards.

3.8 Buyers' pressures for compliance

The dominant buyers of RMG products of Bangladesh include Wal-Mart, H&M, Marks and Spencer, Sears Holdings Global Sourcing Ltd., JC Penney, Tesco International, and Nike Inc., among others. Some of these buyers have initiated special programmes in their source factories to ensure labour compliance, freedom of association, and skills development. Such initiatives are visible in both EPZ and non-EPZ factories. It needs to be mentioned here that all the RMG factories of Bangladesh are free from child labour. This is also an outcome of pressure exerted by the buyers in the mid-1990s.

The main instrument for checking on compliance is an audit. Large buyers' offices carry out their own audits. Smaller buyers tend to engage a local company for the purpose. In any case, most of the staff who carry out the audits are Bangladeshi. The audit checks on matters like prevalence of child labour have worked well at the factory level, but they have not extended their reach into the relatively small informal sector (ICF International, 2012).

Other audits deal with whether workers have contracts and are paid overtime, and the observance of some health and safety precautions, such as whether there are first aid boxes and toilets. These are spot checks that are not usually random. This makes it easy for factories to arrange nominal compliance with these conditions and then withdraw it after the auditors leave.

More important, however, is that audits are in general perfunctory, taking account only of the easily observable. Fire precautions are not something such audits might uncover; they also do not usually check compliance with building regulations. Of course, it can be argued that conforming to building regulations is the government's responsibility. However, given the high level of corruption in Bangladesh, large numbers of factory buildings do not conform to Bangladesh building norms. Even the headquarters of the Bangladesh Garment Manufacturers and Exporters Association (BGMEA) was declared by the High Court to be an illegal construction and ordered to be demolished.

While the Bangladeshi government surely bears the main responsibility for ensuring factory buildings conform to norms, any such measure to improve building standards will involve costs. In the aftermath of the Rana Plaza disaster, a number of international buyers have come forward to put up some money for building improvements. This is a one-off commitment that could be made regular by setting up a quadripartite mechanism for industrial relations in GPNs.

Compliance by factory owners is probably not voluntary but has become a condition of business. However, at the same time, there is little doubt that compliance with labour standards has improved since the early days of the 1980s. Nonetheless, building norms and related safety standards have been neglected in the rush to increase capacity. As the ILO notes, 'In response to a surge in demand for read-made garments from foreign companies, suppliers in Bangladesh have established factories and manufacturing sites without following building and safety codes and the Government of Bangladesh has not provided adequate regulatory oversight and enforcement' (2013, p. 1–2).

3.9 Limits of social upgrading without redoing vertical relations

The advancement of workers' representation and organizations of different types, whether unions or forms of NGOs, including global unions and international NGOs, is important for the development of workers' voice. Workers' organizations deal with direct employers and the government, which often supports the employers, in trying to secure improvements in wages and working conditions. These are, as one might put, it horizontal relations within a GPN, relations between suppliers or direct employers, workers, and government. But the possibility of bargaining within horizontal relations is constrained by the outcome of relations between buyers and suppliers or vertical relations within a GPN.

We look at vertical GPN relations in the Bangladeshi garment industry through Tables 3.6 and 3.7, utilizing data from Miller (2013) and Khatun et al. (2008).

FOB prices as a proportion of retail prices varied from 11 to 24 per cent for different types of garments. Bangladesh's main exports are at the lower end, so FOB prices

Table 3.6 Summary of vertical and horizontal relations in the garment GPN, Bangladesh

Garment style	Retail price ($)	FOB ($)	FOB as % of retail	Labour cost at living wage as % of FOB	Labour cost at living wage as % of retail price
1	2	3	4	5	6
Men's polo	23.00	2.50	10.86	3.6–10.8	1–3
Men's formal shirt	36.00	4.10	11.38	3–9	0.3–1
Men's 5- pocket jeans	22.50	5.50	24.44	6.5–19.5	1–3

Source: Adapted from Miller (2013, Table 4).
Notes: (1) The price data are for 2006.
(2) Living wage has been taken as Tk 5,000, as against the then-existing minimum wage of Tk 1,662 in 2006.
(3) In columns 5 and 6, the first figure is for production at 100 per cent efficiency, while the second figure is for production at 35 per cent efficiency.

Table 3.7 Distribution of costs and profit margin (% per factory)

Indicators	2004	2005	1992 (ISS study)	1995 (BIDS study)
Industrial costs	77.0	77.4	73.0	64.0
Non-industrial costs	3.7	4.44	3.0	5.0
Wage bill	12.3	11.9	11.0	7.0
Profit margin	7.0	6.2	13.0	24.0
Total	100.0	100.0	100.0	100.0

Source: Khatun et al. (2008, Table 21, p. 41).

would tend to be around 11 per cent of retail prices. This low ratio of FOB to retail prices certainly raises a question about the high margins earned by buyers and retailers: 75–88 per cent of retail prices cannot be deemed to be normal design, branding and marketing costs, along with normal profits. The buyers earn a rent from wage arbitrage, which is the difference in wages in destination and manufacturing countries.

At the same time, labour cost as a proportion of FOB price is also low, ranging from about 3 per cent to less than 20 per cent, even at full efficiency. The costs of material inputs have not been separately calculated here, but a calculation by Khatun et al. (2008) gives a profit margin of 6–7 per cent, which is not very high. Given the competitive nature of the suppliers' market, this relatively low margin is not unexpected.

Table 3.7 reveals relatively low margins of Bangladeshi suppliers. In addition, there are problems created by short-term contracts and short delivery times. Short-term contracts inhibit investments by suppliers in increasing capacity. Rather, they encourage forced overtime and other negative labour practices.

Wages are not a large part of costs, but 'factory-owners are hard-faced about paying rotten wages not because they're vital in themselves, but because they're just about the only cost factories can control' (Miller, 2011, p. 12). Given the relatively low margins of Bangladeshi suppliers, the question is: Are the buyers, retailers, or brands jointly responsible along with suppliers and the Bangladeshi government for workers' conditions in Bangladesh? If so, is some redistribution of rents from buyers to Bangladesh needed to improve these conditions? Examining the process through which sweatshops were abolished in the US will be helpful in answering these questions.

3.10   Joint responsibility for factory conditions

Sweatshops existed in the US garment industry right up to the 1950s. In a historical sense, one can see sweatshops as not only the beginnings of industrialization but also the product of two factors—the separation of manufacturing from design and marketing in conjunction with the Lewis-type transfer of surplus labour from agriculture, providing unlimited supplies of labour at a fixed wage, which needs to be just above the opportunity cost, that is, the agricultural income.

In the US, designers initiated the enterprise-based separation of design and marketing, called jobbers, from manufacturing units, or stitchers (Anner et al., 2014). Early retailers such as K-Mart also played a role in this separation of tasks (Hapke, 2004). This separation of tasks enabled the designers and marketers to concentrate rents from the garment industry in their hands. Manufacturing units, which did not require scarce skills, did not have to be given any part of these rents, as would have been the case in integrated garment units. With manufacturing enterprise profits at competitive levels, wages could not be above competitive levels. This was ensured by the Lewis-type transfer of international migrants who were surplus in European agriculture (*ibid.*).

The result of this development of a two-tier supply system was that conditions in the stitcher units deteriorated, leading to sweatshop conditions. The present international system of GPNs extends the two tiers of designers-cum-retailers and stitchers from the national to the international level. It also produces the same type of sweatshop conditions, the difference being that the sweatshops are recreated in far-off countries like Bangladesh, Cambodia, or even China. How did labour in the US deal with sweatshops?

Most stitchers then, as now, were women. In New York and the surrounding areas of New England, they were members of the famous International Ladies Garment Workers Federation (ILGWF). They successfully argued[6] that jobbers, who determined the prices paid to stichers, were also responsible for sweatshop conditions and needed to be brought into the picture. They argued that 'jobbers and contractors were part of an "integrated process of production" and as such, were jointly liable for wages and working conditions in contracting shops' (Anner et al., 2014, p. 11). Tripartite agreements were then entered into between jobbers, stitchers, and workers.

In the contemporary GPN context, the above experience shows that buyers need to be brought into the existing tripartite structure of industrial relations. This is possible at the horizontal level, where manufacturers and workers, with the government, settle work conditions, but is constrained by the vertical relations between manufacturers and global buyers. As argued by Nova (2010), in Miller et al. (2011, p. 9), 'If factories are going to start paying workers properly, protecting their safety in the workplace, providing legally mandated benefits that were previously denied, letting workers go home at a reasonable hour, and so on, costs are going to go up'. These increased costs have to be borne somewhere in the GPN and shared between buyers and suppliers. In this connection, one would need to accept a doctrine of 'joint responsibility' for working conditions. The US Fair Labor Standards Act (FLSA) of 1938 introduces the notion of 'joint employment' of subcontracted workers.[7] With the development of GPNs, it becomes necessary to extend the notion of joint employment and thus joint responsibility for workers' conditions to the international level. Responsibility must necessarily have a financial connotation. If buying practices have an impact on labour conditions, then there would need to be a reform of buying practices. The so far *ad hoc* financial commitments made by buyers after each factory disaster would need to be replaced by regular commitments and a reform of buying practices.

The trinity of 'stable orders, fair prices, and safe factories' (Anner et al., 2014, p. 1) sums up the manner in which vertical and horizontal relations interact

---

[6] This is based on Anner et al. (2014).

[7] See Miller et al. (2011), for a discussion of the relevance of the FLSA to the current GPN situation.

in the GPN. Without the first two, the third becomes difficult, if not impossible. Without overlooking the culpability of local employers and governments, who cut corners supposedly to remain competitive, poor prices and unstable orders certainly contribute to the poor safety situation. Improving safety requires investment, and that is constrained by low prices and unstable orders.

After the Rana Plaza disaster, a number of global buyers have come forward to put up some money to improve factory safety conditions. Different schemes have been proposed by a group of largely European buyers, called the Accord (2013), along with the ILO, and another group of US buyers, called the Alliance (2013). The Accord is based on a binding commitment, which can be subject to arbitration. The Accord is signed by European companies and international unions, with an ILO official to oversee the process. The Alliance, of the main North American retailers and brands, pledges to contribute funds for building renovation to meet safety standards. Being a voluntary contribution, unlike the Accord, it does not have a provision of arbitration. The Accord, with its legally binding commitment, is a step in acknowledging that brands and retailers are accountable for factory conditions in Bangladesh—whatever money is put into either of these schemes is a redistribution of some of the rents they have earned from sweatshop conditions. What is now needed is to make this part of a regular quadripartite system (manufacturers, workers, government, and global buyers) to manage industrial relations in the garment industry in Bangladesh (Nathan, 2013).

Any commitment of funds means an increase in costs. For individual buyers to undertake this increase is difficult, since costs go up. But at one level, the amounts involved are so little: just a few cents per piece of clothing. As Md. Yunus (2013), founder of the Grameen Bank, has suggested, there could be a surcharge of, say, $0.50 per piece, which could be used to invest in improving building conditions. Of course, this could not be done at just a national level, since any such unilateral move would reduce that country's competitiveness as a supplier. There would have to some international agreement for such a tax to be applicable in all supplier countries.

3.11 Conclusion

Wages in Bangladesh are still the lowest of all the major garment manufacturing countries. Incidents of fires and factory building collapses are only symptomatic of overall poor working conditions. But even within this situation, it should be noted here that there is a good number of compliant factories in the country, which have managed to remain profitable even after ensuring decent working conditions.

While wages and working conditions have been improving, they are still some distance from providing living wages and safe working conditions. Enabling conditions for such improvements have been the economic upgrading by suppliers, mainly through functional upgrading. These changes, in turn, have been facilitated by more stable relations with suppliers and have resulted in higher earnings per worker.

Higher earnings for firms, however, have led to some improvements in wages, in large measure because of the transformation of garment workers into a social and political force. More than 4 million workers, of whom 70 per cent are women, form a significant concentration of workers. In addition, the rapid and continuing growth of the garment industry in the country has increased workers' ability to exit from particular factories, certain of getting jobs in other factories. Numbers, and the possibility of getting a job after exiting another factory, could together have increased the voice of garment workers. This, in turn, has forced the Bangladeshi governments and factory owners to accede, at least partially, to demands for higher wages and better working conditions.

A long distance still has to be travelled before working conditions for garment workers in Bangladesh can approach the full extent of decent work conditions. But the improvements that have taken place show that things are not standing still. The concentration of workers and the continuing growth of the industry together have created the conditions for workers to express their voice and secure some responses from governments, buyers, and suppliers. International opinion is influencing buyer behaviour, while the threat of losing business is forcing both Bangladeshi owners and the government to take some action. After the Rana Plaza disaster, the government of Bangladesh has removed the clause requiring that employers certify workers wishing to form a union, which virtually meant that permission was required from employers for workers to register a union.

The improvements that we have noted here are quite limited. Tackling the major issue of building safety will require much more investment. While the European group has agreed to a legally binding agreement, US buyers are not willing to submit themselves to such legal requirements.

But in one way or the other, the money buyers are putting into building improvement comes out of rents that international buyers have earned from using Bangladeshi suppliers and workers. While workers' voice can make an impression on horizontal relations within the GPN, what can be done at this horizontal level is constrained by the vertical relations between buyers and sellers. In a more systematic manner, and not just in terms of *ad hoc* commitment of funds after disasters, there needs to be a redoing of vertical GPN relations so that supplying firms and countries get some part of what now accrues as rent to the buyers. A combination of redoing both vertical and horizontal relations is required to substantially improve wages and working conditions in Bangladesh's garments industry.

References

Accord. 2013. 'On Fire and Building Safety in Bangladesh.' Available at, http://bangladeshaccord.org/wp-content/uploads/2013/10/the_accord.pdf. Accessed on April 30, 2014.

Ahamed, F. 2012. 'Improving Social Compliance in Bangladesh's Ready-made Garment Industry.' Available at, http://www.nla.gov.au/openpublish/index.php/lmd/article/viewFile/2269/3148. Accessed on May 20, 2013.

Ahmed, F. E. 2004. 'The Rise of the Bangladesh Garment Industry: Globalization, Women Workers and Voice.' *Natl Assoc Women's Stud (NAWS) J* 16 (2): 34–45.

Alliance. 2013. 'For Bangladesh Workers' Safety.' Available at, http://www.bangladeshworkersafety.org/about. Accessed on April 30, 2014.

Anner, M., J. Bair, and J. Blasi. 2014. 'Towards Joint Liability in Global Supply Chains: Addressing the Root Causes of Labor Violations in International Subcontracting Networks.' *J Comp Labor Law Policy* 35 (1): 1–43.

Awaj, AMRF Society and Consulting Service International Ltd. 2013. *Workers' Voice Report 2013: Insight into Life and Livelihood of Bangladesh's RMG Workers.* Dhaka: Awaj.

Baral, L. M. 2010. 'Comparative Study of Compliant and Non-compliant RMG Factories in Bangladesh.' *Int J Eng Technol* 10 (2): 93–100.

Bernhardt, T., and W. Milberg. 2011. 'Economic and Social Upgrading in Global Value Chains: Analysis of Horticulture, Apparel, Tourism and Mobile Phones.' *Capturing the Gains Working Paper.*

BGMEA (Bangladesh Garment Manufacturers and Exporters Association). 2013. 'Apparel Statistics of Bangladesh.' Available at, www.BGMEA%20Data.html#.UZhWaiv8-XQ. Accessed May 19, 2013.

BGMEA (Bangladesh Garment Manufacturers and Exporters Association). 2012/13. 'Trade Information.' Available at, www.bgmea.com.bd/home/pages/TradeInformation#.UW5Lwa4xF7E. Accessed May 19, 2013.

Bhaskaran, R., D. Nathan, N. Phillips, and C. Upendranadh. 2010. 'Home-Based Child Labour in Delhi's Garment Production: Contemporary Forms of Unfree Labour in Global Production.' *Ind J Labour Econ.*

Birnbaum, D. 2013. 'Bangladesh and the Failure of Compliance.' Available at, http://www.birnbaumgarment.com/2013/09/26/bangladesh-and-the-failure-of-compliance/. Accessed on May 20, 2013.

BKMEA (Bangladesh Knitwear Manufacturers and Exporters Association) and IART (Institute of Apparel Research & Technology). 2010–2011. 'Apparel

Export Statistics of Bangladesh.' Available at, www.bkmea.com. Accessed on April 10, 2013.

Chandra, V., J. Y. Lin, and Y. Wang. 2013. 'Leading Dragon Phenomenon: New Opportunities for Catch-up in Low-income Countries.' *Asian Develop Rev* 30(1): 52–84.

Chowdhury, N. J., and Md. Hafiz Ullah. 2012. 'Socio-economic Conditions of Garment Workers in Chittagong Metropolitan Area.' *J Bus Technol* 5 (2): 53–70.

Coe, N., and M. Hess. 2012. 'Introduction.' *Global Production Networks, Labour and Development.* Special Issue of *Geoforum* 44: 4–9.

Dannecker, P. 1999. 'Conformity or Resistance? Women Workers in the Garment Factories in Bangladesh.' *Working Paper 326.* Bielefeld: Sociology of Development Research Centre, Universtat Bielefeld.

———. 2000. 'Collective Action, Organization Building and Leadership: Women in the Garment Sector in Bangladesh.' *Gender Develop* 8 (3): 31–39.

Datta, K. 2013. 'Sweatshop Nations.' *The Business Standard,* 23 May 2013.

Frederick, S., and C. Staritz. 2012. 'Developments in the Global Apparel Industry After the MFA Phaseout.' In *Sewing Success: Employment, Wages and Poverty Following the End of the MFA,* edited by G. Lopez-Acevedo and R. Robertson. Washington, D.C.: World Bank.

Hapke, L. 2004. *Sweatshop: History of an American Idea.* New Brunswick, NJ: Rutgers University Press.

ICF International. 2012. 'Child Labor in the Informal Garment Production in Bangladesh.' Washington, D.C.: US Department of Labor.

Impactt. 2012. 'Nice Work: Are Workers Taking the Strain of the Economic Downturn?' Available at, www.impactt.com. Accessed on May 20, 2013.

ILO (International Labour Organization). 2012. 'Decent Work: Indicators and Measurement.' Geneva: ILO.

———. 2013. 'Bangladesh: Seeking Better Employment Conditions for Better Socioeconomic Outcomes.' Geneva: IILS/ILO.

Kabeer, N. 2000. *The Power to Choose: Bangladeshi Garment Workers in London and Dhaka.* London: Verso.

Khatun, F., M. Rahman, D. Bhattacharya, and K. Golam Moazzem. 2008. 'Gender and Trade Liberalization in Bangladesh: The Case of Readymade Garments.' Dhaka: CPD.

McKinsey & Company. 2011. *Bangladesh's Ready-made Garments Landscape: The Challenge of Growth.* Frankfurt: McKinsey & Company.

Miller, D. 2011. 'Regulating the "Wage Effort Bargain" in Outsourced Apparel Production—Two Provocations.' Better Work Research Conference. Washington, DC, 26–28 October.

———. 2012. *Last Nightshift in Savar: The Story of the Spectrum Sweater Factory Collapse.* Newcastle: McNidder and Grace.

———. 2013. 'Towards Sustainable Labour Costing in UK Fashion Retail.' *Capturing the Gains Working Paper.*

Miller, D., S. Tuner, and T. Grinter. 2011. 'A Critical Reflection on Neil Kearney's Mature Systems of Industrial Relations Perspective on the Governance of Outsourced Apparel Supply Chains.' *Capturing the Gains Working Paper.*

Muhammad, A. 2011. 'Wealth Deprivation: Ready-made Garments Industry in Bangladesh.' *Economic and Political Weekly.* 20 August.

Nathan, D. 2013. 'Industrial Relations in a GPN Perspective: From Tripartite to Quadripartite Machinery.' *Economic and Political Weekly* 48 (30): 29–33.

Nielson, J., and B. Pritchard. 2009. *Value Chain Struggles: Institutions and Governance in the Plantation Districts of South India.* London: Wiley Blackwell.

Rehman, R. I., and R. Islam. 2012. 'Trends in Female Labour Force Participation in Bangladesh.' Paper for ILO South Asia Decent Work Team.

Rhee, Y. W. 1990. 'The Catalyst Model of Development: Lessons from Bangladesh's Success with Garment Export.' *World Develop* 18 (2): 316–33.

Rock, M. 2003. 'Labour Conditions in the Export-Oriented Garment Industry in Bangladesh.' *J South Asian Studies* 3 (26): 391–407.

The News Today. 2012. 'Editorial: Government Must Act in RMG Sector Quickly.' Available at, http://www.newstoday.com.bd/index.php?option=details&news_id=2315612&date=2012-06-18. Accessed on August 30, 2013.

Yunus, Md. 2013. 'On 50c surcharge.' Available at, http://www.theguardian.com/world/2013/may/13/fashion-chain-finance-safety-bangladesh-factories. Accessed on August 30, 2013.

World Bank. 2013. *Bangladesh: Poverty Assessment.* Dhaka: World Bank.

4

Bargaining in Garment GVCs

The Asia Floor Wage

Anannya Bhattacharjee and Ashim Roy[1]

4.1 Introduction

The primary concern of trade unions is to improve wages and working conditions of workers in firms owned by capitalists. Wages are a key component of workers' well-being and trade unions are concerned with establishing dignified and decent wages for workers and their families. Their endeavours, through a large part of capitalist history, have been directed at establishing decent working conditions and a living wage within national boundaries. The concern for a decent wage also serves some important social functions, such as reducing gender wage gap and increasing the wage share, that go beyond the physical well-being of workers and their families. As the recent discussion on inequality points out, the fall of wage share in the 1980s and thereafter affects the stability of the international capitalist system (ILO, 2013; Nathan and Sarkar, 2014). Increasing wages and the share of wages in the wealth created from economic growth is an important part of inclusive growth.

The developing countries of Asia possess a large reserve army of labour in agriculture and the urban informal sector, on account of which establishing living wage levels, even in the organized factory sector, has been a hard-fought battle. However, the evolution of contemporary globalization, with the splitting up of production among different countries in the form of global value chains (GVCs), has changed the arena within which the struggle for living wages takes place. Capital, particularly in GVCs, is mobile, while labour is relatively immobile. GVC-based capital, in particular, seeks to take advantage of the possibility of wage arbitrage that results from Global North capital having dual access to low-wage Global South production markets and to high-value Global North retail markets. With GVC-style functioning, manufacturing or cut-make-trim (CMT) functions in the apparel

---

[1] Thanks to Doug Miller for his various suggestions to improve the chapter.

industry is separated from design, branding, and marketing. The CMT segment of the garment industry is shifted to low-wage locations, such as in the developing countries, which also have or can establish basic manufacturing capabilities. With developing country manufacturers competing for contracts with brands and retailers, the latter are able to utilize this competition to push down Freight-on-Board (FoB) prices for manufacturers. As a result, brands and retailers pay increasingly low prices to Global South manufacturers for goods that they sell at high-value Global North retail markets. Manufacturers, in turn try to shift the cost pressure onto wages.

The competition among developing country capitalists for GVC-based investment or contracts has increased after the abolition of the national quota system that existed through the Multi-Fibre Arrangement (MFA). The increasing competition for GVC-based investment in the developing countries of Asia has forced trade unions in the region to rethink their strategies. On what basis then could there be an international strategy and international solidarity among trade unions of countries that were competing for GVC investment?

This chapter deals with the manner in which trade unions and other workers' organizations in a number of Asian developing countries (Bangladesh, Cambodia, China, India, Indonesia, Malaysia, Pakistan, and Sri Lanka) came together to meet the challenge of bargaining and halting a 'race to the bottom' in garment GVCs. They formulated and gave concrete shape to an Asia Floor Wage (AFW), which is now becoming the norm in wage discussions and in the analysis of wage issues in the region and beyond.

4.2 Wage-setting in the garment GVC framework

Garment production occurs primarily in the Global South, in regions like Latin America, Africa, and Asia and in the periphery of the European Union in Eastern Europe. Although present on all continents, garment manufacturing remains concentrated in Asia, which accounts for 60 per cent of the world's clothing. In terms of scale of production, size of workforce, access to raw materials, technology, diversity of skills, and labour cost, Asia offers the most competitive advantage. Within Asia, garment production takes place in many countries such as China, India, Bangladesh, Sri Lanka, Pakistan, Indonesia, Cambodia, Vietnam, and Thailand. The garment GVC is the quintessential buyer-driven chain, where multi-goods retail companies and big brands set the standard, both for products and wage conditions, for the garment global supply chain.

An astonishing phenomenon is that even as prices of most commodities have recently shot upwards, the prices of garments have *fallen* in the Global North.

Moreover, the profits of garment brands have been impressive. This is explained by the fact that the CMT prices that brands pay to the manufacturers in Asia have decreased, possibly reducing the profit margins of Asian manufacturers, and keeping production workers' wages low. As Heintz (2002) notes, 'Much of the emphasis on competitiveness has focused on production costs and, in particular, labour costs. Consumers in affluent nations benefit from low-wage imports when retail prices fall for the goods they purchase'. Global sourcing companies pay approximately the same prices to their supplier factories in Asia: around 25 per cent of the retail price (Miller, 2013). Because garment workers' wages make up a very small proportion of the final retail price for clothes—around 1–3 per cent—substantial wage rises could be achieved without a corresponding increase in retail prices.

Retailers, including brands, are primarily interested in the FOB price of a garment. In arriving at a bargainable FOB price, they cost material inputs and labour. There is some elaborate calculation of labour minutes involved in various tasks (Miller, 2013) and thus of total work that can be done in a working day. This calculation of total work done in a working day can be carried out at various efficiency levels. It is not unusual (*ibid.*) for the calculation to be done in a range from 50 to 75 per cent efficiency. How does this calculation of work translate into a monetary amount, i.e., into wages? This is the crucial aspect of the price-setting equation. The monetary calculation—labour minute value—could be based on a number of standards: it could be that which would provide the worker the minimum wage, or a poverty-level income, or even a living wage. What this would mean is that the piece rate used in pricing decisions should be based on the amount that would give the worker a target wage at the assumed average efficiency level. In principle, this target could be either the existing minimum wage or the living wage.

Buyers are concerned about the production cost of a consignment, while the actual wage level is the responsibility of the seller/manufacturer. Garment wage costing is based on the existing minimum wage. There are three reasons for this. Retailers and brands seek to maximize their profits from wage arbitrage and thus would push FOB prices as low as possible. On the other hand, developing country manufacturers compete to secure orders and so are willing to accept low margins in order to do so. This willingness to accept low margins is buttressed by their knowledge that under the surplus labour conditions prevailing in developing economies, there is a large reserve army of labour which would be willing to accept employment at a wage equal to or just above the existing minimum wage. Developing country governments, as part of supporting employers and employment, also keep minimum wages at a level much below the living wage level. Both suppliers and their governments see low wages as the key competitive advantage in securing investment and orders. This, of course, is the reason why unions are so crucial in securing living wages for workers. Any intervention to benefit production workers in this global garment production structure has to simultaneously consider the interrelated factors of brands' huge profits, low profit margins for Asian manufacturers, and stagnant wages for Asian workers.

4.3 The history of labour rights in the garment industry

Poor working conditions have been an historical feature of supply chains in the global garment industry. Workers' rights activists, at both production and retail ends, have been at the forefront of international accountability campaigns for over a decade, supporting the organizing of workers, publicizing labour rights violations, fighting to hold employers and multinationals accountable to fair labour standards, and organizing consumer-led anti-sweatshop campaigns (Chapters 20 and 21, for a detailed analysis). These campaigns have brought together companies, social organizations, unions, governments, and international institutions in an effort to build multi-stakeholder initiatives focused on accountability. Activists have also extensively documented the working conditions, the global supply chains, consumer attitudes, and other aspects of the industry.

The result of this long history of activism has been the development of various sophisticated mechanisms for corporate monitoring and accountability in the garment industry. One example is the development of codes of conduct, which many multinational companies voluntarily developed under pressure from activists. In a similar vein, codes of labour practices were developed through dialogues initiated by the activist community. These codes have been supplemented by monitoring mechanisms and organizations. SA8000 is a standard developed for certifying companies that are supposedly practising fair labour practices, including that of a living wage. International compliance mechanisms like the OECD mechanism have been painstakingly developed. These mechanisms have established the need for monitoring and have played a major role in developing powerful publicity campaigns to shape public opinion. These activities also help to develop a full understanding of the range of improvements needed for ensuring liveable conditions for workers.

Laudable as this work has been, it has not resulted in improving the protection of workers in the two ways that matter most—economic sustainability of workers and their families and collective voice at the workplace. Economic gains have to be bargained for by workers; no employer will unilaterally share the gains without the articulation of this demand. In order to press for wage and other demands, the collective voice of workers has to be established legally and politically; mere verbal recognition of such a right by the employers does not mean that the conditions exist within which it becomes operational. Frequently, workers who have developed bargaining positions in a given factory and demanded higher wages have done so under the threat of closure and job relocation. They are also often told that their employers' hands are tied by the insufficient prices that they receive from the buyer, that is, the contracting multinational.

There have also been attempts at ensuring fair labour standards through the use of clauses in trade agreements (such as a social clause or labour-side agreement, as was discussed in the context of NAFTA). In an industry like the garment industry, where production is spread out across the globe, such clauses or agreements do not necessarily deliver collective bargaining to workers in a specific country and may actually weaken workers' collective power by dividing them nationally, when in fact they operate within the global production chain of an industry.

Trade unions and labour rights organizations in Asia, after years of experience in the garment industry, came together in 2005 to frame a demand that is negotiable and deliverable, and that is appropriately formulated given the structure and economics of the industry as a whole. Starting with Bangladesh, Cambodia, China, India, Indonesia, Malaysia, and Sri Lanka, the Asia Floor Wage Alliance as it is known, now comprises trade unions, labour and human rights organizations, development NGOs, women's rights groups and academics in over 15 countries across Asia, Europe, and North America (AFW, 2009). The Annex lists countries and organizations involved in the AFW Alliance in 2013.

4.4   Components of the Asia Floor Wage

The Asia Floor Wage was formulated through a combination of top-down and bottom-up processes. The AFW Alliance used data from need-based surveys in India, China, Bangladesh, Sri Lanka, and Indonesia as a basis for the AFW formula. It is based on widely accepted norms that are institutionalized in existing policies, laws, and practices in Asian countries and on Asian governmental figures and international research.

The Asia Floor Wage is composed of two categories of expenditures: food and non-food. Both categories are estimated without subtle internal differentiations, the goal being to provide a robust regional formula which can be further tailored by trade unions in different countries, based on their needs and contexts. The food component of the AFW is expressed through calories rather than food items so as to provide a common basis. The calorie figure is based on studying calorie intake in the

Asia region by governmental and intergovernmental bodies while defining poverty line, living wage, and minimum wage levels. In addition, the two salient issues that the AFW considers are the physical nature of work (sedentary, moderate, or heavy) and the calorific measures prevailing in current discourses. Garment factory work can be described as requiring moderate to heavy physical work.

In a report in June 1999, the Economic and Social Commission for Asia and the Pacific (ESCAP) published that 'the per capita food intake for survival assumed for deriving the food poverty line varied across countries as well as within countries from 2,100 calories to 2,750 calories per capita per day'. Official Chinese statistics plus a study produced by the Food and Agriculture Organization in 2000 show that the calorie requirement of those below the poverty line in China was 2,400 kcal/day (now revised to 2,100 kcal), while that used by the FAO is 1,920 kcal/day. The Indian Labour Conference in 1957 made 2,700 calories the norm for the minimum wage for an adult worker (performing moderate to heavy physical work). The Indonesian government most recently defined 3,000 calories as the intake figure for a living wage for a manufacturing worker (performing moderate to heavy physical work). The AFW Alliance has decided that the floor wage should not result in lowering standards in any country and therefore adopted the Indonesian norm of 3,000 calories as its standard.

Garment workers from Indonesia, India, Bangladesh and elsewhere spend a great deal—frequently around half—of their income just on food. For example, an oft-quoted figure internationally is that food costs amount to 60 per cent of costs at poverty level (Rural Survey Organization, 2004). The Ministry of Labour and Employment in India released working class data in June 2008 where the share of food items was 47.5 per cent of the income. In Thailand, food consumption is assumed to account for 60 per cent of total consumption at poverty lines. The AFW study of various countries, for working-class population, shows an average of 50 per cent of the income being spent on food. Therefore, non-food costs are taken to be the other half of the income, leaving the details of what comprises non-food to be left to the trade unions in local contexts. The 1:1 ratio of food costs to non-food costs was thus calculated based on the ratio that currently exists for the working classes in different garment-producing countries in Asia.

4.5 Family basis

Living wage definitions normally include the notion that wages should support more people than just the individual worker. Minimum wage regulations, by contrast, may (as in India) or may not (as in Indonesia). The AFW unions decided to base the AFW on a family. The AFW Alliance studied the family sizes in key Asian countries and came up with an approximate average figure. The ratio of earner to dependants was calculated based on the family sizes in different countries. For example, the Ministry of Labour in India calculated the average size of a working-class family to be 4.46 in 2008, and the Ministry of Commerce in China calculated the average family size in China to be 3.38 in 2003. In order to account for childcare costs, the AFW posits a single-income family. The AFW defines the formula to be based on three adult consumption units. As a child consumes less than an adult, a child is calculated as half of one consumption unit. The three consumption units can then be configured in various ways: as a family of two adults and two children or one adult and four children or three adults.

4.6 Non-wage benefits

The AFW is a basic wage figure prior to benefits such as health care, pensions and so on. Delivery of other benefits by employers to workers is not the norm in the industry and thus, they have not been made the basis for the AFW. Therefore, if an employer provides dormitory housing or a canteen lunch, the AFW figure is not lowered. This is because not only are the benefits, not the norm, but also that workers should have the option to obtain these basic necessities from the wage, since it is meant to be a minimum living wage with which a worker can support him/herself and dependents. The AFW is a minimum figure that should provide basic costs so that the worker is not at the mercy of the employer for basic needs.

4.7 Hours of work

The AFW Campaign defines the regular work week as a maximum of 48 hours prior to overtime. This definition of a work week and its independence from benefits sends a clear message that workers need to earn a minimum living wage without other humane working conditions being sacrificed.

4.8 Asia Floor Wage currency

The currency through which the AFW is expressed is the imaginary currency of the World Bank, Purchasing Power Parity (PPP). The reasoning for choosing PPP as opposed to a specific national currency is that for comparative purposes and for conversion to an actual wage, the exchange rate is not a good and appropriate measure. Exchange rates are determined by the supply and demand for each currency globally, in other words by the currency market. They are highly volatile and fluctuate on a daily basis and are not reflective of national conditions. PPP, on the other hand, is based upon the consumption of goods and services by people within a country, reflects standards of living and hence is a more appropriate tool for comparing wages. PPP allows one to compare the standard of living between countries by comparing the price of a basket of identical goods and services in terms of the currencies of the two countries.

The PPP system does have some weaknesses. One is that the PPP definition of a basket of goods and services is largely based on habits of consumption in developed countries (buying countries). Also, the PPP reflects overall consumption habits in a country and is not adjusted for the working class population. In short, the PPP-defined basket of goods has a bias towards developed country and middle class habits. The second weakness is that the basket used in the PPP calculation is not the same as that of the AFW. The AFW basket is a variable basket divided only into food and non-food (as a factor of food cost) items based on actual averages of working class food and non-food expenses. The third weakness in the PPP definition is that it is calculated at longer intervals and is not a current reflection. Despite these weaknesses, however, the PPP is the only relevant and stable measure reflecting consumption. If the weaknesses and biases explained above are corrected, the value of the AFW will only be pushed upward.

Thus, the current formulation of the AFW continues to be a conservative estimate for a minimum living wage. Any calculation of living wage has an element of subjectivity, since there can be differences about what expenses should be included. Additionally, the expenses to be included differ based on culture and social situation. But the AFW being conservative meets a minimal criterion put forward more than a hundred years ago, 'We can, at least, produce a limit below which it is wrong to go, while not committing ourselves to the conclusion that the limit is sufficiently high', (John Ryan, in 1906, quoted in Anker, 2011, p. 12).

4.9   Asia Floor Wage formula

The AFW, based on food costs for a family where an adult consumes 3,000 calories per day, was calculated in the local currencies of several Asian countries. This AFW in local currency was converted to PPP$ and the result was a comparable spectrum of values in PPP$. The AFW Alliance unions then discussed the spectrum of values and came to a consensus on AFW in PPP$ for the region. It was determined to be 475 PPP$ as of January 1, 2009, based on 2008 data. The report *Stitching A Decent Wage Across Borders* explains how the AFW was defined and calculated as a minimum living wage benchmark for several Asian countries (AFW, 2009). Naturally, this benchmark figure needs to be regularly adjusted

Table 4.1 Asian Floor Wage in local currency on the basis of PPP 2012–2013

Country name	PPP Conversion factor, 2011	Local currency figure for 540 PPP$, 2012	Local currency figure for 725 PPP$, 2013
Bangladesh	35.43	19,132	25,687
Cambodia	2,182.99	1,178,815	1,582,668
China	4.32	2,333	3,132
India	22.4	12,096	16,240
Indonesia	5,583.76	3,015,230	4,048,226
Malaysia	2.16	1,166	1,566
Nepal	39.11	21,119	28,355
Pakistan	36.38	19,645	26,376
Sri Lanka	63.68	34,387.2	46,168

Source: Asia Floor Wage Alliance, 2013.

Table 4.2 Living wage unit costs in US cents at 50 per cent efficiency using AFW wages

Bangladesh	0.50
China	0.76
India	0.48
Sri Lanka	0.48
Thailand	0.76
Indonesia	0.64

Source: Miller (2013), Table 5.

to account for the price rises in the cost of living (i.e., inflation). The AFW was revised to be 540 PPP$ for 2011.

4.10 Costing with AFW

As mentioned in other parts of this chapter, wage costs account for barely 1–3 per cent of final retail prices, while FOB prices are around 25 per cent of retail prices. What would be the cost difference to garments based on paying living wages? Miller (2013) calculates wage costs on the basis of AFW living wages at 50 per cent efficiency.

Based on this data, it is possible to calculate that, in Bangladesh, for example, the costs of shifting from 2012 wages to the AFW would be just between 1 and 3 per cent of the retail price (Miller, 2013, p. 15). If the cost of implementing an AFW wage-based costing is so low, then why has securing it been so problematic? In brief, the struggle pits trade unions and their supporters against a market-based solution to the wage question. In the age of neoliberal globalization, international and national policy makers accept that wages, as the price of labour power, should be set like the price of any other commodity on the market. Trade unions and other protagonists argue that labour is not a commodity like any other, and that its price should be taken out of the purview of market-based determination.

In the world of GVCs, what this means is that there is a double responsibility on both the buyer (retailer or brand) and supplier (developing country manufacturer). As the late trade unionist Neil Kearney put it, 'A sustainable system would see the employer being responsible for the payment of a living wage and the buyer being responsible for making the payment of a living wage a contractual obligation, paying prices that enable the supplier to fulfil that obligation, and supporting suppliers in bearing the risk of paying higher wages by providing greater stability in orders', (quoted in Miller, 2013, p. 1).

It should be noted here that fashion retailers are not engaged in any systematic costing of the labour input into garment manufacture (Miller, 2013). The imprecise clarification of 'labour minute values' and factory efficiency are significant factors in the chronic persistence of factory non-compliance on wages and overtime. It is possible to calculate labour minute values for any garment that also incorporates a living wage element. It is possible to determine and ring-fence the agreed labour cost and to make this an explicit part of the contractual obligation between the buyer and the supplier, in the same way that fabric is itemized in negotiations. Ring-fencing the labour cost would force brands and suppliers to address the issue of how a factory is operating, since the basic minimum wage would be the same regardless of factory efficiency. Of course, with fixed labour minute value, the pressure could then shift to reducing standard allowed minute.[2]

4.11 The right to a minimum living wage

The AFW is the practical implementation of the original ILO concept of a 'minimum living wage', which is an important qualitative concept, without a concrete quantitative definition. The AFW is intended to function as a quantitative definition of a minimum

---

[2] We owe this point to Doug Miller, personal communication.

living wage for garment workers in the global garment industry. The AFW campaign seeks to define and assert the right to a minimum living wage for garment workers and set a precedent for assertion of the right to a minimum living wage.

The AFW has several other social benefits, including that it will help decrease the gender pay gap by raising the floor. Worldwide, women form the vast majority of garment workers. They are over-represented among low-paid workers and their mobility to move into higher wage work is also lower. The AFW raises the value of women's work to a dignified level, demonstrating to female workers that they are worthy. In fact, some believe that the garment industry has such low wages because it employs predominantly women (unlike, say, the more male automobile industry). Workers work back-breaking overtime hours to earn a minimum living wage, while their family lives, health, and basic humanity are lost in the race. In addition, a new generation of children without parental care or education will only lead to more child labour. Raising workers out of poverty leads to sustainable communities where new generations can lead a better future.

The AFW affirms the principle that the only way to enforcement is through unions. AFW implementation requires the existence of a union, and is not a substitute for unionization. In so far as the AFW is a collective bargaining strategy, the right to 'effective recognition of collective bargaining' is essential, and efforts must be made to secure the necessary legal and institutional framework for this. The ILO makes explicit the link between collective bargaining and wage setting in its *Global Wage Report 2008/09*. It notes that 'higher coverage of collective bargaining ensures that wages are more responsive to economic growth, and also contributes to lower wage inequality'.

Indeed, collective bargaining is not simply a means to various welfare-related ends for workers, but a process by which they assert and realize their rights and expand the scope of their rights and of justice in society. In that it includes an assertion of the right to equal participation in social life and in the project of human development, the AFW can be understood as an essential mechanism for ensuring 'the continuous improvement of living conditions' as envisioned in the Universal Declaration of Human Rights.

4.12   Campaigning for the AFW

The AFW movement carried out an International Public Launch on October 7, 2009. The AFW Alliance wrote letters to almost 60 brands demanding meetings for the delivery of AFW. From 2009 onwards, the AFW Alliance has engaged in numerous debates and dialogues with brands and multi-stakeholder initiatives

(MSIs) and several meetings with the ILO and Global Union Federations (GUFs). Over 2 years, the AFW achieved international credibility and legitimacy and began to be used as a benchmark by some brands/MSIs and semi-government agencies just as it gained currency in ongoing discussions on labour issues world-wide.

The Asia Floor Wage bargaining process targets the brands, the principal employers of the buyer-driven global subcontracting commodity chain, in order to ensure decent wages for workers in the industry, since it is the buyers who exercise maximum influence on the way that production is organized. Central to the demands of the AFW, therefore, is the need for a concerted effort by brands and retailers to address the issue of unfair pricing, as an important first step towards the implementation of a living wage in the garment industry. The AFW is formulated based on the paying capacity of the global industry, whereas national wage definitions arise from an analysis of prevailing wages within the country. The proposed demand is an Asia Floor Wage for Asian garment workers in conjunction with fair pricing that would make Asia Floor Wage possible.

Labour cost is one of the most suppressed costs of production. Other factors of production include quality of infrastructure, access to raw materials, technology, energy, transportation, quality of management, legal systems, etc. Yet another factor in production costs is the purchasing practices of buyers that include lead time, quantity of order, advanced planning, etc. The AFW fixes the labour cost, which would reduce the tendency of both the industry and governments to compete solely on this human factor and make them focus their attention on other factors. This could push for more efficiency, higher productivity, and better production and sourcing systems. As Piore and Sabel (1994) pointed out, when wage competition is taken out of the picture, clusters become more competitive; on the other hand, clusters where wage competition prevails tend to lose competitiveness.

An initiative involving labour costing will require a high degree of transparency and openness between sourcing companies and their suppliers. Some buyers insist unilaterally that their suppliers 'open their books', during price negotiations, a practice which some observers see as naked power play in an attempt to drive prices down. In such circumstances, it is argued, suppliers have no other option but to hedge by distorting their figures. A more cooperative 'open book costing' will require integrity measures on the part of buyers such as price increases, long-term supply agreements, and the offer of productivity expertise where available. Buyers will also require an assurance that the additional amount of money identified as the living or sustainable wage element in excess of the current prevailing unit labour costs is reaching the workers. The AFW Alliance has shown a willingness to participate in helping brands to develop such mechanisms.

Since the Asia Floor Wage was made public on October 7, 2009, then, it has gained recognition as a credible benchmark for a living wage in the industry, in the garment labour movement, and in scholarly discussions. The AFW has become a point of reference for scholarly living wage debates such as by Anker (2011) and Vaughan-Whitehead (2010). Anker pointed out, 'The Asia Floor Wage Alliance is an important recent initiative that has breathed new life into interest in living wages' (2011, p. 38). It has been adopted as a living wage benchmark by the multi-stakeholder forum, the Fair Wear Foundation (2014), and serves as a point of reference for brand-level associations such as the Fair Labor Association. The German development organization GIZ has acclaimed the value of AFW. The AFW has been adopted by a few brands as a comparative benchmark for wage analysis; its credibility and feasibility continue to act as a pressure point. The Workers' Rights Consortium (2014) has used the AFW in a variety of ways in its analysis and benchmarking (e.g., analysis of Alta Gracia, Dominican Republic).

4.13 Bargaining

The AFW bargaining process targets the brands in order to ensure decent wages for workers in the industry. Brands and retailers' financial power is built through the garment global supply chain and sharing a negligible fraction of their profit could dramatically lift millions of workers and families out of poverty. The AFW Alliance has developed the Asia Brand Bargaining Group (ABBG) consisting of a number of Asian unions to enable greater coordination and regional bargaining that complements national priorities and struggles.

The ABBG has four common demands pertaining to the welfare of garment workers in Asia: living wage, freedom of association, abolition/regulation of contract labour, and an end to gender-based discrimination. The AFW Alliance has conducted three National People's Tribunals in India, Sri Lanka, and Cambodia on the issue of a living wage and working conditions in the garment global supply chain. Dozens of women workers have testified, and brands have been asked to testify as well to demonstrate what they have done to deliver a living wage. The jury verdicts that have emerged from these point to shocking deficits in decent labour standards and dangerously low wages. In Cambodia, for example, the mass fainting of women workers in the workplace was clearly attributed to malnutrition and poverty wages. The juries in all three tribunals have unanimously recommended that a living wage needs to be paid immediately and that any other activity of the TNCs (the most popular being further research to learn what is already well known) are only delaying tactics.

The Asia Floor Wage Alliance believes that the Asia Floor Wage must be implemented by brands that possess political and economic power in the global supply chain. A generalized pricing mechanism can be developed, taking into account the unit AFW labour cost of a garment in terms of both FOB and retail costs. AFW would fix the floor for the labour cost so that the FOB costs can be adjusted through other factors and the price agreed upon accordingly. The premise of Asia Floor Wage implementation requires freedom of association to be respected and for unionization to occur, since enforcement can only be done effectively with unions and worker representatives as part of the process. Therefore, the right to organize is central to the ultimate success of the Asia Floor Wage campaign. An AFW is possible only in the presence of dynamic workers' struggles. In fact, the AFW campaign converges national struggles into an Asian framework and so, complements and adds to the power of bargaining at national levels.

4.14 Conclusion: A step on a long road

Garment workers in Asia, the majority of whom are women, currently earn less than half of what they require to meet their own and their families' basic needs, such as for food, water, education, and health care. A recent calculation by the Clean Clothes Campaign gave the following percentages of prevailing minimum wages to the AFW—Bangladesh 19 percent; China 46 per cent; India 26 per cent; Cambodia 25 per cent; Indonesia 31 per cent; Malaysia 54 per cent; and Sri Lanka 19 per cent (Clean Clothes Campaign, 2014). Formulating the AFW and building an AFW Alliance are steps on the way to securing decent work for Asian garment workers.

The Asia Floor Wage concept and its PPP calculation are also important to taking the living wage issue beyond national boundaries. As capital globalizes its operations, workers, even in their struggles for improvements in wage and working conditions, also need to go beyond national boundaries, not just in terms of solidarity but in moving towards common goals. The AFW is one such common goal for workers in Asia. Although formulated with reference to garment workers, it is relevant to all workers in Asia. However, in order to be extended to other regions there would have to be some adjustments to what are considered basic living standards.

International Framework Agreements (IFAs) have so far been restricted to particular brands. The AFW Alliance seeks to go beyond that to secure labour rights across an industry in a region. Such a regional grouping is important to reduce wage-based competition among countries. Since Asia is the largest manufacturer of the world's garments, it is likely that a regional alliance for the AFW could have an effect on wages across the region. In this regard, the AFW demand and process is historic in that it is attempting to develop a global industrial collective bargaining framework for a wage increase for production workers within the garment global supply chain.

References

AFW (Asia Floor Wage). 2009. Stitching a decent wage across borders. Available at www.asiafloorwage.org.

Anker, Richard. 2011. 'Estimating a Living Wage: A Methodological Review.' *Working Paper*. Geneva: ILO.

Barrientos, Stephanie. 2007. 'Global Production Systems and Decent Work.' *Working Paper No. 77*, Policy Integration Department. Geneva: ILO.

Clean Clothes Campaign. 2014. 'Minimum Wage vs. Living Wage.' Available at, http://www.cleanclothes.org/livingwage/living-wage-versus-minimum-wage.

Evans, John, and Euan Gibb. 2009. *Moving from Precarious Employment to Decent Work*. Global Union Research Network, Discussion Paper No. 13. Geneva: ILO. Available at, http://www.gurn.info/en/discussion-papers.

Fair Wear Foundation. 2014. *Living Wage Engineering*. Available at, http://www.fairwear.org/ul/cms/fck-uploaded/documents/fwfpublications_reports/LivingWageEngineering20141.pdf, last accessed October 27, 2014.

Gereffi, Gary, and Olga Memedovic. 2003. *The Global Apparel Value Chain: What Prospects for Upgrading by Developing Countries*. Strategic Research and Economics Branch. Vienna: UNIDO.

Heintz, James. 2002. *Low-wage Manufacturing Exports, Job Creation, and Global Income Inequalities*. Working Paper Series. Amherst: Political Economy Research Institute.

ILO. 2010. *Global Wage Report 2010/11*. Geneva: ILO.

———. 2011. *Global Employment Trends 2011*. Geneva: ILO

———. 2013. *Global Wage Report 2012/13: Wages and Equitable Growth*. Geneva: ILO.

Miller, Doug. 2013. *Towards Sustainable Labour Costing in the UK Fashion Retail: Some Evidence from UK Fashion Retail*. Newcastle: Social Science Research Network, University of Northumbria at Newcastle.

———. 2013. 'Towards a Sustainable Labour Costing in UK Fashion Retail.' *Capturing the Gains Working Paper 14*. www.capturingthegains.org

Nathan, Dev, and Sandip Sarkar. 2014. 'Global Inequality, Rising Powers and Labour Standards.' *Oxford Development Studies*, January.

Ohmae, Kenichi. 1995. *The End of the Nation State: The Rise of Regional Economics*. New York: Harper Collins.

Patnaik, Utsa. 2007. *The Republic of Hunger and Other Essays*. New Delhi: Three Essays Collective.

Piore, Michael, and Charles Sabel. 1986. *The Second Industrial Divide: Possibilities for Prosperity*. New York: Basic Books.

Pollin, Robert, Mark Brenner, Stephanie Luce, and Jeanette Wicks-Lim. 2008. *A Measure of Fairness: The Economics of Living Wages and Minimum Wages in the United States*. Ithaca and London: Cornell University Press.

Ramaswamy, Krishnarajapet V. 2003. *Globalization and Industrial Labor Markets in South Asia: Some Aspects of Adjustment in a Less Integrated Region*. East West Center Working Papers No. 54 (April) Honolulu: East-West Center.

de Regil, Álvaro J. 2010. 'A Comparative Approximation into China's Living-wage Gap.' The Jus Semper Global Alliance. Available at, http://www.jussemper.org.

Rural Survey Organization. 2004. *Poverty Statistics in China*. Beijing: National Bureau of Statistics.

SPN - GARTEKS SBSI SBSI, AKATIGA, FES - TWARO. 2009. 'Living Wage in Textile and Garment Industries in Indonesia.' Available at, http://www.fes.or.id/fes/download/Survey_Result_Indonesia.pdf.

Vaughan-Whitehead, Daniel. 2010. *Fair Wages: Strengthening Corporate Social Responsibility*. Cheltenham and Northampton, MA: Edward Elgar.

Workers' Rights Consortium. 2014. 'WRC Labor Rights Verification and *Alta Gracia* Apparel.' Available at, http://www.workersrights.org/verification/index.asp, accessed on October 27, 2014.

5

Fresh Produce Markets, Standards, and Dynamics of Labour

Grapes in India

Sukhpal Singh

5.1 Introduction

Fresh fruits and vegetables (FFVs) are part of the fresh produce consumption story that began in the 1970s in the Western world as opposed to canned or frozen fruits and vegetables. They are also available year-round in the consuming markets due to global sourcing. Further, they are a 'luxury crop', meaning they are destined for upmarket consumers who place an emphasis on quality, not bulk (Collins, 2000). Fresh produce markets are changing rapidly due to the new quality standards that range from global trade-related compliances like the Sanitary and Phyto-Sanitary Measures (SPSMs) of the World Trade Organization (WTO) to collective standards like Global Good Agricultural Practices (GlobalGAP)[1], to private standards of individual buyers like

---

[1] The original version of GlobalGAP—the EurepGAP (Euro retailers produce working group Good Agricultural Practices) put together in 1997 and made into Eurepgap in 1999 covered only pre-farm gate practices pertaining to fresh produce and required third-party certification. Renamed in September 2007 as GlobalGAP, it has codes regarding consumer food safety, hygiene, labour conditions, animal welfare as well as environmental management on the farm land. Starting with FFVs, now it covers aquaculture and livestock and by September 2008, it embraced 80 countries, 92,000 certified growers, and 100 independent accredited certification bodies across the globe. It has inspired other regional and national GAPs like Chilegap and Mexicogap. By September 2008, 14 countries had aligned their GAP to the GlobalGAP. There are major and minor musts at the all farm level (45), crop-base level (120), and specific product group level (71), to which compliance is required. These altogether totalled to 74 major musts, 125 minor musts, and 37 recommended control points, making a total of 236 in September 2007. There were 34 major and 28 minor musts besides 9 recommended control points in fruits and vegetables alone, making a total of 71 points (Amekawa, 2009). By 2007, there were 250 GlobalGAP members including 31 retailers/food service providers, 111 suppliers, and 108 associate members (Bain, 2010).

Tesco's Nature's Choice and the codes of conduct (CoC)[2] of various types including Ethical Trading Initiative (ETI)[3]. New markets have different product standards. For instance, both the domestic Indian and the Middle Eastern markets do not have the GlobalGAP standard requirements that the European Union (EU) markets have. This is leading to the production of new crops and the introduction of new farming practices in the developing world. New crops interface with existing land and labour relations, which influence and are in turn influenced by such interventions. New sourcing practices lead to a new just-in-space production configuration (Fold, 2008). As the exports of Indian grape production rose, and as exports of Indian grapes shifted from the commoditized markets of the Middle East to the quality product markets of the EU, the role of GlobalGAP standards in Indian grape production has also increased.

In this context, we examine how organizational and institutional changes impact labour in the context of the Global Production Network (GPN) of a developing economy export crop and how local labour regimes influence labour governance and upgrading. We also look at the nature of labour linkage in GPNs, in terms of labour conditions at work both in pack houses and farms, as well as the gender dimensions of labour use. The shift from a commoditized to a quality product market is what is termed economic upgrading[4] (Barrientos et al., 2011). The key question in this paper, then, is: was this economic upgrading accompanied by social upgrading[5], meaning an improvement in the conditions of workers in the GlobalGAP-organized GPN as compared to those in the commoditized production of grapes? If so, why? The related aspects of this research question explored in the paper are: Are there differences in the way labour requirements differ across GPN-driven high-quality export markets

---

[2] These include Ethical Trading Initiative (ETI), ILO's labour code, Fair Trade, Organic, Common Code for the Coffee Community (4C), and Rainforest Alliance and many other multi-stakeholder initiatives like Social Accountability International (US), Clean Clothes Campaign (Netherlands), Workers well as enviroium (US), Fearwear Foundation (Netherlands), Fair Labor Association (US). Better Cotton or Responsible soy production (Muradian and Peluepsy, 2005 and Lund-Thomsen, 2008).

[3] ETI focuses on helping to make substantial improvements to the lives of poor working people around the world and requires the buying companies to bring their supply chains into compliance with ETIs base code which draws on ILOs standards for among other things, working conditions, wage levels, and child labour (Friedberg, 2003).

[4] Economic upgrading refers to capabilities of players within a chain to move to higher value-added activities in production, to improve technology, knowledge and skills, and to increase the benefits or profits deriving from participation in GPNs. It could be product, process, functional, or inter-sectoral or inter-chain upgrading or entire value chain shift (Barrientos et al., 2011).

[5] Social upgrading refers to the process of improvements in the rights and entitlements of workers as social actors, which enhances the quality of their employment. This includes access to better work, better working conditions, social protection, and worker rights (Barrientos et al., 2011).

and domestic-cum-commoditized export markets due to global quality and social standards? What are the gender aspects of labour dynamics in export grape production and processing? How do the skills and expertise of workers matter for quality and therefore affect worker bargaining power within the grape GPN? Finally, how do hiring practices differ between production for commoditized and quality product markets and what are the implications of this for worker upgrading and livelihood improvement?

The chapter draws on primary case studies of GlobalGAP-certified export grape production facilities in western India. The chapter is organized as follows: the next section locates the research questions in an analytical framework drawn from GPN literature. This is followed by a description of the context and research methodology in Section 5.3. Section 5.4 examines the labour dynamics of grape GPNs, including the differences between export and domestic markets, the impact of gender on work and wages, and worker interface in farms and pack houses. It also explores the dynamics of local processes of hiring and sustaining the labour loop, as well as evidence of social upgrading. Section 5.5 concludes the chapter with an examination of the implications for local labour in high value GPNs.

5.2   Analytical framework

The global value chain (GVC) and the global production network (GPN) are the two very influential frameworks within which global trade and development issues may be understood. The GVC analysis focuses on the commercial dynamics between and among firms in different segments of the production chain and examines value creation, differentiation, and value capture in the entire process of production, distribution, and retail (Barrientos et al., 2011). The GPN differs from GVC in that it incorporates 'all kinds of network configuration' and 'all relevant sets of actors and relationships' including labour (Selwyn, 2012). This is important in understanding the processes of upgrading and downgrading of products, processes, and functions for various stakeholders, especially smaller firms, producers, and workers. The literature around GPNs places more emphasis on the institutional or social context of interconnected commercial operations. GPN analysis examines not only the interaction between lead firms and suppliers, but also the whole range of actors that contribute to influencing and shaping global production, such as national governments, multilateral organizations, international trade unions, and non-governmental organizations (NGOs). A GPN approach also emphasizes the social and institutional embeddedness of production, and power relations between actors, which vary as sourcing is spread across multiple developing countries (Barrientos et al., 2011).

The GPN framework allows us to understand how the various actors involved in the production, distribution, and marketing of a product are interrelated and networked even though they may be geographically dispersed over long distances. Further, the framework facilitates the analysis of power relations within GPNs by showing which actors make strategic decisions and which actors have to respond to them (Henderson et al., 2002; Coe et al., 2004; Selwyn, 2007). The labour aspects of a chain/network have often been excluded from the analysis in the past, as these chains/networks often ended at the level of primary producers, i.e., farmers. There are only a few studies located in African and Latin American contexts that have tried to understand labour issues in such networks (Collins, 2000; Dolan and Sutherland, 2002; Barrientos and Kritzinger, 2004). More generally, GVC/network analysis has found it difficult to incorporate class relations into the argument (Barrientos et al., 2011; Selwyn, 2012).

The local operations of value chains/GPNs are tied to sourcing practices and reflect new patterns of rural transformation within privately regulated territories. Even when these value chains are driven by global supermarkets or transnational corporations (TNCs), value chain specificities are still conditioned by the nature of the crops or produce procured at a local level. However, it has been argued that value chain analysis, by focusing on governance and upgrading, neglects the issue of 'space' or territoriality as well as the institutional context. These are better addressed in the GPN framework, wherein the various actors shaping GPN dynamics are anchored in different places and on multiple scales. This creates an explicit link between a given GPN and regional or local development (Fold, 2008).

Further, 'value' needs to be understood not just in terms of creation, enhancement, capture, and upgrading within a GPN, but also in terms of the impact on local areas and communities within the production network. Focusing on the local enables the formulation of national and regional policies based on an analysis of the structure and dynamics of a GPN located within a national territory. Though agro-ecological reasons limit their ability to relocate spaces of production, buyers can still influence, change, or expand these spaces through capital mobility and technological, institutional, and organizational innovations and improvements (Fold, 2008). New crop varieties and processing technologies are the keys to such changes and expansions, in addition to models of procurement like contract farming or out-grower schemes, as they change market preferences and competitive positioning, which, in turn, change production or procurement sources.

Countries, regions, or sub-regions that produce the same product or commodity for the same market may have quite different development trajectories, depending on their local class relations, social structures, and labour dynamics. These factors can influence the operation of a GPN through workers' structural (marketplace and workplace bargaining power) and associational (workers' collective organizational) power (Selwyn, 2012). To understand labour processes and outcomes, therefore, it is important to examine local actors and factors like state-as-regulator, class relations (including caste in countries like India), labour unions, and bargaining power within GPNs (Goto, 2011; Selwyn, 2012).

Governance, or the non-market co-ordination of economic activities, refers to the phenomenon of key actors in the chain determining the inter-firm division of labour and shaping the capacities of participants to upgrade their activities (Gereffi, 2001). This includes defining the products, processes, and standards for suppliers (Gibbon, 2001). Chains differ significantly with respect to how strongly governance is exercised, how concentrated it is in the hands of a single firm and how many lead firms exercise governance over chain members (Gereffi et al., 2001). Governance can be public, private, or collective in terms of actors; facilitative, regulatory, or distributive in terms of impact; and local, national, regional, or global in terms of its domain (Mayer and Pickles, 2010). Governance also deals with the setting of standards, whether of products, production processes, or labour conditions, and their monitoring and compliance in GPNs.

Labour is a crucial input and wages is an important cost in horticulture. Harvest costs often account for half of the total production costs of fruit crops in export-oriented production systems (Rogaly, 2008) as the harvest season is often short and demands a large number of labourers for various harvest-related activities, including grading and packing produce according to international specifications like GlobalGAP. The involvement of labour is expensive and brings with it a host of other concerns. Farmers often seek to manage costs by resorting to employing women workers, who are both cheaper and more efficient—the latter in terms of the 'nimble fingers' argument. Since women have lower opportunity costs, they are paid less than men; women also do not unionize and are considered more honest (Collins, 2000).

In addition, the existence of specifications like GlobalGAP requires the careful monitoring of harvesters to ensure quality and often leads to grower strategies of incentives and innovations in farm practices. It also raises questions about the relevance of piece-rate contracts, which reward quantity and quality of work without any supervision and shirking, but can also lead to careless performance that might be costlier in the long run. Piece-rate contracts also can be problematic when new productivity enhancing technology is introduced, since it would lead to the downward adjustment of rates and potentially cause walkouts and decrease workforce morale (Ortiz and Apraicio, 2006).

The increasing use of labour contractors (also called labour agents, quasi-labour agents or ad-hoc labour contractors in different contexts) in GPNs is another important issue (Barrientos, 2013). Labour contractors can be kinsmen who belong to the worker community but recruit for a farmer and may be involved in recruiting and supplying local, national, or international migrant labour. They may start as workmen, become supervisors, and may eventually be charged with recruiting workers. They are paid by farmers and are not engaged in protecting labour interests. Rather, they often engage in exploitative labour practices and take advantage of the weak bargaining position of those they recruit (Ortiz, 2002; Barrientos, 2013). Labour contractors aid growers in tapping vulnerable labour pools, cheapening wages, reducing recruitment costs, and assuming responsibility for organizing and supervising tasks. But labour contractors are not always preferred, especially by growers whose crops must adhere to high-quality requirements for final markets; growers might choose to avoid them because of the associated risks and costs (Ortiz, 2002).

The gender dimension of labour hiring and use is rooted in the local meanings of women's work. Women are perceived to be residual labour, worth much less than male labour (Ortiz, 2002). Even at the bottom of the GPN, i.e., in farms and pack houses, tasks and wages are gendered, with low-wage, jobs perceived as low-skill being given to women. They receive few non-wage benefits or social protection and CoC apply to them inadequately (Dolan, 2004). There are numerous reasons for this: the pressure of price competition that squeezes exporters' profits, the prevalence of just-in-time production aimed at reducing inventories, demand for new products, and category management at the supermarket level. Thus, workers' gender and ethnic backgrounds may be used to categorize them as lower cost and more efficient in performing many crucial tasks like grading and packing.

It is also argued that the workers are an important group on whom the producers of fruits can offload some of the risk, especially on to seasonal and flexible workers, the category in which the largest number of women are employed (Barrientos, 2001). However, growing demands on producers for cost effectiveness and quality produce (both tangible and intangible, i.e., in terms of the processes and social aspects of production) may lead to a demand for more regular and skilled labour rather than casual and flexible labour (Selwyn, 2009). In addition, supermarket export linkage has led to new process and quality requirements that have given workers structural power, as even short work stoppages could disrupt the entire harvest calendar and prevent farms from producing export quality fruits. Thus, the labour dimensions of GPNs in local regions and economies include issues of gender, intermediaries, local livelihood options and the pressures of quality, alongside the casualization of labour and structural and associational power of workers within the GPN.

5.3 Context and methodology

5.3.1 Context of grape production

Grapes were chosen for this study as the export of grapes is one of the most significant success stories of high value export that adheres to standards like GlobalGAP and other company/supermarket-specific compliances discussed earlier. There are few other fresh agricultural products from India that are grown to global standards and exported in such large volumes to standards-driven markets. The commercial production of grapes in India began only after seedless varieties were introduced in the 1960s in Maharashtra. India has the highest yield of grapes among the 91 major grape-producing countries. Grapes began to be exported in 1991, forming 2.3 per cent of fruit exports in 1999–2000 (Sharma and Jain, 2011). Their share rose to 9.1 per cent of all fruit and nut exports in 2010–2011. The compound annual growth rate in grape export was 14.4 and 17.8 per cent in volume and value terms between 1993–1994 and 2010–2011, respectively, which reflects higher and higher prices being realized at least in nominal terms (based on APEDA data for the period). Grape export volumes doubled and the value of exports tripled (nominal prices) between 2005–06 and 2011–12 (APEDA, 2013).

Though Indian grapes were exported to more than 65 countries during 2008–2009 to 2010–2011, four countries (the Netherlands, Bangladesh, the United Arab Emirates (UAE), and the United Kingdom (UK)) accounted for 80 per cent of the volume of Indian exports and 67–80 per cent of value during the period 2008–2009 to 2010–2011. The Netherlands and the UK (the third-largest grape importer in the world) are quality product markets, where grapes are labelled by the country of origin and according to GlobalGAP standards. On the other hand, Bangladesh and the UAE are commoditized markets (APEDA, 2013). The export market for grapes from India moved from the Gulf countries which accounted for 86 per cent of all grape exports from India in early 1990s to the European markets which came to account for 60 per cent by late 1990s from only 2.5 per cent during the early 1990s (Rath, 2003). This was the shift from commoditized markets to quality product markets the impact of which on labour dynamics is examined in this paper.

For grape exports to commoditized markets, there are no Maximum Residue Limits (MRL) restrictions or GlobalGAP certification requirements. In contrast, for grape exports to quality markets within the EU, both public and private standards normally apply. In relation to public/trade standards, it is essential that fresh table grapes are graded according to the AGMARK standards set by the Department of Marketing and Inspection (DMI) of the Ministry of Agriculture,

Government of India. Only those farmers registered with the Agricultural and Processed Food Export Development Authority (APEDA), which regulates the quality of exports, are allowed to export their produce. This is to ensure that exports to various countries that follow EU food safety norms do not contain chemical residue in excess of the prescribed levels under GlobalGAP which is a private collective standard. The farmers/growers/exporters and any other stakeholders have to comply with the EU MRLs. Compliance with EU regulations on grade, quality, safety, and wholesomeness of fresh table grapes, pre- and post-harvest practices, quarantine, packing, fumigation, certification for wooden pallets, sanitary and phytosanitary measures or any other requirements is the responsibility of the farmers, growers, exporters, and other stakeholders involved in the production of grapes for export.

Pesticide residue was the major reason for grapes being rejected for export to the EU in the 1990s. This was followed by berry size and price. This led to a change in the way production was organized/managed for export markets at the grower level. Rather than individual farmers, it was higher-level organizations-co-operatives, or export companies who took over the tasks of achieving and maintaining compliance with the required standards. The percentage of growers who were part of a collective effort, i.e., a co-operative, informal group, or export company/agency, went up substantially from 5 per cent in 1998 to 19 per cent in 2008. The cost of compliance to standards is up to 10–20 per cent of total costs in most cases, and even up to 20–50 per cent in some cases (Shankar, 2012).

The state of Maharashtra, where this paper's study is located, accounts for 80–90 per cent of India's grape exports in volume and value (Shankar, 2012) and 85 per cent of India's wine grape production. Maharashtra also accounts for 90 per cent of all APEDA recognized pack houses in India. More than two-thirds of all grapes are grown in Nashik district alone (Bhosale, 2001), which makes Nashik district the largest producer of grapes in India with nearly 0.175 million acres under vineyards out of the total grape acreage in Maharashtra of 0.25 million acres. Around 70 per cent of the state's grape exports come from Nashik as it has 75 per cent of the grape farms registered for export in the state (Shankar, 2012). Given Nashik's importance in export grape production, it was an obvious choice as the site of field investigation.

5.3.2 Research methodology

This paper is based on a case study of the grape GPN in Maharashtra carried out in 2012. The study involved key informant interviews to map the export grape value chain, followed by primary interviews with grape farmers, farm workers, harvest workers, and pack house workers from the region. All the major stakeholders in the grape GPN including supermarkets, importers based in EU markets, exporters, and facilitators were interviewed as part of the GPN mapping process, and farmers and workers of various types were interviewed at length during the following fieldwork for the study. Interviews were also conducted with the chief executives of exporting firms, their production and procurement managers, service providers (including pack house and harvest management agencies), farmers supplying to these exporters and farm, harvest and pack house workers. The pack house workers and harvesting workers belonged to the villages (Sakora, Pimplegaon, Mohadi) in Niphad and Dhindhori talukas (sub-districts) of Nashik district. These two talukas accounted for 78 per cent of the area under grapes and 80 per cent of production of grapes in Nashik district (Shankar, 2012). The non-harvesting grape farm workers were also mostly local from villages in Nashik district, with only permanent migrant workers (from other districts) staying on the farms. Table 5.1 provides details of the number of respondents, both farmers and workers, across various categories. Our evidence also comes from field visits to production and packing sites, observation and interaction with various stakeholders, besides some supplementary secondary information.

Table 5.1 Number of farmers, farm workers, harvesting workers and pack house workers interviewed in the grape GPN

Farmers	Non-harvest workers		Harvest workers		Pack house workers		All workers		Total workers
	Men	Women	Men	Women[#]	Men	Women	Men	Women	
25	12	8	22	-	11	14	45	22	67

[#]There are no women harvest workers in grape production, as harvesting is undertaken solely by male workers.

5.4 Labour dynamics in the grape GPN

There are over 10,000 grape growers in Nashik district most of whom were located in two sub-districts of Niphad and Dhinodri (as mentioned above). They were all registered with APEDA for growing export quality produce, though all of them did not necessarily export. This could be on account of being unable to afford the inputs needed, due to the lack of access to finance, lack of a suitable market or price, or failure to meet standards (Shankar, 2012). In Maharashtra, about 15,000 farmers registered for export every year between 2006 and 2012, though the number went up to 22,000 in 2013 due to better export market prospects. In comparison, both Brazil and South Africa, India's competitors in grape exports to the EU, have a fraction of the number of farms and registered exporters (Trienekens and Willems, 2007; Selwyn, 2009). India has an advantage over these two countries, as the Indian grape harvest occurs in a window when few grapes are harvested anywhere else in the world.

In India, there are large individual grower-exporters and organized grower-exporters (through grape growers' co-operatives and their marketing company, and primary marketing organizations (PMOs) under the GlobalGAP certification standards for smallholder groups). Further, most of the exporters do not export directly but are suppliers to wholesalers and food retail supermarkets who actually sell these grapes in those markets. For example, each supermarket in the UK has a few suppliers of grapes from different countries including India to meet market demand in different seasons of the year. In supermarkets, these grapes are sold under the brand name of the supermarket, but the details of the supplying company/ exporter (including small-scale suppliers) may be mentioned, in order to maintain traceability.

Attaining public quality parameters in grape production is critical for export. These take the following attributes into account: bunch size (oblong or conical), berry size, colour, shape, weight of bunch, firmness, sugar content (total soluble solids) acidity, bruises, spots, flavour, odour or taste, packing of berries, pesticide or chemical residue, stem colour, berry shrivelling, berry splitting, damage due to post-harvest water loss, pest damage, wasted or shattered berries, chill damage, temperature, taints, packing quality and average check weight (field research interviews; Collins, 2000; Bhosale, 2001; Roy and Thorat, 2008). The produce quality is checked when it is harvested, in the pack house, and at the time of final dispatch. The Package of Practices (PoPs) recommendations include chemical residue monitoring and lab tests for plant growth promoters.

Fifty per cent of the case study PMO exporter's farms were also compliant for standards of German supermarkets like Metro, Aldi, and NettoPass. The farms and pack houses were also ETI code compliant for legal minimum wages. The exporter also supplied to Asda (now part of Wal-Mart) and Coop supermarkets in the UK. The farms were monitored by 17 quality and procurement staff varying from 10 in Nashik, 5 in Sangali, to 2 in Latur. The pack houses leased for three years were GlobalGAP certified.

At the time of research, a GlobalGAP audit cost Rs. 0.25 million (US$ 4500) per hectare and farmers had to spend Rs. 50,000 (US$ 900) on an average to become GlobalGAP compliant. GlobalGAP certification involves maintaining records of production and input used for each registered grower for each plot in a GlobalGAP record register that must be maintained by each farmer. It includes details of PMO policy on the rational use of plant protection products, the reduction of plant protection products, and chemical fertilizers by 5 per cent through integrated pest management (IPM), adhering to economic threshold limits (ETLs) for pest control and the use of bio/organic manures. It even targets noise pollution on the farm by machines and environmental measures like avoiding killing snakes on the farms and providing drinking water in pots for birds. It has instructions on harvested produce safety and the maintenance of hygiene on the farms and in pack houses. Other conditions for certification include the health and safety of workers at farms, living wage or minimum wages and legal working hours, no child labour on farms and in pack houses, the reduction, reuse and recycling of waste and efficient water management through micro-irrigation. On an average, about 5 per cent of samples failed. Rejected produce could be sold to countries such as the UAE, and Bangladesh which did not demand GlobalGAP certification, and in the Indian local market.

Policy and the state agencies have played a major role in setting up the export grape GPN since as early as the 1990s, when grapes were beginning to be exported as well as when the liberalization of Indian economy occurred. This was also the time when the grape co-operatives were set up. This was further supported by state agencies in the late 1990s when Mahagrapes, a business entity of grape co-operatives under public–private partnership, was set up with support from APEDA, the state Agricultural Marketing Board and the National Co-operative Development Corporation (NCDC). Finally, APEDA stepped in to ensure quality compliance and the adherence to standards. The provision of labs to test chemical residue and subsidies for sample testing for exports are some examples of direct support given to the GPN, besides the roping in of the agricultural research and extension system for monitoring and farmer handholding.

The grape GPN involves multiple stakeholders like rootstock suppliers, farm input and technology companies, R&D centres and agencies, banks, certification agencies, labour contractors, transporters, and state agencies that provide incentives and subsidies, besides those directly involved in growing and exporting, who come together to produce GlobalGAP compliant grapes for export, and it is driven by global buyers. State agencies have played a major role in getting the grape GPN going by enabling production that adheres to standards. But the state seems to be missing from the scene as far as labour standards are concerned. The state interventions were not directly targeted at workers, but more at grape farmers and exporters.

Though there is a prevalence of more informal, flexible market-based exchanges between supermarket buyers and farmers in domestic fresh produce networks, export market buyers prefer more formal contracts with growers, due to the quantity and quality commitment required in fresh produce like export grapes.

The farmer and the pack house interface of the PMO and other exporters is managed by third-party operators. For example, one of the case study service providers (EA) manages harvesting and packing for the export firm that was part of this case study. Grape harvesting and packing is a part-time business for the person who runs the service providing agency, since his services are only required during the harvest season. The number of services offered includes surveying grape farms, scheduling harvests, grading and packing the fruit as well as their pre-cooling, cold storage, and containerization. The latter activities take place in a pack house that is leased for the season from a local owner. Most of the pack house labour force had worked with the service provider for the past 3–4 years. The grape pack houses employ about 30,000 workers across India during the harvest season, with the overwhelming majority (80 per cent) of workers being women. The pack houses operate from early February to the middle of April. A typical pack house operator in Nashik employed 200 harvesting and packing workers and 10 supervisors. In general, the service provider who runs the pack house manages harvesting and packing labour for the export firm, which monitors wages and labour conditions and provides training to workers through videos on harvesting and packing.

The service providers as third parties are the real drivers of local systems for export production, as they belong to local areas and leverage their networks for labour recruitment, supply, and labour management. Service providers often work with multiple firms, and lease a number of pack houses to fulfil the demands of the market. Export companies have minimal contact with farmers, only to the extent needed to fulfil certification system requirements, i.e., smallholder group certification and traceability requirements. In 1992, there were only a few pack houses and a few service providers. In 2012, there were more than 80 pack houses and 25 service providers. This jump in numbers can be attributed to the growth of quality export market opportunities as total production of grapes did not grow that much.

Labour organizers or contractors supply workers on the basis of a piece rate that is agreed upon in advance with service providers, but the latter also often recruit and hire the labour themselves. In the case of service providers, who also act as labour recruiters and suppliers, there have been instances of firms being shelved after they were discovered to have violated labour regulations. One service provider agreed that companies like his also violate labour laws, though that could cause trouble if they were ever caught.

Labour is an important factor in grape production but much more so in export grape production, which is highly labour intensive in both harvesting and packing and requires skill. The labour intensity of grapes is as high as 1500 person-days per hectare, including farm labour, labour supervisors, and skilled labour, as there is no technology that could reduce labour intensity in grape harvesting. Six workers are required for work on an acre of grapes for export for 20 days spread over the season; a worker engaged full-time in grape work gets 160 days of employment in a year. On the significance of labour in general and skilled labour in particular, Rath (2003 p. 481) remarks: 'They (workers) form the fulcrum on which the entire enterprise is balanced … The enterprise of implementing new vine and bunch treatment techniques would have failed but for the existence of this skilled pool of labour. There would have been no big bunches with big grapes to export'.

There is generally no overlap between export and domestic market growers, though growers might shift between these markets over time and rejected/ low-quality produce is usually earmarked for the domestic market. More recently, it has been seen that some farmers have withdrawn from export market as the domestic market is becoming equally or even more lucrative.

There are substantial differences in the various farm and off-farm activities involved in commoditized and quality export market grape handling. Production involves activities like the pruning of vines (twice a year), tilling, fertilizing, trimming non-productive branches, monitoring blemishes and diseases and applying pesticides, selecting the best bunches on each branch and culling the rest, trimming the bunches to quality export size, harvesting, grading and packing. Labour processes differ in terms of activities required in harvesting and packing depending on whether produce is meant for export (quality) or domestic (commoditized) market. This difference in production processes based on whether the produce is intended for export or domestic use has also been observed in other grape contexts like Brazil, where grapes meant for export involved 34 operations per harvest cycle compared with just 9 for the domestic market (Selwyn, 2012).

All of the quality parameters and tasks listed above influence the work regimes on farms and during the harvest. For instance, the processes of thinning (of each bunch with scissors) and dipping (into a solution of chemicals to fatten berries) that help produce large bunches with large grape berries for the EU market are very labour intensive and need care. The need for thinning and dipping as part of the export grape production process increases the employment opportunities for workers on farms; they are also highly skilful operations and determine the tonnage, reject ratio, and value of the produce, depending on how timely and how well they are carried out (Rath, 2003). These two processes are optional for commoditized markets as size is not an issue. Another example is that grapes meant for the domestic market are graded and packed on the farms by local workers composed of men and women. The fruits are sent by truck in crates after being graded and wrapped in paper. No retail packing is done and they are still in loose form. This reduces the number of activities undertaken by workers in grading and packing.

The quality grape production GPN is therefore both more skill and more labour intensive than in the case of commoditized grape production. The differences between labour employed on export quality and commoditized products can be summarized in relation to growing, harvesting, and packing. Quality production requires higher skills and provides more days of employment. This has implications for labour recruitment and retention, which is examined in the following subsection.

5.4.1   Labour recruitment and retention

Grape farms in India rely on two kinds of labour: regular farm labour and harvest labour, with local permanent and migrant workers forming part of both workforces. Local labour is rarely used for skilled work like vine or bunch treatment. Farmers directly employ local labour for harvesting only for the domestic market, as the harvesting of crops intended for export is undertaken by the buying party's service provider. The service provider hires workers from neighbouring villages through a labour leader (who is paid Rs. 50 (US$ 1) more per day than the workers he recruits). The service provider studied for this paper employed an entirely male harvest workforce, and the crop of a farm was harvested in 4–5 days, with work hours running from 4 a.m. to 12 noon. The workforce recruited was mainly local (within a radius of 25 km). Workers were given on-the-job training for specialized activities like plucking and bunch identification, and there were export firm's inspectors who monitored these tasks besides the labour contractor who monitored the harvest labour.

Regular farm labour is undertaken by locals and sometimes also by migrant workers. Most of the individual activities on the farm are done by contract labour in a group. The *toli* or group leaders organize the group: they monitor work, communicate with farmers on work schedules, and manage the payment of wages. They do not receive any payment for these duties, but the position offers social status and political respect. Our field investigations did not reveal any complaints about group leaders taking kick-backs from group members. Workers who are classified as contract migrant labour live on the farms in accommodation provided by farmers during the fruiting and harvesting season (September to May). They either worked on contract for the entire season, mainly from the October (or April) pruning period to just before the harvest, or had activity-specific contracts. The contract rate for an entire season ranged from Rs. 42,000 (US$ 750) per hectare (from October pruning to harvest) to Rs. 72,000 (US$ 1250) per hectare (April pruning to harvest). The group or *toli* leader visited the farm before the onset of the grape season and fixed the wages, and the other terms and conditions with the grower of the crop. Usually, farmers paid 10–15 per cent of the fixed contract amount in advance before the start of the season to avoid non-availability of labour during the peak season.

Migrant workers engaged in non-harvest labour carried out all production operations including April pruning, auxiliary bud removal, sub-caning, pinching, removing failed shoots, dipping, thinning, girdling, paper wrapping and so on, and had flexible work hours. Farmers try to retain the same labour groups over the years as finding good replacements is not easy, especially for critical grape work tasks like pruning, GA (chemical) treatment, thinning, and harvesting, which require skill and experience. There are groups of workers, including some from the neighbouring state of Gujarat, who carry out this work on a contract basis or job-work basis. Farmers use the provision of facilities like accommodation, water, electricity, and free medicines to attract these workers (Bhosale, 2001). Typically, 60 per cent of the on-farm workforce is regular, while the rest is made up of floating labour.

The pack house service provider does not train fresh recruits as workers and prefers to hire those who would have worked in other pack houses. In 2005–2006, EA had only 30 harvest workers but this increased to 60 in 2012, while the number of pack house workers increased from 60 to 190, with women consistently making up two-thirds of the workforce, as the quantity of grapes handled for export also increased manifold. The number of supervisors, both male and female, also increased from only 2–3 in total to 5 men and 5 women each. Permanent employees made up 20 per cent of the workforce in 2005–2006, and this was 35 per cent in 2012, in the case of male employees, but 20 per cent in the case of female employees, since many women move away after marriage.

Due to the skills and efficiency required to maintain quality, the profile of export grape handling workers, especially those in harvesting, was different from those handling commoditized production. Harvest workers were younger on average (about 28 years) than non-harvest workers (men: 31 years and women: about 28 years). There were even younger (up to 17 years) women in grape work than young men. Two-thirds of harvest workers reported being married, as against 75–83 per cent of non-harvest workers. The average number of years of schooling was higher for harvest workers (6.1 years) than non-harvest workers (5.5 years for men and 4.87 for women). Harvest workers had been in farm work for 9.29 years on average and for 4.09 years in harvest work alone, with 45 per cent having been engaged in harvest work for 4–6 years. Among non-harvest workers, these numbers were 10.2 and 12.7 years for men and women in farm work, and 9.8 and 8 years in grape-related work for men and women, respectively. Since grapes for export became a phenomenon only a few years ago, the average experience is lower than in the case of other grape workers. Most harvest workers also engaged in casual labour in non-grape season.

Both harvesting and other grape farm workers came from similar backgrounds and showed similar occupational diversity in their families. On average, 85 per cent of the worker families in areas that supplied labour had at least one worker engaged in grape work. While non-harvest workers were employed under a variety of arrangements, including task contracts, harvest workers were all local and worked for a daily wage.

Pack house workers were, on an average, not very different from the harvest workers in age (women: 32.64 years and men: 26.27 years) and were mostly married (80 per cent of women and 70 per cent of men). They were somewhat better schooled, especially the men, who had an average of 7.5 years of schooling, while 40 per cent of women were illiterate, despite an average 4.9 years of schooling. Generally, women workers had done farm work for an average of 14 years and pack house work for as many as 6 years with the majority having had 4–9 years of experience. In comparison, male workers had 6 years of farm work experience, 3 years of pack house work, with the majority having been engaged in either type of work for less than 3 years.

Both female and male pack house workers had been attracted to the work because it offered better wages, extra income for their families and transportation to and from work, and it was better quality work. Fixed working hours, safety and proximity to their homes also factored into workers' choice to continue working at pack houses, especially for women workers. The above figures show that retention of women is higher despite their not being permanent workers as they are more confined to their local surroundings unlike men who could move further away for better employment. The daily pick up and drop facility for women workers led to their being dominant category of workers in pack houses, among other factors.

Thus, the pack house labour and harvesting labour that are exclusive to export grape production were more educated and younger though they came from similar social backgrounds as the on farm workers. This requires workers to be given various facilities to meet the standards as well as to retain them for next season. In fact, grapes destined for domestic and commoditized export market were graded and packed at the farm level itself without any use of pack house or such workers.

5.4.2 Gendering of tasks and wages in grape work

In terms of work on grape farms, while men mostly worked on grafting, pruning, and girdling as well as land preparation, irrigation, and the application of chemical inputs, women workers were involved in dipping, thinning, berry thinning, and pinching work. Both men and women worked on grading on the farm in the case of domestic market-bound produce. There is no gender gap in wages on grape farms, where men and women are paid the same daily wage or same rate for similar type of work. This is unlike most other farm work in India where there is a definite gender gap in wages with women's wages being at least 30 per cent lower than that of men, if it is not piece-rate-based work.

Women workers on the grape farm (who did not engage in harvest work) were paid Rs. 110 (US$2) per day, of which Rs. 80 (US$1.5) made up the wage and the rest was towards transportation and other deductions. The male workers travelled to the pack house in a shared taxi or on bicycles. The harvest workers worked only 5 hours and were paid Rs. 160 (US$3) per day, of which Rs. 30 (US$0.6) was a transportation allowance.

Higher earnings, including both wages and various allowances, set grape work apart from other farm work available in the same area. Harvest workers took up work on grape farms because of the higher wages it offered and the lower number of work hours. Harvest work (85 days) comprised 30 per cent of their total work days in a year (280). They were directly employed by the service provider. On average, one worker had to harvest about 30 crates in a day, but if there was less produce to harvest on a given day, workers were still paid in full. They were given transport facility their homes to the grape farms. Training was provided by the harvesting supervisor of the service provider.

At pack houses, women performed tasks like bunch cleaning, grading and labelling of punnets, pouch packing, and cleaning of crates. Men performed tasks like sticking labels on punnets, packing and weighing them, pouch packing, moving filled and empty crates and boxes, in addition to loading and unloading produce. Men were usually relied on for weighing and crate lifting in pack houses and for containerization. Women, on average, performed fewer tasks than men: 45 per cent of men reported performing six or seven tasks, while only 26 per cent of women reported performing the same number of tasks (Rath, 2003). The daily wages for female pack house workers at the case study pack house were Rs. 215 (US$3.75) per day, of which Rs. 120 (US$2) made up the wage, with an additional Rs. 15 (US$0.27) for apron cleaning, Rs. 30 (US$0.5) for transportation, and Rs. 50 (US$0.9) towards a provident fund (savings). Male pack house workers were paid Rs. 215 per day, and there were no deductions made towards a provident fund. This must be so because the women were on pay roll and men not so as most of the pack house workers were women. There were seven supervisors in the pack house but none in harvesting teams, where supervision was done by grape farmer and the exporter's team.

Thus, there was gendering of tasks in both export grape production and packing, unlike the domestic market-driven or commoditized production and packing, but no gender differentiation in wages. Export grape production and its packing were attractive to workers of various categories due to higher incomes from it and substantial employment opportunity. Further, harvest and pack house work was considered better than farm-based production work and the need for timely operations with quality led to better facilities and compensation for workers.

5.4.3 Labour upgrading and livelihoods

Labour upgrading for farm workers was seen in the acquisition of job training and movement into pack houses from farms. Better performers were upgraded to supervisory positions. Non-harvest workers in many cases applied chemical pesticides with the tractor-operated sprayer which could be a case of process upgrading. For 25 per cent of men and women workers, grape is the safest crop to work since growers favour biofertilizers and biopesticides to minimize chemical residues in exportable produce, which are safer than conventional chemicals and fertilizers used in non-export grape production. In addition, since they required more frequent application, they also created new work opportunities on the farms.

Fixed work hours and transportation arrangements were reported as being the advantages of working in export grape production. Permanent workers received shelter and food grains, in addition to a number of other free facilities (television, electricity, drinking water). There was an increase of 40–50 per cent in nominal wages over 5 years (2007–2012), and annual work days increased by 35 per cent during the same period. Further, work opportunities in general had increased (workers reported 25 per cent higher work availability), work was more regular now and there were perceived better terms for women than 5 years ago. Therefore, even the National Rural Employment Guarantee Scheme (NREGS; a national level public works program for the rural poor with minimum days of work per year at minimum wage as a legal right under the NREG Act) has not evoked much interest among the grape workers as their wages are much higher than what the scheme provides as daily wage (Rs. 100 per day (US$ 1.75). The wages of workers have also risen, from an average of Rs. 40 (US$ 0.7) in 1992 to Rs. 250 (US$ 4.5) in 2010. Permanent male workers in some cases were appointed to supervise and manage the hired labour, which was much easier work in comparison to the other activities on the farm and could be construed as functional upgrading, but it was limited to a few workers.

On the other hand, many harvest workers reported that all operations in export grape farming except the pesticide application were safer. They were also trained to harvest for export by harvest supervisors, group leaders, and sometimes by a field officer from the export firm. However, they also pointed out that they were held to greater accountability, as all harvested produce could be traced back to them through the unique numbers issued to them by the service provider.

For pack house workers, upgrading has happened in terms of better wages, transportation arrangements, regular hours, and payment for putting in overtime. As part of GlobalGAP certification, pack houses had toilet and washing facilities for workers which can be considered a case of improved working conditions and worker upgrading. In terms of social upgrading, they valued workplace facilities like a 45-minute lunch break, separate toilets for men and women and safe drinking water, besides being able to work under a roof, unlike farm and harvest workers. The respect shown to them by their employer was valued by male workers. Men and women workers reported learning new skills at the pack house, including grading (different from grading at field level) and packing. Due to the higher export demand for grapes, new exporters have come up and thus, the availability of work has increased for workers. Pack house worker wages have gone up by 100 per cent in the case of men and 70 per cent for women over the last 5 years. Some men and women workers reported that they were given more responsibilities at work, on the basis of their skill at grading and packing, which was some indication of workers' functional upgrading.

The pack house workers, who are mainly women, seem to be the major gainers from quality grape exports in terms of better workplace conditions, better wages, and better treatment from employers, although this has come about not because of workers' associational power, but more because of structural power, which is not demonstrated by workers, but perhaps anticipated by employers, that is, pack house operators and export agencies.

In general, it may be concluded that there was a definite improvement in both wages and working conditions for male and female workers in quality grape GPN for the EU, where GlobalGAP standards applied. This is in sharp contrast to commoditized grape production for non-quality conscious export markets (West Asia and Bangladesh) and the domestic market where wages were lower and work conditions poorer. The higher skill requirements for quality products also resulted in employers providing various benefits, such as accommodation and retainers in the off-season, to retain skilled workers. Though there were no gender differences in wages but there was gendering of tasks and, therefore, women were not able to access some of the tasks which fetched better wages, especially in farm work like harvesting or some other farm activities. But, in general, grape export to standards driven markets had led to more employment opportunities for workers with better terms and conditions.

Why did quality grape product workers secure better wage and working conditions than those working for commoditized grape production? Selwyn (2007) analysed a similar type of quality production requirement and concluded that these quality and related standards' requirements increased workers' structural power. In this case, structural power refers to both market place and workplace power. The former is related to the relative shortage of workers with grape-specific skills. The latter is related to the very short season for work and the threat that any disruptions would pose to the ability of exporters to meet quantity and quality commitments in their GPNs.

Despite this increased structural power, Selwyn held that it needed associational power to be translated into wage and other improvements for workers. In our case study, workers were unorganized, rather they were organized not into unions but as labour gangs controlled by brokers. Nevertheless, there is a clear difference between wage and working conditions in GPN-related quality production and commoditized production. A major part of working conditions, such as the prohibition on use of pesticides, is part of the requirement of GlobalGAP. But, the improvements in wages cannot be attributed to technical requirements in standards. We would put forward the thesis that the increase in wages was due to the relative shortage of workers with grape-specific skills sets. In this manner, through labour shortages in the market, workers' structural, market place power can make itself felt even in the absence of any associational power. Such social upgrading due to labour market pressures cannot be ruled out.

The differentiation in quality export and commoditized markets in Indian grape sector led to differences in labour processes and workers' structural power in the network, though in the Indian grape export context, harvest and pack house workers were not able to translate this structural power to their advantage as there were no worker unions. The objective conditions of workers did not permit any major bargaining and agitations as the local wage conditions were poor and the local labour contractors used their personal contacts to recruit and manage the worker-local firm interface. Further, the low opportunity cost for women workers made them accept given wages and work conditions. Since all workers, especially harvest and pack house, were recruited through labour contractors or directly by local firms (service providers), there was not much difference across worker categories or gender in terms of workers' associational power.

The structural power of farm workers was weaker than that of harvest or pack house workers as they were not hired by a legal entity and were under the direct control of local farmers who bonded them with advances, besides the fact that some of them were migrants and, therefore, outsiders in the grape-growing regions.

5.5 Conclusions

The above case study of various stakeholders in the grape GPN shows that the grape GPNs have been locally entrenched for decades and are sophisticated in terms of meeting the quality requirements of export markets. They have leveraged local systems of labour mobilization and management from the existing domestic networks that service other crops such as sugarcane production and management, i.e., harvest workers and *tolis*. But despite the large number of exporters, farmers, and facilitators, there is no major labour shortage problem though labour cost has gone up. The local facilitators and labour contractors have stepped in to meet the challenge of labour supply for export production. This is unlike the case of sugarcane harvesting where, despite the presence of labour contractors for decades, labour issues could not be managed effectively and there were frequent labour struggles and negotiations for better harvest compensation. The sugar mills have more recently resorted to the mechanization of sugarcane harvesting with heavy machines that cannot be owned by individual farmers and therefore are being bought by mills and provided to farmers on a sharing basis.

There is no doubt that the emergence of GPNs in grape production has led to new and better employment opportunities for workers in general and women in particular as there was no similar employment opportunity of a similar quality earlier. Also, since grapes are a long life crop running into 20–30 years, the employment is more stable and workers can hope to specialize and benefit from it for some time. Workers have been able to negotiate a regular annual wage increase, pick-up and drop-off by farmers in jeeps and pickup trucks everyday and regular rest periods during the workday. Permanent male workers in some cases were asked to supervise and manage the hired labour, which is much easier than other activities on the farm. Thus, although issues remain with respect to working conditions for farm work and casualization of work through contractors, in general, grape workers have seen upgrading in terms of more work availability, better wages, more regular employment, and more respect from employers. Further, the better work and wage conditions seem not so much a result of associational power of workers as of their structural power within the grape GPN and its recognition by local facilitators and exporters.

The analysis also shows that though better quality and work standards are being brought into food GPNs by global buyers and development agencies, they are not yet enforced fully at the farm level. Such standards are meant to address, for example, issues such as the gender gap in wages for farm workers, lack of basic work conditions, and minimum wages. Though some aspects like minimum wages or no gender gap in wages have been addressed by global standards, the issues of regular work, work conditions, and social benefits remain to be addressed. At the pack house level, conditions seem somewhat better with wages much higher than minimum wages and women dominating in the workforce. But here too, the supervisors are men.

There are also local conditions like cost pressures on smallholder producers, which do not permit the adequate implementation of such standards. Further, the reliance on contractual labour has also led to poor enforcement of labour and wage standards, as buying agencies (the export firms) do not employ workers directly and, thus, do not feel liable for ensuring labour well-being and conditions of work. The supermarket buyers depend on agencies and formal procedures to enforce standards and do not monitor their compliance. They are more concerned with quality and regular supply and managing the interface with producers. Further, since there is no other standard in the Indian GPN like organic or fair trade or even better or more responsible production requirements, the GlobalGAP is not challenged to improve beyond a point though it includes elements of various standards like the fair trade or organic farming.

In such situations, it is important to bring in the workers' interest through wages being part of the compensation terms for farmers and other intermediaries. Worker organization is the key to achiev better work conditions and wages, but NGOs are not involved in helping to clean up these GPNs or setting up better bargaining positions for workers. The role of the state is not effective, as minimum wages are not enforced in the agricultural sector. NREGS has helped some worker communities in low wage areas but in high value crop work like grapes or vegetables, it does not seem to make a difference.

Further, since women workers predominate in such GPNs at the local level, there is a need to bring in more gendered work conditions like separate toilets for women workers, crèche facilities, and safe transport to and from home, all of which would make women workers feel safer and better cared for, and contribute to the overall performance of the GPN. This could be part of the GPN driver's strategy as well as of the workers' unions or NGOs.

At the same time, while attempting upgrading in networks, the upgrading of workers needs to be provided for alongside that of growers, in order to make them better workers as well as entrepreneurs who could take up part of the network activities. GPNs are not just about value creation and capture by the drivers but also about value sharing with other, especially weaker and smaller stakeholders in the network, from a livelihood perspective.

References

APEDA. 2013. *Procedures for export of fresh table grapes to the EU through control of residues of agrochemicals,* Trade Notice no. QMC/GEN/056/2013-14, Agricultural and Processed Food Exports Development Authority (APEDA) New Delhi.

Bain, C. 2010. 'Governing the Global Value Chain: GlobalGAP and the Chilean Fresh Fruit Industry.' *Int J Sociol Agri Food* 17 (10): 1–23.

Barrientos, S. 2001. 'Gender, Flexibility and Global Value Chains.' *IDS Bull* 32 (3): 3–93.

———. 2013. 'Labour Chains': Analysing the Role of Labour Contractors in Global Production Networks.' *J Develop Stud* 49 (8): 1058–71.

Barrientos, S., and A. Kritzinger. 2004. 'Squaring the Circle Global Production and the Informalisation of Work in South African Fruit Exports.' *J Int Develop* 16 (1): 81–92.

Barrientos, S, Gary Gereffi, and Arianna Rossi. 2011. 'Economic and Social Upgrading in Global Production Networks: A New Paradigm for a Changing World.' *Int Labour Rev* 150 (3–4): 319–40.

Bernhardt, T., and W. Milberg. 2011. 'Economic and Social Upgrading in Global Production Networks: Analysis of Horticulture, Apparel, Tourism and Mobile Telephones.' *Capturing the Gains Working Paper 6*, November.

Bhosale, Suresh. 2001. 'Diagnostic Study SME: Grape Cluster (Maharashtra).' Cluster Development Programme. Ahmedabad: UNIDO/EDII.

Coe, N., M. Hess, H. W. Yeung, P. Dicken and J. Henderson. 2004.'"Globalising" Regional Development: A Global Production Networks Perspective.' *Trans Inst Brit Geograph* 29: 468–84.

Collins, Jane L. 2000. 'Tracing Social Relations in Commodity Chains: The Case of Grapes in Brazil.' In *Commodities and Globalisation: Anthropological Perspectives*, edited by Angelique Haugerud, Priscilla M. Stone and Peter D. Little. New York: Rowman & Littlefield.

Dolan, Catherine S. 2004. 'On Farm and Packhouse: Employment at the Bottom of a Global Value Chain.' *Rural Sociol* 69 (10): 99–126.

Dolan, C., and K. Sutherland. 2002. 'Gender and employment in the Kenya Horticulture Chain.' Available at, http://www.gaperesearch.org/production/finaldraft.pdf, accessed on October 18, 2011.

Fold, Niels. 2008. 'Transnational Sourcing Practices in Ghana's Perennial Crop Sectors.' *J Agrar Change* 8 (1): 94–122.

Gereffi, G. 2001. 'Beyond the Producer-driven/Buyer-driven Dichotomy: The Evolution of Global Value Chains in the Internet Era.' *IDS Bull* 32 (3) July: 30–40.

Gereffi, G., J. Humphrey, R. Kaplinsky, and T. J. Sturgeon, 2001. 'Introduction: Globalization, Value Chains and Development.' *IDS Bull* 32 (3): 1–8.

Gibbon, P. 2001. 'Agro-Commodity Chains: An Introduction.' *IDS Bull* 32 (3): 60–8.

Gibbon, P., and S. Ponte. 2005. *Trading Down: Africa, Value Chains, and the Global Economy*. Philadelphia, PA: Temple University Press.

Goto, K. 2011. Competitiveness and Decent Work in Global Value Chains: Substitutionary or Complementary? *Develop Pract* 21 (7): 943–58.

Henderson, J., P. Dicken, M. Hess, N. Coe, and H. W. Yeung. 2002. 'Global Production Networks and the Analysis of Economic Development.' *Rev Int Polit Econ* 9 (3): 436–64.

Kritzinger, Andrienetta, Stephanie Barrientos, and Hester Rossouw. 2004. 'Global Production and Flexible Employment in South African Horticulture: Experiences of Contract Workers in Fruit Exports.' *Rural Sociol* 44 (1): 17–39.

Lund-Thomsen, P. 2008. 'The Global Sourcing and Codes of Conduct Debate: Five Myths and Five Recommendations.' *Develop Change* 39 (6): 1005–18.

Mayer, F., and J. Pickles. 2010. 'Re-embedding Governance: Global Apparel Value Chains and Decent Work.' *Capturing The Gains Working Paper 1.*

Milberg, W., and D. Winkler. 2011. 'Economic and Social Upgrading in Global Production Networks: Problems of Theory and Measurement.' *Int Labour Rev* 150 (3–4): 341–65.

Muradian, R., and W. Pelupessy. 2005. 'Governing the Coffee Chain: The Role of Voluntary Regulatory Systems.' *World Develop* 33 (12): 2029–44.

Ortiz, Sutti. 2002. 'Labouring in the Factories and in the Fields.' *Ann Rev Anthropol* 31: 395–417.

Ortiz, Sutti, and Susana Aparicio. 2006. 'Management Response to the Demands of Global Fresh Fruit Markets: Rewarding Harvesters with Financial Incentives.' *J Develop Stud* 42 (30): 446–68.

Pietrobelli, C., and R. Rabelloti. 2006. 'Clusters and Value Chains in Latin America: In Search of an Integrated Approach.' In *Up-grading to Compete: Global Value Chains, Clusters, and SMEs in Latin America*, edited by Carlo Pietrobelli and Roberta Rabelloti. Washington, DC: Inter-American Development Bank. 1–40.

Ponte, S., and J. Ewert. 2009. 'Which Way Is Up in Upgrading? Trajectories of Change in the Value Chain for South African Wine.' *World Develop* 37 (10): 1637–50.

Rath, Sharadini. 2003. 'Grape Cultivation for Export: Impact on Vineyard Workers.' *Econ Polit Weekly* 38 (5): 480–89.

Rogaly, Ben. 2008. 'Intensification of Workplace Regimes in British Horticulture: The Role of Migrant Workers.' *Popul, Space Place* 14(6): 497–510.

Roy, Devesh, and Amit Thorat. 2008. 'Success in High Value Horticultural Export Markets for the Small Farmers: The Case of Mahagrapes in India.' *World Develop* 36 (10): 1874–90.

Selwyn, Benjamin. 2007. 'Labour Process and Workers Bargaining Power in Export Grape Production, North East Brazil.' *J Agrar Change* 7 (4): 526–53.

———. 2009. 'Labour Flexibility in Export Horticulture—A Case Study of Northeast Brazilian Grape Production.' *J Peasant Stud* 36 (4): 761–82.

———. 2012. 'Beyond Firm-Centrism: Re-integrating Labour and Capitalism into Global Commodity Chain Analysis.' *J Econ Geogr* 12: 205–26.

Shankar, M. V. 2012. 'The SPS Agreement, Perceptions of Small Farmers and Institutional Response: A Case Study of the Grape Sector in Maharashtra.' *J Int Econ* 3 (2): 97–113.

Sharma, Vijay Paul, and Jain, Dinesh. 2011. 'High Value Agriculture in India: Past Trends and Future Prospects.' *Working Paper No. 2011-07-02*. Ahmedabad: IIM.

Trienekens, Jaques H., and Sabine Willems. 2007. 'Innovation and Governance in International Food Supply Chains: The Case of Ghanian Pineapple and South African Grapes.' *Int Food Agribus Manage Rev* 10 (4): 42–63.

6

The 'Zero-Fee' Tour

Price Competition and Chain Downgrading in Chinese Tourism

Yang Fuquan, Yu Yin and Dev Nathan

6.1 Introduction

Global production network (GPN) analysis is based on the link between product and factor market outcomes. Nathan and Sarkar (2011) and Milberg and Winkler (2013) argued that rents are usually concentrated in one part of the chain, that of the lead firm, while the manufacturers or suppliers received merely competitive or normal profits. Competitive profits result in employees or service providers of supplier firms receiving merely competitive wages, while employees in lead firms could hope to share part of their firms' rents. The result of rents to lead firms and competitive profits to suppliers depends on a particular market structure, i.e., that of oligopolistic-lead firms and competitive suppliers. Oligopolistic-lead firms could be price makers in both final and intermediate product markets. But what if the lead firms were themselves in a highly competitive market? Kaplinsky (2007) pointed out that in such a situation price competition would transform the rents of lead firms into consumer surpluses.

This effect of highly competitive markets at the level of both service suppliers and lead firms is looked at in this paper in the context of the rise of the 'zero-fee' tour in Chinese tourism. An unusual and notable feature of tourism in China has been the rise of the zero-fee tour, or, even more extreme, the buying of tourists, whereby service providers pay the outbound tour operator (OTO) for the tourists provided. Who then pays for the service providers and how is this done? These questions need to be answered if we are to understand this phenomenon. More important, however, is understanding the factors that have led to the rise of this phenomenon, its possible negative or downgrading effects on the tourism services' network and ways of dealing with it. This paper takes up these questions in the light of the GPN analysis mentioned above.[1]

---

[1] The paper is based on our investigations of tourism in Lijiang, Shangri-la and Kunming of Yunnan Province, supplemented by material from Dali, also in Yunnan province. The first Chinese author is

We start by laying out the basic structure of the tourism services' production network, along with its associated cash flow system, and then go on to consider how the zero-fee mode changes the usual cash flow system. This is followed by an analysis of both supply- and demand-side factors and the way they work through the production structure. The fieldwork for this study was conducted in Lijiang and Shangri-la in Yunnan province and at the Great Wall at Badaling. These areas were chosen as representing indigenous, or minority, and mainstream or mass tourism, respectively. However, Yunnan, although an indigenous or minority area, is also an area of mass tourism: the township of Lijiang, with a population of less than 400,000, receives about 10 million visitors in a year.

Initially, our investigations in these areas were on the impact of tourism on poverty reduction, of which we found substantial evidence, as analysed in Chapter 7. But it was also clear that the zero-fee tour was widely prevalent in these areas, albeit less so in Lijiang than in Shangri-la or Badaling. Discussions with scholars who had studied Dali (Bai, 2010), which also falls within Yunnan Province, showed that the zero-fee tour was widespread there. In fact, Dali is historically more famous than Lijiang, having been an important post on the Southern Silk Route to Tibet and India. However, as we discuss later in this paper, overcrowding and poor environmental management contributed to reducing its attractiveness as a tourist destination. Our field investigations in Lijiang, Shangri-la and Badaling are supplemented by published material on Dali, Hong Kong, and other tourist destinations in China, along with various analyses and accounts of zero-fee tours.

6.2 Structure of the Chinese tourism global production network

The tourism global production network (GPN) is what connects customers (tourists) with service providers who offer travel, accommodation, food and beverages, excursions and entertainment and shopping, all of which together provide

---

a member of the Yunnan provincial cultural tourism advisory body. The second Chinese author has also closely observed the development of tourism in Yunnan. The non-Chinese author has visited and carried out fieldwork, often with one or the other of the Chinese authors, over 20 years and about 10 visits to Kunming, Lijiang, Lugu Lake, Shangri-la and other parts of Yunnan. In a more systematic manner, the authors, jointly and separately, conducted interviews with more than 50 persons involved with tourism, including tourism department and local government officials, staff of tour agencies, staff of non-governmental organizations (NGOs), operators of guesthouses and restaurants, tour guides, drivers and taxi operators and providers of horse rides and other village services. The interviews were conducted over 3 weeks each in March–April 2011 and June 2012.

the tourist experience (Figure 6.1). There are usually two levels of intermediation between the tourist and the experience—the OTO and the local operator (LO), who is also called the destination manager (DM). These intermediaries perform two key functions. The first is that of integration: putting together or bundling all the services mentioned above into one package. The second is that of aggregation or accumulating large numbers of tourists so as to secure discounts from service providers (Paraskevas, 2005). A third function that intermediaries have traditionally performed is that of providing information about destination services. Given the availability of information on the Internet and via telephone, however, it is increasingly possible for individual tourists to acquire the requisite information about destinations and services provided rather than acquiring this from intermediaries.

There is also a trust factor in customers' interaction with these intermediaries, as the quality of the destination services purchased remains somewhat unknown. Earlier, besides tour operators' (TOs) own contracts, word of mouth used to be an important way of learning about the quality of services and their reliability. With the Internet, word of mouth is being replaced by customer reviews on various social networking sites. However, it is the younger tourists who tend to use these information access technologies; older tourists tend to rely more on

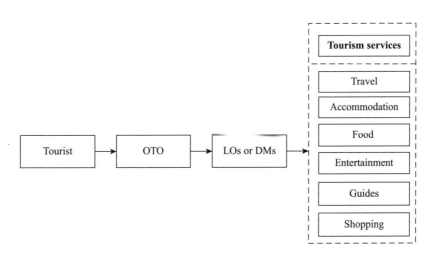

Figure 6.1 Tourism production network

Note: OTO, Overseas tour operators; LO, Local operators; DM, Destination managers.

traditional TOs for both information and trust. What also counts in the use of TOs is that this takes away all the supply chain management hassles. Tourists do not have to individually contract each service, but can just buy an appropriate package.

There are, then, four sets of agents in the tourism GPN: (1) tourists; (2) TOs, who can be sub-divided into OTOs; (3) LOs; and (4) tourism service providers. The business relationships between different segments of service providers (OTOs, LOs, and destination service providers) are usually contracted, which is what justifies the use of the term 'GPN' for tourism. The lead firm in the tourism GPN is the OTO, who controls and provides the tourists for the LOs and service providers. The OTO, on the basis of customers' requirements, decides on the quality requirements of the tour package.

In the case of China, these four agents need to be supplemented by one more—provincial and local governments. In most countries, governments play an enabling role in providing infrastructure and an overall policy framework. In the case of China, governments, both provincial and, in particular, local, play not only supervisory but also substantial and direct roles. Besides licensing various types of operators, they also own key LOs that directly operate in the market. For instance, the tourism corporation owned by the Shangri-la Tourism Department purchases all hotel rooms and then resells them to LOs, some of which are also subsidiaries of the department's holding company.

The tourism GPN can be simplified into the following four stages, shown in Figure 6.1. In the case of inbound international tourists, there may be yet another layer, that of national or principal tour operators (PTOs), who are intermediaries between the OTOs and the LOs. In China, most PTOs are in Beijing, Shanghai, or Guangzhou, which are the usual entry points for foreign tourists. These then subcontract to LOs, in Kunming or Lijiang or elsewhere, but any TO that has the financial capacity and the permission to secure international tourists can become a PTO. More recently, with the development of destinations in Yunnan, Kunming has also become a point of entry for foreign tourists, albeit to a limited extent. TOs in Kunming do put together all-China packages for foreign tourists.

We use the term GPN in the general sense of a production network, recognizing that this production network need not be global but could also be regional or even just domestic. In fact, one of the features of Chinese tourism (Christian and Nathan, 2013 for details) is that domestic tourism far outweighs international tourism in the Chinese tourism market. As seen in Table 6.1, about 88 per cent of total travel and tour expenditure in China is domestic and not foreign.

Table 6.1 Share of domestic visitor spending in tourism and travel, 2011

Country	Share of domestic visitor spending in tourism and travel (%)
China	88.1
India	82.2
Indonesia	79.1
Kenya	39.8
South Africa	56
Uganda	29

Source: WTTC (2011).

The increase in Chinese income per capita means people have more money and leisure time, and tourism, both domestic and international, has become increasingly popular. In 2000, urban residents' annual discretionary income per capita was RMB 6,280 (equivalent to US$ 1,047). In 2011, annual discretionary income per capita had risen more than threefold to RMB 21,810 (equivalent to US$ 3,635). Correspondingly, the total number of domestic tourists increased more than threefold from 744 million in 2000 to 2,641 million in 2011. Travel and tourism spending has also increased proportionately, from RMB 317.6 billion to RMB 1,018.4 billion (about US$ 170 billion). The average travel and tourism spending per capita has also increased, from RMB 426.6 to RMB 731.[2]

6.3 The zero-fee tour

A tourist or a tourist group usually approaches an OTO, who creates a package that includes the cost of transport, accommodation, food and (non-alcoholic) beverages, and excursions, along with a fee for the OTO and for the LO, also sometimes called the DM.[3] The zero-fee tour is a tourism package that just about covers the above costs minus the LOs fees. At times, the package may even be below the above costs. In either case, the LO then recovers its fees through getting the tourists to shop at designated shops or participate in entertainment. Both types of establishments give

---

[2] All data from National Bureau of Statistics (2013).
[3] Some of the analyses of the zero-fee tour phenomenon are, in English, Dai et al. (2011); Zhang and Qi (2009); Zhang et al. (2009); and Zhou and Chan (2012); and, in Chinese, Zhang (2006) and Zhoumin and Liang (2005).

a commission to the tour guides (who take the tourists to the establishments) and the LO. At times, there may even be a 'negative commission' package, whereby the LO pays the OTO for each tourist supplied.

In China, the relationship between the tour agency and tour guides is often not a formal employment arrangement. Tour guides are more like freelance agents who obtain short contracts from tour agencies. Most tour guides are not paid salaries when they deal with Chinese tourists, and they are expected to earn their fees through shopping and related commissions. The shopping commissions for tour guides are about 10 per cent, which they have to share with other staff, such as drivers. Salaries of about RMB 300 per day (US$ 50) are paid only when guides deal with foreign tourists. When working a zero-fee tour, tour guides have to earn not just for themselves but also for the LOs.

The shopping commissions for LOs in the zero-fee tour go up to 60 per cent, as against the normal 30 per cent. The shopping is done in designated shops, with which there are prior arrangements. These designated shops were designed to protect tourists from being sold fake or poor quality products. Initially, they needed to get approval from the local tourism authority in order to cater to tourists. However, these days, they need no such approval. The shops are located either in the suburbs along travel routes or inside scenic spots to facilitate shopping. Most products are jewellery, herbal medicines, amulets, etc. The products have one common characteristic, i.e., that the sellers decide the price and customers lack the knowledge to value them, which leads to customers being induced by sellers to pay high prices. This information asymmetry between seller and buyer in tourist shopping is a key factor in the operations of the zero-fee tour, as also argued in Zhou and Chan (2012).

The stress of meeting local costs, including normal income, in the zero-fee tour is passed on to the tour guides and shopping by tourists. Shopping stops are marked out and tourists are cajoled or even forced to spend a certain amount of time in designated shops. A zero-fee tour is risky, since it depends on the extent of shopping tourists carry out. Sometimes, the LOs further shift the risk on to tour guides, by making them 'buy' the tour. It is then up to the tour guides to recover their costs. One guide who had 'bought' such a group reported making a loss of RMB 1,000 (about US$ 160).

A GPN as a production relationship is also a cash flow relationship. In tourism, the normal cash flow along the GPN is as given in Figure 6.2. The zero-fee tour reverses part of the usual cash flow along the tourism production network, as shown in Figure 6.3. Instead of the OTO paying a commission to the LO, the LO secures a share of shopping commissions through the tour guides. In the case where the LO pays the OTO for the tourists sent, some of the LOs shopping commissions may be passed on to the OTO.

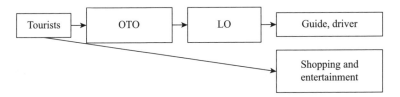

Figure 6.2   Cash flow—normal mode

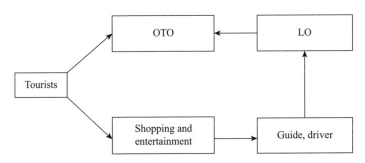

Figure 6.3   Cash flow—zero-fee tour

Source: Adapted from Zhang et al. (2009).

The zero-fee tour seems to have first emerged to boost Chinese outbound international tourism immediately after the 2003 SARS epidemic (Lu, 2006; Zhou and Chan, 2012a)[4], when Chinese tourist numbers declined substantially. Chinese law requires all Chinese tourists to travel abroad only as part of groups (Zhang et al., 2009). When there was a sharp contraction in the market, LOs in Hong Kong, Singapore, etc., did not charge their Chinese business partners the usual commissions, but instituted high shopping commissions to secure their own incomes. Over time, this practice has spread to Chinese domestic tourism, where there is no legal requirement to undertake tours only as part of organized groups. However, local governments prefer group tours, since it is easier both to regulate and provide services for groups than for individual tourists.

The analysis of Zhang et al. links this system with 'group travel as the only permitted travel mode' (2009, p. 369) as one of nine key factors in this mechanism. The appearance and continuation of zero-fee tours in Chinese domestic tourism means this analysis is inadequate and there must be other features of the tourism market and its organization that account for the zero-fee tour. Group travel may promote the zero-fee tour, but it is not a necessary condition for its appearance.

---

[4] In Zhou and Chan (2012), the origin of the zero-fee tour is traced even earlier, back to Thailand.

What, then, are the factors in Chinese tourism that have led to the appearance and persistence of the zero-fee tour?

6.4 Increased competition among tourism service providers

First, the existence of over-capacity in key parts of the tourist service supply network: accommodation, guides, drivers, etc. In the townships of Lijiang and Shangri-la, local government and tourist officials admit that in both places there is over-capacity in hotels.

Some of this over-capacity may be traced back to the usual overinvestment in a period of expansion, when many entrepreneurs see a good business opportunity in a given industry. Another contributing factor is non-commercial investment by government departments. In Lijiang, for instance, customs, forest and other government departments have invested in hotels, since they have both land and a surplus of investible capital. The hotel management in these establishments is under no compulsion to even cover costs. As one official is reported to have pointed out, 'It is unnecessary for hotel managers who are also government officials to worry about the revenue of the hotel, because they do not need to be responsible for the deficits of the business' (quoted in Wang and Ap, 2013). But, leaving aside the amortization of capital, there is not even a requirement to recover staff costs. This is why such government department-run hotels can indulge in price competition.

Besides non-commercial hotels run by various government departments, there is another factor behind over-capacity in tourist accommodation: the proliferation of guesthouses that are converted residences. In the old town of Dayan in Lijiang, the number of guesthouses has been increasing. Similarly, along the shore of Lugu Lake, all residences have given way to guesthouses or larger hotels. These have even spread to interior parts of the villages that are not on the lake shore. Commercial tourism service organizations, government department-run non-commercial hotels and numerous family-owned guesthouses all vie for space in the tourism business. With the township of Lijiang itself receiving 10 million visitors in 2011,[5] there is still a shortage during the peak tourist seasons of spring and summer, but the real problem occurs in winter, when discounts of more than 50 per cent are normal.

The number of tour agencies of various types has also grown. The number of travel agencies in China more than doubled from 8,993 in 2000 to 22,784 in 2010

---

[5] Data from Tourist Department, Lijiang and Kunming. The population of the township of Lijiang was less than 400,000 in 2011.

(National Bureau of Statistics, 2013; Zhou and Chan, 2012). Tour agencies carried out price competition with their own respective customers and LOs reduced or eliminated their charges from OTOs, while OTOs reduced prices charged to tourists. Owing to local protectionism, tour agencies generally cannot operate alone across provinces, and need local tour agencies to provide tourism services. This restricts the growth of tour agencies on a corporate scale. Hence, most tour agencies are small scale and scattered, with weak management and poor service quality. In order for most tour agencies to survive, they try to reduce costs to attract customers, as they know the demand for tourism is highly price elastic.

Other tourism services are also over-supplied. This is so for shops, restaurants, and bars. With an agglomeration effect, whole streets in the town of Dayan and the neighbouring old town are filled with bars, while others streets are almost entirely made up of shops. Surrounding villages compete to supply horse rides and other entertainment services. Educated youth (and all youth are educated at least through middle school) from all over the township have flocked into Dayan town to work as tour guides or in various other tourism-related businesses. Discussions and observations all over the region point to the villages being emptied of youth, who have all taken to tourism-related work.

Being a domestic tour guide is an occupation that almost any Chinese youth can take up, but the investment required to acquire some proficiency in foreign languages restricts the supply of such tour guides. The differences in the investment required for the two types of guides leads to differences in their supply, with a surplus of domestic tourist guides and a shortage of guides for foreign tourists. Remuneration systems are also quite different for the two types of tourist guides.

Guides for foreign tourists get a salary, which they can supplement with tips and regular shopping commissions. Guides for domestic tourists do not get a salary, but have to manage with tips and shopping commissions.

Two factors have contributed to the over-supply of tourism services in the informal sector of small-scale providers. One is the ease of entry into segments of tourism service provision, as not much capital or education is required to provide these services. To be in the horse riding business, a rural family needs a set of two or three horses. For tour guides, middle school education, which all youth have, is sufficient, along with some easily acquired knowledge of local culture and history. As a result, besides accredited guides there are numerous unofficial guides, offering services at reduced prices.

This ease of entry is compounded by the absence of other non-agricultural employment in upland areas. As discussed in more detail in our study of tourism and poverty reduction in upland areas (Nathan et al., Chapter 7), the upland areas of China and India have little manufacturing employment available, which is the traditional route for absorbing surplus rural labour. Tourism has been the only non-farm sector that has developed in these upland regions. It has lifted not only the urban but also the rural population out of poverty; some villages, such as Lashe on Lugu Lake, have even become one of the 10 richest villages in the province. But the absence of other non-farm employment avenues means entrants into tourism are, in a sense, trapped in it, and are not able to shift into other sectors. This works to retain over-supply and thus reduce supply price.

So far, we have dealt with service suppliers within a region. But there is an additional aspect of over-supply, which is that of the proliferation of tourist destinations. Yunnan province has airports in Kunming, Lijiang, Dali and Jing Hong. A new airport is due near Lugu Lake. Railways and expressways also connect these major centres. This is all only within Yunnan province. Other provinces in the poorer west of China, such as Sichuan and Guizhou, have also developed their own tourist centres. These are not as well established on the tourist circuit as Yunnan but they add to the supply of 'me-too' tourist centres, i.e., centres that supply basic tourist services but have no distinguishing historical or environmental features.

As with sun-and-sand centres in South East Asia, there is homogeneity among the minority or indigenous tourist offerings in western China. Even if they try to differentiate themselves, which, as we see later, is an important strategy in trying to reduce competition and increase returns, most tourist offerings are forms of recreational tourism with a minority or indigenous cultural angle. Homogenization of destinations is a factor in increasing competition, and a differentiated product is possible only for a few cases. But it should be noted that the zero-fee tour operates even in unique products, such as the Great Wall and the Xian terracotta armies.

6.5 Technological factors in increased competition

LOs have traditionally played an important role in providing information and overcoming trust deficits in tourism services. Where tourists did not have much information about destination service providers, they had to rely on LOs to create affordable packages. But destination service providers, such as hotels, guesthouses, and transport operators, increasingly have web sites. Even if they do not have facilities for online payment, when supplemented by phones and credit cards, bookings can be carried out. Airlines, railways, and transport operators can be accessed and booked via the Internet, while individual service providers, such as guides and drivers, can also be contacted by mobile phone. In addition, they can also put together local packages, with accommodation, transport, and excursions all taken care of. Once they have gained experience of the various dimensions of tourism packages, providers of a single service have begun to operate as small-scale LOs. The Internet and the mobile phone are therefore together reducing, if not eliminating, the factor of 'incomplete knowledge of the destination held by tourists before departure', which Zhang et al. (2009, p. 370) identify as one of the factors in the rise of the zero-fee tour in China.

Zhou and Chan (2012) also identify information asymmetry as a key factor in promoting the zero-fee tour. The information asymmetry is not about tourist destination services but about prices in retail shops. Particularly in the case of jade, where there are not standard prices, tourists are unlikely to be aware of the extent of mark-up in the retail shops. For this information asymmetry to be a factor in the zero-fee tour, shopping must be an essential component of the tourist experience. This is quite likely to be true with regard to destinations like Hong Kong or Singapore, which are well known for electronics being cheaper than in China. But in domestic tourist destinations, shopping is not a key factor in tourists' choices. Shopping for mementos and gifts are part of tourism, but they may not be very expensive.

Overall, the Internet and mobile phone together, in reducing the information gap, are contributing to reorganizing the tourism industry. Porter wrote about the impact on the Internet on strategy, stating 'Its greatest impact has been to enable the reconfiguration of existing industries that had been constrained by high costs for communicating, gathering information, or accomplishing transactions' (2011, p. 66). The proportion of tourists travelling on their own, without OTOs or even LOs, is increasing. In addition, web-based agencies like Expedia.com are creating a new space for web-based intermediaries. For the purposes of this chapter, we note that the Internet has reduced the information gap, and that this promotes increased competition.

6.6 Competition among lead firms

Tourists in China, even domestic tourists, largely travel in groups. Only younger tourists and the famous 'singles' that throng Lijiang travel as individual families or singly. In the case of international destinations, Chinese tourists are only permitted to travel in groups. This could lead to a kind of cartelization. The OTOs could push down LOs' supply prices, but not pass on the benefits to consumers. In this case, it would be a zero fee for the LOs, but not for tourists. However, the fact that tourists were also passed on the price benefits shows there was competition among OTOs, in both international (outbound) and domestic tourist markets.

With tourist numbers increasing every year, why was there competition among oligopolistic OTOs for tourist customers? When an economy has been consistently growing at above 8 per cent a year, businesses are likely to make their annual plans on the basis of such growth. When that growth does not occur, then the effect could be like that of an actual decline in the market in the case of a slow-growing economy. When business growth is below expectations, it could spark off a price war for customers. The struggle for market share becomes a price war in a stagnant or declining market. The key periods when a decline in tourist numbers sparked off price wars are those of the 2003 SARS decline and the post-2008 global recession.

Table 6.2 shows that the growth rates of domestic tourism varied from over 11 per cent in 2006 to just 1 per cent in 2008. Such variation in rates of growth in an economy growing at above 8 per cent would upset business plans and could trigger competition. Some of the impact of the variation in rates of growth is possibly reflected in a sharp fall in employment (Employment in Table 6.2) of as much as 6.4 per cent in 2008.

Table 6.2 China tourism growth (%)

	2006	2007	2008	2009	2010	2011	2012
Tourism exports	9.5	−1.6	−9.3	−4.3	9.5	−6.3	7.4
Domestic tourism	11.6	7.6	1.0	6.7	2.8	7.7	9.9
Employment	3.6	−3.6	−6.4	0.3	5.0	1.7	1.9

Source: WTTC (2012).

We next deal with the impact of the zero-fee tour on different segments of the tourism GPN.

6.7 Effects of price competition on the tourism production network

With competition among suppliers, LOs often give discounts of up to 70 per cent to the lead buyers, the OTOs. The OTOs in turn pass on some of this discount to tourists. Having given these discounts, LOs then put pressure on tour guides to retrieve the lost income through shopping commissions. Tour guides for their part put pressure on tourists to spend more time and money shopping. This system of recouping tourism chain incomes, through shopping commissions rather than straightforward additions of commissions to tour costs, affects the whole chain in a number of ways.

Commissions on normal shopping by tourists are around 30 per cent, but on zero-fee tours, shops give commissions of 50–60 per cent, although tour guides and drivers together get only 5–8 per cent. The high commissions in 'zero-fee' shopping destinations show the extent to which prices are inflated. Along with price inflation in retail shops, there is also outright cheating. Artificial gems and diamonds are sold as natural, with the cheating covered up by extra-fine print text stating that the stones were made artificially (Zhou and Chan, 2012).

For tourists, with the over-emphasis on shopping there is a deterioration of the tourism experience, key components of which are relaxation and experiencing novel places. While the price of the tour may be low, the tourists lose both in the quality of the experience and in the forced and high-priced shopping. In an important manner, the quality of the tourist product is downgraded. As Zhang and Qi put it, there is a 'dissatisfying and even disastrous travel experience of the tourists' (2009, p. 21).

Various reports in Chinese newspapers[6] have highlighted the abusive behaviour of tour guides when tourists do not shop as they are expected to do. In more than one instance, tour guides have abandoned the tourist party and left them to fend for themselves. In a survey of 2,000 tourists in six Chinese cities, some 68.5 per cent reported unpleasant experiences (Lu, 2006). These frequent incidents show the deleterious effects of the pressure on tour guides to earn commissions for themselves, the drivers, and the LOs.

Sometimes, the LOs 'sell' the tour party to the tour guide. Tour guides may pay about RMB 6 (US$ 1) or more per tourist to get a group. The LO recovers some part of its fees in this manner, and transfers the risk of the tour to the guide. The guide will then bear any loss in case the group fails to buy enough to make up for the amount paid to 'buy' the group. One guide who had to pay for a tourist group reported losing HK$ 1,000 on a tour group (Lu, 2006). Desperate competition to get tourists to buy enough for guides to make a living resulted in strikes by tour guides in both Sichuan and Yunnan provinces (ibid.).

In an integrated tourist agency, where the agency provides all the services, including that of guides, drivers etc., the impact of a zero-fee situation would be felt by the agency as a whole. In a production network, however, one would expect

---

[6] We refer to a few of the reports easily available in the English language press, e.g., Asia Times Online (2007) and China Daily (2011).

the burden of losses or of reductions in profit to fall unevenly on different segments, based on their bargaining power within the network. The production segment, where entry is easy and neither high capabilities nor large amounts of capital are required as with tour guides, is the weakest portion of the production network. They are the ones who get no salary at all but have to entirely depend on commissions. Further, they have to make sure they secure this commission not only for themselves but also for other service providers, such as the LOs. As the buying of tour groups shows, they may end up bearing most of the business risks (Zhou and Chan, 2012).

The need to pay commissions to tour guides and through them to the LOs affects the quality in other segments of the tourism GPN as well. For instance, restaurants are forced to give commissions to tour guides who bring them customers. The result could be that the restaurant gets an effective price of, say, RMB 6 per person for a set meal, while RMB 4 of the customer price of RMB 10 goes to the tour guide and the LO (Dai et al., 2011). With restaurant profit margins cut in this manner, there is bound to be deterioration in food quality.

Hotels and other providers of accommodation also have their margins cut by the commissions they have to pay. Competition does not allow them to raise prices; rather, margins have to be cut. This will affect both the quality of care and the ability of the hotel or guesthouse owners to recoup their investments and earn normal profits. Aside from a fall in the quality of hotel care, there will be a fall in surpluses available for reinvestment, essential to maintaining quality.

What the above points show is that profits all along the chain are likely to fall below normal levels. This could also end with the local tour industry in a debt chain, as tour agencies are unable to pay for the hotel, the tour bus, and restaurants, leading to further deterioration in tour services. This will affect the quality of service and products and of the whole tourism experience, as tourists are forced to increase their time shopping. In effect, there will be a downgrading of the whole network, and price wars will affect ability to carry out renovations, let alone improvements and upgrading. The economic results will affect reinvestment and the sustainability of the tourism network.

The effects of this downgrading on the quality of the tourist experience are clear from the reports mentioned above. But their inevitable impact on earnings along the value chain was not so obvious in our field investigations, which were in Lijiang township and its villages, including Lugu Lake. As discussed in Chapter 7, Lijiang has managed to control the zero-fee tour owing to the success of its branding. As such, the negative impacts of the zero-fee tour on the incomes of various actors along the network did not show up. But analysis of Dali (Dai et al., 2011) and discussions in Shangri-la and Kunming did bring out the negative impacts on incomes along the network.

Table 6.2 showed the impact on employment in tourism and travel. Employment fell by as much as 6.4 per cent in 2008. Such an impact is likely to have been less in the mountain areas, where alternative employment is less available. In such areas, those working in tourism would have stayed on and accepted a decline in income. Discussions with tour guides in Shangri-la pointed to such declines in income, while employment did not change.

The share of zero-fee tours in total tours seems to be rising. For Hong Kong, an estimated 60 per cent of LOs operated zero-fee tours in 2006, and this went up to 90 per cent in 2008 after the global recession set in (Zhou and Chan, 2012). The Hong Kong Tourism Board estimates the proportion of tour groups under the zero-fee system to take 85 per cent of all Chinese tourists. This means just 15 per cent of Chinese tourists to Hong Kong pat for high-quality regular tours (*ibid.*). This would clearly mean serious degradation of the tourism production network.

Deterioration in quality of services, decline in the incomes of service providers and, most importantly, erosion of the ability to reinvest in providing quality services—all these are bound to degrade the network. Destinations that are able to brand themselves and secure some rent may, however, be able to escape such degradation. In addition, there are quality-conscious tourists, who want better service and are willing to pay higher rates. The higher-quality segment would be better maintained, while the zero-fee segment would be degraded.

While there are two different segments of tours, full-cost and zero-fee tours, TOs, whether OTOs or LOs, are not differentiated by the type of service they provide. Both full-cost and zero-fee tours are provided by all operators. There is a difference in TOs by tourism segment only in the case of foreign tourists. Only those TOs registered to deal with foreign tourists are allowed to receive them. And, as pointed out earlier, at the level of tour guides, there is a difference between those who deal with foreign and domestic tourists. A higher-quality product is related to better employment conditions for tour guides.

Our analysis leads to the hypothesis that high levels of competition at both service provider ends, origin and destination, have eroded the overall profitability of the tourism network. To the extent that some profits are retained, this depends on shopping or the limited high-quality segment. At an analytical level, the role of shopping commissions as key to earnings in the tourism production network shows that shopping must be included as part of the tourism network, not as something outside it. Souvenirs and gifts for family and friends are part of the tourism experience. Besides high-end shopping for jewellery, local handicrafts and clothes often play a part. The share of shopping in total expenditures varies from 10 to 40 per cent in China. At one level, budget tourists may well prefer to minimize expenditure on services and maximize expenditure on shopping. The latter provides some goods the tourists can take back; the former is spent just on services, with nothing to show afterwards. The share of shopping expenditure in overall tourist expenditure in different price segments would be an interesting issue to investigate.

6.8   Dealing with the zero-fee tour

Alarmed by the negative effects of the high level of price competition and the spread of zero-fee tours, local governments have taken many administrative steps to try to control competition and stabilize prices. To regulate tourism prices and make the tourism market more orderly, the State Development Planning Commission and Tourism Administration Department in Yunnan issued regulations such as 'On strengthening tourism prices management consolidation order notice' and 'The scenic spots' tickets price management measures'. However, governments are still weak in regulating the intense price competition among tour agencies.

In Shangri-la township, the local government, through its fully owned tourist corporation, bought up all hotel rooms and then resold them to tour operators. This was an attempt to maintain a price level and not allow discounts. In Lijiang, the local government forced hotels to close by rotation in the off-season, which was the period of the deepest discounts. In Dali too, the local government took similar measures to reduce competition in the market for hotel rooms.

In Shangri-la, competition took on an ethnic character of Han–Tibetan conflict: Han hotel operators, with higher financial staying power, were able to out-compete Tibetan operators. Because of this potential for ethnic conflict, the local government was very strict in not allowing formal hotel room prices to fall. But this does not mean hotels may not have been returning commissions in cash. With regard to a similar situation of local government price regulation of accommodation and catering in Dali, 'these establishments still provided cash commissions to tour guides in order to increase their share of the available tourists' (Dai et al., 2011, p. 157). Our field research in Shangri-la also revealed cash commissions being paid to circumvent government controls on prices.

Further, while local governments could to some extent regulate the formal sector, they have not been able to do much about the informal sector. Small guesthouses and small-scale LOs have proliferated in a growing informal sector. These are outside the purview of government regulation and could continue to keep down prices. At times, OTOs, LOs, and informal service providers have colluded to circumvent government regulations. In Dali, when the local government tried to keep hotel prices high, an alliance of these actors set up a half-day sightseeing itinerary and then took the group to Lijiang, skipping any overnight stay in Dali (Dai et al., 2011). This led to the government organizations incurring losses.

Local government regulation of accommodation seems to have been more successful in Lijiang than in either Dali or Shangri-la. One possible factor is the growing importance of young, single men and women in Lijiang tourism. This increases the proportion of tourists who make their own, direct arrangements through the Internet and by mobile phone. There are also two other interrelated reasons for this. The first was that Lijiang had established itself as a differentiated product in a generally homogenized market. It was the preferred Spring Festival destination in China, with its quasi-matrilineal status being a special attraction. Established brand status meant Lijiang could keep its prices higher than, say, Dali or other destinations in Yunnan.

Related to its established brand status was the fact that its surplus of rooms was basically a seasonal phenomenon. In spring and summer, and in fact right till winter, rooms remain in short supply. As mentioned earlier, Lijiang received a total of 10 million visitors in 2011.

It is only in winter that rooms are in surplus. Consequently, the rationing of rooms is not a year-long but only a winter matter, making it easier to implement than if it had been a year-long problem. The main factor in Lijiang being able to withstand competitive pressures better than Dali or Shangri-la is its brand status. Establishing a differentiated product, which need not force its LOs into price competition, was the main strategy to counter intense competition. The differentiated product allows service suppliers to command a higher price. Rents earned in this manner enabled better income conditions all along the network, compared with destinations that were forced into competitive price-cutting.

Even with a homogenized product, at a local, that is, village level, it was possible to establish some control over supply. Controlling supply on the market and thus propping up supply price was the key to combating the zero-price tour. At the destination level, whether in Lijiang, Dali, or Shangri-la, the ability to implement a policy of controlling supply depended on the ability to develop and maintain a differentiated product, a brand that could earn some rents through premium prices on the market. Earning higher returns through branding could control the struggle to secure volume through competitive price-cutting. In a sense, higher-value products, giving higher returns per tourist, could control the struggle to secure higher volume, trying to compensate for lower returns per tourist through increasing market share.

However, in destinations that are not able to break out of the pack of homogenized products, there will have to be some reduction of supply.

Administrative arrangements to restrain completion without reducing supply are not likely to be successful.

As the experiences mentioned above show, such administrative measures are likely to work temporarily but will inevitably be subverted by the various agencies in the network.

6.9 Conclusion

This paper has argued that a combination of competition among service providers and simultaneous competition among lead firms for tourist customers could lead to product prices falling below full cost levels, as reflected in the phenomenon of the zero-fee tour. Rather than different agents in the production network securing and sharing profits produced in the network, these profits are distributed away from producers in the network and, through lower prices of the products, end up as consumer surpluses. Over time, such a dissipation of producer surpluses as consumer surpluses is bound to lead to deterioration in the quality of production in the network. There could be a painful process of adjustment as excess capacity is reduced. Given the ease of entry of small-scale service providers in the informal sector, a reduction of capacity will very much depend on the growth of alternate employment opportunities.

This is an extreme form of the Prebisch–Singer thesis, as extended by Kaplinsky (2005) to manufacturing in global value chains. In Kaplinsky's analysis, the negative effects were felt by the commoditized manufacturers in the commoditized segment, e.g., cut-make-trim garment work. In the zero-fee tour case, the negative effect is felt not only in the lowest segment, namely, tour guides, but also all along the network. There is degradation of the network itself, or at least of a major part of it, the low-price segment. Network degradation or downgrading is likely to be more with single-service providers than with multiple-service providers. What leads to this network degradation effect is the existence of high competition among lead firms too, resulting in at least some of the surpluses being transferred out of the production network to consumers. This degrades the quality of the service.

The major interventions in combating the zero-fee tour have been in terms of controlling supply. Sometimes supply is restricted, so that the supply price does not fall. At other times, supply is restricted and prices are simultaneously controlled, but we have seen that supply restriction is effective in increasing prices only when it is combined with brand building, which helps gain higher prices. These higher prices leading to higher returns can restrict or even eliminate the competitive search for market share.

In addition, supply is affected by the ease with which small-scale suppliers can enter the market. This limits the effectiveness of supply restrictions, which work through the formal organizational structure. Over-crowding at the lower end of the supply chain is a feature of economic regions, viz. the uplands, where there are no alternative, non-farm occupations available. Tourism tends to be the residual sector, absorbing all those who are getting out of agriculture. This problem can be taken care of by the development of other, non-tourist occupations. At some point, a reduction of supply or capacity is needed to reduce price competition.

Supply-side restrictions are difficult to implement, and that too for a long period, when there is already over-capacity and entry is not too difficult, particularly at the lower end of small-scale service delivery and where some units in the market are not commercial or receive local government support to remain in business. Reductions of capacity and brand building are then two ways to deal with the intense competition that has become a ubiquitous feature of the tourism production network in China.

At the theoretical level, the zero-fee tour epitomizes the unusual GVC situation of high competition in both lead firms' and service suppliers' ends of the chain. This reduces returns to all players in the tourism chain. It further results in a downgrading of the tourism chain, manifested in the deterioration of the quality of the tourism service provided. While competition is useful in bringing down prices of services, thus benefitting consumers, at the same time, it could reduce the capacity to reinvest in the chain. Over time, there will have to be some reduction in service suppliers or an increase in demand to make the chain sustainable.

References

Axelrod, Robert. 1984. *The Evolution of Cooperation*. New York: Basic Books.

Bai, Zhi Hong. 2010. *Making A Difference: Bai Identity Construction in Dali*. Kunming: Social Science Academic Press.

China Daily. 2011. 'Zero-Fee Tours on the Rise Again.' *China Daily*, June 8.

Christian, Michelle, and Dev Nathan. 2013. 'Tourism Overview: Changing End Markets and Hyper Competition.' *Capturing the Gains Working Paper No. 24*.

Dai, Shanshan, Honggang Xu, Noel Scott, Peiyi Ding, and Eric Laws. 2011. 'Distortions in Tourism Development in the Dali Autonomous Region, China.' *Asia Pacific J Tour Res* 17 (2): 146–63.

Kaplinsky, Raphael. 2005. *Globalization, Poverty and Inequality*. Cambridge: Polity.

Lu, Joy. 2006. '"Zero-Fee" Practice Damages Travel Industry.' *China Daily*, September 11.

Milberg, William, and Deborah Winkler. 2013. *Outsourcing Economics: Global Value Chains in Capitalist Development*. Cambridge: Cambridge University Press.

Nathan, Dev, and Sandip Sarkar. 2011. 'A Note on Profits, Rents and Wages in Global Production Networks.' *Econ Polit Weekly* 46 (36): 53–7.

National Bureau of Statistics 2013. *China Statistical Yearbook 2012*. Beijing: National Bureau of Statistics (in Chinese).

Olivia Chung, Asia Times Online. 2007. 'Scandals turn Chinese Shoppers off Hong Kong.' *Asia Times Online*, 24 April.

Paraskevas, Alexandros. 2005. 'The Impact of Technological Innovation in Managing Global Value Chains in the Tourism Industry.' Paper Presented at OECD Conference on Global Tourism Growth: A Challenge for SMEs, Gwangju, 6–7 September.

Porter, Michael E. 2011. 'Strategy and the Internet.' In *On Strategy*. Cambridge, MA: Harvard Business Review.

Wang, Dan, and John Ap. 2013. 'Factors Affecting Tourism Policy Implementation: A Conceptual Framework and a Case Study of China.' *Tour Manage* 36: 221–33.

WTTC (World Travel and Tourism Commission). 2011. 'Different Components of Tourism, 2011.' Accessed June–July 2012. www.wwtc.org.

———. 2012. 'Economic Impact of Tourism: China.' Accessed June–July 2012. www.wwtc.org.

Zhang, Hanqin Qiu, and York Qui Yan. 2009. 'Analysing Zero-Fee Tours Through Game Theory.' *The Voice of TIC* 2: 20–23.

Zhang, Hanqin Qiu, Vincent C.S Heung and York Qui Yan. 2009. 'Play or Not to Play: An Analysis of the Mechanism of the Zero-commission Chinese Outbound Tours Through a Game Theory Approach.' *Tour Manage* 30: 366–71.

Zhang, Y. 2006. 'Analysis of Current "Zero-Fee" Group.' *Chinese Tourism Market* November: 227–29 (in Chinese).

Zhou, Wen, and Penelope Chan. 2012. *Zero-fee Tours: An Irresistible Bargain or a Sinkhole?* Hong Kong and Cambridge, MA: Asia Case Research Centre, University of Hong Kong and Harvard Business Review.

Zhuomin, T., and Liang, L. 2005. 'Study of the Formation Mechanism of the "No Charge Tour" and "Minus Fee Tour" and the Countermeasures.' *Financial Trade J* 6: 46–50 (in Chinese).

7

Restricting Competition to Reduce Poverty

Impact of the Tourism Value Chain in an Upland Economy in China

Yang Fuquan, Yu Xiaogang, Yu Yin, Govind Kelkar and Dev Nathan

7.1 Introduction

This is a study of the impacts of the tourism value chain on the upland economy of the indigenous people-dominated Lijiang Prefecture in China's Yunnan Province. Our central concern is with poverty reduction and the ways in which this might be brought about by local segments of the tourism value chain. The extent of benefits arising from these local segments of the value chain depends on the ability of local producers and local governments to restrict competition among tourism service suppliers.

The next section sets out the nature of poverty in the uplands, and the constraints facing economic development of the uplands. This is followed by a discussion of the nature of the tourism value chain and the likely local linkages of tourism. The next section summarizes field findings from Lijiang Prefecture and is followed by a discussion of the precarious nature of tourism jobs and the role of competition-reducing organization of producers and state-provided social security in reducing precarity and increasing the positive impact, in terms of reducing poverty.

This paper is based on field investigations over a number of years in villages and the old town of Dayan in Lijiang Prefecture, including recent field trips in March 2011 and 2012. The details of this field work are mentioned in Chapter 6.

7.2 Economic constraints and poverty in the uplands

Poverty in China, as in much of Asia, is disproportionately concentrated in the uplands. China's indigenous peoples who live in the uplands made up about 40 per cent of the absolute poor in 2000, though they accounted for less than 9 per cent of the population (Nathan et al., 2012). Generally speaking, the potential for the development of agriculture and industry, i.e., two sectors that are usually considered key production sectors, is narrowly limited in upland economies.

In the case of agriculture, mountain soils are thin, water retention capacity is poor, and there is little irrigation. The one type of agriculture in which the uplands can compete with the plains is in the cultivation of temperate fruits and off-season vegetables, or of resource-specific products, such as the highly valued *shitake* mushroom, which only grows alongside oak trees.

In the case of industry, the difficulties of mountain transport mean that even with good road infrastructure, transport costs in the mountains are higher than in the plains. The Government of India tried to offset this disadvantage by offering tax concessions to those investing in the mountain state of Uttarakhand. But it is no surprise that all the resulting investment in the state took place in its two narrow plains districts and not in the mountainous areas.

The lack of viability in agriculture and unfavourable conditions for manufacturing leave services as one sector in which growth might be possible. Services are not as dependent on natural resource extraction as the other two sectors. Some services, such as restaurants or hospitality in general, are also relatively more reliant on labour. Of course, there are different types of services, with varying skill and infrastructure requirements. For instance, the quintessentially modern sectors of IT and IT-enabled services (ITES, such as call centres), allow mountain areas to overcome the disadvantages of distance and poor roads, since broadband connections with reliable power supply are more easily set up than transport infrastructure.

On the other hand, tourism requires good transport and accommodation infrastructure. However much of a mixed bag tourism services might be, depending on local capabilities, the service sector could be developed in upland economies to provide recreational services required by those in external economies, whether domestic or international. Expansion of these services could, in turn, lead to an increase in income in the resource-constrained upland areas.

The scenic and natural resources of the uplands could themselves be turned into a source of income, even of rents or above-normal profits. Lijiang Prefecture in Yunnan Province, China is known as the closest snowline to Southeast Asia. In addition to the scenic beauty of the location, the indigenous peoples' cultures can also be considered a resource. For instance, the matrilineal community of the Moso around Lugu Lake in Lijiang Prefecture is known and even advertised as the 'Land where women rule'. Realizing the rent potential of a scarce natural resource, though, does require a degree of public investment (Kaplinsky, 2005).

At the same time, even scare scenic natural resources are not so unique. In an earlier chapter (Chapter 6), the tourism value chain was analysed and it was seen that a condition of high competition among sellers and the oversupply of services can lead to a complete dissipation of rents in the value chain, resulting in the phenomenon of the 'zero-fee tour'. One way of getting around the dissipation of rents was through the suppliers getting organized and restricting supply.

Given the context outlined above, this chapter examines the poverty-reducing impacts of tourism in Yunnan, China. In Yunnan Province as a whole, the gap between farmers' net per capita incomes in the areas inhabited by indigenous peoples (minority) and majority areas went down from 38 per cent in 1995 to just 10 per cent in 2004 (Nathan et al., 2012). What accounts for this reduction in the income gap between minority and non-minority areas? For the one million people in Lijiang Prefecture, at least, the reduction in this gap is due to the growth of tourism.

In the villages we investigated, tourism now accounts for at least half of village income; for some villages around Lugu Lake, tourism accounts for virtually all village income. Indeed, it accounts for most of the income growth in these villages. Involving most households, the widely distributed income growth from tourism has virtually eliminated poverty from these villages. Of course, the development of tourist income in these areas must be seen in the context of the local government policy of restricting supply (forcing hotels to shut down by rotation in the off-season) and of the local suppliers own self-organization to restrict competition and thus regulate the supply of tourism-related services. In examining the role of tourism, therefore, we start with the nature of local linkages of the tourism value chain.

7.3 Tourism and local linkages

The upland economic regions of China are labour surplus economies, which means the use of labour in tourism services can be carried out without any negative effect on agricultural production. The income from such a Lewisian transfer of surplus labour from agriculture to tourism would provide a net addition to local income, thus contributing to poverty reduction. The extent of poverty reduction would, however, depend on the nature of the link between the local and external segments of the value chain.

The extent to which tourism has an impact depends on the sector's local linkages, which can be in terms of materials and services provided. Accommodation, transport and guides are the key areas of local tourist income. Other forms of destination impacts are through excursions, most commonly white-water rafting, hiking, and horse or mule rides. As proportions of tourist expenditure, they may be quite small, but when there is high volume associated with these activities, then there can be substantial impacts on poverty.

141

Excursions and entertainment are often the key part of the tourism experience, they are what distinguish one destination from another. Inadequate information (about various services, their prices and availability), high transaction costs (in finding adequate quality service providers) and trust deficits (uncertainty over whether services contracted at a distance will in fact be provided) result in tourists seeking intermediaries. The function of the intermediary, or composite tour operator (TO) is to put together or integrate a tourist package, which includes all of the required services. The need to integrate a package as a tourist product leads to a high level of intermediation in tourism. This affects the share of income acquired by service providers in the destination as powerful intermediaries acquire higher shares of the tourism income.

The high share of income acquired by the intermediaries, leads to one strand of analysis that points out that destination segments acquire relatively low shares of the total tourist income (Clancy, 2001), often characterised as adverse inclusion (Phillips, 2013). At the same time, another strand of analysis could point to the increase in local incomes due to tourism and the poverty-reducing impact of local tourist expenditures. Which measure one uses depends on the objective of the analysis. If the objective of the analysis were to explore distribution and inequality, then share of income would be the correct measure to use. However, if the objective of the analysis were to examine absolute poverty, then the correct measure would be the income earned, which can be compared with the poverty benchmark. There is a connection between the distributional and poverty analyses, as a better distribution increases the impact on poverty. In this chapter, since the focus is on the poverty impact of services provided by villagers in the distribution, we concentrate on the incomes earned locally, and not on the shares of tourism income. As we will see, even a relatively minor activity, such as horse riding carried out in sufficiently large volume, can have a substantial impact on poverty.

Thus, it is necessary to look at both the scale and the extent of the impact to assess poverty reduction. Home-stays, for instance, are relatively high income services, but the number of households involved may be limited. In addition, home-stays are likely to benefit the community's better-off households, who may already have incomes that put them above the poverty line. Specialty tourism too tends to be high impact, but of low volume. The amount of money spent per tourist in the destination may be high, but the numbers who benefit from this high expenditure are low. On the other hand, mass tourism is a high volume activity, though the amount of money spent locally per person may be quite limited.

The difference between the benefits of the two types of tourism is illustrated by the circumstances of the initial Moso tourist village on Lugu Lake. Home-stays have substantially increased the income of the initial 43 households who own village guest houses and have resulted in this village becoming one of the 10 richest villages in the Prefecture. On the other hand, the relatively low-paying horse rides, repeated across many villages in the Prefecture, have helped raise many such villages to above poverty levels.

Thus, it is necessary to take both volume and unit price into account when assessing the impact of a tourism segment on poverty reduction. Merely examining the distribution of shares of income across the value chain will not enable such an assessment of poverty impact. As a result of the two different measures of impact, one of relative distribution of income shares and the other of the absolute amounts earned, there may well be two different kinds of statements to be made about the impact of tourism, statements which may both be true at the same time.

7.4 Tourism entrepreneurs in Lijiang villages

There are two main pathways through which tourism can impact the rural economy. One is through the development of destination facilities, such as accommodation, food, and excursions. Instead of this being carried out by TOs, this could be provided and managed by local community organizations in the manner that has come to be called community-based tourism (CBT), or by individual providers of the same services.

The other way in which tourism impacts the rural economy is through the development of facilities for the provision of services (food, rest, etc.) along the route taken by tourists. We will consider both of these in turn, based on field observations in Lijiang.

Provision of accommodation in guest houses is a high-income earning segment of the tourism GVC. However, constructing and managing a guest house is not just a matter of having the capital required, but also of having the know-how to manage one. This management knowledge takes some time to acquire. Discussions with some Naxi guest house owners in Lijiang showed that this knowledge is often acquired through observation. The Naxi owners initially leased out their houses to Han entrepreneurs to run guest houses. They observed what was being done and then, after the lease expired, took the guest houses back in order to run them themselves.

This process was facilitated by the legal restrictions on sales of Naxi-owned houses to non-Naxi individuals. The houses could be leased but not sold, so there was a way to get them back. In the Moso village on Lugu Lake, the village had its own regulation that required a local partner for any outside investor.

These restrictions enabling local control over the guest houses should be contrasted with the situation in the Great Wall region. In the village of Mutyanlu, a company registered in the British Virgin Islands and owned by an American and Chinese couple had bought some peasant homes and redone them as guest houses. Others too had bought such peasant houses. The peasant owners may have been paid a good price, but they had no possibility of subsequently re-establishing control over the houses. This would be fine for those who desired to migrate, but not necessarily for others.

In the Moso village of Luoshui on Lugu Lake, in Yunnan, China, the guest houses in which tourists stay are all owned, most wholly and a few partially, by local villagers. The village of Luoshui[1] had in the 1990s taken action to ensure that tourists would use their residential facilities and not those provided by a nearby government-run hotel. They refused to provide various excursion and entertainment facilities to those who did not stay in village-owned guest houses. Of course, by 2011, tourism had grown to such an extent that such a restriction became meaningless.

By 1996, tourism had replaced farming in Luoshui village as the leading sector and was the main source of income for most households. Luoshui is now known far and wide as a relatively wealthy tourist village and is, in fact, one of the 10 richest villages in Lijiang prefecture. Thirty-two out of thirty-three households located on the lake front have built new wooden houses and acquired telephones, refrigerators, washing machines, and television sets. Small appliances are increasingly popular. Each family has a flush toilet and some households even have water heated by solar energy equipment. This was the situation observed in 2005. In 2012, such developments had spread through most of the village. There were cars in many houses, and motor-cycles in the rest. A few guest houses have also come up in the Naxi village of Yu Hu. They usually offer overnight stays.

Guest houses, however, require a fair amount of investment and there is often a strong inequality factor in their development. Not many of the former peasants would be able to set up guest houses. For instance, the village of Wen Hai got around the inequality problem by forming a cooperative to own and run the guest houses. Having at least one family member working in a good urban job seems an important factor in being able to get the required capital. Once the owners learn how to manage a guest house and provide the necessary services, the returns are potentially quite high.

---

[1] The data on Luoshui village date back to the early 2000s, when it had already become one of the richest villages in Lijiang Prefecture. When we revisited the village in 2012 there seemed to be nothing but tourism in the entire area around Lugu Lake.

On Lugu Lake, the poorer villagers whose houses were not located on the lake shore have not benefited as much from tourism, but they supply most of the other amenities that tourists require, like horse and boat riding. The villages of Shi Hu (at Lashe Lake, near the Prefecture headquarters) and Yu Hu (the village from which the botanist–ethnographer Joseph Rock conducted his studies of the Naxi and Moso in the 1930s and 1940s) are half an hour and an hour away from Lijiang. They both receive large numbers of tourists for horse rides, varying in duration from an hour to 6 hours and costing US$ 50–100 per person. The excursions are mainly organized by tour companies who send the tourists. The tourists pay the company, who in turn pay the villagers every month.

In Shi Hu village, they reported that for eight months of the year they earn Y5,000–6,000 per month and for 4 months Y2,000–3,000. Out of 70 families in the village, 40 participate in the horse rides[2] and own three horses each. They rotate the use of horses for rides and share the income equally. Each family cares for its own set of three horses, which cost about Y16,000 per year to maintain.

Each horse-riding family in Shi Hu gets a net annual income of US$ 5,300–7,300. This is a net addition to their income, which did not exist 5 years ago.

In the village of Yu Hu, which has about 300 households, about 1,000 tourists visit every day in the peak season. Horse-owning villagers earn Y2,000–2,500 and about Y1,000 per month off-season. However, they have just one horse each, so their net earnings from the horse rides are not very different from Shi Hu villagers and come to around $5,000 per year.

There are three points to note about the manner in which the horse-ride enterprise is organized. First, the organization of tourist visits is undertaken by an outside company, which gives just one-third of the list price to the villagers of Y100–400, although the villagers do not know how much the company charges the tourists. Another third is paid as commissions to the TOs, tour guides, and drivers (about 15 per cent, 10 per cent, and 5 per cent, respectively). The company keeps one-third of the price, some of which would be passed on as commission to TOs.

The second point is that the participating villagers share the horse rides and the resulting income equally among themselves. This maintains a manner of equality in sharing the benefits from tourism. In Yu Hu, about 7 years ago, the villagers initially started providing horse rides individually, but the resulting competition led to low prices. As a result, the villagers began working as a group, which not only leads to

---

[2] The 30 families which do not participate in the horse rides all have the main adult(s) working in towns.

Yang Fuquan, Yu Xiaogang, Yu Yin, Govind Kelkar and Dev Nathan

the equal sharing of income, but, importantly, eliminates competition among the villagers and thus keeps prices high. The elimination of competition is an important policy of restricting supply and thus earning rents.

At the same time, however, the maintenance of horses is undertaken individually by each household (or, rather, by the women in the household). This household-based caring for horses means that inter-household free-rider and collective action issues do not crop up in caring for the horses.

7.5   Income impact of excursion segment of tourism

Village income has gone up substantially. Not all of the US$ 5,000 per year from horse rides is additional income, as some lower-income types of activities have been abandoned or reduced, such as collecting non-timber forest products (broom grass or cane). But in both the villages, it was estimated that about 50 per cent of income of participating households now comes from tourism.

An additional source of tourism-based income is that of village youth working in the town. In Shi Hu, which is just across the hill from Lijiang town, almost two-thirds of families have at least one member who works in the town; while in Yu Hu it is about one-third of families. Both in these villages and in Lijiang town, we were constantly told that at least two-thirds of youth in the Prefecture are involved in tourism. Indeed, the only youth who continue to live in the villages were those involved in tourism.

As a result of the increase in income in both villages, we were told that there were no poor families anymore. From discussions conducted in the two villages, we estimated the following well-being distribution of households, shown in Table 7.1.

In both villages, the chief criterion of being poor meant not having enough to eat. As the most educated person from Yu Hu (now working in an international NGO in Lijiang) said, 'We used to be hungry when I was a child. Now we have so much of everything'.

In Yu Hu, we were told that those families who had someone doing well in the town were somewhat better off. The remittances from these children enabled the families to acquire various electronic gadgets, etc. Most households in both the villages had colour TVs, washing machines, rice cookers, private toilets, solar heaters, and even liquid petroleum gas, though they also used firewood to boil water. Many household gadgets were bought in 2008–2009, when the government provided subsidies for rural purchases of these household electronic goods to counteract the effects of the global slowdown.

Table 7.1   Changes in well-being in two villages of Lijiang

	Shi Hu village (70 HHs)		Yu Hu village (300 HHs)	
	1996	**2011**	**1996**	**2011**
Poor	50%	None	100%	None
Not-poor	None	100%	None	100%
Well-off	None	None	None	Few

Note: 1996 is the usual comparison year etched in people's memories, since it was the year of the big earthquake, which destroyed a good part of the Old Town of Lijiang. After that earthquake, the government poured in a lot of money for rebuilding (there was a requirement that all rebuilding in the Old Town of Dayan had to preserve the old exterior architectural style), and into improving infrastructure. In a perverse but beneficial manner, the earthquake drew attention to the architectural, cultural, and scenic attractions of Lijiang. Before 1996, tourism in Lijiang was dominated by foreigners, including overseas Chinese. At present, however, Chinese domestic tourists dominate the market.

The economies of villages around Lugu Lake, as seen in 2012, have become entirely based on tourism. The number of tourists has grown from less than 20,000 in 1994 to almost 500,000 in 2011. Along with this, income too has grown dramatically. When the villages depended on agriculture, fishing, and other natural resource-based economic activities, per capita income was about Y400–500 (less than US$ 100, or US$ 1,200 per year) in 1992. But this has now increased to more than Y40,000 (or US$ 7,000) per year in 2010.[3] The sheer volume of tourists has transformed the area.

Without being able to check the figures, the magnitude of change is visible. All the researchers have visited the villages around Lugu Lake over at least 20 years. The differences in the quality of housing, types of food consumed, clothes, motor vehicles, household appliances—all these changes are dramatic. The villages around Lugu Lake have moved from being among the poorest in Yunnan to being among the richest in the province. In the mid-1990s, only the pioneering tourist village of Luoshe was well off, but now all the villages around Lugu Lake are well off. Large numbers of Han Chinese from Sichuan and other neighbouring provinces have also migrated to work here. From an initial labour-surplus situation, the area now has become a magnet for migrants from other areas.

---

[3] Data supplied by the Tourism Office, Lugu Lake.

In contrast to the major income transformations brought about by mass tourism above, we should note the relative deprivation of a poorly connected village, that of the Yi on the hill above Lashe Lake. In 1998, we had to walk up the hill. But even in 2012, this village was not connected by a road suitable for motor vehicles. We had to cover the last few kilometres by tractor. With such poor communication, the village received only a few 'adventure tourists' or researchers, like us. The village still relies on upland cultivation of buckwheat, livestock, and extraction of forest products as its major sources of income. In 2012, clothes and food are better than they were in the mid-1990s, but most houses are still of the old type. With poor educational levels and lacking urban social networks, there was very little migration to the urban tourist centres. Villagers are eager for their village to be well connected, so that they can also benefit from tourism. In a sense they saw their poverty as being due to not being related to tourism, i.e., as residual rather than relational.

7.6 Gender roles and relations in tourism

How has the development of tourism affected gender roles and relations in the Lijiang villages? Whether in guest houses or horse rides, tourism has increased women's workload. In the guest houses, there is the work of cooking and cleaning, which is done almost entirely by women or hired help. In the case of horses, again it is women who do the job of feeding and otherwise caring for them. Feeding includes cutting and carrying fodder for the horses. In Shi Hu village, we saw some women carrying fodder on their backs, and some in bicycle-vans, so at least some of the income was being used to reduce women's drudgery. But, overall, there has been a substantial increase in women's workload, both in running the guest houses and in caring for horses.

Does the additional income from tourism accrue to women? In the case of horses, it goes directly to the men of the household. Some of them told us that they give about one-third to their wives for household expenses and keep the rest themselves. Some of this portion may be saved or invested, but the men too reported that there was an increase in their expenditure on cigarettes, alcohol, and entertainment.

In the matrilineal Moso village, there were signs of changes in gender roles in household management. External contact was and is the province of men. When the village was still a subsistence economy, external contact played little role in the largely domestic economy. With the development of tourism, external contact has become more important. In particular, loans for investment in guest houses were secured through external contact with the government and banks. Being the conduit for securing loans, even if the property ownership system remained matrilineal and the keys of the house, including the guest house, were with the mother (or the eldest daughter), men had more of a role in managing the commercial affairs of the guest houses. Labour in the guest houses, where it was not done by hired staff, remained the preserve of women. At the same time, the grandmother still remained the head of the household.

In Lijiang, it can be seen that rural women, when they are not owners of land, as in Lugu Lake, are involved in tourism activities, and fall within the category of 'contributing family workers'. They do not upgrade their economic status to either own-account or wage workers. In either of these cases, there is likely to be an improvement in status, as women would be seen as bringing their own income into the household and would thus be recognized as independent income earners. This, as the theory of cooperative conflict in household bargaining predicts, would strengthen women's bargaining position within the household and increase their capacity to increase their own well-being within the household.

Large numbers of young women, however, have become independent income earners, often as tour guides and in organizing various tourist services. This independent income would increase their status in their families and communities. All over these tourist areas one can see an increased self-confidence and assertiveness of young women involved in tourism.

But there is also the growth of sex tourism, involving young women from poor areas surrounding the better-off tourist destinations; and something villages on the shore of Lugu Lake try to deal with by banishing the 'Karaoke' joints to outside village limits. Tourism provides young women many types of jobs; and sex tourism is not the main form of these jobs, but it does exist and is seen to be difficult to deal with.

7.7 Quality of jobs and competition

The jobs in the tourism sector in this case study, are very much of the self-employed or own-account type in the informal sector, or, since services are provided by the household, as contributing family workers. Obviously, the jobs themselves do not provide any kind of insurance or other social protection. But, in China, the workers do have medical insurance, which is provided to the whole rural population. Since tourism is, in the main, seasonal, the jobs are also seasonal. In the case of Lijiang though, there are a fair number of tourists, even in the off-season.

What is important about the jobs is that they are largely of the low-skill variety, being jobs that rural people can take up with their agriculture-based educational levels. This is important in providing an avenue for non-farm employment for low-skilled workers and thus reducing poverty.

What does help to improve earnings is the factor of organization. Where guest house or excursion services are provided individually there is competition among service providers, leading to low rates. For instance, in rafting in Uttarakhand, India, competition has led to high capacity and brought down margins for service providers. The circumstances are similar for the porters and mule-providers along the trekking routes in these areas. In many villages in Lijiang, the villagers initially provided horse rides individually but found that internal competition brought down their prices. They then organized themselves and rotated service supply. Where the service providers are organized, as is the case now in Lijiang generally, they are able to limit entry and keep prices from falling.

In the tourist city of Venice, there is a good example of ancient guild systems being maintained in order to eliminate competition and thus keep prices high.[4] There are only 50 or so families of gondoliers, who take tourists for boat rides in the iconic Venetian canals. This absolute entry barrier enables them to charge as much as €100 for a 30-minute gondola ride, and it is easy to restrict entry into the gondola ride segment. But, in the case of glass-blowing, the Venetians are not able to control the flood of Chinese glass into the city markets. The glass-blowers of Murano thus market their products as high-end artistic works, in comparison to the cheaper Chinese glass pieces.

In value chain segments that are easily entered, as emphasized in Kaplinsky (2005), the normal working of the market-cum-bargaining relationship of value chains would tend to push earnings down to the least possible. Where there is a condition of surplus labour with no other type of employment, as could be the case in upland economies, wages, or earnings could be well below the living wage. However, wages or earnings can be sustained at higher levels and contribute to poverty reduction when organizations of service providers are able to act like 'closed-door' trade unions and keep prices from falling to the lowest possible levels on the market.

7.8 Conclusion

Jobs in tourism, particularly those at tourist destinations, are often characterized as being seasonal and low-paying (Clancy, 2001; Slob and Wilde-Ramsing, 2006). What our case study shows is that even relatively low-paying jobs, such as conducting horse or mule rides or being porters and guides, can have a substantial impact on poverty. Compared to the higher-paying segment of accommodation provision, large numbers of local people (albeit largely men) participate in these

---

[4] Discussions with hotel staff and a gondolier in Venice and personal observation.

end-of-chain tourism activities. Overall, even such seemingly low-end jobs, through mass tourism, can result in a substantial reduction of poverty in upland economies.

Importantly, these jobs are secured by those with little or even no education, rather than the office-based tourism jobs secured by those with higher education and skills.

Both the size of the sector and the share that reaches the poor are important, not just one or the other (Mitchell and Ashley, 2010). A higher share of a small sector, such as community tourism, may not have as much of an impact on poverty as a lower share of a large sector, such as mass tourism. The ability of local workers, particularly the poor, to take up the segments of the value chain that can easily be localized is important in determining the impact of tourism on poverty in the destination areas. The nature of these linkages limits the extent to which tourism can positively impact on well-being in destination areas. This impact, again, can be increased by organization of the workers, which both reduces competition among service providers and could increase their bargaining power *vis-à-vis* the bulk buyers of their services, such as TOs.

The excursion-type jobs in tourism, however, are both heavily male-dominated and carry forward forms of social exclusion. Those in poorly connected villages in the uplands are also excluded from the benefits of tourism. Women, as we have seen, bear an increased work burden in, for instance, looking after horses or providing house-keeping services in guest houses. They undertake this work, however, as contributing family workers and as a result their status within the household or community does not necessarily rise.

Further, since these are largely jobs of the self-employed type, they do not carry social security benefits, nor can social security benefits be provided directly through the TOs. What can be done is to levy a cess on the industry as a whole, in the form of payment to the state made by each tourist. The money from the cess can then be used to provide social security or medical benefits. Alternatively, such benefits could also be provided directly by the state, financed out of general taxes rather than out of an industry cess, as is done in China.

Finally, we should note the importance of tourism as a non-farm economic activity in upland economies with limited agricultural or manufacturing potential. Rather than crowding out other domestic sectors (Dwyer et al., 2000), tourism is the one form of non-farm economic activity that can develop in remote upland economies. Additionally, since tourism relies on a clean environment, there is a stake in encouraging rural hygiene and preserving nature, which is a key asset in tourism.

The benefit of improved environmental conditions follows from the shift from resource extraction economic activities to tourism as the means of livelihood. But this too requires the management of supply of services. For instance, when a cable car system replaced horses in taking tourists up to the legendary Suicide Meadow of the Naxi overlooking the Jade Dragon Mountain, there was an initial degradation of the meadow with the increased numbers of tourists tramping on the meadow. But the local government soon put up a fenced boardwalk, which was the only space open to tourists. This has enabled the meadow to recover and regenerate.

In addition, there is the higher valuation of environmental resources themselves, on which tourism depends. For example, villagers in the lakeside village of Laoshe villagers have abandoned their earlier practice of capturing wild birds for sale. Tourism, in part, depends on the lake being a reserve for migratory birds and would be affected by the elimination or reduction in number of these migratory birds. In addition, many non-traditional fishers have abandoned fishing, as they earn more from tourism-related activities, such as horse rides. As a result, the number of fishing boats has gone down from 500 to just 50. In villages around Lugu Lake, farming has been virtually abandoned as an economic activity. Farm land has been rented to the state for reforestation.

The inverse relationship between the growth of non-farm activities and the continuation of farming has been observed in other contexts too. In Thailand, after the onset of the late 1990s recession, rural migrants were laid-off from their urban jobs. On returning to their villages, they often cleared land to plant cassava or undertook the extraction of non-timber forest products (Nathan and Kelkar, 1998). A fall in urban income led to an increase in resource-extractive farming and collection. On the other hand, the recent construction boom in the forested state of Jharkhand, India, was seen to result in the lowered extraction of non-timber forest products, as wage employment in construction provided a higher income than collection and sale of non-timber forest products (IHD, 2011).

Such concern for nature can also be quite limited, even when beneficial. In Xishuangbanna, in southern Yunnan, a tourist village had protected the forest as it was necessary to attract tourists, especially since the village advertised a 'walk in the rainforest' as its main attraction. But a walk around the hill showed that only the side facing the road was forested, while the other side of the hill was bare! Protection with a commercial objective can thus be quite limited. Of course, the remedy is not to do away with all monetary gain attached to environmental protection but to generalize remuneration for provision of environmental services.

To return to the main point of this analysis, organization of the service providers, either as unions of service providers or workers, is important if returns from tourism are to increase. The *laissez faire* operation of market forces, however, would dissipate the rents and reduce or even eliminate the poverty-reducing impacts of tourism. Nonetheless, rents can be secured by service providers restricting and regulating supply. By securing rents through organized suppliers, the poverty reduction impacts of even otherwise easy to enter value chain segments can be quite substantial.

References

Clancy, M. 2001. 'Mexican Tourism: Export Growth and Structural Change Since 1970.' *Latin Am Res Rev* 36 (1).

Dwyer, L., P. Forsyth, J. Madden, and R. Spurr. 2000. 'Economic Impacts of Inbound Tourism Under Different Assumptions Regarding the Macroeconomy.' *Curr Iss Tourism* 3 (4).

Institute for Human Development (IHD). 2011. *Poverty and Gender Analysis of Jharkhand.* IHD: Ranchi (mimeo).

Kaplinsky, Raphael. 2005. *Globalization, Poverty and Inequality.* Cambridge: Polity Press.

Mitchell, J. and C. Ashley. 2010. *Tourism and Poverty Reduction: Pathways to Prosperity.* London: Earthscan.

Nathan, D., T. Ganesh, K. Govind, and A. Cordone. 2012. *Markets and Indigenous Peoples in Asia: Lessons from Development Projects.* New Delhi: Oxford University Press.

Paraskevas, A. 2005. 'The Impact of Technological Innovation in Managing Global Value Chain in the Tourism Industry' (mimeo). Paper Presented at OECD Conference on Global Tourism Growth: A Challenge for SMEs, Gwangju, Korea, 6–7 September 2005.

Philips, Nicola. 2013. 'Globalization and Development.' In *Global Political Economy*, edited by John Ravenhill. Oxford: Oxford University Press.

Slob, B., and J. Wilde-Ramsing. 2006. 'Tourism and Sustainability in Brazil: The Tourism Value Chain in Porto de Galinhas, Northeast Brazil.' Report. Amsterdam: Center for Research on Multinational Corporations (SOMO).

8

Restructuring of Post-crisis GVCs

Tourism in Bali, Indonesia

Girish Nanda and Keith Hargreaves

8.1 Introduction

Global value chains (GVCs) can change in structure, with a key factor in such changes being shocks. Shocks are defined as occurrences that originate from outside the system, or are exogenous to the GVC. Within the tourism GVC, one of the most powerful factors within the GVC is the tourists, the customers themselves. A shock could affect the composition of tourists, and not all segments of the GVC are likely to be affected equally. For instance, the current global economic crisis has clearly impacted developed economies more than emerging economies. This could result in a shift in the composition of tourists away from the developed economies towards the emerging economies. Tour operators (TOs) from the two sets of countries would correspondingly gain or lose power within the GVC, with domestic TOs gaining proportionately more from new business opportunities as a result.

In the current post-crisis situation, there has been some attention given to the restructuring of GVCs. Cattaneo et al. (2011) point to the shifts in end markets and the growing importance of emerging economies and regional value chains. However, it is not just end markets and product standards that could change, but the structure of GVCs as well. Milberg and Winkler (2011) point to the possibilities of both vertical and horizontal consolidation in value chains. Vertical consolidation could take place when markets shrink, thus reducing the extent of the division of labour and leading to some consolidation of tasks within the remaining tiers of the supply chain. There could also be horizontal consolidation, with the number of firms operating in any tier falling on account of the shrinking market. Milberg and Winkler raise an interesting question about whether there would be symmetry in shrinkage and recovery, with the number of firms being restored in recovery. They expect that the high-productivity suppliers might be better able to expand in recovery, so that there would be a consolidation in the GVC. They also put forward the hypothesis that buyer-driven chains would experience more consolidation than supplier-driven chains.

This paper explores changes in the tourism GVC on the Indonesian islands of Bali and Sulawesi. It looks at a number of recent shocks to tourism in the island economy, starting with the Asian financial crisis of the late 1990s, and taking in the mid-2000s, severe acute respiratory syndrome (SARS) epidemic and tsunami, as well as the Bali bombings in 2002 and 2005, with the latter being where our analysis is concentrated. In analysing changes in GVC structures following shocks, we look at a few crucial factors: the changing composition of tourists, the development of new segments of the industry and the growth or decline of the labour force and related social downgrading before and after these shocks. There is a brief comparison of the experience of Bali with that of Tana Toraja in Sulawesi. While tourism recovered after each shock in Bali, island-based ethnic conflicts in Sulawesi led to a virtual collapse of tourism. The paper also lays out some initial discussion on the differences between the two islands' experiences. This question of coping with shocks has not been addressed in the papers mentioned above (Cattaneo et al., 2011). To this end, we ask the following questions in our paper: what were the coping mechanisms adopted by those who lost employment and income in the aftermath of the shocks? What was the role of the 'family rice bowl' in coping with shocks?

The study is based on a combination of secondary and primary data. Primary data were collected from both enterprises and workers in tourism. Overall, investigations were conducted with 30 enterprises of different types, TOs, hotels, guest houses, shops, and other service providers in the two centres of Bali and Tana Toraja. To understand coping mechanisms, structured interviews were conducted with 21 employees and own-account workers. These interviews and investigations were conducted in Bhasa Indonesia.

Additionally, many interviews were conducted with officials, informed persons, industry associations, and operators at various levels in the industry. Secondary data are from government reports and analyses carried out by national and international agencies.

8.2 Shocks and tourism

Tourism dominates Bali's economy. This includes a large number of economic sectors—accommodation, travel, restaurants, entertainment, etc. Tourism Satellite Accounts (TSAs) estimate the contribution of tourism to GDP using input–output estimates of the various inputs into each unit of tourism. One TSA exercise estimated that tourism accounts for more than 50 per cent of the island's income (Lumaksono, 2007). Bali is also a tourism destination that has faced a history of critical shocks in the recent past, especially the Bali bombings in 2002 and 2005.

The available literature on the effects of external or internal shocks has shown that the tourism sector is particularly vulnerable. The following are two examples that support this notion. In Thailand, 6 months after the occurrence of the tsunami, year-on-year occupancy rates in Phuket fell by 57 per cent, while occupancy rates in the relatively smaller tourist destinations of Phang Na and Krabi fell by 63 per cent. According to a survey conducted by the Asian Development Bank (ADB) in the above three provinces in June 2006, individuals dependent on incomes from tourism were the most severely affected: 92 per cent of Beach Vendors and 86 per cent of Entrepreneurs experienced a decrease in income (Bhanupong, 2007).

During the SARS outbreak of 2003, which originated in Guangdong province in China, anecdotal evidence suggested that the tourism and travel industry in neighbouring Hong Kong was the most severely affected, with the press reporting reductions of 10–50 per cent in the sales of retail and restaurant outlets. Between March and April 2003, visitor arrivals to Hong Kong fell by 63 per cent. Occupancy rates in hotels fell from 79 per cent in March 2003 to 18 per cent in early May 2003. Even though a recovery occurred by July, the short-term effects of the outbreak were severe, as the above statistics suggest (Siu and Wong, 2006). The sharp contraction in tourist numbers immediately after the SARS episode intensified competition among both TOs and service providers in China and facilitated the phenomenon of the 'zero-fee' tour, that is, where the price of a tour at best covers travel and accommodation costs, as discussed in Chapter 6.

Examples of other recent shocks include the September 2001 terrorist attack on the World Trade Centre in New York, the Bali bombings, the Asian financial crises, ethnic/religious tensions and the 2008 global financial crisis, of which the 2002 Bali bombings were the most significant shocks for Indonesia and Bali. The following sections review the effects of these shocks on the tourism industry of Bali in further detail.

8.3   Specific impact of shocks on Bali

Of the two types of external shocks, the case study of Bali strongly suggests that terrorist attacks pose a much stronger risk to the tourism GVC in terms of income, employment, and poverty levels than those resulting from the financial crises. This can be attributed to their unanticipated nature, because of the drastic and immediate reduction they bring about in demand and because of the implied (at least in the short term) threat they pose to the safety of potential tourists. This section first assesses the impacts of each of the Bali bombings and the financial crises that followed. It then explores the strategies firms used to cope with these crises and minimize the economic and social downgrading that occurred after the shocks, and the strategies workers used to cope with such downgrading. Finally, it examines the government's response during these crises.

In the context of the response to the shocks, both annual and monthly timeframes must be analysed closely, as they provide a better perspective of the depth and short-term impact of the shocks. Further, in order to assess post-crisis conditions better, surveys provide an accurate perspective of the strategies both firms and employees use to cope with the crises. Before we discuss the impacts of the crises in detail, we present Figure 8.1, which shows the total number of foreign arrivals in Bali during the period 1997–2010.

Figure 8.1 shows a slight dip after the Asian financial crisis in 1997, but this is followed by quick growth in 1998 and 1999. After the Bali bombings in 2002 and 2005, there were sharp dips in foreign arrivals. But what is noteworthy is the quick recovery in terms of total numbers of foreign tourists: in each case, the year after the dip there are recovery numbers that are higher than the previous highest point. Behind the increase in numbers, as we see later on, is a change in the country-wise composition of tourists. The 2008 global financial crisis had no impact on total foreign arrivals, pointing to the limited scope of this crisis.

While the 1997–1998 Asian financial crisis had a devastating impact on the Indonesian economy as a whole, the impact on Bali's economy was relatively small. In a report by SMERU (an independent research group) on the social impact of the crisis in different regions of Indonesia, Bali was rated 38th out of the 51 regions at

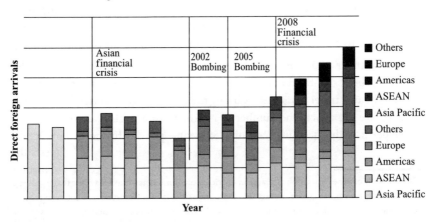

Figure 8.1 Foreign arrivals in Bali, 1997–2010

Source: Bali Tourism Statistics (2011).

the time. The study indicated that parts of Sumatra, Sulawesi, Maluku, and Bali were among the least affected (Wetterburg and Pritchett, 1998).

In a survey of 200 hotels in Bali, over 90 per cent of managers pointed out that the impact of the Asian financial crisis was much less severe as compared with that of the 2002 Bali bombing (World Bank and UNDP, 2003b). The May 1998 riots in Jakarta, which coincided with the Asian financial crisis, led to a 29 per cent reduction in tourist arrivals in May. Within a period of 3 months, however, tourist arrivals had surpassed April 1998 levels by a nominal margin. The initial decline in tourist arrivals in the month of May dropped from 92,936 to 66,326 (*ibid.*).

The quick recovery in the tourism industry can be attributed partially to the drastic devaluation of the rupiah to the dollar from an exchange rate of Rp2,200/US$ 1 to Rp7,500/US$ 1, which in effect made tourist services cheaper for foreigners visiting the island, thus boosting the total number of arrivals. This was even utilized as a tool for promotion, with the local government carrying the slogan, 'Our Loss is Your Gain'. In particular, the number of Australian tourists increased quite substantially after the Asian financial crisis.

In October 2002, the terrorist bombings in the prime tourist area of Kuta came as a rude shock to the people of Bali and the international community. The bombings had a profound impact not only on tourist arrivals to the island but also on the livelihood and employment of the people in Bali. Prior to the 2002 Bali bombing, Bali was finally on the road to recovery from the global slump in tourism caused by the 11 September 2001 attacks. Hotel prices alone had increased to their original levels after falling by 25–50 per cent following the 11 September 2001 attack (World Bank and UNDP, 2003a). Bali had barely begun to recover from the bombings when in April 2003 it was again hit by the impact of the Iraq War and the SARS epidemic, which proved to be a further dampener on tourist arrivals in the island.

In November 2002, the month after the Bali bombing, tourist arrivals had crashed to about one-third of expected levels, exacerbated by many major foreign countries issuing travel advisories[1] warning their citizens to avoid travel to Bali. Two weeks before the attack, the number of international arrivals had averaged 4,650 people per day; this had fallen to only 750 people per day by the end of October

---

[1] The question of the extent to which travel advisories actually influence travel is a topic that needs to be studied. But one cannot ignore the fact that there were clear falls in tourist arrivals following the Bali bombing shocks, which were accompanied by travel advisories. There is a definitely a politics of travel advisories. How many travel advisories were issued regarding travel to the US following 9/11? And how did the US government and businesses respond to any such advisories? As Michelle Christian (personal communication) points out, it would be worthwhile to study the politics of travel advisories.

(UNESCAP, 2005). After the bombing, there was in fact a mass exodus of tourists from the island. Tourism arrivals remained in a slump for the next 8 months, to a large extent because of concerns over the safety of the islands. With Australians representing the largest number of casualties during the 2002 bombing, they also constituted the segment with the most drastic post-bombing decline in terms of foreign direct arrivals of tourists. The security scare also led to a significant reduction in European foreign direct arrivals.

With the first bomb shattering perceptions of Bali as a safe tourist destination, the impact of the second bomb in October 2005 was of much less magnitude, although the method used, that is, suicide bombing, was the same. In 2003, after the first Bali bombings, tourists from both the Americas and the Asia-Pacific region had dropped by 21.8 per cent and 20.60 per cent, respectively. In contrast, after the 2005 Bali bombings, year-on-year reductions were less than half as much, at 10 per cent and 14 per cent, respectively.

A significant proportion of the victims of the second bomb blast were Indonesian nationals. An excerpt from The Bali Update (2005a) stated, 'Of the total 132 casualties at least 61 were Indonesian nationals. Australians suffered 17 casualties, 3 of which numbered among the dead, with Japanese, Koreans, and Americans also listed among those killed or injured in the blasts'. While Western countries were noted to have issued stricter travel advisories in the wake of the second Bali bombing, Australian visitors continued to come to Bali. Japan and Malaysia contributed 10 per cent of the tourists at the time while deciding not to strengthen their travel advisories.

In terms of direct foreign arrivals to Bali, the financial crisis in 2008 has had the least impact as compared with the other crises. There was, in fact, only 1 month, that is, February 2009, wherein monthly arrivals fell below the previous year's levels. With Bali's peak season normally centred around July and August, tourist arrivals in October were equally high. In addition, if we take a look at Australian tourist arrivals to Bali, which account for a major portion of its tourism, revenue growth was over 200 per cent between 2008 and 2010. Such a surge could be attributed partly to the fact that the Australian economy was not overexposed to the 2008 financial crisis. Japan, Bali's other core tourist market, on the other hand, was confronted with a weak economy. Visitor arrivals from Japan are also expected to continue to decline, given its nuclear disaster in March 2011 and the continuing stagnation of the Japanese economy.

Two tourist markets that grew rapidly after the 2008 global economic crisis were those of tourists from China and domestic tourists. While the Chinese do not comprise the majority of foreign tourists and domestic tourists are outnumbered by foreign tourists, Chinese and domestic tourists were the fastest-growing segments of the tourism market. The growing proportion of Chinese and domestic tourists had implications for both spending per day and services provided. Chinese and domestic tourists not only spent less per day than other tourists but also demanded different kinds of services (Hitchcock and Darma Putra, 2007).

8.4 Impact on tourism enterprises

Crisis does not only mean contraction. The Asian financial crisis from 1997 onwards did lead to a severe contraction of more than 20 per cent in the Indonesian economy. But the devaluation following the crisis also sparked off an expansion of the tourism industry in Bali. Tourism operations grew in all segments. Expanding tourism in Bali attracted many entrepreneurs and migrant workers of different types from the other islands.

On the basis of interviews and discussions in the field with practitioners and experts, this crisis can be seen as a catalyst for economic upgrading in the tourism GVC, with an increase in the number of foreign direct arrivals in 1999 and 2000. While there was a slowdown in 2001, a literature review suggests this was caused by the global rise in security fears created by the September 11, 2001 attacks. Therefore, some of the positive impact of this devaluation may have been counteracted by such events.

Bali has been a prime tourism destination for a long time. Opportunities have been driven mainly by preferences for prime tourist segments. But the steep devaluation of the Indonesian currency made Bali more attractive than many other competing destinations, including those in Thailand. The Indonesian government campaigned for foreigners to visit Bali, as we have seen, with the slogan 'Our Loss Is Your Gain'. The subsequent expansion of tourism in Bali could be related to the exchange rate gain brought about by devaluation.

Before going on to consider the economic impacts of the Bali bombing crises on tourism enterprises, it would be useful to summarize the Bali tourism GVC structure as it existed before the bombings. Figure 8.2 represents the Bali tourism GVC. Most foreign tourists came in through TOs or travel agencies located in their own countries. These foreign entities operated through local agents or national arrangers. These national arrangers implemented the tourist packet, arranging for the various tourism services needed other than international travel.

Relations between global and national arrangers were what can be called modular, that is, the foreign tour agencies made up a package and contracted the Indonesian agency to carry it out. The package was quite detailed in its specifications, covering the type of accommodation, transport, excursions. and so on. In this relationship, the Indonesian tour agencies tended to be in a weaker position, as there was substantial competition in that segment. The global buyer was an oligopolistic buyer, with a few

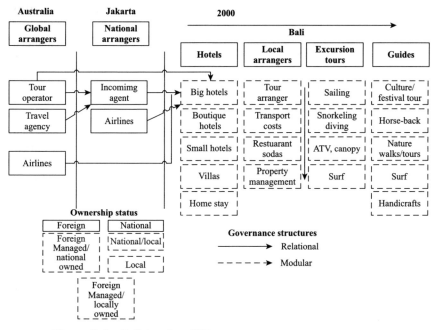

Figure 8.2 Bali tourism GVC

Source: Primary interviews with tourism providers at different levels of the GVC.

from each country being able to choose from many options among the Indonesian sellers. Indonesian sellers were unable to contact tourists directly and had to depend on global TOs to get them customers. This unequal relationship put the buyers in a stronger position in bargaining with sellers.

The national arrangers, in turn, arrange for the provision of various services. There was substantial competition among these service providers. Of course, the major hotel chains with their brand values could command premium prices. But the further down the network one went, and the lower the capital or skill required, the greater was the number of service providers. The high level of competition was among service providers, particularly those for excursions and beach-level services, and the commoditized nature of these services reduced the bargaining capacity of these service providers. With the ease of entry into these tourism segments, these segments could not command premium prices. We will return to the GVC later on to see how it changed through the crises between 2000 and 2010.

The impact of the 2002 bombing on local firms in the tourism industry was devastating, both in terms of numbers and if we look at indicators such as revenue, profits, and size of the workforce. The reduction in the workforce is an indicator of what is being called social downgrading; reductions in revenue and profits are both indicators of economic downgrading.

In the hotel segment of the tourism GVC, starred hotels with pre-bombing occupancy rates ranging from 65 to 100 per cent dropped to below 10 per cent at the end of October. Five-star hotels that had high pre-shock occupancy rates of more than 75 per cent dropped to 20 per cent immediately after the shock. While the hotel industry at the time employed only 3.3 per cent of the workforce, it contributed 21 per cent of Bali's GRDP, or gross regional domestic product (World Bank and UNDP, 2003a).

An industry-level survey of 140 tourism-related producers in the textiles, silver/metal, furniture and wood sectors across several sub-districts in Bali carried out in June 2003 (3 months after the bombing) reveals the extent of the economic impact of the crisis on these tourism-related industries. There was, on an average, a 51.6 per cent reduction in staff across all producer surveys, with the range being 33.9–60 per cent. In each of the sub-districts surveyed, on average 29.3 per cent firms broke even and 15.7 per cent made a loss (Table 8.1).

The same survey suggested that production levels were reduced significantly in response to the crisis, with average declines of 55 per cent (Table 8.2), with the firms adjusting to the crisis by making a significant reduction in staff to avoid major losses. As can be seen from the data, this strategy worked, as a substantial proportion of the firms surveyed did not make a loss in the end. Another important insight from this survey was that micro and small businesses were hit the hardest, suffering up to a 66.6 per cent reduction in staff and a 65.1 per cent reduction in sales. This is illustrated in Table 8.2.

Industries that directly catered to the tourist sector in Bali, including taxi drivers, traders, and handicraft producers, all suffered a loss in demand. Beach vendors and traders in most markets reported declines in turnover of more than 60 per cent. Table 8.3 provides a vivid illustration of the impact of the first Bali bombing on the business of vendors and traders in Bali.

The bombing in 2005 occurred at a time when fuel subsidies were reduced in Indonesia, thereby putting additional pressure on tourism-related industries that rely on fuel, particularly taxi drivers, although all industries rely heavily on fuel prices. Merpati Airlines, Garuda (Indonesia's national airline) and Air Paradise Airlines all faced debt difficulties post-crisis in 2005. Garuda posted a loss of US$ 70.7 million in 2005 (The Bali Update, 2006b). According to the Chairman of the Bali branch of the Indonesian Furniture and Handicraft Association, Mr Dewa Astama, 'the increase in the cost of fuel can be blamed for a 20 per cent reduction in sales and a further 30 per cent drop as the result of the recent bombings' (ibid.). Like the handicraft industry, the Taxi Drivers Union was also hit both by the fuel surcharge as well as a 30–40 per cent drop in night loads.

Table 8.1 Tourism industry-related survey

Product	Labour force			Profitability			Future outlook
	No.	% reducing staff	% reduction in staff	% breaking even	Loss		% not confident business would survive till end of year
Textiles	14	42.9	39.2	35.7	7.1		0.0
Silver/metal	14	92.9	35.8	64.3	7.1		7.1
Textiles	14	7.1	5.0	21.4	21.4		7.7
Furniture/wood	14	84.6	57.0	64.3	28.6		0.0
Furniture	14	69.2	69.4	7.1	7.1		7.1
Wood	14	71.4	57.0	21.4	28.6		0.0
Wood	14	71.4	51.8	21.4	42.9		7.1
Silver/metal	14	57.1	60.0	42.9	7.1		7.1
Wood	14	78.6	57.0	7.1	7.1		7.1
Wood	14	21.4	33.8	7.1	0.0		0.0
All	140	59.4	51.6	29.3	15.7		4.3

Source: World Bank and UNDP (2003b).

163

Table 8.2 Impact on micro and small businesses

Business indicator	Micro	Small	Medium
	1–4 staff	5–20 staff	20+ staff
% production outside of Bali	25.0	39.4	35.0
% reduction in staff	61.4	51.0	29.2
% reduction in production	66.6	54.9	38.6
% reduction in price	21.2	23.3	23.3
% export	18.7	24.5	33.8
% reduction in sales	65.1	55.8	41.4

Source: World Bank and UNDP (2003b).

An indicator of a slowdown in domestic tourism could also be gauged by the reduction in bus transport in Bali. According to the Head of the Kuta Central Parking Terminal, Mr. Haji Agus Bambang Priyanto, the number of buses using his facility in December 2005 totalled 409, down 55.39 per cent from the 917 buses that parked there in December 2004. The Chairman of the Bali Transportation Association (PAWIBA), Bagus Soediana, indicated that post the bombing, only 12 per cent of his Association's fleet was operating actively (The Bali Update, 2006a).

The two Bali bombings resulted in reductions in foreign tourist numbers as a whole. But the 2008 global financial crisis was quite different in that overall tourist numbers did not decline. Tourist numbers fell from those economies most affected by the financial crisis, in particular the North Atlantic economies. But tourist numbers increased from those not affected or not affected as much, such as China, Australia. and even Indonesia itself.

Firm-level interviews in Bali indicate that no one particularly suggested that this 2008 crisis was an issue, given the increase in regional tourism. One fact highlighted during interviews was that firms operating in the tourism segment, which also have heavy investments in the export sector, such as in garments, may have suffered reductions in the market.

8.5 Strategies of firms in tourism GVCs and changes in the composition of tourists

After the 2002 Bali bombing, with drastic reductions in the demand for tourism, discounts were offered by firms in the tourism GVC, including TOs, travel agents, and hotels. One survey indicated that 75 per cent of starred hotels dropped their

Table 8.3 Short-term impacts on beach vendors and traders

Trading location	District	Market type	No.	Average daily sales		Reduction in sales (%)	Average daily profit		Reduction in profit (%)
				Before tragedy Kuta (Rp)	Six months after (Rp)		Before tragedy Kuta (Rp)	Six months after (Rp)	
PantaiKuta	Badung	Tourist	102	1,51,716	60,735	60	48,284	18,578	62
PasarBadung	Badung	General	48	2,94,167	2,00,313	32	83,854	68,021	19
Pasar Sukawati	Gianyar	Tourist	50	5,61,000	1,76,400	69	1,77,000	35,900	80
PasarUbud	Gianyar	Tourist	30	3,98,333	1,16,667	71	1,48,333	43,500	71
PasarAmlapura	Karanga-sem	General	30	7,34,000	2,75,833	62	1,01,333	34,167	66

Source: UniversitasUdayana (Denpasar) Traders' Survey, May 2003, in World Bank and UNDP (2003b).

prices by an average of 37 per cent (World Bank and UNDP, 2003b). In terms of the hotel segment, five-star hotels were in a better position to weather the crisis, and stabilized their occupancy rates to 40 per cent within a period of 6 months. This can be attributed to their wider networks and greater ability to cut prices. Further, five-star hotels, with their global offices and reach, had more of an ability to assure tourists of safety and comfort as compared with the non-star hotels. Owing to such discounts, the five-star hotels in fact succeeded in attracting the former clientele of the one- to three-star establishments.

Firms also significantly shed their workers and reduced the number of working hours for active workers, as the previous section illustrated. In addition to the strategy of heavy discounts, both the government and private actors in the tourism GVC focused on facilitating growth in the domestic segment and regional segment (Association of Southeast Asian Nations—ASEAN) of tourism, which was much more supportive and willing to engage in tourism in Bali. Immediately during the post-crisis period, the government declared an additional national holiday and promoted Bali to its citizens (UNESCAP, 2005). The focus on the domestic sector is illustrated by the fact that, typically, three- to four-star hotels during the pre-crisis period had room occupancy of 25 per cent from domestic guests, while the corresponding figure rose to 85 per cent immediately after the advent of the post-crisis period.

However, domestic tourism was not able to substitute the decline in demand from international tourists. This was because the number of domestic tourists and their per capita expenditure was much lower than that of the foreign tourists. With domestic tourists incurring only one-third of the per day expenditure of foreign tourists and one-sixth of the length of stay, even if the increase in domestic visitor arrivals had compensated for the loss of foreign arrivals the tourism industry would still have been impacted by the various crises. An analysis of the overall number of foreign arrivals, as shown in Figure 8.3, indicates that, while the number of domestic tourists increased by over 600 per cent from November to December 2002, the proportion of domestic guests remained within 5–7 per cent of pre-shock levels during the remaining months until April 2003. As Table 8.4 shows, domestic tourists spent less than one-third (US$ 20) per day of that which foreign tourists spent per day (US$ 62). Regional tourists also spent 50 per cent less than those from Europe, Australia, and Japan (Hitchcock and Darma Putra, 2007).

After the first bombing, discounts were offered across the board to compensate for the short-term decline in arrivals. One such example in the airlines sector was the giving away of 10,000 international tickets by Garuda between 10 November and 31 December, with an additional 5,000 tickets given away in raffles for domestic travellers on board flights (The Bali Update, 2005a).

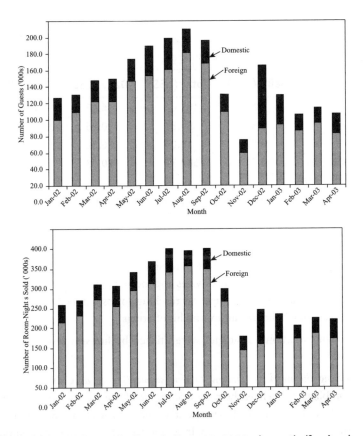

Figure 8.3 Visitor arrivals to Bali, 2002–2003, domestic/foreign break-up

Source: World Bank and UNDP (2003b).

Table 8.4 Foreign and domestic expenditure, 2003

Expenditure type	Foreign		Domestic	
	Daily (US$)	Total (US$)	Daily (US$)	Total (US$)
Accommodation	29.60	324.71	7.38	32.77
Food and drink	11.82	129.67	4.11	18.25
Transport	2.11	23.15	0.64	2.84
Attractions	1.54	16.89	0.97	4.31
Trips	2.81	30.83	0.98	4.35

(Contd)

Table 8.4 (Contd)

Expenditure type	Foreign		Domestic	
	Daily (US$)	Total (US$)	Daily (US$)	Total (US$)
Souvenirs	9.81	107.62	6.02	26.73
Guides	3.63	39.82	0.26	1.15
Other	0.92	10.09	0.32	1.42
Total (daily versus overall stay)	62.24	682.77	20.68	91.82

Source: World Bank and UNDP (2003b); Ministry of Tourism (www.depbudpar.go.id).
Note: The total is a result of daily expenditures and length of the stay.

Anecdotal evidence from interviews in the field confirms offers of such discounting/promotions like 'stay for three days and get one night free', free transport in and around certain areas, free tour services and room discounting, to name a few. One TO claims to have focused more on reaching tourists directly through the Internet by advertising Balinese culture and his offerings.

The following additional strategies were utilized by firms in response to the various crises[2]:

- *Diversifying the market—looking to new segments such as China and India*: The bombings, as well as the potential threat of the global economic crisis eventually leading to a slowdown in tourism, encouraged firms to look to high-growth markets in the Asian region. Interviewees suggested that the bombings as well as the financial crises might have put more pressure on firms to try to diversify markets.
- *Promoting the domestic market to make it grow*: In the case of the first Bali bombing, there was a distinct shift towards promoting the growth of the domestic tourism market, which has also gained prominence over the past 10 years.
- *Increasing packaging options*: After the 2002 bombing, several TOs said they had tried to increase the variety of tour packages to bring tourists back. One tour operator mentioned that, in 2002, Ubud, Tanah Lot, and Kintamani were the three basic offerings; after the crisis, additional tours were added, to Besakih, Ujung, and King's Palace.
- *Use of technology to help in the 2005 recovery*: Some respondents said the wider use of the Internet in 2005 increased firms' ability to reach tourists and

---

[2] This is based on firm and association interviews conducted by Strategic Asia.

focus on marketing. In addition, a former head of the Bali Hotels Association pointed out in an interview that the media was much more organized during the second bombing, thereby allowing starred hotels to recover more quickly in terms of regaining the confidence of tourists.

- *Cooperating under the aegis of the Bali Tourism Board*: The chairman of the Bali Tourism Board was officially asked to lead the recovery after the 2005 crisis, even though it played only a participatory role in the recovery after the first bombing. This umbrella organization of major tourist associations in Bali effectively monitored and utilized US$ 7.5 million of support money provided by the government. The success of this organization can perhaps be highlighted by Law No. 9 on Tourism of 2010, which made it a government entity, with the goal of duplicating it in the other provinces of Indonesia. The vice-chairman of the organization indicated that, although it had been in existence for over 20 years, it became more active especially after the two Bali bombings.
- *Focusing on quality*: An interview with a member of the Wood Handicrafts Association indicated that, after the first Bali bombing, with assistance from the government, there was a focus on increasing the quality of the handicraft products being manufactured. The association also emphasized the selection of high-quality material. The government offered its cooperation through three departments: the Department of Commerce, to help with the sales and promotion strategy; the Department of Industry, to promote techniques on how better to incorporate machinery and make the production process more efficient; and the Bali Government Tourism Office, which helped promote handicraft firms by organizing conventions and festivals, among other events.

The one general point that does emerge in the response to all shocks is that there was a post-shock search for markets. These new markets, however, were different from the older, established markets. In the tourism GVC, TOs from growing markets looked likely to gain strength, while those from declining or stagnant markets looked likely to lose strength.

8.6 Government response to the crises

The government, foreign donor agencies and countries, as well as the community in Bali, made a concerted effort to respond to the downturn in the local economy in the wake of the Bali bombings in 2002. Naturally, the first focus of these efforts was to strengthen security, because it was the fear of terrorist activity that was keeping tourists away from Bali. Security was strengthened by ramping up police presence in key tourist areas such as Kuta, as well as by setting up a specific working group for security in tourist areas to address the key concerns and vulnerabilities at the time.

Next came the relief for victims of the Bali bombings, and attempts were made to start addressing the socioeconomic impact of the bombing. The latter task was, however, the slowest to take off, because of administrative delays and the time needed to mobilize government machinery. Community-level organizations in Bali, notably the strong *adat* (traditional village government) institutions, responded swiftly to the crisis. Their efforts were aimed at supporting other security measures and mobilizing cash resources.

Emergency relief support to victims and assistance to police investigations were quickly made available from domestic and international sources. Donors and the government agreed to set up a monitoring system to assess the socioeconomic impact of the bombings and to identify the short-term needs of the local economy and society. There was early recognition of the fact that a successful strategy for recovery would need not only to resolve the socioeconomic impact of the bombings but also restore the image of Bali as an attractive and safe tourist destination. The central government allocated a sum of US$ 12 million for the efforts, which included tourism campaigns and security improvement. The victims of the bombings were given preferential access to healthcare and education. There was also a focus on developing new or more income-generating activities and enhanced access to social services.

The slow government response to the crisis was due to the unanticipated nature of the bombings as well as the system of decentralization, which was only 4 years old at the time. There were simply no local budget allocations for such shocks. Ensuring coordination among different levels of the government in implementing the proposed programmes proved to be a challenging task.

The main donor programmes were the Australian Agency for International Development (AusAID) Bali Rehabilitation Fund, the World Bank's Kecamatan Development Programme, the US Agency for International Development (USAID) Bali Response, the UN Development Programme (UNDP) Community Recovery Programme, the World Bank Bali Urban Infrastructure Project, and the World Bank Dutch Trust Fund to support grants to schools. The donor focus on Bali was new, since prior to the bombings, Bali had not been a major recipient of assistance, given its relative prosperity.

Not all the donor activity was directed at contributing to the recovery of the economy in Bali after the bombings. Many donor governments issued travel advisories and stressed the continued risk to their citizens visiting Bali.

The Indonesian government was concerned with these advisories, as they had a negative impact on the image of Indonesia, and, of course, on tourism in Bali.

The response to the second Bali bombing was along similar lines as the first, with the government increasing the allocation of funds for tourism promotion and swiftly acting to arrest the people behind the bombings. The primary difference between the first and second Bali bombings was that, after the second bombing, the Bali Tourism Board took a more active lead. In an interview, the vice-chairman of the Bali Tourism Board indicated that the vice-president of Indonesia himself had asked him to lead the recovery efforts. He revealed that while approximately US$ 15 million was spent on recovery efforts after the first Bali bombing, after the 2005 bombing an amount of US$ 7.5 million was utilized. The focus again was on increasing security and promotional efforts, as after the previous bombing. One such example of promotion was in June 2006, when the visa on arrival facility was expanded to 52 additional countries in an effort to promote tourism.

While the effects of the 1998 Asian crisis on the tourism industry were short-lived, and the effects of the most recent 2008 global crisis were minimal, the government still felt the need to continue promoting the destination through campaigns such as 'Visit Indonesia 2008' and 'Wonderful Indonesia 2010'.

8.7 Impact on social conditions

According to the International Labour Organization (ILO) in 2003, informal estimates suggest that 40 per cent of the island's jobs depend on tourism. Other estimates indicate that 80 per cent of households depend on tourism. This fact highlights the extent to which a crisis can have an impact on the working population.

If we analyse Tables 8.2 and 8.3, the first trend noticed is that, in the short term, there was a significant shedding of workers (Table 8.2) and a significant reduction in salaries (Table 8.3). With an average reduction of 51.6 per cent in staff combined with a reduction in sales ranging from 32 to 71 per cent, the data suggest that workers faced a significant struggle in the short term.

The following statistics from the World Bank and UNDP (2003b) further elaborate on the impact of the crisis in terms of social downgrading in the tourism GVC:

- Across Bali, an estimated 29 per cent of workers were affected by job losses within a year.
- Around 50,000 people employed in the hotel sector were made redundant. Small and medium enterprises (SMEs) reduced their staff by 52 per cent, with some SMEs facing a decline of up to 60 per cent in their revenue.

- Casa Grande, an association of 35 four- and five-star hotels in Bali, found that bookings had declined steeply, and a total of 878 staff members were made redundant, including 600 in Denpasar, accounting for a total of approximately 1,400 job losses.
- In a survey of district leaders, cited in World Bank and UNDP (2003b), 94 per cent of respondents reported a drop in income and 70 per cent a drop in employment by May 2003. Average incomes were reported to have dropped by 40 per cent and 20 per cent of the people lost their jobs. The highest declines in income were observed in Karangasem, Gianyar, and Buleleng. In the same survey, 70 per cent of community respondents suggested that handicrafts were important to their livelihood; of these, 84 per cent said their incomes had decreased severely during the year.
- The main local financial institutions in Bali are the state-owned Bank Rakyat Indonesia, the privately owned Bank Perkreditan Rakyat and the Lembaga Perkreditan Desa. Immediately after the bombings, many families entered into a debt crisis owing to declining incomes, and were forced to sell assets to meet their debt obligations.

The key respondent survey also shed light on the coping mechanisms of the community in response to the crisis, as Table 8.5 indicates.

While decreased expenditures, taking of loans for daily consumption, delay in debt payments, and sale of assets are suggested as the most significant coping methods, 46.4 per cent of respondents changed professions. This suggests redundant workers found other jobs outside of the tourism GVC to cope with the crisis. While a reduction in meals was not reported as a coping method by a majority of the respondents, this response was concentrated in poorer areas such as Karangasem.

In a Kecamatan Development Programme survey conducted in May 2003, 76 per cent of respondents indicated that the family was the first group to help in crisis, with 66 per cent indicating that a friend would be the second most important candidate to look for assistance.

A worker-level survey of 21 labourers was conducted by Strategic Asia for this study across the various segments of the GVC. Since the selection of labourers was geared towards incorporating a balanced gender ratio, only those labourers who had worked in the industry since 2002 (when the first Bali bombing took place) were interviewed. Most of the findings in this survey in relation to the first Bali bombing correspond with the report completed by the World Bank and UNDP in 2003 (World Bank and UNDP, 2003a; 2003b).

Table 8.5   Coping mechanisms in the crisis in order of importance

Various mechanisms		Yes	No	Do not know	(%)
(1)	Decreased expenditures	827	41	16	93.6
(2)	Delay in debt repayments	612	235	36	69.3
(3)	Postponement/decrease in facilities/infrastructure maintenance	527	317	31	60.2
(4)	Pawning of assets	528	311	45	59.7
(5)	Sale of assets	431	403	50	48.8
(6)	Changing professions	395	411	46	46.4
(7)	Loans for daily consumption	405	435	43	45.9
(8)	Putting other family members to work	349	474	58	39.6
(9)	Change of business	311	514	48	35.6
(10)	Decrease in artisan participation	228	592	63	25.8
(11)	Decrease in contributions to village	222	616	45	25.1
(12)	Change in staple diet	213	617	53	24.1
(13)	Postponement/decrease in religious practices	48	809	25	5.4
(14)	Reduction in number of meals	46	791	45	5.2

Sources: Udayana University Key Respondent Survey, in World Bank and UNDP (2003b).

The survey was geared towards determining if new opportunities were being considered as a result of each crisis in order to explore the impact and coping mechanisms utilized after each crisis as well as to understand if there were any differences in the new opportunities based on gender. In the context of this survey, the 2002 bombing in Bali was the most severe, with several interviewees indicating a reduction of more than 60 per cent in income. For some people, the wage rate remained the same, but the number of working hours had reduced from eight to four. In the case of certain interviewees, a reduction was noted in both income and working hours. One respondent working in the guides sector took the opportunity after the first bombing to upgrade his skills by learning Korean. This allowed him to avail himself of further opportunities when the market recovered. One woman working at a garment and handicraft shop near the site of the bombing left the industry for 6 years during the crisis. It is thus possible that some people also left the industry entirely right after the crisis. In the context of this survey, most of the labourers stayed within their segments despite the first Bali bombing. In terms of differences in conditions by gender, only one respondent noted a differential in wages; the others claimed there was no difference in working conditions. It is important to keep in mind that the sample size was limited and thus may not be reflective of the total labour force.

In the context of the 2005 Bali bombing, the Strategic Asia survey of 21 workers suggests that the impact of the crisis was less severe than in the case of the first bombing. Many of the respondents noticed no changes in working conditions during this crisis. One respondent attributed the lack of reduction in income to the increase in the regional markets. For those who did experience reductions in income, these were of the magnitude of 20–30 per cent. Little or no variation was noted among the range of five- to three-star hotels this second time.

With regard to the economic recession in 1998, in view of the existence of a more vibrant tourism sector up to the first Bali bombing, it is likely that this created new job opportunities in the sector and, therefore, had a positive impact in terms of social upgrading. On the other hand, in response to the 2008 economic crisis, no particular social impact was noted. As pointed out earlier, there was a change in the composition of tourists, with Chinese and domestic tourists both becoming more important. No particular impact with relation to social downgrading was attributed to this crisis on the basis of stakeholder interviews.

8.8 Shocks and poverty

Given that Bali is highly reliant on the tourism industry, it is important to look at changes in the poverty levels in both the urban and rural areas after the shocks. Table 8.6 shows a decline in urban poverty and an increase in rural poverty from 2000 to 2001. As previously indicated, higher rates of unemployment in Bali can be attributed to return migration from Java, thus possibly accounting for the increase in the rural poverty rate. For the 2002 bombings, there was an approximately 6.5 per cent increase in the percentage of the total population below the poverty line between 2002 and 2003; after the 2005 bombings, there was an approximately 5 per cent increase in the percentage of the population below the poverty line during the year 2005/2006. However, one nuance to be noted is that, after the 2005 bombings, although urban poverty increased, rural poverty declined by approximately half a percentage point. This could suggest that the impact of the bombing did not have a significant impact

Table 8.6 People in Bali under the poverty line, 2000–2010

	No. of poor people ('00,000)			% of poor people (as % of population)		
	Urban	Rural	Total	Urban	Rural	Total
2000	80.1	96.7	176.8	5.49	5.85	5.68
2001	67.1	181.3	248.4	4.3	11.35	7.87
2002	98.9	122.9	221.8	5.72	8.25	6.89
2003	99.7	146.4	246.1	6.14	8.48	7.34
2004	87.0	144.9	231.9	5.05	8.71	6.85
2005	105.9	122.5	228.4	5.4	8.51	6.72
2006	127.4	116.0	243.4	6.4	8.03	7.08
2007	119.8	109.3	229.1	6.01	7.47	6.63
2008	115.1	100.6	215.7	5.7	6.81	6.17
2009	92.1	89.7	181.8	4.5	5.98	5.13
2010	83.6	91.3	174.9	4.04	6.02	4.88

Source: Central Statistics Agency (2010).

on the rural areas of Bali. Between 2008 and 2010, there was a clear declining trend in the population below the poverty line from approximately 6 to 4.8 per cent, suggesting that the impacts of the 2008 financial crisis on poverty in Bali were minimal.

8.9 Crises and the family rice bowl

A feature of the coping mechanism is strong reliance on the community and family. Policy stressed the role of the traditional village community organization, *adat*, in helping families through the crisis. The survey reported in Table 8.5 points out that almost half of those affected took to other professions. Some of these other professions could have been, say, nursing for young women. But, given that most Balinese have some rural links, it is likely that the 'other professions' were mainly in agriculture. Anecdotal evidence suggests much going back to the village in times of slowdown. This is in line with experiences of other Southeast Asian countries (e.g., Thailand) where 'recent' and commuting migrants have continuing rural links. When urban jobs go down, workers return to family farms. This is the type of agrarian involution first analysed by Clifford Geertz for Java (1963).

One may link Geertz's involution analysis with that of Lewis's (1954) unlimited supplies of labour. During the expansion of tourism in Bali, the rural economy supplied its surplus labour at real wages that needed to be just a little above what could be earned in agriculture. But during a downturn, the now redundant urban labour returns to the rural hinterland. However, the additional labour may not result in an increase in production, resulting in involution and thus a sharing of poverty.

In the Bali case, there was an attempt to increase agricultural production. After the 2002 bombings, many meetings were held to promote a development of agriculture, in particular to cultivate many of the fruits that were now being imported. But it was also pointed out that, with tourism having become the mainstay of the Bali economy, there had been neglect of the irrigation system and a quick development of agriculture would not be possible. The government did allocate money for improving the irrigation systems (Hitchcock and Darma Putra, 2007 for a discussion of these issues). However, with the quick recovery of tourism in just about a year, all such talk of developing agriculture quickly receded into the background.

The important point for our analysis, however, is that the family and the rural economy provided the safety mechanism that helped people absorb the shock of the tourism downturn. As was revealed widely across Southeast Asia during the 1990s crisis, the 'family rice bowl' was the safety net during economic downturns (Nathan and Kelkar, 1999). The family rice bowl, in turn, largely depends on the labour contribution of women, which would mean the burden of coping with the crisis falls disproportionately on women. This was a feature of East Asian adjustment during the late 1990s financial crisis and continued to remain a feature of adjustment in Bali through the tourism shocks. It is only now that Indonesia is moving towards a state-provided safety net. A minimum social floor for all citizens is being set up, and this should reduce the burden on the family rice bowl and women during economic crises.

8.10   Changes in GVC structures

Compared with 2000, the tourism GVC in 2010 shows a few changes. The governance structures did not change. The only modular governance structures were those between the foreign TO or tour agency and the incoming agent, and they remained modular. All other governance structures are relational, and remained so.

The structural changes were mainly in the growth of two new segments, those of villas and spas. Villas utilized local houses for tourism, thus increasing the revenue to local owners. Villas often did not pay taxes and were thus able to offer discounts.

In addition, being relatively small and gated, they could be more secure than large hotels.

The growth of spas to provide relaxation is in line with the international trend in the growth of such units. What is interesting, however, is that they developed from having been part of hotel offerings to being specialized units. Clearly, the growth of the market led to the increase in specialization, in the manner analysed by Adam Smith, where 'the division of labour is limited by the extent of the market' (Milberg and Winkler, 2011).

With the growth of the market, there was an increase in the number of suppliers, with spa activity, earlier a part of hotel services, becoming a specialized service. Villas too enter the GVC as a new segment in accommodation services.

On the other side, the number of local TOs declined from 628 licensed operators in 2000 to 307 in 2011. This is a form of horizontal consolidation, a reduction in the number of units operating in a GVC segment (Milberg and Winkler, 2011). The decline in the number of TOs occurred through the various crises. But with the recovery of the tourist industry, there was not a corresponding increase in TOs. The consolidation in TOs must have led to the remaining ones having a large enough capacity to handle the increased volume. This could be seen as a form of economic upgrading for those able to absorb the extra business. Additionally, the earlier experiences of operators bearing losses could have reduced the attempts of service providers to become TOs. This points to a manner of hysteresis in the evolution of horizontal consolidation. The horizontal consolidation in the TO segment during the downturn is not offset by horizontal expansion after recovery. Rather, the units remaining in operation seem to have grown in capacity. Have entry barriers increased? Since the volume of tourism has not gone down, it could be that the remaining TOs enjoy economies of scale, similar to what Milberg and Winkler (2011) point out, which makes it difficult for newcomers to enter the market.

The horizontal consolidation of destination tour agencies during the shock-induced contractions was not mirrored by an increase in these numbers after the recovery.

Finally, the growing end-markets are those of Chinese tourists and domestic tourism. This would obviously increase the strength of tour agencies from these areas of origin. Tourists from China and the ASEAN countries increased in numbers, but even by 2011, these numbers did not add up to more than one-third of the total. Domestic tourists also increased and were about 20 per cent of the total. At the same time, per capita spending by tourists from both Asia and Indonesia was only about 20 per cent that of tourists from the developed economies. When the number of tourists from Asia began to grow, Bali hoteliers complained that they did not spend much money, for instance, in their restaurants (Hitchcock and Darma Putra, 2007).

8.11 Ethnic conflict and the collapse of tourism in Tana Toraja

In contrast with the repeated and quick recovery of Bali from shocks, another site in Indonesia has seen the collapse of tourism in the same period. Tana Toraja on the island of Sulawesi is a centre of indigenous tourism. It is a designated UN Educational, Scientific and Cultural Organization (UNESCO) World Heritage Site that preserves traditional architecture and burial sites. But the area does not have a direct air link. The nearest airport is a whole day's drive away. Consequently, it is an area that only intrepid travellers or those interested in its archaeological–anthropological–cultural significance would visit.

Despite such limitations, tourism to Tana Toraja did increase over the later 1990s and early 2000s. The shock it suffered was in the form of inter-ethnic clashes on the island. This was compounded by the Bali bombings, which had an impact on tourism in Indonesia as a whole.

With the downturn, many workers left tourism-related work and took up other livelihoods. Those who combined farming with tourism now took to farming alone. At the height of Tana Toraja tourism, many young people had trained as guides. Obviously, there was not much work for these guides, who either migrated to other islands or retrained for other professions, such as nursing. The number of TOs went down. There was a clear horizontal consolidation in the tourism GVC, with numbers falling in the various tourism segments. It is not clear if there was vertical shrinking too, with those remaining taking on those functions that had been specialized earlier on.

Why did Tana Toraja collapse while Bali rebounded and even went ahead after each shock? The reason must lie in the limited attractions of Tana Toraja and the difficulty of access. Undertaking a whole day's drive for what is just a day's excursion to the main village is not something that tourists are likely to do. This would need to be combined with other features, such as the beach and related activities, for an extended stay. But as a beach, it would have to compete with established centres, not only Bali but also other Southeast Asian beach spots.

The differences in the post-shock experiences of Bali and Tana Toraja are most apparent when we examine the role of local government. In Bali, the degree to which the local government supported the post-shock recovery was far greater than in

Tana Toraja, where most people in the industry felt sorely let down by the (lack of) government response. This study extrapolates that the main reason for this is that, as a percentage of regional income, tourism in Tana Toraja is relatively small compared with other sources of income, particularly agriculture and remittances from abroad. On the other hand, Bali's tourism income is more than half of the island's GDP. The local government there had much more reason to intervene energetically to support tourism after each crisis.

8.12   Conclusions

The shocks looked at in this chapter are of three types. The Bali bombings were generalized shocks to the whole tourist economy. They affected tourist numbers as a whole, without any clear bias for or against particular national groups. There was a general reduction in demand for Bali tourism. The Tana Toraja ethnic conflict shock, while of a different nature again, was more in line with that of a generalized shock.

But in the case of the two economic crises, the 1990s Asian financial crisis and the 2008 recession, there were clear regional differences in demand responses. After the Asian financial crisis, there was a sharp devaluation of the Indonesian currency, boosting foreign demand, particularly from the non-Asian countries that did not go into recession. In the current recession, on the other hand, there has been a reduction in demand from non-Asian economies, while demand from Asian economies has grown. Chinese and domestic Indonesian tourists have been the growing segment of Bali tourism.

What this means is that one has to look at the specific type of shock and the manner in which they impact demand from different regions. There cannot be just a general analysis of shocks. A terrorist attack is a non-specific shock affecting all tourists, but economic crises may affect particular demand segments and thus result in a change in the overall composition of tourists.

However, one general point does emerge in the response to all shocks—there is a post-shock search for markets. The search for new markets could be different from an attempt to increase flows from existing markets. The latter is likely to require price discounts to attract those who wish to spend less. But in a bombing-related security crisis, price discounts may not have much of an effect on volumes. Rather, the search is for new markets from among those less likely to be affected by the bombing-related security scares. Given that non-Asian foreigners were understood to be the targets of bombings, there was an expansion of the market among both Asian and domestic markets. Thus, the new markets were different from the older, established markets. Correspondingly, in the tourism GVC, TOs from the growing markets gained strength, while TOs from the declining or stagnant markets lost strength.

The results of this study suggest that Bali has really been the motor of tourism in Indonesia, and shocks that threaten its prominence can have a significant impact on tourism in other regions, especially ones that are more nascent tourist destinations, including those such as Tana Toraja. The appreciation of the Indonesian currency during the 1997 Asian financial crisis and the booming Australian industry in recent years have to some extent cushioned the effects of the financial crises of 1998 and 2008, respectively. However, in the case of the bombings, there were more adverse short-term effects, especially because of the perceived threat to the safety of tourists. The first bombing was more severe than the latter owing to its novelty and the fact that it occurred soon after the September 2001 attacks, which acted as a huge shock to the psyche of global tourists at the time. The World Bank study on the Bali bombings of 2002 highlights the fact that the impact within the tourism GVC was not evenly felt, with smaller firms hit the hardest.

In Bali, post-crisis GVC structures changed to an extent. At present, the growing end-markets are those of China and domestic tourism. This would obviously increase the strength of tour agencies from these areas of origin. As predicted in the Milberg–Winkler analysis (2011), the horizontal consolidation of destination tour agencies during the shock-induced contractions was not mirrored by an increase in these numbers after the recovery. This may be due to scale effects, making it difficult for newcomers to enter the market during the expansion. But expansion of the market post-recovery has seen the growth of vertical specialization or vertical expansion. The number of segments has increased with the creation of two new specialized niches, those of villas and spas. There was hysteresis in the case of horizontal consolidation, but not so in the case of vertical specialization. Specialization, as Adam Smith would have expected, did increase with the growth of the market.

With regard to workers, the reduction of staff and the use of more part-time workers are a consistent part of the strategies being devised to cope with external shocks. But the main burden of the shock fell in terms of the sharing of poverty in the so-called family rice bowl, in which women's labour predominates. With the growing vulnerabilities connected to globalization, including the vulnerability to terrorist attacks, the local economy did not have the institutional structures for state-provided social security and had to fall back on the traditional family-based security network. The newly passed bill on social security may minimize the short-term impact of future shocks.

Acknowledgements

Thanks to Michelle Christian and Dev Nathan for very substantial comments that have helped sharpen the analysis of the paper. Needless to say, responsibility for any errors and omissions is that of the authors alone.

References

Bhanupong, Nidhiprabha. 2007. *Adjustment and Recovery in Thailand Two Years After the Tsunami.* Discussion Paper No. 72. Manila: ADB Institute.

Braithwaite, John, Valerie Braithwaite, Michael Cookson, and Leah Dunn. 2010. *Anomie and Violence; Non-truth and Reconciliation in Indonesian Peace-building.* Canberra: ANU Press.

Cattaneo, Olivier, Gary Gereffi, and Cornelia Staritz. 2011. *Global Value Chains in a Post-crisis World: Resilience, Consolidation and Shifting End Markets.* New Delhi: Academic Foundation and the World Bank.

Central Statistics Agency. 2010. *Bali in Figures, 2010.* Bali: Central Statistics Agency.

Cole, S. 2008. 'Living in Hope: Tourism and Poverty Alleviation in Flores.' In *Tourism Development: Growth, Myths and Realities,* edited by P. Burns and M. Novelli. Oxford: CABI.

Geertz, Clifford. 1963. *Agrarian Involution: The Processes of Ecological Change in Indonesia.* Berkeley and Los Angeles, CA: University of California Press.

Hitchcock, Michael and Nyoman Darma Putra. 2007. *Tourism, Development and Terrorism in Bali.* Aldershot: Ashgate Publications.

ILO (International Labour Organization). 2003. 'Employment and Human Resources in the Tourist Industry in Asia and the Pacific.' Briefing Paper for Tripartite Regional Meeting.

Institut Pertanian Bogor. 2008. 'A Sustainable Tourist Destination in Toraja: A Value Chain Approach.' Bappeda and BPS Toraja, mimeo.

Lewis, W.A. 1954. 'Economic Development with Unlimited Supplies of Labour.' *The Manchester School* 28 (2): 139–91.

Lumaksono, A. 2009. 'Bali Tourism Satellite Account.' Fifth UNWTO International Conference on Tourism Statistics, Bali, 30 March–2 April.

Milberg, William, and Deborah Winkler. 2010. 'Trade, Crisis and Recovery: Restructuring Global Value Chains.' In *Global Value Chains in a Postcrisis World: A Development Perspective,* edited by Olivier Cattaneo, Gary Gereffi, and Cornelia Staritz. Washington, DC: The World Bank.

Nathan, Dev, and Govind Kelkar. 1999. 'Agrarian Involution, Domestic Economy and Women: Rural Dimensions of the Asian Crisis.' *Economic and Political Weekly,* 8 May, 1135–41. New Delhi: Academic Foundation and the World Bank.

Pongpaichit, Pasuk, and Chris Baker. 1998. *Thailand's Boom and Bust*. Chiang Mai: Silkworm Books.

Siu, Alan, and Y. C Richard Wong. 2006. 'Economic Impact of SARS: The Case of Hong Kong.' Hong Kong: University of Hong Kong.

The Bali Update. 2005a. 'More on Garuda Ticket Giveaway.' 14 November.

———. 2005b. 'Handicraft Sales Down 50%.' 24 November.

———. 2006a. 'Only 12% of Bali's Tourism Transport Opening.' 16 January.

———. 2006b. 'Garuda Posts a US$ 70.7 Million Loss for 2005.' 30 January.

The Jakarta Post. 2011. 'Bali Tourism Industry must Diversify.' 28 March.

UNESCAP (UN Economic and Social Commission for Asia and the Pacific). 2005. 'Review of accomplishments and the plan of action for sustainable tourism development.' High-level Intergovernmental Meeting on Sustainable Tourism Development, Jakarta, November.

Wetterburg, S., and Pritchett. 1998. 'The Social Impact of the Crisis in Indonesia: Results from a Nationwide Kecamatan Survey.' Jakarta: SMERU.

World Bank and UNDP (UN Development Programme). 2003a. *Confronting Crisis: Impacts and Response to the Bali Tragedy. Brief for the Consultative Group on Indonesia*. Jakarta: World Bank.

———. 2003b. *Bali Beyond the Tragedy: Impact and Challenges for Tourism-led Development in Indonesia*. Jakarta: World Bank.

Yang, F., Yin, Y, and Nathan, D. 2015. *The Zero-fee Tour: Price Competition and Network Downgrading in Chinese Tourism*. Chapter 7, this book.

9

Dynamics of Labour-intensive Clusters in China

Wage Costs and Moving Inland

Lixia Mei and Jici Wang

9.1 Introduction[1]

Unlike innovative clusters which rely on innovative capability based on flexible specialization, as in Italy (Muscio and Scarpinato, 2007, p. 774–775), China's manufacturing clusters mostly compete on the basis of low price, cheap materials, numerical labour flexibility and low-cost labour. This situation has been extensively criticized and suggestions for Chinese clusters to upgrade from the bottom of global value chains to upper levels has been a hot topic among both Chinese and international scholars (Humphrey, 1995; Schmitz and Nadvi, 1999; Gereffi, 1999; Wang, 2007).

Given the above, the purpose of this chapter is to take a step further in exploring the labour dynamics of labour-intensive industrial clusters of China in recent years, in terms of changes in China's international competitive advantage. We suggest that there are limits to China's competitiveness in global markets being based continually on low-wage labour. The massive migration of workers from rural agriculture to urban industry keeps wages low in the low-skill, labour-intensive clusters. However, at some time, as the Lewis model (1954) predicts, migration will have exhausted all available surplus labour. Wages will then begin to rise both nationally and locally, eroding the low-wage basis of labour-intensive clusters. Our analysis stresses the role of local labour shortages in leading to higher wages and shorter working hours, both of which would increase wage costs. However, we differ from the usual demographic analysis of labour shortages, by arguing

[1] This research has been funded in part by the ILO and in part by the National Natural Science Foundation of China under grant No. 40535027 and No. 71103202. We wish to thank the referees for their valuable criticisms and comments on earlier versions of this article. We extend special thanks to Anne Posthuma, Stephanie Barrientos, and Cindy C. Fan, for their comments on earlier versions and to Ren Bao, Pan Fenghua and Li Pengfei at Peking University for data collection and map drawing.

that it is the deficit in decent work conditions and the simultaneous improvement in rural conditions, that together account for this labour shortage.

Can China continue with competitive advantage based on low wages, or does erosion of this advantage push for these labour-intensive segments to be re-located away from the coastal clusters to lower wage regions, such as in China's inner or Western provinces? Or push the development of innovative capability in order to help upgrade these clusters from their current dependence upon low-cost production capability? These are the dynamics of China's labour-intensive clusters that we explore in this chapter.

While the chapter is based on investigations and secondary data from the middle to late years of the last decade, the trends we discuss have continued since then. If anything, labour shortages have intensified in the coastal provinces. This has led to both relocation to the inland and Western provinces, even to other countries in South-east Asia, such as Vietnam, Cambodia and Lao PDR. There are also concerted attempts to carry out both process innovations to reduce costs, and functional upgrading to move up the value chain. All of these trends were already visible in the second half of the last decade, which is the reason that this analysis of the causes and impacts of labour shortages continues to remain relevant even in today's China. As can be seen in Table 9.1, minimum wages have more than doubled from 2007–08 to 2015, further intensifying the trends of relocation, process innovations and functional upgrading mentioned in this chapter.

The chapter is organized as follows: In Section 9.2, the features of Chinese clusters, including the formation, distribution, and local division of labour within them, are discussed, with an emphasis upon labour dynamics. In order to further examine

Table 9.1 Minimum wages in selected provinces and cities of China, 2007–08 and 2015

City/Province	Minimum wages (Unit: *Yuan* RMB)					Starting date (yyyy/mm/dd)
Beijing	730	–	–	–	–	2007/07/01
Shanghai	840	–	–	–	–	2007/09/01
Shenzhen	850	750	–	–	–	2007/10/01
Jiangsu	850	700	590	–	–	2008/02/20
Zhejiang	850	750	700	620	–	2007/09/01
Guangdong	860	770	670	580	530	2008/02/20

(*Contd*)

Table 9.1 (Contd)

City/Province	Minimum wages (Unit: *Yuan* RMB)					Starting date (yyyy/mm/dd)
Beijing	1720	–	–	–	–	2015/04/01
Shanghai	2020	–	–	–	–	2015/04/01
Shenzhen	2030		–	–	–	2015/03/01
Jiangsu	1630	1460	1270	–	–	2014/11/01
Zhejiang	1860	1660	1530	1380	–	2015/11/01
Guangdong	1895	1510	1350	1210	–	2015/05/01

Source: Ministry of Labour and Social Security, PRC, 2008 and 2015.
Notes: 1. The reason for one location having more than one minimum wage relates to local geographical disparity in income and prices.
2. Exchange rate between US\$ and RMB on 2007/07/01 was 100:760.75; on 2007/09/01 was 100:756.07; on 2007/10/01 was 100:751.06; and on 2008/02/20 was 100:714.52.

changes in patterns of labour supply and utilization, two case studies are presented— the Wenzhou footwear cluster and the Lecong furniture cluster. Section 9.3 describes the trend toward industrial relocation of the clustered firms from the coastal clusters to the inner provinces, as well as its implication for both clustered firms and their workers, in terms of rising labour costs and the labour shortage in those old industrial cluster areas. A general conclusion and discussion follow in the final section.

9.2 Features and dynamics of labour-intensive clusters in China

Clustering in the manufacturing sector is pervasive in China in the sectors of apparel, footwear, furniture, TV sets, home electrical appliances, toys, motorcycles, and the like, most of which are labour-intensive sectors. The literature highlights the success of China's clusters at the grassroots[2] and analyses the factors contributing to their impressive economic performance. They are an important part of the story behind China's 'weapons of mass production', and newspapers describe them as the 'niche cities':

> Buyers from New York to Tokyo want to be able to buy 500,000 pairs of socks all at once, or 300,000 neckties, 100,000 children's jackets, or 50,000 size 36B bras. Increasingly, the places that best accommodate orders are China's giant

---

[2] Grassroots, means the local peasant-entrepreneurs, like the globally distributed Wenzhou businessmen, who were born in local places as peasants and don't have much education, but are very successful in business.

new specialty cities. The niche cities reflect China's ability to form 'lump' economies', where clusters or networks of businesses feed off each other, building technologies and enjoying the benefits of concentrated support centers. (Barboza, 2004)

This general characterization does not capture the whole range of industrial agglomerations existing in China. There are other clusters in the auto industry and information and communications technology (ICT) industry, as well as in cultural and creative industries. Furthermore, economically significant agglomerations of SMEs are found in the metalworking industry, as in Tangshan or in Handan (Hebei Province, Northern China). Nevertheless, they are very heterogeneous clusters and it would thus go beyond the scope of this chapter to attempt to discuss labour and employment in this diverse range of clusters found in China[3].

The extreme diversity among China's regions adds a geographic dimension to the process of capability building (Rawski, 2005). Foreign investment, industrial exports, and expansion of manufacturing capability were all concentrated in China's dynamic coastal areas, creating numerous labour-intensive clusters largely in provinces such as Guangdong, Zhejiang, Jiangsu and Fujian, most of which are located in South-east coastal areas of China.

Labour-intensive clusters are unevenly distributed across provinces and are mainly concentrated in the provinces with higher GDP. Zhejiang Province hosts some 136 industrial clusters, followed by Guangdong, Jiangsu and Shandong, with 73, 70 and 54 industrial clusters (districts), respectively. Demonstrating poor economic performance and lagging behind other provinces in economic reforms, the inland provinces such as Anhui and Shaanxi have only a few industrial clusters. Zhejiang, Jiangsu and Guangdong provinces of China are the production sites for most of the low-cost, labour-intensive products usually associated with Chinese export industries, such as apparel, toys, bicycles, shoes, etc.

In terms of labour, Guangdong Province accommodates the largest migrant workforce from other provinces of China. According to the Fifth Population Census of China, even in the year 2000, there were 15 million migrant workers from other provinces working in Guangdong, which accounted for 17.4 per cent of

---

[3] In a debate on the Italian model of industrial districts, Markusen (1996, p. 297) rejected the dominance of the Marshallian industrial districts in regional development. She identified three additional types of industrial districts, that is, the hub-and-spoke districts; the satellite platform; and the state-anchored districts. The industrial clusters in China in this paper refer to the Marshallian industrial districts or the Italian model of industrial districts.

the total population of 86.42 million in Guangdong Province[4]. This large number of workers was distributed mainly in the labour-intensive clusters.

It is worth noting that 60 per cent of the migrant workers in Guangdong province at that time were young women aged between 18 and 25 years, who are referred to as 'Dagongmei' or 'working girls' (Pun, 2005), and later the so-called 'new rural daughters' (Zhang, 2007) in the literature on China's migration. According to Pun Ngai (2005),

> Cheap labour and low prices for land are not the only reasons for the current relocation of transnational capital to China. Diligent, well-educated Chinese women workers who are willing to toil for twelve hours each day, who are suitable for just-in-time global production, and who are potential consumers for global products are all factors that contribute to tempting transnational capital to relocate to China. (2005, p. 4)

This may be another story beyond this paper, in terms of the massive rural migrant workers and their social lives. However, the situation is different in Zhejiang Province, which is home to the largest number of clusters in China. Small- and medium-sized firms, mainly from former rural households, are clustered in neighbourhoods, usually around a marketplace, for their production. Starting with simple manufacturing products such as food, apparel, footwear, and ball pens, and learning by doing, the rural, grassroots firms in Zhejiang Province are now creating brand name products at home and abroad.

9.2.1 Formation mechanisms of China's clusters

Were these Chinese clusters formed by internal or external forces or by the interaction between both? Research in the developed countries generally argues that clusters have been bred by internal forces, from the bottom-up. However, for the formation of Chinese clusters, the effect of rapid cross-border dispersion due to international outsourcing by multinational corporations (MNCs) co-exists with local effects of external economies. These clusters are associated not only with sector-specific activity in the same area, but also associated with institutional and social features that support their creation, survival and growth.

Unlike the Marshallian industrial districts, where the so-called 'labour pool' usually comes from local areas, China's industrial clusters usually present

[4] Development and Reform Commission of Guangdong Province, 2002-07-19: http://www.gddpc. gov.cn/common_file/show_file.asp?id=14369&lanmu=39

diversified labour sources. Especially for those clusters based on Export Processing Zones (EPZs) and industrial parks, a majority of these workers in clustered firms come from inland provinces of China, such as Sichuan, Hunan, Henan, Hebei, Jiangxi, Guangxi, and so on, as migrant workers (Wong et al., 2007, p. 32–34). Nearly 70 per cent of these migrant workers move to East and South coastal areas of China, where agglomerated labour-intensive clusters provide them possible job opportunities.

Global Perspective

The emergence and development of clusters in China should be understood above all from the global perspective. It is important to pay attention to the concentrated dispersion caused by offshore outsourcing (Guerrieri and Pietrobelli, 2004). It is China's participation in the global economy that enabled the rise of these clusters. Chinese clusters were the product of the fragmentation of production associated with the 'global factory' concept related to the global shift of international manufacturing (Dicken, 2003), as well as the offshoring of global jobs (Gereffi, 2006) from advanced nations.

The clusters of firms in China have been increasingly involved in the international fragmentation of production. This fragmentation of production, as well as knowledge, into different industrial activities carried out by great numbers of firms in different places, brings opportunities for learning and upgrading (Schmitz and Knorringa, 2000). Given the rich components of any single cluster, it may either occupy a single segment (e.g., manufacturing of parts and components in a particular industry, or their assembly) or cover multiple segments (R&D, completion of a high-value-added product, marketing) of a value chain anchored to a locality (Chen, 2006). Generally speaking, Chinese production is located primarily at the bottom of global value chains, typically involving assembling, processing, and manufacturing.

Local Perspective

However, the location of existing manufacturing capacities in China refutes the conventional wisdom that low labour costs are the sole source of manufacturing advantage. While the impact of global outsourcing is important, local agglomeration economies also continue to matter, creating, in turn, the path-dependent nature of the evolution of localized clusters. The Marshallian 'labour pool' effect can best be seen within China's clustered regions.

In a context of increasing integration with global networks, the origins of local clusters in China differ from case to case, reflecting the complex transition of China's reform. The development process of many clusters in coastal China begins in the 1980s but each cluster shows distinctive features that have contributed to take-off. These clusters serve both domestic and foreign markets (Wang, 2007).

The tension between localization and globalization is shown in each cluster's development. Capital investment originating from Hong Kong and Taiwan accounted for nearly two-thirds of FDI in China and was the initial impetus to the formation of clusters in Guangdong Province and Fujian Province; however, many clusters in Zhejiang Province originated from the economic strength of local peasant-entrepreneurs and have developed through consanguinity, affinity and geographic ties with Chinese characteristics. Due to the combined effects of global outsourcing for low-priced land and labour and peasant-entrepreneurs, a great number of labour-intensive clusters thrive not only in the Export Processing Zones located in coastal opening cities, but also in the many inland villages and small towns, where local peasant-entrepreneurs are very active in starting their own businesses. For instance, a hundred clusters of textile and apparel industry production have grown along coastal townships and are export-oriented.

In Guangdong Province, hundreds of export-oriented 'Specialty Towns (industrial clusters)' have emerged. With the policy advantages of reform[5] and opening early, such regions started their business with 'processing and compensation trades' (*Sanlai Yibu*) in the late 1970s. Firms in such labour-intensive clusters usually provide processing trade or original equipment manufacture (OEM) for global buyers and rely on the global market. Guangdong's initial development relied on clusters of local and overseas firms that employed unskilled, mainly immigrant workers and were funded by foreign capital (mainly from Hong Kong and Taiwan), and firms created by local entrepreneurs. These clusters made Guangdong and, more specifically, the Pearl River Delta, a region that achieved one of the fastest growth rates in the world, with its degree of foreign trade dependence as high as 161.6 per cent in 2005. The net GDP of Guangdong Province grew from RMB 24.965 billion *Yuan* in 1980 (approximately US$ 16.64 billion)[6], to RMB 2237 billion *Yuan* (approximately US$ 279 billion) in 2005, which means a nearly

---

[5] Policy advantages of reform in China's coastal areas usually include tax exemption and favourable land use advantages and infrastructure, relatively loose labour regulation, and similar measures, all in favour of attracting new investment, especially foreign direct investment (FDI). In the early years of China's economic reform, only those Special Economic Zones, like Shenzhen, Zhuhai, Xiamen, Shantou, and Hainan enjoyed such policy advantages; afterwards, most of China's inland cities were opened to the world market and such policy advantages became all-pervasive.

[6] The exchange rate between US$ and RMB in 1980 was 100:150, while in 2005 was 100:807.9.

90 times growth in terms of nominal GDP during the 25 years, giving it the No. 1 rank in mainland China in terms of GDP.

In Zhejiang Province, however, nearly 95 per cent of the production values came not from state-owned enterprises (SOEs) or FDI, but rather, from local private peasant-owned firms, set up and operated with the help of Shanghai engineers. Take the case of Wenzhou, the Shoe Capital of China, as an example, which was described by Cody (2006):

> Wenzhou people only want to be the boss … you will never see a Wenzhou person in the factory making a shoe. They would rather be the head of a small company than a worker in a big one.(Cody, 2006, p. 30)

This quotation reflects the strong business spirit of local entrepreneurship in Zhejiang Province. This leads us to expect that, at least in Wenzhou city, the majority of labour working in clustered firms are not local, but instead, migrant workers from other provinces, though most of the employers are local peasant-entrepreneurs.

The Formation of Apparel Clusters in Guangdong and Zhejiang

Firms in the Dalang wool spinning cluster in Dongguan, Guangdong Province, and in the Ningbo apparel cluster in Zhejiang Province (Tan, 2007), respectively, received global outsourcing orders from Hong Kong and Shanghai firms and dispersed the orders from there to supplier firms. Afterwards, a local division of labour between clustered firms emerged.

After the 1980s, the apparel industry in East Asia lost its cost advantage gradually and began to transfer overseas. At that time, mainland China started its reform process and open door policy, so the Pearl River Delta became the export-oriented area of Hong Kong-based apparel firms. The main pattern of participation in global production networks was by 'receiving orders from Hong Kong or Taiwan, producing in the mainland, transiting through Hong Kong, and selling overseas' (Chen, 2006). The formation of the Dalang textile apparel cluster benefited from accepting materials from Hong Kong firms for processing.

In 1979, the first Hong Kong-based woollen factory was established in Dalang Town, and many farmers started to work there. Some of these workers accumulated capital to start their own business and set up various mills around the town. Thus, the division of labour of 'receiving orders from Hong Kong and producing in Dalang' came into being. The woollen mills did not only

---

receive orders from Hong Kong, but also set up shops, which finally formed a specialized sweater market. Thereafter, fabric and woollen firms began to set up their sales bases. Now nearly 3,000 woollen firms are operating in this cluster, employing over 160,000 workers, producing over 250 million sets of sweaters a year and supplying 30 per cent of the domestic market. In 2005, the total output value of Dalang wool and sweater industry was RMB 8.4 billion *Yuan* (approximately US$ 1.04 billion)[7], and export value surpassed US$ 490 million, with products exported to Europe, America, Russia, East and South Asia and Hong Kong. Dalang received the title of 'China's Famous Sweater Township' from the China Wool Textile Association (CWTA)[8].

Distinct from the Dongguan cluster originating from Hong Kong, the Ningbo apparel cluster originated from Shanghai. 'Apparel stores in Shanghai, apparel factories in Ningbo', as the Chinese phrase goes. The origin of the Ningbo apparel cluster is due to the township apparel start-ups, which mostly had the experience of processing for state-owned firms in Shanghai. However, after China's admission to the WTO, Ningbo apparel cluster rapidly improved its global market share and become an export-oriented sector. In 2004, the Ningbo apparel cluster exported RMB 15.2 billion *Yuan* (approximately US$ 1.84 billion)[9], about 74 per cent of the total textile production value of Ningbo city (Tan, 2007).

At the end of the 1970s and the beginning of the 1980s, there was a popular saying in the Shanghai apparel sector, 'work depends on the bumpkins'. These firms received orders from overseas and carried out the sales; they subcontracted production to rural firms, factories and family workshops. With local governments' support, many township firms and local state-owned firms, like Youngor, Shanshan and Romon, smoothly transformed into private firms, and implemented the 'joint stock system reform'[10] in the early 1990s (Tan, 2007).

In Ningbo, 439 of the total 2,000 apparel firms in the cluster in 2004 reached the annual revenue of RMB 5 million *Yuan* (approximately US$ 0.6

---

[7] According to Bank of China, the exchange rate between US Dollars and Chinese RMB on Dec. 30, 2005, was 100:807.09, www.boc.cn

[8] Brief introduction and primary data for Dalang wool and sweater cluster, "Dalang: China's Famous Sweater Township", http://www.cwta.org.cn/mz_4.htm

[9] According to Bank of China, the exchange rate between US Dollars and Chinese RMB on Dec. 30, 2004, was 100:827.65, www.boc.cn

[10] In terms of the "Joint-stock system reform" of China, please refer to the introduction from *Reform* magazine, 2007-06-06, http://www.reform.net.cn/book_r.php?bid=6&tid=37

million in 2004). Among these, national brand name firms numbered less than 40. Most of the firms were engaged in doing only processing work. The small processing firms were generally unable to directly receive large orders from foreign buyers, so they mainly received processing orders from brand firms, foreign trade companies and the nearby processing firms via personal relationships. However, the large-scale processing firms had already founded their own foreign trade companies with export rights. So these large-scale processing firms not only directly accept processing orders, but also traded directly. Even famous brand firms like Youngor, Shanshan and Romon similarly undertook massive processing services. These brand firms generally received large orders, and directed these to their own outsourcing factories, that generally number over 20. In order to guarantee quality, these firms generally sent their own technicians to the processing factories for a long time.

Around certain large firms in Ningbo, it is easy to find dozens of processing firms. For instance, there is an apparel firm with the trademark of 'Orient-hongye' in Ningbo and it is linked with more than 30 embroidery factories, 20 printing and dyeing plants and 10 laundering factories within a radius of 5 km. The bosses and managers were very familiar with each other, so they often needed no official contract, but instead made deals via telephone calls or through social activity. Therefore, transaction costs could be reduced and the transaction process shortened, thus reducing information loss and raising reaction speed to market.

Many similar examples could be found of a detailed local division of labour between clustered firms, such as the labour-intensive clusters of Ningbo and Dongguan cities. For another instance, in Cangnan County, South-west of Zhejiang Province, there emerged a label and badge cluster. Local producers divided the production procedures into tens of independent but inter-related activities, and coordinated all activities in the production process, from the raw material to the finished product, including the design, melting, writing, engraving of the mould, plate copying, hammering, drilling, making the needle, assembly, packing and so on, which involved more than 10 working procedures. This entire process was undertaken by over 800 independent firms and workshops, and each procedure's semi-manufactured goods were exchanged through the market, which formed the entire local production system, producing 89 per cent of the country's cafeteria magnetic cards, 91 per cent of the unit credentials, most of the famous white spirits bottle marks and packing boxes in China, even the labels and badges for 340,000 US policemen, the UN peacekeeping force and China's troops in Hong Kong.

9.2.2 Labour dynamics within Chinese clusters

As described earlier, clusters in China are highly specific in terms of location, emergence, and path dependence. Together with the geographical agglomeration of clustered firms in China, is the agglomeration of labour. The thickly dotted clusters distributed along China's coastal areas not only provide the world market with massive consumer products that are 'Made-in-China', but also provide nearly two-thirds of China's labour-intensive employment. Here, we focus on the most typical clusters in Zhejiang and Guangdong provinces, with the aim of identifying the labour dynamics that lie behind the well-reported industrial dynamics of clustered firms. In doing so, we must place the labour dynamics of clusters under the broader context of the evolution of China's employment structure in general.

Evolution of China's employment structure evolution as a whole

China has been experiencing rapid industrialization and mass urbanization, with the employment structure evolving according to the theorem of Petty (1899) and Clarke (1940), which states that the labour proportion of primary sector (agriculture) will continually decrease, while in the secondary sector (industry), it will increase for some time and then decrease, and that of the tertiary sector (services) will gradually and continually go up. China's employment structure evolution over the past two decades follows a very similar trajectory to this theorem, as shown in Figure 9.1.

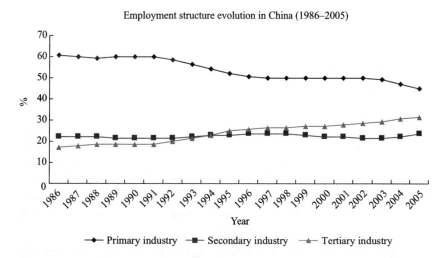

Figure 9.1 Employment structure evolution by industrial sectors (1986–2005)
Source: China Labour Statistical Yearbook (2006).

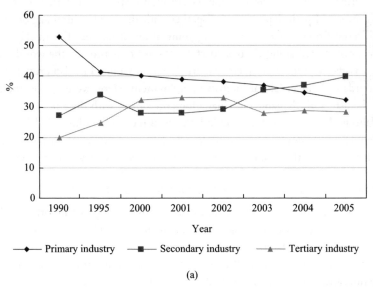

Employment structure evolution in
Guangdong Province (1990–2005)

(a)

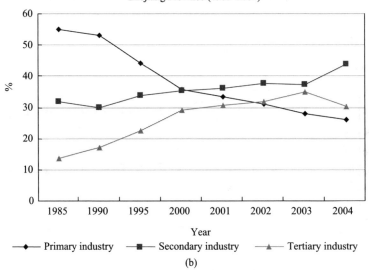

Employment structure evolution in
Zhejiang Province (1985–2004)

(b)

Figure 9.2 Employment structure evolution in Guangdong Province
(1990–2005) and Zhejiang Province (1985–2004)

Source: Guangdong Statistical Yearbook (2006) and Zhejiang Statistical Yearbook (2005).

In Guangdong and Zhejiang provinces, where most of China's labour-intensive clusters are located, the employment structure evolution matched the general dynamics of China, although the secondary sector (industry) based on clusters in Guangdong and Zhejiang grew much faster than the Chinese average (See Figures 9.2a and b).

Labour shortages: What has happened to labour-intensive clusters and the labour force?

Starting from around 2002, factories in Southern China were facing difficulties in securing a sufficient number of workers, and the shortage rapidly intensified after the spring of 2004 (Inagaki, 2006). At that time, media over the world reported on China's labour shortage and its impact upon the labour-intensive firms, especially around the Pearl River Delta (PRD) region[11]. This labour shortage of mainly young women workers was felt most acutely among apparel-related manufacturers (Inagaki, 2006).

> That kind of behavior (the labour shortage) was unheard-of as recently as three years ago, when millions of young people were still flooding into booming Shenzhen searching for any type of work.
>
> —The New York Times
> (Labour Shortage in China May Lead to Trade Shift, April 03, 2006)

It seems quite difficult to explain the problem of labour shortage with regard to China's huge population and massive migration of workers from rural to city areas. Yet, a great deal of clustered firms were working without enough workers. This happened around 2004 for the first time in China's history of economic growth after 1978. According to statistical analyses from the Guangdong Bureau of Labour and Social Security, the supply and demand of occupations in Guangdong Province in the 3rd quarter of 2007 showed that labour shortage in Pearl River Delta areas was really severe. According to a 2005 survey conducted in Guangdong Province, although a third of the manufacturers there tried to solve the labour shortage by raising wages and benefits, overall demand still exceeded supply with more than one million job vacancies.

---

[11] China Daily, 25 August 2004. 'Labour shortage puzzles experts'. http://www.chinadaily.com.cn/english/doc/2004-08/25/content_368566.htm;
The New York Time, 3 April 2006. 'Labour Shortage in China May Lead to Trade Shift'. http://www.nytimes.com/2006/04/03/business/03labor.html?pagewanted=1&_r=1&th&emc=th

Lixia Mei and Jici Wang

The top 10 occupations short of workers are shown in Figure 9.3, where the job opening rates ranged from 1.23 to 3.92: electronic parts manufacturing workers (job opening rate: 3.92), manual workers (2.66), insurance service workers (1.88), cold processing technicians (2.58), cutting/sewing workers (3.19), restaurant workers/ chefs (1.98), real estate clerks (2.35), departmental managers (2.40), salesman (1.42), and shop clerks/cashiers (1.23).

Top 10 occupations short of applicants in GD Province (Jul–Sep 2007)

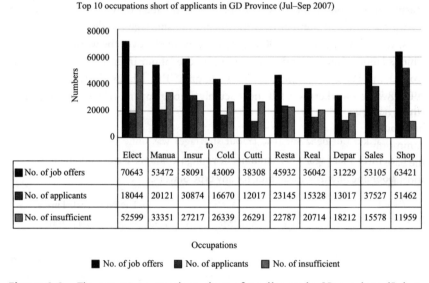

	Elect	Manua	Insur	Cold	Cutti	Resta	Real	Depar	Sales	Shop
■ No. of job offers	70643	53472	58091	43009	38308	45932	36042	31229	53105	63421
■ No. of applicants	18044	20121	30874	16670	12017	23145	15328	13017	37527	51462
■ No. of insufficient	52599	33351	27217	26339	26291	22787	20714	18212	15578	11959

Occupations

■ No. of job offers   ■ No. of applicants   ■ No. of insufficient

Figure 9.3   The top 10 occupations short of applicants in GD province (July to September, 2007)

Source: Guangdong Bureau of Labour and Social Security, Analysis of the Supply and Demand of Occupations in Guangdong Labour Market in July to September, 2007.

What had happened to China's labour market? Why did a labour shortage of more than 150 million migrant workers appear? Why was this taking place in Guangdong Province, which used to be the very place where millions of young people came from all around the country in search of any type of work, and where firms now could not recruit enough low-cost labour?

Population economists tend to ascribe the labour shortage to the so-called 'structural shortage', which sheds light on the shortage of skilled labour; and the decline of the 'population dividend', which has much to do with structural changes of China's population along with the high-speed economic development process.

The most frequently cited explanations with regard to the labour shortage in Eastern and Southern China include the following (Inagaki, 2006):

1. Low wages and adverse working conditions of factories;
2. The sharp rise in demand for labour in the manufacturing sectors;
3. The economic development model of China reached a turning point;
4. The rise of job opportunities in the services sector and the rising preference among workers for jobs in services;
5. The spread of mobile telephones facilitating the exchange of information among workers;
6. The decline of the youth population, due to the 'One Child Policy' of China; and
7. The increasing popularity of agriculture, given the rise of incomes.[12]

Among the above factors, 'low wages and adverse working conditions' ranks first, which has much to do with the extensive form of economic development that had been pursued, as well as the social transition process taking place in China. It was commonly believed that China had an inexhaustible supply of cheap labour, providing the base for the neoclassical analysis of 'comparative advantage'; however, the labour shortage appeared to challenge what was once held as conventional wisdom.

At a national level, many economists hold that China has passed the Lewisian turning point, where migrant labour no longer becomes available at a constant wage rate. For example, 'When the movement of the labour force out of rural areas and the outcomes of demographic transition are translated into the labour market, it can be seen that China has passed the Lewisian turning point, as evidenced by frequent labour shortages and rising wages for unskilled workers' (Yang, 2013, p. 94).

However, according to our observations on China's industrial clusters, we would like to argue that the labour shortage that appeared in Eastern and Southern China was rather a relative and structural shortage because of low wages, lack of training and promotion, and the decent work deficit, but not an absolute shortage because of the gap between overall labour supply and demand. However, there could also be a connection between the national situation and local shortages, with rising wages at the national level being reflected in shortages where local wages are held low.

---

[12] To improve China's rural and peasants' income became a key theme for China's government. A series of 'No.1 Documents' in favour of policies to increase rural income were released since 2000 by China's central government, including the policy of cancelling agricultural taxes, enhancing agricultural subsidies, augmenting transfer payments to rural areas, and 'Building New Socialist Countryside', and so on. These policies really bettered and improved rural people's incomes to a certain extent.

In addition, the shortage of migrant labour could also be caused by a rise in agricultural incomes, which took place after the 2006 abolition of agricultural taxes. When agricultural incomes rise, the reserve price of labour, i.e., the price at which labour will migrate for wage employment, will go up. Finally, what matters for employers are the shortages that might occur at their own local levels. These changes may be connected to national developments, but what introduces a dynamic into cluster development are the local manifestations of labour shortages. We will look at these two factors, decent work deficits for migrant workers and rising rural incomes, in the next two sub-sections.

9.2.3 Decent work deficits within labour-intensive clusters

In early 2004, the China State Council proclaimed that 'migrant farmer workers have become an important part of the industrial labour force of China'.[13] However, as migrant labour in cities, these workers can hardly attain decent work, and fall into a kind of 'decent work deficit', as defined by the ILO (1999), in China for some of the reasons considered below.

Low-wages as a factor of labour shortages

In early 2004, China's Minimum Wage Order (*Zuidi Gongzi Guiding*) was enacted, and took effect from March 1, 2004. In view of price rises, the Order required that each province or city adjust the monthly minimum wages every 2 years. In Table 9.1, we display the official monthly minimum wages in some provinces and cities of China, mainly in clustering areas, to provide a general view of average wage levels in China at that time.

Although the aim of the 'minimum wage' is to protect basic wage rights for workers, a majority of employers, or bosses, only pay their workers at or even under the minimum level in cluster areas.

A research report on 'China's rural migrant workers' conducted by the Research Office of the State Council of China (2005) concluded that the average monthly wage of rural migrant workers was between 500 and 800 *Yuan* RMB (about US $60–100). However, even for that small sum, workers within the most labour-intensive clusters worked more than 10 hours a day, and either 6 or 7 days a week, in some cases without overtime pay, which reduced their average hourly wage significantly. That should be compared with the US minimum wage of $5.15 per hour, prior to July 24, 2007 when the US minimum wage was raised (US Department of Labour 2007).

---

[13] Chinese State Council Policy on the Promotion of Farmers' Income Growth (Zhonggong Zhongyang Guowuyuan Guanyu Cujin Nongmin Zengjia Shouru Ruogan Zhengce de Yijian), February 8, 2004. http://www.china.com.cn/chinese/PI-c/493311.htm

Delayed wage payment was so widespread in nearly all locations and sectors, that in 2004 Premier Wen Jiabao signed a series of official documents designed to protect rural migrants' basic right to receive their wages on time. This central government intervention was effective in helping large numbers of rural migrant workers in China to receive their earned wages.

The literature on China's rural migrant workers (Fan, 2004; Pun, 2005) indicates that, in addition to earning low wages, laws that linked civil rights to where one is born made it difficult for rural migrant workers to obtain urban household rights (*Hukou*) or social security benefits in the area where they have migrated to work. As a result, these migrant workers faced great hardship in obtaining access to basic services such as housing, medical insurance and education, for both their children and themselves. Without the rights of an urban household, these migrant workers could hardly gain the fundamental rights of citizens in the location where they may have worked for years. Few migrant workers within clusters had access to job training and career education, and they were poorly informed about labour legislation meant to protect their labour rights.

9.2.4 Rising rural incomes

While focusing on building an 'Innovation-oriented Economy', China's central government did not forget the existence of its huge labour force of migrant workers. From 2004 to 2006, even while labour shortages began to emerge in some parts of China's coastal provinces, the Chinese central government paid much more attention to improve rural rights and livelihoods. On January 1, 2006, China's central government abolished the Agriculture Tax—an unprecedented act in more than 2600 years of Chinese agricultural history. As a result, more and more rural farmers who used to be migrant workers looking for jobs in the cities now preferred to stay in their hometown.

> Now the national policy for agriculture is better and better. The agriculture tax has been abolished. Why not stay at home farming? Why should I go so far away to find a job in the city? In cities we have to work long-hours everyday, and often extra work without pay; even worse is that we always received the salary with a delay.
>
> —A former migrant worker from Hunan Province

It is only to be expected that a rise in rural incomes would push up the reserve wage of migrant labour. In the absence of an adequate increase in wages in the coastal belt, there was a fall in migration, leading to labour shortages.

9.3 Case studies

We now turn to an examination of the labour shortage and its effects in two case studies: the Wenzhou shoe cluster and the Lecong furniture cluster.

Case 1: Wenzhou footwear cluster and labour force transformations

The city of Wenzhou, in Zhejiang province, is located nearly 500 km from Shanghai and is famous for its grassroots entrepreneurship. Wenzhou was named 'the Shoe Capital of China' in 2001 by the China Light Industry Association, as the footwear produced in Wenzhou accounts for nearly 25 per cent of total Chinese output of footwear, including the output for export and for the domestic market, with over 4,500 shoemaking firms located within the Wenzhou footwear cluster.

The annual output of leather shoes in the Wenzhou footwear cluster increased from 60 million pairs in 1998 to 460 million pairs in 2005. Along with production growth, the number of firms and employment has also grown; by 2005, more than 420,000 workers were employed in the factories comprising the Wenzhou footwear cluster.

At present, it is difficult to obtain reliable employment data on an annual basis for the Wenzhou footwear cluster. Nevertheless, it is possible to note an important labour force transformation. The majority of workers in the footwear cluster became local people, and not migrant labour. These migrant workers used to come from Western China; but when some industries relocated from Eastern to Western China, these workers could now find employment in their own home locations. Employers too could get local labour at a wage lower than they used to pay migrant labour, as will be described in greater detail below.

Firms move from Eastern to Western China and shift from migrants to local workers

After 2004, Zhejiang Province began to feel the impacts of labour shortage, making it difficult to continue producing low-cost shoes because of rising labour costs, as well as other price pressures arising from limited land, water, electricity, and raw materials. A large number of clustered firms relocated from Eastern to Western areas of China in search of lower production costs, especially to those provinces that originally were the source of out-going migrant workers such as Sichuan, Hunan, Jiangxi provinces and Chongqing City (the fourth largest Municipality of China, after Beijing, Shanghai, and Tianjin), as they offered acres of undeveloped land, a large and low-cost local labour force, and favourable investment policies. The antidumping taxes imposed by the European Union against Chinese leather shoes which started on October 7, 2006 added further pressure for footwear firms to transfer their production from Eastern to Western China in order to reduce costs. Already in 2006, over 300 footwear producers had relocated to Chengdu, Sichuan Province.

Two leading firms within the Wenzhou footwear cluster, Aokang and Red Dragon, relocated, respectively, to Bishan and Tongliang, Chongqing City, in 2003. The former invested more than 1 billion *Yuan* (approximately US$ 120 million) RMB in Bishan County to build a 'Shoe Capital of the West'; and the latter invested 200 million *Yuan* (approximately US$ 24 million) in Tongliang County to build a 'Western Shoe Production Base'. As two of the largest firms in the Wenzhou footwear cluster, both Aokang and Red Dragon persuaded a group of supplier firms in Wenzhou City to relocate to Chongqing City. For instance, Aokang succeeded in persuading 27 inter-related shoemaking firms and Red Dragon brought over 30 supplier firms to Chongqing City, in which several new footwear clusters came into being.

In addition to this relocation of leading firms from within the Wenzhou footwear cluster to inner provinces in China, there was a similar trend of skilled labour moving from the economically developed provinces on the Eastern coastal area back to their rural hometowns, where more local and low-wage workers could also find work in the shoe factories without migrating to other places. Soon there were some 120,000 shoe workers in Chongqing City and most were local labour.

> We have to pay more than 1000 Yuan each month to those skilled workers [in Wenzhou], however, we only pay 500 Yuan each month for the same kind of labour here (in Chongqing city).
>
> —A Wenzhou footwear producer

Indeed, it was reported by some local TV stations that some of these returning workers, called 'local entrepreneurs', began to set up their own business, either as shoe merchants or small suppliers for larger firms. However, we do not have more detailed information about whether these returning workers were considered 'skilled workers' and received a higher wage than the other unskilled rural workers or not.

In a nutshell, the case of Wenzhou footwear cluster firms relocation implies that it was not the gap between supply and demand of labour in Wenzhou City that was driving the relocation strategy of the clustered firms; rather, they were relocating to reduce costs and explore inner labour markets. Of course the low-cost advantages may also have declined in the Western and middle areas of China. However, clustered firms relocated to inner provinces actually faced more difficulties, given a less developed supplier network. As a result, upgrading and building innovative capacity could be the only way to remain competitive. At the same time, with the geographical shift of clustered firms, workers whether from the local area or migrant workers from inner provinces, both faced more challenges, even as they had more opportunities.

Case 2: Lecong furniture cluster and the labour changes

Lecong is a small town located in the Shunde District of Foshan city, South-west of Guangzhou, Guangdong Province. This place is regarded as a 'World Furniture Centre'. In fact, Lecong is not a furniture production centre, but a trade centre with more than 4,000 furniture merchants and surrounded by a succession of furniture 'supply chain cities' (Gereffi, 2006). In 2004, Lecong Town was given the title of 'Capital of the Furniture Trade of China' by China Light Industrial Association.

In this small town with a local population of no more than 100,000 people, there were over 110,000 migrant workers, nearly half of them working in the furniture industry. After 2004, labour shortage also began to trouble the Lecong furniture cluster. It was reported that 30 per cent of the migrant workers who used to work in the Lecong furniture cluster did not return to work after the 2006 Spring Festival. This forced employers to raise wages and also recruit un-skilled labour, in order to avoid a possible delay in delivery of their foreign orders, which would have caused huge losses.

In the face of a labour shortage, as well as other cost inflation factors, such as rising raw material prices, limited land available, antidumping taxes, RMB appreciation, etc., a few of the Lecong furniture cluster firms moved to inland China to reduce costs.

> I have to work for more than 12 hours a day in very adverse condition, to get only about 1,000 Yuan in Lecong; however, now that the Central Government has abolished agricultural taxes, I can earn almost 1,000 Yuan in my hometown without any transport expense, and what's more, I can stay with my family more often. Of course I prefer to work locally.
>
> —A migrant worker from Sichuan Province

Thus, former migrant workers benefited from this relocation. However, the suppliers could not find a sufficient number of related industrial chains as existed in the integrated production environment of the Lecong Town cluster. Despite lower wages, the absence of supplier units made it even more difficult for them to control costs. As a result, after a few months, they returned to Lecong.

Therefore, what we can conclude from the case of the Lecong furniture cluster's failed relocation is that cheap labour and policy subsidies are not sufficient for firms to stay competitive on the global market. They also require the advantages of clustering, of being in close proximity to low-cost and efficient suppliers in a competitive market. However, in order to remain within the cluster and to deal with the labour shortages, the employers surely had to start paying their workers better and improving their working and living conditions. This was the only way to go, especially for those big leading firms inside clusters, because, in doing so, not only could the massive cheap labour reproduce themselves as a better labour force, but also the clustered firms could improve the human capital in their industries. This is the only way for labour-intensive industries of developing countries to increase productivity, accumulate innovative capacities and then upgrade in global value chains. We now look in a little more detail at the impacts of labour shortages on the clusters.

9.4 The impacts of labour shortages within clusters

The impacts of labour shortages upon labour-intensive clusters can be classified as both direct and indirect impacts, with the former having implications primarily for clustered firms and labour, and the latter aspects having implications for local and national government and global buyers and their governments.

9.4.1 The direct impacts of labour shortages in China

Firms in clusters: Relocation to keep racing to the bottom or innovation to stay rooted at home?

From the cases described above, we can see that many clustered firms considered relocation as a solution to the problem of the labour shortage and rising cost pressures, rather than considering investment in labour-saving machinery, or improved training for a smaller but better-paid and higher-skilled labour force.

Firms agglomerate in special spaces in order to benefit from the labour pool and knowledge spill-over effects; as Marshall put it, 'Employers are apt to resort to any place where they are likely to find a good choice of workers with the special skill which they require; while men seeking employment naturally go to places where there are many employers who need such skill as theirs and where therefore it is likely to find a good market' (Marshall, 1920, 271); however, the labour shortage that emerged in China broke up the low-cost labour basis on which many Chinese clusters based their competitive advantage. The labour shortage created intense competition for workers.

Most enterprises in industrialized countries replace human labour with advanced machines in the face of labour shortage or rising wages. However, this posed a difficulty in China's labour-intensive clusters, as their narrow profit margins provided little capital to invest in new machinery.

Scholars (e.g., Gereffi, 1999; Humphrey and Schmitz, 2000) suggest that clustered firms should innovate and upgrade from original equipment manufacture (OEM) to original design manufacture (ODM) and even own brand manufacture (OBM) to change the basis of their competitive advantage from low-cost production to innovative capability. This seems to be an ideal and reasonable way to solve the problem of labour dynamics within China's clusters in the long run, in particular for the big leading firms in clusters.

However, most small firms with an average lifespan no more than 5 years are vulnerable to market fluctuations and preferred to relocate to other low cost areas for cheaper labour, rather than invest more on R&D to improve innovative capability. For these firms, the options were either 'move or die'. Hundreds of small labour-intensive clustered firms reportedly closed in the PRD area. By moving to an inland province, such firms could obtain cheaper land, favourable taxes, and proximity to local labour and product markets, which provided them with new opportunities. On the other hand, if they persisted with a low-cost strategy that is vulnerable to the race to the bottom in the global game, perhaps such firms may need to relocate again and again.

According to data from the Federation of Hong Kong Industries, 37.3 per cent of Hong Kong firms already located in the Pearl River Delta (PRD) area were planning in 2007 to transfer all or part of their business to inland China. With the leading footwear firms relocating from Zhejiang province to Western areas of China, more upstream and downstream suppliers would also have to transfer. A similar phenomenon occurred in early 1990s when a flock of Taiwanese lead firms relocated to mainland China, bringing their supplier networks that relocated together with the leading firm.

However, industrial relocation in search of low-cost labour is not a long-term solution to the labour shortage facing China's labour-intensive clusters. Rather, only improvement in the clusters' innovative capability can unleash a process of both economic upgrading for firms and social upgrading for labour. What is more, big leading firms and small following firms, had to take on different roles in the light of their different market positions and capacities. Big leading firms had to take more responsibility in terms of improving workers' welfare and carrying out firm R&D, thus enhancing innovation capability. At this point, social upgrading is in line with the economic upgrading of clustered firms.

Government intervention: Different concerns at central and local levels

China's central government enacted a new *Labour Law (Laodong Fa)* in early 2008, which extended the protection of legal rights for labour, particularly as regards overtime, delayed wage payment, and labour security. Workers, especially rural migrant workers in labour-intensive clusters, expected that this new legislation would help them to attain stable wage growth and recognition of social rights to access basic services in order to lead a decent life.

At the same time, China's central government also positively encouraged industrial relocation from the Eastern and Southern coastal areas to the middle and Western provinces, with the macroeconomic objective of improving inland development, as well as reducing the economic gap between advanced coastal areas and undeveloped inland areas. For example, the No. 44 Document promulgated by China's Ministry of Commerce and China Customs, with the title of 'List of Restricted Commodities in Processing Trade' (*Jiagong Maoyi Xianzhilei Shangpin Mulu*), came into effect on August 23 of 2007. According to this new trade policy, in a large number of labour-intensive products, production was restricted in coastal areas, but their production could be expanded in middle and Western China, where the local economies were lagging and required more foreign and private investments. This policy caused companies in the coastal areas to grapple with the final painful decision: either to upgrade from low-cost to high-value-added production, or transfer to inland regions to continue low-cost production.

Local governments in coastal provinces and inland provinces had different policy priorities because they had different concerns. In coastal provinces from which firms were relocating, local governments tried to persuade firms to leave their headquarters or R&D centres in the areas and just move the low-value-added, low-tech, and labour-intensive activities to other places. Some local governments encouraged firms to transfer within the province. For instance, Guangdong provincial government set up 23 government-driven 'Industrial transfer parks' within the geographical range of Guangdong Province, mostly located in undeveloped and mountainous areas of Guangdong, beyond the advanced cities of Guangzhou, Shenzhen, Dongguan, Foshan, etc.

However, the situation was different for inland provinces to which firms were trying to move. For these undeveloped areas, industrial transfer undoubtedly provided a good opportunity to attract investment and new firms. Officials from inland and neighbouring provinces, such as Hunan, Jiangxi, Guangxi, Sichuan, Anhui, Yunnan, Hubei, all went to the coastal areas, PRD and YRD areas, to invite business and attract investment, even with their provincial governors or mayors leading the teams. In order to win the race of attracting firms and investments, these inland provinces emulated the coastal zone strategies by offering acres of cheap land and favourable investment policies to firms that were willing to relocate.

In this context, many labour-intensive firms relocated to inland areas. For example, the Foxconn Group, one of the largest leading labour-intensive firms in the electronics industrial cluster of PRD and the world's largest Contract Manufacturer providing EMS (Electrical Manufacturing Services) to Apple, Motorola and others global brands, which employs more than 100,000 workers in mainland China, planned to relocate from its original location in Guangdong to Hubei, Guangxi, and Hebei provinces. Its relocation strategy, on the one hand, favoured inland areas, while, on the other hand, the impact of this relocation on local GDP and employment loss was a source of worry for the Guangdong government.

Clustered labour: Rising wages and more job opportunities

The direct impact of the labour shortage within China's clusters is seen in rising wages. According to the sample survey based on 3,086 worker interviews in the PRD area conducted by Zhongshan University (Wu, Zhao, Li, et al., 2007), the advent of the 'labour shortage', meant that the delay in wage payment became less, and most importantly, the average monthly wages for migrant workers in 2006 increased to RMB 166.53 *Yuan* (approximately US$ 20.61), which is 17.9 per cent higher than it was in 2005 (Wu, Zhao, Li, et al., 2007).

Aside from rising wages and shorter working hours, migrant workers now have more job opportunities in other provinces, such as Beijing, Jiangsu, Fujian, Shandong and even in their hometowns such as in Jiangxi, Hunan, Guangxi, and Henan. More importantly, many migrant workers recognize that professional education and training can help them improve their skills and incomes, so they invest money in joining evening school, training classes, and English courses. Many local governments are offering free training projects for migrant workers, as part of the 'Sunshine Project' (*Yangguang Gongcheng*).

Some migrant workers chose to stay at home, others opened their own business and others went back to farming with the Chinese government's new policies and incentives to encourage farmers in modern agriculture and to help them improve incomes.

9.4.2 The indirect impact inside and outside China

The indirect impacts of the labour shortage within Chinese clusters could be felt both inside and outside China, as discussed below.

External impacts: The labour shortage may weaken China's competitiveness on world markets?

The international media present different concerns with regard to China's labour shortage. According to the *New York Times,* the labour shortage may to some extent weaken China's competitiveness as a world production centre, and many trades will shift away:

> The shortage of workers is pushing up wages and swelling the ranks of the country's middle class, and it could make Chinese-made products less of a bargain worldwide. International manufacturers are already talking about moving factories to lower-cost countries like Vietnam.
>
> —The New York Times
> ('Labour Shortage in China May Lead to Trade Shift', 3 April 2006)

On the other side of the coin, optimistic economists regard the changes within China's labour structure as progress, thinking that China is moving up the economic ladder, or upgrading in global value chains. Migrant workers may see more opportunities beyond simply being unskilled assemblers of the world's goods. Rising wages may also prompt Chinese consumers to start buying more products from other countries, helping to balance China's huge trade surpluses. The labour shortage may also spur Chinese clustered firms to improve labour conditions and to more aggressively recruit workers with more incentives and benefits.

Internal impacts: Industrial relocation, upgrading and indigenous innovation in China

Over the past 30 years, China has achieved fast and stable growth as part of its economic development, as well as attracted foreign and domestic investments. However, wages and working conditions have not necessarily improved along the economic upgrading path. Though the labour shortage within clusters may to some extent, in the short run, impair Chinas' export competitiveness in low-end products, in the long run, it is going to catalyse the transformation of China's economic structure, promoting industrial upgrading, with more emphasis on indigenous innovative capability.

The relocation of clusters to Central, Western and Northern China in search of lower labour costs is leading to a new internal division of labour between the developed and undeveloped regions. The coastal zones will become the locus of higher technology production and R&D centres and the outsourcers to lower-cost inner provinces. In turn, the inner areas will compete in attracting investments and industrial transfer from Eastern and Southern China, which may result in more complicated dynamics of labour movements in China. It remains to be seen whether the relocation of firms from the Eastern and Southern coastal clusters to inland and Western provinces, implies upgrading and convergence between regions, or divergence between regions at different developmental levels.

For the massive low-wage labour force, in other words, primarily the large number of rural migrant workers in China, what they need most urgently is definitely not only temporary wage increases, but greater access and opportunities to get training and education, therefore to improve their human capital which will also promote the innovative capacity of clustered firms, and finally build competitive advantage based on the country's indigenous innovation capability.

9.5 Conclusion

In this chapter, we have briefly analysed China's numerous labour-intensive clusters, in terms of their formation, and distribution, and then the division of labour between different regions of China from both global and local perspectives.

The labour dynamics within these clusters has been highlighted and structural changes, especially the labour shortage, its causes and impacts within clusters, analysed by way of case studies of the Wenzhou footwear cluster and the Lecong furniture cluster. The main finding is that the labour shortage reflected a deep-seated economic and social problem of contemporary China: most attention was directed toward attracting investment and stimulating economic development, while too little attention was given to improving labour conditions and meeting social challenges, notably in terms of upgrading the social and regional impacts of clusters. Only when the labour shortage broke out, did clustered firms, local governments, and scholars become aware of its profound implications.

We now turn to the question posed at the beginning of this paper: the extent to which China's competitive position in global markets will continue to be based on low-wage labour. The significant labour shortage within China's clusters reduces the case for this option, i.e., low wages can no longer be the key pillar of sustainable growth in China. This reinforces the role of investments in R&D, education and training as key drivers of future growth. Though there is still is a long way to go, such a strategy would provide a viable alternative to the low-wage growth model.

Industrial clusters used to be considered as a new universal model for industrial growth and regional development in China. These labour-intensive clusters distributed along China's Eastern and Southern coasts promoted China's industrialization and helped employ a large number of migrant workers. However, experience from successful clusters in the industrialized countries shows that clusters are not necessarily innovative because of clustering, but indeed industries that get into an innovative dynamic can be additionally supported by the clustering process. This innovative process cannot be separated from labour dynamics within clusters, where labour shortages and increases in wages force a reformation of the value chains with an emphasis on upgrading. This process of industrial upgrading must be accompanied by a process of social upgrading for labour, which should involve improved working conditions for workers, as well as providing them with social recognition and greater opportunities for education and professional training that would improve their skills, incomes, and human capital. This will also result in an increased consumption capacity, thus supporting a more balanced, domestic-demand led, economic growth model for the country.

References

Bair, J., and G. Gereffi. 2001. 'Local Clusters in Global Chains: The Causes and Consequences of Export Dynamism in Torreon's Blue Jeans Industry.' *World Develop* 29 (11): 1885–903.

Barboza D. 2004. 'Textile Enclaves: In Roaring China, Sweaters Are West of Socks City.' *New York Times*, December 24.

Chen, X. 2006. 'Regionalizing the Global-Local Economic Nexus: A Tale of Two Regions in China.' University of Illinois at Chicago.

China State Council. 2006. *Guojia Zhongchangqi Kexue he Jishu Fazhan Guihua Gangyao* [国家中长期科学和技术发展规划纲要", National Medium and Long term Science and Technology Development Plan: 2006–2020). Accessed February 9, 2006. http://www.gov.cn/jrzg/2006-02/09/content_183787.htm

Clark C. 2001 (1940). *The Conditions of Economic Progress*. London: Macmillan.

Cody, D. 2006. 'The Adaptation and Advancement of the International Industrial District Model in Wenzhou: A Case Study of the Footwear Industry.' Lund University.

Dicken, P. 2003. *Global Shift: Reshaping the Global Economic Map in the 21st Century*. 4th ed., London: Sage Publications Ltd.

Fan, C. C. 2004. 'The State, the Migrant Labour Regime, and Maiden Workers in China.' *Polit Geogr* 23: 283–303.

Gereffi, G. 1999. 'International Trade and Industrial Upgrading in the Apparel Commodity Chain.' *J Int Econ* 48 (1): 37–70.

———. 2005. *The New Offshoring of Jobs and Global Development. ILO Social Policy Lectures*. Jamaica: International Institute for Labour Studies.

Guerrieri, P., and C. Pietrobelli. 2004. 'Industrial Districts' Evolution and Technological Regimes: Italy and Taiwan.' *Technovation* 24: 899–914.

He, Canfei. 2003. 'Entry Mode and Location of Foreign Manufacturing Enterprises in China.' *Eur Geogr Econ* 44 (1): 399–417.

Humphrey, J. 1995. 'Industrial Reorganization in Developing Countries: From Models to Trajectories.' *World Develop* 23 (1): 149–62.

Humphrey, J., and H. Schmitz. 2000. 'Governance and Upgrading: Linking Industrial Cluster and Global Value Chain Research.' *IDS Working Paper No. 120*. Brighton: Institute of Development Studies, University of Sussex.

International Labour Organization. ILO. 1999. *Decent Work*. Geneva: Report of the Director General.

Inagaki, H. 2006. *South China's Labour Shortage: Will the Current Worker Shortage Escalate?* Tokyo: Mizuho Research Institute.

Lewis, W. A. 1954. 'Economic Development with Unlimited Supplies of Labour.' *The Manchester School* May: 400–449.

Marshall, A. 1920. *Principles of Economics*. 8th ed., Cambridge: Cambridge University Press.

Markusen, A. 1996. 'Sticky Places in Slippery Space: A Typology of Industrial Districts.' *Econ Geogr* 72 (3): 293–313.

Muscio, A., and M. Scarpinato. 2007. 'Employment and Wage Dynamics in Italian Industrial Districts.' *Reg Stud* 41 (6): 765–77.

National Bureau of Statistics of China. 2006. *Guanyu Woguo Guonei Shengchan Zongzhi Lishi Shuju Xiuding Jieguo de Gonggao* ["关于我国国内生产总值历史数据修订结果的公告", Bulletin of China's Historical GDP Data Revision]. Accessed on January 9, 2006. Available at, http://gy.sc.stats.gov.cn/Article_Show. asp?ArticleID=3850.

Petty, Sir William. 1899. *The Economic Writings of Sir William Petty*, edited by Charles Hull. Cambridge: Cambridge University Press. Available at, https:// books.google.com/books/about/The_Economic_Writings_of_Sir_William_ Pet.html?id=7kdJAAAAYAAJ.

Pun, N. 2005. *Made in China: Women Factory Workers in A Global Workplace*. Durham: Duke University Press.

Rawski, T. 2005. 'China as Producer: Chinese Industry after 25 Years of Reform.' Conference Paper presented at the China and the World Economy Workshop, December 2005.

Schmitz, H., and P. Knorringa. 2000. 'Learning from Global Buyers.' *J Develop Stud* 37 (2): 177–205.

Schmitz, H., and K. Nadvi. 1999. 'Clustering and Industrialization: Introduction.' *World Develop* 27 (9): 1505–14.

Tan, W. 2007. 'Upgrading of Apparel clusters in Global Production Network: The Case of Ningbo.' PhD diss., Peking University.

Yang, Du. 2013. 'Labour Market and Social Protection in China: Experiences and Issues.' In *Aligning Economic and Social Goals in Emerging Economies: Employment and Social Protection in Brazil, China, India and South Africa,* edited by Gerry Rodgers. New Delhi: Academic Foundation.

Wang, J. 2007. 'Clusters in China: The Low Road Versus the High Road in Cluster Development.' In *Development on the Ground: Clusters, Networks and Regions in Emerging Economies,* edited by A. Scott and G. Garofoli. London: Routledge.

Wong, D. F. K., C. Y. Li, and X. H. Song. 2007. 'Rural Migrant Workers in Urban China: Living a Marginalised Life.' *Int J Soc Welfare* 16: 32–40.

Wu X., X. Zhao, C. Li, et al. 2007. *Zhujiang Sanjiaozhou Nongmingong Wenjuan Diaocha Baogao* [Survey Report of Migrant Workers in Pearl River Delta Area], *Zhujiang Jingji* (Zhujiang Economy) Issue 8.

Zhang, H. 2007. 'China's New Rural Daughters Coming of Age: Downsizing the Family and Firing Up Cash-Earning Power in the New Economy.' *J Women Cult Soc* 32 (2): 671–98.

10

Migrant Labour in Global Value Chains in Asia

Yuko Hamada[1,2]

10.1 Introduction

The expansion of GVCs in Asia has resulted in a significant labour demand in the region and opportunities for greater diversification. Occupations that require higher skill and offer higher remuneration have become more popular than labour-intensive segments in upstream supply chains, which are considered '3D' (dirty, demeaning, and dangerous) activities. The conditions faced by workers, especially foreign workers, tend to be worse when they are engaged in labour-intensive segments. Countries that are unable to supply labour to these GVC segments often opt to recruit workers from overseas. This trend has been further fuelled by increasingly ageing societies in developed countries in Asia, as well as the economic disparities between developed and developing countries.

This chapter examines labour issues within GVCs with a particular focus on labour migration in Asia. The chapter gives an overview of foreign employment in GVCs, before discussing the main challenges that foreign workers face within GVCs. Finally, the chapter suggests policy options for countries that deal with foreign employment in GVCs.

10.2 Foreign employment in GVCs

It has become increasingly common in Asia as well as other parts of the world to recruit foreign labour from developing countries to form part of GVCs in more developed countries. The growth of GVCs contributes to an increase in demand for

[1] The author would like to thank Sanam Rahman, Chris Foulkes and Nissara Spence from International Organization for Migration for their assistance in researching and editing this paper as well as providing valuable inputs.

[2] The analyses presented in this paper are the views of the author and do not reflect the views of the International Organization for Migration (IOM).

labour, as labour-intensive sectors grow. Within the academic discourse, the different job categories in GVCs are clearly distinguished, and these distinctions are based on the availability of information technology enabled services (ITES), meaning that business processes are information technology-based. Despite increased innovations and access to ITES, GVCs still rely on different levels of human resources. Wage differences reflect different levels or job skills. Due to the demographic and economic complexities in the region, some developed countries face shortages of native-born workers willing to undertake labour-intensive, low-skilled work. There is a growing trend of foreign workers filling these positions in some countries.

10.2.1 Horizontal diversification of production

The horizontal diversification of production is a form of supply chain management which may manifest in a 'build-where-you-sell' strategy (World Trade Organization and Institute of Developing Economies-Japan External Trade Organization, 2011). This style of production is often seen in the automobile industry, where automobiles are built where they are sold. Japan and Korea are examples of two countries that recruit and employ foreign workers in their supply chains.

Japan has experienced labour shortages since the 1980s, and invited large numbers of foreign workers from Latin America, Southeast Asia, and South Asia. Japanese employers favoured Peruvians and Brazilians of Japanese ancestry to work in the automobile industry. Often, most workers in Japan from foreign countries work in the manufacturing sector. By the end of October 2009, a total of 218,900 foreign workers were employed in the manufacturing sector in Japan (Yamada, 2010). Yasushi (2012) claimed that the concentration of diaspora populations in Japan working in the manufacturing sector areas is as high as 36.2 per cent, of which 70.4 per cent for Vietnamese, 66.6 per cent Peruvian, 63.8 per cent Brazilian, 59.4 per cent Indonesian, and 44.9 per cent Chinese. This concentration reflects mainly low-skilled foreign labour, dispatched or subcontracted workers (Brazilians and Peruvians), and technical intern trainees (Vietnamese, Indonesians, and Chinese).

Korea recorded over 49,000 foreign workers in the manufacturing sector (Jung, 2011) and has signed Memoranda of Understanding (MOUs) with 15 countries from which it recruits foreign workers. Table 10.1 highlights the numbers of foreign migrant workers in Korea due to these MOUs.

Another example of the horizontal diversification of production is the fishing industry in Thailand. In 2009, the GDP value added by industry for the fishing industry in Thailand stood at THB 68,020[3] million at constant prices, and the percentage share

---

[3] Approximately equal to USD 2027, based on Google currency conversion dated May 8, 2015.

Table 10.1 Migrant workers' countries of origin under employment permit system in manufacturing in Korea

Country	Numbers
Philippines	39,044
China	7,216
East Timor	429
Kyrgyz	922
Pakistan	5,360
Myanmar	2,322
Bangladesh	5,364
Nepal	6,753
Uzbekistan	11,438
Cambodia	7,641
Mongolia	23,082
Sri Lanka	23,150
Indonesia	31,822
Thailand	41,249
Vietnam	68,306
Total	274,098

Source: Jung (2011).

in total value added to GDP was 1.6 per cent (International Labour Organization n.d.). The Thai fishing industry is an example of an industry where foreign workers fill the supply gaps in the labour market. Locals are reluctant to engage in fishing and fish processing jobs that keep them away from home for long periods of time, and involve working irregular hours and piece-rate wages. Consequently, the fishing and fish processing industries employ approximately 15 per cent of Thailand's migrant workers from neighbouring countries, while they only employ approximately 2 per cent of the Thai workforce (Martin, 2007). As shown below, Thailand depends heavily on migrant workers for catching fish, making nets, and fish processing. The fisheries industry has contributed directly to the growth of other related industrial activities such as ice manufacturing, cold storage, and ship building (Food and Agricultural Organization, 2009). In 2011, the International Organization for Migration estimated that there were over 247,000 migrant workers from the neighbouring countries of Lao PDR, Myanmar and Cambodia in the Thai fishing industry (International Organization for Migration, 2011) (Table 10.2 and Figure 10.1).

Table 10.2   Migrant workers in fishing industry in Thailand

Work	Total of three nationalities	Cambodia	Lao PDR	Myanmar
Fishing	56,578	14,969	1,800	39,809
Seafood processing	136,973	6,020	1,180	129,773
Food sales	54,225	4,483	13,074	36,668

Source: International Organization for Migration (2011, p. 12).

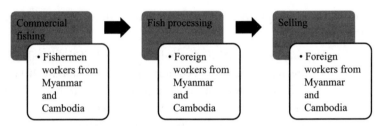

Figure 10.1   Supply chain of fishing industry

Source: International Organization for Migration (2011, p. 12).

10.2.2   Vertical specialization

A second significant form of supply chain management requiring overseas labour is the vertical specialization of the global supply chain. Vertical specialization seeks to stage production along a global supply chain, where each part of the process is undertaken in the most efficient geography available (World Trade Organization and Institute of Developing Economies-Japan External Trade Organization, 2011, p. 16). Vertical specialization applies to the production of consumer goods such as electronics and designer clothes where parts are assembled in low-cost countries across the world and then sold in developed markets. Hennes and Mauritz (H&M), ZARA, and the Southeast Asian palm oil industry are good examples of companies and industries which use this approach.

ZARA, the fashion retailer, is owned by Inditex, a Spanish company. When Inditex outsources production, it uses Asian and European countries with low production costs. A total of 34 per cent of Inditex's manufacturing is outsourced to Asia and 14 per cent to parts of Europe including Turkey (Economist, 2011). Fabrics are cut in-house at the headquarters and then sent to cooperatives for sewing and packaging (inserting price tags and hangers). Following this, the products are

Table 10.3   Palm oil industry in Malaysia, 2010

Country	Palm oil exports (1) (USD bil.)	Agricultural exports (2) (USD bil.)	(1)/ (2) (per cent)	Foreign exports (3) (USD bil.)	(2)/(3) (per cent)	GDP (4) (USD bil.)	(3)/ (4) (per cent)	(1)/ (4) (per cent)
Malaysia	18.6	25.9	51.1	199.0	13.0	430.9	46.2	4.3

Source: Accenture for Humanity United (2013).

then returned to the headquarters to be driven and flown to ZARA retail outlets around the world (*ibid.*).

A similar thing happens at H&M. Around 65 per cent of the Sweden-based products by H&M are made in lower-cost countries in Asia (Economist, 2011). The business model that H&M follows includes having a team of 100 in-house designers develop the clothing in coordination with buyers and then outsourcing these to their network of 700 suppliers (Capell, 2008). Over two-thirds of these suppliers are located in low-cost Asian countries (*ibid.*).

Southeast Asia leads the globe in the export of palm oil globally. In 2010, Malaysia earned over 18.6 million USD through the palm oil industry; this accounted for more than half of the agricultural exports of Malaysia (Accenture for Humanity United, 2013), as shown in Table 10.3.

Activities in this industry are labour-intensive and physically challenging. Human resource requirements change according to the phase of production in which workers are employed. 'Upstream production', activities at the bottom of the supply chain, depend on foreign workers as these activities are not popular amongst nationals. Upstream activities in the agricultural sector including clearing and preparing the land for seed plantations, planting seed crops, spraying seed crops with insecticides and other petrochemicals for fertilization, harvesting crops, and delivering them to the mills for further processing. The wage rate is another discouraging factor. Companies try to minimize staff costs in order to maximize profits. Hence, the dependency on foreign workers is increasing. In the oil palm industry, foreign labourers comprise 70 per cent of employees (Accenture for Humanity United, 2013). Bangladesh sent 3,853 workers to Malaysia in 2013 (Bureau of Manpower, Employment and Training, 2014). Following a meeting with Malaysian authorities in Kuala Lumpur, the secretary of Bangladesh's Ministry of Expatriates' Welfare and Overseas Employment claimed that 12,000 workers will be hired for plantation jobs in Sarawak province, at Sarawak Plantation Berhad in 2014 (Monitor Global Outlook, 2014).

10.3 Main challenges of labour migration in GVCs

These figures raise the question: what kind of labour issues are migrant workers confronted with when engaged in work in supply chains? Reportedly, scholars find more vulnerability in workers who are involved in upstream activities of GVCs compared to those who are in downstream activities. Duarte (2013) argued that while flexibility in production aims at reducing costs, lower levels of unemployment and overall economic performance, it has led to an increased number of informal workers, especially in the beginning of chains; informality is associated with insecurity and vulnerability (Duarte, 2013). Barrientos and Barrientos (2002) looked into social protection issues of informal workers in horticulture GVCs, specifically the fruit exports from Chile and South Africa to the United Kingdom. They explored the horticulture value chains to identify and analyse issues of employment and social protection, as well as any risks that are transferred down to informal workers at the bottom of the chain (Barrientos and Barrientos, 2002). They identified that the risks faced by these workers include job insecurity, low wages, risk of poverty, and health and safety risks. Most migrant workers engaged in GVCs fall into the low skilled category. Issues can be categorized into four areas according to the migration processes.

10.3.1 Pre-migration phase

Before their departure, migrant workers pay high recruitment fees in their countries of origin. In many cases throughout Asia, the workers bear virtually all migration-related costs such as transportation, commission fee for recruitment intermediaries, visa fees, as well as medical charges. In this region, malpractice in recruitment practices is a serious problem resulting in many migrants paying high fees to recruitment intermediaries. Recruitment intermediaries play a significant role in hiring workers from labour-sending countries, as they have contacts with employers or other intermediaries in receiving countries. Their presence and involvement in the migration process often raises the costs of migration, despite the limits set on recruitment fees in many origin countries. For instance, in Bangladesh, the maximum migration cost for low-skilled male and female migrants has been fixed, by the Ministry of Expatriates' Welfare and Overseas Employment (MoEWOE) at BDT 84,000 (USD 1,027) and BDT 20,000 (USD 245), respectively (Agunias, 2012). However, interviews with migrants reveal that on an average workers pay brokers around BDT 200,000 (USD 2,445) (*ibid.*).

This suggests that the cost of the middlemen and the profits of the licensed recruiters are as high as BDT 150,000 (USD 1,833) or almost two-thirds of the total cost to the migrant (*ibid.*).

Procedures for recruitment are often time-consuming and complicated. In Nepal, for example, foreign employers are required to recruit through licensed agencies registered with the Department of Labour and Employment Promotion, Government of Nepal (Embassy of Nepal n.d.). This department is in charge of overseeing the recruitment process of agencies and providing permission to send Nepali workers overseas. The licensed recruiting agencies can communicate directly with the overseas employers, and once they receive valid vacancy demands from the employers, they can apply to the Director General of Labour Department for permission to recruit, with the following documents (Embassy of Nepal n.d.):

- A copy of the Power of Attorney issued by a foreign employer in favour of the recruiting agent to act on his behalf.
- A copy of the demand letter from the employer containing details of the vacancies.
- A copy of the employment contract or service agreement.
- Guarantee letter to the DG of the Department of Labour & Employment Promotion.
- Inter-party agreement between the manpower demanding employer and the recruitment agency in Nepal.
- Guarantee and Undertaking to the Embassy of Nepal (*ibid.*).

Permission to recruit is only granted if the department is satisfied with the validity of the demand letter, and if the terms and conditions stated are in line with government regulations (Cosmos Nepal Human Resource Pvt. Ltd., 2014). Upon obtaining permission, the recruitment company can advertise the position in local and national newspapers and start the recruitment process. Although this process has been designed to ensure that potential migrant workers are protected from fraud and abuse, it has been observed that bureaucratic delay and 'too many' requirements often goad recruiters into unethical practices, and workers to opt for unregistered recruiters who promise quicker work placements abroad.

Another problem faced by migrant workers is that they have little access to information about their employment conditions and their rights in their destination countries. Migrants often do not have adequate information about countries of destinations and leave without knowledge of the rights they can exercise in countries of destination. They can leave without acquiring the basic language skills needed for work in destination countries, and often without having a proper employment contract outlining the conditions of work and remuneration. In many cases, migrant workers end up performing completely different jobs than what they had been promised prior to departure. For those workers who have contracts, these are normally short-term contracts limited to no more than 1 year. Some migrant workers bring their families, and their spouses end up working illegally alongside them.

10.3.2 During employment

Migrant workers arriving in destination countries without proper information regarding their employment and living conditions can face a variety of issues. Many migrant workers are not aware of the terms, conditions, and responsibilities of work or work environment. Since migrant workers leave their homes, logistical arrangements such as accommodations, meals, or living conditions can become an issue. It was reported in The Guardian, a leading UK newspaper, that the world's largest prawn farmer, the Thailand-based Charoen Pokphand (CP) Foods, buys fishmeal for its farmed prawns from some suppliers that are directly or indirectly involved in business with fishing boats staffed with 'large numbers of men bought and sold like animals and held against their will on fishing boats in Thailand' (Hodal, Kelly and Lawrence, 2014). These men are purportedly forced to take part in the production of prawns sold globally, including by the top four retailers, Walmart, Carrefour, Costco, and Tesco (*ibid*). As reported by the few workers who were able to escape, workers have to work 20-hour shifts, and can be beaten, tortured, and even murdered (*ibid.*). Many of the workers come from neighbouring countries such as Myanmar and Cambodia or other countries in the Greater Mekong Subregion, and have been sold to boat captains, despite paying brokers to help them find work in Thai factories or on building sites (*ibid.*).

One of the main problems is the wage rate, as mentioned previously. According to an interview conducted with migrant workers in palm oil industry in Malaysia, many migrant workers engaged in low or unskilled work are only paid less than or around minimum wage. Modes of payment vary from fixed day rates or piece-rates. Migrant workers who work in the palm oil industry very often work by piece-rate. Some workers are paid based on tonnage of product (anonymous, personal communication, April 14, 2014). However, these modes of payment are not negotiated with employees; rather they are decided by employers and announced verbally. Very often, payment is in cash without the provision of any pay slips. Migrant workers are also often forced to work in poor employment conditions. Workers engaged in upstream production work physically challenging hours, often in difficult weather or temperatures. For instance, workers engaged in construction have challenging working environments, which require certain rest hours and adjustment of working hours (anonymous, personal communication, April 14, 2014).

The absence of employment contracts prior to departure can often lead to a violation of labour rights, exploitation, lack of protection, forced labour, child labour, confiscation of documents, and human trafficking. The confiscation of passports or other relevant private documentation by employers is raised as one of the biggest problems. Employers often retain these documents to ensure that the migrant workers will not abscond. Without proper documentation, it is often extremely difficult for migrants to secure justice and legal recourse when problems arise.

The lack of proper documentation can also lead to difficulties in availing social services and welfare support. Cases become serious when migrant workers are without any documents such as passports or work permits. While some countries in Asia have started to introduce insurance schemes for migrant workers, ensuring occupational health and safety is still an important issue that needs more attention from employers who hire migrant workers. Lack of proper documentation can also mean that there is little prospect for migrant workers to improve their skills. Lack of documentation can be problematic for migrant workers engaged in upstream production in GVCs; without skill improvements, they are not likely to be able to move to mid- and high-skilled occupations in GVCs.

There are only a few countries in Asia that provide migrant workers and their family members with the same access to medical facilities and education as nationals. Although the majority of labour migration policies do not permit families to accompany the workers, the reality is that people find ways to be close to their family, and in the process the families of migrant workers often end up facing the same risks and vulnerabilities as the migrant workers themselves.

The lack of documentation, absence of contracts or recourse to any formal mechanisms - all these features have led to some forms of migrant employment being called 'modern slavery'. The condition of undocumented migrants, even those who are initially documented but have their passports seized, working under conditions of debt or other bondage, and the transfer, even sale of migrant workers from one employer to another, certainly amounts to an extreme form of unfree labour or forced labour. But when forced labour is combined with undocumented existence in a foreign country, the worker can be transferred from one employer to another, and work is carried out in conditions of physical force and verbal, even sexual abuse, it is the closest modern equivalent to slavery. What distinguishes this modern day variety is that it is a form of short-term control as against long-term, even life-long, ownership (Bales, 1999) of previous forms of slavery.

10.3.3 Upon return/integration

Migrant workers in Asia often opt to undertake the migration process again and return to work abroad. A number of factors contribute to this. First, migrant workers are sometimes unable to find employment upon their return to their countries of origin. Many countries of origin still suffer from high unemployment rates. There are not enough job opportunities that would meet skills and experiences that were acquired during employment abroad. There is inadequate recognition of acquired skills and experiences and lack of opportunities, which could contribute to the sustainability of job prospects in countries of origin. Moreover, returned migrants may find it difficult to find salary packages that are better than what they used to obtain abroad. There is a lack of support for integration not only with regard to jobs, but also efforts to welcome migrants back to their home communities. Due to the high dependence on remittances created by migration, families often want migrant workers to go back to work abroad and to continue to remit money.

10.3.4 Families left behind

In addition to these migration cycles, it is important to take into consideration families left behind. Migration can have both positive and negative consequences for families left behind. One positive consequence is that remittance, being a source of income, has enabled many recipient households to emerge out of poverty. According to Ratha (2013) 'unlike some publicly-funded social safety nets, remittance receivers can identify their greatest needs and can allocate the remittance income accordingly'. Consequently, many studies argue that households that receive remittances fare much better than those that do not; these households have higher levels of consumer spending and lower incidences of extreme poverty (*ibid.*).

Imai et al. (2012), for example, examined the impact of remittances on poverty in 24 Asian countries. They found that remittance contributes to reductions in poverty. Their results indicated that in Bangladesh, a 50 per cent rise in the share of remittances in GDP (from 11.78 to 17.67 per cent) would raise the GDP per capita growth rate from 4.30 to 4.97 per cent, and decrease the poverty headcount[4] from 49.60 to 38.69 per cent for the lower cut-off of US$ 1.25 a day; and for the higher cut-off (US$ 2.00 a day) from 81.30 to 71.54 per cent (Imai et al., 2012). These results prove that remittances alleviate poverty substantially, particularly extreme poverty. Other results that strengthen this finding include results for India where an increase in the share of remittances in GDP were found to accelerate

---

[4] The poverty headcount measure can be defined at the percentage of population living on less than US$ 1.25 a day at 2005 international prices (World Bank, 2015).

economic growth and reduce poverty (*ibid.*). Similar results were also obtained for Nepal, the Philippines and Sri Lanka (*ibid.*).

In other regions, household survey data revealed declines in the percentage of the populations below the national poverty line—for example, by 11 percentage points in Uganda and 5 in Ghana (Ratha, 2007; Sharma, 2009). Hence, a question that naturally follows from the analysis of the remittance–poverty relationship is whether remittances are spent on consumer goods by the recipient families or used to finance human and/or physical investments.

Various studies strongly support the view that remittances, being a transitory form of income for households, are spent on human and physical investments (Rahman, 2012). These include Edwards and Ureta (2003), Yang (2006), and Osili (2004), whose analysis focused on El Salvador, Philippines, and Nigeria, respectively (*ibid.*). In El Salvador and Philippines international remittances were found to have a large positive impact on retention rates in schools and education, respectively, while in Nigeria a large share of remittance earnings is spent on housing (*ibid.*). Such use of remittance income can contribute positively towards economic development as it ensures sustained growth and improvement in peoples' socioeconomic conditions.

When migrant workers opt to leave home for employment abroad, they are forced to choose between economic gains to secure a home and better future for their families and physical presence required to strengthen emotional and familial ties. Absence of one or both parents can be very difficult for children to cope with, and many grow up without knowing their parents and are often raised by grandparents or family members. There are many case studies and reports on the 'left-behind' children of migrant workers and the issues faced by them. One example of the above is the study conducted by Reyes (2008) on the children of women labour migrants from the Philippines.

The Philippines is a leading global supplier of women labour migrants who work as domestic helpers, nurses, and caregivers. Reyes (2008) estimated the number of children left behind by these women at 9 million or 27 per cent of the total youth. It was claimed that children's acceptance and tolerance of being left behind by their mothers depends on their 'cognitive development[5]' (*ibid.*). Given that younger children have not yet built strong bonds with their mothers, they may find it easy to accept the absence of their mother simply as abandonment. On the other hand, adolescents can become embittered and psychologically affected. Another study by Graham and Jordan (2011) analysed the psychological well-being of left-behind

---

[5] Cognitive development is the construction of thought processes, including remembering, problem solving, and decision-making, from childhood through adolescence to adulthood (Encyclopedia of Children's Health, 2015).

children in Indonesia, the Philippines, Thailand, and Vietnam. Using multivariate models, they showed that children of migrant fathers in Indonesia and Thailand were more likely to have poor psychological well-being, compared to children in non-migrant households. Similar findings, however, could not be established for the Philippines or Vietnam, and hence they concluded that more research should be undertaken (*ibid.*). Other examples of studies include a national survey conducted by the Government of Sri Lanka to examine the links between the health status of spouses, children, and caregivers left behind. The study established many significant findings, among which are the facts that 25.4 per cent of children left behind are underweight, 44 per cent of children left behind suffered from some form of psychopathology, depression was higher amongst spouses left behind compared to those in non-migrant households, and that caregivers are worst affected, both physically and psychologically (Government of Sri Lanka and International Organization for Migration n.d.). In addition, for countries that are suffering due to ageing societies, taking care of elderly family members is becoming a pressing issue.

10.4 Policy options of labour migration in GVCs

These complexities of human resources in GVCs lead to policy challenges for governments in countries that provide human resources to other countries, as well as countries that receive the workers. There are four priority areas in dealing with labour migration issues in GVCs. They are (1) to increase access to global labour markets in GVCs; (2) to improve the efficiency and effectiveness of the process prior to employment in GVCs; (3) to enhance protection through travel, work and return to their home countries; and (4) to maximize the development potential of foreign employment in GVCs.

10.4.1 Access to labour markets for migrant workers

One of the essential components of getting people working within GVCs is the creation of greater access to labour markets for potential migrants. Migration policy can promote better research into the labour markets of receiving countries and analysis of the kinds of skills and qualifications that are in demand in overseas labour markets. One way in which research efforts can be promoted and institutionalized in migrant-sending countries is through the creation of research agencies such as Market Research Units (MRUs) within relevant ministries.[6] In addition to

---

[6] Market Research Unit (MRU) is a government office designed to undertake a research program to promote the country's overseas employment program (IOM, 2007). A MRU can be used to effectively identify human resource profiles that destination countries are looking for. According

gathering information on labour markets, migration policy in sending countries can aim at studying destination countries' experiences and regulations regarding the acceptance and overall conditions for foreign workers.

Once labour markets are identified, negotiation can be encouraged between countries of origin and countries of destination. Bilateral labour arrangements are often the result of such negotiations. Labour arrangements such as bilateral agreements and MOUs formalize labour mobility arrangements between countries. In some contexts, bilateral labour arrangements may take the form of 'economic partnership agreements' (such as those between Japan, Indonesia, and the Philippines).[7] Such arrangements can outline the scope of migration flows in terms of the number of migrants permitted; the duration of stay allowed; the type of employment allowed, and any further conditions relating to work. Bilateral labour arrangements also clarify the responsibilities of the country of origin and the country of destination, and often outline the way in which both sending and receiving countries can collaborate to strengthen protection mechanisms. For example, Sri Lanka's MoU with Qatar for the regulation of Sri Lankan labour in Qatar prohibits the recruiting agency from collecting any sum from the worker, and also requires the employer to pay the worker's transportation both to and from Qatar, at the beginning and end of the work period (International Organization for Migration, 2008). Such arrangements may also often specify the roles that labour attaches from sending countries should play.

Given that labour agreements formalize each side's commitment to ensure that migration takes place in accordance with agreed principles and procedures, they may lead to orderly migration. However, the effectiveness of these agreements is not easy to evaluate due to the plethora of objectives. Multiple objectives may end up creating trade-offs among goals and some objectives may in fact conflict (Organisation for Economic Cooperation and Development, 2004). Consequently, the effectiveness of agreements will depend on the weight assigned to each goal. For instance, if the goal is to facilitate rapid labour market adjustment, the lack of information on newly arrived migrant workers may give rise to security problems in the destination country; simultaneously, there may be concerns of 'brain drain' and loss of potential economic development in the sending country (*ibid.*). Thus, it is essential to promote social dialogue by involving social partners in developing and monitoring migration agreements so that benefits to all stakeholders can be ensured. Overall, agreements

---

to these profiles, sending countries can design skills trainings to increase their labour migrants' competitiveness.

[7] The Government of Japan state that these acceptances are conducted as enhancement of economic partnerships, not as a response to a labour shortage.

should be flexible if their full benefits are to be reaped (*ibid.*). Bureaucratic and costly agreements are in danger of failing to produce the desired outcomes.

It is also important to note migrants' motivation to look beyond national labour markets. The prime motivation for migrating for work throughout the different decades has been migrants' desires to carve out a better future for themselves and their families. In this regard, the advent of the twenty-first century and all its geopolitical and socio-economic changes have given potential migrants and their families' reason to factor in many different considerations when deciding between competing job prospects and career opportunities, nationally and internationally. These include but are not limited to education prospects of migrants' children, possibility of citizenship, existence of social support networks/communities, and political stability in both countries of origin and destination.

At the same time, migrants can also explore a variety of labour migration schemes (often based on skill level) offered by countries of destination who find that admission of foreign labour aligns with their national development goals. The main types of admission policies revolve around employment-based immigration systems and temporary labour migration systems. The following paragraphs discuss these policies in details.

Employment-based immigration schemes are mainly aimed at skilled migrants and are typically designed to promote economic growth in receiving countries, and to ensure a stable population and labour force there (International Organization for Migration (IOM) and Organization for Security and Co-operation in Europe (OSCE), 2010, p. 278). Such policies are often used by countries such as Australia, Canada, New Zealand, and the United States (*ibid*). The two main ways for selecting permanent immigrants under this system are (International Organization for Migration (IOM) and Organization for Security and Co-operation in Europe (OSCE), 2010, p. 279):

- The points system, based on supply: potential migrants have to score a minimum number of points according to a number of criteria in order to apply for admission.
- The demand system, where the procedure for admission relies on the initiative of the employer.

Examples of employment-based immigration schemes include 'SkillSelect', an online service set up by the Department of Immigration and Border Protection from the Government of Australia. This system helps Australia manage its skilled migration programme by ensuring that the skilled migration programme is based on Australia's economic needs and also addresses regional skills shortages (Commonwealth of

Australia, 2015). Potential migrants can indicate if they are interested in living and working in Australia, and the Government can manage the applications.

Temporary labour migration systems refer to temporary admission with, or without a possibility of settlement in the country (International Organization for Migration (IOM) and Organization for Security and Co-operation in Europe (OSCE), 2010, p. 287). Such policies are notably implemented by EU Member States (*ibid.*). In the Netherlands, for example, the Pilot Circular Migration Programme was launched in 2009 (European Migration Network, 2011, p. 50). Recognized as the 'Blue Birds' programme, under it, 160 semi-skilled workers from South Africa and Indonesia are employed in the Netherlands based on their education and skills, and return to their countries after a temporary stay (*ibid.*). Germany has two similar schemes—Contract Worker Agreements and Guest Worker Agreements—through which migrant workers can live and work in Germany for a short period of time. In the former case, companies in partner EU Member States and third countries can send employees to Germany for a short time to complete a project in cooperation with a German company. In the latter case, workers from 14 Central and Eastern European states can be employed for up to 18 months for the purpose of vocational or language-related training.

Particular to Asia, there is one scheme which should be highlighted as a good example of efficient, effective, and ethical recruitment practice from the region. This scheme is the Korean Employment Permit System. Introduced in 2004, the Employment Permit System (EPS) allows Korean employers to hire foreign workers in industries suffering from labour shortages. As of 2010, 15 countries have signed MOUs with Korea: Vietnam, the Philippines, Thailand, Indonesia, Sri Lanka, Mongolia, Uzbekistan, Bangladesh, Cambodia, Pakistan, Kyrgyzstan, China, Nepal, Myanmar, and Timor-Leste (So, 2012).

A total of 579,223 foreign workers had been hired through EPS by the end of July 2010 (International Organization for Migration (IOM), 2011, p. 51). The recruitment process is conducted through designated agencies in Korea and the sending countries to guarantee transparency. Agencies in sending countries select suitable candidates based on work experience, skills, and proficiency in the Korean language; the job seekers are then approved by the Republic of Korea Human Resources Development service. Korean job centres then match employers and candidates.

In the countries of origin, workers are required to undergo 45 hours of basic Korean language and culture training and are also given information pertaining to their trade; this is supplemented by 20 hours of employment training on arrival. Additionally, the Korean government has created eight Support Centres for Foreign Workers to handle grievances and provide training in Korean language and orientation regarding customs and laws. In this scheme, migrant workers enjoy the same rights as locals and are given employment contracts, health insurance, industrial accidental compensation, and a guaranteed minimum salary. They are not tied to a single employer and may seek new employment up to three times over a period of 3 years.

10.4.2 Effectiveness of the migration process prior to employment abroad

For many countries of origin, policies that ensure a safe, transparent, and cost-effective migration process are essential to ensure that labour migration contributes to economic growth. Such policies aim to regulate recruitment agencies in order to reduce migration costs, increase transparency, and improve efficiency. These systems frequently ascribe the regulation and monitoring of private employment agencies to a particular public body. Indonesia, Pakistan, the Philippines, India, Sri Lanka, and Thailand have regulated employment agencies for over 25 years (International Organization for Migration, 2012). These government agencies are tasked with handling recruitment processes, which can include registration of private employment agencies, providing them with licenses, monitoring their performance, and applying sanctions if there are legitimate complaints raised by nationals. For instance, Pakistan established the Emigration Ordinance and Emigration rules in 1979. The ordinance regulates activities of overseas employment promoters and agencies by establishing procedures for licensing, recruitment, and protection of workers against malpractices, as well as to redress of workers' grievances (International Labour Oragnization (ILO), 2008).

These systems have at least three benefits. First, they allow the government to pre-screen private employment agencies' capabilities and professional experience in job-placement activities. Second, they create transparency by identifying companies and outlining the scope of their overall activities. Third, a licensing system makes it possible for governments to track the essential and critical information, such as an agency's business address, as well as the types of services the agency offers (International Organization for Migration, 2012).

10.4.3 Protection mechanisms prior to and during employment abroad

Many countries of origin provide information to their nationals prior to work abroad. Practitioners and policy makers nearly universally agree that migrants need accurate and relevant information to make informed decisions at every stage of the migration process (International Organization for Migration, 2012). The former is also likely to contribute to fostering a 'triple win' situation for migrants and their families, for countries of origin, and for employers and host countries. Two standard information provision tools used in sending countries are 1) pre-departure orientation and training for migrant workers and members of their family and 2) the establishment of Migrant Resource Centres (MRC).[8]

Migrant workers, who are moving within the framework of bilateral agreements, often have access to pre-departure orientation and sometimes also to pre-employment orientation seminars (PEOS). Pre-departure orientation courses have typically been designed for workers in lower-skilled occupations but could be expanded to more highly skilled recruitment. The information disseminated through these training programmes often includes information on migrants' rights, work, and living conditions in countries of destination; conditions of admission, stay and employment, and relevant immigration laws; information concerning the issuance of travel documents, airport procedures, and travel tips; health awareness; cultural differences; support services offered by public authorities and non-governmental actors; and so on.

MRCs are facilities dedicated in providing information and other services such as language training courses for migrants and their families to facilitate their integration in the workplace and host society and raise awareness of their future living and working environment prior to their departure. They also inform migrant workers about the risks and realities associated with labour migration and work to improve migrants' access to information on immigration and labour legislation.

Out of the eleven Colombo Process Member Countries,[9] nine currently require some or all migrants to attend a pre-departure orientation or training programme prior to departure (International Organization for Migration, 2012). MRCs serve as 'one-stop shops' for information and services for migrants in both source and host countries (International Organization for Migration, 2010). MRCs offer a neutral space for potential and actual migrants to obtain accurate information on legal migration procedures and required documentation, the risks of irregular migration, health and safety, and migrants' rights and responsibilities. MRCs can also play a role in helping migrants to understand how they can become active contributors to the development of their countries of origin. Migrants are often enthusiastic about undertaking or contributing to philanthropic activities in their communities or engaging in business ventures to assist communities in their countries of origin. MRCs

---

[8] Examples of countries where MRC is established include Czech Republic, Finland, and Portugal.

[9] The Colombo Process is a Regional Consultative Process (RCP) on the management of overseas employment and contractual labour for countries of origin in Asia. Eleven Members Countries are Afghanistan, Bangladesh, China, India, Indonesia, Nepal, Pakistan, the Philippines, Sri Lanka, Thailand, and Vietnam.

can fill in gaps by providing information on potential means of leveraging the benefits of their migration or return for the development of their countries of origin (*ibid*).

10.4.4 Mechanisms to maximize development potential of migration

Recently, more and more migrant-sending countries have integrated migration into their national development plans and strategies. This has been the result of both the recognition of the role of remittances as a critical contributor to the economic development of sending nations, and the recognition that the skills that migrant workers acquire or strengthen while abroad can contribute to the socio-economic growth of their country of origin.

Many countries of origin have established policies to reduce remittance transfer costs in order to encourage migrants to remit through formal channels and increase the capital available in formal financial institutions for the further stimulation of the economies. For instance, Bangladeshi migrants can open a Non-resident Investor's Taka Account (NITA) using money remitted from abroad for investment in shares and securities in Bangladesh capital markets (Trust Bank Limited, 2013). The balance from NITA can also be used to buy shares and securities in the stock exchange (*ibid*). Likewise, the Philippines' central government has successfully directed remittance funds to development projects through establishing the Philippine Sectorial Development and Needs Profiling System (PHILNEED), which provides information on projects gathered from Local Government Units and NGOs to potential Filipino contributors abroad. The Link for Philippine Development Assistance (LINKAPIL) also contributes to development goals by working through local embassies and consulates to mobilize migrants' savings, and channel them into education, healthcare, small-scale infrastructure, and livelihood support projects (Economist Intelligence Unit, 2008).

While remittances are given priority in discussions on migration policies, many countries of origin have also started to look at how the skills their nationals acquire abroad can contribute to the economic growth of their countries. As an example, Taiwan, Province of China, has adopted a return approach. Taiwan experienced a substantial loss of qualified persons in the 1960s and 1970s. However, when Taiwan's high-tech sector took off, it was able to attract back these skilled professionals, mostly from the USA and Canada. These returning migrants brought with them the expertise and work experience they had gained overseas. This return of migrants contributed to Taiwan's rapid economic growth beginning in the 1980s. Similarly, India started setting up Institutes of Technology from the 1950s to support national development. Many graduates from these Institutes emigrated to the USA and other developed countries in search of higher paid jobs and a better standard of living. However, large numbers of IT experts later returned to help establish India's fast-growing IT sector (Khadria, 2005).

10.4.5 Good governance in labour migration and human resource development

These migration policy areas form the foundations for good governance of labour mobility, which ultimately contributes to the economic development of both receiving and sending countries. These areas of migration policy in labour-sending countries are interdependent. Every element is necessary to ensure that migration realises its potential for economic growth. Migration policies should take a holistic approach; from integrating measures pertaining to the access to labour markets for migrant workers, to improving the effectiveness of the migration process prior to employment abroad, to strengthening the protection mechanisms along the migratory cycle, and to increasing mechanisms to maximize the development potential of migration.

In order to pursue the mainstreaming of migration into sustainable development, it is critical to enhance international cooperation. The region has established an international framework to support good governance of international migration. One of the important mechanisms for promoting cooperation amongst the labour-sending countries is the Colombo Process. The Colombo Process is a Regional Consultative Process on the management of overseas employment and contractual labour for countries of origin in Asia (International Organization for Migration, 2015). The Process provides Member States with a non-binding and informal environment within which to engage in dialogue, exchange of views, and cooperate on issues related to contractual labour migration. Moreover, the region has been making efforts to bring countries of destination in discussion. One of the platforms for this is the Abu Dhabi Dialogue, which promotes cooperation between countries of destination and countries of origin. Furthermore, there are sub-regional settings through regional organizations such as ASEAN or Greater Mekong Subregion that can and have been utilized for these purposes.

10.5 Conclusion

In Asia, globalization of trade and the increasing numbers of multinational and transnational corporations have contributed to the expansion of GVCs through FDI. While it is recognized that the service sector creates job opportunities for mid- and high-level professions, in Asia the majority of migrant workers are still low-skilled and temporary workers who are the primary human resource for upstream production in GVCs. Due to the nature of their situations, migrant workers face numerous challenges not only during the employment phase, but also prior to departure as well as in the post-employment period. Countries of destination prohibit workers from coming with their families, and there have been numbers of problems with families left behind such as taking care of children and the elderly.

Migrant workers bring many benefits too. For countries of origin, emigrants ease unemployment rates, bring remittances, and often bring back skills from their migration experiences. For countries of destination, migrant labour can fill positions or vacancies which nationals are reluctant to take up for a number of reasons including low pay compared to other professions, physically challenging nature of the tasks involved, etc. those unpopular professions that nationals do not want to be engaged in. Additionally, many ageing countries simply do not have young labourers to work in their upstream production industries; their demographic compositions mainly consist of ageing people.

Labour-sending countries establish policies and infrastructures to encourage international labour migration as an integral component of their economy and to earn revenue through remittances (Hamada, 2011). Encouragingly, bilateral, multilateral, and regional cooperation is emerging and is resulting in international labour migration policies, albeit primarily non-binding ones. The non-binding nature of these policies may be a reason why they are yet to be appropriately implemented at the national levels. However, as migration for employment grows, international cooperation could be increased at the multilateral and regional levels.

The formulation of a policy that establishes and strengthens good governance of international labour migration requires cooperation between more than two countries to strengthen relationships and achieve shared objectives. Encouraging this cooperation can result in appropriate national-level policy formulation. Enforcement remains a strong challenge.

The private sector should play a significant role in this. Multinational companies who employ foreign workers need to examine their policies and ensure that labour rights apply equally to foreign workers as they do to local employees. Promoting pre-departure orientation prior to departure from origin countries has become essential to ensuring that migrant workers are well informed about the nature of employment and their living conditions in destination countries.

Responsibility for labour conditions in GVCs, however, extends beyond FDI units. The GVC is a form of non-investment influence on labour conditions. Most GVC relationships are contracted relationships between buyers and sellers of products and services. The contracting relationship not only benefits the lead firms but also provides them varying degrees of influence over labour and working conditions in the supplying entities. Labour contracting is itself a form of out-sourcing (Barrientos, 2011), and it does not absolve the GVC-lead firms of responsibility for conditions of contracted labour.

The Tripartite Declaration of Principles concerning Multinational Enterprises and Social Policy of the ILO, the UN's Global Compact, and the OECD's MNE Declaration are all beginnings in dealing with labour conditions in global operations. The California Transparency in Supply Chains Act (2012) requires all businesses operating in California and having global business in excess of $200 million to carry out due diligence on issues of trafficking and forced labour in entities in the supply chain. The OECD Guidelines (2013) also requires lead firms to conduct due diligence all along the supply chains of minerals from conflict-affected and high-risk areas. One should add, not only from such high-risk areas but also in high-risk employment in backward linkages of the value chains, particularly where low-skill, low-paid labour is performed in procuring raw materials, whether agricultural raw materials or fish.

The increasing complexity of labour migration renders bilateral negotiations less efficient and more tilted toward labour-receiving countries, which can seek different 'suppliers' if the terms are not favourable. As a result, there should be greater collaboration between public and private sector actors at the supranational, regional, and global levels in order to promote and facilitate safe and regular migration.

In this chapter, it has been seen that there are benefits from migration, even for work in low-skill, low-wage segments of value chains. Such migration has drawn labour from labour-surplus economies and helped reduce poverty, both through making the labour market tighter in source countries and through remittances. But in reducing the risks of bondage often associated with unsafe migration, besides the governments of involved countries and international organizations, it is also necessary to extend governance responsibilities in GVCs to include overseeing the elimination of forced labour anywhere in the chain.

References

Accenture for Humanity United. 2013. 'Exploitative Labor Practices in the Global Palm Oil Industry.'

Agunias, Dovelyn R. 2012. *Regulating Private Recruitment in the Asia-Middle East Labour Migration Corridor.* Issue-in-Brief, Bangkok and Washington, D.C.: International Organization for Migration and Migration Policy Institute.

Bales, K. 1999. *Disposable People: New Slaves in the Global Economy.* Berkeley, CA: University of California Press.

Barrientos, Armando, and Stephanie W. Barrientos. 2002. *Extending Social Protection to Informal Workers in the Horticulture Global Value Chain*. Discussion Paper, Washington: World Bank.

Barrientos, Stephanie. 2011. 'Labour Chains': Analysing the Role of Labour Contractors in Global Production Networks. Accessed on June 20, 2014. Available at, http://wiego.org/sites/wiego.org/files/publications/files/Barrientos_Labour_Chains.pdf.

Bureau of Manpower, Employment and Training. 2014. Government of the People's Republic of Bangladesh Ministry of Expatriate's Welfare and Overseas Employment. Accessed on July 17, 2014. Available at, http://www.bmet.gov.bd/BMET/viewStatReport.action?reportnumber=35.

Commonwealth of Australia. 2015. *SkillSelect*. Accessed on March 16, 2015. Available at, http://www.immi.gov.au/Work/Pages/SkillSelect/SkillSelect.aspx.

Cosmos Nepal Human Resource Pvt. Ltd. 2014. *About Recruitment Process*. Accessed on November 24, 2014. Available at, http://cosmosnepalhr.com/About-Recruitment-Process.html.

Duarte, Renata Nunes. 2013. 'Flexibility Is Good for Workers? An Evaluation of Global Value Chains.' *Acad J Int Relations* 1 (3): 121–36.

Economist Intelligence Unit. 2008. *Building a Future Back Home: Leveraging Migrant Worker Remittances for Development in Asia*. Economist Intelligence Unit White Paper, New York: Economist Intelligence Unit.

Edwards, Alejandra C., and Manuelita Ureta. 2003. 'International Migration, Remittances, and Schooling: Evidence from El Salvador.' *J Develop Econ* 72 (2): 429–61.

Embassy of Nepal. 2014. *Embassy of Nepal, Doha, State of Qatar*. Accessed on November 24. Available at, 2014. http://www.nembdoha.com/pages.php?cid=4.

Encyclopedia of Children's Health. 2015. *Cognitive Development*. Accessed on May 11, 2015. Available at, http://www.healthofchildren.com/C/Cognitive-Development.html.

European Migration Network. 2011. *Temporary and Circular Migration: Empirical Evidence, Current Policy Practice and Future Options in EU Member States*. Synthesis Report, European Migration Network.

Food and Agricultural Organization. 2009. *National Fishery Sector Overview-Thailand*.

Government of Sri Lanka and International Organization for Migration. 2012. *Sri Lankan Migration Health Study: Study on Families Left Behind*. Colombo: IOM. Accessed on June 26, 2015. Available at, http://srilanka.iom.int/iom/sites/default/files/IOMSL%20Migration%20Report%20-%20Families%20left%20behind%20IDF%20MA0221.pdf.

Graham, Elspeth, and Lucy P. Jordan. 2011. 'Migrant Parents and the Psychological Well-Being of Left-Behind Children in Southeast Asia.' *J Marriage Family* 2011: 763–87.

Hamada, Yuko. 2011. 'Global Governance and International Migration: A Bridge too Far?' In *Limits of Good Governance in Developing Countries*, by Hirotsune Kimura, Suharko, Aser B. Javier and Ake Tangsupvattana, 517–54. Yogyakarta: Gadjah Mada University Press.

Hodal, Kate, Chris Kelly, and Felicity Lawrence. 2014. 'Revealed: Asian Slave Labour Producing Prawns for Supermarkets in US, UK.' *The Guardian*. 10 June 2014. Accessed on November 24, 2014. Available at, http://www.the guardian.com/global-development/2014/jun/10/supermarket-prawns-thailand-produced-slave-labour.

Imai, Katsushi, Raghav Gaiha, Ali Abdilahi, and Nidhi Kaicker. 2012. *Remittances, Growth and Poverty. New Evidence from Asian Countries*. Occasional Paper, Rome: IFAD.

International Labour Organization. 2005. *Global Alliance Against Forced Labour*. Geneva: ILO.

———. 2008. *Labour Administration in Selected Asian Countries*. Geneva.

———. 2013. *Employment Practices and Working Conditions in Thailand's Fishing Sector*. Thailand: ILO.

International Organization for Migration. 2007. *The Roadmap to Developing the Market Research Unit of the Countries of Origin of Labour Migrants*. 2007. Geneva: International Organization for Migration.

———. 2008. *Compendium of Good Practice Policy Elements in Bilateral Temporary Labour Arrangements*. Geneva: IOM.

———. 2010. *Fact-Sheet on Migrant Integration*. Geneva: International Organization for Migration.

———. 2011. *Thailand Migration Report 2011*. Bangkok: IOM.

———. 2012. *Pre-departure Orientation Training Manual*. New Delhi: International Organization for Migration.

International Organization for Migration and Organization for Security and Co-operation in Europe. 2010. *Training Modules on Labour Migration Management Trainer's Manual*. Vienna and Geneva: OSCE and IOM.

Jung, Bong Su. 2011. 'Employment Permit System (EPS).' Accessed on June 20, 2014. Available at, http://www.adbi.org/files/2011.01.18.cpp.sess2.3.jung. employment.permit.system.pdf.

Khadria, Binod. 2005. *Migration in South and South-West Asia*. Policy and Research Paper, Geneva: Global Commission on International Migration.

Martin, Phillip. 2007. *The Economic Contribution of Migrant Workers to Thailand: Towards Policy Development*. Bangkok: International Labour Organization.

Monitor Global Outlook. 2014. *Labor Curbs Hit Remittances, Spur Illegal Migration*. 28 July 2014. Accessed on November 12, 2014. Available at, http://webcache.googleusercontent.com/search?q=cache:Kb_gJEkvMSUJ:

www.monitorglobaloutlook.com/Briefings/2014/07/Labor-curbs-hit-remittances-spur-illegal-migration+&cd=1&hl=en&ct=clnk&gl=th.

Organisation for Economic Cooperation and Development. 2004. 'Executive Summary.' In *Migration for Employment Bilateral Agreements at a Crossroads*, by Organisation for Economic Cooperation and Development, 7–8. Paris: OECD.

Osili, Una. 2004. 'Migrants and Housing Investments: Theory and Evidence from Nigeria.' *Econ Develop Cult Change* 52 (4): 821–49.

Rahman, Sanam R. 2012. *Labouring Away: The Remittance and Growth Story of Bangladesh*. M.Sc diss., Unpublished.

Ratha, Dilip. 2007. *Leveraging Remittances for Development*. Washington: Migration Policy Institute.

———. 2013. *The Impact of Remittances on Economic Growth and Poverty Reduction*. Policy Brief, Washington: Migration Policy Institute.

Reyes, Melanie M. 2008. *Migration and Filipino Children Left-Behind: A Literature Review*. Synthesis Study, UNICEF.

Sharma, Krishnan. 2009. 'The Impact of Remittances on Economic Insecurity.' *DESA Working Paper No.78*. New York: United Nations.

So, Byung Gyu. 2012. 'Introduction to EPS.' Siem Reap.

Trust Bank Limited. 2013. *Non-Resident Investors Taka Account (NITA)*. Accessed on November 27, 2014. Available at, http://www.trustbank.com.bd/international-banking/non-resident-investors-taka-account.

World Bank. 2013. *Developing Countries to Receive Over $410 Billion in Remittances in 2013, Says World Bank*. Press Release, Washington: World Bank.

World Trade Organization IDE-JETRO. 2014. 'Trade Patterns and Global Value Chain in East Asia: From Trade in Goods to Trade in Tasks.' Accessed on June 19, 2014. Available at, http://www.wto.org/english/res_e/booksp_e/stat_tradepat_globvalchains_e.pdf.

Yamada, Masahiko. 2010. 'The Current Issues on Foreign Workers in Japan.' *Jap Lab Rev* 7 (3): 5–18.

Yang, Dean. 2006. 'International Migration, Remittances, and Household Investment: Evidence from Philippine Migrants' Exchange Rate Shocks.' *National Bureau of Research, Inc.* Accessed on March 16, 2015. Available at, http://www.nber.org/papers/w12325.pdf.

Yasushi, Iguchi. 2012. 'What Role do Low-Skilled Migrants Play in the Japanese Labour Markets?' *Am Behav Sci* 56 (8): 1029–57.

Modular Governance

11

From Disposable to Empowered

Rearticulating Labour in Sri Lankan Apparel Factories

Annelies M. Goger

11.1 Introduction

Sitting around a conference room table, three male mid-level managers at Finewear Garments[1] delivered a presentation about their factory, which employs 2900 people in Sri Lanka.[2] The conversation started out as a heavily scripted, technical description of their transition to lean manufacturing, but gradually the managers inserted anecdotes that conveyed their enthusiasm. One manager interrupted the presenter to say:

> Actually, Finewear Garments is called Finewear University [within the larger company]! So people come and have a look at the practices and they copy things from us.

Indeed, there was a large banner on the shop floor that said, in large print, 'FINEWEAR UNIVERSITY: Learning to Achieve Higher Performance', and underneath it was an oversized training schedule. The managers told me, with great pride, how they had reorganized production in ways that empowered employees to make decisions that they would not have been involved in previously.

The managers spoke with particular passion about their efforts to change the negative perception of garment workers in Sri Lankan society and among global buyers (their 'customers'). For instance, managers described how they put up banners around town so that their employees would 'feel powerful when they are walking with their families', and to ensure that 'even family members know they have

---

[1] The name of the plant has been changed for confidentiality.

[2] This chapter reprinted (with minor revisions) with permission from Pion Ltd., London. It was originally published in 2013 with the same title and author in *Environment and Planning A* 45(11): 2628–45. The original article is available from www.pion.co.uk and www.envplan.com

been given due respect for their jobs.' They expressed frustration with visitors who, upon seeing the headscarves and hearing the title 'machine operator', think that Sri Lanka has the same 'adverse practices as other countries'. 'This is not the case', one of the managers exclaimed, 'Because they are ... bringing in 54 per cent of foreign exchange in Sri Lanka, so we need to recognize that!'

Having male garment factory managers decry the undervaluation of women's work was striking, given that it seems to contradict the feminist literature on the systemic devaluation of women's labour in globalized production (Fernandez-Kelly, 1983; Mills, 1999; Ong, 1987; Salzinger, 2003; Wright, 2006). This devaluation, which Wright (2006) calls a 'myth of disposability', is deployed through management discourses and practices that reproduce the 'disposable third world woman' as a normalized subject and reaffirm systems of power and hierarchy that enable the production of value. So, if Sri Lankan managers are strategically disrupting (or disarticulating) the disposability myth as they try to upgrade (or 'move up') in global value chains (GVCs), how are they rearticulating labour and reconfiguring industrial relations to produce value?

Upgrading is normally analysed in the GVC literature[3] as an attempt to improve a firm's or a nation's position in international trade networks by, for example, making better products, adopting more efficient production processes, or adding higher skilled functions (Gereffi, 1999; Humphrey and Schmitz, 2002). Since 2002, Sri Lankan apparel firms have pursued an extensive set of competitiveness strategies with the aim of transforming into a full-package, knowledge-based, ethical sourcing destination (JAAF, 2002; Ruwanpura and Wrigley, 2011; Wijayasiri and Dissanayake, 2009). Here, I draw on the feminist literature to analyse upgrading by exploring how it also resubjectifies female workers through the labour process. Specifically, I analyse how the mid-level managers in Sri Lanka deploy legitimating ideologies to rearticulate worker subjectivities and workplace culture in an effort to address a labour shortage and to upgrade to lean production models. I show how, in global circuits of production, the production of value[4] hinges on these everyday moments of instability and dis/articulation. Drawing on Wright's (2006) research on disposability discourses, I argue

---

[3] Although I use the GVC framework in this chapter since it is increasingly adopted by mainstream development institutions, it is important to acknowledge that the global production network (GPN) framework offers a more relational understanding of power. Drawing on the GPN framework to reconceptualize or critique upgrading is a promising area for theoretical development, but this is a larger endeavor that exceeds the scope of this chapter. For a summary of debates, Bair (2008) and Coe et al. (2010).

[4] 'Value', in this context, means the financial returns from upgrading, which include profit margins, but also higher market shares and purchase-order quantities.

that value is not only produced through inter-firm or firm-state relations, but is also determined by the labour process, as it is shaped by legacies of colonialism, persisting hierarchies, and the everyday reproduction of social difference.

This research suggests that upgrading cannot be reduced to an economic logic of value generation and capture in the form of disembodied technical or functional interventions. Instead, upgrading should be rethought as a complex process of disarticulation and rearticulation that occurs through an embodied labour and management process. This matters because upgrading is often deployed as a generalizable technical fix for promoting global competitiveness and development, without adequate attention being paid to the nuances and contradictions of actually existing upgrading processes and their effects on people and places (Pickles et al., 2006; Schrank, 2004; Tokatli, 2012; Werner, 2012). Doing so can help address the question that has been taken up in this volume about how labour benefits (or not) from the expansion of apparel GVCs in Asia, specifically shedding light on the management dynamics of process upgrading.

This chapter examines three key moments of instability in the labour process that occurred in the Sri Lankan garment sector (Sections 5, 7, and 8). In Sections 2 and 3, I provide the theoretical framework for the chapter, situating it in the dis/articulations perspective and exploring the potential contributions of feminist industrial ethnography literature. In Section 4, I contextualize the rise of antidisposability discourses in Sri Lanka, and in Section 5, I specifically analyse women's empowerment programmes as a key moment of disruption and rearticulation. I then shift from worker subjectivities to examine the shift towards adopting lean manufacturing in three factories. In Section 6, I situate lean manufacturing in a changing global landscape of apparel trade, and in Section 7, I examine a key moment in which managers were rearticulating industrial relations and workplace culture to make this transition. In Section 8, I examine a third key moment that shows how the managers' attempts to disrupt and restructure hierarchies were themselves, disrupted and contested.

This chapter is based on a multi-sited[5] research project on ethical manufacturing initiatives in Sri Lankan apparel supply chains, which included a wide range of informants and was conducted in the summer of 2008 and from August 2010 to November 2011. However, this chapter draws most heavily on multi-sited ethnographic fieldwork with 65 mid-level managers, to whom I refer herein as 'managers', meaning that they are not the owners or top executives but, rather, the people on the shop floor or in the corporate headquarters who transform

---

[5] See Marcus (1998) and Burawoy (2001) on multi-sited research methods and global ethnography.

Annelies M. Goger

management ideas into practice.[6] I visited nine factories of various sizes in Sri Lanka; respondents included managers from nine different companies and included factory directors, human resources managers, production managers, trainers, and team leaders. I also conducted key-informant interviews with industry-association representatives, worker organizations, and government officials. This chapter focuses on managers as embodied subjects—a perspective that tends to be overlooked in the GVC literature but that is well developed in the feminist ethnographies of global production (Ong, 1987; Salzinger, 2003; Wright, 2006). By studying managers across several firms, it also addresses a lack of meso-level studies of the apparel industry in Sri Lanka [an exception is Ruwanpura and Wrigley (2011)], while building on extended ethnographic research conducted in individual factory sites in Sri Lanka (Hewamanne, 2008; Lynch, 2007).

A focus on managers allows an analysis of how they navigate a variety of constraints and translate ideas of 'good' management into practice in embodied and contradictory ways. In that sense, this chapter utilizes an 'ethnography of circulations' rather than an 'ethnography of locations', meaning that the focus is on how worlds are created by policy ideas on-the-move (Appadurai, 2001; Peck and Theodore, 2010; Roy, 2012). Lean manufacturing is a flexible, just-in-time production method that has increasingly becoming a normative philosophy of 'good' manufacturing, and this chapter draws out how it is variegated and mobile in practice. The dis/articulations perspective provides an opening to use the analytical tools of feminist geography, cultural studies, and economic anthropology to critically engage with the concept of upgrading as a management practice and a value-creation opportunity. This, in turn, enables an analysis of how value is distributed through GVC structures from some new angles.

11.2 Upgrading as a process of everyday dis/articulations

The dis/articulations perspective came out of a critique of the GVC literatures (Bair and Werner, 2011; Bair et al., 2013). GVCs are globally dispersed inter-firm networks of production that are coordinated by lead firms, and they are buyer-driven in the case of apparel (Gereffi and Memedovic, 2003). The dominant themes in the GVC literature include analysing the dynamics of inter-firm coordination, or governance, assessing the opportunities for upgrading, and creating recommendations for states and other institutions to enter into global production circuits (Bair, 2005; Gereffi et al., 2005; Humphrey and Schmitz, 2002). While this chapter draws upon the GVC concept of governance because of the strong role that global buyers play in shaping

---

[6] In smaller firms, I consider owners in this category given that they are heavily engaged in day-to-day operations as well. All interviews with managers were conducted in English.

supplier practices, it engages critically with the GVC concept of upgrading and the assertion that industrial upgrading will necessarily lead to global competitiveness and national development (Schrank, 2004; Tokatli, 2012).

Although the dis/articulations perspective critiques the GVC literature for downplaying moments of exclusion and displacement from global chains (the 'inclusionary bias'), these authors are not just calling for more commodity chain studies of excluded people and places:

> [What] is needed ... is closer analytical attention to the relationship between inclusion and exclusion as ongoing processes that are constitutive of commodity chains. Thus, we call for a deeper engagement with the processes that engender the forging and breaking of links between circuits of commodity production, people, and places (Bair and Werner, 2011, p. 992).

Thus, they emphasize the dialectical processes of inclusion and exclusion (articulation and disarticulation) as constitutive of GVCs and the need for more research on how everyday struggles over value rework and reproduce the uneven geographies of capitalism. In this chapter, I aim to do this by getting inside the labour process to deeply engage with how moments of disarticulation and rearticulation produce social worlds, including the economy and value. It is hard to understand how labour has benefited from upgrading in GVCs without such analysis.

The dialectical aspect of dis/articulation was central to Hall's (1980) understanding of articulation, on which the dis/articulations perspective is based (Bair and Werner, 2011). Hall uses the concept of 'articulation' to explore how capitalist and non-capitalist modes of production are theoretically connected and mutually constituted in an ongoing fashion. Drawing on the work of Wolpe (1975), he argues that the mode of political domination and content of legitimating ideologies assume racial, ethnic, and cultural forms (Hall, 1980, p. 322). This way of thinking about disarticulation and rearticulation also has origins in the political economies of development literature, specifically the work of Rey (1973), who asserts that once capitalism has taken root, it tends to enlarge at the expense of precapitalist relations (as cited in Bradby, 1980; Wolpe, 1980). Hall stresses that the relationship between the cultural and the economic realms of production is not a necessary relation—meaning the relationship cannot be assumed *a priori*. Thus, in the emerging dis/articulations literature, this chapter foregrounds how legitimating ideologies help forge the ongoing production of value through the labour process. It analyses three moments of rupture and recombination to examine how value is produced through the disarticulation of the disposable worker, the rearticulation of an empowered team member, and moments in which these articulations were disrupted or constrained. This understanding of the labour process as involving an ongoing process of dis/rearticulation contrasts with the GVC literature's analytical emphasis on articulating better: providing strategies for insertion into and 'moving up' global chains.

It is important to situate everyday articulation processes in the broader context in Sri Lanka. Specifically, industry leaders in Sri Lanka were explicitly embracing upgrading as a sector-wide, national development strategy. In response to the phase-out of quotas,[7] Sri Lankan apparel industry associations formed the Joint Apparel Association Forum (JAAF) in 2002, which launched an aggressive, well-organized action plan for the country to become a knowledge-intensive, ethical, and full-service apparel manufacturing hub (JAAF, 2002; Wijayasiri and Dissanayake, 2009). This involved several forms of upgrading, outsourcing, consolidation, and diversification (Staritz and Frederick, 2012; Wijayasiri and Dissanayake, 2009). The upgrading strategies emphasized stronger partnerships with buyers (e.g., Nike, Marks & Spencer, Victoria's Secret), specializing in higher value products, adding functional capacity (such as fabric research), and increasing efficiency, quality, and turnaround times (including lean production). Large, well-resourced firms have spearheaded these efforts, leveraging partnerships with buyers, joint-venture partners, and the government (Wijayasiri and Dissanayake, 2009). As an overarching component, JAAF extensively promoted human resources by developing and investing in management training institutions and curricula at universities, efficiency and productivity-enhancement programmes, and labour-recruitment and turnover-reduction strategies (Wijayasiri and Dissanayake, 2009). Therefore, this was a comprehensive effort that extended well beyond the largest firms. This elevation of human resources contradicts the established research on the global apparel sector, described in the next section.

11.3   Logics of disposability in globalized production

Feminist ethnographies of labour in global production circuits have, since the early 1980s, analysed how the global labour process articulates with existing structures of domination and subordination (e.g., gender, class, ethnicity) to shape the everyday lives and identities of female workers (Fernandez-Kelly, 1983; Hewamanne, 2008; Lynch, 2007; Mills, 1999; Ong, 1987; Salzinger, 2003; Wolf, 1992). Comprehensive reviews of this literature have highlighted the variegated ways in which capital uses gendered ideologies to recruit and discipline workers, discursively emphasizing the 'cheapness' of women's labour, their subordination as 'daughters', their roles as wives and mothers, their potential to become feminized consumers, and/or their

---

[7] Since the 1970s the Multi-Fibre Arrangement (MFA) controlled global trade in textile and apparel through a quota system, but the Agreement on Textiles and Clothing replaced the MFA in a phase-out process from 1995 to 2005.

sexualized bodies (Bair, 2010; Mills, 2003). Feminist inquiry, in general, is attentive to the ways in which difference shapes the organization of social worlds, including the economic, in particular conjunctures (Bair, 2010). Therefore, this literature informs present debates about dis/articulation in globalized production in many ways—especially by emphasizing subjectivity as a mechanism for interpellating particular forms and bodies of labour into global commodity production.

In this literature, 'subjectivity' refers to how capital uses ideologies of social difference to recruit and discipline workers. Management and executive discourses about work and workers are the keys because they are tools of interpellation that continually reproduce capitalist subjects and configure systems of power—albeit in ways that are incomplete, contradictory, and possible to disrupt (Ong, 1987; Salzinger, 2003; Schoenberger, 1997; Wright, 2006). Drawing on Butler (1997), Wright (2006, p. 5) considers the 'myth of the disposable third world woman' as a tool of interpellation because 'it establishes the expectations both for identifying disposable third world women within specific populations and for determining how those subjects, so identified, should behave in relation to those who do the identifying'. Interpellation, disruption, and rearticulation are conceptualized as ongoing processes that are never complete. Because of its focus on how gendered practices and subjects are constitutive of globalized production, this scholarship is key for the further conceptual and theoretical development of the dis/articulations perspective. This is why management discourses about work and worker subjectivity are at the centre of the analysis in this chapter.

At the same time, because of its ethnographic emphasis on being grounded in particular factory settings, the feminist industrial ethnographies so far do not thoroughly incorporate hierarchical dynamics of power that operate through firm networks, which is what the GVC approach has focused much of its analysis on (Gereffi, 1994; Gereffi et al., 2005). Apparel chains are buyer-driven—meaning that large multinational buyers and retailers such as Wal-Mart or Nike have a high degree of market power and influence over suppliers down the chain (Gereffi and Memedovic, 2003). Wright's (2006) study of the deployment of the disposable third world woman subjectivity in Mexican *maquiladoras* was one of the few studies in the feminist literature to start bringing these global dynamics into the analysis (Bair, 2010). Wright calls the disposable third world woman subjectivity 'endemic' to the organization of globalized production, a global logic that is expressed through locally specific tropes (2006, p. 10–11).

I extend this work by putting it in conversation with GVC analysis of buyer-driven governance structures. In doing so, one of the contributions of this research—and the dis/articulations perspective more generally—is to demonstrate the ways in which the global/local and the economic/social are mutually constitutive, rather than separating the analysis of economic globalization into one strand of literature that is global and economic and another that is local and cultural (Nagar et al., 2002). Thinking about globalized production in this way requires an attentiveness to how value is produced not only through firm–firm or firm–state relations, but also through the labour process. Upgrading is an embodied process and, as such, it involves a rearticulation of the social formation that is not driven exclusively by economic or state-led regulatory logics.[8]

11.4   Background: Disposability logics and moral panic contribute to a labour shortage

One of the important moments of rupture and reconfiguration in the upgrading process in Sri Lanka, as noted in the introduction, has been a targeted effort to change the negative perception of garment work in Sri Lankan society. This section contextualizes the emergence of a set of specific initiatives to rearticulate worker subjectivities as valuable and respectable, which I refer to as 'women's empowerment programs'. These programmes were not only implemented in factories that were adopting lean production but were part of a more widespread phenomenon that was contemporaneous with industry-wide efforts to upgrade and were largely precipitated by a labour shortage.

One of the dominant tensions in Sri Lankan political discourse is the question of how to reconcile modernization and economic development with the preservation of established cultural traditions and moral codes (Hewamanne, 2008; Lynch, 2007). There is a distinctly nationalist and postcolonial tone to these debates, because economic liberalization was accompanied by two perceived threats to the nation: the insurgency movements within Sri Lanka and Westernization (Lynch, 2007). In this context, many Sinhalese Buddhists (the dominant social group) consider women to be agents of cultural and national preservation, especially the 'pure' and 'innocent' women from rural villages who were recruited for employment in the nascent garment industry (Lynch, 2007). As men were recruited into the war effort, many garment workers felt that they were doing their part to serve the country by generating foreign exchange earnings (Lynch, 2007). Nevertheless, widespread social concern and 'moral panic' ensued, especially over the migration of young women to the Katunayake export processing zone (EPZ), where the media widely reported workers living in unsanitary boarding houses, an absence of parental control, and a preponderance of social problems such as prostitution, premarital sex, rape, and abortion (Hewamanne, 2008; Lynch, 2007).

---

[8] The GPN framework theorizes de-centred power relations (Coe et al., 2010); however, none of the commodity-chain frameworks have adequately incorporated the social embodiment of production.

Therefore, in Sri Lanka, disposability discourses manifested primarily through the stigmatization of garment workers as a threat to Sri Lankan morality and national identity (Hewamanne, 2008; Lynch, 2007). In other words, the moral panic was not only about the working conditions of the jobs themselves, it was also about what the presence of 'our girls' in modern factories and Westernized spaces represented—a threat to societal norms and the virtue of the nation (Lynch, 2007). Debates in the popular media and national politics portrayed the area outside Katunayake as the 'Zone of Prostitutes' and the 'City of Women' (Hewamanne, 2008; Lynch, 2007). Garment workers were labelled 'Juki girls' (after the Japanese brand of sewing machine) and portrayed as promiscuous, aggressive, and 'bad' women (Hewamanne, 2008, p. 33). By contrast, girls in villages were portrayed as 'good' girls who were innocent, submissive, obedient, and sexually chaste until marriage (Hewamanne, 2008).

These portrayals of female garment workers helped to legitimate the incorporation of young women into export-oriented production in low-paying, unskilled positions, despite their relatively high levels of education. The garment industry was the first and the largest industry to attract foreign capital to Sri Lanka after liberalization, and it still contributes over 40 per cent of industrial production (Staritz and Frederick, 2012). Even though they were considered 'bad' jobs, many young women were pushed into these jobs because neoliberal development policies eroded previous forms of livelihood by, for example, removing crop subsidies and closing state-owned textile mills in the 1980s (Jayaweera, 2003; Shaw, 2004). However, by employing 80–90 per cent women (Jayaweera, 2003), the garment industry came to represent the feminization of the nation as society grappled with its engagement with globalization (Hewamanne, 2008; Lynch, 2007).

Because families were reluctant to send their daughters to work in garment factories, the industry began to face labour shortages. Both the state and the industry were then compelled to address these contradictory effects of the disposability logic. In the early years of liberalization (1977–1993), the Sri Lankan state created the EPZs that made some areas more available to foreign investment than others (Ong, 2006). To address rural unemployment and to quell the moral panic, the Sri Lankan state reversed its zoning strategy in 1994 with a rural industrialization programme called the 200 Garment Factory Program (200 GFP) (Lynch, 2007). This programme incentivized garment manufacturers to locate factories in each of the 200 administrative areas of the country. The government also equalized trade policies, making the entire country open to foreign investment.

Although many of the 200 GFP factories have now closed, a variety of stakeholders (including worker NGOs and trade unions) praised this programme because it made garment companies 'give back' to local communities, enabled garment workers to live at home, and revitalized villages. Some of the largest and most innovative garment factories on the island are located in rural or semirural areas that are a 3-hour or 4-hour drive from Colombo, including the factories that first piloted lean manufacturing. In addition to meeting the demands of global buyers to be ethically compliant, suppliers had to meet local demands that were consistent with Sinhalese Buddhist norms to be deemed 'good' employers (Goger, 2014). They needed to treat workers with dignity, establish safe environments, and show generosity—for example, by donating to local schools and providing housing assistance after natural disasters. Basically, employers came to see their image as a problem that they needed to fix.

11.5 Moment 1: Disarticulating disposability by advancing women

When a global buyer, Gap Inc., expressed interest in funding women's empowerment programmes to improve its own ethical reputation in the mid-2000s, Sri Lankan suppliers were well positioned to partner with Gap in this regard because they could meet two goals at the same time: enhancing buyer partnerships and securing a workforce. In at least three very large firms in Sri Lanka, there are specific programmes designed to empower female workers. These programmes include workshops and modules for workers on topics such as work–life balance, sexual and reproductive health, how to dress professionally, and how to manage finances.

When questioned about why his company was focusing on this, one manager explained that they wanted to change the stigma, especially in rural factories:

> On a girl going down the road, the people used to call, "garment girl", "Juki girl", right? It's a "garment piece", or "Juki piece". That image, we thought that, first off, we had to break that image, with Gap. Then, we proposed the subject called "professional grooming and lifestyle standard" for the apparel sector: how to do makeup, how to talk in public, how to use mobile phones, how to speak with friends in public areas ... So those things we educate them [about], so they know what to purchase.

Thus, this 'professional woman' discourse was deployed to establish how garment workers should behave. Yet it was also contradictory, because the disarticulation of 'Juki girls' through specific programme modules and discourses of professional standards was accompanied by the rearticulation of a need for patriarchal control. For example, the assumption is that these women cannot be trusted to decide what handbag to purchase without instruction modules. The manager went on to say:

> Our theme is, you know, rather than producing good supervisors, good executives, good production managers—our main theme is to produce the perfect woman for society. Not for [our company], the perfect woman for society.

With prompting, he clarified what he meant by the 'perfect woman':

> Groomed, financially conscious, having a dream, having targets, and career progress as well, and sexually and health-wise confident, and a wise woman who can resolve problems, and legally confident through the legal module. So she knows everything, basically. *Not like garment industry workers*, she's qualified (emphasis added).

This 'perfect woman' helps them recruit, retain, and motivate their workforce. She abides by local norms in some respects because she performs respectability and is dutiful to her family, but she challenges them in others because she is working and 'qualified'. Thus, as the companies tried to improve their ethical image in Sri Lankan society and among image-conscious buyers, this 'professional woman', a model citizen, was an important figure in keeping the industry and the nation in good moral standing and securing a labour force.

This 'professional woman' subjectivity suggests that an antidisposability logic is at work in these upgrading projects in several respects. In contrast to the situations of 'unlimited supplies of labour' (Wright, 2006), in Sri Lanka, the labour shortage was getting worse as alternative job opportunities expanded after the end of the war in 2009. Thus, employers had reduced bargaining power and lower supplies of the type of labour they desired (female, young, experienced, motivated, model citizen, career-oriented). Similarly, rather than seeking an ideal rate of turnover of around 7 per cent (Wright, 2006, p. 28), Sri Lankan employers wanted to minimize this as much as possible, with an intermediate goal of around 4 per cent. Their main concern was getting women to stay on after marriage and having children, rather than getting them to leave once their value declined. Third, female workers were not seen as untrainable. Instead, the managers saw their role as inclusive of educating or modernizing the young rural people who worked for them. As one manager put it:

> A [rural] mindset ... [is] really challenging. It's an overall mindset of a young, of a teenager—or a female or male between the ages of 18 to 25—needs to be guided well. So, you need to have more ... that's where the CSR comes in.

So, the CSR[9] intervention is justified by women's lack of development, and in Sri Lanka a paternalistic discourse is deployed to legitimize these modernizing endeavours. In other words, they may not be disposable, but they are third world women who need to be educated.[10]

Thus, these discourses show that forms of subjugation are still occurring—just under a different guise. Exactly who gets included/excluded and how they are interpellated is overdetermined, meaning that disposability, per se, is not an inexorable consequence of global capital–labour relations (Bair, 2010). Managers internalize a neocolonial logic of development, in which women are seen as lacking development, in order to maintain discipline in the labour process. This is how the managers are deploying ideologies of social difference in ways that make the ongoing production of value in global chains possible. The two sections that follow focus on the emergence of lean management practices in Sri Lanka, which triggered a second important moment of disarticulation and rearticulation.

11.6   Background: The global impetus for lean restructuring in Sri Lanka

The global landscape of the apparel trade has become increasingly volatile and more competitive. To survive, Sri Lankan firms have re-examined their work processes with a view to make them as efficient as possible. At least two of the largest and wealthiest firms in Sri Lanka[11] have devoted substantial resources to the adoption of lean manufacturing, a reorganization of work processes that aims to 'eliminate waste' (Plankey-Videla, 2012). In this section, I situate these process-upgrading endeavours in the changing global patterns of apparel sourcing.

The way in which buyers decide where to place orders has changed since the early 2000s. Since the phase-out of quotas in 2005, China's share of world apparel exports has increased from 23 per cent in 2003 to 41 per cent in 2011.[12] More generally, quota phase-out led to consolidation, increased barriers to entry, and intensified competition (Staritz, 2011). In addition, the global economic crisis of 2008–2009 and the rising price of oil have triggered reduced consumer demand in the US and Europe and unstable input prices, respectively. With increased volatility, global apparel value chains

---

[9] CSR—corporate social responsibility.

[10] Plankey-Videla (2012) observed similar forms of paternalism in lean factories in Mexico.

[11] Three of the nine factories in this study were in more advanced stages of this shift to lean production.

[12] My calculation based on UN COMTRADE data, adding import flows of HS codes 61 and 62 (as reported) from partner codes 0 (world) and 156 (China), and using reporter code 12398 (world aggregate), http://comtrade.un.org/db/

are bearing higher risk at the same time that access to finance capital—especially for small- and medium-sized enterprises (SMEs)—has decreased. In response to these changes, US and European retailers, such as H&M, Next, and Nike, are increasingly adopting the 'fast fashion' model of just-in-time production (pioneered by Zara in the late, 1990s) in their value-chain management, and consumers increasingly demand 'value for values' (Hughes, 2012; Tokatli, 2008). Part of a lean philosophy, just-in-time emphasizes small batch production, demand management, quick changeovers, and efficient inventory management (Plankey-Videla, 2012; Womack et al., 1991).

Buyers' sourcing strategies once focused mainly on production costs, reliability, and quality; but now they include additional criteria such as faster lead times, social and environmental compliance, design capability, and inventory management (Staritz, 2011). Some call this 'lean retailing', the goal being to make the whole value chain more efficient (Abernathy et al., 1999; Pickles and Smith, 2010). This has also led to the rise of large intermediaries and first-tier suppliers who take on additional functions and allow buyers to shift the burden of risk down the value chain (Appelbaum, 2008). One of the main goals of the JAAF in Sri Lanka is to transform the sector into one of these 'full-service' manufacturing hubs (JAAF, 2002). Increasingly, buyers have engaged in capacity building with strategic partners, consolidated their supply chains, and encouraged suppliers to adopt lean.

The Sri Lankan apparel industry has explicitly relied on upgrading and other strategic manoeuvres to survive in this volatile landscape. Compared with other garment-producing countries, Sri Lanka has a highly educated workforce, a small but relatively stable set of buyers, and more domestic ownership—by 1999 the industry was 80 to 85 per cent Sri Lankan owned (Kelegama and Wijayasiri, 2004). As a well-organized and politically powerful industry, Sri Lankan apparel firms have aggressively pursued the upgrading strategies that they set out through JAAF in 2002. As a result, the industry has maintained a stable share of world trade despite the global economic crisis (Staritz and Frederick, 2012). Since the phase-out of quotas in 2005, exports have gradually increased (except from 2008 to 2009) and employment has been stable at around 280,000 (Staritz and Frederick, 2012). However, the number of factories has decreased over time from a high of 1061 in 2001 to only 300 in 2009 (Staritz and Frederick, 2012). Even in 2001, the industry was highly concentrated, with 12 per cent of exporters generating 72 per cent of industry revenue (Kelegama and Wijayasiri, 2004), and since then it has consolidated further. These trends indicate that the sector is undergoing a shake-out process in which large companies are expanding and SMEs are closing (Staritz and Frederick, 2012; Wijayasiri and Dissanayake, 2009). The lean reorganization analysed below is occurring in this context of consolidation.

11.7 Moment 2: The cultural politics of a lean transformation

Even though the lean reorganization is, in large part, a response to changing global dynamics, the actually existing practices of lean transformation occur through (and are shaped by) the power geometries of particular places (Collins, 2003; Plankey-Videla, 2012). In this section, I show how managers primarily saw the transition to lean as a cultural change, much like Plankey-Videla (2012) observed in Mexico. The managers continually emphasized the importance of how it 'evolved the people' in the factory and represented a path towards modernization that extricated 'Western' influence. By showing how managers articulated these shifts, my aim is to demonstrate how upgrading, in the specific form of lean production, involved an embodied rearticulation of social differences.

As in many other places throughout the world (Plankey-Videla, 2012; Womack et al., 1991), the lean restructuring involved the following factory-level changes:

- Reorganizing workers into small teams or 'modules' rather than assembly lines;
- Having workers to do multiple operations, rather than one task repeatedly;
- Training workers in multiple skills and establishing career paths;
- Changing the roles of management and workers—workers self-manage;
- Performance measurement, problem-solving, and kaizen (continuous improvement);
- Shifting to small, customized, just-in-time production batches.

These forms of 'flexible' production differ from Fordist mass production in many respects. Most importantly, flexible suppliers respond more rapidly to changing consumer demands. In short, lean requires a different labour process and a different kind of workforce: 'Flexible workers are valued for their brains as well as for their brawn' (Wright, 2006, p. 50). This section focuses on two key aspects of these changes as Sri Lankan suppliers adopted lean: (1) organizing consent, or gaining buy-in, and (2) creating a learning-oriented workplace culture.

The managers framed lean as 'journey' that is never complete, and they have implemented it gradually to ensure sufficient buy-in. Therefore, the political nature of changing the labour process is explicitly acknowledged and incorporated into the lean training curriculum (Plankey-Videla, 2012).[13]

---

[13] Because one supplier's pilot lean teams were so successful, Nike opened an Apparel Innovation and Training Center in Sri Lanka in 2009. Managers come to Sri Lanka from around the world to take courses in lean manufacturing, and they earn belts similar to those in karate (yellow, green, black, etc.) upon completion of these courses.

The Sri Lankan managers took several steps to organize consent through the labour process, and these were consistent across all three plants shifting to lean in this study. For example, they replaced the label 'worker' with that of 'team member'. At one firm, a general manager interrupted an interview to say, 'Actually, we don't use "worker" .... We don't use that word. We call it "*samajikaya*". *Samajikaya* is a member.' Later, he added: 'Our goal is to get people to think of the organisation, not just of themselves, to have ownership'. A corporate-level manager at another firm articulated the rejection of the 'worker' label as an effort to restructure the hierarchy:

> You would have heard that there's a "team member" in a line, which we used to call a "worker". Now we have taken off that name. If someone says "worker" to me, I really get annoyed and I will say "Oh, there are no workers here. There are only team members". So, that means if a person is a worker, then you should be a non-worker—what's the definition? ... What we are doing with the restructuring is we're trying to take apart all of this hierarchy, trying to structure it in a proper manner, a standard manner across [the company]. That is one of the biggest challenges we have .... And so what we are trying to do here is we are trying to get even our team members to do problem solving.

Here, the manager wants to situate team members as constitutive of management, not separate from it. For him the team dynamic was a foundation for building a problem-solving workplace culture that valued everyone's ideas.

Another way in which the managers organized consent was by rearticulating their own roles as managers. Participants said that 'good' managers do not yell. They have patience, want to hear suggestions, explain things well, train team members to self-manage, and motivate people. This discourse about management contradicted the 'professional woman' discourse of the empowerment programmes because it focused more on improving managers' rather than workers' behaviours. For example, one manager said:

> What I believe is operators are really good. There are no bad operators. It's about management. If you guide them well, they will be good always.

Other managers framed this shift in terms of creating a teacher–learner relationship, portraying labour in positive terms as self-enhancement rather than as self-deprecation.

These attempts to rearticulate the role of management are consistent with how Wright and Plankey-Videla characterized flexible production as, in some ways, placing more value on the workers' intellectual contributions. On the other hand, they depart from Wright's observations in Mexico in other respects, because the female team members in Sri Lanka were not seen as untrainable. Their relatively high education levels were a source of national pride. The managers said that their main challenge was convincing them to see garment work as a career rather than a temporary job. Therefore, the production of value in Sri Lanka's lean factories hinged on the managers' abilities to motivate team members, recognize their intellectual contributions, and cultivate a sense of ownership over the production process. This led them to disarticulate the disposability logic and rearticulate a logic of self-management and empowerment. This indicates that upgrading, as it is articulated through the labour management process in GVCs, must negotiate power geometries at multiple scales (global, national, local, etc.).

Managers saw the creation of a culture of learning and leadership as a cornerstone not only for the shop floor, but also for the Sri Lankan society. By drawing on locally relevant master tropes, such as the generosity and connectedness of 'Sri Lankan culture',[14] they empowered themselves and the team members as important agents in securing a better future for the nation. Here, a corporate-level manager conveys this desire to recuperate 'Sri Lankan values':

> I mean the part that people miss is the people. That's the most important thing. Because it's a different culture, it's a different DNA that we bring into this organization. I mean, if you look at five–six years back, there were certain concepts and philosophies engrained in this organization—especially things that come from the apparel sector, which has migrated from places like the US, I mean, more than US—UK. I mean, people like Sara Lee and all that bringing in these things. So, they had certain paradigms ... and the challenge for us was how we challenge those paradigms.

Stabilizing this anticolonial/postcolonial identity in this way was common, and it is consistent with Sri Lanka's historically conflicted relationship with the West (Hewamanne, 2008; Lynch, 2007). By invoking 'DNA', the participant naturalizes the distinction, and positions his firm as an emancipatory agent that is freeing Sri Lankans from the previous, more Western, regimes of accumulation. In this rearticulation, the company uses lean to formulate a viable modern regime of

---

[14] As Lynch (2007) demonstrated, 'Sri Lankan culture' is often conflated with the hegemonic Sinhala-Buddhist culture and this generates contradictions and moral anxieties as Sri Lankans struggle to stabilize a 'Sri Lankan' national identity in the wake of colonialism and violent conflict.

accumulation that also has Sri Lankan characteristics. At the same time, they do so with the contradiction that the idea of lean originated in Japan (with Toyota) and has, now, been adopted in many Western countries as well (Plankey-Videla, 2012). So, this identification of lean production as 'Sri Lankan' reproduces difference at the same time that it attempts to rearticulate garment production as valuable and respectable for the nation.

In response to a question about whether the idea of promoting a learning culture was from 'outside' or from inside Sri Lanka, one manager said:

> [It's] from the Toyota culture book ... It's also a Sri Lankan way of management. We don't have a hire and fire culture. We have a more emotionally engaged, connected culture, right? So, ah, it's how you transcend to that culture, cultural values of reaping the benefits with your investments.

This participant seems to see Toyota, and possibly Japan, as having a culture that is more aligned with Sri Lankan values than the previous models of industrial relations—presumably Fordist models of mass production originating in the US. Therefore, again, there is an emphasis on articulating the home-grown characteristics of lean manufacturing and disarticulating the West from export-oriented production. These examples of how managers selectively deployed 'Sri Lankan culture' to legitimate the dramatic changes to the labour process show how complex it is to forge an upgrading process in practice, and how important the political and the cultural realms are for stabilizing new forms of value appropriation in GVCs. The next section shows this was not a smooth process for the managers.

11.8 Moment 3: Disruptions to the managers' efforts to rearticulate work and workers

Up to this point, the managers' efforts to disrupt the disposability logic, to dislodge the label 'worker', and to displace Western cultures of production have been analysed without much attention to how effective they were. Despite the zeal which many of the managers had for this new culture of work, they encountered several problems. For example, in rural factories, managers reported increased domestic violence and some husbands or fathers forbidding their wives or daughters from returning to work. One manager said that husbands and fathers of workers have told him that he is 'empowering them too much'. In response, the managers invited families to the factory to 'educate' them, gave them access to factory facilities such as an on-site gym, and offered counselling services to workers.

Other managers pointed out that despite all of their investments in training, engaging, and motivating the workers, they were having less success than they had hoped in getting workers to stay on after marriage. One manager expressed his frustrations with this:

> After getting married, their husbands, spouses, don't want to send them ... .
> That is their culture, of course. They really don't want to send their wives
> to jobs. That is in our culture, which we need to change as much as possible.

The way he switches from 'their' to 'our' reveals some of the friction and difficulty he is experiencing as he negotiates various fields of social difference. Managers spent a lot of time and effort trying to navigate the bargaining power that workers had to leave. Although they valued previously existing social norms in many respects, they delicately tried to change them because they were constraining the transformation to lean and, by extension, their global competitiveness. Hence, their efforts to upgrade were conflicted.

When questioned about why they did not recruit more men, given the challenges in getting women to stay, a common response was that men did not have the right temperament, were harder to control, and might unionise. Therefore, the displacement of the label 'worker', emphasis on teams, and reorganization of the hierarchy may also be a part of a strategy to reduce the role of workers' councils or the likelihood of unionization. Along these lines, managers in the lean factories introduced a new position: the 'mentor'. Mentors are liaisons between the team members and the team leader (who focuses on production goals), to ensure that the workers get support if they are sick, etc, and to report problems or tensions to human resources. These mentors, in effect, play an important role in addressing grievances—a function typically carried out by workers' councils and/or unions.

Meanwhile, managers consistently expressed their opposition to the idea of having unions in their factories.[15] They said Sri Lankan unions were too 'political', had ulterior motives, were driven by 'outsiders' (international union federations), and would not be present in Sri Lankan factories unless there was a problem with the management.[16] For example, an industry association staff person said that the idea of a union is 'perfect' but that, in Sri Lanka, unions had motivations other

---

[15] There were no unions in the factories visited for this study. Unions are practically non-existent in rural factories, but they have a larger presence near the EPZs. The factories have worker councils, but these are not the same as unions (Ruwanpura, 2012). The landscape of unions and unionization in Sri Lanka is problematic in many respects, but there is insufficient space to analyse it in depth here.

[16] To them, 'bad' managers displayed violent, impatient, or antagonistic behaviour or did not treat people with respect.

than helping the workers. Therefore, changing the job title from 'worker' to 'team member', embedding mentors into the production process, and continuing to focus recruitment efforts on women could also be interpreted as ways for managers to consolidate their power and keep collective organizing outside the realm of production. In other words, this may be a threat to worker bargaining power, despite the empowerment rhetoric.

Another significant contradiction to the claim that they were restructuring hierarchies was the limited mobility from the highest levels of shop-floor work to the lowest level of management (the production executive), a move that was still extremely rare. This jump is accompanied by a significant pay increase, from approximately 20,000 rupees per month to 40,000 or more, and the barrier is policed by a number of factors both inside and outside the factory. The most direct form of policing occurs, as one female manager in a factory reported, when male managers threaten a female manager, intimidate her, or undermine her ability to do her job. Other forms of gendered policing occur through the naturalization of particular job categories as 'women's work', and others as 'men's work'. For example, management-level jobs at the factory were frequently considered too stressful for women; especially women with child-care responsibilities. Indeed, in the rural factories, management teams are typically brought in each week from Colombo by vanpool and this kind of travel was widely considered very hard to do for a woman with a family. Because it is often harder to earn promotion without taking a position far from Colombo, this seems to counteract their efforts to produce 'professional women'.

In addition, class distinctions were policed with preferences for high educational attainments and English fluency. Although there were shop-floor workers with college degrees, typically this was not enough for promotion to management. Almost all of the managers in this study were very fluent in English (many had attended an elite, private, English-only secondary school or had lived overseas), possessed prestigious university degrees, or had significant experience in a leadership role—such as in the military. Given the mobile nature of management teams in rural factories, the fact that the management team was almost entirely from Colombo and was considered more Westernised also contributed to a sense that management positions were not normatively appropriate for local people.

I observed rare cases of female managers who had been promoted from the shop floor, but only after decades of work. Some managers (both female and male) expressed concern and frustration over this glass ceiling, while others maintained that gender-based discrimination does not exist in Sri Lanka—or, at least, it is less of a problem there than elsewhere. Thus, the processes of trying to articulate an empowered, professional woman are fraught with contestation. The power of managers is constrained by lateral and vertical structures of domination and subordination (Ruwanpura, 2013).

Suppliers also expressed anxiety and frustration about the continued downward pressure on prices from global buyers (Ruwanpura and Wrigley, 2011). Managers frequently questioned the ethics of buyers who do not pay a fair price for the effort required. As a result, some managers took a pessimistic view of the future of apparel manufacturing in Sri Lanka, and the collapse in the number of firms seems to support this. One owner of a medium-sized garment company said that as surviving garment firms develop 'full-solution capabilities', the actual manufacturing would start to shift overseas where labour was cheaper. Two large firms have recently opened large industrial parks in India—a diversification strategy of outsourcing. Other managers said that their newest upgrading efforts were focused on automation, which could also decrease employment. This potential for future displacement of labour-intensive activities following an intense period of consolidation and upgrading suggests that it is important to couch these articulation processes in the context of long-term industry life cycles.

11.9 Conclusion

In this chapter I have engaged with the dis/articulations analytic to explore upgrading as an embodied process occurring in everyday settings, rather than a disembodied technical fix. I have presented management narratives that highlight the importance of contextually relevant legitimating ideologies in shaping the labour process and making ongoing capitalist accumulation possible. For example, suppliers are using discourses of 'empowering' or 'advancing' women to disarticulate the myth of disposability and to rearticulate worker subjects as professional, modern, and respectable. Doing this helps the garment firms please buyers and overcome stigma so that they can recruit, retain, and train a more highly skilled and experienced workforce. Likewise, the managers are disarticulating the West from export-oriented production and selectively rearticulating Sri Lankan culture by emphasizing how lean production aligns better with social norms in Sri Lanka. Portraying 'work' as 'learning', and 'workers' as 'team members', enables managers to get buy-in for pursuing more fast-paced, flexible, and efficient production. Because these narratives are also rife with contradictions and instabilities, they suggest that the economic logics of upgrading are mutually constituted by cultural and political logics that operate in specific conjunctures.

This research contributes to debates about value in the GVC literature, suggesting that the emphasis on the production of value through inter-firm and firm-state relations obscures other forms of value creation and appropriation that occur through the ongoing reproduction of the labour process. For example, the labour shortage and the need for producing and retaining an experienced, highly skilled, problem-solving, capable workforce led the managers to advocate in surrounding communities for greater respect for female garment workers and to train workers in skills that gave them greater bargaining power over time. For the feminist literature on globalized production, this research suggests that the logic of disposability is not a necessary relation but, rather, that it is produced and reproduced through specific historical and geographical contexts of social difference. To the contrary, this case shows that certain kinds of product value chains and labour market contexts operate through antidisposability logics—meaning that multiple global logics of interpellating labour in global production circuits coexist and interact.

Methodologically, in this chapter I have drawn on feminist ethnographies of labour to analyse how managers shape and are shaped by social worlds, in the material spaces of the factory and beyond. For example, they were not only trying to articulate the 'perfect woman' for the factory, but they also wanted to shape the imaginaries of a modern future and secure a place for the garment industry in that future. In this way, analysing management discourses about worker subjectivity offers an opening for commodity-chain studies to more deeply engage with the politics of production—such as how upgrading in practice often ends up reproducing uneven power relations more than it challenges them. Fruitful avenues for future research include both 'studying up' the value chain to trace how ideas of 'good' management circulate and travel and 'studying down' the value chain to see how workers and their families negotiate lean manufacturing and empowerment programmes.

Considering the central question of this chapter is how labour has benefitted from the expansion of apparel manufacturing in Sri Lanka, this research suggests that the answer is highly influenced by gender relations and other contextually embedded forms of power. Garment employment and industrial upgrading in Sri Lanka have, literally, put more earnings in the hands of female workers and threatened previously existing patriarchal power relations in significant ways. In other respects, however, the labour process reproduces and rearticulates new forms of patriarchal control over female bodies and exposes them to risks, such as stigmatization and gender-based violence. Therefore, identifying ways to enable labour to benefit more from GVC participation is not simply a matter of transferring knowledge or technologies to enhance supplier capabilities, but it also requires more careful attention to how the labour-management process is articulating, disarticulating, and rearticulating through situated micro-level spaces of production. Given the complex dynamics observed in this case, how effective will management be in the long run at recruiting, promoting, and retaining labour in a volatile macro-level trading environment? How will continued consolidation of the national industry sector in Sri Lanka shape employment opportunities and labour's bargaining power? These are key questions for understanding the long-term implications of the GVC structure for labour.

Ultimately, by showing how these efforts at disarticulation and rearticulation came up against other cultural and political structures of power, in this chapter I highlight that the economic realm of production is not the only determinant of social worlds. For example, lean production has to be politically and culturally viable—both inside and outside the factory—to succeed as an accumulation strategy. Therefore, the ongoing production of social worlds is a contested project that is never complete. These instabilities, limitations, and contradictions open up new possibilities for social change and resistance, which sometimes may be found in unexpected places.

Acknowledgements

This research was supported by the Social Science Research Council International Dissertation Research Fellowship (with funding from the Andrew W. Mellon foundation), a National Science Foundation Doctoral Dissertation Research Improvement Grant, the Fulbright US Student Program in Sri Lanka, the American Institute for Sri Lankan Studies, and the Carolina Asia Center at the University of North Carolina at Chapel Hill. I am grateful to Joshua Barkan, Jennifer Bair, Elizabeth Havice, Kanchana Ruwanpura, Elizabeth Hennessey, Murat Es, John Pickles, Dev Nathan, and five anonymous reviewers for helpful comments. An earlier version was published in the journal Environment and Planning A, 2013, Vol. 45, 2628–2645, a publication of Pion Ltd, London, www.pion.co.uk, www.envplan.com

References

Abernathy, Frederick H., John T. Dunlop, Janice H. Hammond, and David Weil. 1999. *A Stitch in Time: Lean Retailing and the Transformation of Manufacturing—Lessons from the Apparel and Textile Industries.* New York: Oxford University Press.

Appadurai, Arjun. 2001. 'Deep Democracy: Urban Governmentality and the Horizon of Politics.' *Environ Urban* 13 (2): 23–43.

Appelbaum, Richard. 2008. 'Giant Transnational Contractors in East Asia: Emergent Trends in Global Supply Chains.' *Comp Change* 12 (1): 69–87.

Bair, Jennifer. 2005. 'Global Capitalism and Commodity Chains: Looking Back, Going Forward.' *Comp Change* 9 (2): 153–80.

Bair, Jennifer. 2008. 'Analysing Global Economic Organization: Embedded Networks and Global Chains Compared.' *Econ Soc* 37 (3): 339–64.

Bair, Jennifer. 2010. 'On Difference and Capital: Gender and the Globalization of Production.' *Signs* 36 (1): 203–26.

Bair, Jennifer, and Marion Werner. 2011. 'Commodity Chains and the Uneven Geographies of Global Capitalism: A Disarticulations Perspective.' *Environ Plan A* 43 (5): 988–97.

Bair, Jennifer, Christian Berndt, Marc Boeckler, and Marion Werner. 2013. 'Dis/articulating Producers, Markets, and Regions: New Directions in Critical Studies of Commodity Chains.' *Environ Plan A* 45 (11): 2544–52.

Bradby, Barbara. 1980. 'The Destruction of Natural Economy.' In *The Articulation of Modes of Production: Essays from Economy and Society*, edited by Harold Wolpe, 93–127. London: Routledge and Kegan Paul.

Burawoy, Michael. 2001. 'Manufacturing the Global.' *Ethnography* 2 (2): 147–59.

Butler, Judith. 1997. *The Psychic Life of Power: Theories in Subjection.* Stanford, CA: Stanford University Press.

Coe, Neil M., Peter Dicken, Martin Hess, and Henry Wai-Cheung Yeung. 2010. 'Making Connections: Global Production Networks and World City Networks.' *Global Netw* 10 (1): 138–49.

Collins, Jane L. 2003. *Threads: Gender, Labor, and Power in the Global Apparel Industry.* Chicago: University of Chicago Press.

Fernandez-Kelly, Maria Patricia. 1983. *For We are Sold, I and My People: Women and Industry in Mexico's Frontier.* Albany: State University of New York Press.

Gereffi, Gary. 1994. 'The Organization of Buyer-Driven Global Commodity Chains: How U.S. Retailers Shape Overseas Production Networks.' In *Commodity Chains and Global Capitalism*, edited by Gary Gereffi and Miguel Korzeniewicz, 93–122. Praeger: Westport Press.

———. 1999. 'International Trade and Industrial Upgrading in the Apparel Commodity Chain.' *J Int Econ* 48 (1): 37–70.

Gereffi, Gary, and Olga Memedovic. 2003. *The Global Apparel Value Chain: What Prospects for Upgrading by Developing Countries?* Vienna: UNIDO.

Gereffi, Gary, John Humphrey, and Timothy Sturgeon. 2005. 'The Governance of Global Value Chains.' *Rev Int Polit Econ* 12 (1): 78–104.

Goger, Annelies. 2014. 'Ethical Branding in Sri Lanka: A Case Study of Garments Without Guilt.' In *Workers' Rights and Labor Compliance in Global Supply Chains: Is a Social Label the Answer?* edited by Jennifer Bair, Marsha Dickson and Doug Miller, 47–68. New York: Routledge.

Hall, Stuart. 1980. 'Race, Articulation and Societies Structured in Dominance.' In *Sociological Theories: Race and Colonialism*, 305–45. Paris: UNESCO.

Hewamanne, Sandya. 2008. *Stitching Identities in a Free Trade Zone: Gender and Politics in Sri Lanka*. Philadelphia: University of Pennsylvania Press.

Hughes, Alex. 2012. 'Corporate Ethical Trading in an Economic Downturn: Recessionary Pressures and Refracted Responsibilities.' *J Econ Geogr* 12 (1): 33–54.

Humphrey, John, and Hubert Schmitz. 2002. 'How Does Insertion in Global Value Chains Affect Upgrading in Industrial Clusters?' *Reg Stud* 36 (9): 1017–27.

JAAF. 2002. *Sri Lanka Apparel Industry Five Year Strategy*. Colombo: Joint Apparel Association Forum.

Jayaweera, Swara. 2003. 'Continuity and Change: Women Workers in Garment and Textile Industries in Sri Lanka.' In *Tracking Gender Equity Under Economic Reforms: Continuity and Change in South Asia*, edited by Swapna Mukhopadhyay and Ratna Sudarshan, 196–226. Ottawa: International Development Research Centre.

Kelegama, Saman, and Janaka Wijayasiri. 2004. 'Overview of the Garment Industry in Sri Lanka.' In *Ready-made Garment Industry in Sri Lanka: Facing the Global Challenge*, edited by Saman Kelegama, 13–45. Colombo: Institute of Policy Studies of Sri Lanka.

Lynch, Caitrin. 2007. *Juki Girls, Good Girls: Gender and Cultural Politics in Sri Lanka's Global Garment Industry*. Ithaca, NY: Cornell University Press.

Marcus, George E. 1998. *Ethnography Through Thick and Thin*. Princeton, NJ: Princeton University Press.

Mills, Mary Beth. 1999. *Thai Women in the Global Labor Force: Consuming Desires, Contested Selves*. New Brunswick, NJ: Rutgers University Press.

———. 2003. 'Gender and Inequality in the Global Labour Force.' *Ann Rev Anthropol* 32: 41–62.

Nagar, Richa, Victoria Lawson, Linda McDowell, and Susan Hanson. 2002. 'Locating Globalization: Feminist (Re)readings of the Subjects and Spaces of Globalization.' *Econ Geogr* 78 (3): 257–84.

Ong, Aihwa. 1987. *Spirits of Resistance and Capitalist Discipline: Factory Women in Malaysia*. Albany, NY: State University of New York Press.

———. 2006. *Neoliberalism as Exception: Mutations in Citizenship and Sovereignty*. Durham, NC: Duke University Press.

Peck, Jamie, and Nik Theodore. 2010. 'Mobilizing Policy: Models, Methods, and Mutations.' *Geoforum* 41 (2): 169–74.

Pickles, John, and Adrian Smith. 2010. 'Clothing Workers after Worker States: The Consequences for Work and Labour of Outsourcing, Nearshoring and Delocalisation in Postsocialist Europe.' In *Handbook of Employment and*

Society: Working Space, edited by Andrew Herod, Susan McGrath-Champ and Al Rainnie, 106–23. Cheltenham: Edward Elgar.

Pickles, John, Adrian Smith, Milan Buček, Poli Roukova, and Robert Begg. 2006. 'Upgrading, Changing Competitive Pressures, and Diverse Practices in the East and Central European Apparel Industry.' *Environ Plan A* 38 (12): 2305–24.

Plankey-Videla, Nancy. 2012. *We are in This Dance Together: Gender, Power, and Globalization at a Mexican Garment Firm*. New Brunswick, NJ: Rutgers University Press.

Rey, Pierre-Philippe. 1973. *Les Alliance des Classes*. Paris: Maspero.

Roy, Ananya. 2012. 'Ethnographic Circulations: Space–Time Relations in the Worlds of Poverty Management.' *Environ Plan A* 44 (1): 31–41.

Ruwanpura, Kanchana N. 2012. *Ethical Codes: Reality and Rhetoric: A Study of Sri Lanka's Apparel Sector*. Swindon: University of Southampton and Economic and Social Research Council.

———. 2013. 'Scripted Performances? Local Readings of "Global" Health and Safety Standards (The Apparel Sector in Sri Lanka).' *Global Labour J* 4 (2): 88–108.

Ruwanpura, Kanchana N., and Neil Wrigley. 2011. 'The Costs of Compliance? Views of Sri Lankan Apparel Manufacturers in Times of Global Economic Crisis.' *J Econ Geogr* 11 (6): 1031–49.

Salzinger, Leslie. 2003. *Genders in Production: Making Workers in Mexico's Global Factories*. Berkeley: University of California Press.

Schoenberger, Erica. 1997. *The Cultural Crisis of the Firm*. Oxford: Blackwell.

Schrank, Andrew. 2004. 'Ready-to-Wear Development? Foreign Investment, Technology Transfer, and Learning by Watching in the Apparel Trade.' *Social Forces* 83 (1): 123–56.

Shaw, Judith. 2004. 'Decent Work or Distress Adaptation? Employment Choice and Job Satisfaction in the Sri Lankan Garment Industry.' In *Women and Work: Current RMIT Research*, edited by Sara Charlesworth and Maureen Fastenau, 50–64. Melbourne: RMIT Publishing.

Staritz, Cornelia. 2011. *Making the Cut? Low-income Countries and the Global Clothing Value Chain in a Post-quota and Post-crisis World*. Washington, D.C.: World Bank.

Staritz, Cornelia, and Frederick S. 2012. 'Sri Lanka.' In *Sewing Success: Employment, Wages, and Poverty Following the End of the Multi-fibre Arrangement*, edited by Gladys Lopez-Acevedo and Raymond Robertson, 441–69. Washington, D.C.: World Bank.

Tokatli, Nebahat. 2008. 'Global Sourcing: Insights from the Global Clothing Industry—The Case of Zara, a Fast Fashion Retailer.' *J Econ Geogr* 8 (1): 21–38.

———. 2012. 'Toward a Better Understanding of the Apparel Industry: A Critique of the Upgrading Literature.' *J Econ Geogr*. doi: 10.1093/jeg/165043.

Werner, Marion. 2012. 'Beyond Upgrading: Gendered Labour and the Restructuring of Firms in the Dominican Republic.' *Econ Geogr* 88 (4): 403–22.

Wijayasiri, Janaka, and Jagath Dissanayake. 2009. 'The Ending of the Multi-Fibre Agreement and Innovation in the Sri Lankan Textile and Clothing Industry.' *OECD J: General Papers* 4: 157–88.

Wolf, Diane Laren. 1992. *Factory Daughters: Gender, Household Dynamics, and Rural Industrialization in Java*. Berkeley: University of California Press.

Wolpe, Harold. 1975. 'The Theory of Internal Colonialism.' In *Beyond the Sociology of Development*, edited by Ivaar Oxaal, Tony Barnett, David Booth, 229–52. London: Routledge and Kegan Paul.

———. 1980. 'Capitalism and Cheap Labour-Power in South Africa: From Segregation to Apartheid.' In *The Articulation of Modes of Production: Essays from Economy and Society*, edited by Harold Wolpe, 289–320. London: Routledge and Kegan Paul.

Womack, James P., Daniel T. Jones, and Daniel Roos. 1991. *The Machine that Changed the World: How Japan's Secret Weapon in the Global Auto Wars will Revolutionize Western Industry*. New York: Harper Perennial.

Wright, Melissa W. 2006. *Disposable Women and Other Myths of Global Capitalism*. New York: Routledge.

12

Scripted Performances? Local Readings of 'Global' Health and Safety Standards in the Apparel Sector in Sri Lanka[1]

Kanchana N. Ruwanpura

12.1 Introduction

Safe working places are a cornerstone for enabling worker welfare in factory settings. Occupational health and safety (OHS) is perceived as most 'straightforward' for implementation and where forward movement has been made under voluntary global governance regimes (Brown, 2009; Barrientos and Smith, 2007). OHS, however, is a disputed arena as it essentially encapsulates the perennial conflict between state, capital, and labour.

Ethical codes are an important instrument of global governance in the garment trade, where the issue of OHS has evolved rapidly because of its auditable nature (Barrientos and Smith, 2007; Clean Clothes Campaign, 2005). However, growing evidence suggests that problems abound in OHS systems in global supply chains. For example, factories generally lack on-site OHS professionals, and there have been significant challenges to the implementation and effectiveness of monitoring mechanisms (Brown, 2009; Miller, 2011; O'Rourke, 2000). Consequently, factory fires and collapses continue to plague the industry with devastating and deadly

[1] Acknowledgements: The support of a 3-year Economic and Social Research Council (ESRC) Council Grant (RES-061-25-0181) is acknowledged for making this research possible. This paper is a revised version of an article, which initially appeared in *Global Labour Journal* (2013, Vol. 4, 2: 88–108) under the Creative Commons Copyright, and their openness to have it republished in this edited volume is greatly appreciated. An early version of this paper was presented at a workshop at the University of Sussex on July 2010, where numerous academic colleagues generously offered constructive comments. Grace Carswell, Nick Clarke, Malathi De Alwis, Geert De Neve, Geoff Deverteuil, Annelies Goger, Doug Miller, Gale Raj-Reichert and Peter Sunley deserve a special mention for the time they took through the paper's life cycle to help shape and strengthen it.

consequences for workers, especially in Bangladesh and Pakistan, as the collapse of Spectrum Factory and Rana Plaza testified (Brown, 2011, 2012; Day, 2010; Miller, 2009, 2011). In contrast, neighbouring Sri Lanka has evaded this negative publicity, and the media tends to portray the Sri Lankan apparel industry as an 'ethical' supplier that takes global governance regimes seriously—an image that the industry has strategically cultivated (Karp, 1999; O'Leary, 2009). The idea that labour's health and safety fare well in these settings is very much taken for granted.

De Neve (2009), however, rightly reminds us that there is also a politics of compliance—in so far as 'ethical corporate regulations are shaped by and constitutive of power relations in the global market' (2009, p. 63). His interventions underscore the point that the neoliberal global economy is 'rooted in, and shaped by, particular social practices, cultural mores and institutional frameworks', which result in erratic distinctions in myriad spatial locations (Wills, 1999, p. 446). This particular grounding, as labour geographers have suggested, matters for worker agency but also requires appreciating their spatial choices within 'capitalisms unevenly developed geography' (Herod, 2012, p. 21; Castree, 2007). Moreover, Castree (2007) notes the need to be attentive to the social and cultural tapestry of workers' social lives, signalling that how workers live outside workplaces also matters for labour geography. My contention is that these sociocultural spheres are never neatly left behind when labour enters workplaces. As I show in this paper, sociocultural politics within factory sites is also an important lens through which to appreciate the workings of labour agency. Hence, unravelling how workers encounter corporate codes in the global garment industry requires considering not simply how capital embeds locally (Herod, 2012; Mezzadri, 2012), but also how labour negotiates industrial relations.

This research focuses on how global governance circulates, or takes on a life of its own worldwide and is put into practice in local settings in one area of ethical codes, i.e., health and safety. By zooming in on the realm of health and safety, this paper brings to the fore discussions about how global governance regimes are mutually constituted by local contexts. Using Sri Lanka's apparel sector as a case study, this paper aims to show the divergent ways in which health and safety measures constructed in the Global North are implemented in factory settings in the Global South.[2] The paper illustrates how OHS measures cannot be separated out from uneven development processes. Instead, I argue that global efforts to improve the health and safety of workers and create healthy work settings needs to incorporate place and space through a greater understanding of how the relationship between global governance and uneven

---

[2] See Humphries (2010) for a historical evaluation of the central import of various types of labour conditions, including in the realm of health and safety, in the spread of capitalism in industrial Britain.

development is co-constituted. This focus enables a more situated analysis of capital and labour relations, positioning them within wider sociocultural relations and uneven development processes (Carswell and De Neve, 2013; Herod, 2012). It also fulfils a lacuna identified by Herod (2012) in labour geography regarding the absence of empirical study outside of industrial capitalist societies.

12.2 The Sri Lankan sociality

Sri Lanka in the late 1970s embarked on open trade policies, with Sri Lanka's first free trade zone set up in 1978 (Gunawardana, 2007, p. 80). The industry has witnessed phenomenal growth since the 1970s, with the garment sector accounting for over 45 per cent of exports by 2005 and employing nearly 275,000 workers (Sluiter, 2009, p. 53). Although the phase-out of World Trade Organization quotas in 2005, the global recession of 2008, and the removal of GSP+ trade preferences from the EU in 2010 created oscillations within the industry, as of 2008 it remains a significant source of employment for workers with the sector employing 49.9 per cent of the workforce according to the Census and Statistics data (Ruwanpura, 2012). The 200 Garment Factory Programme of 1992 lies at the helm of current employment trends, because it was implemented to redress rural unemployment and attend to latent nationalist anxieties (Lynch, 2007). While the cultural politics of Sri Lanka's garment industry workers have been subject to scholarly scrutiny (Lynch, 2007; Hewamanne, 2008), our awareness of labour-management responses to global governance initiatives is limited. This is unlike neighbouring countries in South Asia, where there is coverage on the politics of global labour standards and compliance in the apparel industry (De Neve, 2009; Mezzadri, 2012; Miller, 2012). Because there are limited studies about how the garment sector in Sri Lanka has responded to the demands of consumers and retailers to provide safe and hygienic working environments, this paper seeks to address a significant gap.

Sri Lanka's ability to evade negative media scandals is often attributed to the high health and education levels of its workforce, such that the social development of the country places a degree of responsibility on managers to be attentive to worker welfare (Sluiter, 2009). In more recent times, in response to ethical trade efforts promoted via consumer campaigns and multi-stakeholder initiatives, the Sri Lankan apparel industry has positioned itself as an ethical sourcing destination. The apparel sector has thus taken great strides to ensure that the built environment and landscapes of factories adhere and aspire to the health and safety standards required of them. Some factories set the industrial standard not just for Sri Lanka, but also for South Asia and the world—and in this regard, surpass industrial expectations by leaps and bounds (O'Leary, 2009).

Notwithstanding these laudable efforts, worker health in the industry is not without blemish. Attanapola (2004) explored the health status of women workers in the largest Free Trade Zone (FTZ) in Sri Lanka through qualitative fieldwork and life histories. She points to the health impacts of changing gender roles and practices, which include muscular–skeletal disorders and recurrent headaches, noting how workers normalize illness and poor health—which constrains their ability to seek appropriate medical treatment (2004, p. 2307).[3] Similarly, Hewamanne's (2008) careful analysis of factory life in Sri Lanka points to the ways in which the medical care offered within the workplace is deployed as an instrument of 'disciplining agents who control 'unnecessary' disruptions to the assembly-line work' (2008, p. 115; also Lynch 2007). Because workers are under the watchful eye of the penalizing role of medical power within factory settings, illness gets normalized and working while ill is commonplace. More importantly, her work hints at how certain OHS standards are neglected either because of worker discomfort or management leniency. For instance, when workers are using toxic glues, they are unlikely to use protective covering because they perceive it as a hindrance to easy breathing. Management is equally at fault because it turns a blind eye (*ibid*, p. 54). Occupational hazards are potentially created not necessarily through wilful neglect but also through the ways in which workers and management prioritize health and safety issues. Even though there is a commitment backed up with initiatives set in place by the Sri Lankan apparel industry, the need to pay attention to persisting aberrations is evident. These gaps present an opportunity to better understand what is at stake in the disjuncture between global OHS discourses and local practices—and the consequent implications for labour conditions, rights, and agency. These interventions also highlight how these efforts cannot be separated from inequities embedded in the global economy and macro processes of dominance and subordination.

12.3 Fieldwork in a Sri Lankan setting

The research for this article springs from a 3-year Economic and Social Research Council (ESRC grant number 0161-25-0181) project on how labour responds to ethical trading codes at sites of production. Initial fieldwork for the research included interviewing 25 senior and mid-ranking managers drawn from buying offices and producers in the apparel trade of Sri Lanka (Ruwanpura and Wrigley, 2011). These initial interviews lead to serendipitous connections, and two senior factory managers expressed willingness to having us conduct an extended ethnography in

---

[3] Attanapola's fieldwork settings include both apparel and non-apparel industries within the FTZ and she does not distinguish between the type of health problems in the two sectors.

their factory. Since global multi-stakeholder initiatives have been critical of their lack of openness to labour rights organizations, they reasoned that being open to a seemingly trustworthy and independent researcher would work to their benefit. Their only request was that I maintain anonymity of the suppliers' names and details.

The two factories I was based at produced apparel for the export markets, primarily in the United Kingdom and the United States, with the variety of garments made ranging from lingerie to outerwear. Their buyers included high street brands, such as Marks & Spencer, Debenhams, BHS, Tesco, American Eagle, George, and Matalan, as well as more exclusive retailers like Eddie Bauer, Calvin Klein, Tommy Hilfiger, Levi Strauss, and Lily Pulitzer. Given this retail clientele, both factories were regularly audited by local commercial auditing bodies such as the Ethical Trading Initiative (ETI), Fair Labour Association (FLA), Worldwide Responsible Accredited Production (WRAP), or retailer-commissioned auditors.

This paper is based on seven-and-a-half months of fieldwork between early August 2009 and end February 2010. During this time, I conducted participant observation and in-depth interviews with 60 factory workers at these two factories. The factories employed 1,500 and 800 workers, respectively, hence relatively large production facilities. In order to acquaint and familiarize myself with the workers, I visited the two factories daily. Prior to this, a Research Assistant who came on board at the start of April 2009 was embedded at the two research sites to create an enabling context for long-term (2 years) interactions with workers. Since both of us were women and were of a similar age to the bulk of women workers, who were in their 20s or 30s, and were proficient in the vernacular, after 2–3 weeks of routine visits we were able to break the ice and build an excellent rapport.[4] We were always aware that our class location and positioning was different. However, as a feminist scholar in the manner of Lynch (2007), I 'was attentive to the myriad power dynamics within the factories of supervisors, workers and managers, and between myself and all of them' (2007, p. 15). My positionality meant that I negotiated the data gathering conscientiously and delicately.

Moreover, once I had developed a particular rapport and familiarity with workers, alongside my regular placement at the two factories, I also did one- or two-day visits to a range of other factories in the apparel sector. These visits were to medium- and large-sized factories producing for both high- and low-end retailers,

---

[4] Initially, the workers were suspicious, cautious, or curious about our presence and would inquire whether we were working for the buyers or auditors. However, these concerns were soon assuaged because we visited the factories daily for several weeks, which would never happen in the case of auditors or buyers. The eventual friendships that were built with workers have led the researchers to keep in touch with a good number of workers after the research was completed.

which offered me an informed sense of the conditions and practices at factories across the country.

My time at the two factories meant the opportunity to observe and sometimes participate in the daily working realities of factory life. Using participant-observation data, I can also speak to changes and events over a period of time. The dissonance between the purported goals and practices of OHS are unlikely to be captured through management and worker interviews unless a catastrophic crisis has occurred (Brown, 2011; Miller, 2011). Hence, thick description helps illustrate the everyday factory setting in the realm of OHS. This is supplemented by accounts given by workers to consolidate the multiple, seemingly incongruous ways in which workers perceive and negotiate occupational hazards.

12.4   Compliant factories of Sri Lanka

Against a backdrop of exporting to the global market as an 'ethical' supplier, adherence to ethical codes includes providing workers with a working environment that is safe and hygienic. All managers noted the many accomplishments the Sri Lankan industry has made in this regard (Ruwanpura and Wrigley, 2011), and constant improvements remain an aspiration of local management. While each corporate or multi-stake initiative has its own points of emphasis and orientation, the ETI base code suggests that safe working places are a priority for clothing retailers. By instituting these measures, supplier factories are supposed to protect worker welfare. The factories in this study, likewise, had taken the necessary steps to create visibly pleasant and purpose-built plants, paying attention to health and safety requirements. The allocation of outdoor space for gathering in case of a fire, fire extinguishers allocated at appropriate locations, fire exits, ample glass windows, skylights and doors for proper light, air circulation and ventilation, air-conditioning, clean and sufficient toilet facilities, and needle rooms are provisions provided to create a safe working environment. All workers are given training in health and safety during their induction period, usually lasting between 2–3 weeks.[5]

Management at both plants claim to record all minor and major incidents that take place, because it offers auditors a paper trail to follow when conducting

---

[5] While both factories I was based at offered the necessary health and safety training to new workers during their training period, there was variation in the manner in which repeated training for assigned workers took place. There was diligence on the part of one factory about offering the repeated training to workers *in situ*, while at the other the recurrence of health and safety training to current workers was undertaken via select OHS worker representatives—who in turn were expected to apprise their colleagues of any new knowledge learned.

inspections.[6] In factory X, this recording takes place through the medical centre, with three nurses—two women and one man—held responsible for noting injuries, recurrent ailments, or ill-health. A medical doctor also visits weekly to meet workers who have enduring health issues. Workers see the medical practitioners through appointments, although urgent incidents are seen the same day. The records kept serve as part of the audit trail. Additionally, there is an in-house counsellor whom workers can access routinely, with both personal and health-related problems that affect their ability and capacity to work.[7]

Factory Y went about this audit-driven promotion of a safe working environment differently. Every production line is placed with a First-Aid Cross with dates of the month, which are colour coded—green for no incident, orange for a minor incident, and red for a major incident—on a daily basis by the line supervisor or the health and welfare worker representative for the production zone. These First-Aid Crosses are then filed away for inspection and further interrogation during appraisals; the mechanics of the auditing process with a paper trail are duly in place.

Procedural systems in place signal the commitment on part of factories to comply and uphold health and safety. But what of the ground-level realities? Which OHS measures get translated and implemented and how is this done? The next section offers accounts of two incidents that shed light on grounded dynamics shaped by socio-economic inequities, class relations, and gendered positions.

12.5   Unrecorded, but supported (just-about)

Karthika, a 39-year-old woman worker, had been in the trade for the past decade, and her employment experience spanned working abroad in the Middle East. She was unmarried—a rarity in her age group and cohort—and acutely aware of

---

[6] Elsewhere, I have documented the politics of paper trails and auditing mechanisms and what implies for worker welfare in a specific realm of OHS (Ruwanpura, 2014).

[7] In contrast to the workers' praise of the medical facilities, their attitude towards the counsellor was by and large ambivalent. Often they noted that they could not trust the counsellor because they felt she was the ears for the management; workers who had accessed her thought the support was of limited use because she simply narrates the management line rather than genuinely taking initiative to resolve their problems. My sense is that this rather suspicious view of the counsellor and her role has much to do with cultural factors, where personal problems and issues are dealt with speaking to extended kin and close friends rather than a stranger with whom there is no or limited rapport. Moreover, somewhat unfortunately, the counsellor usually limited herself to her office space—located in the canteen area next to the medical centre—with regular visits to the Human Resources division, and had limited interaction with workers. These factors combined together did not create an enabling context for the counsellor to develop a trusting relationship with workers.

all codes, another rarity. Her knowledge stemmed from having a niece who had conducted a pilot audit for a local organization, as well as partly from the fact that she had been working in the sector for a decade. Her role on the line was that of a jumper; namely, a multi-skilled worker who is called upon to attend to diverse tasks, depending upon the needs of the line. Because of this, at no time did I see her on the same line, operation, or task for more than a week; she was constantly moving around—similar to other jumpers. All jumpers had the necessary training for various activities during the production process, positioning them at a higher pay scale, and position in the ladder than workers doing single-task operations. Some of these skills were obtained on the job through years of work. Other tasks—using the snap-button attach, button attach, buttonhole, keyhole, and rivet attach machines—required formal training and a licensed certificate to carry them out.

I got to know *Karthika* during my initial days at Factory Y. She hailed me during my many rounds of ambling along the lines and started talking to me, inquiring about my presence there, the nature of the research, and so forth. While she is someone I had initially wanted to conduct a semi-structured interview with during my fieldwork, for one reason or the other this never happened. This, however, did not prevent me having lengthy conversations with *Karthika* both inside and outside the factory setting.

One day in early October 2009, my research assistant (RA) called to inform me that *Karthika* had been taken to hospital because of a workplace injury. She let me know that her finger had been badly injured and because her bleeding had not stopped they had taken her to the local state hospital. I was spending the day at Factory X and was heading to Factory Y,[8] where the incident had taken place, the next day. I suggested to the RA that she touch base with *Karthika* and make arrangements to visit her in hospital.

The next day, when I visited Factory Y, I was curious to see what arrangements were made to record the incident in the colour-coded First Aid Cross diagrams. This ought to have been a red-coloured event. I sought out the line that *Karthika* had been working on the day the injury had happened. Because she is a jumper, it took some investigation. Once I located it, her colleagues narrated how the injury had taken place. Because operating the snap-button machine is deemed risky they stressed how many, although not all, had undergone the necessary training. They also pointed out how having their nails chipped was a fairly typical occurrence, which they did not even report to the line supervisor, and after a quick trip to the medical centre to get a plaster around their nail, it was back to work again. However,

---

[8] The distance between the two factories was approximately 17 km and while I was staying near Factory Y, which was about a 20-minute walk, commuting to Factory X required driving to the place as it was about a 30-minute drive through pot-holed roads of rural Sri Lanka.

they said that *Karthika's* injury was more serious, as her nail had got removed and the bleeding did not stop even after she was taken to the medical centre. Her friend, who had accompanied her to the medical centre, said that by the time they arrived *Karthika* had felt terribly weak and her bleeding was incessant. The nurses, in the absence of a full-time doctor, had informed the Human Resources office that she needed to go to the hospital. The HR office had transported *Karthika* to the hospital, to which a nurse and a junior HR manager accompanied her. They admitted her into the hospital, ensured that she secured a bed, got her lunch, informed her family, and then left her in the care of the hospital medical staff.[9]

The HR office's involvement in taking all of these steps to ensure that *Karthika* was appropriately cared for medically might lead one to believe that Factory Y also followed procedures for recording the event. After my conversations with *Karthika's* workmates, I looked around for the First-Aid Cross; it was hanging in its usual place on the line. There was, however, no red marking; for that matter was not even an orange marking on the First-Aid Cross—just the low-level green marking. This was perplexing, given the management's active role in responding to the incident. When I asked the other workers on the line, some of them said 'May be the Production Floor manager will make a note of it later on', while another said

'Sister, they never make note of such accidents. If they think they are at fault, they will offer all the medical attention. Otherwise, they will get us to see the nurse, she will treat the wound, and they will put a plaster on our finger. Back to work again! These incidents never get recorded. You can always walk this way for the next few days and see if the marking on the First-Aid Cross has changed'.

True to the word of these workers, no recording of the accident was ever made in the First-Aid Cross put in place for this purpose. Moreover, *Karthika* mentioned that when she returned from 3 weeks of medical leave on the recommendation of the hospital, she had been informed by the Human Resources Department that she would not be entitled to paid medical leave and this period would be deemed no-pay leave. She sought informal legal advice and even though she found out that she was legally permitted to receive paid medical leave, she told me 'There is no point talking to them, x, they will not heed. Unless I leave the job, there is not much point asking'.

Karthika's experience is not a one-off and an unusual incident. Since that time, two male workers were also injured while using the snap-button machines. Although their injuries were less severe, they had taken 14 days medical leave. In these cases too, the factory had given reduced-pay leave: a mere 4 days of paid leave.

---

[9] While *Karthika* was still in hospital, she narrated to me how the management took care of her at the factory and hospital after the accident.

The two injured men were really upset about this outcome. Their concern was not only a loss of income but also that it meant disqualification for tri-annual bonuses that are determined by their absence record.[10] In this way, the management used socio-economic vulnerabilities and power differentials to manipulate workers into deciding either to return to work sooner than advised by medical professionals or to sacrifice their pay, incentives, and/or bonuses.

Brooks (2010) notes the lack of compensation for workplace injuries in a Sino-owned apparel sector of Zambia as '... illegal and inhumane actions undertaken to ensure profits would not be depleted' (2010, p. 125). Aside from the cost savings from such a human resource policy, I contend that with regards to ethical codes, the HR department also doubly ensures that there is no paper trial of an extended leave period that may look dubious to auditors and signal possible workplace accidents. It thus reduces the likelihood of 'prying' and cross-examination by auditors. The lack of offering paid medical leave is contrary to the spirit and letter of Sri Lankan law with regard to mishaps in work environments. Yet the management is absolved from further scrutiny because 'care' has been shown to the workers. Performing to a script gets inflected with endeavours 'to create a work environment that [is] intensely personal, paternalistic ... and localized' (Lynch, 2007, p. 206). Thus, management behaviour is continually scripted with limited space for labour to respond or resist these encroachments. Under the guise of the organizational fix of ethical governance, management is then not without shrewd armoury that continually finds ways to constrain the welfare of workers when it affects their profit margins— and hence the suppression of labour agency (Carswell and De Neve, 2013; Harvey, 2011). This cache of management tactics was not limited to extraordinary moments of workplace accidents; the everyday labour process was also subject to similar constraints on labour agency, as the account below shows. While it shows that changes sometimes come about accidently, it also demonstrates that workers' efforts to make their concerns heard at times yield unanticipated consequences.

12.6 From 'Best' practice to debatable change

The recurrent image conjured up in our imagination about apparel sector workers is of young, single, women workers between 17–25 years toiling away as machine

---

[10] More recently, the factory has invested in three new snap button machines with finger guards, where the button is fed into the machine automatically via a button box; all the worker has to do is to feed buttons into the box. Three snap button machines with finger guards in a factory employing approximately 1,500 workers and about 22 production lines is not a remarkable shift—especially as most lines continue to use the older snap-button machines with health risks to workers.

operators. It is a symbol that is in no small part reproduced through the existing academic literature, and in particular to feminist contributions that honed in on young women workers and their lives (Elson and Pearson, 1981; Hale and Wills, 2005). Rarely do we consider, hear, or think about women workers in the apparel sector who are at different stages of the life cycle and how that affects their capacity to carry out machine work. Indeed Humphries (2011) notes how we need to focus on exceptional moments, since they reveal as much about capitalism as does the norm.

When I began visiting Factory X, one thing I noticed was that there were a number of visibly pregnant workers on the production floor. They were, however, not working on the machines; they tended to assist the machine operators with numerous tasks, which ranged from trimming and cutting to undoing the damage in stitched clothing items. Coined 'helpers', they often were found seated next to a machine operator, or as a group of workers undoing a defect in a garment. The assistant production managers, together with the line supervisors, decided which tasks workers were assigned to and to balance the line according to the targets set for the day and week.

I befriended a number of pregnant women at Factory X—whose ages ranged from 22 to 34 years. For some women this was their first pregnancy, while for others it was not. Almost all of them unanimously spoke highly of the practices in place at the factory for protecting their welfare as pregnant women. They appreciated the less strenuous work they were assigned to do as well as the mid-morning and mid-afternoon breaks of about 30 minutes, which included toilet usage, and not having to do night shifts or overtime at night. Additionally, during the first year after their babies were born, they were entitled to 2 hours of nursing time after their return to work. *Nitya*, a 34-year-old woman expecting her second child, had been working at Factory X for about 8 years. According to her, 'They have always looked after pregnant women workers well and it is much better than other factories that we hear about. From the moment we inform them that we are pregnant, they take us off operating the machines on the production floor. I think this practice came through the previous British management policies and practices—they had the interest of the worker at heart. The current management simply follows these rules. I wouldn't have worked here for so long if I felt that my health and safety was at risk when I was pregnant—and last time, I worked through my pregnancy right until the time of delivery. I plan doing the same this time too'. *Nitya* was not alone in commending these practices, as similar sentiments were echoed by many other workers too.

They were, however, also quick to point out that despite some positive practices, the factory was less than diligent about giving them the full maternity leave time that they were entitled to. Indeed, some of our conversations revolved around them asking me to clarify the laws on it. *Chandrika*, a 31-year-old expecting her (unplanned) third child, once asked me, '*Aney mey* (here, please) will you find out for us what maternity leave policies and leave are applicable to us? They tell us different things about our entitlements when it comes to maternity leave. If you can find out for us, it will be a great help—some of us can then speak with the management directly about this'. Once I researched this and gave *Chandrika* the information, it became apparent that the state's policy maintaining divergent thresholds of maternity leave policies for different groups of workers leads to confusion and uncertainty amongst workers as to their entitlements. The Factory Ordinance Act of 1956 under the Wages Board covers pregnant women workers in the manufacturing sector by offering them 12 weeks (84 days) of maternity leave, inclusive of Saturdays, Sundays and other public, bank and mercantile holidays. Amendments introduced in 1985 via the Maternity Benefits Ordinance provide 2 hours of milk time per day afterwards, until the child is a year old, unless on-site crèche facilities are provided—in which case a 30-minute feeding time is offered. By contrast, service sector workers, covered by the Shop and Office Act, and public sector workers, covered by the Public Sector Workers Act, have more generous maternity leave policies (see also Brooks, 2010).[11]

Despite pregnant women workers' unease with unfair maternity laws, reflecting the gendered and class position of apparel labourers, they appreciated the factory policy of taking them off heavy machinery work protected their long-term health and safety. Conversely, it meant taking home lower wages, because they were no longer eligible for productivity incentive payments associated with operators.[12] Lack of income security is a very real pressure for these women and their families. A minority of pregnant women mentioned that they wished they had the option to choose whether to work as operators or take on the less laborious task of being a helper. *Inari* was a 24-year-old who had found out about her pregnancy around mid-September. We had begun to casually converse from the start of my fieldwork at Factory X and when one day I saw her seated as a helper, I was perplexed and

---

[11] The Shop and Office Act gives 84 working days of maternity leave, excluding Sundays and public, bank and mercantile holidays and with a half-day for each Saturday counting towards the maternity leave period. The Public Sector Workers Act is more generous giving 96 working days of maternity leave. Despite ILO interventions on the discriminatory nature of different thresholds for maternity laws in Sri Lanka, the state has taken little initiative to make necessary amendments and meet international obligations on protecting all women workers alike.

[12] The lack of involvement in the production process for them means not getting target-based incentive payments as well as overtime wages for night shift work; during their pregnancy, this leads to a much lower wage packet and a reliance only on their basic pay. More often than not, when this results in nearly a one-third decline of their average monthly pay packet, the dent on their income and household security becomes an obvious concern.

inquired why she was doing a different task that day. She shared her news about her pregnancy and then went onto say 'I know it is for the best for me to do this work and not be at the machines. But sometimes, I think it would be good for us if the managers and supervisors gave us the chance to decide whether we felt fit to undertake operating tasks or if we should become helpers. We have financial pressures too, which we have to think about. If the management was aware and let us decide, then we have the choice—the way it is now we have to undergo financial stresses. I am saying this, even though I know it is best for me and my baby (and she touches her belly area) to be a helper'.

Since some pregnant women shared sentiments similar to *Inari*, a few women were hopeful that a request could be taken to the Worker Council. Their proposal to management was to give workers an option to be either machine operators or helpers during pregnancy. This was not the dominant view; yet, it was a perspective and a critical one given their economic insecurities. While it was unclear whether this proposal ever made it to the Worker Council (and via this to the management), before *Inari* shared her news with me, a '*case*' occurred (in the language of the factory setting) that ultimately signalled the changes that took place.

I walked into the canteen around mid-morning looking for a worker. Coincidently, a number of pregnant workers were swiftly walking out of the canteen, when a few of them who I was well acquainted with said 'Aiyo, miss ... can't stop to chat with you. A case has happened. We will let you know later what happened'. I was intrigued, but because they seemed frazzled I didn't broach the subject with them on the floor. That evening I spoke with *Chandrika*, who had previously requested that I make necessary inquiries about their legal entitlements to maternity leave. Her narrative, which was subsequently confirmed by a number of other pregnant workers, is noted below. Other workers talked about the incident for a number of days, because they were bitterly disappointed and annoyed by it.

A group of pregnant women workers had been taking their mid-morning rest when the HR manager had walked in. When he saw them having tea in a near-empty canteen, he scolded them for loitering about the canteen without being on the production floor. They were upset and scared by the unexpected scolding, because they were on their 30-minute tiffin break and had not exceeded the stipulated time. Because they were upset, a few of them mentioned that they were going to complain to the HR office and a put a complaint in the suggestion box about the HR manager's lack of consideration. This episode suggests that gender relations coupled with social hierarchies enabled the manager to rebuke workers erroneously without consequence. As a pregnant worker said to me, 'He is a man. He may not know what it is like to walk around with a child in the stomach when you are eight months pregnant. We don't walk, we waddle—and we do everything slower than is normal. Surely, he must have noticed this with his wife?' Their grievance and annoyance made its way to the HR office, because the next day a meeting was summoned by the counsellor to convey the HR manager's apologies to the pregnant workers. It had been an irrational and thoughtless moment of rebuke. However, he was under the impression that they were aware of new rules that pregnant workers could only spend 15 minutes in the canteen during their tiffin with the remaining 5 minutes to be used for using the toilets and drinking water. A new rule with a shorter and more regimented rest period was thus introduced in a rather sloppy and oblique fashion.

This alteration of factory rules with regard to pregnant workers was the first of a series of steps in which their health and safety protections were gradually eroded. By the start of January 2010, the HR office decided that newly pregnant workers were to continue their work as machine operators in the first two trimesters. They could request to work as helpers during this time; however, the default position was to continue as operators until their pregnancy was more advanced. From the seventh month onwards, pregnant workers were required to work as helpers to protect the health of both mother and baby. When I queried about the rationale for the shift of policy from the HR office, they mentioned that this was a response to complaints by pregnant workers because of the lower monthly salary for helpers. Because they realized the financial stresses these working women underwent and the request had come from the pregnant workers, they felt that this was a correct decision to make. They also quickly pointed out that the pregnant workers could always opt to work as helpers if they wanted to, from the beginning of their pregnancy, but this would no longer be the default position.

Floor-level managers mentioned that the decision was not merely a response to the request made by some pregnant workers; it also coincided with production pressures and meeting targets. *Ekanath*, a floor-level manager, acknowledged that there could be health risks associated with pregnant operators and that their challenge was to weigh this against the production targets. In this way, a request by a segment of pregnant women workers coincided with increased production pressures, resulting in a change of internal policy without due consideration for factory social hierarchies (De Neve, 2001).

By the time I left Sri Lanka after completing my *in situ* fieldwork, the policy had changed again. Any woman worker who became pregnant would continue as an operator unless they elected not to. Amongst the workers I knew, two recently pregnant young women opted for different options against this new policy. *Imani*, is a 25-year-old who found that she had conceived in early February, while *Sayuri*, a 22-year-old had found out about her pregnancy in January. While *Sayuri* opted to work as a helper and communicated her preference for this to the management, *Imani* made the decision to leave her job because she did not think that it would be good for her to be working as a machine operator while pregnant. When I mentioned to her that she could switch to a helper position, she quipped, 'That is what they say, miss', implying that she did not quite trust their word. I asked *Sayuri* if she thought her peers would feel comfortable requesting to be a helper like she did. She replied, 'Most often probably not, miss. Not all of us feel comfortable going to the HR to talking to them openly and making requests; added to that Mr T comes across as quite strict. I made the request because my midwife at the clinic thought that I would be taking unnecessary risks during my pregnancy if I worked as an operator, especially because I'm thin and anaemic'. Their sentiments suggest that power dynamics between management and workers have made redundant offering 'choices' to pregnant workers, despite the fact that some pregnant workers had previously requested these options.

Is the newly instituted default position of continuing as operators likely to pose medium- to long-term health and safety risks to pregnant workers? Some pregnant workers acknowledged the likely health risks and yet recognized that it is because some pregnant workers had given undue emphasis to their economic pressures that the shift in human resource policy had taken place. Offering a choice to pregnant workers is likely to give management the credence on paper that attention is paid to both OHS and the economic imperatives of workers. However, the claim that pregnant workers could continue as operators without it impinging upon their health and welfare is medically debatable. It is medically acknowledged that pregnancy is not an illness but a condition where any woman can continue with her usual work routine so long as her physical state permits her to do so, but this medical advice presupposes that pregnant workers have the latitude to take necessary breaks. During an 8-hour shift pregnant workers ought to be given a break every hour for about 2–3 minutes to walk around, to relax their legs and muscles, use the toilet, and drink plenty of liquids.[13] As an operator on a line or module with set targets, any frequent disruption is unlikely to help the pregnant worker meet incentive targets or for a module to reach its daily and weekly production goals. Whether there was careful attention paid to these realities is unclear, in which case production targets for pregnant workers would have to be drastically reduced in recognition of their condition. Where pregnant women were

---

[13] According to the information I have obtained from medical doctors, a lack of such breaks is likely to cause numerous medical risks to the pregnant mother and the foetus, including the risks of IUGR (Intra-Uterine Growth Restriction). [My thanks to medical doctors Bhathiya Alagoda, Oliver Morris, and Eashika Knox for explaining the health risks associated with pregnancy and working on sedentary repetitive tasks without regular work stoppages and rest.]

aware of the health risks posed by undertaking repeated machinery tasks, whether they would always navigate a power-laden terrain to request for the non-default option to work as a helper is uncertain. What is clear, however, is that there was a gradual shift away from practices that promoted the health of pregnant workers to a less than expedient human resource management decision that is likely to go against the health of pregnant workers. The claim that this change was a response to workers' complaints about the economic hardship of switching to a helper position ignores other possible ways of addressing the problem, such as equalizing pay for pregnant helpers.[14] Deploying a discourse of 'choices' also ignores the sociality of the workplace politics, through which gendered hierarchies and authority thwart workers' actual perceptions of their options (De Neve, 2001; Mezzadri, 2012).

12.7 Global efforts, local labour practices

The ways in which global efforts take on a life of their own as they journey worldwide across uneven development spaces and through local settings in one area of ethical codes, i.e., health and safety, is the focus of this research. By investigating shop floor health and safety practices, this paper shows how global governance regimes take on situated meanings in the context of apparel production in Sri Lanka. O'Rourke (2001) already draws our attention to situations in which major labour problems in the realm of health and safety hazards occur and calls for gathering detailed information to build alternative systems. Perhaps as a partial response to this challenge, the Sri Lankan apparel industry has taken laudable steps to meet OHS requirements. However, the fine-tuned ways in which the global and local interact through actually existing compliance practices to shape labour agency are often left out of the analysis. In other words, exploring global–local connections helps unpack the ways in which the global political economy has a bearing on labour agency (Carswell and De Neve, 2013; Miller, 2011; Wills, 1999). This paper shows that the flux engendered by global

---

[14] This shift when contextualized against the backdrop of labour practices at other apparel sector factories in Sri Lanka is no different from other factories. In Factory Y, for instance, pregnant workers were expected to work as operators throughout pregnancy unless they had a medical note advising against such work. Many of the other factories I visited stated that they consider pregnancy part of a 'natural cycle' for women workers and not as an illness as such and therefore, the expectation was that they continue as operators unless they (the workers) requested for lighter work. Pregnant workers, however, could be distinguished from their cohort because they either wore an arm band or a different coloured scarf denoting their pregnant condition—so that the line supervisors, production assistants, or managers could be visually informed. The exception was a large-scale factory, considered a leader in the trade for compliance and a commitment to worker welfare, which got pregnant workers to only do light work throughout their pregnancy.

capitalisms' governance regimes shape labour agency within the factory floor in messy, complex ways. Pregnant workers collectively raised concerns to management and had unexpected success, but they also found that their disquiet does not necessarily yield desired results. Injured workers get the medical care and attention they need, but they are not able to collect the unpaid leave for recuperation that they are entitled to and their injuries are not adequately recorded for auditing purposes. Existing management–labour power dynamics, gender relations, and social hierarchies in the workplace suggest that the spaces of rupture in the implementation of ethical codes are continuously constrained by wider social and material relations, in this case the increasing pressures on managers to meet production targets (Brooks, 2010; De Neve, 2001; Mezzadri, 2012). Adopting an ethnographic approach to the study of health and safety allows us to recognize that codes are 'always provisional – never stable, and never fixed' and as 'social products ... their meaning becomes realized in specific *places*' (Prentice, 2010, p. 10). This realization of ethical trading codes, however, continues to be informed by considerations of political economy and global capitalism. As processes they are not simply unstable and continuously in flux but also implicated in social hierarchies and cultural mores of places that constrain labour agency.

The paper trail processes and the mechanisms for social auditing with regards to health and safety standards in both factories are well in place with sound articulation of intentions—and sometimes even best practices. Yet the ways in which local realities shape and transform practical responses are not merely shaped by production imperatives and the favourable social and human development context of Sri Lanka; they are also shaped by economic inequities, gender relations, and social hierarchies at the workplace (Brooks, 2010; De Neve, 2001; Mezzadri, 2012; Prentice, 2010). Workers who had workplace injuries were offered the necessary care, support, and were even given 'compassionate' (unpaid) extended leave (see also Lynch, 2007); there was, however, neither a trace of the wounds the workers suffered nor were they offered compensated medical leave. Moral tropes of caring factory employers are then freely used as a distinguishing marker of an ethically sourced destination (Perry et al., 2014). Humphries (2010) notes how 'violence [was] less widespread in factories and workshops where other mechanisms of control were available' in an emergent industrial Britain (2010, p. 245). Similar sentiments are echoed for contemporary factory life in Sri Lanka (Gunawardana, 2007; Hewamanne, 2008; Lynch, 2007). Similarly, through a simple diktat, the HR manager changes protective measures in place to care for pregnant workers with regards to their rest periods within a day. This becomes an incipient step in transforming health and safety provisions for pregnant workers. Within months the manager proceeds to 'respond' to noises from a group of pregnant women workers—thus apparently taking into account their economic hardship. Nonetheless, most labourers interpreted these adjustments as a regressive move against the health and safety concerns of pregnant women workers. Standards thus respond to the local realities of production pressures and economic imperatives, and yet such shifts ought not to prevent us from reading the local for its incongruities too. The HR staff point to the economic hardships of workers as the triggering factor that made them let pregnant workers continue as operators during the initial 6 months of pregnancy—a very 'local' concern, if one ignores the economic inequities and the lack of a living wage in the sector. Similarly, HR management neglects the social hierarchies and power dynamics, also local factors, which shape the capacity for pregnant workers to exercise their notional choice of continuing as a sewing operator or becoming a helper.

Workers initiate and are cognizant of their agency in relation to the multiple geographies intersecting with their working lives, whether it is local labour laws, global governance regimes, or social auditing methods. The material conditions and social relations within which they are embedded suggest that they may be resilient and even develop strategies of resistance, but it does not necessarily lead to a reworking of material inequalities which makes them seek out work in the apparel sector (see also Lynch, 2007). The absence of a living wage, freedom of association, and collective bargaining in the Sri Lankan apparel industry means that the capacity of workers to exercise their collective agency is continuously frustrated (Ruwanpura, 2012). Even as there are moments of rupture shedding light on multiple social relations and material conditions, they also reveal the asymmetries between labour and capital. Health and safety standards purport to create spaces for betterment as they navigate across uneven development spaces, yet workers' ability to benefit from them remain embedded in a politics of inequity, with implications for labour conditions and agency. Observing how contemporary discourse on global governance regimes matters to workers, the evidence is differentiated and patchy as to its success in making a sustained difference to worker welfare. It reminds us that too often tropes of worker empowerment and social justice via voluntary ethical codes remain business speak and are mobilized without the necessary traction (see also De Neve, 2009; Mezzadri, 2012; Wills, 1999, 2000). Using thick description illustrates how 'webs of significance' signalled through the adoption of ethical trade regimes also results in 'webs of power' that need disentangling (Geertz, 1993). Global governance regimes are then not only negotiable as forms of cultural political life, but also serve to legitimate global capitalism and lead to clever manipulation of inherent inconsistencies within codes for the hidden gain of global capitalism.

12.8   Conclusion: Hazardous endings?

The apparel sector in Sri Lanka is taking multiple steps to move into high value-added and upmarket production processes; one way it does this is by paying attention to the built environment and safety codes in these spaces. In this paper, I have attempted to uncover whether these shifts represent a palpable difference for labourers' health and safety. Even in the case of ethically compliant factories, the scrutiny afforded to what these ethical codes mean for labour agency remains an under-researched area. Wills (1999) makes the evident point that as old certainties vanish, it is important to highlight 'the interconnections of development in different parts of the world' where we do not lose sight of the political edge of our analysis (1999, p. 448). While ethical codes and global governance regimes have a two-decade long run in global production systems, the evidence is scanty—at best—that the agency of labour has found a more gratifying space within which to articulate its bargaining power.

De Neve (2009) notes that the politics of compliance leads to the 'consolidation of the power of standard-setting actors by facilitating the devolution of risks, uncertainty and responsibility to the weaker 'partners' in the chain' (2009, p. 71). In his work, he shows how this 'partnership' plays out between buyers and suppliers. My fieldwork shifts to another scale to show how labour negotiates the global governance terrain, highlighting that the power dynamics between capital and labour implicated in corporate codes need equal scrutiny too. The codes of reality that emerge in respect of health and safety illustrate that the cultural hegemony of corporate codes still continues to short change workers (Elling, 1989). Labour geographers point to how labour is a constitutive agent facilitating the spread, breadth, and accumulation of global capitalism (Castree, 2007; Herod, 2012). Yet to understand the ways in which labour agency shapes and is transformed in the process, it is also important to record the disjuncture between the rhetoric and practice of capital's latest armoury, global voluntary corporate codes. As ethical codes are deployed, the realities of labour practices at production sites suggest that to rely on an instrument without teeth is to also curtail the potential of labour's agency. This paper makes a modest attempt at pointing to these gaps in the domain of one code—health and safety standards. It shows that health and safety codes in practice are embedded socioculturally and travel across uneven capitalist production spaces, leading to irregular application, which has implications for labour practices, conditions, and agency.

References

Armbruster, Heidi. 2010. 'The Ethics of Taking Sides.' In *Taking Sides: Ethics, Politics and Fieldwork in Anthropology*, edited by Heidi Armbruster and Anna Laerke. Oxford: Berghahn Books.

Attanapola, Chamila. 2004. 'Changing Gender Roles and Health Impacts Among Female Workers in Export-Processing Industries in Sri Lanka.' *Soc Sci Med* 58 (11): 2301–312.

Barrientos, Stephanie and Sally Smith. 2007. 'Do Workers Benefit from Ethical Trade? Assessing Codes of Labour Practice in Global Production Systems.' *Third World Quarterly* 28 (4): 713–29.

Brooks, Andrew. 2010. 'Spinning and Weaving Discontent: Labour Relations and the Production of Meaning at Zambia-China Mulungishi Textiles.' *J Southern Afr Stud* 36 (1): 113–32.

Brown, Garrett. 2009. 'Genuine Worker Participation—An Indispensable Key to Effective Global OHS.' *New Solutions* 19 (3): 315–33.

———. 2011. 'Corporate Social Responsibility; What is it Good For? Factory Fires in Bangladesh: Again and Again and Again.' *Ind Safety Hygiene News* 45 (5): 34–5.

Carswell, Grace and Geert De Neve. 2013. 'Labouring for Global Markets: Conceptualizing Labour Agency in Global Production Networks.' *Geoforum* 44: 62–70.

Castree, Noel. 2007. 'Labour Geography: A Work in Progress.' *Int J Urban Reg Res* 31 (4): 853–62.

Clean Clothes Campaign. 2005. *Looking for a Quick Fix: How Weak Social Auditing is Keeping Workers in Sweatshops.* The Netherlands: CCC.

Day, Peter. 2010. 'Ready to Wear.' *In Business.* BBC Radio 4, January 21, 2010. Available at, http://www.bbc.co.uk/radio4/features/in-business/peter-days-comment/20100121/.

De Neve, Geert. 2001. 'Towards an Ethnography of the Workplace: Hierarchy, Authority and Sociability on the South Indian Textile Shop-Floor.' *South Asia Res* 21 (2): 133–60.

———. 2009. 'Power, Inequality and Corporate Social Responsibility: The Politics of Ethical Compliance in the South Indian Garment Industry.' *Econ Polit Weekly*, 44 (22): 63–71.

Elling, Ray H. 1989. 'The Political Economy of Workers' Health & Safety.' *Soc Sci Med* 28 (11): 1171–82.

Elson, Diane and Ruth Pearson. 1981. 'Nimble Fingers Make Cheap Workers: An Analysis of Women's Employment in Third World Export Manufacturing.' *Feminist Rev* 7 (Spring): 87–107.

Geertz, Clifford. 1993. 'Thick Description: Toward an Interpretive Theory of Culture.' In *The Interpretation of Cultures: Selected Essays,* edited by Clifford Geertz. New York: Fontana Press.

Gunawardana, Samanthi. 2007. 'Perseverance, Struggle and Organization in Sri Lanka's Export Processing Zones: 1978–2003.' In *Global Unions: Challenging Transnational Capital through Cross-Border Campaigns,* edited by Kate Bronfenbrenner. Ithaca: Cornell University Press.

Hale, Angela and Jane Wills. 2005. *Threads of Labour: Garment Industry Supply Chains from the Workers' Perspective.* Oxford: Blackwell Publishing.

Harvey, David. 2011. *The Enigma of Capital and the Crisis of Capitalism*. London: Profile Books.

Herod, Andrew. 2012. 'Labour Geography: Where Have We Been? Where Should We Go? In *Missing Links in Labour Geographies*, edited by Hege Merete Knutsen, Ann Cecilie Bergene and Sylvi B. Endesen. Farnham: Ashgate.

Hewamanne, Sandya. 2008. *Stitching Identities in a Free Trade Zone: Gender and Politics in Sri Lanka*. Philadelphia: University of Pennsylvania Press.

Humphries, Jane. 2010. *Childhood and Child Labour in the British Industrial Revolution*. Cambridge: Cambridge University Press.

Karp, Jonathan. 1999. 'Sri Lanka Keeps Victoria's Secret: Island Workers Produce Panties in Cool Comfort.' *Wall Street J.* 13 (July): B1, B4.

Lynch, Caitrin. 2007. *Juki Girls, Good Girls: Gender and Cultural Politics in Sri Lanka's Global Garment Industry*. Ithaca: Cornell University Press.

Mezzadri, Alessandra. 2012. 'Reflections on Global and Labour Standards in the Indian Garment Industry: Codes of Conduct versus 'Codes of Practice' Imposed by the Firm.' *Glob Lab J* 3 (1): 40–62.

Miller, Doug. 2009. 'Neil Kearney Obituary—Inspirational Trade Union Leader with International Influence.' *The Guardian*, November 26. Available at, http://www.guardian.co.uk/politics/2009/nov/26/neil-kearney-obituary.

———. 2011. 'Global Social Relations and Corporate Social Responsibility in Outsourced Apparel Supply Chains: The Inditex Global Framework.' In *Shaping Global Industrial Relations: The Impact of Cross Border Social Dialogue and Agreements*, edited by Konstantinos Papadakis. Geneva: ILO/Palgrave.

———. 2012. *Last Nightshift in Savar: The Story of the Spectrum Sweater Factory Collapse*. London: McNidder & Grace.

O'Leary, Michael. 2009. 'Responsible Garment Management.' *Serendib*. (2009 November–December): 68–70.

O'Rourke, Dara. 2000. *Monitoring the Monitors: A Critique of PWC Labour Monitoring*. Unpublished Working Paper.

———. 2001. 'Sweatshops 101: Lessons in Monitoring Apparel Production around the World.' *Dollars and Sense: The Magazine of Economic Justice* September/October.

Perry, Patsy, Steve Wood and James Fernie. 2014. 'Corporate Social Responsibility in Garment Sourcing Networks: Management Perspectives on Ethical Trade in Sri Lanka.' *J Busi Ethics*. doi: 10.1007/s10551-014-2252-2.

Prentice, Rebecca. 2010. 'Ethnographic Approaches to Health and Development Research: The Contributions of Anthropology.' In *The SAGE Handbook of Qualitative Methods in Health Research*, edited by Ivy Bourgeault, Robert Dingwall and Ray de Vries. London: Sage.

Ruwanpura, Kanchana N. 2014. 'Metal Free Factories: Straddling Worker Rights and Consumer Safety?' *Geoforum* 51(January): 224–32.

———. 2012. 'Ethical Codes: Reality and Rhetoric—A Study of Sri Lanka's Apparel Sector.' *Working Paper*. University of Southampton.

Ruwanpura, Kanchana N., and Neil Wrigley. 2011. 'The Costs of Compliance? Views of Sri Lankan Apparel Manufacturers in times of Global Economic Crises.' *J Econ Geogr* 11 (6): 1031–49.

Sluiter, Liesbeth. 2009. *Clean Clothes: A Global Movement to End Sweatshops.* London: Pluto Press.

Wills, Jane. 1999. 'Political Economy I: Global Crisis, Learning and Labour.' *Progr Hum Geogr* 23: 443–51.

———. 2000. 'Political Economy II: The Politics and Geography of Capitalism.' *Prog Hum Geogr* 24: 641–52.

13

Diffusing Labour Standards Down and Beyond the Value Chain

Lessons from the Mewat Experiment

Meenu Tewari[1]

'Minimizing the role of the middlemen—that is actually the whole Mewat model' (Gap DGP Interview, 2011).

13.1 Introduction

In the early hours of a bright Sunday morning on the 25th of November 2012, an unexpected ripple of shock spread through a gathering of academics, policy makers, and social activists who had gathered in Dhaka, Bangladesh to discuss inclusive development in global value chains—such as those in the clothing industry that have helped generate $20 billion annually in foreign exchange for Bangladesh from garment exports to major markets such as the US and the EU. The shock was caused by the disturbing news that a horrific fire had broken out in a garment factory outside Dhaka, and over 120 workers, mostly women, were feared dead. A few hours later, news channels confirmed the fire and the official number of lives lost was placed at 112, the majority of them women.

The investigations that followed revealed huge safety gaps at the factory and pointed to a number of probable causes for the conflagration—missing fire safety certification, a missing external fire exit, no fire extinguishers, illegal construction of six extra floors on top of a building that had structural clearance for only three, poor circulation, unsafe wiring, cramped working conditions, doorways that were locked or blocked with piles

[1] Funding from the Capturing the Gains Project of the University of Manchester for the field work on which this paper is based is gratefully acknowledged. Rachel Alexander and Manjeeta Singh provided valuable research assistance. I thank Stephanie Barrientos for introducing me to the Gap official involved in the project. I am grateful to all participants in interviews and focus groups for their insights and time. All errors of fact and interpretation are my responsibility. The names of interviewees have been abbreviated at their request.

of clothing and most egregiously, coercion—the supervisors had paid no heed to the fire alarm, calling it a test and ordering the women who tried to leave the 5th floor (where the fire first broke out) back to their workstations even as they complained of the smell of smoke and suffocation (Yardley, 2012, Manik and Yardley, 2012).

Contrary to what these poor working conditions might suggest, Tazreen Fashions, the factory where the fire broke out, was not a small sweatshop churning out cheap clothing for non-descript low-end local markets. This factory of 1400 workers was a supplier to some of the world's most powerful brands—Walmart and Sears, among others—each of which had their own well-established, well-publicized, and third-party-audited codes of conduct. Yet, the presence of these codes and elaborate protocols of inspection had failed to ensure safer working conditions that could have prevented the blaze. Why did the company codes not filter down to Tazreen? Even as Walmart denied any direct dealings with the company, subcontractors of at least three of Walmart's suppliers were getting portions of their orders produced at Tazreen (Greenhouse, 2012): Walmart contracted out to first-tier suppliers, who in turn subcontracted out portions of their orders to smaller suppliers, who in turn subcontracted to suppliers like Tazreen.

On the face of it, the presence of cascading layers of contractual ties among multiple actors across the supply chain appeared to have disrupted the chain of accountability between the final buyer and the supplier at the base of its own chain. Even when the company's codes required that all its orders be executed by company-approved suppliers in accordance with specified standards governing quality, labour conditions, and safety regulations meant to prevent just such outcomes; informal processes at the bottom of the chain remained invisible. The costs of this broken down chain of accountability were evident in even starker proportions in April 2013, just months after the Tazreen fire, when Rana Plaza, an eight-storey building collapsed in Greater Dhaka with 3,500 workers inside, 1,100 of whom lost their lives (Manik and Yardley, 2013; Burke, 2014; O'Connor, 2014).

These examples are part of a mounting body of evidence on the growing limits of private governance and their adequacy in regulating working conditions in a world of global value chains. After nearly two decades of the rise and dominance of private voluntary regulation (in its myriad forms), there is fresh debate about their effectiveness (Locke, 2008, 2013). Indeed, private regulation grew out of the need to reconcile the demands of an increasingly internationalized, multi-sited production system with the jurisdictional limitations of national labour laws in monitoring and regulating cross-border economic activity. But there are questions today about the ability of private self-regulation to reach the workers it is meant to target, or penetrate far enough down the chain to protect the most vulnerable workers such as those under coercive conditions at places like Tazreen (Nadvi, 2008); there are questions about the cherry-picking of benefits[2] and their piece-meal diffusion to subsets of workers, such as improved working conditions for some workers but not others[3] in complex production networks (Barrientos and Smith, 2007; Barrientos, 2008; Barrientos et al., 2011; Posthuma and Nathan, 2010), and concerns over the potential for widespread gaming of the system of inspections and monitoring by some companies and contractors (O'Rourke, 2002). At the same time, it is also true that *without* any private regulation and company codes of conduct, there would be many more Tazreens or Rana Plazas—given the weakness of public sector regulation, or at least their weak enforcement in many supplier countries. Therein lies the dilemma for the world of private governance: how to ensure a wider socialization of safe and improved working conditions that can reach further and deeper down the value chain, and even beyond it, in the face of intensified competition, tight lead times, low margins, relentless price pressures and the powerful search for low costs? What are the conditions under which economic gains to companies at the firm level can be combined with benefits to workers, within and beyond the firm?[4]

Finding ways to reconcile the interests of firms and workers to improve conditions of work for the most vulnerable workers is especially pressing today because new pressures on price in the current business environment appear to be eroding even those gains that private regulation has achieved since the 1990s. On the one hand, competition over stagnant demand in the post-recession era has intensified the squeeze on prices that was a result of the post-MFA consolidation within global supply chains in the mid-2000s. On the other hand, deepening consolidation within global aggregators such as Li & Fung who disperse production even more widely and opaquely to low cost sites, and the rise of new business models such as 'fast fashion', with its low margins and dramatically short turnaround times, is pushing competitors to further cut costs. Most notably these competitive pressures are leading to cuts in compliance budgets even in companies that were at the forefront of ethical trade, social responsibility, and innovation in compliance as reported by a former social accountability officer at a major US garment brand (LB interview, 2011). Together, these pressures have *increased*, rather than decreased incentives to outsource to multiple suppliers further down the value chain resulting

---

[2] For example, 'measurable standards' such as space between stations, number of toilets, light and space standards versus 'enabling rights' such as fair wages and benefits (Barrientos and Smith, 2007).

[3] Such as between full time, permanent workers versus contract workers on the same shop floor.

[4] These were some of the questions at the heart of the Capturing the Gains research collaboration anchored at Manchester University and Duke University, of which some of the research reported here, and in this volume, was a part.

in a large pool of contracts associated with labour that is precarious, contingent, and largely out of reach of private company codes of conduct. Evidence is thus building that firm-led initiatives are necessary, but not sufficient to link corporate growth with sustained social upgrading and improved labour conditions in the global economy.

It is in this context that some companies, buyers, labour advocates, unions, and segments of the state have begun to experiment with other models of regulation to supplement company-based approaches to private governance as well as national regulations. This experimentation is often triggered by incidents such as the Tazreen fire and Rana Plaza or individual public shaming of brands in the context of serious violations in their supply chains, such as the presence of child labour or trafficked labour, or by the squeeze on budgets and deepening competitive pressure. These new experiments are collaborative efforts, and often focus not only on the factory floor, but also beyond it. By focusing on the places and communities where workers live, the aim is to try and mitigate the risks of child labour, for example, or other violations in the labour catchment area itself. Examples include the work of corporations like IKEA in the carpet-making belt in North India, the work of independent unions (such as NTUI in India) and others (Tewari, 2010).

In this chapter, I examine the workings of one such effort that was led jointly by Gap Inc., and the government of India, in partnership with exporters, buyers, and key local allies to provide more transparent and broader-based protection to workers engaged in embroidery and handwork. This kind of work, which has traditionally been dominated by home-based workers, who are largely (but not exclusively) women, is mostly carried out in informal segments of the garment chain and has proven to be among the hardest to regulate. Beadwork and handcrafted embellishments that add significant value to high-end garments sold by upmarket brands across the world often represent some of the most unstable, low-paid, exploitative and precarious employment and is riven by problems of child labour (Mezzadari, 2011; Jeemol Unni and Scaria, 2009). Labouring behind walls of multiple middlemen and contractors, handworkers often have no idea whom the product they produce is ultimately meant for. Working informally and out of sight of both the state and final buyers, they have little recourse in the event of exploitation.

The Case: Between December 2008 and mid-2011, Gap Inc., together with the government of India's Ministry of Women and Child Development, and key partners— a major buying house, two exporters, and a local NGO—piloted a novel institutional arrangement in a desperately poor region, Mewat, located in Haryana, India that would eliminate middlemen and link local handworkers directly to markets. The women were trained by the factories that placed the orders and paid decent wages, under broad oversight of Gap and the government, which went straight to their bank accounts—accounts that the experiment's NGO partner, SPYM had helped organize over 15 years of work in the region. To eliminate the possibility of child labour, the women worked in a common work area in a community centre and crèche managed by the NGO partner, and in close proximity to where they lived. Within the first 6 months of the program, the women who participated in it had collectively earned Rs. 2 million, with individual women taking home between Rs. 1500 to Rs. 5000 per month. Many of the women were participating in the labour market and earning incomes for the first time. By the end of the first year, leadership structures had emerged among the women and they had taken charge of negotiating rates with the exporters, often rejecting work that fetched lower rates than they were willing to work for. The BBC ran a documentary on the program in 2010, it was written up in government documents as an innovation, featured prominently in Gap's annual reports, presentations, and website and showcased by a number of other labour-related organizations such as the ILO and the UNODC in their own annual reports and case documents. By 2011, there was talk of replicating the Mewat model in other states and even in other sectors—including agriculture (Government of India, VK interview, 2011). In this paper I analyse the initiative's origins, operations, and outcomes to draw institutional lessons from it for the prospects of diffusing labour standards across and beyond global value chains in ways that benefit both firms and workers.

The Mewat experiment is not the only novel program where global buyers and brands have linked handworkers directly with the market—Gap itself has a long history of working with SEWA, a trade union of self-employed women in India, to successfully source handwork in safe ways. What is novel and interesting in the Mewat model is the involvement of the *government* in co-producing workplace protections for informal workers in hitherto unregulated segments of the supply chain and linking them to export markets in partnership with brands, exporters, and civic actors. The return of the state in the diffusion of labour standards and protections to *less formal* segments of the labour market in export value chains in active partnership with global brands is a significant departure from the recent dominance of private governance in the regulation of labour practices in global value chains. Understanding these and the conditions under which the involvement of the state is occurring, how these partnerships work, and the circumstances under which they are sustained can help push forward our understanding of the transitions that are currently taking place in the structure of private governance and in the involvement of the state in fostering workplace protections to vulnerable workers.

Argument: My findings suggest that diffusing good labour standards down and beyond individual value chains requires an active role of the 'grounded' state, especially in a context where 90 per cent of employment is in the informal sector and outside the reach of both labour laws enshrined in rulebooks as well as the monitoring protocols and codes of conduct of buyers and private companies. Neither the state nor private companies nor civil society organizations can work alone, as each has a clear and important role in co-creating and seeding processes that can benefit both firms and labour and further the state's goal of creating good jobs. It is significant that these experiments do not turn away from past efforts, but build upon them and transform them by using existing resources in new ways. This involved a layering in of the private on the public, as others have also found elsewhere (Locke, 2013; Bartley, 2011), where the new, spatially rooted experiments were anchored in the trust and prior engagement of the local community in the creation of institutional supports (community banking and self-help groups in this case) that had been built over many years by civic actors with assistance from the state. Tapping into these civic networks was crucial to the success of the government and Gap's collaborative initiative. The Mewat case also shows that when sustainable work can be created in poor communities, especially for women, the earnings find their way into more stable consumption, retiring of punishing debts, children's education, and more confident lives.

Yet significant challenges to sustaining these emergent practices remain. The same micropolitics around intensified price competition and jurisdictional limitations (between states, lead firms, and their value chains) that placed the standard compliance model in stress, and created the conditions for experimentation, can sap the room to manoeuvre of the old actors as they try to do things in new ways. These pressures, for instance, are leading many brands—even those that were once pioneers of social responsibility—to gradually withdraw from core CSR investments (LB Interview, 2011). Similarly, while reformist bureaucrats can help initiate experiments, continued support for them can face pressure to scale up, or jurisdictional challenges may arise if the officers who incubated an experiment get transferred. Moreover, ensuring that these experiments last is a labour-intensive, hands-on process that it is not cost-less. In an environment, where there is churn within bureaucracies and corporations and price pressures are resurgent, and where government departments interpret sustainability in terms of scale of impact, it is quite possible that the old logics, expectations, and behavioural norms of standard institutional practices may derail these decentralized experiments even before their benefits and efficacy can fully percolate.

Under these conditions, it would seem that in order to survive long enough for their merits to become more widely visible, such programs would need the capacity to transform, evolve, and flexibly adapt to external and internal pressures. In the Mewat case, it appears that this might involve shifting from a sole focus on export demand and global buyers, to also looking at domestic demand and large buyers (global or domestic) in the rapidly growing home market. Still, with changes at Gap and within the state, questions remain about who will be at the helm of this process.

But this much is clear: the state's role is going to be critical if these spatialized experiments are to succeed. But the state alone cannot provide the stability and the economic viability necessary without commitment from firms that can link workers to the market, and the grounding presence of locally rooted civic actors, or self-organized worker associations, that can maintain operational continuity.

My analysis draws on 24 interviews that I conducted in Mewat and in the National Capital Region (NCR) of North India in 2011 and 2013 through a purposive, snowball sampling method. It also draws on two focus groups with a subset of women workers involved in the Mewat program in 2011, including five key informant interviews. I also include interviews with two key government of India officials in the Ministry of Women and Child Development (MWCD) and in the Ministry of Rural Development (MRD), with Gap Inc.'s former Director of Global Partnerships and Social Responsibility, who was responsible for spearheading and leading the project for its first year and half of operation, with a key officer at Impulse, the buying house that partnered with Gap on the business side of the project, and with the leader of the Society for the Promotion of Youth and Masses (SPYM), the NGO that helped run the project on a daily basis. Additional interviews were conducted with firms (Radnik, Orient Clothing) who were part of the project, other firms in the NCR region (and beyond, such as in Tamil Nadu) to understand firm perspectives on the emergence of new vulnerabilities in the garment chain, an officer in the Department of Labour, and three field workers of SPYM in Mewat. These open-ended qualitative interviews and focus groups were supplemented by analysis of reports on the program prepared by Gap and its NGO partner, as well as by published scholarly accounts of other embroidery clusters (Mezzadari, 2011; Unni and Scaria, 2009).

The rest of the paper is organized as follows: Section 13.2 explores the origins of the Mewat program and its micro-politics. It explores why Gap and the government got involved, and why they decided to partner with each other at this point in time. Section 13.3 examines how the model actually played out on the ground and its initial 'success'. Section 13.4 analyses the post-recession turning point and explores the model's seeming stagnation by examining shifts in the roles of the partners (brands, exporters, government, and the community) and the evolution of workers' attitudes over the course of this lull. Section 13.5 briefly examines the current shifts in the model and its portability to other places, while Section 13.6 concludes the chapter.

13.2   Shock of public embarrassment as trigger

The Mewat innovation arose out of a process of public shaming and its aftermath. In October 2007, the BBC aired a damning account of child labour in Gap's clothing supply chain in New Delhi, India, uncovered by reporter Dan MacDougall. This widely publicized account sent shockwaves through a company that had prided itself on upholding some of the strictest compliance standards in the industry and was regarded as a leader in ethical trade by consumers and peers alike since the early 2000s. Gap immediately withdrew the item allegedly produced using child labour, banned the supplier responsible for the violation, worked to rehabilitate the children, and vowed to investigate the matter: 'We have a strict prohibition on child labour, and we are taking this very seriously. This is very upsetting and we intend to investigate thoroughly' (BBC, 2007, quoting the head of compliance, Dan Henkle).

The then Director of Global Partnerships and Social Responsibility at Gap (henceforth Gap DGP), who had been at the centre of Gap Inc.'s CSR team since 1997, was asked to lead the investigation. 'The internal discussion within Gap was that ... we do know that the children could be somewhere in the informal part of the supply chain, so instead of trying to take a legalistic stand, let us deal with this proactively', (Gap DGP Interview, 2011).

The results of the internal investigations revealed surprises that the company had not anticipated. It was not just that child labour had been used in its supplier factory or that the children were working long hours under terrible conditions, but that they were trafficked. They had been 'bought' by contractors from their families in Bihar and brought to work in Delhi under dismal conditions for virtually no pay. As the Gap DGP noted, 'I thought this makes no sense, ten years I have been here, I have not had a single crisis in India. Here I am about to leave and we have our worst ever media story in Delhi ... Then getting into this with these children we realised that these children were trafficked' (Gap DGP Interview, June 2011). The challenge of dealing with child labour was now complicated by the problem of dealing with trafficking, a complex issue with deeper roots and wider causes. There was also the difficulty of reaching into the labyrinthine informal segments of the supply chain where vulnerable labour could enter at almost any point.

The intensification of competition in the post-MFA period and the consequent squeeze on prices had unleashed vulnerabilities that were becoming manifest even in the more formalized segments of the value chain: 'We had practically ended the contract worker system in [our supply chains in India] the early 2000's; we had more permanent workers with better benefits and systems and all of that had now been dismantled. [O]ver 80 per cent of your workforce [in the Indian garment industry] is on contract and easy come and easy go', (Gap DGP Interview, 2011). The problem was not of one country alone, but widespread, and was beginning to '[undermine the] gains that CSR had produced since the early 2000s'. The consequence was an enlargement of informality within the garment chain, and an expansion of impermanent, vulnerable, and unprotected spaces within it (LB interview, 2011).

Realizing that the problem was bigger than they could handle alone, Gap turned to the state. Gap's DGP reached out to the Ministry of Women and Child Development (MWCD), the department in the national government charged with the social and economic welfare of women in the country and also of children. Interestingly, MWCD, along with a group of committed young bureaucrats in the Ministry of Rural Development, had been working for over a decade on programs that sought to reach out to poor and vulnerable women, often in violence affected districts (such as in the Naxal belts of Andhra Pradesh) to organize them, upgrade their skills, and connect them to government programs that could help augment their sources of income and livelihoods. One of the focus areas was organizing women into networks of Self-Help Groups that could serve as the backbone for other initiatives. This had laid a strong organizational foundation in many parts of the country, such as in AP and Mewat, where the project would eventually be piloted.

At MWCD, the Gap DGP made contact with MK, a dedicated young officer who was part of the larger group of reformist bureaucrats. Her work with poor and vulnerable women brought her in regular contact with issues of trafficking. Trafficking referred not only to conditions where people who had been abducted or unlawfully displaced, but also where people had been lured into, or due to their own poverty forced into, exploitative conditions of work.

> I was looking at livelihoods for women and also ... at issues relating to violence and other social impacts on women [as a result of] unsafe migration, trafficking, exploitation of women and children for labour and for various other purposes. So we were looking at partnerships with community based organisations, NGOs, to work with us in developing community capacity, awareness and also imparting some amount of skill building as well as income generating opportunities, and linking them with [public] programs. For example, in the Ministry of Women and Child Development we have four or five schemes which focus solely on developing skills of women, training, access to credit, micro-credit especially, and also mobilising them into self-help groups initially and then hand-holding them till such time that they are able to take off on their own or develop into larger cooperatives and federations, or find stable [links to] markets (MK Interview, 2011).

However, the government had found that despite its efforts, it was not easy to augment women's livelihoods in a sustained and stable manner. The weak link was access to markets. The NGOs who organized and trained the women on MWCD's behalf, 'did not know the market ... or even understand what is required, what skills are required of these women or what kind of products are required ... so it was just like, whatever they could do they did, whatever sales they could manage they managed. It did not go beyond that' (MK interview, 2011). If the NGOs turned to middlemen or contractors to mediate market access, it was another form of exploitation. 'There is a lot of money that goes through the middle person. He is paying them something but not the full amount, and giving them highly exploitative working conditions ... So you need the corporate sector, you need the companies to be helping you out in [creating links to the market]' (MK interview, 2011). These circumstances explain why the MWCD was receptive to the idea of partnering with Gap and the exporters when they reached out to the government in early 2008.

The collaboration began with a joint conference that MWCD co-organized with Gap and UNODC[5] in New Delhi on March 15, 2008, 5 months after the child labour incident. The conference focused on 'Issues of Trafficking in the Garment Supply Chain', and over 150 people attended it. There were international brands sourcing from India, their key suppliers, buying houses, exporters, the Apparel Export Promotion Council, other industry associations, NGOs, and civic groups working in the garment sector. Special attention was paid to tackling exploitation within the most vulnerable, less visible, and largely informal segments of formalized clothing chains, such as handwork, embroidery, and subcontracted home-based work.

The involvement of so many brands in the conference was not just a reflection of concerns that child labour had resurfaced even in some of the most 'monitored' Indian garment chains but also of unease over deeper vulnerabilities that were beginning to creep into global garment chains, including less understood threats like trafficking.

> [I]t is [a problem] not just in the garment industry. What we have seen increasingly and especially post-2008 is the re-entry into the formalised supply chains of the most vulnerable workers globally. These are children, these are trafficked women, these are migrant workers, all of them had made a reappearance in the most robust, so-called monitored supply chains and it is to do with cost (Gap DGP interview, 2011).

In this highly uncertain environment, companies had begun to feel that brand-based compliance efforts were no longer enough, said the Gap DGP who organized the

---

[5] United Nations Office of Drugs and Crime (UNODC) works on issues of human trafficking among other problems.

conference; partnering with the government was going to be key. Foreshadowing some of the more recent concerns over the limits of private governance of working conditions within GVCs and multinational production and calls for a renewed involvement of the state in promoting labour rights and labour standards (Locke, 2013, Mosley, 2010, Schrank, 2009) discussions at the 2008 conference centred on collaborations with the government:

> It is so critical for the private sector to actually join hands with the government because if we talk about scale, if you kind of look at the last decade and a half there is so much that has happened in the name of effort [by brands] but how much can we actually see in the name of impact? So it is time we stop measuring effort and started measuring impact, this is very very critical. Which means you have got to look at doing things differently ... We need to use our sphere of influence to be that catalyst of change, not replace governments but support it and bring in the other stakeholders. So that is the space ... I think this is what the future is all about (Gap DGP Interview, 2011).

At the conference, the government of India (MWCD) announced the formation of a think tank for the garment industry that brought together several brands active in India, garment exporters, representatives of the Indian garment and textile industry, government organizations, NGOs linked to the industry and representatives of international organizations such as the ILO and UNODC to develop 'short, medium, and long-term' collaborative strategies to strengthen workforce protections and tackle the problem of child labour, forced labour, and trafficking (MK interview, 2011 UNODC India Country Report, 2009). Two months later, the government (MWCD) operationalized the work of the think tank by deputing a taskforce on the issue of human trafficking, that was charged with developing a pilot project to link women garment workers in vulnerable areas to export markets. The taskforce began meeting immediately in June 2008 and was led by Gap on the side of the brands and MWCD officials on the side of government and members of the industry, UNODC, and select NGOs participated.

The idea of piloting the project in Mewat came from the MWCD official who had driven this collaboration all along. Mewat is a large, desperately poor district in Haryana, one of the most prosperous states of India. Spread over many communities, villages, and towns, Mewat's one million residents have historically relied on rain-fed agriculture that has dwindled over the years due to chronic droughts and environmental degradation. The region's residents are urgently in need of jobs and alternate sources of development. The region is dominated by the Meo-Muslim community, and the local women have a tradition of embroidery skills. These skills have never been exploited even though Mewat is just hours from a major garment export cluster in the neighbouring NCR-Gurgaon region. An NGO, the Society for the Promotion of Youth and Masses (SPYM) had been working with the Ministry of Women and Child Development in Mewat for a decade organizing local women in self-help (savings) groups (SHGs). MK's idea was that if the brands and exporters could build on the existing efforts by the government and its NGO partner where the women had already become organized through the formation of SHGs, the pilot project could get a head start as. Gap thus decided to locate the pilot in Mewat, upgrade the women's traditional skills, and connect them to exporters.

13.3   The Mewat model: A relational approach to organizational design

This was not Gap's first effort at organizing ethical handwork production networks in India. Since 2005, it had funded SEWA (Self Employed Women's Association) and other organizations that worked with women in the informal sector to carry out embroidery for export markets. It had also worked with the UK's trade craft cooperative model and had worked with organizations dealing with the social conditions that generated child labour and other vulnerabilities, such as the Bachpan Bachao Andolan (Save the Child Movement). How was Mewat different?

A major difference between the Mewat model and other models that Gap had supported previously was that Mewat was not a membership-based approach but a 'modular' approach where a loosely coupled alliance of civic, government, and industry actors (brands, exporters, government and existing NGOs) could come together with a clear division of labour to connect the local labour force directly to export markets. Access to work was not restricted to members of any particular organization, but was open to the entire community. Mewat was a potentially 'self-organizing', relatively portable model where partners with clearly defined roles could layer onto existing organizational initiatives (public or civic) to directly mobilize local workers and link them with existing sources of demand (MK interview, 2011).

> The Mewat model is basically [about organizing] a direct linkage between the community and the manufacturer who is catering to the export industry using *existing business drivers and demands* ... [there are] no riders ... We said here is the community, here is the manufacturer, you guys get together, see what can work ... the only rule is that the systems must be very very transparent when it came to payments ... and they are. If you go to the women, each of them has a passbook ... there is daily entry of how many

pieces are produced. They have bank accounts [developed by SPYM] ... The [payment] goes into the bank ... it [is] a very direct intervention.' (Gap DGP Interview, 2011, emphasis added).

Most of the other models that Gap had worked on earlier were, in the DGPs words, 'alternate marketing models instead of actually trying to leverage the mainstream business drivers' (Gap DGP Interview, 2011). These alternative models generally worked through membership-based organizations and took time to put in place as they involved adjustments on both sides—the exporters and the NGOs they worked with: 'It was a difficult struggle for them because to really understand the demands of an export market is not easy for an NGO which feels it needs to adhere to its [own] processes ... It has taken 5-6 years of adjustment and learning, but they have morphed and continue to work with factories ... with a fair amount of success' that has been sustained over time (Gap DGP Interview, 2011).

In Mewat, four principles shaped the project's organizational design: (1) cutting out middlemen; (2) curtailing competition between buyers to prevent undercutting of prices; (3) providing a safe, easy to monitor working environment that was free of child labour and human trafficking; and (4) a system that ensured workers were paid fair and transparent wages. These principles in turn generated a set of 'rules' and a specific division of labour that anchored the program organizationally, as we see next. This division of labour and the different roles of the different actors in the partnership were not written down in the form of formal legal contracts but emerged out of many discussions among the partners and were agreed to and clearly understood by all, even if the rules stayed unwritten.

13.3.1 Specific roles and a new institutional division of labour

In order to cut out middlemen, Gap stepped in to link the workers directly to the market by partnering with a large Indian buying house, Impulse, which sourced for European brands and was interested in developing an assured pool of child-labour-free handworkers proximate to NCR where most of its suppliers were located. Together, both partners picked two regions in Mewat—Hathin and Nagina—where the NGO, SPYM, had a presence, and connected each community directly to a supplier each from their export network. Gap brought in OCCL, an exporter, into Hathin and Impulse linked one of its exporters, Radnik, to Nagina. SPYM facilitated this relationship by opening up their offices to create community work centres in each location where the women could come and work. Gap and Impulse oversaw the program to ensure that minimum wages were paid, but placed no direct orders—only the selected exporters did. They also did not micromanage the process of placing orders, the volume of orders that the exporters placed, or the negotiations around rates beyond clarifying that the minimum wage rule was a condition of participation.[6]

The exporters whom Gap and Impulse brought in were both based in the NCR region—just over an hour from the worksites in Mewat. Their role in the project was to train the local workers in their community, upgrade their skills to the levels required for the products they intended to outsource to them, and then place direct orders with them through SPYM, whose local staff ran the community work centres on a daily basis. The factories directly assessed capabilities and figured out which skills could be upgraded most directly before orders could be placed, and which skills would be learned on the job or later (Gap DGP Interview, 2011).

The motivation behind this arrangement where the buyer/exporter trained and prepared the workers in the communities they sourced from was that the investment by the factory of its own time, money, and effort to train and provide the workers plant-specific skills would serve as an incentive to build long-term, relational ties between the workers and exporters. This would help develop the community by providing steady work that enhanced livelihoods and in the process help create a permanent handwork supply base in the region. But why link only one exporter to one community? Why did Gap and Impulse not invite any interested exporter from their network to place orders in the two communities in Mewat for their handwork and embroidery needs?

Gap and Impulse decided to bring in only one exporter each and link them to separate communities within Mewat district, they argued, to prevent competition between buyers (Gap DGP Interview, 2011). The spatial division of labour was in part based on the kinds of products each factory produced and the nature of skills that each community had. OCCL was mainly looking for handwork and relatively simple embroidery on women's clothing, a skill that the women in Hathin traditionally had and could be upgraded with a little training, while Radnik was looking for more specialized large frame embroidery work ('*Adda* work') in addition to handwork. The workers in Nagina had the potential to develop these skills. As SPYM, the NGO that ran the project in Mewat explained, 'The idea was that we will not bring in any company [into the two work centres] without the consent of these two organisations, [because] GAP and Impulse who were mobilising their suppliers to bring work' (SPYM Interview, 2011).

---

[6] But of course, to the extent that the exporters were part of supply network of Gap and Impulse, there was significant pressure on them to comply with the rules of transparency set up by the project (AK Interview, 2013).

While Gap and Impulse brought in exporters from their own supply networks, it is important to note that neither OCCL nor Radnik were sole suppliers to them. They supplied to many other brands as well (Next, Debenhams, George, Monsoon, Esprit), and that was the project's intention—that even when only one supplier (exporter) was placing orders in each community the project would go beyond dependence on orders from a single brand. This reflected in part the brand's effort to hedge against uncertainties in their sourcing patterns. 'We did not want this to be dependent only on Gap. Especially today when you have no guarantees the way supply chains shift' (Gap DGP Interview, 2011). But it also reflected a return on investment in skills for the investing firms—in return for training the workers and developing local skills the investing firm got the benefit of sole access to an assured pool of handworkers in close proximity to their factories without the threat of rate increases or being outbid by other interested factories.

To provide the workers a safe and child-labour free environment the project turned to SPYM. From its prior work with SEWA's handwork centres, Gap knew that to ensure there was no child labour in the work system, women workers would have to be brought out of their homes and into safe and transparent community work spaces. SPYM used its long history of work in the region and the social capital and trust it had built in local communities to help provide and anchor these community centres in each of the two sites. Over the 15 years that SPYM had worked in the region it had organized more than 20,000 women into SHGs across Mewat. To manage this growing network of SHGs, SPYM had set up a CBO in 2003 with local chapters in each community to oversee local activities. Each local chapter operated from rented spaces embedded in community buildings or in cultural centres in the heart of the local community; these centres became the 'common workplaces' for the new project.

In Hathin, the site that I visited in 2011, the project's community centre was located in a temple in the centre of town. SPYM had a large hall that served as the workspace, a small office, and a crèche upstairs and I was told that none 'of the women have to walk more than 10 minutes from their homes to reach these community centers', (SPYM Interview, 2011). These familiar institutional spaces, SPYM's long years of work with the government in the region, and its embeddedness in the community gave the project a legitimacy in the eyes of the local community that Gap, Impulse, or their exporters working on their own would have had a hard time achieving at the outset of the project.

SPYM hired and paid a local team of two men and one woman [a skilled worker from the community] to run the work centres. Gap gave SPYM a small grant to support management costs at the start of the program—$5000 annually for the first 2 years—but the financial model envisioned for the project was that SPYM would cover its administrative costs by retaining 20 per cent of the value of the orders that the factories would place through the centre and 80 per cent would be disbursed to the women workers according to the hours they put in. If the volume and pace of the orders were consistent, the expectation was that this arrangement would make the operation fairly self-sustained, as happened over the first year and a half of the project (SPYM Interview, 2011). How realistic this was in an industry characterized by fluctuations of fashion and seasonality we shall examine in the next section.

A second way in which SPYM invested in the project was to commit to paying a monthly wage to the women who worked through the centre. Since the exporter would pay only after the product was delivered and sometimes not until 2–3 months after delivery, and timely payments were a priority for the project, Gap, Impulse, and SPYM agreed to pay the workers on the 7th of each month for the hours they had put in over the previous month. Each worker maintained a passbook where she noted the hours worked, as did SPYM. Most women workers already had a bank account through the SHGs. The monthly payments by SPYM deposited into their bank account based on the hours recorded in the passbook. SPYM would later recoup these funds when the exporters released their payment. This 'pre-payment' by SPYM was supported in part by the grant that it got from Gap, and in part by its own funds. Its primary intent was to shield workers from delays in buyer payments that plague most subcontracting arrangements by maintaining a regular payment cycle. We will see in the next section how this worked when the scale of the work grew, and what happened during downturns.

The final difference between Mewat and Gap's previous programs around handwork was its partnership with the government in this program. This was the first time Gap had partnered directly with the state in India. The involvement of the government in Mewat in a tripartite alliance with the brands and civic institutions repositioned the role of the state as an important actor in shaping the labour standards in export chains and extending them to informal workers at the lowest levels. In the process, it reoriented private governance towards a more actively collaborative public process. The involvement of the state with a prominent brand such as Gap gave new levels of visibility to the project that initially created quite a buzz around the partnership, drawing in many interested exporters and buyers who had been reluctant to engage with Mewat. Several retailers visited the centres to see how it worked, and the government for its part later sought to extend it to other states (AP, Bihar) and even to other sectors—such as natural, zero-budget farming of specialty crops (AK interview, VK Interview, 2011).

What made this collaboration potentially portable to other places was the specificity of each partner's role. As the MWCD official noted, 'We had the government as facilitator, we had the NGO which had actually developed the community at the grassroots level, and we had the corporate sector where GAP came in and said we will [partner with you on] this, we will bring ... in our exporters, we will teach the women the specific skills that the particular company requires and this company will then pick up all the garments from them that they can produce ... so it was a tie-up which was perfect. There was a hundred percent market, there was also the company which would come and actually teach them what to do, how to do it ... [W]e ensured that that they were paid the minimum wage [of the state of Haryana] if not more ... and ... there was no middleman, that was the biggest benefit' (MK Interview, 2011).

The active presence of the Ministry was also crucial because initially it brought the local elite along. The local administration and elected councillors who would otherwise be wary of outside influences in the region did not oppose the project. The leaders of the dominant local Muslim community as well as the minority Hindu community were strongly socially conservative and closely monitored the interaction of outsiders with women in their community. The Ministry itself was sensitive to these concerns and for its own part used its internal and informal channels to keep the local elected elite informed of the project's activities.

The state's role in the project was noteworthy for two additional reasons. First, the state did interfere with structuring the workers' (and community's) link to the market. In contrast to cases where the government sometimes becomes a direct 'buyer' of products produced by artisans or vulnerable groups for sale through government-run stores or emporia, in Mewat, the buying and selling was left entirely to the brands and the exporters whom they brought in. The fact that the government stayed away from direct involvement with marketing decisions and left it to the brands and their suppliers was precisely because the government was already an active partner in shaping the design of the project all along.

Second, the state did not put any money directly into the project beyond in-kind facilitation of the partnership and the prior support it had given to the community and SPYM for the development of SHGs in the district. By contrast, the brands, exporters, and the NGO did put their own money into the project directly or indirectly. As noted above, Gap gave $10,000 to SPYM over a 2-year period to help set the project up, the exporters who placed orders invested time to train the women before they began placing orders (and during the lean season beyond that), and SPYM used its own space as the community work centre. The project's main financial model, however, was to leverage existing resources and finance the costs of administering the program by having SPYM retain 20 per cent of the cost of every consignment into a collective administrative fund. The state's funding would come later if and when the project was scaled up.

13.4 Fitting informal workers into export chains

Export value chains are notoriously tight, shifting at short notice, with increasingly short turnaround times and penalties for delays and mistakes. Furthermore, garment chains are marked by seasonality, fluctuations in fashion, style, and design—even more so for hand-embellished products. In standard handwork sourcing decisions, it is the subcontractor who manages the ups and downs of these processes. How did the project actually fit Mewat's handworkers directly into the factories own export commitments? Who negotiated the contracts? How were rates set? How were production deadlines met? How was quality assured, how were rejections handled and how were finished goods transported to the exporters?

In the early days of the program, a lot rested on three aspects of the Mewat project: its proximity to the NCR garment cluster—which allowed staff from the export factories to visit the worksites on a regular basis; the assigning of a community to a particular exporter to develop skills and build a supply base, which had the unintended consequence of building a collective image around the women's work in each community; and the prior history of skill in the region. There was also a high degree of personal coaching, hand-holding, and investment of time by the factories not only in developing worker skills, but in explaining them the importance of timeliness and quality and how the embroidery portion of the work that they did fitted into the factory's production process. This lasted well into the first year of the program and was an important contribution—a form of institutional support—from the program to the workers in the community that had wider consequences to the workers understanding of their own role and went beyond fulfilling orders. As we will see, it led to leadership emerging among the women who soon took over the process of negotiating rates and deciding which orders to take on (Focus group, Hathin, 2011).

About 90 per cent of the work that came to Mewat was for fashion garments for women and children (beading work, sequins, thread embroidery) and some home textiles. The work ranged from relatively simple embroidery to work of mid-range complexity. But all the work that the exporters gave to the region's workers was targeted to the skill levels they had and to the levels to which their skills were upgraded by the training offered by the factories in the preparatory stage. Before the first formal orders were placed in December 2008, the two exporters OCCL and Radnik sent their production supervisors to the communities to carry out detailed assessments of existing skill levels. The supervisors conducted time-studies on simple orders and then targeted training to bring the workers up to the basic skill levels that they needed the workers to get to. The supervisors spent 2–3 hours every day for about a month, training the women workers in the kinds of embroidery they would outsource to the region. In Nagina, Impulse worked with their exporter Radnik to train women in the more complex large frame embroidery: 'Gap subsidised it. We paid actually for two people from Bareilly [an established center for frame embroidery in a neighboring state] to come and train these workers. And while work was continuing in Hathin [on basic embroidery], some people from there were being trained [on frames] as well' (Gap DGP Interview, 2011). Although some simple orders began within 10 days of training—especially in Hathin where the embroidery was more basic, the supervision continued well beyond the first month of training and into the first year of the program. Indeed, the idea was to use seasonality to the program's advantage and provide training upgrades to the women in the slack season (Gap DGP Interview, 2011).

The point of this relatively intense interaction with the workers was also to understand their work-habits and to get a better sense of their social constraints and the social structure of work in the region besides estimating their capabilities. For example, the supervisors found that even minimal training went a long way given the women's existing skills. This was evident in the unusually low rejection rates even in the earliest orders that were placed during the testing phase—a pattern that has continued (Impulse Interview, 2011). But the supervisors also realized that the women would need very flexible work hours. While the work centres opened at 8:30 a.m. and continued till 7:00 p.m. (or even longer when necessary), none of the women worked 8–5; the women came after their duties at home were over. Some worked till 2 p.m. and left when their children came home from school, others worked 2–3 hours in the morning and 2–3 hours in the afternoons, and some worked only 1–3 hours per day. To cope with fluctuating and flexible work hours and yet meet their production deadlines, the factories realized they would need to train a large pool of workers with similar skill levels whom they could draw on based on availability to fulfil their orders on time. By the time, the formal orders were placed in late 2008 to early 2009, about 6–800 women had been trained across the two sites (MK Interview, 2011; AK Interview, 2013).

By the time, regular orders began to be placed the exporters knew what to expect and what size of order they could place in Mewat. When a new order came in, the production supervisor of the factories brought it to SPYM. The exporter would have already carried out work-time studies to estimate the time it would take the women in the region to complete the order. Given the number of pieces in the order, the level of complexity of the work, and an estimate of the time it would take to complete each piece, the supervisor, along with SPYM, converted the monthly minimum wage into hourly rates and then into piece rates. If the hourly rate came to Rs. 20 per hour by this calculation, SPYM would try to negotiate the rate to say Rs. 24 to ensure that after it kept 20 per cent of it for overhead costs, the women would still get the minimum wage rate. The exporter sometimes agreed and sometimes not, but the deal rarely slipped below a gross minimum hourly rate (SPYM Interview, 2011). SPYMs staff would then spread the word among the women that work was available and the women who were interested and had the time would come to the centre. If one worker said she would do 10 pieces total for the order in 3 hours, another might commit to 30 pieces or more, and on that basis SPYMs staff drew up the workpool for the entire order. Then, once the price was agreed on and the work was distributed, the women carried out the work, recording in their passbooks the number of pieces produced and the hours worked. At any given time, in the first year when there was a regular flow of orders, 60–100 to 150 women worked at the centre (AK Interview; Focus group, Hathin, 2011).

Although the women workers worked flexibly according to the time available to them, a collective sense of the community's work emerged soon. In the focus group at Hathin, the women reported that they worked on different quantities individually, but together they and SPYM staff tried to ensure that the order was completed on time, 'because it was about the image [reputation] of our community' (Focus group, Hathin, 2011). On occasion, longer hours would be needed and the women collectively worked out strategies to meet the deadline. Gap and Impulse both said that delays in the completion of orders were rare and rejection rates low. To reinforce this sense of 'community responsibility' and explain to the women how export chains worked and why timeliness was important, as well as quality, Gap brought in students and professors from the Pearl Academy School of Fashion in New Delhi to the work centres as interns (students) or as speakers (professors) who explained the processes of production and export to the workers, emphasizing the importance of timeliness, as well as providing some organizational training to SPYM. Impulse also clarified that the exporters did not penalize the workers for mistakes or rejections, although SPYM and the women felt that it was not always so and there were mysterious deductions in the total payment which they did not understand. These differences were inchoate in the early excitement of success, but surfaced later, as we will see in the next section.

13.5 The Janus-faced nature of success

The early success of the Mewat project was striking. Formally launched at the end of 2008, by the time the factories began placing regular orders in early 2009, about 800 women had been trained in basic embroidery skills across the two worksites (about 500–600 in Hathin and 200–300 in Nagina). Depending on the size of the orders, 100–150 women worked at the centre at any given time. Despite the great recession that had begun to take a toll on global trade by late 2008, the first 18–19 months were good. The women associated with the project produced roughly 200,000 pieces between 2009 and mid-2010 or 10,000–12,000 per month on average (Impulse Interview, 2013) with individual workers earning between Rs. 1000 and 5000 per month depending on the work hours and more than Rs. 20 lakhs [Rs. 2 million] came into the community in the first 8 months of the program (Gap DGP Interview, 2011).

Throughout the first year of its operation, Impulse, Gap and the factories, OCCL and Radnik made presentations about it to the retailers and others, and several factories and retailers visited the worksites to see how the project was working. In 2010, the BBC made a brief documentary on how Mewat's hand-embellishment centres had changed the lives of the women there. It interviewed the women and documented how they invested their earnings in their children's education (several had shifted their children to better schools), nutrition, and debt-relief (BBC, 2010; Impulse, 2013; SPYM studies, 2013). Some of these themes were echoed by women in the focus group I conducted in Hathin. Though the outcomes varied for different women depending on their involvement with the project, they pointed to improved incomes and how they had invested their earnings into education for their children, home repairs, loan repayment and consumption. They wanted the project to continue.

More importantly, as the government official associated with the project as well as SPYM and Gap noted, it had nurtured leadership within the women who worked on the project: 'Initially OCCL [the exporter working with Hathin] paid the women what it would have paid to any embroidery sub-contractors about two seasons into this, the women started negotiating for better prices'. During my own focus group with the workers several women made clear that awareness of alternative options had improved their bargaining power: '[The] factories are always trying to get you to work for less. But if I know that MNREGA [a government-run rural employment guarantee program that provides 100 days of work to unemployed rural workers and was an alternative employment option for Mewat's women] is paying more than Rs. 110 a day, why would I work for any less than that for them [the exporters]?' (Focus group interview, Hathin, 2011).

However, by the time I went to the field, the pace of the project had slowed down substantially and after a lean season with no orders, they had only one order of home textiles (quilts) at the Hathin work centre in the summer of 2011. Barely 50–60 women had work at the centre. Despite the powerful success of the project between 2009 and mid-2010, why had work slowed down? When I returned to the field again 2 years later, in 2013, the program was in its fifth year of operation. It was still running, SPYM still had its work centres and the women still worked there when there were orders, but the orders were erratic and much had changed. Gap for one had practically left the project. Impulse and the two exporters, OCCL and Radnik, still remained and discussed of continuing the orders and were very happy to have the option of working out of Mewat, but then why were orders down, despite the exporters' professed happiness with Mewat's low reject rates and quick turnaround times?

Four factors, each related to the very traits that gave the project its innovative success also explain the challenges it has faced. In addition, external factors such as the aftermath of the recession also impacted performance. These faced effects of program design illustrate the challenges of institutionally anchoring supports that can safely incorporate informal workers into rapidly shifting export chains within the broad context of the drawing down of CSR in many large corporations. These factors also illustrate the growing importance of the role of the state in providing continuity to labour supports at a time of flux within supply chains and when buyer commitments are fragile. What is interesting is that despite these challenges the project persists and has transformed itself in the process. From focusing solely on export markets, it has begun to diversify into the domestic market as was evident when I returned to the project in 2013. Moreover, aspects of the model and lessons from it are being diffused to other places, such as Andhra Pradesh and other sectors (agriculture).

13.5.1 The recession breaks the momentum

In hindsight, the timing of the launch of the project was unfortunate—right on the cusp of the great global recession of 2008. Yet, as we saw, the first year and a half was very good for the project. Embellished work was in vogue in the global markets in 2009–2010 and orders flowed in consistently. The lean season was used for home textiles and training. But in early 2010, one of OCCLs major buyers in the UK market went bankrupt. Others cut back on orders. The cascading effect of this was that OCCL itself nearly went bankrupt and work ground to a trickle. It not only stopped sending orders to Hathin but payments for completed work were delayed. Initially, Gap stepped in with its second grant of $5000 to SPYM to maintain payments while OCCL recovered—which it did by early 2011. But the momentum had been stopped and some of the trust was eroded because the workers and SPYM were never clear about what to expect, in part because OCCL was in fire-fighting mode. When work began in 2011, the workers were reluctant to work with OCCL for fear that they would renege again. To make matters worse, by 2011, embellishment was not in great demand and the orders were lower value and smaller.

The early success of the program depended upon having a large pool of trained workers and on limiting the number of exporters that could access them. During OCCLs crisis, this came back to haunt the project. The large number of women who had been trained and who had come to expect a few hours of work daily or every week were stranded. Because SPYM could not bring in another exporter to the region—since that was the responsibility of Gap and Impulse, and both felt OCCL would recover and return, the hiatus could have been avoided if MOUs had been signed with more exporters.

13.5.2 Institutional costs and contractual ties

However, the larger issues this revealed was about who would bear the institutional burden of ensuring program continuity during times of slack as well as ironically, during times of rapid growth. At first, when the exporters were sending in their supervisors to place orders, oversee work and bring orders back, transport costs were not an issue for SPYM or the workers. However, when the volume of orders grew and work was steady, the hour and a half of daily commute began to add up for the exporters and they stopped sending their people to deliver and fetch the pieces. SPYM had to arrange for the transportation to pick and deliver pieces—and this took place on a daily basis at the peak of the program's success. Technically the 20 per cent that was meant for overhead costs—and was used to pay the rent of the community centre, utilities, crèche, staff salaries and some transport costs—did not cover these daily trips. In addition to having to pay the workers their regular monthly salaries despite 3–4 month delays from OCCL, this became a burden for SPYM. This created tensions between the factory and the NGO.

In standard sourcing practices, as an informant at Impulse explained, 'the subcontractor chases the factory' for orders and for delivery. Even at SEWA, the NGO manages to pick up and deliver and sustain itself. In Mewat, the 'marketing ability of the NGO was limited' (AK Interview, 2013). With all the personal investment in training, delivery, pick up, the costs added up for OCCL— in contrast to the ease of handing over the orders to subcontractors at the factory doorstep and receiving the completed orders without having to worry about training, preparing or monitoring the workers. That is why, my informant explained, companies find it easier to default this option. Why was the exporter not able to charge the retailers they supplied to for the extra cost of maintaining safe handwork practices? The informant at Impulse said, when they made this case to their buyers, the buyers lauded the effort and wished to see it continue but did not agree to help pay for it. 'You are still fighting over 2–3 cents a piece. The retailers want a clean supply chain, but they look the other way in terms of pricing' (AK Interview, 2013).

13.5.3   Scale, local political economy and withdrawal of CSR

At the opposite end of the spectrum from the dampening effects of the recession was the effect of success itself, which brought surprising challenges. First, the MWCD responded to the success of the program over the first 18–19 months by suggesting that they scale up the project to cover not just two villages, but the entire district of Mewat, across all its 400 communities. They had the funds for it, and according to government norms, these funds could only be used for large-scale efforts. MWCD initiated talks with Gap, Impulse and with the local district administration in Mewat and the elected officials there. They even discussed the possibility of inviting a factory to come and locate a branch in Mewat. But the personal hand-holding and coaching that was the hallmark of Mewat-I was too labour-intensive to carry out pan-state. For that, the Apparel Export Promotion Council (AEPC) would have to step in and train the workers. AEPC had a training centre 90 minutes away from the site. The government offered to pay to take the women there and bring them back, but the men in the community, particularly elected leaders balked at that and the effort to scale up the project's success backfired.

Simultaneously, at the same time as this subtle pushback was emerging, the BBC made a documentary in May 2010, which was aired on Channel 4, where interviews with the women workers showed how delighted they were to dress up and go to a common place to work and how these had built social supports besides augmenting their incomes and had given them confidence. The airing of the documentary, coupled with the government's efforts to help scale up the project led to serious backlash in the community and its socially conservative leaders. Gap's DGP was sent death threats and warnings that outsiders should stay out of Mewat. The government departments involved and the district administration counselled the program to step back and let the controversy blow over. This stepping back compounded the effect of the recession into a prolonged slowdown.

Meanwhile, the Gap DGP finally decided to leave at the end of 2010. Part of the reason for her departure was wider shifts in CSR and restructuring within the company. Other old-school colleagues also moved on as budgets were cut and reporting lines re-aligned in ways that made CSR subsidiary to procurement. A second person who was appointed by Gap to look after the Mewat project also moved shortly after (in, 2011), and by 2013 Gap had still to appoint a replacement. Meanwhile the official at MWCD who had championed the project also moved to a different department, but remains broadly interested and is in touch with SPYM.

In her new department (Rural Development), she and her colleagues are working to replicate the Mewat model in other states—Andhra Pradesh and Bihar, where there exists a network of SHGs on which to layer the Mewat approach.

This organizational churn has left Impulse, OCCL, Radnik and SPYM in the project. SPYM still has offices and the community centre, the women remain interested and do whatever work OCCL and Radnik give them from time to time— about 60 workers were working at the time I last visited the program in 2013, but OCCL was preparing to ramp up orders as it was expecting embellishment to once again be in fashion in 2014. While all parties believe the program will continue, the structure of the model is changing and evolving. SPYM has begun to explore linkages with domestic buyers and it remains to be seen how the overlay of domestic work alongside export work will change the rules and the division of labour for the women of Mewat.

13.6   Conclusions

In the context of growing evidence about the limits of CSR, the private voluntary codes of conduct that have dominated the governance of global value chains over the past two decades, new experiments of extending labour protections are emerging where the state and the community are key actors alongside private firms. Private governance produced many gains that were valuable in the absence of the state's intervention in the cross-border regulation of production chains. However, deepening price pressures, intensified competition and the post-recession structuring of production chains in the context of shrinking global demand has opened up fresh vulnerabilities in formalized global value chains. These include the return of child labour, human trafficking and worker safety challenges in the context of the informalization of parts of the global garment chain.

This chapter examined an innovative new model aimed at providing decent wages and safe working conditions to women handworkers in Mewat, India, by linking them directly to garment exporters. This approach was anchored within a relational collaboration between global brands, the state and a community based organization, each with a specific role and clear set of functions. This modular, relatively portable model involved layering market linkage on top of prior institution building that had taken place as a result of government support in the community. The striking departure of the model from other approaches to thinking about global value chains was that it was structured around the spatialization of work, in that it focused on the community where the workers lived, and not just on workplaces. After striking initial success that lasted a year and a half, the model faced internal and external challenges—of organizational churn within its private and public partners, as well as effects of the great recession—to which it appears to be adapting.

The Mewat experiment, now in its fifth year of operation remains a work in progress. Its progress so far offers at least three lessons. First, a focus on 'place'—linked to, yet beyond the value chain—is important in efforts to extend labour standards and worker protections to informal workers labouring in less visible segments of global value chains, including those who become incorporated into formalized export networks. Place is important in terms of how it reflects the institutional relationships which link workers to workplaces. If we can create security in these places, the benefits will spill over into the wider labour market beyond individual chains. As the Mewat case showed, we will need to pay attention to the places where workers live and work and to the communities in which they are located to achieve greater impact. As precariousness and fragility grow in formalized segments of global value chains, and as migration and mobility, a lot of it unsafe, grows within these chains, the places that become the receptacles of where people move to and where the chains touchdown in space become important areas to pay attention to.

Second, firms are crucial links between workers and global markets, but they are not sufficient to diffuse good working conditions down and beyond the chain—the state will need to get involved, together with locally embedded civic actors. The Mewat case pointed to the importance of a layered approach to building public and private partnerships on top of institutional supports built over long years of work on the ground. But the Mewat case also sheds light on how material involvement of the state might be of critical importance to provide continuity to the connections of local workers with highly unpredictable and shifting private actors—brands, buyers and exporters—in today's volatile, price-driven, value chain world. As the Mewat case shows, a financial model whose sustainability relies on a continuous flow of orders in an industry marked by seasonality and fluctuations in fashion and in demand was unrealistic and institutionally incomplete. As Sabel noted in a different context (1982), the division of labour that the partners designed, and which was the program's strength initially was analytically acceptable to all partners at the start because of its relevance to the strengths of each. But it did not translate into any clear cut division of longer term responsibility between the organizations involved. When crisis hit, the most powerful actors withdrew. In future iterations of the program, it will be crucial to ensure that the components whose presence and coordination are indispensably required for the project to function are recognized and provided for (Hirschman, 1967).

Finally, the handholding, tutelage and coaching of the workers by the firms was of critical importance to the early success of the program, but left unresolved the question of how financially sustainable this approach was as production scaled up. The pressures that latter plagued the project highlighted why companies tend to fall back on the subcontractor model. Yet, the program has survived for over 5 years, albeit at reduced intensity. Moreover, despite the churn in the organizational partnerships and the division of labour envisaged at the outset, the program has evolved and adjusted to changes in its internal and external environment by turning to the domestic market in addition to exports. The most hopeful sign, perhaps, is the state's interest in extending the Mewat model to other regions and sectors. Even though a major brand, Gap, was a crucial co-originator of the program, the program's resilience is perhaps most clearly demonstrated by the fact that the experiment has survived its exit.

References

Bannerji, Abhijit, and Esther Duflo. 2007. 'The Economic Lives of the Poor'. *J Econ Persp* 21 (1): 141–67.

Barrientos, Stephanie. 2008. 'Contract Labour: The "Achilles Heel" of Corporate Codes in Commercial Value Chains'. *Develop Change* 39 (6): 977–90. doi: 10.1111/j.1467-7660.2008.00524.x.

Barrientos, S., G. Gereffi, and A. Rossi. 2011. 'Economic and Social Upgrading in Global Production Networks: A New Paradigm for a Changing World'. *Int Lab Rev* 150 (3–4): 319–40. doi: 1111/j.1564-913X.2011.00119.x.

Barrientos, Stephanie, and Sally Smith. 2007. 'Do Workers Benefit from Ethical Trade? Assessing Codes of Labor Practice in Global Production Systems'. *Third World Quart* 28 (4): 713–29. doi: 10.1080/01436590701336580.

BBC. 2007. 'Gap Pulls 'Child Labor' Clothing'. Accessed on April 16, 2015. Available at, http://news.bbc.co.uk/2/hi/south_asia/7066019.stm.

Bartley, Tim. 2011. 'Transnational Governance as the Layering of Rules: Intersection of Public and Private Standards. *Theor Inquir Law* 12 (2): 517–42.

Burke, Jason. 2014. 'Rana Plaza: One Year on from the Bangladesh Factory Disaster'. *The Guardian*, April 19.

Greenhouse, Steven. 2012. 'Documents Reveal New Details About Walmart's Connection Tazreen Factory Fire'. *New York Times*, October 2012.

Hirschman, Alfred O. 1967. *Development Projects Observed*. Brookings Institution.

Locke, Richard. 2013. *The Promise and Limits of Private Power.* Cambridge: MIT Press.

Locke, Richard, F. Quin, and A. Brause. 2007. 'Does Monitoring Improve Labor Standards? Lessons from Nike'. *Ind Labor Relat Rev* 61 (1): 3–31.

Manik, Julfikar Ali, and Jim Yardley. 2012. 'Bangladesh Finds Gross Negligence in Factory Fire'. *The New York Times*, December 17.

———. 'Building Collapse in Bangladesh Leaves Scores Dead'. *The New York Times*, April 24.

Mezzadari, Alessandra. 2011. 'Indian Garment Clusters and CSR Norms: Incompatible Agendas at the Bottom of the Garment Value Chain'. *mimeo*; SOAS.

McDougall, Dan. 2007. 'Child Sweatshop Shame Threatens Gap's Ethical Image'. *The Observer*, October 28. Accessed on February 11, 2015. Available at, http://www.theguardian.com/business/2007/oct/28/ethicalbusiness.india.

Nadvi, Khalid. 2008. 'Global Standards, Global Governance, and the Organization of Global Value Chains'. *J Econ Geogr* 8: 323–43.

O'Connor, Clare. 2014. 'These Retailers Involved in Bangladesh Factory Disaster Have Yet to Compensate Victims'. *Forbes*, April 26.

O' Rourke, Dana. 2002. 'Monitoring the Monitors: A Critique of Corporate Third Party Labor Monitoring'. In *Corporate Social Responsibility and Labor Rights: Codes of Conduct in the Global Economy*, edited by R. Jenkins, R. Pearson, and G. Seyfang. London: Earthscan.

Sabel, Charles. 1982. 'The Structure of the Labor Market'. In *Work and Politics, the Division of Labor in Industry*. Cambridge University Press. pp. 31–77.

Tewari, Meenu. 2010. 'Footloose Capital, Intermediation and the Search for the "High-Road" in Low Wage Industries'. In *Labour in Global Production Networks in India*, edited by Anne Posthuma and Dev Nathan, 31–77. New Delhi: Oxford University.

Unni, Jeemol and S. Scaria. 2009. 'Governance, Structure and Labor Market Outcomes in Garment Embellishment Chains'. *Working Paper 194*, Gujarat Institute for Development Research.

Yardley, Jim. 2012. 'Horrific Fire Revealed a Gap in Safety for Global Brands'. *The New York Times*, December 6.

14

Social Upgrading in Mobile Phone GVCs

Firm-level Comparisons of Working Conditions and Labour Rights

Joonkoo Lee, Gary Gereffi and Sang-Hoon Lee

14.1 Introduction

In developing countries, more and better jobs have been a key goal of economic development based on the integration of local firms and workers into global value chains (GVCs). As global production is increasingly organized by multinational lead firms through a dense web of inter-firm relationships across national boundaries, the participation of local producers in GVCs is widely considered to be an effective way to create new employment, generate incomes, and therefore reduce poverty in developing countries. Such optimism is premised on the expectation that, as firms and countries move up the value chain into high value-added activities through varied forms of economic upgrading, workers will benefit through higher wages and better working conditions. In other words, economic upgrading is expected to lead to improved workers' conditions and entitlement in GVCs.

Over the last several years, however, there has been a growing concern about the disjuncture between the gains from GVC integration and economic upgrading, and what is captured by workers and their families and communities surrounding them (Barrientos et al., 2012; Posthuma and Nathan, 2010). This concern has been reinforced by a growing body of evidence and a plethora of news reports and public exposés showing that workers in developing countries catering to global buyers, from Chinese electronics workers to Bangladeshi apparel workers, are not given a fair share of the gains from export growth.[1] This has prompted GVC researchers to propose the concept of social upgrading, which entails an enhancement of the

---

[1] Different concepts, such as 'living wages' and 'fair wages', have been proposed to define a fair share of the gains for workers in GVCs beyond the minimum wage. According to Vaughan-Whitehead (2014, p. 69), 'fair wages' refer to 'wage levels, wage progression and wage-fixing mechanisms that

quality of employment and working conditions and an improvement in the rights and entitlements of workers (Barrientos et al., 2011). The Capturing the Gains research program has been a notable effort to examine the conditions under which economic and social upgrading in GVCs might be combined.[2]

Building upon this effort, our study attempts to investigate the relationship between economic and social upgrading by comparing labour conditions at the firm and factory levels in mobile phone GVCs. Specifically, it asks three comparative questions:

1. A vertical comparison (VC): Are working conditions better in higher value-added segments of the mobile phone value chain?
2. A horizontal comparison (HC): Do some firms do better in social upgrading than others in the same segment of the chain?
3. A temporal comparison (TC): Have working conditions gotten better (or worse) over time in our focal firms?

To address these questions, we use data from multiple reports on investigations, published by various non-governmental organizations (NGOs) and labour watchdogs, which document working conditions in mobile phone (and electronics) factories in China and India. We focus on the GVCs driven by two original equipment manufacturers (OEMs) in the mobile phone GVC, Nokia and Samsung Electronics Co. (SEC), and their major suppliers. China and India are particularly relevant when investigating labour conditions in mobile phone GVCs because China is the world's largest producer and exporter of mobile phones and India has emerged as one of the major production hubs for mobile phone firms (Lee and Gereffi, 2013).

The rest of the chapter is organized as follows. First, we discuss labour issues in GVCs and the concept of social upgrading. Second, the data, comparative methods and profiles of the case firms used in this study are introduced. Third, we present our findings in terms of the vertical, horizontal and temporal comparisons outlined above. Finally, this chapter discusses the implications of our key findings and the limitations of this study.

14.2 Global value chains, labour and social upgrading

Labour is an integral part of a capitalist system. Workers are key productive agents in the operation of the system. Labour unions and workers are influential as pressure groups and as consumers, respectively. Differences in the size and quality of the workforce,

---

provide a living wage floor for workers, while complying with national wage regulations and lead to balanced wage developments within the company'.

[2] For more information on the program, see http://www.capturingthegains.org/

wages, and workers' bargaining power *vis-à-vis* employers across countries and regions have been major driving forces in shaping the uneven geographies of production and trade in the global economy (Bair and Werner, 2011; Dicken, 2011). There is also an overarching concern with unequalization and the 'race to the bottom,' i.e., downward pressure on working conditions (Kaplinsky, 2000; Schmitz, 2004). While the global commodity chain, a conceptual precursor of GVCs, refers to 'a network of labour and production processes whose end result is a finished commodity' (Hopkins and Wallerstein, 1986, p. 159), labour has been relatively neglected as an object of study from a GVC perspective until recently (Barrientos et al., 2011; Coe et al., 2008; Rainnie et al., 2011; Selwyn, 2012). More attention has been paid to the role of relatively skilled workers in moving up the value chain to higher value-added activities, or 'economic upgrading' (Gereffi et al., 2011) than to the consequences for various types of workers across the chains and their social conditions (Barrientos et al., 2011).

Creating more and better jobs is a central objective of economic development strategies centred on GVC integration. Since global production is increasingly organized through a dense web of inter-firm relationships across national boundaries, the participation of local producers in GVCs is widely considered an effective way to generate employment and reduce poverty in developing countries. Indeed, the sectors integrated into GVCs have become important sources of job creation for low-income countries, many of which lack significant job-creating manufacturing sectors (Gereffi and Fernandez-Stark, 2011). Historically, in newly industrializing countries in Asia, export-driven light manufacturing, such as textiles, apparel and toys, provided a launching pad for generating a large number of manufacturing jobs with decent wages and working conditions (Gereffi and Wyman, 1990), and workers in the export sector became a key agent for large-scale social change, like democratization (Koo, 2001). This is still the case, as exemplified by the apparel industry. The expansion of the apparel GVC into low-income countries has played a critical role in employment generation because these countries represent three-fourths of world clothing exports, and the sector's formal employment amounts to 25 million in low- to mid-income economies (ILO, 2005).

There is concern, however, about the growing disjuncture between the gains from GVC integration and economic upgrading, and what is captured by workers and their families and communities surrounding them (Barrientos et al., 2012; Posthuma and Nathan, 2010). The initial presumption of the GVC-based economic development strategy was, explicitly or implicitly, that as firms and countries moved up the value chain into high value-added activities, workers would also benefit from economic upgrading with higher wages and better working conditions. It was expected that economic upgrading would lead to an improvement in the well-being of workers in GVCs (Milberg and Winkler, 2010). Such optimism, however, has been overshadowed during the last decade by a mounting body of evidence and a plethora of news reports and public exposés showing that workers linked to global buyers do not receive a fair share of the gains from export growth. Public concerns have escalated after revelations about young Chinese migrant workers in electronics factories who jumped from dormitory buildings and killed themselves (Chan, 2013), Bangladeshi garment workers who lost their lives in a series of factory fires and building collapses (Miller, 2012) and children who work in horrible conditions to mine minerals for multinationals in many developing countries (Nathan and Sarkar, 2011).

For a long time, undesirable working conditions in export-driven sectors and special economic zones (SEZs) have been studied and reported (Freeman, 2000; McKay, 2006). However, a distinctive feature of a GVC-driven global economy is that more and more large and well-known global brands have become implicated in these labour issues (Locke et al., 2013). Nike, a pioneer of 'factory-less' branded manufacturing, whose competitive edge lies in design, branding and marketing (Donaghu and Barff, 1990), is among the companies that have faced intense scrutiny and public outrage for labour wrongdoings in their suppliers' factories in Asia (Locke 2003). As offshore outsourcing has become an industry norm among global brands, from apparel to electronics to grocery retailing, they have found themselves under an intense spotlight with regard to labour problems in their global supply chains. At the same time, several factors, including the expansion of GVCs into low-income economies, the fine-slicing of value chain activities, and the rise of multiple-tier, complex supply chain structures, have generated numerous blind spots in GVCs, in terms of enforcing and monitoring labour laws and standards (Lim and Phillips, 2008; Locke, 2013). As the chains reach down to lower-tier suppliers and countries with weaker law enforcement capabilities, workers in those firms or countries are stuck in zones where transparency is, at best, limited. This presents new challenges in ensuring decent working conditions across GVCs, along with significant business risks to global brands.

Although many of these workers are often not direct employees of global brands or their independent suppliers, global buyers have the incentive to care about labour conditions in their supply chains for several reasons. Any wrongdoing would lead to far greater damage to their business than that of their suppliers, given the higher visibility of the brands to consumers and the public. In addition, any disruption caused by labour unrest in one segment of the supply chain could impact the operation of the entire chain by creating a ripple effect, as exemplified in the disruption of Japanese carmaker Honda's supply chains by Chinese workers' strikes in 2010 (Bradsher, 2010). Furthermore, global buyers and manufacturers are fully aware that workers play a critical role in ensuring the quality of products and implementing a variety of social and environmental standards, which have become more important in a consolidated market (Barrientos and Visser, 2012).

In recent years, research on the labour dimension of GVCs has begun to gain traction (Barrientos et al., 2011; Coe, 2013; Rainnie et al., 2011). Its interest and focus have been expanded to include a variety of labour issues, including child labour (Phillips et al., 2014), labour staffing agencies (Barrientos, 2008), labour regulations (Lan et al., 2015), and labour standards (Locke and Romis, 2010). The effects of various governance forms and actors on labour conditions have also been examined (Gereffi and Lee, 2016; Locke, 2013; Mayer, 2014). One of the most notable efforts to address labour in GVCs is the introduction of the concept of 'social upgrading', which addresses the quality of employment and improvement in the rights and entitlements of workers (Barrientos et al., 2011).

Social upgrading can be subdivided into two components: measurable standards and enabling rights (Elliott and Freeman, 2003, Barrientos and Smith, 2007). Measurable standards are those aspects of worker well-being that are more easily observed and quantifiable. This includes different aspects, such as the type of employment (regular or irregular), wage level, social protection and working hours. Enabling rights of workers are those that are less easily quantified, such as freedom of association and the right to collective bargaining, non-discrimination, voice and empowerment. Lack of access to enabling rights undermines the ability of workers (or specific groups of workers, such as women and migrants) to negotiate improvements to their working conditions that could enhance their well-being. The Capturing the Gains research program, as noted, focuses on the relationship between economic and social upgrading in GVCs. The core question of the research is under what conditions economic upgrading is likely to lead to social upgrading. In other words, how does a firm's position in GVCs affect the conditions of the workers in the firm? Under what circumstances could one expect economic upgrading to lead to better working conditions in GVCs?

In an attempt to answer these larger questions, this paper poses three types of comparative questions: vertical, horizontal and temporal. Figure 14.1 illustrates the mobile phone GVC and the three modes of comparison.

The first question is whether a firm located in a higher value-added segment of the mobile phone value chain provides better working conditions than its counterpart at the lower value-added segments. This vertical question compares firms located at two different nodes of the value chain in terms of their working conditions. In the case of mobile phone GVCs, the following two nodes are critical: branded manufacturers (or OEMs) like Samsung and Apple, and their suppliers and assemblers of parts and components (Lee and Gereffi, 2013). It is known that OEMs, which produce and sell mobile phones of their own brands, tend to capture much higher value than their suppliers, although the value position of various suppliers may vary (Dedrick et al., 2011). In addition, OEMs are likely to face stronger pressures for social upgrading from NGOs and consumers given that their brands are more recognizable than their suppliers are (Mayer and Gereffi, 2010). Thus, we should expect better working conditions in an OEM's factory than the factories of its suppliers.

The second question is horizontal in nature, i.e., whether and how much working conditions vary between firms in the same GVC segment. On the one hand, firms can provide working conditions that are different from those of their peers in the same value chain position; this is influenced by various firm-level factors, ranging from structural (e.g., firm size) and financial attributes (e.g., profits) to ownership (e.g., country origin) and managerial characteristics (e.g., human resource management practices). On the other hand, suppliers linked to the same buyer (or a similar group of buyers) may provide relatively homogenous conditions for their workers if the amount of value captured by the suppliers *vis-à-vis* the buyers is more or less same. The fact that all of the case firms in our horizontal comparison were suppliers for Nokia that were located close to one another and relied on almost the same regional labour markets leads us to expect relatively similar working conditions across the suppliers.

The final comparison question involves a temporal change, i.e., whether working conditions in GVCs have improved over time in a given firm or factory. Several factors lead us to expect improvement in some, if not all, aspects of labour conditions. During the period of our observation, many mobile phone firms experienced considerable growth and economic upgrading, which provided them more resources that could be used for such improvement. In addition, market and value chain concentration in the post-crisis mobile phone GVC (Lee and Gereffi, 2013) likely put a higher level of public pressure for social upgrading on consolidated firms with greater visibility, as exemplified by Apple. The leading smartphone brand came under intense public scrutiny after labour wrongdoings were revealed in the Chinese factories of Foxconn, its key supplier (Duhigg and Barboza, 2012). Thus, we should expect that labour conditions in a given factory improved over time although the degree of improvement may vary by upgrading areas.

In short, we would expect working conditions: (a) to be better in higher value-added segments of the chain, specifically in OEMs rather than their suppliers (vertical comparison); (b) to be relatively similar in the same GVC segment (horizontal comparison); and (c) in terms of the temporal comparison, we expect working conditions in a given factory to be better over time, i.e., at t_2 than t_1 in Figure 14.1.

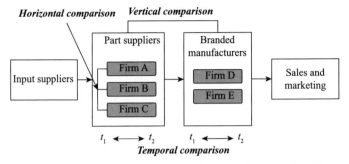

Figure 14.1 Mobile phone global value chains and three modes of comparison
Source: Authors.

14.3 Data, methods and cases

To address these questions, we examined multiple reports that document working conditions in mobile phone (and electronics) factories in China and India. These investigation reports were published by various NGOs and labour watchdogs. While they are not the ideal data set to analyse contemporary labour conditions, our use of secondary data was shaped by the well-recognized difficulty of collecting systematic and comparable data on working conditions in mobile phone factories across different factories and/or over time. The ideal research design would be a cross-factory/firm comparative study conducted over time with a well-defined, consistently applied framework to assess the various aspects of labour conditions in multiple firms. However, this would only be possible with active cooperation from the firms and workers in study, which is generally lacking.[3]

Our choice has advantages and disadvantages. The downside involves the issue of cross-case comparability and reliability. The investigations these reports were grounded on were not designed under a single research scheme and conducted independently, and because of a general lack of access to these factories, researchers gathered information through whatever means were available, with little or no consideration to potential data collection biases. Thus, different reports often use distinct categories to assess various aspects of working conditions in the factories. Critical information (e.g., wages) is missing for some cases or not comparable across the cases even in the same report, constraining

---

[3] By far, the most rigorous effort to analyse certain aspects of labour conditions in global supply chains is the recent book by Richard Locke (2013). For a discussion of the strengths and shortcomings of Locke's analysis, see the Review Symposium of his book in the journal *Socio-Economic Review* (Gereffi et al., 2014). Locke's book focuses on the limitations of voluntary corporate codes of conduct and factory-level capability-building approaches, and thus it does not address the full range of social upgrading conditions addressed in this paper.

our ability to make systematic comparisons. Another drawback is the reliability of the data. Due to the extremely limited access to workers and managers through official channels, these reports largely relied on a small number of off-site worker interviews (and even fewer when it comes to our particular firms of interest). Furthermore, the claims of workers were not independently verified in most cases.

Despite all the downsides, we believe our study is a worthwhile effort for advancing our understanding of this important topic because the current state of available data is unlikely to improve in the near future. We have a rather modest goal, i.e., providing the best possible answer to the topic in a few specific cases, and controlling for industry and factory locations by country. Moreover, our design has several advantages over the case-based or cross-sectional studies. First, our data, albeit secondary and with the aforementioned flaws, allow us to capture temporal changes in working conditions that might otherwise be difficult to pin down. The publication of the earliest report that we utilized dates back to 2005, when the relocation of mobile phone manufacturing to countries like China and India began to take off, with scant attention given to the implications of the production shift on labour conditions in developing countries. Second, these reports enable us to conduct a series of controlled comparisons of multiple OEM firms and supplier factories without collecting first-hand data for each of them, which would be a daunting task. We deliberately chose our firm cases among the ones best documented in the reports, controlling as best we could for differences among the cases that might affect the outcomes.

We have examined the relationship between economic and social upgrading at the firm, and more specifically the factory, levels. Our specific questions are summarized as follows:

- Vertical (cross-chain segment) comparison (VC): Are working conditions better in one segment of the chain than others? For example, does an OEM (higher value-added segment) provide better working conditions than its suppliers (lower value-added segments)?
- Horizontal (within-chain segment) comparison (HC): In the same segment of the chain, do some firms do better in social upgrading than others? For example, between Flextronics and Foxconn, two leading contract manufacturers, which is better at social upgrading?
- Temporal (cross-period) comparison (TC): Have working conditions gotten better (or worse) over time in a given firm? For example, do Samsung or Foxconn provide better working conditions now than a decade ago?

Table 14.1 introduces the profiles of case firms and factories in our paper. They include two global OEMs in mobile phones: Nokia (now Microsoft Mobile) from Finland

Table 14.1 Profile of case firms and factories

Company (Headquarters)	Factory location	Establishment year	Main activities	Main buyers	VC				HC			TC	
					1	2	3	4	1	2	3	1	2
Dongguan Nokia Mobile Phones Co., Ltd. (Finland)*	Dongguan, China	1995	Assembly	Nokia	•								
Nokia India (Finland)*	Chennai, India	2006	Mobile phone manufacturing	Nokia		•	•					•	
Foxconn Electronics Inc. (Taiwan)	Shenzhen, China	1988	Component manufacturing (cases)	Nokia, Motorola	0				0				
Foxconn Electronics Inc. (Taiwan)	Chennai, India	2007	Components (cell phone plastic covers, panels)	Nokia		0	0			0	0	0	
Flextronics (Singapore)	Chennai, India	2006	Components (cell phone chargers, mechanical closures, PCB assemblies)	Nokia, Alcatel, Sony Ericsson			0				0		
Salcomp (Shenzhen) Co., Ltd. (Finland)	Shenzhen, China	2002–2003	Accessories (battery chargers)	Nokia	0				0				

Company	Location	Year	Main products/activities	Customers	2014	2007
Salcomp (Finland)	Chennai, India	2007	Accessories (cell phone chargers)	Nokia, Samsung, LG	0	0
Perlos Engineering Plastics Company, Ltd. (Finland)*	Guangzhou, China	2000	Components (housings, plastic components)	Nokia	0	0
Perlos Engineering Plastics Company, Ltd. (Finland)*	Chennai, India	2007	Components (casings)	N/A	0	0
Shenzhen Samsung Kejian Mobile Communication Technology Co., Ltd. (South Korea)	Shenzhen, China	2002	CDMA mobile phone manufacturing	Samsung	•	•
Tianjin Samsung Telecommunications Co. (South Korea)	Tianjin, China	2001	GSM, CDMA mobile phone manufacturing	Samsung		•
Tianjin Samsung Mobile Display (South Korea)	Tianjin, China	2004	Components (mobile display devices)	Samsung	0	0

Source: see Data Sources below.

Note: • OEMs; 0 component suppliers;

*Nokia and Perlos were acquired, respectively, by Microsoft and LiteOn Technology (Taiwan) in 2014 and 2007.

and Samsung Electronics (SEC) from South Korea (Korea hereafter); and two major contract manufacturers, Foxconn (Taiwan) and Flextronics (Singapore). While the latter two firms, also known as electronics manufacturing service (EMS) firms, provide assembly services for major OEMs, their factories studied here functioned as component suppliers for the OEMs. Other factories are component suppliers that have close or special relationships with their OEM buyers. During the period under study, Perlos (now part of LiteOn Technology) and Salcomp were Finnish component suppliers for Nokia, although they supplied other OEMs. Tianjin Samsung Mobile Display (TSMD) was affiliated to Samsung Group, along with its main buyer, SEC.[4]

First, our four vertical comparison (VC) cases compare one OEM (either Nokia or Samsung) and the suppliers in its supply chains. Three of the cases involve Nokia's supply chains located in China and India, and the other one involves SEC's two Chinese assembly factories in Shenzhen and Tianjin, and their display supplier (also affiliated to Samsung Group). The question is whether Nokia or Samsung provided better working conditions than their suppliers. Second, our three horizontal comparison (HC) cases overlap with the VC cases, but we highlight the differences among the suppliers. We look at several three-firm sets arrayed for vertical comparison in different locational and temporal settings with a focus on the differences between the firms at the same chain segment. Finally, two temporal comparison (TC) cases involve two sets of companies whose working conditions are analysed at two different points in time.

For each case, we examined the following aspects of working conditions in the factories: (1) working hours, wages and overtimes; (2) hiring and contract practices (e.g., internship, temporary workers, and benefits); and (3) health and safety conditions. In addition, labour rights were assessed in terms of unionization and the presence of collective bargaining, along with the presence and effectiveness of communication channels between workers and the management. Other aspects (e.g., discrimination and harassment) are included if related information is available in the sources.

14.4 Working conditions and labour rights in mobile phone GVCs: Comparative findings

In this section, we discuss the main findings from our comparative research. The first four cases involve vertical comparison (VC), two OEMs and their suppliers: three for Nokia and one for SEC (Tables 14.2 through 14.5). The discussion for

---

[4] Nokia's mobile phone unit was acquired by Microsoft and has become part of Microsoft Mobile since April 2014. Perlos was acquired by Taiwan-based LiteOn Technology Co. in 2007.

Joonkoo Lee, Gary Gereffi and Sang-Hoon Lee

Table 14.2 Working conditions in China: Nokia, Salcomp, Perlos, Foxconn, China, c2004 (re: VC#1 & HC#1)

	OEM		Suppliers	
	Dongguan Nokia Mobile Phones	Salcomp (Shenzhen)	Perlos (Guangzhou) Engineering Plastics	Foxconn Electronics (Longhua)
Employment	500	4,500	1,200	70,000
Composition of workers	Migrant: N/A; Female: approx. 50%; Contract: N/A	Migrant: 85%; Female: 78%; Contract: N/A	Migrant: 75%; Female: 50%; Contract: 46%	Migrant: 85%; Female: 70%; Contract: N/A
Hiring	Direct hiring for perm. workers	Through local staffing agencies (no deposits for workers)	Through local staffing agencies (fee deduction from wages)	Hiring part-timers through a local staffing agency
Working hours Working days	a. 12-hr, two shifts; b. 4 workdays and 3 days off	a. 12-hr, two shifts; b. 6 workdays and 1 day off	a. 8-hr, three shifts; switches every 2 weeks; b. one day off in 7 days	a. 12-hr, two shifts; b. one day off every 3 weeks
Probation period	N/A	1 month	2 months	6 months
Overtime	Strong restriction on overtime (dampening actual earnings)	2-hr/day; frequent and compulsory	3-hr/day; not compulsory	3-hr/day; pressures for overtime due to high production quota
Wages (permanent workers, RMB/month)	No exact figure available; above legal minimum	Dropped from RMB 1,400 to 1,000 (Mar 2004) for 3-year workers (went up after strikes in July 2004 by an unspecified amount)	More than minimum wage (RMB 510 and 684 since Dec. 2004)	Basic: RMB 600 (minimum wage: 450)+overtime; Overall: RMB 1,000+/month

(Contd)

326

Table 14.2 (Contd)

	OEM	Suppliers		
	Dongguan Nokia Mobile Phones	Salcomp (Shenzhen)	Perlos (Guangzhou) Engineering Plastics	Foxconn Electronics (Longhua)
Social insurance	Covered	Only for permanent workers	No social insurance (monthly social insurance supplement provided)	Only for permanent workers
Housing and other benefits	Company housing for permanent workers - 8–9 per room; air-conditioned	Company-rented housing + bus transport; - 12 per room ('crowded') - no hot water or drinking in the rooms (see company reaction)	Company housing + housing allowance + bus transport only for permanent workers - 5 per room (30 sqm) - hot and cold water, internet	Company housing: 8 per room (25 sqm)
Punitive measures (financial)	Extra training without pay for mistakes	Reprimanded by supervisors for mistakes (see company reaction)	N/A	Recurring mistakes: - falling asleep (20 yuan or more) + verbal reprimand
Health and safety	a. Minimum contact with hazardous materials b. Complying with Chinese standards c. Fire training 4 times a year;	a. Air-conditioned b. Protective gears provided c. Irregular fire drills (1–4 times a year) d. 1–2 days introductory safety training (see company reaction)	a. Factory halls air-conditioned b. Minimal noise and dust c. Facility fully or partially automated d. Specially designed seats for manual workers	a. Little or no training after introductory one b. Some parts of the factory not air-conditioned

	d. Regular equipment inspection		e. Rigorous introductory training; own safety handbook; f. Twice-a-year fire drills	None
Labour union	None	None (2-day strikes on July 2004)	None	None
Communication channels	Suggestion box	a. Suggestion box (management responds) b. Monthly newsletter	Suggestion board (management responds)	Suggestion box (limited or no impact; only reaches lower managers)
Code of conduct (CoC)	Not effective measures to monitor compliance	Nokia's CoC posted; Nokia inspected twice a month, but not about workers' rights (see company reaction)	Nokia's CoC received but not distributed in the factory; treated it as a confidential document	Not aware of Nokia's code of conduct; client visits focused on quality and efficiency, not workers' rights

Source: FinnWatch et al. (2005).
Note: 'N/A' denotes that the source has no information in the given factory.

Table 14.3 Working conditions comparison in Nokia, Salcomp, Perlos, Foxconn, India, c2008 (re: VC#2 & HC#2 & TC#1)

	OEM		Suppliers	
	Nokia India	Salcomp	Perlos	Foxconn
Employment	8,000	1,800 (2008); 2,500 (2009)	770 (2008); 2,000 (2009)	2,500–3,000 (2009)
Composition of workers	Female: approx. 50%	Female: 85% No contract workers	Female: 40%	Female: 50–60%
Working hours Working days	Three 8-hr shifts	Three 8-hr shifts on 6 workdays	Three 8-hr shifts on 6 workdays	N/A
Trainee period	N/A	14 months	N/A	1.5–2 years
Overtime	Very rare	No overtime work	Very rare	a. No overtime work (management's stance) b. Overtime almost everyday, even on Sundays; threatened with dismissal if they refuse (workers' claims)
Wages (permanent workers, rupees/month)	a. Average range: Rs. 4,500–5,500 b. Trainees (1-yr): Rs. 2,500–3,000	a. Starting: more than minimum wage (Rs. 3,700) b. Average: Rs. 5,500 c. Lowest take-home: Rs. 4,500	Average: Rs. 3,600 (just at minimum wage)	Average: Rs. 4,500 (overtime included)

				Employee state insurance (management's stance)
Social insurance	N/A	a. Provident fund, employees' state insurance, retirement fund (management's stance); b. ESI dispensary; access limited (workers' claims)	State social security and health insurance, Provident Fund	
Other benefits	a. Wedding (Rs. 5000) and birthday (Rs. 500) allowances b. Various in-house skill training	a. Subsidise food (85%) b. Free transportation	a. Free transportation b. Workers paid for food	a. Free shuttle bus b. Canteen food
Discrimination	a. Committee against Sexual Harassment b. Women workers' grievance attended c. Local youth around the SEZ denied employment d. Unfavourable working conditions for pregnant women	Surrounding community complains about gender-based employment	N/A	Discriminatory actions against local workers
Health and safety	a. Experienced back pain, aches in legs, and exhaustion b. Varying degree of skill ailments reported	a. Use of potentially harmful chemicals (workers' report)	Limited health service	N/A

(Contd)

Table 14.3 (Contd)

	OEM		Suppliers	
	Nokia India	**Salcomp**	**Perlos**	**Foxconn**
	c. 1–2 times a year medical check-up (records not accessible)	b. Use of chemicals limited and meets all legal standards (management response)		
	d. Very few undergone fire drills and first aid training	c. Report could not verify either claim		
Labour union	Unionized (2009–2010) following a series of strikes and workers' suspension and reinstatement	None	None	None
Communication channels	Workers' council; set up by the management in 2009	a. Company committees on health & safety, canteen, transport, work	No workers' council or any other forum for grievances	N/A
		b. Grievance process		
		c. Regular meetings		

Code of conduct	N/A	a. No participation in any social audit in India	N/A	a. EMS Electronic Manufacturing Standards and Nokia's standards; ISO 9000 b. Two internal and one outside auditing per year; Nokia conducts supplier audits

Source: CIVIDEP-SOMO (2009; 2010).
Note: 'N/A' denotes that the source has no information in the given factory. ESI: Employees State Insurance; ISO: International Organization for Standardization; SEZ: special economic zone.

Table 14.4 Working conditions in Nokia, Salcomp, Foxconn, Flextronics, India, c2011 (re: VC#3 & HC#3 & TC#1)

	OEM	Suppliers		
	Nokia	**Salcomp**	**Foxconn**	**Flextronics**
Employment	15,300	4,000	5,000	1,700
Working hours Working days	Four, 8-hr shift (one shift is always off)	Three, 8-hr shift per day, 6 days a week	N/A	Three, 8-hr shift per day, 6 days a week
Probation period	6 months	6 months	6 months	6 months
Training	a. 50% of workers: no special training for trainees b. 30% of workers: estimated training; 15 days to 1 month, including a 1-week class w/pay about work-related safety c. Remained trainee status for 15 months	a. Worked as trainees for the first 18 months b. Managers admitted that a new operator can learn the necessary skills in 4–6 weeks	a. Even after 2 years of trainee period, no permanent order given b. Trainees assessed at the end of the year and put on probationary status c. Workers with no performance problems in the training period automatically confirmed as permanent status	a. No separate 'trainee' category b. Preliminary training: 3–6 days (classroom-based and practice at model work stations) c. Contract workers: gained training on the job and appointed as permanent workers after assessment

Wages (Permanent workers, Rs/month)	Rs. 4,820–11,666 - 0–15 months: 4,820 - 2–3 years: 6,420 - 4 + years; 11,666	Rs. 4,600–6,000	Rs. 8,000–9,500 - 2–3 years: 8,000 - 3–4 years: 9,000 - 4 + years: 9,500+	Rs. 5,300–6,000 - 4 + years: 53% pay increase on average
Wages (Contract workers, Rs/month)	Rs. 3,600–6,000 - Length of employment - 25% above minimum wage but below a living wage	Rs. 4,200	Rs. 5,000 (w/PF and ESI included) - Contract workers must pay for uniforms around Rs. 750 per year	Rs. 4,130–5,500
Wages (Trainees, Rs/month)	Rs. 4,820	Rs. 4,200	Rs. 5,000	N/A
Social insurance	Employer's contributions (incl. contract workers) - Provident Fund (PF) - Employee State Insurance (ESI)	Advice on employees state insurance (ESI)	N/A	Medical insurance provided for employees and family
Health and safety	a. Long hours of standing in assembly line;	a. Three nurses	a. No regular health check-ups (only for the new employees)	Complies w/EICC standards and implements 'Flex-pledge'

(Contd)

Table 14.4 (Contd)

	OEM	Suppliers		
	Nokia	**Salcomp**	**Foxconn**	**Flextronics**
	b. Rest area provided c. Medical clinic only in the SEZ; will be a bigger clinic during 2011	b. Training in first aid, counselling, emergency preparedness, health and hygiene education, safety classes	b. Health centre only has an un-trained nurse who gives the same pill regardless of the symptoms c. Workers attend private medical clinics	(part of workers' rights program)
Discrimination	N/A	N/A	Preferential treatment of newly recruited workers over more experienced workers involved in the strike	N/A
Standing orders	Referred to standing orders to justify the suspension of workers after strikes	Framed on the basis of a common format used by all companies in the Nokia Telecom SEZ	a. Accused workers of breaking various company rules in relation to strikes in 2010 b. Workers did not know what the orders were, but got a thick document copy in English, as part of the 'hearings'	N/A

Labour union	Nokia employees union – recognized as an 'independent' union – in process of getting formally registered – 60 members including women (open to contract workers)	No union (rebuked for forming groups and approaching the management)	– Formed in April 2010 – LPF represented workers, signed a 3-year wage settlement – Some workers disappointed w/LPF decision to affiliate with CITU, which Foxconn refused to recognize as a union	N/A
Communication channels	N/A	a. Three core workers' committees in place of unions to handle workers' issues (committee members selected annually by workers) b. Human resource manager receives grievances, shares phone number	N/A	a. Workers' committees b. Quarterly 'town hall' meeting, monthly shop-floor conclaves, 'skip level' meetings

Source: Finnwatch et al. (2011).

Note: 'N/A' denotes that the source has no information in the given factory. CITU: Centre of Indian Trade Unions; LPF: Labour Progressive Federation; SEZ: special economic zone.

Table 14.5 Working conditions in Samsung Shenzhen, Samsung Tianjin and Tianjin Samsung Mobile Display, China, c2004 (VC#4, TC#2)

	OEM	Supplier	
	Shenzhen Samsung Kejian Mobile Communication Technology	**Tianjin Samsung Telecommunications**	**Tianjin Samsung Mobile Display**
Employment	1,000	4,500	1,200
Working hours/days	a. Three 8-hr shifts b. 5 working days/week (1 day off/week in peak time)	a. Three, 8 -hour shifts, b. 5 working days/week (1 day off/week in peak season); annual leave, maternity leave	a. Three, 8-hour shifts b. 5 working days/week (1 day off/week in low season); annual leave, maternity leave
Recruitment channels	Vocational schools and labour agents (RMB 1,000/placement)	Vocational schools all over China	Vocational schools all over China
Hiring and labour contract	a. 3-month probation; b. 1-year, annually renewable contract	a. 3-month apprentice (legal minimum) b. 2-month probation (80% regular wage); c. 1-year, annually renewable, regular contract; no accumulation of seniority	a. 3-month apprentice (legal minimum) b. 2-month probation (80% regular wage) c. 1-year, annually renewable, contract; no accumulation of seniority
Overtime	N/A	Less than 2 days/week in peak time	Less than 2 days/week in peak time

Wages (permanent workers, RMB/month)	a. RMB 1,000 (Basic wage RMB 750 + Full attendance bonus RMB 100 + Travel allowance RMB 150) b. Overtime wage: RMB 1,300 (low)—1,600 (high)	a. RMB 1,150 (Basic wage RMB 530 + Incentives RMB 420 + Welfare RMB 200) b. Overtime wage: RMB 1,000 (low)—1,800 (high)	a. RMB 1,150 (Basic wage RMB 530 + Incentives RMB 420 + Welfare RMB 200) b. Overtime wage: RMB 1,000 (low)—RMB 1,600 (high)
Wages (apprentice/probation workers, RMB/month)	a. Basic wage: RMB 690 b. Overtime: RMB 6–8/hour	First 2 months: RMB 630 Third month: RMB 730	First 2 months: RMB 630 Third month: RMB 730
Housing	Six-person dormitory rooms - housing deduction RMB 200/month	Six-to-eight-person dormitory rooms - For migrant workers (RMB 80/month) - locals and some migrant workers rent places nearby	Six-to-eight-person dormitory rooms - For migrant workers (RMB 80/month) - locals and some migrant workers rent places nearby
Social security	a. RMB 60/month for old age b. Work injury insurance	a. Old age b. Work injury insurance	a. Old age b. Work injury insurance

Source: AMRC (2006).
Note: 'N/A' denotes that the source has no information in the given factory.

VC centres on the difference between the OEM and its suppliers. The differences between the latter are highlighted further when we present the findings from the horizontal comparisons.

14.4.1 Vertical comparison: Does an OEM provide better working conditions than its suppliers?

The first case (VC#1) compares working conditions in Nokia's mobile phone assembly factory in Dongguan, China and those of its three suppliers, Salcomp, Perlos and Foxconn, located in the same city. Each supplied Nokia with battery chargers, housings and plastic components and mobile phone cases, respectively. Overall, Nokia provided better conditions for workers than its suppliers (Table 14.2). Two aspects stand out: First, compared to its suppliers, Nokia's Dongguan factory was reported by interviewees to put strong restrictions on overtime, although the details are not available.[5] In China, a few hours of overtime were prevalent, and in some factories, as shown in the cases of Salcomp and Foxconn, working overtime was 'involuntary', in the sense that workers felt heavily pressured to work for extra hours in the face of high daily production quotas. Second, workers in the Nokia factory had more days off, particularly compared to Foxconn, where workers had only one day off every 3 weeks.

In certain aspects, however, Nokia did not perform better than its suppliers. For example, it only had suggestion boxes as communication channels between workers and management. Its factory did not have labour unions (nor did its three suppliers). Moreover, Nokia's codes of conduct were ineffective in many respects. Some suppliers received the codes of conduct, yet the workers did not have access to them (e.g., Perlos in China), and Foxconn in China was not aware of them. Visits to supplier factories by Nokia representatives appeared to be frequent, but they mainly focused on the production side (e.g., efficiency and product quality), not on the social aspects (e.g., working conditions and workers' rights). The comparison also highlights a common issue for workers in China. While migrant workers appeared to be prevalent, accounting for 75–85 per cent of employees in Nokia's supplier factories, these workers' well-being was negatively affected by public governance measures like the family registration (*hukou*) system, which prevented them from accessing social services.

The second VC case (VC#2) involves Nokia and the same three suppliers around 2008 in India. Nokia established its first Indian mobile phone factory in 2006 at the Sriperumbudur SEZ near Chennai, where other component suppliers were co-located to cater to Nokia. It is hard to assess all of the four equally because

---

[5] The unintended consequence of such restriction is to further depress the actual wages that workers bring home, when the company pays them only slightly above the minimum wage.

of insufficient comparable information (Table 14.3). One aspect that clearly stands out, however, is that Nokia's factory in India was unionized in 2009–2010 following a series of strikes. In contrast, labour rights were not supported in Nokia's supplier factories, in terms of the rights of free association and collective bargaining. Meanwhile, compared to the China case, overtime in Nokia's factory appeared to be less prevalent at the time when the study was conducted (2008–2009), as well as in some of its suppliers like Salcomp and Perlos. This might well have to do with shrinking orders caused by the global recession more than any country-specific factor, such as tighter working-hour regulations in India.

There are several areas of concern across these factories. First, Indian workers appeared to be better covered by social insurance without restrictions than workers in China. However, access was still an issue because workers often did not have information on how to acquire such benefits. Second, in India, there was discrimination against local communities. Firms in SEZs near Chennai in the state of Tamil Nadu preferred hiring commuting workers from the city or migrant workers from other parts of the state instead of young people living in the surrounding communities. Finally, the widespread use of interns and student workers and their long training period (e.g., 1.5–2 years for Foxconn India) is problematic. This practice often negatively affects wages because workers tend to get paid less during the probation period (e.g., trainee operators in Nokia India are paid 14 per cent less than their regular peers).

The third vertical comparison (VC#3) involves Nokia and its three component suppliers, i.e., Salcomp, Foxconn and Flextronics, located in the same Indian SEZ in 2011 (Table 14.4). Overall, Nokia provided better working conditions than its suppliers, in terms of wages, training periods, and health services. First, Nokia's workers received higher wages compared with their peers in its supplier factories when working for more than 4 years, although first-year wages were higher in Foxconn and Flextronics.[6] Second, the training period was shorter in the Nokia factory than in Salcomp and Foxconn, and Flextronics did not have a separate category for 'trainees'. While a longer training period may indicate higher skill requirements or a greater investment in skill development, it was also a reality that the trainee stage often lasts longer than it should, as admitted by a manager at Salcomp, only to be used to suppress wages for entry-level workers. Finally, Nokia provided better health services, with its own medical clinic and nurses available within the factory site, whereas health services in its supplier factories were provided by untrained

---

[6] Due to the lack of data on the average tenure of workers in these firms, it is not possible to measure the exact impact of the higher wages for longer-tenured workers. The social upgrading impact would probably be limited if many of the workers leave the factory in less than 4 years.

nurses, or worse, health check-ups were not even provided. However, the gap between Nokia and its suppliers has apparently narrowed since the 2008–2009 study (Table 14.3). We later discuss whether this is attributable to the worsening of working conditions in Nokia's factory or an improvement in the conditions in the suppliers' factories.

The final set of vertical comparisons (VC#4) concerns two SEC factories located in China circa 2004, Shenzhen Samsung Kejian Mobile Communication Technology and Tianjin Samsung Telecommunications, and one of its suppliers, Tianjin Samsung Mobile Display (Table 14.5). The most notable finding is that all three companies showed very similar characteristics in labour conditions. This may indicate a potential company effect, considering that all three companies were affiliated to the Samsung Group. Commonalities worth mentioning are equivalent working hours and overtime, similar housing conditions and social security benefits, the existence of a non-bargaining committee that handles workers' complaints, and even identical management practices, such as morning gatherings, daily production quotas, and discipline linked to an incentive scale.

Despite these similarities, disparities did exist in terms of wages, probation periods and the use of labour agents in recruitment. Regional differences played a larger role than firms' value chain positions in this comparative case. In the case of wages for permanent and apprentice/probation workers, using the basic wage as a standard for comparison, workers in Shenzhen Samsung had nearly 50 per cent higher wages compared to the other two firms in Tianjin, likely on account of higher living costs in Shenzhen. In addition, the probation period in Shenzhen was a month longer than at the two Tianjin-based firms, but when a 2-month apprenticeship is added, the total entry period is longer in the Tianjin firms. Finally, all three firms used vocational schools in their recruitment process, but Shenzhen Samsung also used labour agents for recruitment, which meant workers incurred placement fees.

14.4.2 Horizontal comparison: Do some suppliers do better in social upgrading than others?

The horizontal comparison consists of three cases in different locations and time periods, nested within the previous vertical comparison. The first two comparisons include three component suppliers—Salcomp, Perlos, and Foxconn—in distinct settings: China in 2004 (Table 14.2) and India in 2008–2009 (Table 14.3), respectively. The last comparison involves a slightly different set of Nokia suppliers, Salcomp, Foxconn, and Flextronics, in India circa 2011 (Table 14.4). Despite the differences, all three comparisons were linked to Nokia's value chains. Our findings indicate that the overall working conditions were quite similar across these suppliers, with no firm having a general advantage over the others. Each has different areas of concern, and there are also some common problems, notably lack of unionization.

The first comparison (HC#1) shows minor differences in working conditions between the case suppliers (Table 14.2 above). They include the length of probation periods, working hours and overtime, punitive financial measures, and housing conditions for employees. For example, Foxconn employees experienced exceptionally long probation periods of 6 months, compared to just 2 or 3 months at its counterparts. In addition, Foxconn workers were given far fewer days off than employees of the other suppliers, and faced greater pressure to work overtime. Lastly, all three companies provided housing, with Perlos offering this benefit only to its permanent workers and Salcomp having the least favourable conditions. Meanwhile, the common areas of concern include the possible breach of workers' rights through financial punishment for workers' mistakes, the semi-compulsory nature of overtime work, the lack of labour unions and other effective communication channels between employees and management, and the ineffectiveness of the buyer's codes of conduct in improving workplace conditions.

The comparison of the same three suppliers in India (HC#2) also shows relatively similar conditions, with no firm having an advantage over the others: there were equivalent working hours, little or no official overtime work, the nonexistence of labour unions, and similar base wages (Table 14.3). However, there is a disagreement between managers and workers in Foxconn over the existence of overtime; while management stated that there was no overtime work at all, workers reported the presence of extensive overtime work. In addition, Salcomp had extensive communication channels for the employees compared to the other two.

In the final set of horizontal comparisons (HC#3), we examined three suppliers in India, circa 2011: Salcomp, Foxconn, and Flextronics (Table 14.4). Differences between the suppliers were relatively marginal, with varied areas of concern. For example, Flextronics provided better social and fringe benefits and a favourable training environment for employees compared to the other two. Wages at Foxconn appeared to be 50–100 per cent higher for its regular and contract workers relative to those employed by the other two suppliers. Given that Foxconn's wages were not much higher in 2008–2009 (Table 14.3), this is likely the effect of a newly formed labour union, which was recognized in April 2010 and made a 3-year wage settlement with management. This upside, however, was offset by still inadequate services for workers' health and safety at Foxconn: no regular health check-ups and the use of an untrained nurse. The common areas of concern include the still lengthy period of probation (6 months at all the firms) and the limited role of codes of conduct.

14.4.3   Temporal comparison: Have working conditions improved over time?

The final comparison involves temporal difference in two different settings: (1) Nokia, Salcomp, and Foxconn in 2008 and 2011 in India and (2) Samsung Shenzhen and Tianjin Samsung Mobile Display in 2004 and 2012 in China. The question is whether working conditions improved in these companies over time.

In the first comparison (TC#1), there was significant improvement in several social upgrading dimensions in each of the three Indian factories between 2008 and 2011 (Tables 14.3 and 14.4). First, in all three factories, the size of the workforce nearly doubled: from 8,000 to 15,300 in Nokia, 1,800 to 4,000 in Salcomp, and 2,500 to 5,000 in Foxconn. This likely reflects increasing mobile phone production at Nokia's Indian operation and a ripple effect on its suppliers (Lee and Gereffi, 2013). Second, the probation period for workers became shorter. In Salcomp, it came down from 14 to 6 months, and Foxconn workers' probation period was shortened from one and a half or 2 years to 6 months. However, workers still had to go through a lengthy trainee period, 15 months in Nokia and 18 months in Salcomp. One positive sign is that the wage gap between permanent and trainee workers appeared to shrink over the period.

Third, the overall level of wages did not increase much during the period, although comparable data are limited. All three firms seemingly paid more than the minimum wage, but it is questionable whether the workers' standard of living actually improved considering the rise of living costs in many urban areas. Yet, it appeared that Foxconn had caught up with or surpassed the others in wages; for example, workers with 2–3 years of experience got paid more in Foxconn than in Nokia (Table 14.4). As noted above, this could be the effect of the wage settlement signed by a new labour union and the company. Fourth, health services seemingly improved overall, especially in terms of the number of qualified nurses and the quality of clinics available despite several concerns reported about the health services in Foxconn's factory. Finally, another big step that Nokia and Foxconn took was acknowledging labour unions, which did not exist in 2008, although there was some turbulence in labour relations. Overall, although the gap between Nokia and its suppliers was reduced between 2008 and 2011, Nokia still provided relatively better working conditions (see VC#3).

The second temporal comparison (TC#2) involves the studies of two Samsung factories in China, Samsung Keijian Shenzhen (mobile phone manufacturing) and Tianjin Samsung Mobile Display (mobile display manufacturing), with an 8-year gap, leading us to expect relatively substantial improvements in working conditions. Indeed, various improvements were made in some of the social upgrading categories, from contract practices to welfare benefits for workers (Tables 14.5 and 14.6).

Table 14.6 Working conditions comparison in China: Samsung Group, c2012 (VC#4, TC#2)

	Samsung Kejian Mobile Telecommunication (Shenzhen)	Samsung Mobile Display (Tianjin)
Employment	500	3,500
Workers composition	Female workers: 40%	N/A
Recruitment channels	a. Direct recruitment: through schools (never publicly) b. Required age: 16–20 years old	a. 70% from schools, employment agencies, labour dispatch companies – 16–23 years old, w/technical secondary school, high school graduation b. Direct recruitment limited
Labour contract	Signs 3-year labour contracts every July	a. Workers (schools): internship contract w/schools (first year) and factory (after first year, 2 year contract, 3-month probation period) b. Workers (employment agencies): contracts w/agencies
Probation period	N/A	3 months
Working hours overtime	4 different types of 8–9 hr shifts a. Peak season (Oct–Feb): 40–50 hrs/month b. Non-peak: 10 hours/month	2 12-hour shifts (day and night, 1 hr meal time) a. Long day shift works until 8 p.m. or 10 p.m. b. Day shift and night shift: 3 hours (in case of labour shortage: 4–5 hours) c. Average working hours: 12–13 hrs/day
Wages (permanent workers, RMB/month)	a. Average salary: RMB 2000 b. Hardship allowance: RMB 120 (March to October)	a. Based on time (RMB 1,600+ during probation; RMB 1,800+ after probation) b. Overtime wages: 1.5, 2, 3 times minimum wage c. Bonuses: RMB 200–1,000; RMB 500 average (work period: 6 months–)

(*Contd*)

Table 14.6 (Contd)

	Samsung Kejian Mobile Telecommunication (Shenzhen)	Samsung Mobile Display (Tianjin)
Wages (contract workers)	N/A	Contract workers (RMB 1,800–2,200/month)
Health and safety	a. Free health checks; 24/7 clinic in factory, emergency aid might be available b. No contact w/harmful chemicals; anti-static clothing provided	a. Stands constantly while working
Social insurance	Five insurances	Five insurances
Housing and Living conditions	a. Meal: RMB 1 (no meal allowances for off-factory eating) b. Dorm: Free (electricity and water fee RMB 30–100 per workers; 6 to 4 persons/room; leisure amenities available) c. Free transportation to shopping centres and entertainment places on weekends (10 a.m. to 3 p.m.)	a. RMB 50 access card deposit, RMB 20–30 for damage or loss of card b. Dining halls in factory (free meals for day and night shifts) c. Dorms: Free (water and electricity RMB 10/worker; usually 6 workers/room, TV room, shower room, no electronics allowed) d. Free transportation for commuters
Labour union	N/A	No union or similar worker organization
Communication channels	Workers aware of environment, health and safety committee	a. No effective channel to respond or make a report of mean treatment b. Managers very mean to workers; use very loud, abusive language to reprimand the workers in question

Source: China Labour Watch (2012).
Note: 'N/A' denotes that the source has no information in the given factory.

One of the most notable changes was in the labour contracts. Samsung Keijian workers usually signed 3-year contracts, according to the 2012 report, instead of 1-year, annually renewed contracts as in 2004, providing extended job security for workers. As for Samsung Mobile Display, apprentice periods were abolished and 2-year, instead of 1-year, contracts were introduced, which meant a relatively better, if not ideal, contractual situation for workers. Instead, the probation period was extended to 3 months, possibly to give management a longer time to evaluate new workers. However, such improvements only extended to regular workers recruited from vocational schools and employment agencies after an internship period. Contract workers hired through employment agencies were not allowed to sign contracts with Samsung Mobile Display, and faced job insecurity and possibly worse treatment within Samsung. This confirms the importance of a formal contract status for workers in social upgrading (Barrientos et al., 2011).

Other changes include improved health services and various welfare benefits. The availability of free health checks in Samsung Keijian and various facilities and benefits provided by both companies were added to improve worker welfare, along with workers being exempt from dormitory fees. In addition, the extensive insurance coverage provided by Samsung Keijian, which increased from two to five items in 2012, was added to better living standards. The increased wages in nominal value should be unsurprising, given the 8-year gap between the 2 observations. In both factories, the level of wages went up approximately two to three times, as compared to 2004. The exact nature of the wage increase and its impact on social upgrading should be further investigated, based on the rate of inflation and the change of living costs in the region where the factories were located.

However, there are other areas that showed little or no signs of progress. Communication is one of them. For example, no effective channels were reported in Samsung Mobile Display. In addition, despite the existence of a committee for environment, health and safety in Samsung Kejian, it is not clear how other concerns of workers like wages and discrimination were handled. To make matters worse, there were no labour unions in both Samsung factories, which is typical for the Samsung Group at home and abroad (AMRC, 2006). This would further limit the exercise of workers' rights in many important workplace issues.

14.5   Discussion and conclusion

This chapter has examined working conditions in mobile phone GVCs, focusing on three comparative questions: vertical, horizontal and temporal. It has asked, respectively: (1) Do OEMs provide better working conditions than its suppliers?

(2) Do some suppliers perform better in social upgrading than others? (3) Have working conditions improved over time? To answer these questions, we have used secondary data derived from multiple NGO reports that document changing working conditions in the factories of mobile phone manufacturers and their suppliers in China and India since the mid-2000s. Given the constraints of the data for our research, the findings of this paper should be considered as preliminary, limited answers to the questions and read with extra caution.

Despite the paper's rather modest goal, i.e., providing the best possible answer based on the comparable data across different countries and factories as well as over time, our findings suggest a complicated picture of social upgrading. First, each OEM provided better working conditions than its suppliers did, but the differences varied according to specific social upgrading dimensions, although a fuller assessment was not possible because of patchy data. Second, differences between suppliers appeared to be rather marginal, and few systematic patterns emerged. One notable, albeit preliminary, finding is that the gap between each OEM and its suppliers has become narrower in some cases, as shown in the Nokia value chain in India. Finally, our temporal comparison shows that while the firms have improved working conditions in their factories over time, the improvements were limited to certain dimensions, particularly health services and welfare benefits.

One common finding across the cases is the widespread use of non-regular workers. These include contract and temporary workers, various forms of trainees, and student workers and interns. These irregular workers tend to be subject to wage discrimination. Either they get paid less for the same work or they end up getting less because temporary workers are the last ones hired when demand is slack (e.g., Perlos in China). The latter case could be more serious during recession periods, although India and China fared better than other mobile phone exporting countries in 2008–2009 (Lee and Gereffi, 2013). The prevalence of non-regular workers is likely to lower the possibility of social upgrading, as reported in other studies (Barrientos and Visser, 2012; Christian and Mwaura, 2013). Other forms of discrimination towards these workers were also found. For example, contract/ temporary workers are often hired through third-party staffing agencies and usually have to pay placement fees to the agency. They tend to be excluded from other benefits available to regular, permanent workers, such as social insurance and housing allowance. This shows a clear impact of employment status on labour conditions.

Another notable finding across the cases is the extremely low level of unionization in the mobile phone GVC. Unlike other working conditions, where there is more variability across firms and factories, the enhancing of labour rights should be a concern across the entire value chain. In addition, the companies generally lacked communication channels with workers. While the suggestion box was widely used, the effectiveness of the method is questionable, particularly in terms of whether high-level managers were attentive to workers' grievances expressed through such channels. The limited use of codes of conduct in the case factories was also notable, suggesting that private governance played little role. A positive sign, however, is that labour unions were formed in two of our case factories in India.

Despite the main focus of this paper on the value chain positions of firms, other possible factors might affect social upgrading outcomes. The similarities between the three Samsung firms in China in their factory conditions may be attributed to similar human resource and labour management practices in place across the affiliated firms, pointing to a company effect. In addition, the Samsung cases also illustrated regional difference between Shenzhen and Tianjin. Some social upgrading dimensions, such as wages, may be significantly affected by local labour market conditions. In addition, our study indicates that country-level factors can play a role in social upgrading outcomes, such as the role of a government regulation on migrant workers accessing social services in China, whose impact goes beyond any specific workplace, city, or region. While our case-based study does not allow us to tease out these effects, it is a promising topic for future research.

Finally, a recent development exhibits the fragility of improvements reported in the paper in the face of rapidly changing market environments. After acquiring Nokia's mobile phone business in September 2013, Microsoft announced the largest layoffs in the company's history in July 2014: about 14 per cent of its employees and mostly from the Nokia unit it acquired (Wingfield, 2014). In India, Nokia (now Microsoft Mobile) started to lay off its workers beginning in April, creating a ripple effect of downsizing across its suppliers, including Foxconn, which was already hit by Nokia's recent struggle in the market. Nokia's employment in South India has drastically declined from over 10,000 at its peak in 2011 to less than 1,000, with a looming possibility of moving production to Vietnam. Foxconn plans to cut its employment by half, citing declining production volumes in the Nokia's factory (GoodElectronics, 2014). This dramatically illustrates that even hard-fought improvements in social upgrading can be wiped away quickly by market shifts in GVCs, suggesting that the changing geographies of global production involve constant shifts between booms and busts, and inclusion and exclusion, in different places (Bair and Werner, 2011). It also highlights that the value chains play a key role in rapidly transmitting the effects of such changes across firms.

Data sources

AMRC. 2006. *Labour In Globalising Asian Corporations: A Portrait of Struggle.* Hong Kong: Asia Monitor Resource Centre. Available at, http://www.amrc.org.hk/ publication_for_download/publication_for_download/labour_in_globalising_ asian_corporations_a_potrait.

China Labour Watch. 2012. *An Investigation of Eight Samsung Factories in China: Is Samsung Infringing Upon Apple's Patent to Bully Workers?*, September. Available at, http://chinalabourwatch.org/pro/proshow-177.html.

CIVIDEP-SOMO. 2009. *Corporate Geography, Labour Conditions and Environmental Standards in the Mobile Phone Manufacturing in India.* Available at, http://somo. nl/publications-en/Publication_3218.

CIVIDEP-SOMO. 2010. *Changing Industrial Relations in India's Mobile Phone Manufacturing Industry.* Available at, http://somo.nl/publications-en/Publication_ 3580.

Finnwatch, ICA, & Finnish ECA Reform Campaign. 2005. *Day and Night at the Factory: Working Conditions of Temporary Workers in the Factories of Nokia and its Suppliers in Southern China.* Available at, http://www.corporatejustice.org/day-and-night-at-the-factory,099.html.

Finnwatch, CIVIDEP, & SOMO. 2011. *Phony Equality: Labour Standards of Mobile Phone Manufacturers in India.* Available at, http://electronicswatch.org/phony-equality_3565.pdf.

References

Bair, Jennifer, and Marion Werner. 2011. 'Guest Editorial. Commodity Chains and the Uneven Geographies of Global Capitalism: A Disarticulations Perspective.' *Environ Plan A* 43 (5): 988–97.

Barrientos, Stephanie 2008. 'Contract Labour: The "Achilles Heel" of Corporate Codes in Commercial Value Chains.' *Develop Change* 39 (6): 977–90.

Barrientos, Stephanie, Gary Gereffi and Dev Nathan. 2012. 'Economic and Social Upgrading in Global Value Chains: Emerging Trends and Pressures.' Capturing the Gains Summit Briefing, University of Manchester. Available at, http://www. capturingthegains.org/pdf/CTG-GVC.pdf.

Barrientos, Stephanie, Gary Gereffi and Arianna Rossi. 2011. 'Economic and Social Upgrading in Global Production Networks: A New Paradigm for a Changing World.' *Int Labour Rev* 150 (3–4): 319–40.

Barrientos, Stephanie and Margareet Visser. 2012. 'South African Horticulture: Opportunities and Challenges for Economic and Social Upgrading in Value Chains.' *Capturing the Gains Working Paper 2012/12*, University of Manchester.

Available at, http://www.capturingthegains.org/publications/workingpapers/wp_201212.htm.

Bradsher, Keith. 2010. 'Strike Forces Honda to Shut Plants in China.' *The New York Times*, May 28. Available at, http://www.nytimes.com/2010/05/28/business/global/28honda.html?_r=0.

Chan, Jenny. 2013. 'A Suicide Survivor: The Life of a Chinese Worker.' *New Technology, Work and Employment* 28 (2): 84–99.

Christian, Michelle, and Francis Mwaura. 2013. 'Economic and Social Upgrading in Tourism Global Production Networks: Findings from Uganda.' *Capturing the Gains Working Paper 2013/19*. Available at, http://www.capturingthegains.org/publications/workingpapers/wp_201319.htm.

Coe, Neil M. 2013. 'Geographies of Production III: Making Space for Labour.' *Prog Hum Geogr* 37 (2): 271–84.

Coe, Neil M., Peter Dicken, and Martin Hess. 2008. 'Global Production Networks: Realizing the Potential.' *J Econ Geogr* 8 (3): 271–95.

Dedrick, Jason, Kenneth L. Kraemer, and Greg Linden. 2011. 'The Distribution of Value in the Mobile Phone Supply Chain.' *Telecommunications Policy* 35 (6): 505–21.

Dicken, Peter. 2011. *Global Shift: Mapping the Changing Contours of the World Economy*. New York: Guilford Press.

Donaghu, Michael T., and Richard Barff. 1990. 'Nike Just Did It: International Subcontracting and Flexibility in Athletic Footwear Production.' *Reg Studies* 24 (6): 537–52.

Duhigg, Charles, and David Barboza. 2012. 'In China, Human Costs Are Built into an iPad.' *The New York Times*, January 25. Available at, http://www.nytimes.com/2012/01/26/business/ieconomy-apples-ipad-and-the-human-costs-for-workers-in-china.html.

Freeman, Carla. 2000. *High Tech and High Heels in the Global Economy: Women, Work, and Pink-Collar Identities in the Caribbean*. Durham, NC: Duke University Press.

Gereffi, Gary, and Donald Wyman. 1990. *Manufacturing Miracles: Paths of Industrialization in Latin America and East Asia*. Princeton, NJ: Princeton University Press.

Gereffi, Gary, and Karina Fernandez-Stark. 2011. 'Global Value Chain Analysis: A Primer.' Durham, NC: Center on Globalization, Governance & Competitiveness. Available at, http://www.cggc.duke.edu/pdfs/2011-05-31_GVC_analysis_a_primer.pdf.

Gereffi, Gary, Karina Fernandez-Stark, and Phil Psilos, eds. 2011. *Skills for Upgrading: Workforce Development and Global Value Chains in Developing Countries*. Durham, NC: Center on Globalization, Governance & Competitiveness.

Gereffi, Gary, John Humphrey, and Timothy Sturgeon. 2005. 'The Governance of Global Value Chains.' *Rev Int Pol Econ* 12 (1): 78–104.

Gereffi, Gary, and Joonkoo Lee. 2016. 'Economic and Social Upgrading in Global Value Chains and Industrial Clusters: Why Governance Matters.' *J Busi Ethics* 133 (1): 25–38.

Gereffi, Gary, Marino Regini, and Charles F. Sabel. 2014. 'On Richard M. Locke, *The Promise and Limits of Private Power: Promoting Labor Standards in a Global Economy*, New York, Cambridge University Press, 2013.' *Socio-Econ Rev* 12 (1): 219–35.

GoodElectronics. 2014. 'GoodElectronics, Cividep Concerned About Mass Retrenchment of Nokia Workers in India.' July 7. Available at, http://goodelectronics.org/news-en/goodelectronics-cividep-concerned-about-mass-retrenchment-of-nokia-workers-in-india.

Hopkins, Terence K., and Immanuel Wallerstein. 1986. 'Commodity Chains in the World-Economy Prior to 1800.' *Review* 10 (1): 157–70.

ILO. 2005. 'Promoting Fair Globalization in Textiles and Clothing in a Post-MFA Environment.' Geneva: International Labour Organization. Available at, http://www.ilo.org/wcmsp5/groups/public/---ed_dialogue/---sector/documents/meetingdocument/wcms_161673.pdf.

Kaplinsky, Raphael. 2000. 'Globalisation and Unequalisation: What Can Be Learned from Value Chain Analysis?' *J Develop Studies* 37 (2): 117–46.

Koo, Hagen. 2001. *Korean Workers: The Culture and Politics of Class Formation.* Ithaca, NY: Cornell University Press.

Lan, Tu, John Pickles, and Shengjun Zhu. 2015. 'State Regulation, Economic Reform and Worker Rights: The Contingent Effects of China's Labour Contract Law.' *J Contemp Asia* 45 (2): 266–93.

Lee, Joonkoo, and Gary Gereffi. 2013. 'The Co-Evolution of Concentration in Mobile Phone Global Value Chains and Its Impact on Social Upgrading in Developing Countries.' *Capturing the Gains Working Paper 2013/25*, University of Manchester. Available at, http://www.capturingthegains.org/publications/workingpapers/wp_201325.htm.

Lim, Suk-Jun, and Joe Phillips. 2008. 'Embedding CSR Values: The Global Footwear Industry's Evolving Governance Structure.' *J Busi Ethics* 81 (1): 143–56.

Locke, Richard M. 2003. 'The Promise and Perils of Globalization: The Case of Nike.' In *Management: Inventing and Delivering Its Future*, edited by Thomas A. Kochan and Richard Schmalensee, 39–70. Cambridge, MA: MIT Press.

———. 2013. *The Promise and Limits of Private Power: Promoting Labor Standards in a Global Economy.* New York: Cambridge University Press.

Locke, Richard M., Tim Bartley, Gary Gereffi, Pamela Passman, Aseem Prakash, Isaac Shapiro, Jodi L. Short, Michael W. Toffel, Hannah Jones, Drusilla Brown, and Layna Mosley. 2013. 'Can Global Brands Create Just Supply Chains?' *Boston Review*, May/June. Available at, http://www.bostonreview.net/forum/can-global-brands-create-just-supply-chains-richard-locke.

Mayer, Frederick. 2014. 'Leveraging Private Governance for Public Purpose: Business, Civil Society and the State in Labour Regulation.' In *Handbook on the International Political Economy of Governance*, edited by Anthony Payne and Nicola Philips, 344–60. Cheltenham, UK: Edward Elgar.

Mayer, Frederick W., and Gary Gereffi. 2010. 'Regulation and Economic Globalization: Prospects and Limits of Private Governance.' *Busi Polit* 12 (3): 1–25.

McKay, Steven C. 2006. *Satanic Mills or Silicon Islands?: The Politics of High-Tech Production in the Philippines.* Ithaca, NY: Cornell University Press.

Milberg, William, and Deborah Winkler. 2010. 'Economic and Social Upgrading in Global Production Networks: Problems of Theory and Measurement.' *Capturing the Gains Working Paper 2010/4*, University of Manchester. Available at, http://www.capturingthegains.org/publications/workingpapers/wp_201004.htm.

Miller, Doug. 2012. *Last Nightshift in Savar: The Story of the Spectrum Sweater Factory Collapse.* Alnwick: McNidder & Grace.

Nathan, Dev, and Sarkar, Sandip. 2011. 'Blood on Your Mobile Phone? Capturing the Gains for Artisanal Miners, Poor Workers and Women.' Capturing the Gains Briefing Note, No. 2. Available at, http://www.capturingthegains.org/publications/briefingnotes/bp_02.htm.

Phillips, Nicola, Resmi Bhaskaran, Dev Nathan, and C. Upendranadh. 2014. 'The Social Foundations of Global Production Networks: Towards a Global Political Economy of Child Labour.' *Third World Q* 35 (3): 428–46.

Posthuma, Anne and Dev Nathan, eds. 2010. *Labour in Global Production Networks in India.* New Delhi; New York: Oxford University Press.

Rainnie, Al, Andrew Herod, and Susan McGrath-Champ. 2011. 'Review and Positions: Global Production Networks and Labour.' *Compet Change* 15 (2): 155–69.

Schmitz, Hubert. 2004. 'Globalized Localities: Introduction.' In *Local Enterprises in the Global Economy: Issues of Governance and Upgrading*, edited by H. Schmitz, 1–19. Cheltenham, UK: Edward Elgar.

Selwyn, Ben. 2012. 'Beyond Firm-Centrism: Re-Integrating Labour and Capitalism into Global Commodity Chain Analysis.' *J Econ Geogr* 12 (1): 205–26.

Vaughan-Whitehead, Daniel. 2014. 'How 'Fair' Are Wage Practices Along the Supply Chain? A Global Assessment.' In *Towards Better Work: Understanding Labour in Apparel Global Value Chains*, edited by Arianna Rossi, Amy Luinstra and John Pickles, 68–102. Basingstoke: Palgrave Macmillan.

Wingfield, Nick. 2014. 'Microsoft to Lay Off Thousands, Most from Nokia Unit.' *The New York Times.* July 18. Available at, http://www.nytimes.com/2014/07/18/business/microsoft-to-cut-up-to-18000-jobs.html.

15

The Politics of Global Production

Apple, Foxconn and China's New Working Class[1]

Jenny Chan, Ngai Pun and Mark Selden

15.1 Introduction

The magnitude of Apple's commercial success is paralleled by, and based upon, the scale of production in its supply chain factories, the most important of them located in Asia (Apple, 2012a, p. 7). As the principal manufacturer of products and components for Apple, Taiwanese company Foxconn currently employs 1.4 million workers in China alone. Arguably, then, just as Apple has achieved a globally dominant position, described as 'the world's most valuable brand' (Brand Finance Global 500, 2013), so too have the fortunes of Foxconn been entwined with Apple's success, facilitating Foxconn's rise to become the world's largest electronics contractor (Dinges, 2010). This chapter explores the contradictions between capital and labour in the context of the global production chains of the consumer electronics industry. Drawing on concepts from the Global Commodity Chains and Global Value Chain frameworks (Gereffi and Korzeniewicz, 1994; Bair, 2005; Gereffi et al., 2005), the article analyses the power dynamics of the buyer-driven supply chain and the national terrains that mediate or even accentuate global pressures.

The principal focus is on labour in the electronics supply chain, including working conditions and labour as agency, consistent with recent studies of labour as the key element in global production chains or networks (McKay, 2006; Smith et al., 2006; Taylor and Bain, 2008; Webster et al., 2008; Taylor et al., 2013). In particular, the concentration of capital in China and the important roles played by Asian contractors open up new terrains of labour struggle (Silver, 2003; Appelbaum, 2008; Silver and Zhang, 2009). This inquiry evaluates the incentives for Apple

---

[1] This chapter is reprinted with permission from *The Asia-Pacific Journal*, Vol. 11, Issue 32, No. 2, August 12, 2013, http://japanfocus.org/-Jenny-Chan/3981.

to outsource and to concentrate production in a small number of final-assembly facilities in China. It also examines the potential risks or disincentives that might compel Apple to respond more directly, or responsibly, to negative publicity surrounding labour conditions and the collective actions of workers in its supply chain. While the specific detail is concerned with the interaction between Apple and Foxconn, the article briefly considers the relationship between other buyers (e.g., Dell) and contractors (e.g., Pegatron). Consequently, it locates emergent labour struggles more broadly in the electronics sector as a whole.

The authors draw on interviews with 14 managers and 43 workers outside of major Foxconn factory complexes, where employees were not subjected to company surveillance. The manager interviewees were responsible for production management (four persons), commodity procurement (three persons), product engineering (two persons) and human resources (five persons). All workers interviewed were rural migrants aged 16–28, who worked in assembly (semi-finished and finished products), quality testing (functionality and audiovisual appearance), metal processing and packaging. These interview data are complemented by fieldwork observations conducted between June 2010 and May 2013 in Shenzhen (Guangdong), Taiyuan (Shanxi) and Chengdu (Sichuan), which are major industrial centres in coastal, northern central and south-western China. New enterprise-level data have provided evidence of the replication of Foxconn's management methods across its plants, the tensions between Foxconn and its largest corporate buyers, the working experiences and discontents of workers, and explosive episodes of labour protest. Primary evidence is supplemented by company annual reports, scholarly studies, reports from labour rights' groups and journalistic accounts.

The chapter is structured as follows. First, the literature on global outsourcing and the challenges to labour will be reviewed. The next section will consider the growth of China as an industrial power and the emergence and distinctive character of a new working class. These discussions will be followed by an analysis of the Apple–Foxconn business relationship, and the responses of workers to heightened production demands in the 'just-in-time' regime. The concluding part will consider the future of the young generation of China's rural migrant workers who are struggling to define and defend their rights and dignity in the multilayered network of corporate interests and state power.

15.2 Politics of global production

The corporate search for higher profits has been enhanced by efficient transportation and communications technologies, neoliberal trade policies and international financial services, as well as access to immigrants and surplus labour. Multinationals have reduced, if not eliminated, major barriers to capital mobility across spaces of uneven development (Harrison, 1997; Harvey, 2010). Within contemporary global supply chains, scholars (Henderson and Nadvi, 2011; Sturgeon et al., 2011) highlight the power asymmetry between buyers and contractors, in which giant retailers and branded merchandisers play decisive roles in establishing and dominating global networks of production and distribution. Under buyer-driven commodity chains, Lichtenstein (2009) and Chan (2011) find that American retailers and branded merchandisers constantly pressure factories as well as logistic service providers to lower costs and raise efficiency and speed: 'The determination of retailers to cut costs to the bare bone leaves little room for [China-based] contractors to maintain labour standards' (Bonacich and Hamilton, 2011, p. 225). The distinction between retailers and merchandisers in their control over suppliers has become insignificant when 'most global retailers have successfully developed private-label (or store-label) programs, where they arrange with manufacturers or contractors to produce their own label' (Bonacich and Hamilton, 2011, p. 218). In the electronics industry, Lüthje (2006, pp. 17–18) observes that brand-name firms have focused on 'product development, design, and marketing', gaining a larger share of the value created than hardware manufacturing, which is mostly outsourced and performed by formally independent contractors. 'Contract manufacturers' have emerged to provide final-assembly and value-added services to technology firms and giant retailers (Starosta, 2010; Dedrick and Kraemer, 2011).

Asian contractors have been upgrading and growing in size and scale. Lee and Gereffi (2013) explain the co-evolution process that capital concentration and consolidation of branded smartphone leaders in China and other global supply bases has advanced alongside the expansion of and innovation within their large assemblers, notably Foxconn and Flextronics. Appelbaum (2008) finds that East Asian contractors, ranging from footwear and garments to electronics, have been integrating vertically in the supply chains. Starosta (2010) focuses on the rise of 'highly concentrated global contractors' in the electronics industry, in which they serve multiple brand-name firms in different product markets. Not only production tasks, but also inventory management, are being increasingly undertaken by strategic factories, resulting in ever stronger mutually dependent relations between buyers and suppliers. Giant manufacturers, rather than smaller workshops, are more able to 'respond to shortening product cycles and increasing product complexity' (Starosta, 2010, p. 546). Nevertheless, Yue Yuen, the world's largest footwear producer, could only 'pass on less than a third of the cost increase to its customers', including Nike, when 'costs rose sharply' (Appelbaum, 2008, p. 74). Intense bargaining by big buyers over costs and profits has kept a tight rein over producers, frequently slashing profit margins.

In global outsourcing, electronics suppliers are compelled to compete against each other to meet rigorous specifications of price, product quality and time-to-market, generating wage pressure as well as health and safety hazards at the factory level while shaving profit margins (Smith et al., 2006; Chen, 2011). Brown (2010) argues that 'contractor factories' are often not provided with any financial support for corporate responsibility programmes required by brands; 'instead they face slashed profit margins and additional costs that can be made up only by further squeezing their own labour force'. High-tech commodity producers therefore 'focus their labour concerns on cost, availability, quality, and controllability' to enhance profitability in the export market (McKay, 2006, p. 42).

Workers' adaptation, or resistance, to capitalist control has to be understood in this new context of global production, in which concentration of capital at the country, sectoral and/or firm level has reconfigured the class and labour politics. In her longitudinal survey of world labour movements since 1870, Silver (2003) documents the rise of new working class forces in sites of capital investment for the automobile industry in the twentieth century. She defines 'workplace bargaining power' as the power that 'accrues to workers who are enmeshed in tightly integrated production processes, where a localized work stoppage in a key node can cause disruptions on a much wider scale than the stoppage itself' (Wright, 2000; Silver 2003, p. 13). Recently, Butollo and ten Brink (2012) and Hui and Chan (2012) reported the factory-wide strike at an auto parts supplier in Nanhai, Guangdong, which paralyzed Honda's entire supply chain in South China, resulting in wage hikes and increased worker participation in trade union elections. Periodic and limited worker victories aside, managerial assault and/or state repression of labour protests are still commonplace.

A neoliberal state collaborates with private entrepreneurial elites by providing infrastructural support and ensuring law and order, thereby facilitating capital accumulation and economic growth. In China's capitalist transformation, on the one hand, the state has stimulated employment and industrial development through large-scale financial investment and favourable policy implementation (Hung, 2009; Chu, 2010; Naughton, 2010). On the other hand, it has severely restricted workers' self-organization capacity and fragmented labour and citizenship rights among worker subgroups, despite ongoing pro-labour legal reforms (Solinger, 1999; 2009; Perry, 2002; Lee, 2007; 2010; Pun et al., 2010; Selden and Perry, 2010). In our sociological research, we explore the dialectics of domination and labour resistance within the political economy of global electronics production.

15.3 Global production and a new working class: Japan, China and East Asia

Between 1990 and 2006, the expansion of intra-Asia trade accounted for about 40 per cent of the total increase in world trade (Arrighi, 2009, p. 22). China's growing dominance has reshaped regional production networks previously dominated by Japan and its former colonies Taiwan and South Korea. The rise of Japan and East Asian capitalism in the 1950s and 1960s was integral to the Cold War geopolitical order. To contain the spread of Communism and consolidate its global economic reach, the United States provided military and economic resources to its 'client states', encouraged Taiwan and South Korea to open up their markets to Japanese trade and investment, and fostered the growth of a regional power centred on Japan's export-oriented industrialization (Evans, 1995, pp. 47–60; Selden, 1997). Japanese firms received subsidised loans to create new industries and exported finished products to Western markets. In the 1960s, Toshiba, Hitachi, Panasonic, Sanyo, Ricoh, Mitsubishi, Casio and others moved to Taiwan to start operations (Hamilton and Kao, 2011, pp. 191–193). Similarly, Japanese trading companies began sourcing garments and footwear from Taiwan, South Korea and Hong Kong.

From the mid-1960s, IBM, the leader in business computing, shifted its labour-intensive production from the United States and Europe to Asia in order to cut costs. The microelectronics components of IBM System 360 computers were assembled by workers in Japan and then Taiwan because 'the cost of labour there was so low' that it was cheaper than automated production in New York (Ernst, 1997, p. 40). RCA, the consumer electronics giant, swiftly moved to 'take advantage of Taiwan's cheap labour and loose regulatory environment' in the export-processing zones in the late 1960s (Ku, 2006; Ross, 2006, pp. 243–244; Chen, 2011). Electronics assembly grew rapidly in Taiwan, South Korea, Singapore and Hong Kong ('the Asian Tigers'), and later Malaysia, Thailand, Indonesia and India. In the early 1970s, the Philippines hosted manufacturing plants for semiconductor firms such as Intel and Texas Instruments. In these newly industrializing countries, most factory workers were young women migrants from the countryside (Ong, [1987] 2010; Deyo, 1989; Koo, 2001; McKay, 2006).

In the late 1970s, China set up special economic zones to attract foreign capital and boost exports as the means to integrate regional and global economies. The inflow of overseas Chinese capital has long been significant, combined with growing capital from Japan, the United States, Europe and other countries since the early 1990s (Huang, 2003). Hong Kong and Taiwanese entrepreneurs, ranging from low-end component processing to sophisticated microchip assembly, invested in the Pearl River Delta and the Greater Shanghai region (Leng, 2005). By the mid-1990s, Beijing's Zhongguancun Science Park and Shanghai's Zhangjiang Hi-Tech Park became prominent technology powerhouses, building on foundations of industrial development and local government support (Segal, 2003; Zhou, 2008). Over two decades, the Chinese national economy underwent a transformation from one based on domestically oriented heavy industry, with guaranteed lifetime employment and generous welfare for urban state sector workers, to one that relies heavily on foreign and private investments and massive use of rural migrant labourers in light, export-oriented industries (Friedman and Lee, 2010; Kuruvilla et al., 2011).

Foxconn became China's leading exporter in 2001 following the country's accession to the World Trade Organization and further liberalization of international trade. It has maintained this position ever since (Foxconn Technology Group, 2009, p. 6). Foxconn's expansion is intertwined with the Chinese state's development through market reforms, and it has followed the national trajectory from coastal to inland locations in recent years. The Chinese state attempted to rebalance the economy by initiating the 'go west' project, through which financial capital and human resources were channelled to the central and western provinces (Goodman, 2004; McNally, 2004). Taking advantage of lower wage levels, the strategy was designed to stimulate employment and promote ethnic unity while obtaining foreign investment. Ross (2006, p. 218) concludes that in Chengdu, Sichuan's provincial capital, 'it was impossible not to come across evidence of the state's hand in the fostering of high-tech industry'.

The creation of a new rural migrant-centred industrial class by domestic and transnational capital, with the collaboration of the Chinese state at all levels, lies behind the growing protest, driven by multiple factors. Compared with older workers, this generation of employees, the vast majority being rural migrants born since the 1980s, has strong expectations of higher wages, better working conditions and prospects for career advancement (Pun and Lu, 2010). From the mid-2000s, labour shortages[2] have driven up wages and strengthened workers' power in the market, although wage gains resulting from higher state minimum wage levels and strike victories have been undermined by inflation (Selden and Wu, 2011). Foxconn, not unlike other foreign-invested factories, adjusts basic wages and recruits mostly teens and young adults to run the assembly lines. 'Over 85 percent

---

[2] Gu and Cai (2011) conclude that Chinese fertility is presently 1.6 children per woman, down from around 2.5 children per woman in the 1980s. In the next few years, the number of young labourers aged 20–24 years will peak. China's 2010 Population Census, moreover, showed that the age group 0–14 comprised 16.6 per cent of the total population, down 6.29 per cent compared with the 2000 census data.

of Foxconn's employees are rural migrant workers between 16 and 29 years old,' according to a senior human resources manager in Shenzhen (*Interview*, 14 October 2011). By comparison, 2009 national data showed that 42 per cent of rural migrants were between 16 and 25 years old and another 20 per cent were between 26 and 30 (China's National Bureau of Statistics, 2010).

In recent years, Foxconn has adapted to local labour market changes to employ more male than female workers as fewer young women become available as a result of female infanticide,[3] reversing the historical pattern of a feminized workforce in electronics. Company statistics show that male employees increased from 59 to 64 per cent between 2009 and 2011 (Foxconn Technology Group, 2012e, p. 12). This labour is employed in a production network in which vertical integration, flexible coordination across different facilities and 24-hour continuous assembly bolster its market competitiveness. It manufactures hardware components and assembles products for a very large number of global companies, with Apple being its largest client (Chan, 2013).

15.4   Apple–Foxconn business relationship

Apple, Foxconn and China's workers are at the centre of high-tech production, but relations among them are highly unequal. Apple Computer (later Apple Inc.) was incorporated in 1977 and is headquartered in Cupertino, California in Silicon Valley. In 1981, Apple, which had initially produced its own computers, started to contract offshore facilities in Singapore, along with onshore final-assembly contractors, to ramp up upgraded Apple II personal computers (Ernst, 1997, pp. 49–52). From the early years, it outsourced most component processing, assembly and packaging to contractors, above all in South Korea, Japan, and China. In 1982 Apple Computer President Mike Scott commented: 'Our business was designing, educating and marketing. I thought that Apple should do the least amount of work that it could and ... let the subcontractors have the problems' (Ernst, 1997, p. 49). In the 1990s, Apple, Lucent, Nortel, Alcatel and Ericsson 'sold off most, if not all, of their in-house manufacturing capacity—both at home and abroad—to a cadre of large and highly capable US-based contract manufacturers, including Solectron, Flextronics, Jabil Circuit, Celestica, and Sanmina-SCI' (Sturgeon et al., 2011, p. 236). Today, Apple retains its only Macintosh computer manufacturing complex in Cork, Ireland (Apple, 2013a).

If Apple's competitive advantage lies in the combination of corporate leadership, technological innovation, design and marketing (Lashinsky, 2012),

---

[3] The National Bureau of Statistics has acknowledged that the gender imbalance had reached 119:100 in 2009 before dipping slightly to just under 118:100 in 2010. The 2011 data reported 117.78 baby boys for every 100 girls (*China Daily*, 2012).

its financial success is inseparable from its globally dispersed network of efficient suppliers based mainly in Asia. Pivotal to Apple's growth is effective management of production by its suppliers, including final assemblers. Apple's 2012 annual report filed to the United States Securities and Exchange Commission describes a challenge to its highly profitable business:

> Substantially all of the Company's hardware products are manufactured by outsourcing partners that are located primarily in Asia. A significant concentration of this manufacturing is currently performed by a small number of outsourcing partners, often in single locations. Certain of these outsourcing partners are the sole-sourced suppliers of components and manufacturers for many of the Company's products (Apple, 2012a, p. 7).

Apple identifies the concentration of its manufacturing base 'in single locations' and in the hands of 'a small number of outsourcing partners' as a potential risk. However, analysts observed that, 'because of its volume'—and its ruthlessness—'Apple gets big discounts on parts, manufacturing capacity, and air freight' (Satariano and Burrows, 2011). Group interviews with two mid-level production managers at Foxconn's Shenzhen industrial town reveal that during the 2008–09 global financial crisis, Foxconn cut prices on components, such as connectors and printed circuit boards, and assembly, to retain high-volume orders.

> Margins were cut. But the rock bottom line was kept, that is, Foxconn did not report a loss on the iPhone contract. [How?] By charging a premium on customized engineering service and quality assurance. The upgrading of the iPhones has in part relied on our senior product engineers' research analyses and constructive suggestions (*Interviews*, 10 November 2011; 19 November 2011).

In 2009, in the wake of recession, the Chinese government froze the minimum wage across the country. Foxconn accommodated Apple's and other corporate buyers' squeeze while continuing to reduce labour expenditures, including cuts in wages (mainly overtime premiums) and benefits (*Interview*, 9 November 2011).

Foxconn's operating margins—the proportion of revenues remaining after paying operating costs such as wages, raw materials and administrative expenses—has declined steadily over the past 6 years, from 3.7 per cent in the first quarter of 2007 to a mere 1.5 per cent in the third quarter of 2012, even as total revenues rose in the same period with the expansion of orders (Figure 15.1).[4] By contrast,

---

[4] Foxconn's revenues or net sales increased from US$ 51.8 billion in 2007 (Foxconn Technology Group, 2009, p. 11) to US$ 131 billion in 2012 (Foxconn Technology Group, 2013b). During the same period, the net sales of Apple soared from US$ 24.6 billion (Apple, 2011, p. 24) to US$ 156.5 billion (Apple, 2012a, p. 24).

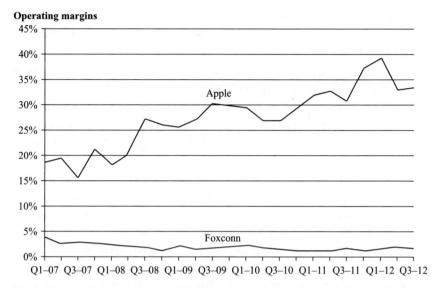

Operating margins

Figure 15.1 Operating margins: Apple and Foxconn compared, 2007–2012

Sources: From Q1 2007 to Q3 2011, see Bloomberg (2012); From Q4 2011 to Q3 2012, see Wikinvest
(2013) for Apple; From Q4 2011 to Q3 2012, see Foxconn Technology Group (2012a;
2012b; 2012c; 2012d).
Note: Data from January 2007 to September 2012 were non-consolidated results for Foxconn.
Starting from Q4 2012, Foxconn announced consolidated results.

Apple's operating margins peaked at 39.3 per cent in early 2012 from initial levels
of 18.7 per cent in 2007. The changes indicate Apple's increased ability to pressure
Foxconn to accept lower margins while acceding to Apple's demands for technical
changes and large orders. Foxconn's margins are constantly squeezed by technology
giants including, but not limited to, Apple. As Foxconn expanded its plants in
interior China (and other countries), expansion costs and rising wages further
impacted revenues.

Twelve major business groups within Foxconn compete on 'speed, quality,
engineering service, efficiency and added value' to maximize profits (Foxconn
Technology Group, 2009, p. 8). 'Two "Apple business groups," iDPBG [integrated Digital
Product Business Group] and iDSBG [innovation Digital System Business Group], are
rising stars in these past few years', stated a Foxconn Chengdu production manager:

> iDPBG was established in 2002. At the beginning, it was only a small business
> group handling Apple's contracts. We assembled Macs and shipped them to
> Apple retail stores in the United States and elsewhere. Later we had more orders

of Macs and iPods from Apple. In 2007, we began to assemble the first-generation iPhone. From 2010, we also packed iPads, at the Shenzhen and new Chengdu facilities (*Interview*, 6 March 2011).

iDPBG currently generates 20–25 per cent of Foxconn's business. To increase its competitiveness, Foxconn Founder and CEO Terry Gou established iDSBG in 2010 when the company won the iPad contracts. iDSBG now primarily manufactures Macs and iPads, contributing 15 to 20 per cent of company revenues. 'Approximately 40 percent of Foxconn revenues are from Apple, its biggest client' (*Interview*, 10 March 2011).

Dedrick and Kraemer (2011, p. 303) find that computer companies currently 'engage in long-term relationships' with their main contractors but sometimes shift contracts to those who can offer better quality, lower cost or greater capabilities. Foxconn's vice president Cheng Tianzong told journalists, 'Some major clients are very concerned with the Foxconn employee suicides, but many of them are our long-term partners. So it doesn't affect Foxconn's orders' (quoted in Zhao, 2010). However, soon after the spate of suicides at Foxconn's facilities in spring 2010, Apple did 'shift some iPhone and iPad orders to Pegatron to diversify risks', according to a Foxconn commodity manager at Chengdu's factory (*Interview*, 13 March 2011). Apple has tightened controls over Foxconn by splitting contracts with another Taiwanese-owned firm, Pegatron. This diversification demonstrates the power asymmetries between Apple and its manufacturers as Foxconn and others seek to retain market position as producers of the iPhone and iPad.

Apple (2013b) obtains products and services 'within tight time frames' and 'at a cost that represents the best possible value' to its customers and shareholders. Figure 15.2 shows the breakdown of value for the iPhone between Apple and its suppliers. Apple's strength is well illustrated by its ability to capture an extraordinary

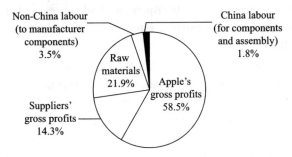

Figure 15.2 Distribution of value for the iPhone, 2010

Source: Adapted from Kraemer et al. (2011, p. 5).

58.5 per cent of the value of the iPhone despite the fact that manufacture of the product is entirely outsourced. Particularly notable is that labour costs in China account for the smallest share, only 1.8 per cent or nearly US$ 10, of the US$ 549 retail price of the iPhone. This ineluctable drive to reduce costs and maximize profits is the source of the pressure placed on Chinese workers employed by Foxconn, many of them producing signature Apple products. While Apple and Foxconn together squeeze Chinese workers and demand 12-hour working days to meet demand, the costs of Chinese labour in processing and assembly are virtually invisible in Apple's balance sheets. Other major component providers (such as Samsung and LG) captured slightly over 14 per cent of the value of the iPhone. The cost of raw materials was just over one-fifth of the total value (21.9 per cent).

Representatives from Apple and other major clients regularly monitor onsite quality processes and production time to market. A mid-level Foxconn production manager recalled: 'Since 2007, Apple has dispatched engineering managers to work at Foxconn's Longhua and Guanlan factories in Shenzhen to oversee our product development and assembly work' (*Interview*, 29 November 2011). A Foxconn human resources manager provided this eyewitness account of Apple's hands-on supervision:

> When Apple CEO Steve Jobs decided to revamp the screen to strengthen the glass on iPhone four weeks before it was scheduled to shelf in stores in June 2007, it required an assembly overhaul and production speedup in the Longhua facility in Shenzhen. Naturally, Apple's supplier code on worker safety and workplace standards and China's labour laws are all put aside. We'd like to make sure that the readers can follow the quote. First, the manager recalled what happened in 2007. Then, we skipped some details. He continued to describe an incident in July 2009. In July 2009, this produced a suicide. When Sun Danyong, 25 years old, was held responsible for losing one of the iPhone 4 prototypes, he jumped from the 12th floor to his death. Not only the short delivery deadline but also Apple's secretive culture and business approach, centred on creating great surprise in the market and thereby adding sales value to its products, have sent extreme pressure all the way down to its Chinese suppliers and workers (*Interview*, 7 March 2011).

Attention to procurement and production detail, including last-minute changes of product design and tight control over prices, assures super-profits for Apple. The purchasing and marketing policy adopted by Apple, the 'chain driver', conflicts directly with its own supply-chain labour standards and the Chinese law.

Tracking demand worldwide, Apple adjusts production forecasts on a daily basis. As Apple CEO Tim Cook puts it, 'Nobody wants to buy sour milk' (quoted in Satariano and Burrows, 2011); 'Inventory … is fundamentally evil. You want to manage it like you're in the dairy business: if it gets past its freshness date, you have a problem' (quoted in Lashinsky, 2012, p. 95). Streamlining the global supply chain on the principle of market efficiency and 'competition against time' is Apple's goal.

Consequently, excessive overtime at final-assemblers and other suppliers is required to meet increased work schedules. Two major sources of production-time pressure commonly felt by factory and logistic workers are well documented by Apple.

> The company has historically experienced higher net sales in its first fiscal quarter [from September to December] compared to other quarters in its fiscal year due in part to holiday seasonal demand. Actual and anticipated timing of new product introductions by the company can also significantly impact the level of net sales experienced by the company in any particular quarter (Apple, 2012a, p. 8).

In a rare moment of truth, Foxconn CEO's Special Assistant Louis Woo, explained in an April 2012 American media program the production pressures that Apple or Dell apply:

> The overtime problem—when a company like Apple or Dell needs to ramp up production by 20 per cent for a new product launch, Foxconn has two choices: hire more workers or give more hours to the workers you already have. When demand is very high, it is very difficult to suddenly hire 20 per cent more people. Especially when you have a million workers—that would mean hiring 200,000 people at once (quoted in *Marketplace,* 2012).

The dominance of giant technology firms, notably Apple, in terms of price setting, onsite production process surveillance, and timing of product delivery, has profound consequences on labour processes. Foxconn's competitive advantage, the basis for securing contracts with Apple and other brand-name multinationals, hinges on its ability to maintain flexibility. The mega factory has to reorganize its production lines, staffing and logistics in a very short time to be demand-responsive. Whereas transnational suppliers, such as Foxconn, have grown rapidly through 'internal development and acquisition' (Sturgeon et al., 2011, p. 235), their drive for profits and higher positions along the global value chains tend to go with the same pattern: the emergence of powerful 'market makers', or leading firms, in their supply networks (Hamilton et al., 2011). The results in competitive manufacturing have been coercive factory conditions and, contentious labour relations, on the ground, to which we now turn.

15.5   Chinese workers' collective actions

Foxconn not only has factory complexes in Shenzhen and all four major Chinese municipalities of Beijing, Shanghai, Tianjin and Chongqing, but also in 16 provinces throughout the country (Figure 15.3). Foxconn Taiyuan in north China's Shanxi province, with 80,000 workers, specializes in metal processing and assembly.

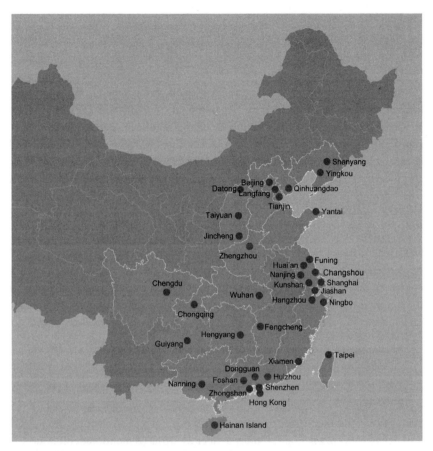

Figure 15.3 Foxconn locations in greater China (1974–2016)

Source: Foxconn Technology Group news and websites.

It manufactures iPhone casings and other components in the upstream supply chain and sends the semi-finished products to a larger Foxconn Zhengzhou complex in adjacent Henan province for final assembly. In 2012, the subtle shift in production requirements from iPhone 4S to iPhone 5 and the speedup to meet Apple's delivery time placed Foxconn and its workers under intense pressure. However, this tightly integrated production regime simultaneously provided workers with leverage, enabling them to demonstrate their collective strength in the fight for their own interests.

Foxconn Taiyuan erupted in factory-wide protests on September 23–24, 2012. 'At about 11 p.m. on 23 September 2012', a 20-year-old worker reported, 'a number of security officers severely beat two workers for failing to show their staff IDs.

They kicked them until they fell' (*Interview*, 26 September 2012). At the male dormitory, workers passing by were alerted by screams in the darkness. An eyewitness said, 'We cursed the security officers and demanded that they stop. There were more than thirty of us so they ran away' (*Interview*, 27 September 2012).

Soon after, a squad of 50 company security officers marched to the dormitory, infuriating the assembled workers. At midnight, tens of thousands of workers smashed security offices, production facilities, shuttle buses, motorbikes, cars, shops and canteens in the factory complex. Others broke windows, demolished company fences and pillaged factory supermarkets and convenience stores. Workers also overturned police cars and set them ablaze. The company security chief used a patrol car public address system to order the workers to end their 'illegal activities'. The situation was getting out of control as more workers joined the roaring crowd.

By 3 a.m., senior government officials, riot police officers, special security forces and medical staff were stationed at the factory. Workers used their cell phones to send images to local media outlets in real time. Over the next two hours, the police contained the labour unrest, detained the most defiant workers and took control of the factory gates. The factory announced a special day off for all production workers, on September 24, Monday. A 21-year-old worker recalled:

> We demanded higher pay and better treatment. In my view, the protest was caused by very unsatisfactory working conditions. It was merely sparked by the abuses of the security guards. Over these past two months, we couldn't even get paid leave when we were sick (*Interview*, 28 September 2012).

With global consumer demand for the new iPhone 5 at a peak, shipping delays were a source of concern for Apple. On September 21, 2012 (8 months after iPhone 4S's China release), Apple launched the iPhone 5 and sold over five million units during that weekend. CEO Tim Cook stated, 'we are working hard to get an iPhone 5 into the hands of every customer who wants one as quickly as possible' (Apple, 2012b). The ever-tightening shorter production cycle pressurizes workers and managerial staff, so that Foxconn Taiyuan workers could not even take one day off in a week, and the sick were compelled to continue to work. At the same time, with Apple demanding fulfilment of impossible targets, the power of workers to display their power peaked.

As justification for its use of paramilitary force, Foxconn blamed the workers, alleging that they were fighting among themselves. The company statement read:

> A personal dispute between several employees escalated into an incident involving some 2,000 workers. The cause of this dispute is under investigation by local authorities and we are working closely with them in this process, but it appears not to have been work-related (quoted in Nunns, 2012).

The underlying cause was that workers are subjected to an oppressive management regime driving them to meet the extreme production demands (Ruggie, 2012). Foxconn, Apple and many other multinational corporations, as well as the Chinese government, have thus far shown little interest in understanding the direct relationship between companies' purchasing practices and labour problems in the workplace. 'On the factory floor', an 18-year-old worker informed us, 'the metal-processing section supervisor's attitude is very bad … We're coerced to meet the extremely tight production deadline' (*Interview*, 29 September 2012). Foxconn leaders' investigation of the 'personal dispute' necessitated turning their eyes away from shop floor conditions.

Less than two weeks later, on October 5, 2012, over 3,000 Foxconn Zhengzhou workers protested collectively against unreasonably strict control over product quality on the line at Zone K. From late September to early October 2012, consumers in the United States and elsewhere complained about scratches on the casing of a particular batch of the new iPhone 5, leading to product quality control investigations of final assembly at the 160,000-strong Foxconn Zhengzhou plant. According to testimony, new quality standards for not exceeding a 0.02 mm appearance defect in iPhone 5 were contributing to workers suffering eye strain and headache. When workers were penalized for not meeting the new standards, quarrels erupted between workers and quality control team leaders on Friday afternoon, resulting in group fighting and injuries.

Production managers yelled at the assembly-line workers and threatened to fire them if they did not 'cooperate and concentrate at work'. Li Meixia (a pseudonym) posted on her Sina microblog that she and her co-workers were angered and walked out of the workshop. In response, another worker posted a statement, which was quickly removed by October 6:

> We had no holidays during the National Day celebrations and now we're forced to fix the defective products. The new requirement of a precision level [of iPhone 5 screen structure] measured in two-hundredths of a millimeter cannot be detected by human eyes. We use microscopes to check the product appearance. It's impossibly strict.

In the case-manufacturing process, workers were also instructed to use protective cases to prevent scratches of the ultra-thin iPhone 5, and close attention to the most minute detail at the fast pace was and remains a major source of work stress, according to testimony. The strike at one workshop eventually paralyzed dozens of production lines in Zones K and L. Senior managers threatened to fire the leading strikers and the quality control team leaders, and demanded that night-shift workers adhere to stringent quality standards. The brief strike did not win workers' demand for reasonable rest.

Given the nature of company unions (Traub-Merz, 2012) and strict corporate controls over workers in both plant and dormitory, Foxconn workers at the Taiyuan and Zhengzhou factories have not organized across factories on a large scale in a coordinated manner. Workers were, however, acquiring public communication skills and raising their consciousness about the need for joint struggle to achieve basic rights. Soon after the September 2012 protest, a 21-year-old high-school graduate with two years' work experience at Foxconn Taiyuan wrote an open letter to Foxconn CEO Terry Gou and circulated it on weblogs (the following excerpt is translated by the authors):

A Letter to Foxconn CEO, Terry Gou

If you don't wish to again be loudly woken at night from deep sleep,

If you don't wish to constantly rush about again by airplane,

If you don't wish to again be investigated by the Fair Labor Association,

If you don't wish your company to again be called by people a sweatshop,

Please use the last bit of a humanitarian eye to observe us.

Please allow us the last bit of human self-esteem.

Don't let your hired ruffians hunt for our bodies and belongings,

Don't let your hired ruffians harass female workers,

Don't let your lackeys take every worker for the enemy,

Don't arbitrarily berate or, worse, beat workers for one little error.

In the densely populated factory-cum-dormitory setting, many rural migrant workers as young as 16 or 17 years old, spoke of their involvement in collective labour protests (Pun and Chan, 2013). If the language of strikes and worker participation is new for some, it is not for others. The testimony of a teenage female worker at Foxconn's Shenzhen Longhua plant is illustrative:

> I didn't know that it was a strike. One day my co-workers stopped work, ran out of the workshop and assembled on the grounds. I followed them. They had disputes over the under-reporting of overtime hours and the resulting underpayment of overtime wages. After half a day, the human resources managers agreed to look into the problems and promised to pay back the wages if there was a company mistake. At night, in the dormitory, our 'big sister' explained to me that I had participated in a strike (*Interview*, 15 October 2011)!

The labour strikes and protests at Foxconn form part of a broader spectrum of labour action throughout China over recent decades (Pringle, 2013). The Taiyuan worker's open letter to Foxconn CEO Terry Gou closes with the following paragraph:

You should understand that working in your factories, workers live on the lowest level of Chinese society, tolerating the highest work intensity, earning the lowest pay, accepting the strictest regulation, and enduring discrimination everywhere. Even though you are my boss, and I am a worker:

I have the right to speak to you on an equal footing.

The sense in which 'right' is used is not narrowly confined to that of legal right. Chinese workers, facing pressure from the company, the local state and their own 'union', are demanding to bargain with their employers 'on an equal footing'. They are calling for dignified treatment and respect at work and for a living wage.

15.6   Conclusion

Marx and Engels ([1848] 2002, p. 223) analysed capital's irresistible impulse to create new markets globally. 'All old-established national industries have been destroyed or are daily being destroyed. They are dislodged by new industries … In place of the old wants, satisfied by the productions of the country, we find new wants …' Production, distribution and consumption must continue in perpetuity if profits are to be made and capital accumulated. Barriers to trade at all levels have to be drastically reduced. In the twenty-first century, consumer electronics has grown to become one of the leading global industries, and Chinese labour is central to its development. An ever quicker and newer product release, accompanied by shorter product finishing time, places new pressures on outsourced factory workers in the Apple production network. At the workplace level, very short delivery times imposed by Foxconn in response to the demands of Apple and other multinational corporations make it difficult for suppliers to comply with legal overtime limits. Price pressures lead firms to compromise workers' health and safety and the provision of a decent living wage. The absence of fundamental labour rights within the global production regime driven by Apple and its principal supplier Foxconn have become a central concern for Chinese rural migrant workers, who form the core of the most rapidly growing sector of the new industrial working class.

The integration of Asian manufacturers in global and regional production networks, tight delivery schedules for coveted products, and the growing shortage of young workers as a result of China's demographic changes have enhanced workers' bargaining power. The ascent of 'global neoliberal capitalism' has created 'opportunities for counter-organization' (Evans, 2010, p. 352), as attested not only by the rise of transnational labour movements and global anti-sweatshop campaigns but specifically by growing labour unrest in China. Increasingly aware of the opportunities presented by the demand by Apple and other technology giants to meet quotas for new models and holiday season purchases, workers have come together at the dormitory, workshop or factory level to voice demands. Internet and social networking technology enables workers to disseminate open letters and urgent appeals for support (Qiu, 2009). The question remains whether workers will be able to win the right to freedom of association and ultimately strengthen a nascent labour movement that is capable of challenging the unfettered power of capital in a milieu in which fundamental labour rights such as the right to strike are lacking.

A historical counterweight to global capital, West and East, exists in workers' and civil society's response. Under public pressure, in February 2013, Foxconn proclaimed that workers would hold direct elections for union representatives. If implemented fairly, and if the unions are organized to uphold the rights enshrined in the Chinese Trade Union Law, Labour Contract Law and the international labour conventions, this would impact upon the balance of power between management and workers. At present, the vast labour force at Foxconn and many workplaces are striving to expand social and economic rights, bypassing the state- and management-controlled unions. A new generation of workers, above all rural migrant workers, is standing up to assert their dignity and rights. Workers' direct actions have been perceived by political leaders and elites as so threatening to social stability that government and employers have been forced to grant certain policy concessions, including higher wages. The Chinese state is also seeking to raise domestic consumption and hence living standards, in part in response to the struggle of aggrieved workers and farmers (Hung, 2009; Carrillo and Goodman, 2012). Apple and Foxconn now find themselves in a limelight that challenges their corporate images and symbolic capital, hence requiring at least lip service in support of progressive labour policy reforms. If the new generation of Chinese workers succeeds in building autonomous unions and worker organizations, their struggles will shape the future of labour and democracy not only in China but throughout the world.

Acknowledgements

We are very grateful to Phil Taylor, Debra Howcroft and four reviewers for their insightful comments. We also thank the independent University Research Group on Foxconn, SACOM (Students and Scholars Against Corporate Misbehavior), GoodElectronics Network, Jeffery Hermanson, Gregory Fay, Amanda Bell, Dev Nathan, Meenu Tewari and Sandip Sarkar. An earlier version of this paper was presented at the Center for East Asian Studies in the University of Bristol on November 15, 2012, where Jenny Chan enjoyed constructive discussions with Jeffrey Henderson and the seminar's participants.

References

Appelbaum, R. P. 2008. 'Giant Transnational Contractors in East Asia: Emergent Trends in Global Supply Chain.' *Comp Change* 12 (1): 69–87.

Apple. 2011. 'Annual Report for the Fiscal Year Ended September 24, 2011.' Accessed December 31, 2011.

———. 2012a. 'Annual Report for the Fiscal Year Ended September 29, 2012.' Accessed December 31, 2012.

———. 2012b. 'iPhone 5 First Weekend Sales Top Five Million.' 24 September. Accessed September 25, 2012.

———. 2013a. 'Our Suppliers.' Accessed March 1, 2013.

———. 2013b. 'Apple and Procurement.' Accessed March 1, 2013.

Arrighi, G. 2009. 'China's Market Economy in the Long Run.' In *China and the Transformation of Global Capitalism*, edited by H. Hung. Baltimore, MD: The Johns Hopkins University Press.

Bair, J. 2005. 'Global Capitalism and Commodity Chains: Looking Back, Going Forward.' *Comp Change* 9 (2): 153–80.

Bloomberg. 2012. 'Apple Profit Margins Rise at Foxconn's Expense.' 5 January. Accessed on January 6, 2012.

Bonacich, E., and G. G. Hamilton. 2011. 'Global Logistics, Global Labor.' In *The Market Makers: How Retailers are Reshaping the Global Economy*, edited by G. G. Hamilton, M. Petrovic and B. Senauer. Oxford: Oxford University Press.

Brand Finance Global 500. 2013. 'Apple Pips Samsung but Ferrari World's Most Powerful Brand.' 18 February. Accessed on February 19, 2013.

Brown, G. 2010. 'Global Electronics Factories in Spotlight.' *Occupational Health and Safety*. 4 August. Accessed on August 5, 2010.

Butollo, F., and T. ten Brink. 2012. 'Challenging the Atomization of Discontent: Patterns of Migrant-Worker Protest in China during the Series of Strikes in 2010.' *Critical Asian Studies* 44 (3): 419–40.

Carrillo, B., and D. S. G. Goodman, eds. 2012. *China's Peasants and Workers: Changing Class Identities*. Cheltenham: Edward Elgar.

Chan, A, ed. 2011. *Walmart in China*. Ithaca, NY: Cornell University Press.

Chan, J. 2013. 'A Suicide Survivor: The Life of a Chinese Worker.' *New Technol Worker Employ* 28 (2): 84–99.

Chen, H. H. 2011. 'Professionals, Students, and Activists in Taiwan Mobilize for An Unprecedented Collective-Action Lawsuit against A Former Top American Electronics Company.' *East Asian Science, Technology and Society* 5 (4): 555–65.

China Daily. 2012. 'China's Gender Imbalance Still Grave.' 29 March. Accessed on March 30, 2012.

China's National Bureau of Statistics. 2010. 'Monitoring and Investigation Report on the Rural Migrant Workers in 2009.' (In Chinese). Accessed on March 20, 2010.

Chu, Y., ed. 2010. *Chinese Capitalisms: Historical Emergence and Political Implications.* Basingstoke: Palgrave Macmillan.

Dedrick, J., and K. L. Kraemer. 2011. 'Market Making in the Personal Computer Industry.' In *The Market Makers: How Retailers are Reshaping the Global Economy,* edited G. G. Hamilton, M. Petrovic and B. Senauer. Oxford: Oxford University Press.

Deyo, F. C. 1989. *Beneath the Miracle: Labor Subordination in the New Asian Industrialism.* Berkeley, CA: University of California Press.

Dinges, T. 2010. 'Foxconn Rides Partnership with Apple to Take 50 Percent of EMS [Electronic Manufacturing Services] Market in 2011.' iSuppli. Accessed July 28, 2010.

Ernst, D. 1997. 'From Partial to Systemic Globalization: International Production Networks in the Electronics Industry.' Berkeley Roundtable on the International Economy, *Working Paper 98.* Accessed on August 1, 2012.

Evans, P. 1995. *Embedded Autonomy: States and Industrial Transformation.* Princeton, NJ: Princeton University Press.

———. 2010. 'Is It Labor's Turn to Globalize? Twenty-First Century Opportunities and Strategic Responses.' *Glob Labour J* 1 (3): 352–79.

Foxconn Technology Group. 2009. '2008 Corporate Social and Environmental Responsibility Annual Report.' Accessed on February 1, 2013.

———. 2012a. 'Non-Consolidated Results for the Twelve Month Periods Ended December 31, 2011.' 27 March (Printed version).

———. 2012b. 'Non-Consolidated Results for the Three Month Periods Ended March 31, 2012.' 14 May (Printed version).

———. 2012c. 'Non-Consolidated Results for the Six Month Periods Ended June 30, 2012.' 31 August (Printed version).

———. 2012d. 'Non-Consolidated Results for the Nine Month Periods Ended September 30, 2012.' 30 October (Printed version).

———. 2012e. '2011 Corporate Social and Environmental Responsibility Annual Report.' Accessed on February 1, 2013.

———. 2013a. 'Global Distribution.' Accessed on February 10, 2013.

———. 2013b. 'Consolidated Results for the Twelve Month Periods Ended December 31, 2012.' 25 March (Printed version).

Friedman, E., and C. K. Lee. 2010. 'Remaking the World of Chinese Labour: A 30-Year Retrospective.' *Brit J Ind Relat* 48 (3): 507–33.

Gereffi, G., J. Humphrey, and T. Sturgeon. 2005. 'The Governance of Global Value Chains.' *Rev Int Polit Econ* 12 (1): 78–104.

Gereffi, G., and M. Korzeniewicz, eds. 1994. *Commodity Chains and Global Capitalism.* Westport, CT: Praeger.

Goodman, D. S. G. 2004. 'The Campaign to "Open Up the West": National, Provincial-Level and Local Perspectives.' *China Q.* 178: 317–34.

Gu, B., and Y. Cai. 2011. 'Fertility Prospects in China.' United Nations Population Division, Expert Paper No. 2011/14. Accessed on April 20, 2012.

Hamilton, G. G., and C. Kao. 2011. 'The Asia Miracle and the Rise of Demand-Responsive Economies', In *The Market Makers: How Retailers are Reshaping the Global Economy*, edited by G. G. Hamilton, M. Petrovic and B. Senauer. Oxford: Oxford University Press.

Hamilton, G. G., M. Petrovic, and B. Senauer, eds. 2011. *The Market Makers: How Retailers are Reshaping the Global Economy*. Oxford: Oxford University Press.

Harrison, B. 1997. *Lean and Mean: The Changing Landscape of Corporate Power in the Age of Flexibility*. New York: The Guilford Press.

Harvey, D. 2010. *The Enigma of Capital and the Crises of Capitalism*. New York: Oxford University Press.

Henderson, J., and K. Nadvi. 2011. 'Greater China, the Challenges of Global Production Networks and the Dynamics of Transformation.' *Glob Netw* 11 (3): 285–97.

Huang, Y. 2003. *Selling China: Foreign Direct Investment during the Reform Era*. Cambridge: Cambridge University Press.

Hui, E. S., and C. K. Chan. 2012. 'The Prospect of Trade Union Reform in China: The Cases of Wal-Mart and Honda.' In *Industrial Democracy in China: With Additional Studies on Germany, South-Korea and Vietnam*, edited by R. Traub-Merz and K. Ngok. Beijing: China Social Sciences Press.

Hung, H., ed. 2009. *China and the Transformation of Global Capitalism*. Baltimore, MD: The Johns Hopkins University Press.

Koo, H. 2001. *Korean Workers: The Culture and Politics of Class Formation*. Ithaca, NY: Cornell University Press.

Kraemer, K. L., G. Linden, and J. Dedrick. 2011. 'Capturing Value in Global Networks: Apple's iPad and iPhone.' Accessed on October 1, 2011.

Ku, Y. 2006. 'Human Lives Valued Less Than Dirt: Former RCA Workers Contaminated by Pollution Fighting Worldwide for Justice (Taiwan).' In *Challenging the Chip: Labor Rights and Environmental Justice in the Global Electronics Industry*, edited by T. Smith, D. A. Sonnenfeld and D. N. Pellow. Philadelphia, PA: Temple University Press.

Kuruvilla, S., C. K. Lee, and M. E. Gallagher, eds. 2011. *From Iron Rice Bowl to Informalization: Markets, Workers, and the State in a Changing China*. Ithaca, NY: Cornell University Press.

Lashinsky, A. 2012. *Inside Apple: The Secrets Behind the Past and Future Success of Steve Jobs's Iconic Brand*. London: John Murray.

Lee, C. K. 2007. *Against the Law: Labor Protests in China's Rustbelt and Sunbelt*. Berkeley, CA: University of California Press.

———. 2010. 'Pathways of Labor Activism.' In *Chinese Society: Change, Conflict and Resistance*, 3rd ed., edited by E. J. Perry and M. Selden. London: Routledge.

Lee, J., and G. Gereffi. 2013. 'The Co-Evolution of Concentration in Mobile Phone Value Chains and its Impact on Social Upgrading in Developing Countries.' *Capturing the Gains Working Paper 25*. Accessed on April 1, 2013.

Leng, T.-K. 2005. 'State and Business in the Era of Globalization: The Case of Cross-Strait Linkages in the Computer Industry.' *China J* 53: 63–79.

Lichtenstein, N. 2009. *The Retail Revolution: How Wal-Mart Created a Brave New World of Business.* New York: Metropolitan Books.

Lüthje, B. 2006. 'The Changing Map of Global Electronics: Networks of Mass Production in the New Economy.' In *Challenging the Chip: Labor Rights and Environmental Justice in the Global Electronics Industry,* edited by T. Smith, D. A. Sonnenfeld and D. N. Pellow. Philadelphia, PA: Temple University Press.

Marketplace (American Public Media). 2012. 'The People Behind your iPad.' 12 April. Accessed on April 13, 2012.

Marx, K., and F. Engels. [1848] 2002. *The Communist Manifesto.* London: Penguin Classics.

McKay, S. C. 2006. *Satanic Mills Or Silicon Islands? The Politics of High-Tech Production in the Philippines.* Ithaca, NY: Cornell University Press.

McNally, C. A. 2004. 'Sichuan: Driving Capitalist Development Westward.' *China Q* 178: 426–47.

Naughton, B. 2010. 'China's Distinctive System: Can It Be A Model for Others?' *J Contemp China* 19 (65): 437–60.

Nunns, C. 2012. 'Apple Profits Unharmed by Foxconn Factory Riots.' *GlobalPost.* 26 September. Accessed on September 27, 2012.

Ong, A. [1987] 2010. *Spirits of Resistance and Capitalist Discipline: Factory Women in Malaysia,* 2nd ed. Albany, NY: State University of New York.

Perry, E. J. 2002. *Challenging the Mandate of Heaven: Social Protest and State Power in China.* Armonk, NY: M. E. Sharpe.

Pringle, T. 2013. 'Reflections on Labor in China: From a Moment to a Movement.' *South Atlantic Q* 112 (1): 191–202.

Pun, N., and H. Lu. 2010. 'Unfinished Proletarianization: Self, Anger and Class Action of the Second Generation of Peasant-Workers in Reform China.' Modern China 36 (5): 493–519.

Pun, N., and J. Chan. 2013. 'The Spatial Politics of Labor in China: Life, Labor, and a New Generation of Migrant Workers.' *South Atlantic Q* 112 (1): 179–90.

Pun, N., C. K. Chan, and J. Chan. 2010. 'The Role of the State, Labour Policy and Migrant Workers' Struggles in Globalized China.' Glob Labour J 1 (1): 132–51.

Qiu, J. L. 2009. *Working-Class Network Society: Communication Technology and the Information Have-Less in China.* Cambridge: MIT Press.

Ross, A. 2006. *Fast Boat to China: Corporate Flight and the Consequences of Free Trade—Lessons from Shanghai.* New York: Pantheon Books.

Ruggie, J. G. 2012. 'Working Conditions at Apple's Overseas Factories.' *The New York Times.* 4 April. Accessed on April 5, 2012.

Satariano, A., and P. Burrows. 2011. 'Apple's Supply-Chain Secret?' Hoard Lasers, *Bloomberg Businessweek*. 3 November. Accessed on March 17, 2013.

Segal, A. 2003. *Digital Dragon: High-Technology Enterprises in China*. Ithaca, NY: Cornell University Press.

Selden, M., 1997. 'China, Japan, and the Regional Political Economy of East Asia, 1945–1995.' In *Network Power: Japan and Asia*, edited by P. J. Katzenstein and T. Shiraishi. Ithaca, NY: Cornell University Press.

Selden, M., and E.J. Perry. 2010. 'Introduction.' In *Chinese Society: Change, Conflict and Resistance*, 3rd ed., edited by E. J. Perry and M. Selden. London: Routledge.

Selden, M., and J. Wu. 2011. 'The Chinese State, Incomplete Proletarianization and Structures of Inequality in Two Epochs.' *Asia-Pacific J* 9 (5): 1–35.

Silver, B. J. 2003. *Forces of Labor: Workers' Movements and Globalization Since 1870*. Cambridge: Cambridge University Press.

Silver, B. J., and L. Zhang. 2009. 'China as an Emerging Epicenter of World Labour Unrest.' In *China and the Transformation of Global Capitalism*, edited by H. Hung. Baltimore, MD: The Johns Hopkins University Press.

Smith, T. D. A. Sonnenfeld, and D. N. Pellow, eds. 2006. *Challenging the Chip: Labor Rights and Environmental Justice in the Global Electronics Industry*. Philadelphia, PA: Temple University Press.

Solinger, D. J. 1999. *Contesting Citizenship in Urban China: Peasant Migrants, the State, and the Logic of the Market*. Berkeley, CA: University of California Press.

———. 2009. *States' Gains, Labor's Losses: China, France, and Mexico Choose Global Liaisons, 1980–2000*. Ithaca, NY: Cornell University Press.

Starosta, G. 2010. 'The Outsourcing of Manufacturing and the Rise of Giant Global Contractors: A Marxian Approach to Some Recent Transformations of Global Value Chains.' *New Polit Econ* 15 (4): 543–63.

Sturgeon, T., J. Humphrey, and G. Gereffi. 2011. 'Making the Global Supply Base.' In *The Market Makers: How Retailers are Reshaping the Global Economy*, edited by G. G. Hamilton, M. Petrovic, and B. Senauer. Oxford: Oxford University Press.

Taylor, P., and P. Bain. 2008. 'United by A Common Language?' *Antipode: Radical J Geogr* 40 (1): 131–54.

Taylor, P., K. Newsome, and A. Rainnie. 2013. 'Putting Labour in Its Place: Global Value Chains and Labour Process Analysis.' *Compet Change* 17 (1): 1–5.

Traub-Merz, R. 2012. 'All-China Federation of Trade Unions: Structure, Functions and the Challenge of Collective Bargaining.' In *Industrial Democracy in China: With Additional Studies on Germany, South-Korea and Vietnam*, edited by R. Traub-Merz and K. Ngok. Beijing: China Social Sciences Press. Accessed on January 2, 2013.

Webster, E., R. Lambert, and A. Bezuidenhout. 2008. *Grounding Globalization: Labour in the Age of Insecurity.* Malden, MA: Blackwell Publishing.

Wikinvest. 2013. 'Apple: Operating Margin.' Accessed on January 10, 2013.

Wright, E. O. 2000. 'Working-Class Power, Capitalist-Class Interests, and Class Compromise.' *Am J Sociol* 105 (4): 957–1002.

Zhao, J. 2010. 'Suicide Occurs after Foxconn Ceo's Visit.' *Caixin.* 27 May. Accessed on May 28, 2010.

Zhou, Y. 2008. *The Inside Story of China's Hi-Tech Industry: Making Silicon Valley in Beijing.* Lanham: Rowman and Littlefield.

16

New Strategies of Industrial Organization and Labour in the Mobile Telecom Sector in India[1]

Sumangala Damodaran[2]

16.1 Introduction

It has been argued for several years now that the phenomenon of 'global production sharing' through global value chains (GVCs) has helped developing countries expand export-oriented manufacturing activity. GVCs represent the significant unit of organization of international production, wherein 'lead firms', largely multinational corporations (MNCs), coordinate production across international borders through extensive networks of suppliers spread across large numbers of countries. This has resulted in a significant change in the structure of international trade, leading to a domination of what has been referred to as the 'trade in tasks', that is, trade is no longer characteristically undertaken in goods, but rather in particular production segments of a production chain (Grossman and Rossi-Hansberg, 2006). The 'trade in tasks', empirically measured in terms of trade in intermediate goods, reflects this phenomenon, and the increased involvement of low- and middle-income countries in trade is clearly seen here, with their share constituting more than 35 per cent of the world's intermediate goods trade during the latter half of the 2000s (UNCTAD, 2013).

[1] This chapter is an output from a project funded by the UK Department for International Development (DFID), the Sustainable Consumption Institute (SCI), the Chronic Poverty Research Centre (CPRC) and the Economic and Social Research Council (ESRC). However, the views expressed and information contained in it are not necessarily those of or endorsed by the funding organizations, which can accept no responsibility for such views or information or for any reliance placed on them.

[2] The author wrote this paper with substantial research assistance from Anindita Chatterjee and Vikas Dalal, who conducted the field study and collected the information that was necessary. Thanks are owed to Joonkoo Lee and Dev Nathan for their comments and suggestions, which have helped improve the paper. Thanks also go to Balwant Singh Mehta for generously making available his calculations of financial and other performance data of Bharti Airtel.

However, it has also been noted extensively that, despite increases in export shares, involvement in GVC-coordinated activities has often not led to any significant increase in value added from those activities over previous commodity-based export regimes, because lead firms in global production networks (GPNs) outsource lower value-added activities while retaining control over production in the higher value-added areas of their 'core competency'. These areas, often characterized by higher technological and skill requirements, are also commonly oligopolistic and subject to significant barriers to entry, whereas the lower value-added segments of many GVCs have low entry barriers and constitute ongoing entry by firms into countries that previously did not produce those products (Milberg, 2004; Milberg and Winkler, 2013). To what extent is it possible for developing countries to counter the tendencies towards lower-end concentration in GVCs, often characterized by poor employment conditions and wage stagnation, which affects the standard of living of people engaged in the sector? To what extent is it possible to capture rents in different segments and thus allow for the reinvestment that is one of the major challenges in longer-term economic development? Even if the former, commonly referred to as 'economic upgrading', happens, what is required for it to translate into social upgrading, or the expansion of employment accompanied by improvement in its quality?

While these are important questions that need to be addressed with regard to the lower-end concentration of developing country firms in typical GVCs, in a vastly changing landscape of industrial organization the overlap between manufacturing and service provision on the one hand and the emergence of lead firms from developing countries has complicated the question of evaluating gains. For example, in India, complex relationships between large corporations, both domestic and foreign, through outsourcing in a high technology sector like mobile telecom, have resulted in an industrial organizational form in the sector where the Indian lead firm, in this case Airtel, has been seen to be substantially capturing rents in the network. This is considered a new pioneering model of outsourcing, subsequently followed by other mobile phone companies as well. In such agreements, typically, the mobile phone company retains authority over only the technology strategy and the determination of the quality parameters of mobile telecom operations, while outsourcing everything else to other large corporations and in turn maintaining its competitive advantage over the long term. How can an experience such as this be understood within the GVC/GPN framework and what are the implications for the whole range of domestic firms and labour involved in the sector?

This paper examines the structures of value chains and production networks in the different segments of the mobile telecom sector in India and evaluates the impact of the industrial organizational structure that has emerged, dominated as it is by what has come to be known as the 'Airtel Model' in the industrial organization literature. It is based on the information gathered through secondary literature, company and industry documents and interviews with managers, contractors, engineers, salesmen and workers in different segments of the sector[3].

The paper is organized as follows: Section 16.2 outlines the industrial organization of the mobile telecom network in India. Section 16.3 uses the case study of Bharti Airtel to describe the features of what has come to be known as the 'Airtel model' of complete outsourcing in the sector, and draw out its implications. Section 16.4 looks at the features of labour markets and employment conditions to assess whether involvement in a high technology sector such as mobile telecom has resulted in social upgrading for those employed in it. Section 16.5 summarizes the issues that come up with the stretching of the limits of outsourcing like in the Airtel model discussed in the paper.

16.2 The mobile telecom network—Industrial organization

The mobile telecom sector consists of a number of 'segments' that are interconnected through a myriad of relationships or multiple sub-chains, which function to bring mobile telecommunication devices and services to the customer. Overall, the sector is associated with high capital investment, high costs of running and maintaining mobile service and communication networks and the need to maintain flexibility, given the volatile and globalized nature of markets. Figure 16.1 provides a pictorial overview of the sector. The key segments of the industry are components; infrastructure like towers; handset manufacture; mobile service provision; and value-added services.

The *components* segment consists of products like chipsets and microcontrollers, which embody a very high-technology component of the sector and are entirely imported. Almost wholly dominated by foreign corporations like Qual Comm, Intel, Texas Instruments and ARM, the production for this segment is undertaken and controlled by companies outside India, mostly in developed countries.

---

[3] The interviews were all conducted between March and July 2012 in different areas in Delhi. Two marketing managers (one each from Airtel and Vodafone) and one personnel manager from Airtel were interviewed to understand the significance of the outsourcing arrangements. In total, 4 engineers, 3 contractors and 15 workers were interviewed at two tower erection sites in Dwarka and Noida, respectively. Eight salesmen were interviewed in two different Airtel retail outlets in Mayur Vihar I and Patparganj.

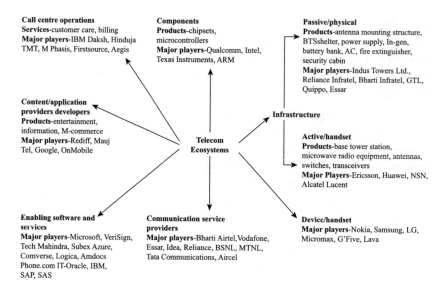

Call centre operations
Services-customer care, billing
Major players-IBM Daksh, Hinduja
TMT, M Phasis, Firstsource, Aegis

Components
Products-chipsets,
microcontrollers
Major players-Qualcomm, Intel,
Texas Instruments, ARM

Passive/physical
Products-antenna mounting structure,
BTSshelter, power supply, In-gen,
battery bank, AC, fire extinguisher,
security cabin
Major players-Indus Towers Ltd.,
Reliance Infratel, Bharti Infratel, GTL,
Quippo, Essar

**Content/application
providers developers**
Products-entertainment,
information, M-commerce
Major players-Rediff, Mauj
Tel, Google, OnMobile

Infrastructure

**Telecom
Ecosystems**

Active/handset
Products-base tower station,
microwave radio equipment, antennas,
switches, transceivers
Major Players-Ericsson, Huawei, NSN,
Alcatel Lucent

**Enabling software and
services**
Major players-Microsoft, VeriSign,
Tech Mahindra, Subex Azure,
Comverse, Logica, Amdocs
Phone.com IT-Oracle, IBM,
SAP, SAS

**Communication service
providers**
Major players-Bharti Airtel,Vodafone,
Essar, Idea, Reliance, BSNL, MTNL,
Tata Communications, Aircel

Device/handset
Major players-Nokia, Samsung, LG,
Micromax, G'Five, Lava

Figure 16.1   Mobile telecom GPN

Source: Representation by Anindita Chatterjee.

16.2.1   Handset/device manufacturers

The value chain of mobile phone manufacturing is long and complicated, consisting of a variety of activities ranging from acquiring input materials and putting together hundreds of components and sophisticated software into increasingly smaller devices to distributing and marketing phones across the world. The manufacturing of each of these products occurs through networks of Original Equipment Manufacturers[4] (OEMs) like Nokia, Motorola, Samsung, LG and Sony-Ericsson, Electronics Manufacturing Services (EMSs) and Original Design Manufacturers (ODMs). The latter two types of companies are generally known as Contract Manufacturers (CMs)[5] (Wilde and de Haan, 2006).

The leading device manufacturers in India are Nokia, Sony Ericsson, HTC, Motorola, Apple Inc. (iPhone), Samsung, LG and Blackberry. Of late, Asian players

---

[4]   OEMs are companies that build products bearing their names.

[5]   CMs offer full-scale manufacturing and supply chain management. EMSs are contract manufacturing services companies that produce the brand name products designed by the brands. EMSs do not own the intellectual property of the products they produce. Most EMSs are based in Western countries, but an increasing number of them are emerging in Asia (mainly China). Prominent examples of EMS are Flextronics and Hon Hai (Foxconn). ODMs, on the other hand, are manufacturers that both design and manufacture products.

like Lava and Micromax (Indian) and G'Five (China) have also started capturing market share. Most of the manufacturing and assembling takes place in three East Asian economies: China, Taiwan and South Korea. In 2010, more than a half of the total exports (58 per cent) of the handsets was accounted for by these countries, indicating the importance of Asia in mobile phone GPNs. Mobile phone exports became more concentrated; the five largest exporting countries represented 74 per cent of the world's exports (Lee and Gereffi, 2012).

The level of outsourcing is considered low in mobile phone manufacture as compared with the manufacture of personal computers (PCs). For example, in their study of handset manufacturing, Lee and Gereffi (2012) note that fragmentation in mobile phone manufacturing is new, becoming significant only since the early 2000s, when lead firms, or OEMs, began to outsource or move manufacturing to locations outside advanced economies. Given rapidly changing markets and technologies, OEMs are under constant pressure to increase flexibility by scaling production volumes up or down and by reducing manufacturing costs. In this regard, outsourcing production to CMs (both EMSs and ODMs) has a number of advantages for OEMs, such as a reduction in production costs, allowing them to focus on the core competencies of marketing and sales, and accelerating their products' time to market. Thus, despite the relatively low level of outsourcing, the phenomenon is on the rise and as part of this, only a few countries and firms have managed to upgrade economically in 'manufacturing hotspots' built around regionalized supply chains.

Further, leading firms display divergence in their GVC governance strategy, ranging from a modular form to vertical integration, and lead firms tend to capture the largest portion of value created in mobile phone chains while CMs and low-end component suppliers capture a much smaller share of value (Chapter 15). Finally, even in the successful production hubs in South East Asia, it has been found that the relationship between economic upgrading and social upgrading, such as increasing wages, improving working conditions and promoting labour rights, has been limited (Lee and Gereffi, 2013).

For developing countries, major phone manufacturers have moved distinctly towards the production of low-cost handsets since 2006, thereby reflecting the industry's shift toward the low-end segment and low-cost geographies. When such production facilities have been set up, India's low-wage cost advantage and favourable demographic profile (the fact that about half the population, which forms the prime low-cost working group, is below 25 years of age and can constitute potential domestic demand) have been seen to be favourable factors allowing for the expansion of mobile phone production. Thus, despite the general level of outsourcing being low, it is different with low-end production, as in the Indian case, where handset majors are gradually looking towards more decentralized production. However, most of the production facilities are highly import-intensive and are in the nature of mere assembling plants, with very little component sourcing occurring within the country at the moment. Only electrical and mechanical parts are being locally sourced, whereas all the electronic components are imported.

Indian firms that sell mobile handsets under their own names, like Micromax, Karbonn and Lava, source their phone components mainly from China and assemble the phones in India. Major international manufacturers employ the same practice but the quality of their finished products is much better in comparison with the local/Indian brands. However, mobile phones bearing Indian brand names and other 'Chinese' phones are cheaper (mostly with the same and sometimes even better features than the imported ones) and attract a large number of customers from low-income groups. For ease of understanding, we denote the major international manufacturers as 'Class I' and others as 'Class II'.

The exercise of a mobile phone reaching a customer is quite complex and depends on the demand for a particular brand. Normally, mobile phone shops are located in urban areas like cities and towns, which feed both urban and rural demand. The primary suppliers or the dealers (closest to the customer) are located in such places. National-level distributors are closest to the manufacturing firm. In between national-level distributors and city-/town-based dealers, there are sub-distributors or local distributors who handle bigger geographical markets (for states or zones). Sub-distributors are sometimes replaced by direct contact with dealers by national-level distributors in many cases, in order to save time and cost, for example, in the case of LG.

All the Class I manufacturers depend on outsourcing the supply chain. For example, Nokia has HCL as its national distributor for India, whereas Samsung and Sony Ericsson have Ingram, HTC has Bright Point and the iPhone is sold through Aircel in the National Capital Region (NCR) and by Airtel elsewhere. Class II manufacturers have set up their own distribution channels with smaller firms or depend on self-distribution. Onida and Videocon also follow this practice.

For Class I manufacturers, all the services related to mobile phones, like marketing, maintenance and the running of service centres, are handled by other firms. For example, the sales and marketing and service activities of Nokia phones are handled by Hindustan Computers Limited (HCL). City-based service centres, under the name 'Nokia Care', are given out as franchises. These employ local people, who are paid low wages, to handle small problems. Serious faults in handsets are, however, handled by central offices that are managed by HCL.

The revenues for both national and local distributors are based on a system of sharing a small percentage of total sales (up to 5–6 per cent of the total sales made). Dealers are incentivized through a system of slabs for a particular volume of sales plus a fixed amount by the national distributor. The system works a lot like the wholesale and retail business in other commodities.

16.2.2 Infrastructure

The infrastructure segment is what is known as the mobile networking segment, that is, the segment that makes the transmission of data and communication physically possible. Its constituents, in turn, are passive/non-electronic infrastructure; and active/electronic infrastructure. The components of passive infrastructure include antenna-mounting structures, base tower station shelters, power supply sources, DG sets for power back-up, air conditioners, battery banks, invertors, fire extinguishers and security cabins, among others. The components of active infrastructure include base tower stations, microwave radio equipment, antennas, switches and transceivers. The major players in the infrastructure segment are NSN (Nokia-Siemens), Ericsson, Huawei, Alcatel Lucent and IBM, to name a few.

There are four kinds of operator models in the network infrastructure sub-segment of the industry, of which network sharing, exemplified by the third and fourth options below, is considered an innovation in industrial organization:

- The first is the infrastructure model with no sharing of resources among operators, with operators investing in infrastructure and managing it internally.
- The second model is one where infrastructure subsidiaries with 100 per cent ownership are set up by a single telecom operator, with the subsidiary company building and managing tower infrastructure. The subsidiary company serves the infrastructure needs of the host (owner–operator) and tenants. For example, Bharti Infratel (excluding Indus Towers) is owned wholly by Bharti Airtel and has a tower portfolio of roughly 27,000 towers (ICRA, 2009). Similarly, Reliance Infratel, owned by Reliance Communications, has a portfolio of 44,000 towers.
- The third model is one where an independent tower infrastructure company, jointly set up by a group of telecom operators, under a joint venture (JV) agreement, spins off as an independent entity for managing tower infrastructure. Each operator contributes infrastructure to the JV and enjoys rights to shared resources. The independent entities are guaranteed occupancy from parent

companies and also serve other entities. For example, Indus Towers is jointly owned by Vodafone Essar, Bharti Airtel and Idea Cellular, and has the largest tower portfolio in the country, of around 85,000 towers (ICRA, 2009).

- The fourth model is that of independent tower infrastructure companies, which build and manage tower infrastructure that is leased out to operators under long-term contracts, such as GTL, Essar and Quippo. Some operators hive off their tower infrastructure to independent companies to unlock value. In 2010, Airtel hived off 17,500 towers to GTL and recovered nearly Rs. 8,400 crores in the process (Business Standard, 2010).

The reason for the emergence of this system of network sharing is that mobile phone markets, which have traditionally been oligopolistic, with their origins in industrialized countries, started experiencing increasingly intense competition as a result of which the per-minute prices earned have been continuously falling, which is not entirely compensated for by increasing mobile phone usage, thereby resulting in a decline in revenue per customer. Along with increased capacity requirements, this trend means that every mobile phone provider is being forced to cut costs. Declining call tariffs in conjunction with favourable regulatory policies have led to a tremendous increase in the subscriber base, which has had a positive impact on industry revenues, but, simultaneously, operator margins have also shrunk, pulling down the 'average revenue per user' (ARPU)[6]. Further, with networks at the centre of the system and network infrastructure procurement costs accounting for an estimated average of about 60–80 per cent of the total investment for a mobile phone company, network sharing has emerged as one of the strategies for cutting costs (ICRA, 2009). Indus Towers, jointly owned by Vodafone Essar, Bharti Airtel and Idea Cellular, is an example of a venture whereby operators compete at the front end of the business, while cooperating in back-end operations, signifying a certain kind of 'cooperative competition' through network sharing.

It is clear that network sharing, where multiple mobile phone companies share common network infrastructure and operations[7], goes a step further

---

[6] For example, the total number of mobile handsets in India was estimated at 881 million, of which 213 million were added only in 2011, indicating the high rate of market expansion. It is estimated that the domestic demand for handsets will touch 350 million units per year by 2020, and it has been predicted that the number of handsets exported during the same year will reach 300 million units. With India being the world's fastest-growing cellular market in terms of subscriber additions, the wireless subscriber base here is expected to reach 1.5 billion by 2020 (Sen, 2012; Wilde and de Haan, 2006).

[7] See http://www.oliverwyman.com/pr-117.html

than outsourcing. While outsourcing uses a classic customer service provider relationship, sharing requires companies to cooperate with their direct competitors to create shared synergies. Of course, a network provider can also initiate such shared usage. Sharing can result in savings not only on operating costs but also on most network investment expenditures.[8]

The phenomenon of network sharing for cutting costs is a significant means of generating flexibility within large-sized corporations, with implications for employment and labour conditions, as can be seen in the following section.

16.2.3 Mobile communication service/network providers/operators

Another important type of company in the mobile phone industry is the mobile network/service operator (MNO).[9] Although MNOs, also known as mobile service providers, do not directly manufacture handsets themselves, they have a significant influence on the mobile telephone market because they provide the telecommunication service that allows people to communicate by using their mobile telephone handsets.

Often, mobile phone suppliers get into arrangements with MNOs, who are, in a sense, large-scale consumers (and resellers) of mobile handsets. As a result, though only a fraction of their revenues comes from handset sales, network operators often see handset manufacturers as their most important suppliers (Wilde and de Haan, 2006), and this sets up inter-firm linkages between them, as between Tata Indicom and Samsung in India. In addition, internationally, a trend over the past few years has been the increasing involvement of mobile network operators in handset development. Mobile network operators such as Vodafone and Orange are increasingly bypassing the OEM node in the supply chain and using outsourced ODM production to market their own line of mobile phones.

---

[8] However, cooperating with competitors is fraught with many potential conflicts of interest that must be considered in the cooperative agreement. Sharing networks also requires defining the split for potential additional costs and depreciation as well as determining termination and compensation payments.

[9] MNOs, also known as wireless service providers, wireless carriers, mobile phone operators or cellular companies, are telephone companies that provide services for mobile phone subscribers. In order to become an MNO within a country, it is necessary to acquire a radio spectrum licence from the government. The precise spectrum obtained depends on the type of mobile phone technology the operator intends to deploy. For example, a Global System for Mobile Communications (GSM) network would require a GSM frequency range. The government may allocate a spectrum using whichever method it chooses, although the most common method is an auction.

The mobile telecom sector, taken as a whole, is thus an interesting one to analyse from the perspective of upgrading in GPNs because its structure and evolution show up complexities that have not yet been analysed in GPN studies. First, the mobile telecom sector straddles manufacturing and services, with the production of a product (the mobile phone), the establishment of network infrastructure for the transmission of signals and the delivery of the service (telecom as well as various other value-added services) being the main segments, of which the first and the third go into fulfilling customer service and satisfaction. So, unlike most other sectors wherein firms would be engaged in either manufacturing activity or service provision, in this case the characteristics of both as well as the ability to combine both determine industrial organization in the sector. This is significant, especially from the point of view of employment, because the question of whether tangible physical output is being produced or not is important in determining the extent and kinds of work–worker–workplace dynamics that exist.

Second, in a sector like mobile telecom, the production of physical products and services entails technological requirements that are very wide ranging, from extremely complex and advanced to very simple, with structures of production and service provision consequently spanning a wide range as well. Industrial organization, with specific characteristics *vis-à-vis* the 'make-or-buy' decisions that firms take, governs the conditions of employment significantly in the sector.

Third, with production and service provision in mobile telecom being globalized from the beginning, the production system that has evolved has typical features of globalized production networks and has been one of the key areas wherein upgrading issues have been in the forefront from the outset. Among the major advantages, employment, especially quality employment, is projected as one, but in this case specifically, employment issues cannot be studied without understanding the tendencies of industrial organization in the sector. At the same time, given that technology and design constitute significant components of the sector, issues of large-scale, heavy investments and the production and use of advanced technology result in a significant part of the production still being concentrated in developed countries, and also in a situation whereby the nature of markets has a very wide ambit, ranging between developed and developing countries. Further, in a country like India, the nature of the domestic market and the presence of large domestic firms with significant market power affect the dynamics of value chain incorporation and the resultant employment conditions.

The nature of India's market, therefore, is an important determinant of how the value chain or the production networks have emerged and is also an important example of how the sector has penetrated developing country markets. As far as the consumer segment is concerned, the market (for mobile phones and for services) is characterized by high volumes, very low margins and potentially high turnover. In this context, developing countries are both lucrative as well as problematic destinations for the same reasons. As ARPU declines and voice gets 'commoditized', the challenge, as per industry documents, will be to retain customers, develop alternative revenue streams and create a basis for differentiation in the high-churning markets. However, the market consists largely of unsophisticated segments, wherein the largest numbers of customers in a country like India need low-end phones with basic services, and therefore large rents cannot be realized. Thus, the mobile phone and telecom domestic market in India, as in many developing countries, largely resembles the market for cheap garments, despite the high levels of technological sophistication involved. Handset manufacturers adopt a strategy of capturing market share by reducing costs, on the one hand, and planning for exporting phones as well as telecom-related services from India, on the other. Thus, one of the main issues with regard to the possibilities for upgrading is whether, despite the low-end nature of India's domestic market, India can become a centre where some of the higher-end telephones as well as higher-end services are produced, for a small segment of the domestic market as well as for the international market.

Despite the labour-intensive consumer goods type of market for mobile telephones and services in India, a large segment of the sector involves expensive and heavy infrastructure provision, in contrast with typical low-value consumer goods production, which necessitates the involvement of large infrastructure companies. In this situation, supervision, centralization of functions and largeness become crucial, making it a sector that is controlled almost entirely by large players, both domestic and MNCs. Therefore, the strategy that has been evolving, thus determining industrial organization, is that of maximum outsourcing and capacity/network sharing, driven by the mobile service provider firms, combined with vertical specialization and consolidation across segments. The outsourcing and network-sharing strategy is one of establishing tie-ups between different large players in each segment, characterized by complexities that are hard to decipher.

What are the areas in which these tie-ups take place and what is the significance of these tie-ups between essentially large players for devising an industrial organization strategy? What is the role of smaller entities in this process and in the value chains or networks that are generated? In a sector that is technology-intensive and that also involves large and heavy infrastructure, how can industrial organization allow for maximum flexibility to cope with volatile, fragmented and varied markets?

It is in this context that the supposedly unique 'Total Outsourcing' model—developed by Airtel first and now also being followed by Vodafone, Idea and other MNOs in India—acquires significance. Increasingly, since about the year 2005 or so, mobile phone companies have turned to far-reaching outsourcing agreements internationally to represent the entire technological make-or-buy value-added chain. Typically, in such agreements, a single outsourcing partner, that is, a large corporation handles the planning and design, development, operation and maintenance of the network. The mobile phone company retains authority over only the technology strategy and the determination of the quality parameters to ensure it maintains its competitive advantage over the long term. The arrangement between Price-buster E-Plus and Alcatel-Lucent, with the latter operating a large part of the E-Plus network as well as absorbing more than 750 E-Plus employees in Germany and H3G in Italy, became an important example of such an arrangement. While network outsourcing began with the networks of smaller mobile phone providers with 1–2 million customers, it soon became common even for the large operators with over 10 million customers, like the examples given above. It is argued that the key factor encouraging the trend towards outsourcing is the fact that large providers like Ericsson, Nokia Siemens Networks and Alcatel-Lucent, thanks to their increasing experience and order volume, can offer cost savings that are attractive for even large mobile phone companies. In the process, service providers are trying to ensure sustained cost savings over the long-term via stringent process optimization based on international best practices, centralization of responsibilities and the associated improved utilization of employees and resources across countries and individual mobile phone companies (Oliver Wyman Report, 2007).

The Airtel 'total outsourcing' model in India, however, went further, making the strategy closer to that of a buyer-driven GVC type, with outsourcing involving several partners, on the one hand, and Airtel focusing exclusively on expanding its customer base, but not bearing the costs of large fixed investments in an otherwise technology-intensive and capital-intensive sector, on the other. The strategy, as such, came to be known as the 'Airtel Model' because it was pioneered in India by Bharti Airtel and it also succeeded in driving a substantial increase in its subsequent earning of rents. It has also been adopted in a more generic sense by other mobile telecom companies like Vodafone and Idea. The features of the 'model' as well as details from Airtel's specific case are discussed in the following section.

16.3 Total outsourcing: The Bharti Airtel model

What does the total outsourcing model involve, in terms of the 'core' and 'non-core' functions of firms, costs and employment? The provision of the service of mobile telecom and other services delivered through companies like Airtel involves the following: (a) provision of enabling software and services, (b) content development/ application provision, (c) call centre operations, wherein the services offered include customer care and billing, among others, and (d) network or infrastructure provision.

The core functions that are performed by a typical MNO like Airtel include the provision of 'mobility', that is, 'selling' a Subscriber Identity Module (SIM)—this means activation and deactivation of a SIM card and ensuring quality network coverage. It is also involved in providing 'solutions', that is, the MNO ties up with content developers to enable SIM cards to perform various tasks like monitoring the inventory, monitoring Television Rating Points (TRPs) and monitoring the Global Positioning System (GPS), among others. Apart from this, it is involved in 'branding', and everything else from the above list, involving content and application development, software development, call centre operations and network infrastructure provision and maintenance, is contracted out. In other words, the only actual operations it gets involved in directly have to do with creating a customer base, ensuring falling caller fees for them and maintaining quality.

Airtel, for example, first outsourced all business processes[10] to IBM[11] to manage. By using IBMs information technology (IT) infrastructure and standardized business frameworks, it reduced capital expenses and increased the quality of customer experience. Further, it outsourced telecom networks to Ericsson and Nokia. Ericsson agreed to receive payment through the usage of its network infrastructure instead of upfront payment. This again reduced Airtel's capital expenses. By adding new customers without having to incur increased fixed costs, Airtel reduced the service fee for its customers. In addition to network infrastructure outsourcing, arrangements have also been made with software service providers, including those providing 'value-added services'[12] (the major players include Microsoft, VeriSign, Tech Mahindra, Subex Azure, Logica, CanvasM and Amdocs), content developers (like Rediff, Mauj Tel, Google, Onmobile), which provide services under three broad categories—entertainment, information and

---

[10] See http://outsourceportfolio.com/benefits-of-business-process-standards-in-bpo/

[11] See http://www.scribd.com/doc/24805146/Bharti-Airtel-Case-Study

[12] Value-added services are supposed to constitute an area where there is great demand and which are expected to grow significantly. Examples of such services, produced by one of the value-added service provider firms, CanvasM, include Saral Rozgar—a platform where blue collar workers call in and get their resumes made and where interested employers can contact them; queue management solutions – a programme that can alert people with appointments about delays in case there is a long queue at a particular office; traffic alerts; and so on.

m-commerce, and call centre operators (like IBM Daksh, Hinduja TMT, Mphasis, Aegis, and Firstsource, among others).

A key feature of the Airtel outsourcing arrangement has to do with the payment structure for outsourcing. Rather than paying for services based on the number of hours worked or some other standard method, the payments to outsourcing partners are based on Airtel's revenue growth, which implies that, as it grows and the demands on its service providers expand, their compensation increases in lock step. Further, the customer base expands without necessitating any greater employment by Airtel, which has only a few hundred employees.

By undertaking the kind of outsourcing detailed above, the MNO, in this case Airtel, which was soon followed by others,[13] first and foremost reduces capital expenditures, as noted earlier. In the case of networks, it saved on the capital cost of the buffer of 30 per cent it would otherwise have had to install. Instead of 32 million lines, including the buffer, it paid for only the 25 million lines it actually used (Subramanyam, 2011). The network suppliers/managers must have managed to absorb this buffer cost because they provided similar services to other telecom operators and could use the higher volume to reduce total buffering, provided the buffering percentage required went down with higher volume.

Second, it expands its focus on customers and shares the revenue growth owing to its expanding customer base with the partners, thus incentivizing them. Third, it keeps employment to the minimum, with a small number of direct Airtel employees coordinating the tie-up with the partners and their large numbers of employees.

Fourth, it brings specialized knowledge into its operations. Instead of Airtel managing the network with its own engineers, whose knowledge would be limited, outsourcing network management brings in engineering services from manufacturers and suppliers. As the Chairman of Airtel put it:

> If something goes wrong with my switch, there's no way anyone from Bharti can do anything about it. An Ericsson guy is going to have to come and fix. I don't manufacture it; I can't maintain or upgrade it. So, I'm thinking, 'This doesn't really belong to me. Let's throw it out' (Sunil Mittal, quoted in Subramanyam, 2011, p. 404).

---

[13] For example, the following major outsourcing deals between MNOs and software providers in the past few years, following Airtel's lead, made news: (a) Vodafone outsourced its operations to IBM for $1.2 billion; (b) IDEA outsourced its operations to IBM for $0.8 billion; (c) Aircel outsourced to Wipro for $0.6 billion; (d) Unitech outsourced to Wipro for $0.5 billion; and (e) Tata Teleservices outsourced to TCS for $0.25 billion.

So, Airtel signed separate contracts with Ericsson, Nokia Networks and Siemens to set up and manage networks in various circles.

Fifth, it hands over management of a whole supply chain to a service provider. Before the IBM contract, Airtel had to deal with a dozen IT service suppliers— billing systems from Kenan Systems, customer care from Oracle, hardware management from Sun Microsystems and HP, storage systems from EMC, fraud management from Subex, data warehousing from NCR Terradata, interconnect systems from Intec and mediation systems from Hughes Software and Comptel (Subramanyam, 2011). Now it deals with just one contract.

A final aspect of industrial organization in sectors such as that of mobile telecom pertains to strategies for striking a balance between global and local markets, which is encouraging a growing number of companies to develop hubs that can provide shared services or resources for local, in-country operations, resulting in increasing levels of regionalization. Thus, with the advent of network sharing as well as full outsourcing, regionalization becomes important, leading to the provision of key functions such as procurement and finance being provided from the same hub, by grouping adjoining markets, yet still being close enough to the end customers to understand their specific needs and challenges. This has often resulted in mergers of different companies within large groups, which have had serious implications for employment. For example, Bharti Airtel, the key Indian example, embarked recently on a restructuring exercise to merge three separate businesses, its mobile, satellite TV (Direct-to-Home (DTH)) and fixed-line and broadband telemedia business, which jointly account for about 90 per cent of the company's revenues and the vast majority of its workforce, into a single entity. It was expected that Bharti's move could provide the trigger for similar action by rival corporations. It was also feared that the restructuring could result in 20–30 per cent of Airtel's 16,830 employees losing their jobs.

It should be pointed out that the sharing of facilities, as, for instance, networks between different mobile telecom service providers, is not confined to mobile telecom services.[14] In the manufacture of mobile phones, competitors such as Apple and Nokia share the manufacturing services of Foxconn. There are clear economies of scale at play over here. Network or manufacturing capacity sharing would seem to be becoming a feature of many players in both electronics and communications. Specialized service providers, whether of manufacturing services or network services, come up as the market expands and provides scope for a finer division of labour, as emphasized in Milberg and Winkler (2010).

---

[14] I owe this point to Joonkoo Lee.

In industrial organization terms, the Airtel 'model' has been vindicated because of its success in the market for mobile telecom services. Its subscriber base expanded rapidly from 2005 onwards, from about 714,000 subscribers in 2004 to more than 39,000,000 in 2007 and 184,550,000 in 2012. The financial statements for the company show a dramatic increase in several parameters that indicate this success from 2005, the year in which the outsourcing strategy was initiated. Thus, sales turnover increased from a meagre Rs. 63 crores in March 2004 to Rs. 8,142 crores the following year, with the figure jumping between 35 and 40 per cent every year to touch Rs. 41,603 crores in March 2012. Similarly, operating profits, which stood at Rs. 27 crores in March 2004, jumped to almost Rs. 3,000 crores in the following year, with the most recent figures for March 2012 standing at more than Rs. 13,000 crores.[15]

This brings us to a key question: given the drastic changes in the industrial organization strategy in the mobile telecom sector, what is the impact on labour markets, employment and conditions of work? Has the growth of the sector resulted in social upgrading? This is discussed below.

16.4 Issues of employment and labour conditions

Given the above discussion on the evolving structure of the mobile telecom industry, what is the kind of labour process that is employed in the different segments? It may be hypothesized that, for the largest part of the sector, the conditions of employment emerge as a residual, determined by the dynamics of inter-firm relationships between the different segments in the sector.

For example, given the need to 'centralize responsibilities' through outsourcing to large, established firms, it is an established practice to 'share employees' through a loose arrangement known as 'rebadging', wherein those employed in one firm get deployed into one where work is outsourced, allowing both firms to avoid longer-term commitments or payouts. This takes advantage of ambiguities involved with employer–work–workplace congruence, typified by service industries. Thus, when an MNO outsources its networking or customer service operations to other corporations, it is the practice to transfer employees as well. For example, Airtel transferred 1,000 of its engineers to the contracted network managers (Subramanyam, 2011). In Africa, where Airtel is now a major player, it transferred its customer care staff to an Indian business processing outsourcing (BPO) firm, Spanco, in Kenya, where it (Airtel) is the second-largest mobile operator. Those transferred stated that the transfer was extremely quick and they were not given enough time to read through

---

[15] All data are from the annual reports of Bharti Airtel, various years, as calculated by Balwant Singh Mehta.

the contracts before signing. Despite assurances by Airtel that their benefits would be protected in the firm to which they were transferred, and that they could return to Airtel within 2 years if they were dissatisfied with the new company, in practice the employees were not permitted to return. In 2011, the transferred employees went on strike in the wake of a court case filed by 51 former Airtel employees against their transfer. Similarly, in the case of the merger cited in the previous section, Airtel has argued that retrenched employees would be allowed to move to its Africa destinations if they wanted, with perhaps similar ambiguities in practice.

In segments that involve physical production, employment arrangements are quite informal, reflecting general informalization trends in the economy. During our fieldwork, it was found that, even in the high-technology segment of infrastructure provision, like in tower erection for communication, the market for which, as detailed above, is controlled entirely by large players, the chain downwards is quite informal. Again, most equipment is imported, but local contractors are hired for actual jobs. For example, in a tower that was constructed for Vodafone by Indus in the Dwarka area in Delhi, where the total cost was reported to be Rs. 10 million, it was found that different contractors were employed to do different types of work. The entire set-up of a telecom tower is broken into segments and specific contractors deal with each of the segments. Earlier, service providers like Airtel and Vodafone dealt directly with them for such work, but now they have come under Indus, which erects and maintains the tower for them. Indus, in turn, pays less for doing the same type of work as compared with direct contracts with Airtel or Vodafone. For example, in the case of a small staircase, it was stated that it had to be constructed within a budget of Rs. 2,500 under Indus, whereas earlier the budget was Rs. 5,000 when the contractor dealt directly with the service provider. Each of these contractors who work for Indus and other infrastructure firms has multiple teams to work at different locations. On average, for those working on contract, the monthly wages are around Rs. 3,000–4,000, with some allowances.

An engineering company was undertaking the civil and electrical work for the tower. Three riggers were constructing the tower meant for placing antennas; they belonged to a different contractor firm. Workers were working with agility and skill but there was very low concern for safety, even though they were wearing safety harnesses. The wages were being paid on a daily basis, amounting to Rs. 150 per day. Various towers are worked on simultaneously, and there are many teams (15 for Delhi for the particular contractor we contacted) under the contractor working on towers at different locations, with each having two to three riggers. There was a technician for every 15–20 towers, again employed informally for Rs. 4,000–5,000 per month, to troubleshoot problems. In some cases, brick kiln workers, who are used to climb great heights, are specifically used for the difficult jobs. Engineers, who work as labour contractors, agents and installers, are often hired for Rs. 5,000–7,000.

Thus, it appears as if the telecom infrastructure set-up, on the ground, functions just like the construction industry elsewhere.

We also conducted interviews at Airtel and Vodafone, to get an idea of how the value chain in mobile telecom functions. An interview with a dealer of SIM cards revealed the following supply chain—from the mobile service provider to the distributor to the local dealer, for both the purchase of SIM cards and the recharge of the balance. To elaborate, in the case of the latter (recharge of talk time), the distributor gets a talk time to the tune of Rs. 0.5–0.6 million deposited in his or her cell phone account from the service provider, which then is sold to local dealers. A dealer may buy talk time worth, say, Rs. 10,000. He or she deals with an agent of the distributor, who collects the money and deposits the talk time. The process works on commission. The dealer's commission is roughly 2 per cent, while that of the distributor is about 1 per cent. It appears that distributors operate on the basis of areas, with a cluster of areas making up the zone of a distributor.

In the case of selling a connection (SIM card), the chain remains the same while the reward for the local dealer is apparently different. Selling a SIM card leads to a 'point', and then the collection of a particular number of 'points' (say, about 0.2 million points) entitles the dealer to a particular product like a camera or a bike.

Clearly, there is no evidence to show any substantial social upgrading as a result of participation in the telecom value chain. There is a substantial growth of employment with the rapid expansion of the telecommunications sector, and wages too have increased in this sector (data in Sarkar et al., 2013). But the varieties of outsourcing result in the spread of precarious forms of employment, contract and casual labour or informalization of employment across various segments of the labour market. Given the prevalence of such a structure, combined with the perceived vulnerabilities of operating in low-margin markets such as India, it is the labour market that provides the guarantee of maximum flexibility. However, centralization necessitates the employment of large workforces and, consequently, labour process control, employment flexibility and increased automation, among other things. In other words, with the characteristics of service provision requiring large numbers of 'feet on the ground', the conditions of employment are informal, to a very large extent. This hypothesis needs to be further examined with systematic research on the different segments in the mobile telecom value chain.

At the same time, the cheapening of mobile phone service provision has clearly been of great benefit to the Indian consumer and has driven the unprecedentedly rapid expansion of mobile phone services. In this manner, because of oligopolistic competition among the handful of telecom majors, at least some of the benefits of outsourcing have been passed on as consumers' surplus to hundreds of millions of Indian users of mobile phones. This, in turn, has made its own contributions to economic and social development in the country, including rural India, as discussed in a study by Mehta (2013). However, it is a matter of great concern that this has meant the polarization of benefits between consumers and workers in the industry.

16.5 Conclusion: What are the limits of outsourcing?

The Airtel outsourcing model brings up an important question of industrial organiza-tion in GVCs: what are the limits of outsourcing? Following the analysis of Prahalad and Hammel (1990), outsourcing was supposed to be about everything other than a firm's core competence. Manufacturing, for instance, has been separated from design, branding and marketing in many consumer products, such as garments and shoes. But the continued codification of substantial parts of knowledge, along with the modularization of tasks (Contractor et al., 2011) has made it possible to finely slice what were integrated tasks into parts that could be outsourced. For instance, in the research and development processes in pharmaceutical companies, 'knowledge-intensive projects are more likely to be assigned to internal teams, while data-intensive projects are more likely to be outsourced' (Azoulay, 2004, quoted in Contractor et al., 2011, p. 26). In contract manufacturing, as is ubiquitous in consumer electronics, lead companies keep design, branding and marketing to themselves, but outsource all manufacturing.

The modularization of tasks in providing telecom services (network management, IT service management) has made it possible to outsource what would earlier have been considered part of the telecom service providers' core activities. Managing networks and IT services were considered part of the skills that constitute a telecom company's core competence. But the Airtel example shows that even these services could be outsourced. The telecom service provider could then further narrowly define itself as one that owns the bandwidth and manages the bundle of services that provide mobile telecom. Of course, there would be limits to outsourcing, and the factors determining those limits need to be explored. But the point here is that the Bharti Airtel networking model has pushed the limits of outsourcing in mobile telecom to a new level.

A final point: what does the outsourcing of such critical parts of GVCs mean for national development, when the firms are MNCs of various origins?[16] This question of national development is complicated by the fact that companies such as Bharti Airtel are themselves new multinationals from among the emerging BRICS (Brazil, Russia, India, China and South Africa) economies. The decisions of such

---

[16] This point is also owed to Jookoo Lee in his review of the draft of this chapter.

new MNCs do not seem to take account of national development concerns; rather, they are business decisions based on cost reduction considerations. It is worth noting that, in providing IT services, Bharti Airtel preferred not one of the Indian IT companies but IBM. The forward linkages, in provision of higher-level expertise, and backward linkages, in providing hardware, are to IBM in the US. Such backward and forward linkages in GVCs have national development implications, but these obviously do not enter into firm-level calculations. This raises major issues about the nature of development policy in a wildly outsourced world.

References

'GTL to acquire Aircel's 17,500 towers for Rs 8,400 cr.' *Business Standard*. 2010. 1 January.

Contractor, F. J., V. Kumar, S. K. Kundu, and T. Pedersen. 2011. *Global Outsourcing and Offshoring: An Integrated Approach to Theory and Corporate Strategy*. Cambridge: Cambridge University Press.

Ernst and Young. 2012. 'The World Is Bumpy—Globalisation and New Strategies for Growth.' Available at, www.ey.com/Publication/.../Globalization%20report%20FINAL.pdf. Accessed on April 27, 2013.

FICCI (Federation of Indian Chambers of Commerce and Industry) and Ernst and Young. 2010. 'Enabling the Next Wave of Telecom Growth in India—Industry Inputs for the National Telecom Policy 2011.' New Delhi: FICCI and Ernst and Young.

Grossman, G. M., and E. Rossi-Hansberg. 2006. 'Trading Tasks: A Simple Theory of Offshoring.' *NBER Working Paper No. 12721*.

ICRA (Indian Credit Rating Agency). 2009. 'Telecom Infrastructure Industry in India.' New Delhi: ICRA.

Lee, J., and G. Gereffi. 2013. 'Economic and Social Upgrading in Mobile Phone Manufacturing Production Networks.' *Capturing the Gains Working Paper*.

Mehta, B. S. 2013. 'Capabilities, Costs and Networks: Impact of Mobile Phones in Rural India.' *Capturing the Gains Working Paper*.

Milberg, W., 2004. 'The Changing Structure of Trade Linked to Global Production Systems: What Are the Policy Implications?' *Int Labour Rev* 143 (1–2): 45–90.

Milberg, W., and D. Winkler. 2010. 'Trade, Crisis, and Recovery: Restructuring Global Value Chains.' *Policy Research Working Paper 5294*. Washington, D.C.: World Bank.

———. 2013. *Outsourcing Economics: Global Value Chains in Capitalist Development*. Cambridge: Cambridge University Press.

Prahalad, C. K., and G. Hamel. 1990. 'The Core Competence of the Corporation.' *Harvard Busi Rev* 68 (3): 79–91.

Sarkar, S., B. S. Mehta and D. Nathan. 2013. 'How Social Upgrading Drives Economic Upgrading by Indian IT Majors: The Case of Telecom Services.' *Capturing the Gains Working Paper 27.*

Sen, S. 2012. 'Handset Manufacturing Value Chain—What Would it Take for India to Actualise Its Potential?' *Electronics Bazaar,* January.

Subramanyam, R. 2011. 'Managing Core Outsourcing to Address Fast Market Growth: A Case Study of an Indian Mobile Telecom Service Provider.' In Contractor et al. (2011).

UNCTAD. 2013. *World Investment Report: GVCs, Investment and Trade for Development.* Geneva: UNCTAD.

Wilde, J. and E. de Haan. 2006. 'Critical Issues in the Mobile Phone Industry—High Cost of Calling.' Report prepared by SOMO.

17

Global Production Networks and Labour Process

Praveen Jha and Amit Chakraborty[1]

17.1 Introduction

In the last few decades, the modus operandi of global capitalism has been subject to significant restructuring. One major aspect of this is the transnationalization of production, i.e., the separation and segmentation of production processes across different regions or factories all over the globe. This phenomenon is often described as the ascendancy of global production networks (henceforth GPN). The different ways of conceptualizing such 'functionally integrated but geographically dispersed' (Gereffi and Korzeniewicz, 1994) systems of production—global commodity chains (GCCs), global value chains (GVCs) and global production networks—explain the production, distribution and consumption of goods and services in similar terms, i.e., as networks of interconnected functions and operations (Coe et al., 2008). In our view, the GPN framework best captures the complex (and often non-linear) dynamics of global capitalist production embedded in socio-spatiality. The framework's scope allows the location of the agency of various actors in the transnational space, to see how they shape the economic and political context around them. Because of its greater analytical openness to a complex reality, this framework also allows for productive dialogues with different branches of heterodox economics and beyond, including labour process theory[2], which is of particular importance in this paper.

---

[1] This is a revised version of the paper presented at the International Workshop on 'New Spatialities and Labour', 6–8 July, 2012, IGIDR, Mumbai. The authors are grateful to the participants at the workshop and the editors of this volume for their helpful inputs.

[2] The concept of 'labour process' as an analytical category received significant attention in Karl Marx's writings, and subsequent literature, particularly in the industrial sociology of the 1970s–1980s inspired by Marxist tradition, with the intervention of Harry Braverman (1974), Marglin (1974), Burawoy (1977, 1985) and others.

Underpinning the GPN framework is the idea that there is increasing global competition between multinational companies to tap into new markets, use cheap labour to exploit economies of scale and to cut down the cost of production (Gereffi et al., 2001; Humphrey, 2003). Further, a substantial strand in the literature views this as a positive development on the grounds that it leads to economic, technical, and social upgrading in the firms that work within a GPN. This in turn is often seen to lead to the acquisition of advanced manufacturing technology (AMT) in host countries, as well as increasing workers' skill levels and affording them greater autonomy in the production process (Womack et al., 1990; 2007). However, there are also arguments that suggest that instead of improving conditions for workers, GPNs may result in worsening their conditions of work and well-being (Harvey, 2010; Foster et al., 2011; Bose, 2012).

Another issue worth highlighting here is that a significant strand of the literature tends to treat capital as autonomous, if not all powerful, in its ability to shape the entire process, rendering the agency of labour almost negligible. In other words, the agency of labour has been inadequately accommodated, except for cases where the collective power of workers in terms of global or regional trade unions (which often do not exist or at most have minimal impact) is examined within the unfolding dynamics of GPNs (Herod, 2001; Coe et al., 2008; Cumber et al., 2008; Selwyn, 2012). However, in recent years, an alternative strand of the relevant literature has emerged. This tends not to view labour in a passive manner and our own understanding resonates analytically with such an approach. Therefore, we try in this paper to understand GPNs from a political economy perspective, in terms of the dynamic interaction of capital strategy and the agency of labour, which in turn articulates the labour process within a GPN. For reasons of space, we refrain from delving into a detailed discussion of the GCC-GVC-GPN and labour process literature here.

In this chapter, we examine automobile production in the Gurgaon-Manesar industrial cluster located in the National Capital Region (NCR) of Haryana. We focus on India's leading car manufacturer Maruti Suzuki's Manesar plant. As it happens, the Manesar plant is a major node in Maruti's production network, and has also recently been a hub of serious worker unrest. This paper is divided into two major sections. The first section, based on fieldwork conducted at two different points of time, seeks to understand the production and labour processes in operation in Maruti Suzuki's Manesar plant. It explores several issues, including the rise of contractualization and the informalization of the workforce even in core production processes, the prospect for skill enhancement, questions of control *vis-à-vis* the labour process, increased workload on the shop floor in a just-in-time production regime, formal and real subsumption of labour under capital[3] and the transfer of crisis in a context of combined and uneven development. The second major section studies the genesis and anatomy of the recent wave of strikes in the Gurgaon-Manesar cluster and elsewhere in the automobile industry, with special emphasis on the 2011 strike in the Maruti Suzuki Manesar unit. The core concern of this section is to understand the significance of resistance by labour and the strategic response of capital, while also exploring issues of workers' organizations and the restructuring of production arrangements.

17.2 The Indian automobile industry GPN: A study of the Gurgaon-Manesar cluster

There was significant restructuring in the Indian automobile industry in the 1980s, in collaboration with Japanese MNCs. One of these is Maruti Udyog Limited (MUL), a joint venture of the Government of India and the Suzuki Motor Corporation. Government policy, aimed at promoting indigenization required manufacturers to adopt a phased manufacturing programme (PMP), with a target of 92 per cent localization of components within 5 years from the start of production. To reduce production vulnerability, MUL tried to develop a strong base of vendor companies and encouraged its local suppliers to adopt flexible practices and advanced technology (Bhargava, 2010). Market liberalization measures were introduced in the 1990s, including the de-licensing of car production (in 1994), and a change in policy (in 1997) that allowed companies to localize 50 per cent of production within 3 years and 70 per cent of production within 7 years (Bhargava, 2010). Companies were also allowed to export components and ancillaries, and this further promoted the integration of Indian automobile sector into global production networks.

Import duties on components have fallen from 60 per cent in the 1980s to 10 per cent today. Since 2008, the export of parts has grown faster than the export of

---

[3] Viewed historically, Marx described 'formal subsumption' of labour under capital as the process where capitalist production emerged from the earlier modes of production with a straightforward distinction between capital and wage labour. From the simple co-operation of workers grew the complex co-operation of the manufacturing division of labour. However, it was with the advent of large-scale industry that the labour process was revolutionized, and the 'real subsumption' of labour under capital began taking place, where instead of prolonging the working day (to increase the appropriation of absolute surplus value), increased productivity through intensification of work, revolutionizing the production techniques (to increase the appropriation of relative surplus value) becomes the centrepiece of labour process. We understand formal and real subsumption of labour under capital here not simply as a matter of chronology but as powerful analytical categories which help us comprehend the dynamics of the present capitalist production process.

assembled cars (ACMA, 2011–2012). At the same time, car part imports for local assembly—mainly from Thailand and South Korea—have grown much faster than local parts manufacturing since 2009. This shows that assembly plants in India use parts from abroad, while manufacturers of parts in India increasingly send more parts abroad than to local assembly plants. In the last several years, there has been an observable extension and re-linking of the supply chain between north and south India, as well as within Asia, thus integrating the Indian automobile industry into complex global production networks. The establishment of assembly plants for big firms like Maruti Suzuki and Hero Honda in Gurgaon (and later another plant in Manesar), Honda in Dharuhera, alongside numerous first-tier, second-tier or third-tier component suppliers, has made the Gurgaon-Manesar-Dharuhera industrial region the most significant automobile manufacturing cluster in India. The changes effected by the ascendency of GPNs in the last few decades in the global auto industry have also influenced and restructured this cluster.

In the production network, just-in-time delivery of material and inventory reduction under lean production become crucial, and so proximity is an increasingly important factor, leading to follow sourcing and the sophistication and integration of component industries. In the case of the Gurgaon-Manesar-Dharuhera cluster, first-tier suppliers like Rico and Omax have emerged as global suppliers of auto components, in addition to supplying the factories of lead firms in the region. The fact that global players like Denso, Delphi or Bosch are establishing production units here delineates this cluster as a destination for the global auto component industry. In order to understand this GPN better, we examined the production process of a lead firm, namely Maruti Suzuki, and some important features of the supply chain operating in the industrial cluster.

17.2.1 Key elements in the production process of the Maruti Suzuki Manesar plant and the supply chain

Production at this assembly plant begins in the press shop, where sheet-metal is cut or pressed, generally one day in advance under a just-in-time production system, meaning what is pressed today will be assembled tomorrow.[4] The power presses are automated, and the press-tools of these machines change without human intervention, according to the different types of parts to be pressed. The press shop runs three shifts and employs almost 40–50 permanent workers in each shift, as well as apprentices, trainees and almost as many contract workers as permanent ones. More difficult tasks, such as removing pressed parts from the machines, are performed

---

[4] This description of labour process corresponds to May–June, 2012, i.e., before the violent clash took place on 18th July, 2012. Many changes took place thereafter and continue to take place.

by contract workers and apprentices. However, press shop work is generally seen as less difficult overall, as most workstations here are machine stations, and workers have a little breathing space while the machines work. Working in the weld shop or assembly line, which are the next steps in the process, is significantly more laborious.

The Manesar production facility includes two plants, A-plant, which employs 250–300 hand-welders (of which nearly 200 are contract workers), and B-plant, which is fully automated. Since 2006, the number of workstations in A-plant has been brought down from 16 to 8, and since June 2011, this has gone from 8 to 4, thanks to an increased degree of automation and the use of robots (in general, one robot substitutes 10 workers; these workers are then reassigned rather than being laid off). However, the mechanization of processes in the weld shop does not necessarily mean a reduced workload. For instance, each worker needs to carry 70–80 sheets that make up the body of the cars up and down the stairs and sometimes works overtime without pay if their work is incomplete at the end of the shift. From the weld shop, the cars are sent to the sealer line. There are about 38–40 workstations there, with two workers at each station. Most workers on the line are either temporary or casual workers, or trainees. The plastic moulding of bumpers is done here, after which lights and other parts are attached to it. Bumper shop workers fix the bumper to the car, which is the next step in the assembly line. Out of almost 250 workers in the bumper department, only 20–25 workers are permanent workers, most are either trainees or contract workers.

In general, there are not many stoppages along the assembly line: they occur once or twice a day, if at all, and generally do not last longer than 1 or 2 minutes. There are about 200 workstations along the long-block assembly line, attended to by one worker each. Once the engine block arrives on the line, it is washed: a single worker uses a crane to clamp the engine block, operates the washing machine, and takes the engine out. All these tasks are completed in 45–50 seconds, but do not involve acquiring a skill in any substantive sense. Following this, data on the engine model must be entered: a worker attaches a barcode and punches in the engine numbers. He also fits the crankshafts, which are checked, washed, and then fitted manually. This fitting is one of the most physically demanding tasks in the production process, as the crankshaft weighs 15–20 kg. In the context of a developing country like India, the availability of cheap labour determines, to a great extent, the organization of work. Much less mechanization is involved in the completion of tasks that do not have an impact on standardization or quality; however, strenuous the work may be.

The pistons, which are sourced from multiple vendors, are attached next and the cars are sent to the dressing line. There are around 12 stations on the dressing line, manned by one worker each. This is where attachments, like starter motors and compressors, are fitted. These parts come from first-tier suppliers. During this part of the production process, heavier tasks, like lifting crankshafts off trolleys or testing them mechanically, are generally done by contract workers, while permanent workers are engaged in relatively lighter and supervisory work, like data entry or final checks. The internal labour market and the segmentation of the workforce take shape in such a way that capital pushes the maximum workload of production to the least organized segment of the workforce.

Workers of vendor companies work on the factory premises. In total, 600 contract workers and 40–45 trainees of Belsonica work two shifts of 12 hours each (on Sundays as well), making smaller sheet metal parts. They are compelled to work longer, and overtime goes up to 150–200 hours per month at the rate of only 24 rupees per hour. This clearly shows the strategy of capital to divide the workforce at their convenience to extract both absolute and relative surplus value.

Maruti Suzuki adheres to a strict 'no single source' policy: supplies arrive at the plants from the company's 250 odd first-tier component suppliers, including 20 global suppliers, and hundreds of lower tier suppliers. Maruti receives many supplies within a single day, which is a radical transformation from the earlier 30-day or 15-day cycles, enabling the plants to produce 4,600 cars a day. Along with methods like electronic flow, modern technologies and materials (like plastic in place of a metal fuel tank) are continuously adopted. Increased competitiveness in the late 1990s led global suppliers to India, many of whose components Maruti uses in the production of its cars.

The main automobile companies in the production network try to outsource not only stock and some production steps, but financial risks too. Local component suppliers down the supply chain face a financial squeeze due to a price pressure from both sides, as steel and rubber prices continue to rise and big firms demand lower prices. The final assembling plants are bound to increase capacity and to continue running to keep up with market demand, while those lower down the supply chain face extreme work pressure. This is passed on to the workers by prolonging the working day, running more and more overtime and forcing shop floor workers to work harder.

17.2.2 Contractualzation and casualization of core production

Workers at Maruti Suzuki's Manesar plant went on strike three times in 2011, in June, September and October.[5] On 18 July, 2012 a clash between the workers and management personnel took place on the company premises. One HR manager died of smoke inhalation when the room caught fire. These incidents ensured that the organization of production and the conditions of work at the plant changed considerably. Company management announced that the contract system would be

---

[5] This description is of November–December, 2013, after the restructuring of workforce following the clash.

abolished in the Manesar plant and that all discharged contract workers would be made regular. A letter submitted to the Labour Department a few months ago claimed to have achieved this, but the present situation is that less than 5 per cent of them have been taken back. After 18 July, 2012, 546 regular workers and all 1,800 contract workers were dismissed without a domestic enquiry. Contract workers had previously been 65–70 per cent of total workforce and had shouldered the major burden of regular production. Now, the company directly employed 'casual' workers, a new tag with the same old rules.

There are nearly 500 permanent workers who have been retained and another 100–150 workers from the Gurgaon plant, altogether almost half that before. There are around 300 trainees, very few apprentice workers and 2,500–3,000 casual workers. Those who are employed as 'casual' workers get a salary of 11,000 rupees, in comparison to the salary of 32,000 rupees paid to permanent workers, though they both do similar work in all departments, including the press shop, weld shop, paint shop and assembly line. The work is 'similar' in terms of participation in the core production processes, like working in the same line, side by side with permanent employees. The tasks performed are slightly different, some are heavier and some are lighter, and in most cases, the contract workers perform the heavier tasks. However, according to the Industrial Disputes Act 1947 and Contract Labour Regulation (and Abolition) Act 1970, contract workers can only work as helpers and should not participate in core production processes.

Casual workers are supposed to be trained for a period of 28 days when they join, but actually receive only 5–6 days of training, after which they work without guidance and must learn on the job. Casual workers, in particular, are victims of market volatility, and face increasing workloads alongside increasing job insecurity. In each new batch of casual workers, fewer workers are taken on than in the previous batch for the same quantum of work. All the casual workers are ITI holders and they come from Himachal Pradesh, Punjab, Uttar Pradesh, Rajasthan and Orissa. This 'company casual' system acts as a useful camouflage of the erstwhile contract system, proving that it has not at all been abolished. Under two contractors, BGR and Gulab Singh, around 600–700 contract workers work in the material supply department. They perform loading and trolley work, and other physically demanding jobs, earning a salary of 5,500–6,000 rupees. After being on the job for 7 months, casual workers are discharged, and a new batch of casual workers is employed for the next 7-month period[6]. Regular workers are pressured by the threat that the reserve army of discharged casual workers will be called back to take their places if they agitate

---

[6] According to the Industrial disputes Act, 1947, if a casual worker works for 240 days in a year, he/she can claim to be made permanent. That is why the management is discharging the casual workers after 7 months.

against management. In addition to this, regular workers face an increased workload, since management refuses to hire new regular workers. For instance, there used to be relievers in each line, to help run the process of production if someone working on the assembly line was on leave—there is no provision for relievers any more. Across all departments, there are fewer workers and supervisors doing the same or more work than before, effectively resulting in a body of over-worked employees.

Maruti Suzuki's Gurgaon plant[7] employs around 2,500 permanent workers, around 3,000 contract workers from 5–6 contractors and nearly 400 trainees. Contract workers usually work at the plant for anything between a few months to a few years, but there is a deliberate gap in their renewal of employment every 6 months, so that they cannot claim to be permanent employees. While contract workers are spread out across the various departments of the production process, there are more of them in a few departments, like the machine shop or engine shop. Contract workers are all ITI holders and get around 11,000 rupees, much less compared to the permanent workers. Contract workers are also flexibly employed to pick up any overtime requirements. In addition, a sub-category of contract workers are the 'helpers', who are mostly non-ITI and get paid 5,500–6,000 rupees.

17.2.3 Production networks and labour process in the Gurgaon-Manesar auto cluster: Some general observations

In our study of Gurgaon-Manesar cluster, we found a complex web of interactions between lead firms and the different tiers of suppliers. To be more precise, polarization and power relations in this sphere do not seem to exactly reflect the rigid vertical order of original equipment manufacturers (OEMs), first-tier suppliers, second-tier suppliers and third-tier suppliers. A kind of complex interdependence and de-verticalization seems to be relevant where a single firm can supply parts to OEMs or to component assemblers. The spatial and institutional dimensions of the GPN framework are well adapted to capture this network complexity within the automobile manufacturing cluster.

On the one side there are OEMs like Maruti Suzuki, Honda and Hero Honda, and global component suppliers like Delphi, Denso, Bosch, Rico, Pricol and so on who have linkages with the lead firms. The labour process, work organization and

---

[7] Apart from the one in Manesar, the other plant of Maruti Suzuki is in Gurgaon; both these plants are almost similar in terms of organization of production, labour condition etc. In passing, we may note that almost all the major manufacturing companies tend to have stark differences in production and labour conditions across developed and developing countries, which tend to be significantly inferior in the latter. By all accounts, Suzuki's plants in Japan are on a completely different plane compared to their Indian counterparts.

technology in use at these lead firms are broadly similar and they have in-house R&D. They are the main players in the GPN and benefit from increasing integration with the global market. In the middle there are large enterprises that operate as first- or second-tier vendors. They benefit from the domestic growth of the automobile industry and are important players in regional production networks. Increasing global competition creates further polarization in this segment. At the bottom, there are large numbers of tiny, small and medium enterprises (SMEs) that do not practice lean production or technological upgrading and struggle to survive.

Working conditions are poor across the board. Internal segmentation of the working class is increasing, alongside growing contractualization. Even at the upper levels of the production chain, 60–80 per cent of the workforce is made up of contract workers performing key production activities. At the bottom of the chain, the notion of permanence in labour terms is often hazy (Bose, 2012). At the bottom of the production chain in the cluster, tiny, small and medium manufacturing enterprises run on very low profit, which means these companies are unable to expand their capacities or upgrade the technology. In this context, the main source of survival is the maximum possible extraction of absolute surplus value of the workers (GurgaonWorkersNews, 2012). Often the operation of these enterprises is located in the informal sector, allowing them to sidestep legal necessities. The lead firms in the production cluster, including Maruti Suzuki, integrate the low-wage low-price regime into their supply chain by outsourcing operations like heat treatment, machining and so on (GurgaonWorkersNews, 2010).

17.2.4 Issues of workers' autonomy and skill

The use of microelectronics in the GNP era has revolutionized the process of control, both over individual machines and in the coordination of other processes[8]. In fact, it is worth emphasizing that the labour process at the current juncture is dramatically different from the Fordist mass production regime and is quite amenable to flexibilities of various kinds. There is a major opinion that lean production (Womack et al., 1990, 2007) as a generalized concept has brought together the best elements of craft production and mass production and has ushered in a new era of workers' autonomy and democracy on the shop floor in the modern automobile industry (considered a cornerstone of work organization in GPNs). However, while it is true that workers' greater participation is represented in the production process in the form of quality

---

[8] These include mechanization of transformation processes, like introducing new capital-intensive, quality-enhancing, cost-cutting, technologies to transform the raw materials into semi-finished products and the semi-finished products to finished products and transfer of material processes, like the development of a conveyor system and assembly-line production.

circles or 'cells' in the upper strata of the production network, this occurs only in so far as it enables a company to appropriate 'local' knowledge, which they might not otherwise have access to. Such knowledge is also integral to gaining greater control over the production process, which is why companies promote a partial integration of conceptual and executive labour processes, for example, the linking of computer-aided design (CAD) with computer-aided manufacturing (CAM). However, even that kind of participation is also very rare, observable only in a very few companies, and for a very small section of workers. For the majority of workers, with contract workers making up the lion's share of the workforce, coercion and subjugation rather than hegemonic control is the main expression of just-in-time production. There seems to be a growing clash between technocratic logic and democratic logic.

There are different views regarding the impact of new technology upon workers' skills. There is a celebration of new work organization with a view that advanced manufacturing technology (AMT) is a means to free workers from boredom by reducing the repetitive or physically demanding parts of the job. This would allow workers a chance to pursue the more fulfilling aspects of work, such as the development of skill as the worker in the labour process interacts with more sophisticated machinery. On the other hand, Braverman's (1974) deskilling hypothesis suggests that the technical change shows a secular trend in the direction of reduction of skills and makes crafts redundant, as we discussed earlier.

We found the question of skill to be quite complex: it has to be understood in manifold terms, including craft-input, knowhow, experience, market value of skill, and so on. There seems to be a general decline in terms of craft input in the labour process. Knowhow increases or decreases depending on the specific changes in the labour process in terms of technological shifts or the reorganization of production. Experience seems to be less and less important, as it is now easily replaced by suitable training. Computer Numerical Controlled (CNC) machines are controlled by microprocessors and are programmed to carry out a detailed sequence of machinery operations, thus offering a comparatively narrow choice of tasks for workers. The use of CNC machines transfers responsibility from the operator, i.e., the worker, to the computer. The skills required to handle new machines are minimal and can be learned by anyone in a matter of days, which increases the disposability of workers. With the evaporation of conventional skills, the possession of a devalued skill and the fear of inability to cope with new technology contribute to undermining job security among workers. Only a few workers are required to be supervisors with the experience to identify a fault when it occurs in the process of production.

From the earlier discussion of the mechanised labour process at Maruti Suzuki's plants and the above discussion, it becomes clear that the promise of re-skilling is more of an ideological campaign than a practical process. This understanding has significant implications for the ongoing process of real subsumption with increasing mechanization, where the general tendency of deskilling, alienation and suffocation on the shop floor increase the cost of reproduction of labour. Capital in the present process of accumulation is not ready to provide the cost of reproduction of labour. Thus, the demands of workers for better working conditions, and greater subsistence wages for the reproduction of labour power, become the cornerstones of new waves of workers' struggle in developing countries.

17.2.5 The coexistence of primitive and modern: The 'unity of opposites' embedded in a 'combined and uneven development'

Even in the most sophisticated segment of production networks, there is ample evidence of dismal work conditions, the exploitation of cheap labour and job insecurity due to the existence of a huge reserve of labour.[9] For example, the paint shop at Maruti Suzuki's Manesar plant reflects a curious combination of sophisticated robotic technology and physical labour of a brutal nature. For instance, 10–12 painting robots are employed at one end, but simultaneously at the other end, workers carry 25–30 kilo loads up and down flights of stairs, and are expected to work an extra hour with no pay if their tasks are not completed by the end of their shift. This unevenness exists apart from the mechanization of a segment of production that has direct implications on quality or standardization; firms operating in low-wage regimes thus find it cost-effective to maximize the use of cheap labour in other segments of production.

Due to the availability of cheap labour and a huge labour reserve, the lower segment of the supply chain, apart from lead firms and global auto component manufacturers in the first tier, becomes the main source of absolute surplus value from workers, through prolonged working hours, overtime at a dismal wage rate and often precarious working conditions, to contribute to the value added in the production network. The firms in this segment absorb the main burden of cost cutting and pressure due to profit squeezing from the upper levels. This results in structural unevenness along the supply chain.

As the Gurgaon-Manesar automobile cluster developed over time, it developed strong backward linkages extending to informal slum production, which has

---

[9] The expression 'combined and uneven development' comes from Marxist literature. It was popularized by Leon Trotsky and later used by dependency theorists and others to refer to a process where both the development of some parts of it and the underdevelopment of the remaining parts are integral to process, as both are outcomes of the same process.

led to regional unevenness. The older industrial areas or workers' *jhuggis,* which emerged as the centre of industrial activities in the 1970s or 1980s in Faridabad or Ghaziabad, were overshadowed and eroded when the centre of industrial activity shifted to Gurgaon or Noida. They were eventually co-opted in the extended labour process of automobile production centred in the Gurgaon-Manesar cluster (GurgaonWorkersNews, 2012). This provides a low-wage, labour-intensive regime with minimal bargaining power for workers, in terms of the outsourcing of hazardous or labour-intensive work from the Gurgaon cluster. Thus, the automobile GPN feeds on the backwardness of its periphery, and the labour process of an old and eroded industrial base is formally subsumed under the new capital.

17.2.6   Transfer of crisis

With the extension of production networks with deep backward linkages, it has been smoother for lead firms and global component manufacturers to siphon off profits and transfer crises onto other segments of the production network with less bargaining power. A crisis can be internal or external to a firm's production process. An internal crisis may arise due to strikes or the increased bargaining power of shop floor workers, leading to a profit squeeze or an erosion of hegemony or control over workers. An external crisis may be generated by a sudden change in demand in domestic or global markets, leading to shortage of capacity or overcapacity; it may also occur due to a rise in oil prices or adverse changes in interest rates, leading to a fall in profit margins. For example, the Indian car industry was impacted by the global economic slowdown from October 2008 to March/April 2009. Firms sacked temporary workers and reduced their capacities accordingly. However, when they faced a sudden rise in demand, most of the lead firms and component assemblers had to deal with overstretched production capacities and supply networks.

Thus, the mechanism of ensuring profit margins and the transfer of crises exploits the combined and uneven development embedded in the production network. This may take various forms. In early 2010, when Maruti Suzuki was recovering from the slump in car sales over the last 2 years, there was a sudden rise in demand, a 30 per cent jump year-on-year in car bookings. The situation was dire, as the company had not invested in increasing production capacity during the slump. The extended wait period for most models meant Maruti's rival companies would start capturing their market share. The compulsion to rapidly increase production resulted in more regular maintenance of machineries, reprogramming robots for better control of the assembly line and increase in speed, productivity and efficiency, and implementation of a 'flexi-line' alongside the main assembly line, to produce multiple models simultaneously. These measures saved Maruti Suzuki the cost of opening a new assembly line (Sruthijith and Chauhan, 2011). Its Manesar plant, which had an installed capacity of producing 250,000 cars a year, began manufacturing 350,000 cars. To contain workers' resistance and to ensure their participation, workers' incentives were linked to production. However, life on the shop floor had become miserable. While production at the Gurgaon plant increased by 17 per cent, Manesar was pushed much harder, resulting in a 40 per cent rise (*ibid.*). This rise in production affected workers, who bore the brunt of it. We argue later that this transfer of crisis onto the workers and subsequent intensification and coercion in the labour process laid the groundwork for the strikes at Manesar beginning in June 2011, as well as the wave of labour unrest elsewhere in the cluster.

In addition, the increasing contractualization of the workforce and shifting the main burden of production onto contract workers or trainees, who have very low bargaining power and lack the right to unionize, helps firms to weaken the bargaining power of permanent workers. Management attempts to co-opt the relatively small number of permanent workers in lead firms and first-tier suppliers by offering them more supervisory roles, thus resulting in deeper division within the workforce. Contract workers, who already perform the more laborious tasks within the production process, also bear the brunt of an increase in the intensity of work that comes with a rise in demand, or have to face layoffs when there is an under-utilization of capacity.

In times of crisis, to maintain a markup of profit, lead firms often pressurize vendor companies lower down in the value chain to set up cost-cutting mechanisms, thus attempting to shift the burden. After the strike in Manesar and the fall in profits, which were also affected by foreign exchange fluctuations, higher interest rates and higher input costs, Maruti Suzuki has begun attempting to reduce its buying costs by 3 per cent every year to increase profit margins. It is simultaneously consolidating its vendor base to increase supply from a more stable and smaller base of first-tier suppliers to bring down logistics costs, while also pressuring supplier companies to reduce their own cost of production. In addition, opening a new plant and shifting the major volume of production to a location where the lower bargaining power of workers can be exploited can weaken the resistance of labour confined to the earlier location of unrest. During the Maruti Suzuki strike in 2011, the company management put pressure on the workers by threatening that the company would shift its production to Gujarat.

17.3 Workers' response: The genealogy and anatomy of strike waves

This section examines the nature of workers' assertion, *vis-à-vis* the changes taking place in the production process, which has time and again expressed itself both locally and globally through factory occupations, strikes, or other forms of labour unrest. A Marxist understanding enables us to appreciate the active role of workers in the emerging dynamics of labour process and GPNs.

In the Gurgaon-Manesar cluster, the automobile industry has seen waves of strikes in recent times. After the 89-day strike by Maruti workers in Gurgaon in 2000 was crushed by the management, it was the spirited struggle of Honda workers in Manesar in 2005 and their success in forming a workers' union that triggered a series of moments when labour went on the offensive against capital. Contract workers have sporadically risen up against their dismal working conditions and low wages across the entire belt, including the Hero Honda factory occupation of April 2006, the Honda HMSI wildcat strike in September 2006, the strike at Delphi in January 2007, unrest in the Hero Honda Dharuhera plant in May 2008, and another wildcat strike at Honda HMSI in December 2010. Workers at Napino Auto (November 2009), Omax Auto (December 2009), Denso (February 2010), Sunbeam and Rico Auto (September 2009), Maruti Suzuki's Manesar plant (in three phases from June 2011 to October 2011), Munjal Kiriu, Autofit (2013–2014), Shriram Piston, Posco ITDC, Ahresty, Minda Furukawa (2014) staged sustained unrest or strikes demanding their right to unionize, for better working conditions or higher wages. The upheaval in the entire belt shows some emerging trends which demand closer attention. We will try to explore these trends, while focusing on the recent experience of the Maruti Suzuki workers' strike at the Manesar plant.

In our view, one important dimension of the new waves of workers' struggle in the automobile GPN is that these are deeply grounded in labour process and in shop floor work experience. The basis of unity among the contract and permanent workers was also the shared experience of the shop floor labour process. Most of the strikes and instances of labour unrest do not put forward documented or concrete economic demands when negotiating with the management. Striking with prior notice appears to be the last resort of collective bargaining in the traditional trade union framework. Sometimes the demands are initially disarticulated as they are linked to different dimensions of working conditions and the aspiration for dignity and workplace democracy, and they gradually take shape during the course of the struggle. Sometimes, demands are semi-articulated, and a plethora of demands might come together in a demand to form a union of workers, where the union symbolizes a united assertion of workers.

In the case of Maruti Suzuki, the workers staged a sudden occupation of the factory on June 4, 2011, demanding recognition of their own union. However, the actual genesis of this strike can be traced back to the worsening of their working conditions, increased managerial and supervisory control and intensification of work to meet the increased demand post-2008 all of which were discussed above.

411

Almost half the wages of permanent workers were designated as variables like production incentives and attendance awards. A leave of absence of one day cost a worker 25 per cent of the attendance award, resulting in a deduction of 1,200–1,500 rupees, while a 3-day absence in a month cost a worker the entire award. Some important points of contention were a 7.5-minute tea break, a 30-minute lunch break and the speed of assembly line, all issues linked to the organization of work. After the partial success of the first phase of the strike, the sudden upsurge in the feeling of collective strength among the workers helped to spread workplace democracy: compelled by the new situation, supervisors were friendlier, no one was harassed for a fault in assembly line, work intensity reduced. The positive atmosphere did not include management and the increased collective strength of workers on the shop floor meant reduced control for management over production. On the one hand, workers tried to ensure and enhance their collective strength, bargaining power and control of production, while the management tried to reassert their control over production back through various attempts to diminish workers' collective assertion. In these circumstances, the truce between workers and management proved to be fragile. The leaders were suspended and workers were asked to sign a 'good conduct bond' before entering the factory. This led to the second phase of labour unrest.

Another important dimension of these struggles is the use of strategies that go beyond the traditional legal trade unionist framework of the workers' struggle, and make capital vulnerable in a new way. At Maruti Suzuki, the workers' struggle in the first and third phases took the form of a 'go-slow' and factory occupation, which made it impossible for management to continue production by employing and training a new workforce. Workers at other factories (Suzuki Powertrain, Suzuki Casting, Suzuki Motorcycle) chose to participate in a sustained solidarity strike, while workers at seven other companies (Satyam Auto, Bajaj Motor, Endurance, Hi-lex, Lumax) participated in a 1-day solidarity strike on October 8, 2011. All these—occupation, go-slow, solidarity strike—are 'illegal', but in a production network that features strong interdependence among firms, these forms of struggle show the disruptive capacity of workers against the strategy of capital.

But labour in the neoliberal era in a GPN faces serious constraints when it comes to collective bargaining. The shift in work organization, use of new technology, increasing contractualization and the increased bargaining power of capital *vis-à-vis* labour due to mobility and shifting of production activity within the GPN have all undermined the effectiveness of trade unions, which are comprised of only permanent workers and act at the factory level. When contract workers form the majority of the workforce and run production, and firms are interdependent both regionally and globally, this becomes a serious constraint. Another problem is that the technological shift, in terms of adopting advanced manufacturing technology (AMT), has rarely been considered an area of workers' struggle within the traditional trade union framework. In many cases, where permanent workers get production incentives, any technological shift that enhances production is considered beneficial, and its impact on labour process is overlooked.[10] However, flexibility and redeployment are crucial to the successful implementation of AMT, so redeploying workers from one job to another, one line to another or one department to another is not considered as a part of collective bargaining and thus the localized resistance of workers against redeployment or intensification of work due to new technology is not properly articulated *vis-à-vis* the 'lack of discipline' accusation of management. Another problem is that the staff, supervisors, and members of the lower and middle ranks of management have historically been outside of labour unions, even antagonistic to them, and vice versa. On the one hand, the reorganization of production under this old job classification divides a section whose work is very close to or the same as the workers, while on the other hand, the creation of an internal labour market and the internal segmentation of workers by management sometimes separates skilled and experienced workers from the rest by designating the latter as supervisors.

To undermine the collective assertion of labour, capital has shown different strategies. One way is to crush the workers' movement and damage the confidence of workers and then restructure work, technology and the production process without any significant resistance, so that the previous objectives of the workers' struggle are changed and undermined. After the 3-month long workers' strike of 2000, the Maruti Suzuki management could crush the resistance and terminate the main leadership. They then introduced a voluntary retirement scheme to reduce the workforce, increased the number of contract workers to undermine the strength of permanent workers, restructured production where contract workers would run the main work, and co-opted a section of workers and formed a separate union. Often, capital is forced to make a compromise with labour to avoid larger damage: thus the struggles of Hero Honda workers in late 1980, Honda workers in 2005 or Maruti Suzuki workers in Manesar in 2011–2012 achieved their right to form unions. But, in due course, at Hero Honda, and partially at Honda, the management

---

[10] Permanent workers receive incentives proportional to the amount of increase in production from a fixed target level. So, the technological shifts that raise the level of production by intensifying labour process and increasing workload, give rise to a material 'production incentive' due to the increase in production. In traditional trade union bargaining, only economic issues are settled in the process of collective bargaining, but issues of increased workload due to technological shifts are rarely addressed. So, in traditional trade union bargaining, the permanent workers' union leaders, often detached from shop floor experiences, seem to accept all those changes that increase production, as on paper they receive a permanent increased incentive.

was successful in containing the union, so that it represented the interests of only permanent workers, whereas the main burden of production is on contract workers.

If we study the post-strike events that unfolded after the struggle at Maruti Suzuki in 2011, we see that the management was forced to increase the workers' tea break from 7.5 minutes to 15 minutes, to decrease the speed of the assembly line, to increase transport facilities for workers, to employ more workers, so that relievers can take a worker's place if they need to leave the line. An average wage increase took place for ITI holding contract workers (from 6,500 rupees to about 8,500 rupees per month). However, all of this means that in order to maintain its profit margin, capital has to transfer the crisis elsewhere, and one option is further down the value chain. As part of a cost-cutting exercise, the company initiated measures to step up localization levels and to pare down the number of first-tier suppliers over the next 2 or 3 years. It also decided to 'discipline' vendors by consolidating its supplier base and increasing sourcing from a smaller and more stable base of first-tier vendors to bring down logistics costs. To secure the supply side, Maruti Suzuki made a deal with FIAT to obtain 100,000 engines per year and also merged with Suzuki Powertrain to ensure the supply of diesel engines (Thakkar, 2012). In addition, B-plant at Manesar became operational during the strike, which meant that management could shift workers hired during the lock-out there. They introduced a different ratio between workers and machinery in the plan: B-plant is more mechanised (for instance, its weld shop is fully automated, unlike A-plant's weld shop). Maruti also adopted 40 ITI colleges in Gujarat (Nanda and Rai, 2012), to ensure a steady supply of labour. By outsourcing work to companies such as Belsonica, FMI, Krishna Maruti, SKH Metal which operate on the company premises, a formal division is created between workers in the same factory. The full significance of this interaction of capital's strategy, assertion of labour and technology is yet to be revealed.

Despite all these constraints, labour unrest in firms that operate in a GPN exposes the vulnerability of this new regime of production. A strike at any point can result in a ripple effect upward or downward along the supply chain, with regional or even global disruptive effects. The 44-day Rico Auto workers' strike saw the killing of a worker in a clash and resulted in a 1-day general strike across the Gurgaon-Manesar automobile cluster, in which almost one lakh workers participated. The resulting shortage of parts brought production to a halt for 3 days in General Motors plants in the US and Canada. The Satyam Auto strike in Haridwar in 2012 disrupted production in the Hero Honda plant in Gurgaon. The strike at the Maruti Suzuki Manesar plant in 2011 halted production at a number of vendor companies, and had damaging effects on production along the supply chain. The strike at Suzuki Powertrain, which supplies engines to the assembly lines of Maruti Suzuki, brought the Maruti Suzuki Gurgaon plant to halt last year. This shows that labour unrest anywhere within the GPN has consequences for other actors both up and down the supply chain. The Maruti Suzuki workers' struggle saw an embryonic form of plant-level workers' self-organization unfold. It included workers of other Suzuki plants as well as a few other companies. However, the question regarding the nature of organization and conscious strategy which the labour movement requires in this new objectivity to forge a unity of workers across production networks remains mostly unanswered.

When we examine important automobile clusters in developing countries that are part of GPNs, there appear to be similar waves of strikes that display similar trends. In China, workers went on strike on May 17, 2010 at Nanhai Honda Lock's transmission factory in Foshan (south-eastern China) near Guangzhou and shut down all four of the Japanese car maker's mainland factories. This strike was followed by a wave of strikes in other car assembly plants (Honda and Toyota). These struggles are an important factor in the relocation of auto production units from southeast to west China, with another factor being a reserve of labour whose wages cost less. Temporary workers at Hyundai's Ulsan plant in South Korea went on a wildcat strike and occupation in November 2010. In Mexico, unrest developed at Honda's El Salto plant in December 2010. A transition from formal to real subsumption of labour under capital, from appropriation of absolute surplus value to relative surplus value in labour process in the new assembly points and automobile clusters in GPNs is giving birth to a young, militant, skilled workforce globally (Silver, 1993). Silver further argues that workers' agency is a key element in the global restructuring of automobile industry, and that the number of global 'labour struggles have prompted managerial responses, including the restructuring of production and the relocation of capital. And each round of restructuring and relocation has undermined workers' bargaining power in the sites of disinvestment/restructuring at the same time that it has created and strengthened new working classes in the sites of new investment'. It is thus important to ask how workers' responses will influence the contemporary operation of GPNs and the new regime of accumulation.

17.3.1 Conceptualizing the struggles

The struggles outlined above show a dynamic contradiction between capital and labour, and that the complete subsumption of labour is never possible in the labour process[11]. These workers' struggles—and particularly the experience of the different

---

[11] An important Marxist category within which to understand this dynamic is 'variable capital' (Nichols, 1980). Workers' wages constitute variable capital and are 'variable' because the necessary labour time and hence wages are not determined in a mechanical, a priori, asocial manner, but rather through an ongoing process of bargaining between workers and capitalists. It is affected by the duration of work,

phases of the struggle at Maruti Suzuki—demonstrate how 'class' is 'formed' through contradictions in the sphere of production. E. P. Thompson emphasized this in his 1963 work, by stating that this experiential and subjective aspect of 'class formation' is determined by the relations of production in which women and men enter often involuntarily.

The entire local workforce in Gurgaon has a rural background. The history of workers' movements and profitability has shown that capital can take on the responsibility of social reproduction of labour power through dispensing various social securities, including shelter, health, education, etc. In the era of globalized production and the exploitation of low-wage regimes, capital does not want to take on similar responsibilities in developing countries, in terms of providing shelter, health facilities or schools. The extremity of extraction of relative surplus value that workers face in factories run by Maruti Suzuki, Hyundai, Delphi, Denso, Honda, where real subsumption of labour under capital dominates, creates workers' struggle because of their dismal experiences in the similar labour process.

When this process of self-reproduction is blocked by a regime of capital accumulation in the sphere of production, and traditional trade unions cannot relate to the crisis emerging from shop floor experience of labour process and the crisis of workers' self-reproduction, the workers' struggle in the arena of production may be expressed through occasional violence. This has its roots in changing class relations, and the erosion of the effectiveness of old institutions and progressive legal and social protections. This is a bitter form of class struggle found in the heart of main assembly points of GPNs in the developing world, whether at Maruti Suzuki in 2011 and 2012, Hyundai in 2009 in India or Honda in 2010 in China.

In this context, it is very important to understand the various dimensions of workers' power to influence capitalist accumulation. Eric Olin Wright (2000) distinguishes between two sources of bargaining power for workers capable of disrupting capitalist production: structural and associational power. Workers possess structural power on the basis of their position in the productive process and their capacity to disrupt it. It is thus determined by the type and importance of the commodity produced and the governance structure of the production chain. For instance, the impact of the workers at Powertrain (who produce engines for different Maruti Suzuki models) was crucial to the Maruti struggle because of the

---

where the worker's fight against the extension of work as a resistance against the squeezing of more absolute surplus value out of the labour process becomes important. Again, for most instances in modern industry, this is affected by the intensity of labour in the labour process, where the workers' resistance can restrict the extraction of relative surplus value.

workers' structural power within the production chain. Similarly, the impact of the 2009 Rico strike was heightened because of their specific location within the global auto production network. In terms of structural power, workers who are now part of global production networks, by virtue of working at specific important locations or making important parts that are integral to a larger production chain, have more of a capacity for disruption than before. Associational power is the unified expression of different forms of powers generated from the collective organization of workers: the trade union is an expression of associational power. Local workers from various villages in Haryana enjoy a social collectivity which allows for associational power in their struggles.

Silver (2003) builds on Wright's division of powers by describing two kinds of structural powers: marketplace bargaining power and workplace bargaining power. Marketplace bargaining power results from tight labour markets due to relatively high levels of employment and the ability of labourers to quit jobs and survive on other sources of income. Workplace bargaining power arises from 'the strategic location of a particular group of workers within a key industrial sector' (Silver, 2003). The interrelation of these two powers *vis-à-vis* the strategies of capital determines the trajectories of working class movements and their capacity to sustain their agency within the dynamics of GPNs. Thus, it is important to identify the sources of the structural power of workers in a specific spatial–temporal context of a GPN, to mobilize it through associational power and to utilize it to shape dynamics that favour labour.

17.4   Concluding

The GPN framework seems to be useful in terms of capturing the spatial-economic and institutional dimensions of contemporary globalized automobile production and the complex interdependence of firms of different tiers, their relational or captive linkages, power relations and governance in the clusters like Gurgaon-Manesar. This cluster, as we have seen, includes broadly three categories of firms who are integrated, to different degrees, into global or regional production networks. This has put in place a trajectory of combined and uneven development, where the tendency of concentration and centralization of capital in large enterprises simultaneously creates conditions for SMEs to be trapped in primitiveness and immiseration.

Next, the claims of a new work regime of lean and flexible production in terms of re-association of conceptualization and execution, workers' autonomy, multi-skilling and the end of Fordist-Taylorist production regime seem to be more of an ideological campaign from our experience with the workers. As we discussed earlier, the general tendency is towards de-skilling for the majority of the workers, even in the arena of modernized production.

Third, due to the wide range of possible combinations of cheap labour and modernized technology in the labour process, there is strong internal segmentation of the working class and both contractualization and informalization of work are evident. This has weakened the traditional forms of trade unions based on associational power of a relatively homogenized permanent workforce. But, due to the increasing prevalence of de-skilled, homogenized work on the shop floor, a new objectivity of unity between permanent and contract workers, grounded in the labour process to increase their associational power seems to be developing in embryonic form, as for example, in the Maruti Manesar plant's workers' struggle.

Fourth, it is clear that a new working class is forming, which has structural power in the context of regional and global production networks and aspires to develop associational power primarily at the plant level in the form of workers' unions. This new tendency is deeply grounded in the shop floor experience of continuously transforming the labour process in global production networks. Due to the increased structural power in the context of GPNs and just-in-time production, workers can make capital vulnerable across the production chain, regional and global, with their disruptive power. This does not automatically transform into associational power, as there is a strong countertendency to weaken the associational power of workers in GPNs. Thanks to a reserve of labour on the global level and particularly in the context of developing countries, capital is far more mobile *vis-à-vis* labour, and this makes the bargaining power of labour weaker and makes workers vulnerable. The interplay of this tendency and countertendency determines the nature of the accumulation regime of capital, and the trajectory and operation of GPNs, as well as the agency of labour in the automobile industry in India.

Fifth, the traditional institutions of the welfare state that offered workers a degree of social and workplace protection seem to be undermined in the contemporary globalized production regime. Legal protection has been withdrawn, to the extent that even the constitutional right to form unions is hardly afforded to workers. In order to ensure the availability of cheap labour to attract investment, the government (regional or national), has increasingly been compelled to stand against the interests of labour. Competition among different states like Gujarat, Uttarakhand, Haryana and Tamil Nadu has increased the bargaining power of capital. Most importantly, traditional trade unions seem to be unable to cope with the changing context within which they operate. This has led to the dominance of capital with less effective institutional mediation between capital and labour. The results are stagnant or falling real wages, intensification of work, worsening of working conditions and no social security or support. The response to these issues has been of an escalating magnitude: factory occupations, violent clashes or in extreme cases even murder of the managerial cadres.

References

ACMA. *Status of Indian Automotive Industry.* Annual Reports: 2011–12.

Bhargava, R. C., and Seetha. 2010. *The Maruti Story: How a Public Sector Company put India on Wheel.* Collins Business.

Bose, A. J. C. 2012. 'Labour Relations in a Liberalized Industry: A Study of Indian Automobile Workers.' Ph.D diss., B. R. Ambedkar Bihar University, Muzaffarpur.

Braverman, Harry. 1974. *Labour and Monopoly Capital.* NY: Monthly Review Press.

Burawoy, Michael. 1979. *Manufacturing Consent: Changes in the Labour Process Under Monopoly Capitalism.* Chicago Press.

Coe, Neil M., and David C. Jordhus-Lier. 2011. 'Constrained Agency? Re-evaluating the Geographies of Labour.' *Prog Hum Geogr* 35 (2): 211–33.

Coe, Neil M., Peter Dicken and Martin Hess. 2008. 'Global Production Networks: Realizing the Potential.' *J Econ Geogr* 8 (3): 271–95.

———. 2008. 'Global Production Networks—Debates and Challenges.' *J Econ Geogr* 8 (3): 267–69.

Cumbers, Andy, Corinne Nativel, and Paul Routledge. 2008. 'Labour Agency and Union Positionalities in Global Production Networks.' *J Econ Geogr* 8 (3): 369–87.

Foster, John Bellamy, Robert W. McChesney, and R. Jamil Jonna. 2011. 'The Global Reserve Army of Labour and the New Imperialism.' *Monthly Rev* 63 (6).

Gereffi, Gary, John Humphrey, Raphael Kapilinsky, and Tim Sturgeon. 2001. 'Globalization, Value Chains and Development.' Institute of Development Studies Bulletin 32.3.

Gereffi, Gary, and Miguel Korzeniewicz, eds. 1994. *Commodity Chains and Global Capitalism.* Westport, CT: Praeger.

GurgaonWorkersNews. Newsletter 51. 2012. Available at, http://gurgaonworkersnews. wordpress.com/gurgaonworkersnews-no-951/.

———. Newsletter 33. 2010. Available at, http://gurgaonworkersnews.wordpress. com/gurgaonworkersnews-no-933/.

Harvey, David. 2010. *A Brief History of Neoliberalism.* Oxford University Press.

Herod, Andrew. 2001. *Labor Geographies: Workers and the Landscape of Capitalism.* New York: Guilford Press.

Humphrey, John. 2003. 'Globalization and the Supply Chain: The Auto Industry in Brazil and India.' *Global Netw* 3 (2): 121–41.

Marglin, Stephen A. 1974. 'What do Bosses Do?.' *Rev Radical Polit Econ* 6 (2).

Marx, Karl. 1976. *Capital, Volume I.* New York: Penguin Books.

Marx, K. 1986. 'Economic Manuscripts of 1857–58 [the Grundrisse]'. In *Collected Works:* Volume 28, edited by Karl Marx and Friedrich Engels. New York, International Publishers.

Nanda, Prashant K., and Amrit Raj. 'Maruti Suzuki to Adopt 40 ITIs to Create Customized Labour Pool.' Mint, July 1, 2012.

Nichols, Theo (ed.). 1980. *Capital and Labour: Studies in the Capitalist Labour Process.* London: Athlone Press.

Selwyn, Ben. 2012. 'Beyond Firm-Centrism: Re-integrating Labour and Capitalism into Global Commodity Chain Analysis.' *J Econ Geogr* 12 (1): 205–26.

Silver, Beverly J. 1995. 'World-Scale Patterns of Labor-Capital Conflict: Labor Unrest, Long Waves and Cycles of World Hegemony.' *Review (Farnand Braudel Centre)* 18 (1): 155–92.

———. 2003. *Forces of Labour: Workers' Movement and Globalization Since 1870.* Cambridge University Press.

Sruthijith KK, and Chanchal Pal Chauhan. 'Workers Strike Thrice in Five Months: How Maruti Suzuki Lost Connect with Them.' *The Economic Times*, October 7, 2010.

Thakkar, Ketan. 'Fiat Signs Deal to Supply Diesel Engines to Maruti Suzuki India.' *The Economic Times,* January 19, 2012.

Thompson, E. P. 1963. *The Making of the English Working Class.* London: Penguin.

Womack, James P., Daniel T. Jones, and Daniel Roos. 2007. *The Machine that Changed the World: The Story of Lean Production.* NY: Simon and Schuster.

Wright, Eric Olin. 2000. 'Working-class Power, Capitalist-class Interests, and Class Compromise.' *Am J Sociol* 105 (4): 957–1002.

Relational Governance

18

Still a Distance to Go

Social Upgrading in the Indian ITO-BPO-KPO Sector

Ernesto Noronha and Premilla D'Cruz

18.1 Introduction

India is the worldwide offshore services market leader, with a share of 58 per cent of the global outsourcing industry. The aggregate revenues in FY 2013 were about $108 billion with exports contributing 75.8 billion of the total industry revenues. As a proportion of national GDP, the sector has grown from 1.2 to 8 per cent and with regard to the share in the total exports from 4 to 25 per cent between 1998 to 2013, providing direct employment to 3 million and indirect employment to 9.5 million (NASSCOM, 2013).

On this road to becoming a market leader, some argue that Indian IT firms, over the past decades, have upgraded to offer all services in the value chain, including information technology outsourcing (ITO), business process outsourcing (BPO), knowledge process outsourcing (KPO), and a significant number of advanced services for specific industries such as finance and health care that were once strictly considered to be the preserve of the industrialized world (Fernandez-Stark et al., 2011). In doing so, they have made a steady movement along the knowledge continuum in the direction of increasing expertise and information-intensiveness in the nature of the work that is outsourced (Thatchenkery et al., 2004).

This emergence of 'high-end' or 'up the value chain' services, besides being a key driver in changing the face of India's outsourcing industry (Raman et al., 2007) has widened the labour market in terms of the skills and the educational backgrounds of those employed in the sector. For instance, engineers, MBAs, PhDs, CFAs, lawyers, etc., are groups now sought after for employment in KPO organizations. Further, the Indian ITO-BPO-KPO sector is considered to be a prime example of global production networks providing high-quality employment opportunities replete with the privileges of high salaries, career development opportunities, comfortable working conditions and a range of employee friendly HR policies (Fernandez-Stark et al., 2011). In short, some argue that 'decent work' does not appear to be a relevant issue for this industry (Upadhya, 2010).

On the other hand, others argue that though the industry claims that it is 'moving up the value chain' towards providing end-to-end software development and consultancy, most companies still depend on low-end work and labour cost arbitrage for their survival (Balakrishnan, 2006). This uneven development is further reinforced by the off-shore production of BPOs that entail the digitization of various financial, retail and other service-oriented transactions, online information and help support through call centres, telemarketing, data entry and conversion, back office data processing, airline reservations, medical transcription, insurance claims, web content development, and so on that are subject to quick learning and future competition based on wage arbitrage (D'Costa, 2011).

Based on a review of the literature and the authors' own substantial fieldwork over many years in the industry, this chapter argues that economic upgrading may have taken place from the perspective of the industry, but the predominance of low-end work across the ITO, BPO and KPO sectors questions the claim of moving up the value chain while simultaneously asserting the limits that may accrue to social upgrading. We therefore begin with reviewing the literature on employment in GPNs, following which we provide evidence for economic upgrading in the ITO-BPO-KPO sector in India. In the final section, we critically examine social upgrading from the perspective of wages and salaries, quality of jobs and employee voice.

18.2 Employment relations in GPNs

The emergence of global commodity chains (GCCs), global value chains (GVCs) and more recently global production networks (GPNs) is part of an important shift from 'the development project' to 'the globalization project' manifest in the move from state-led import substituting industrialization in favour of an export-oriented development strategy (Bair, 2005; Barrientos et al., 2011b; Gereffi, 2001). This shift to export-oriented development models was made possible by rapid advances in transport, data communications and information technology fragmenting production and enabling its relocation across international borders, thus providing the much needed impetus to global production networks that were coordinated and controlled rather than owned by MNCs (Barrientos et al., 2011b; Gereffi and Mayer, 2006; Helg and Tajoli, 2005) governing from a distance (Neilson et al., 2014; Gereffi et al., 2001).

Accordingly, many emerging economies have shifted their development strategies from simple export-oriented industrialization to gaining access to higher value activities in global value chains (Gereffi et al., 2001). Developing countries can now industrialize by joining GVCs instead of building their own value chain from scratch (Gereffi, 2014; Taglioni and Winkler, 2014). However, some evidence suggests that the higher-value-added portions of value chains are located in developed countries, while the commodified and cost-driven portions of the value chains are situated in developing economies (Gereffi and Mayer, 2006). Thus, the real concern is whether the gains from participation in the global economy are effectively disseminated to a broader set of countries or whether there is a further concentration of gains among a handful of countries and their suppliers (Gereffi, 2006). The challenge of economic upgrading in GPNs, is precisely to identify the conditions under which developing as well as developed countries and firms can 'climb the value chain' from low-value assembly activities to relatively high-value activities enhancing competitiveness (Gereffi, 2005) along four economic dimensions: product, process, functional, and chain (Barrientos et al., 2011a)[1].

The initial literature focused on issues of economic governance that sustained accumulation with little mention about the broader network of forces and the role of labour that impacted the capacity of firms to move up the value chain (Davies et al., 2011; Posthuma and Nathan, 2010). The 'firm focus' treated labour as a factor of production, restricting the analysis of labour to the aggregate number of workers at different nodes of the chain (Barrientos et al., 2011a). It was assumed that social upgrading outcomes could follow economic upgrading and it typically benefits permanent workers in mass production sectors, independent artisan groups, entrepreneurs, and communities who are strongly connected with the GPN (Christian, 2012). However, several contributions highlight the possible tension between economic and social upgrading (Bettiol et al., n/d). In fact, the connection between economic and social upgrading is weaker than the connection between export growth and economic upgrading (Milberg and Winkler, 2011). It cannot be assumed that moving up the value chain in GPNs will automatically translate into social upgrading through good jobs, stable employment, better wages and working conditions (Barrientos et al., 2011a; Bettiol et al., n/d; Christian, 2012; Goger et al., 2014; Siegmann et al., 2014). In the worst case, the kind of jobs that could be created are low-skilled manual tasks that are casual and flexible often associated with poor working conditions and low incomes (Barrientos et al., 2011b; Gereffi, 2006, 2014).

More recently, scholars have addressed the labour blindness of the concept of upgrading by distinguishing between economic upgrading and social upgrading

---

[1] There are four types of economic upgrading: (1) process upgrading makes the production process more efficient by substituting capital for labour; (2) product upgrading introduces more advanced product types that enhance the features of the product; (3) functional upgrading changes the mix of activities performed; (4) chain upgrading shifts to more technologically advanced production chains requiring them to move to new industries or product markets that utilize different marketing channels and manufacturing technologies (Barrientos et al., 2010).

(Siegmann et al., 2014). Accordingly, social upgrading refers to three aspects: (1) increasing employment and wages; (2) measureable standards that include aspects that are easier to quantify, such as working hours, health and safety standards, and terms of employment (formal or informal); and (3) enabling rights such as non-discrimination and freedom of association (Barrientos et al., 2011a). Of these, the most commonly used criterion for analysing social upgrading is change in employment and wages (for example, Bernhardt and Milberg, 2011; Goger et al., 2014; Lee and Gereffi, 2013) and 'measurable standards' such as working hours (Butollo, 2013). However, others argue that training and skills development are also a crucial aspect of social upgrading (Startz and Morris, 2013) and should include skills enhancement and degree of autonomy (Bettiol et al., n/d). Moreover, social upgrading could also occur through broader government economic and social policies (Rossi, 2011), the formal and informal social protection networks, the labour codes of large global buyers, the private system of monitoring and auditing (Barrientos et al., 2011a), the structure of labour and land policies and historical embedded environments, like gender and ethnic norms (Christian, 2012).

Nonetheless, the above discussion by and large represents a top-down approach to social upgrading (Selwyn, 2013), with workers seen as passive victims of the new international division of labour posing an occasional short-term impediment to capitalism which could be overcome (Cumbers et al., 2008). On the other hand, the bottom-up approach emphasizes that changes in working conditions are determined by balance of power between capital and labour. Labour-led social upgrading 'prioritizes workers' struggles to ameliorate their conditions through collective action' (Selwyn, 2013) in which trade union associations play a principal role (Christian, 2012) in enhancing opportunities for social upgrading by improving workers' bargaining positions (Goger et al., 2014).

However, in political economic terms, the spread of GPNs has transnationalized the arena of labour relations and introduced new conflicts of interest (Raj-Reichert, 2013). GPNs have not only allowed firms to network various places across the globe into a highly integrated production and distribution system, but at the same time have also enabled them to play off workers in one place against those in another (Rainnie et al., 2011) given that some groups of workers are likely to have material interests that coincide with the strategies of their employers, even if they lead to the exploitation and abuse of workers elsewhere. This uneven organizational and political geography within the union movement means that some union actors become empowered through GPNs while others become marginalized, leading to considerable conflict and internal tensions within global union networks (GUN) (Cumbers et al., 2008), reviving the old scalar dilemma of representing the local and national interests of workers, as against developing more internationalist strategies (Wills, 1998). As a result, union actors have to be sensitive to their complex positionalities in dealing with the dialectical relations of capital and labour, particularly when trying to translate national practices to the transnational scale (Cumbers et al., 2008). International framework agreements (IFAs) or global framework agreements (GFA) are one instance in this broader strategy where unions not only aim to extend labour rights within the global operations of a particular MNC, but beyond its organizational boundaries to subcontractors and suppliers (Davies et al., 2011). Increasingly, IFAs/GFAs are regarded as a primary means of creating space at the local level for organizing and strengthening unions in the subsidiaries and suppliers of Transnational Corporations (TNCs) while at the same time bestowing greater legitimacy upon Global Union Federations (GUFs), in the process overcoming their historical disability of having a negotiated arrangement with an 'opponent' at the global level (Helfen and Fichter, 2013).

To summarize, the impetus behind the move from state-led import substituting industrialization in favour of an export-oriented development strategy was to gain access to higher value activities in global value chains on the assumption that social upgrading outcomes follow economic upgrading. However, it was soon realized that there is a tension between economic and social upgrading and therefore a need to distinguish between the two terms with economic upgrading referred to as product, process, functional, and chain upgrading while social upgrading is defined as employment and wages, measureable standards and enabling rights. This, by and large, represents a top-down approach to social upgrading with workers seen as passive victims of the new international division of labour; on the other hand, the bottom-up approach prioritizes workers struggles to ameliorate their conditions through collective action.

We will now examine how mainly functional and process economic upgrading unfolded in the ITO-BPO-KPO sector and then examine social upgrading from the perspective of wages, terms of employment, skill enhancement, degree of autonomy and enabling rights.

18.3   Economic upgrading of the ITO-BPO-KPO sector in India

In the early phases of the industry, software and hardware developments were both undertaken by a single firm and sold as a complete system (Rothboeck et al., 2001). This model came under pressure as user firms had diverse requirements ranging from generating a product for a specific purpose that could vary from a PC application to developing embedded software (Duran, 2006), thus forcing hardware firms to spin off their software divisions (Rothboeck et al., 2001). Accordingly, the software value chain changed significantly from being vertically integrated with hardware to become a decentralized system based on object-oriented programming and distributed programming breaking down the highly skilled work of software development into a series of relatively standardized production steps starting with the analysis of the problem, design, coding, testing, delivery and installation and finally maintenance of the software (Heeks, 1996). Clearly, these activities involved in software production could be broadly classified into conception and execution tasks. The conception stages of analysis and design require higher level of skills and experience while the execution tasks such as coding and testing are relatively less skill intensive but more labour-intensive (Heeks, 1996; Illavarsan, 2008; Rothboeck et al., 2001). New and innovative work involves heterogeneity at the early stages of conceptualization and design, but this declines at stages of testing and implementation (Sahay et al., 2003). This fragmentation provided two options: one, the (local) value chain could be integrated with the global value chain or could simply exist independently as part of a national chain by addressing domestic software needs associated with the production of customized software. In developed countries, the focus has been on software development for the domestic market, whereas in India and other developing countries, the emphasis has been on export where production is associated with what has been termed outsourcing, either offshore or near shore (Durán, 2006). Thus, the decoupling of hardware from software, and the pronounced human capital intensity of software, together with the rapid improvements in communications technologies and globalization, opened a window of opportunity for countries rich in human capital (Arora et al., 2001b) to get involved in the IT value chain.

With regard to India, by the late 1980s and early 1990s, most software companies acted as sub-contractors, executing assignments onsite (at client's premises) through manpower contracts popularly known as body shopping (Nath and Hazra, 2002; Xiang, 2007). The Indian software firm largely provided software programmers and analysts on a temporary basis to the client who managed and supervised them (Arora and Asundi, 1999). Gradually, first-generation Indian engineers working in the Silicon Valley convinced the senior management of large American corporations to take advantage of wage arbitrage for software skill and establish operations in India (Saxenian, 2002; Nath and Hazra, 2002). As a result, lead firms first established captive centres (i.e., wholly owned subsidiaries) in developing countries to provide low-cost services to their operations in the developed world. These early captive centres were then closely followed by global providers, such as IBM and Accenture, with Indian firms growing alongside these firms to become important sources of competition in the industry. Indian third-party providers—including Tata

Consultancy Services (TCS), Infosys and Wipro – as well as other entrepreneurial IT companies began a phase of rapid growth, offering IT services related to Y2K and ecommerce during the technology boom (Fernandez-Stark et al., 2011). This resulted in the onsite-offshore model emerging as the better value-added model of software service delivery (Athreya, 2004), with companies sending a few software professionals to the client's site for requirement analysis or training in a particular system. These professionals then bring back to India the specifications for the software, where a bigger team develops the software offshore (Arora et al., 2001a). When the project is large, one or more members from the project team work onsite with the client to coordinate on a regular basis between the client and the offshore team in India (Agarwal et al., 2012). Thus, the Global Service Delivery (GSD) model is created in which Indian firms maintained headquarters in India, delivery centres in developing countries and customer support offices near their clients in the developed world (Fernandez-Stark et al., 2011).

However, the GSD model was not enough to overcome separation of production and consumption in software work, and as a result there was a pressure to standardize products so that they could be recognized as reliable by purchasers removed from the place of production (Prasad, 1998). Further, standardization was critical to disembedding and fragmentation of software processes to impart structure and predictability to it (Rothboeck et al., 2001; Sahay et al., 2003; Gereffi, 2006). As a result, processes such as the ISO, CMM (Capability Maturity Model), Six Sigma, etc. were held to be necessary for creating unambiguous and uniformly understood sets of conventions and practices (Fernandez-Stark et al., 2011) and to meet international standards to increase their competitiveness in the global market (Durán, 2006). Moreover, Indian firms saw certification as a marketing tool to distinguish themselves from competitors and to demand a higher price per unit of effort (Arora and Asundi, 1999) which made it possible to capture turnkey contracts, particularly in domains such as banking and retailing (Parthasarthy, 2004; Parthasarathy and Aoyama 2006). Nonetheless, the adoption of these standards had a multiplier effect as several organizations got themselves certified (Prasad, 1998). For instance, in 2002, while 20 companies in the United States held CMM Level 5 certification (the highest rating awarded by the Software Engineering Institute (SEI) that measures the quality and reliability of the software production), there were 50 in India, the highest for any country in the world (Thatchenkery et al., 2004). To this effect, MNCs played a significant role in 'process' and 'functional' upgrading as the Indian software industry began to shift from bodyshopping to offshore services (Parthasarathy and Aoyama, 2006).

Nonetheless, based on the success of the software model, technology firms in particular began to outsource more general business, resulting in the growth of BPOs (Arora and Athreye, 2002; Robertson, 2011). However, it was only in the early 2000s that the BPO segment began to take off in India. The burst of the internet bubble in 2001 forced the IT sector to embark into BPO services such as call centres, payroll, finance and accounting, human resource (HR) activities in the low and middle segments to diversify revenue streams. In the second phase, the country also upgraded to KPO activities which include market intelligence, business analytics and legal services in the highest-value segment of the chain (Gereffi and Fernandez-Stark, 2011). Hence, India entered the value chain first through the ITO segment, followed by simultaneous upgrading into BPO and KPO services, and finally specialization in industry-specific segments (Fernandez-Stark et al., 2011). The software model was easily transposed and almost identically replicated on to the KPO-BPO sector. Thus, though the most frequently observed way to enter the offshore services value chain is by first establishing call centre operations, India's offshore services industry began with the IT segment offering simple IT support services followed by BPO and KPO service contributions (Fernandez-Stark et al., 2011) as clients in the developed world become increasingly comfortable with the concept of outsourcing (Robertson, 2011).

In short, both functional and process upgrading may have taken place in the ITO-KPO-BPO sector, but the impact on social upgrading, as we shall see, was mixed with employees benefiting with regard to wages, terms of employment and skill enhancement but losing in terms of autonomy and enabling rights.

18.4 Two sides to social upgrading of the Indian ITO-BPO-KPO sector

Key drivers in locating offshore services are educational level and skills in the local workforce available at low wages (Arora and Asundi, 1999; Fernandez-Stark et al., 2011). The 4.4 million graduates and post-graduates produced in India in 2012 with a ready-to-hire pool of 4,00,000 to 5,00,000 at one of the lowest fulltime employee (FTE) costs in the world, makes the country an attractive option (NASSCOM, 2012). Further, in the case of India, the linkages with the US and UK, due to the language and the network of skilled immigrants, also favoured it as locations of outsourced activities for both IT and non-IT firms (Arora et al., 2001b). Nonetheless, formal education is used as a preliminary screening measure for potential recruits, which is complemented by further competency evaluations (Wadhwa et al., 2008). For instance, a consistently good record was required to be eligible to take one company's aptitude test and be shortlisted for an interview (Fuller and Haripriya, 2007). In general, ITO-BPO-KPO companies seek employees with good general communication, problem-solving skills, basic computer skills and language ability. These competencies differ according to the service performed in the value chain. In higher-value IT and KPO activities [including Legal Process Outsourcing (LPO)], for example, know-how, innovation and specialized university education are more important as there is more interaction between the client and colleagues based abroad (Fernandez-Stark et al., 2011) while BPOs employ any graduates.

The ITO-BPO-KPO sector firms recruit graduates through campus placement, internal referral programmes, internship programmes, placement agencies, walk-ins or advertisements. Candidates undergo written tests, group discussions, aptitude tests and tests on communication skills and language ability. More specifically, in the LPO sector, firms like QuisLex, Bodhi Global Services, and the Clutch Group used the specially designed Global Legal Professional (GLP) exam to screen candidates. The GLP tests candidates in areas of English fluency, technology, professional skills, personal effectiveness and legal knowledge (Schultz, 2010), while in the BPO sector recruiters wanted employees to display fluency with spoken and written English, multi-tasking ability, computer skills, possessing a pleasant voice, persuasive ability, neutral accent, good attitude, high energy levels and ability to enact emotional labour (Noronha and D'Cruz, 2009a). Some firms adhered to stringent standards of interviewing 10 per cent of all those applying and selecting only 20 per cent of all those interviewed. Finally, a dossier which included the resumes and certificates of the prospective employees to be employed on the project was sent to the clients for their approval. Some clients then completed their own extensive employee background checks, while others gave their approval of those selected to work on the project after examining their dossiers (Noronha et al., 2016).

18.5 The race to the top

The reality was that the quality levels expected by clients often far exceed those of domestic markets in the developing world and hence specific additional workforce development measures were required to be undertaken by firms to meet demand for services and maintain their position in the market (Fernandez-Stark et al., 2011). For instance, Penfold (2009) states that those wishing to work in the BPO sector are often not those suitable or ready for this work. Hence, the private sector had to fill the gap by developing significant in-house training practices to match the specific skills development to client needs (Fernandez-Stark et al., 2011).

Therefore, post-selection, training takes place both in-house and through customized programmes with different science, technology and management institutions in India. In-house training is divided between formal training, on-the-job training, and online e-learning modules (Fernandez-Stark et al., 2011). These modules could be conducted by in-house trainers and experienced employees or be subcontracted to adult education sites where individuals themselves pay for the training they receive (Budhwar et al., 2006; McMillin, 2006; Mirchandani, 2004; Ramesh, 2004). Moreover, the e-learning mode offers both scale and flexibility, allowing employees to access the online system during down periods at work. Further, many firms have begun to provide their employees with a broad range of additional training and education programs, including mentoring, career planning and providing access to formal degree programs, such as MBAs or other Master's programs to retain employees (Fernandez-Stark et al., 2011).

Nonetheless, retaining employees is one of the most significant challenges faced by the ITO-BPO-KPO industry. The explosive growth of the industry gives these professionals the ability to negotiate aggressively and demand high concessions in terms of compensation and career advancement from companies. These problems have prompted firms in the ITO-BPO-KPO sector to explicitly introduce human capital management strategies such as high salaries, opportunities to work abroad, quick promotions, flexi-time, parental leave, provide more congenial and satisfying work environments, transport facilities, the option to telecommute from home, stock option plans, cafeterias, sports facilities, de-stress rooms, on-site childcare and health facilities comparable to those of their strongest competitors in the US and elsewhere (Arora and Athreye, 2002; D'Cruz and Noronha, 2006). Most employer organizations sought to provide physical work environments of international standards resembling those in the West. There was also an effort to create fun in the workplace, particularly in the BPO sector with cultural activities and get-togethers such as team outings, team parties and office gatherings organized frequently (Noronha and D'Cruz, 2009a). The ITO-BPO-KPO sector is also often applauded for providing exceptionally good grievance redressal procedures via open forum meetings, open door policies, intranet discussions counselling and suggestion schemes, non-hierarchical structures, informal work culture, merit-based promotions, career growth through tie-ups with educational institutions and gender equality (Noronha and D'Cruz, 2009a; D'Cruz and Noronha, 2012; Sahay et al., 2003) challenging the hegemonic traditional management practices, which were both overly paternalistic and hierarchical often employing caste in their working (D'Mello and Eriksen, 2010). Thus, Barrientos et al. (2011a) conclude that workers in this sector move both towards better paid employment associated with progressive social upgrading—a clear instance of a 'race to the top' (Arora and Athreye, 2002).

These standards set by employers resulted in the contention that labour laws are irrelevant to this sector (Noronha and D'Cruz, 2009a). However, in terms of other parameters like job security, working with constant deadlines, annual leave with pay, freedom of association, etc., the sector fares badly against comparable jobs in other sectors (Sarkar et al., 2013). Further, lack of opportunities to work in new domains and technologies, routine nature of maintenance and legacy work and reluctance of leaders to invest in the growth of team members have contributed to the high attrition in software firms (Agarwal et al., 2012). Thus, despite paying substantially above Indian standards and providing employees with numerous employee benefits, the difficulty in retaining talented professionals was linked to dead-end jobs.

18.6   Stuck in low value dead-end jobs

Clearly, though functional upgrading from bodyshopping to offshoring integrated India into the international division of labour for software production, and not just as a supplier of low-cost, high-skill labour for low value-added services (Parthasarthy, 2004) there are few signs of high value-added, innovative products or technologies as in the Silicon Valley (Parthasarthy, 2000). Even in the case of turnkey projects entailing design and high-level systems integration, the work done in India is of low-value such as coding, conversions, debugging, testing, and customization of multinational products, most of which are carried out offshore for cost reasons (D'Costa, 2003; Veloso et al., 2003). Quite naturally, with the shift from the onsite to the offshore model the tedious, the unrelentingly monotonous and low-paying execution tasks of maintenance and testing performed by Indian IT workers migrating through body shopping (Xiang, 2007) were among the first to be outsourced, while early life cycle tasks such as design and user requirement analysis were considered more difficult to outsource, as they required more intimate knowledge of the firms work practices (Sahay et al., 2003) and were often tacit and difficult to convey over long distances (Parthasarathy, 2000). Not surprisingly, from a global value chain perspective, many of the software and other IT jobs in India are routine, monotonous, non-innovative, tedious, uncreative, less skilled, low-end involving activities such as offshore development, maintenance, testing, coding, low-level design, data conversion and on-line technical support based on the instructions and specifications given by the client (Agarwal et al., 2012; Arora et al., 2001a; Arora et al., 2001b; Arora an Asundi, 1999; D'Costa, 2004; D'Costa, 2003; Gereffi, 2006; Lakha, 1994; Nath and Hazra, 2002; Rothboeck et al., 2001).

Similarly, Noronha et al. (2016) hold that LPO organizations concentrate on low-end, low value document review and routine support functions that have limited scope while the more sophisticated and strategic work is performed by lawyers in the client's country. From the clients' perspective, document review became the perfect and safe task to be outsourced, since it was simple and less complex, having lower legal and ethical risks while allowing US lawyers to concentrate on high-end work (Hanson, 2009; Regan and Heenan, 2010). Thus, majority of the work outsourced to foreign attorneys constitutes 'low-end' or 'commodity' legal work (Woffinden, 2007) that are divisible and generic in nature, requiring only minimal firm-specific knowledge (Regan and Heenan, 2010). Even with regard to BPO work, Taylor (2010) holds that companies commonly route to India only the 'mass market' calls, with premium or privileged customers, serviced domestically. Higher-value calls or those requiring considerable empathy (e.g., cross-selling), deep tacit knowledge or a 'very good understanding of the vernacular', are retained onshore as 'core competencies' suggesting certain limitations on the ability of India to 'move up the value chain'. Thus, essentially only lower-end basic voice services and simple transactional business processes which are highly standardized, codified and routinized are outsourced to India (Taylor and Bain, 2006).

This pre-dominance of low-end work outsourced to India can thus be traced back to the fact that the Indian firms do not participate in the early stages of conceptualization and high-level design in IT (Nath and Hazra, 2002) as they were condemned only to those market spaces which were non-critical, low value and labour-intensive (D'Costa, 2004). In fact, sophisticated and well-established competitors located in the leading clusters stood in the way of innovative Indian firms reaching the market niches where competition is based on quality and technology rather than price (Arora et al., 2001b). Further, majority of Indian firms are stuck at the lower-end of the business because the thick vertical and horizontal relationships that sustain innovation and growth in successful IT clusters such as the Silicon Valley were missing in India. The software industry in India has been unable to create a domestic market strategy to give firms an opportunity to develop their expertise locally before serving global markets (Arora et al., 2001b; Parthasarathy, 2000). Thus, with the exception of a few firms, the local Indian industry remains on a low-innovation trajectory due to a weak 'ecosystem' for research and development. Besides this, India's heavy reliance on the US has also undercut opportunities in other major markets such as Japan (D'Costa, 2011).

Consequently, since much of the work tends to consist of fairly low levels of technical complexity requiring logical and methodical aptitude and familiarity with software development tools and languages but no in-depth knowledge of computer architecture or operating systems (Arora et al., 2001a), many software engineers feel that they are overqualified for their jobs (Upadhya, 2010) resulting in boredom and attrition (Fuller and Haripriya, 2007). Nonetheless, the preference for engineering graduates or computer science degree or a Masters in Computer Applications (MCA) even though the job did not require such high qualifications, can be explained as an attempt by Indian IT companies to 'signal quality' of their processes and people, and when possible, their experience (Athreye, 2005; Arora et al., 2001a). Similarly, to counter the pre-existing prejudice on the part of onshore clients towards LPO vendors and to meet ethical standards, LPO firms employed only those who had a Bachelor of Law (LLB) degree, even though the tasks involved could be carried out by non-lawyers or paralegals or just graduates with good literacy and numeracy skills. This was done to reassure clients and to impress upon them that the work outsourced would be handled by well-trained Indian lawyers at lower costs (Noronha et al., 2016). Even with regard to Indian call centres, Batt et al. (2005) observe that Indian employees had higher levels of formal education than those in the West but had no opportunities to use their high levels of education because the work was designed to limit independent decision-making or innovative problem-solving resulting in high attrition.

In addition, defining and documenting the software development methodology (Prasad, 1998) did not help matters. Instead it made the difference between IT and ITES work fuzzy (Upadhya, 2010). In fact, the recent focus on ITES as a driver of software exports, reinforces the low-wage segment of the value chain (D'Costa, 2004). Even KPOs who some argued (see Taylor and Bain, 2006) entails genuine complexity and high value services have been subjected to standardized processes solutions rather than being customized (Noronha et al., 2016). For instance, Sako (2010) states that the application of six sigma techniques to legal work disintegrates the value chain namely knowledge and information management (KIM) from consultative advice and representation. While Fernandez-Stark et al. (2011) argue that process upgrading facilitate workforce development and industry upgrading, Prasad (1998) holds that the pressures to standardize products has resulted in deskilling and breaking of the individual employee's monopoly of knowledge over the labour process. This rationalization has turned software work into a mechanical activity that is constantly monitored and measured in terms of time, effort and productivity (Upadhya, 2010). Similarly, the application of six sigma techniques to the LPO process made work monotonous, routine, boring, mundane, repetitive, mechanical and low on variety (Noronha et al., 2016).

The service-level agreements (SLAs) between these lead firms and their clients are further routinizing work. SLAs define every parameter that governs the relationship between client and the vendor, such as work to be done, billable items or units, deliverables, productivity and quality benchmarks, reporting requirements, project management methodology, pricing and terms for payment and adjustments. Emanating from the SLAs are service-level matrices used to evaluate the performance of employees (Noronha et al., 2016). While companies have instituted a team-based appraisal system, individual performance has always been closely monitored and directly linked to monetary and non-monetary benefits and growth opportunities. Various means to control and monitor employee performance on projects include data on project quality, efficiency, productivity, response time, idle time aggregated from weekly status reports which are regularly assessed against the contract with the customer. In addition, feedback from customers is solicited through periodic satisfaction surveys forming a critical source of input into individual and project ratings and incentives for the project team (D'Mello and Eriksen, 2010). Inability to meet these parameters resulted in punishments. While punishments ranged from warnings, retraining and suspension to termination and dismissal, the degree of punishment awarded depended on the nature and frequency of the offence. With termination and dismissal being used even in the cases of confirmed employees, the primacy of transactional psychological contracts was evident (Noronha and D'Cruz, 2009a). Poor performers were counselled and put on to performance improvement plans. If despite these efforts the performance did not improve, they were dismissed (Noronha and D'Cruz, 2009a) in some cases illustrating depersonalized bullying (D'Cruz and Noronha, 2009; D'Cruz, 2012). The predominance of the organizational agenda that was embodied in the 'sacrificial HR strategy' only exacerbated the existing rate of attrition arising from job design elements. The rhetoric of non-hierarchical organizational structures, career advancement, workplace ambience and transparency designed to strengthen employee commitment to organizational goals and reduce incidence of absenteeism and intention to quit failed due to lack of any meaningful consultation with employees or their representatives (D'Cruz and Noronha, 2012). In fact, far from consulting employees, high commitment management practices are advocated as a means to ensure union avoidance (Noronha and D'Cruz, 2009b).

Besides resembling feudalistic set-ups which privilege the informal organization (allowing favouritism, discrimination and manipulative behaviours) (D'Cruz and Noronha, 2012), the project-oriented characteristics of the software services industry in India and the nature of the work posed some other unique challenges for professionals in the industry. Pressure of work was a result of the underestimation of human hours for the project, crisis emanating from the project, client interaction outside traditional working hours, long hours of work, competition for recognition amongst peers and subtle control used by managers (D'Mello and Eriksen, 2010; Upadhya, 2010). Moreover, in the IT sector working late did not imply being paid overtime. The salary was fixed, regardless of the hours worked. Likewise, since American companies had not just outsourced their IT needs, but also their own nightshift a night allowance should have been paid (Baas, 2007). This caused internal strife in the arena of work–life balance (D'Mello, 2005) and in their private lives (Baas, 2007). Similarly, call centres operate round the clock all through the year (i.e., 24/7/365), relying on night shifts to service overseas geographies whose time zones are ahead or behind that of India (McMillin, 2006; Noronha and D'Cruz, 2006; Ramesh, 2004). Odd working hours usually led to disturbance in personal and social life and significantly impacting their health, as manifest in several symptoms of mental and physical illness such as nervousness, chronic fatigue, stiff neck, sore eyes, backaches and headaches, impaired vision, numbness in fingers, bodyache, fever, asthma, sore throats, nausea, dizziness, rashes, insomnia, anxiety, restlessness, irritability, depression, drowsiness, loss of appetite, changes in body weight, decreasing vigilance and gastrointestinal problems (McMillin, 2006; Noronha and D'Cruz, 2006; Poster, 2007; Ramesh, 2004). It was also noticed that employees develop poor eating habits, overeating, smoking and drinking excessive coffee and so on to cope up with the psychological and physical strain (McMillin, 2006; Ramesh, 2004; Singh and Pandey, 2005). Upadhya (2010) concludes that from the perspective of decent work job security, social protection, working hours and work–life balance resulted in high attrition.

18.7 Challenging through individual resistance

This high attrition in the sector is indicative of individual resistance (see Noronha and D'Cruz, 2012). Besides this, notwithstanding their ambivalence to the oppressive work environment (D'Cruz and Noronha, 2015), employees in call centres described a range of breathers, releases, outlets and pauses as manifestations of disorganized coaction, collegial coping and concertive (quasi)supervision, subsuming several variants that some of them and/or their colleagues occasionally resorted to (D'Cruz and Noronha, 2013b). Employees underscored that these activities and behaviours provided them with means of gaining some respite from and power over their stringent work context and did not symbolize any anti-work or anti-employer sentiment. Specifically, breathers, releases, outlets and pauses not only provided employees with some slack time but also allowed them to maintain their performance records. In other words, employees engage in these activities despite their sense of professionalism while also knowing that if their employers discovered their behaviour, they would face punishment up to the level of dismissal. Disorganized coaction was of three types, namely, bounded performance, feedback diversions and vacillations. Bounded performance that refers to employees limiting the quantum of their work in terms of output and temporality in order to gain some breathing space included tactics like extending the call wrap-up time, altering their position in the call distribution queue, extending restroom breaks, unnecessarily transferring customers' calls and delaying the disconnection of calls. With feedback diversion, employees deliberately entered wrong customer email addresses into the system if the call had not proceeded satisfactorily so that feedback could not be obtained from that particular customer. Employees also displayed vacillation which entailed alternating between role embracement and role distancing. Employees were able to decipher when their calls were being monitored either because of an echoing or beeping sound that accompanied such activity or from the call monitoring data sheet, and they would take special care to ensure their optimal performance during that time, indicating role embracement. At other times, when they knew that their calls were not being monitored, they did not perform with as much interest and care, indicating role distancing. When it came to collegial coping, turning the tables on the customer helped employees deal with customer abuse. During the course of customer abuse, some employees would place the phone in mute mode and curse the customer aloud. Team members would respond to this either verbally or non-verbally depending upon the activity they were involved in. Other employees would press the mute button and enable the loudspeaker so that the team could collectively listen to, jeer at and enjoy the customer's tirade.

In contrast to disorganized coaction which was individualistic and largely covert, collegial coping had social and more overt features. Engagement in collegial coping generally occurred when TLs and other supervisors were not present on the call floor or when their attention was diverted elsewhere. When employees filled in for TLs, who for some reason, could not monitor calls, they manipulated the entire system by telling their team members to give a list of calls on which they had performed well or on a round-robin basis such that they relieved each team member in turn for a short period of time at least once during a shift. While concertive (quasi)supervision entailed complicity and co-ordination between the acting supervisor and the employees, it did not embody collectivist sentiments. In spite of the multiplicity of people and synchrony involved, concertive (quasi)supervision remained largely covert and socially fragmented (Noronha and D'Cruz, 2013b). Yet, given their largely individualized, covert, informal, spontaneous and reactive as well as sporadic, fragmented and sequestered nature, these activities represent routine and diffuse resistance micropractices (Ashforth and Mael, 1998; Prasad and Prasad, 1998), partially mirroring subtle subversions and disengagement by Prasad and Prasad (1998) and Lutgen-Sandvik's (2006) subversive (dis)obedience. While undoubtedly indicative of unauthorized and oppositional resistance (Ashforth and

Mael, 1998), these behaviours stand in contrast to traditional and conventional forms of resistance such as protests and mass movements that are formal, active, organized, overt, targeted, sustained, collective and intentionally disruptive working class revolutions (Noronha and D'Cruz, 2013b).

18.8   Collective voice deficit

Several attempts to organize the employees in this sector were backed by international unions. One of the first attempts to organize Indian IT employees was initiated in the 1990s supported by the International Federation of Commercial, Clerical, Professional and Technical Employees (FIET). However, these earlier efforts did not make much headway. Subsequently, in November 2000, the ITPF was formed at Hyderabad and Bangalore with trade unionists from the telecom industry taking the lead. The initial financial support for this endeavour was provided by the Swedish Union for Technical and Clerical Employees (SIF). A vision of a new type of professional association, different from traditional Indian trade unions, was envisaged. The organization was primarily meant to help IT professionals to network and discuss technology trends, identify skills and areas for further training, exchange experiences about the quality of training courses, locate job opportunities and provide tips about career development (Hirschfeld, 2003). Subsequently, with the growth of the BPO sector some of the leaders of ITPF established the Centre for Call Centre and BPO Professionals (CBPOP), under the aegis of UNI-APRO given that employees' work conditions in this sector were sufficiently distinct from those of IT professionals (Taylor et al., 2008). Hence, CBPOP tried to establish contact with BPO employees, convince them about the need for collective representation by creating awareness of and appreciation for trade unionism and to finally consolidate such network of professionals into a trade union which came to be called UNITES professional in 2005 (Noronha and D'Cruz, 2009a,b).

Overall, it was difficult to convince ITO-BPO-KPO employees about the need for a union. They saw no relevance for unions which they associated with blue-collar workers. Slogan shouting on the streets and picketing ITES organizations was seen as detrimental to their professional image. In their view, intelligent, qualified, motivated, responsible and upwardly mobile professionals like themselves, whose jobs provided good returns, whose work environments were modern and chic and whose employers looked after their well-being, were not in the same category as factory workers. Sophisticated human resource management (HRM) strategies had a significant potential to take care of the interests of educated 'executives' who have a voice of their own. In employees' views, unions were relevant in workplaces where workers' interests were being compromised and basic facilities including redressal mechanisms were not in place or not functional (Noronha and D'Cruz, 2006; Noronha and D'Cruz, 2009b). In contrast, IT organizations had developed an elaborate email system for conflict resolution allowing access to top management (Rothboeck et al., 2001). Believing in the relevance of merit as the means of career progress, employees feared that the presence of unions would reverse these trends by introducing a levelling effect through attempts to protect the less capable (Noronha and D'Cruz, 2006; Noronha and D'Cruz, 2009b). The highly individualized wages linked to performance system and the lack of time and space hampered the development of long-term relationships and collective mobilization (Rothboeck et al., 2001). In fact, perceiving themselves as professionals was the primary reason why employees did not wish to associate with trade unions (Noronha and D'Cruz, 2006; Noronha and D'Cruz, 2009b).

Employees also harboured the view that a collectivist agenda is at odds with business interests, and pursuing such a path would unleash conflict. Indeed, management's subtle references to conflict that the presence of unions creates tension, anxiety and disruption because of the use of strike and job action paid off. Employees also believed that the formation of unions would only threaten the flow of foreign direct investments into India, spelling disaster for the industry in the country. By juxtaposing the unsavoury picture of union-related conflict and its consequences with the attractive image of peace, co-operation in the absence of unions, employers tried to avert union formation. Undoubtedly, the very nature of capital being able to shift to low-cost destinations enabled employer organizations to propagate this view among employees. It is not surprising, then, that employees in this sector came to believe that union formation would only precipitate problems for employer organizations, clients and employees themselves, threatening the continuity of the industry and, in turn, of their own employment (Noronha and D'Cruz, 2006; Noronha and D'Cruz, 2009a,b). Staying away from unions and avoiding conflict, even in instances where their rights were violated, was the preferred option, and hence it was not uncommon to find employees quitting their current jobs and seeking fresh appointments within India's booming sector rather than engaging third-party intervention to redress their grievances (Noronha and D'Cruz, 2009a; Penfold, 2009).

Besides being influenced by the anti-union position espoused by their employers, employees feared adverse reactions, including dismissal, should their employers learn about their links with a union. Employees expressed reluctance to be publicly associated with unions and those who attended union meetings strove to maintain the secrecy of their association with the union (Noronha and D'Cruz, 2009a,b).

Responding to these circumstances, unionists acknowledged the need to move away from the conventional protest and grievance handling functions of unions to engage in partnership with management. They foresaw unions as having a much larger role to play in solving a wide variety of workplace problems, including attrition. UNITES was to operate from the standpoint of co-operation and responsibility, rather than militancy and aggression, so that 'mutual gains' were secured for all the stakeholders. The interest of the industry and the workers went hand in hand, and employees had to be flexible and accommodating of employers' needs for the industry to survive. Accordingly, productivity was emphasized and extreme Leftist leanings were denounced. This strategy was expected to rebuild the credibility of Indian unions as respectable, credible, dignified and responsible groups which ITES-BPO employees would be proud to be a part of (Noronha and D'Cruz, 2009a,b).

Emphasis on social dialogue rather than protest as means to resolve disputes formed a significant part of UNITES's agenda. The main goal of social dialogue was to promote consensus building and democratic involvement among the main stakeholders in the world of work. Successful social dialogue structures and processes had the potential to resolve important economic and social issues, encourage good governance, advance social and industrial peace and stability and boost economic progress. UNITES further believed that dialoguing with NASSCOM was required to make India's ITES-BPO industry more sustainable (Noronha and D'Cruz, 2009a,b).

At the same time, globalization required employees to have a strong voice and UNITES remained committed to this end. Since offshoring had pitted employees of different nationalities against each other, UNITES believed that the only way forward was for employees to come together and convince employers to rethink their strategies in favour of development that was sustainable for all. Present policies that suggested a race to the bottom were not in the best interests of employees, customers, national economies or sustainable development. Instead of responding to employer initiatives to relocate work overseas with arguments that could be misconstrued as racist, xenophobic or protectionist, the thrust required was that of decent work for all. This stance seems quite natural given that the issue of outsourcing jobs abroad stirs great emotion among employees in the West (Krishnan, 2007). American union representatives wanted to protect the jobs of their members and consequently did not support the outsourcing to low-wage countries such as India, China, Philippines, etc. In fact unionists visiting India were surprised that

Ernesto Noronha and Premilla D'Cruz

Indian IT workers did not seem to be overly concerned about workers displaced by outsourcing (Tisza, 2005).

Therefore, according to UNITES, the only way to ensure compliance with decent labour standards was for employer organizations and UNI to establish GFAs which included clauses on employees' rights, union rights, health and safety, elimination of discrimination, minimum wages and working conditions, employment stability, respect for others at work and respect for the environment (Noronha and D'Cruz, 2009a,b). In this way, UNI-APRO strived to move from individual corporate standards to general sectoral standards as a means of overcoming structural and associational weakness by organizing and building new unions (Helfen and Fichter, 2013). However, despite untiring efforts to sign a GFA with HSBC worldwide the initiative has not paid off. As a part of the global campaign for GFA when UNITES leaders in India went to hand over a written representation to HSBC Hyderabad they were stopped, with the bank retorting that at HSBC they were committed to fair employment practices and they did not see the need for any global agreement.

18.9 Conclusion

Though product and process upgrading may have taken place from the perspective of the industry, with regard to social upgrading the results are mixed. Employees across the ITO, BPO and KPO industry have benefited in terms of higher salaries, better working conditions and mobility in terms of status in society but given that the work outsourced to India is at the lower end of the value chain, a highly educated workforce has been relegated to mundane and dead-end jobs in terms of employment. As a result, there is high attrition arising out of the nature of the work which cannot be resolved only by sophisticated HR policies. To address this issue of attrition job design elements also need to be reconfigured, besides analysing the problematic areas of job security, social protection, working hours and work–life balance. With regard to enabling rights, employers with their subtle and overt aversion to unions dissuade employees from forming unions. Further, the efforts to sign a GFA did not pay off, leaving individuals to fend for themselves.

References

Agrawal, N. M., N. Khatri, and R. Srinivasan. 2012. 'Managing Growth: Human Resource Management Challenges Facing the Indian Software Industry.' *J World Busi* 47: 159–66.

Arora, A., and J. Asundi. 1999. 'Quality Certification and the Economics of Contract Software Development: A Study of the Indian Software Service Companies.' *Working Paper 7260*. Cambridge, MA: National Bureau of Economic Research.

Arora, A., and S. Athreye. 2002. 'The Software Industry and India's Economic Development.' *Inform Econ Policy* 14: 253–73.

Arora, A., V. S. Arunachalam, J. Asundi, and R. Fernandes. 2001a. 'The Indian Software Services Industry.' *Res Policy* 30: 1267–87.

Arora, A., A. Gambardella, and S. Torrisi. 2001b. 'In the Footsteps of Silicon Valley? Indian and Irish Software in the International Division of Labour.' *SIEPR Discussion Paper No. 00–41.*

Ashforth, B. E., and F. A. Mael. 1998. 'The Power of Resistance: Sustaining Valued Identities.' In *Power and Influence in Organizations*, edited by R. M. Kramer and M. A. Neale. Thousand Oaks, CA: Sage.

Athreye, S. S. 2004. 'Role of Transnational Corporations in the Evolution of a High-tech Industry: The Case of India's Software Industry—A Comment.' *World Development* 32 (3): 555–60.

———. 2005. The Indian Software Industry and its Evolving Service. *Industrial and Corporate Change* 14 (3): 393–418.

Baas, M. 2007. 'Bangalore @ Night: Indian IT Professionals and the Global Clock Ticking.' *Etnofoor* 20 (2): 59–72.

Balakrishnan, P. 2006. 'Benign Neglect or Strategic Intent? Contested Lineage of Indian Software Industry.' *Econ Polit Weekly* 41: 3865–72.

Bair, Jennifer. 2005. 'Global Capitalism and Commodity Chains: Looking Back, Going Forward.' *Comp Change* 9 (2): 153–80.

Barrientos, Stephanie, Gary Gereffi, and Ariana Rossi. 2011a. 'Economic and Social Upgrading in Global Production Networks: A New Paradigm for a Changing World.' *Int Lab Rev* 150 (3–4): 319–40.

Barrientos, Stephanie, Frederick Mayer, John Pickles, and Anne Posthuma. 2011b. 'Decent Work in Global Production Networks: Framing the Policy Debate.' *Int Labour Rev* 150 (3–4).

Batt, R., V. Doellgast, and H. Kwon. 2005. *The Indian Call Centre Industry: National Benchmarking Report.* Ithaca, New York: Cornell University.

Bernhardt, T., and W. Milberg. 2011. Economic and Social Upgrading in Global Value Chains: Analysis of Horticulture, Apparel, Tourism and Mobile Telephones. *Capturing the Gains Working paper 2011/06.*

Bettiol, M., V. D. Marchi, E. D. Maria, and S. Micelli. (n/d). 'Economic, Social and Environmental Upgrading in Emerging Economies: Evidence from India.' 1–38.

Budhwar, P., A. Varma, V. Singh, and R. Dhar. 2006. 'HRM Systems of Indian Call Centres: An Exploratory Study.' *Int J Human Res Manage* 17 (5): 881–97.

Butollo, Florian. 2013. 'Moving Beyond Cheap Labour? Industrial and Social Upgrading in the Garment and LED Industries of the Pearl River Delta.' *Journal of Current Chinese Affairs* 42(4): 139–70.

Christian, M. 2012. 'Economic and Social Up (down) grading in Tourism Global Production Networks: Findings from Kenya and Uganda.' *Capturing the Gains Working Paper No. 11.*

Cumbers, A., C. Nativel, and P. Routledge. 2008. 'Labour Agency and Union Positionalities in Global Production Networks.' *J Econ Geogr* 8 (3): 369–87.

D'Costa, A. P. 2003. 'Uneven and Combined Development: Understanding India's Software Exports.' *World Develop* 31 (1): 211–26.

———. 2004. 'The Indian Software Industry in the Global Division of Labour.' In *India in the Global Software Industry: Innovation, Firm Strategies and Development*, edited by A. P. D'Costa and E. Sridharan. Basingstoke: Palgrave Macmillan.

———. 2011. 'Geography, Uneven Development and Distributive Justice: The Political Economy of IT Growth in India.' *Camb J Reg, Econ Soc* 4: 237–51.

D'Cruz, P. 2012. *Workplace Bullying in India*. New Delhi: Routledge.

D'Cruz, P., and E. Noronha. 2006. 'Being Professional: Organizational Control in Indian Call Centers.' *Soc Sci Comp Rev* 24 (3): 342–61.

———. 2009. 'Experiencing Depersonalized Bullying: A Study of Indian Call Centre Agents.' *Work Organ Lab Global* 3 (1): 26–46.

———. 2012. 'High Commitment Management Practices Re-examined: The Case of Indian Call Centres.' *Econ Indus Democracy* 33 (2): 185–205.

———. 2013b. 'Breathers, Releases, Outlets and Pauses: Employee Resistance in the Context of Depersonalized Bullying.' *The Qualitative Report* 18 (72): 1–24. Available at, http://www.nova.edu/ssss/QR/QR18/dcruz72.pdf.

———. 2015. 'Ambivalence: Employee Responses to Depersonalized Bullying at Work.' *Economic and Industrial Democracy*, 36 (1): 123–45.

D'Mello, M. 2005. '"Thinking Local, Acting Global": Issues of Identity and Related Tensions in Global Software Organizations in India.' *The Electronic Journal on Information Systems in Developing Countries.*

D'Mello, M., and T. H. Eriksen. 2010. 'Software, Sports Day and Sheera: Culture and Identity Processes within a Global Software Organization in India.' *Information and Organization* 20 (2): 81–110.

Davies, S., N. Hammer, and G. Williams. 2011. 'Labour Standards and Capacity in Global Subcontracting Chains: Evidence from a Construction MNC.' *Indus Relat J* 42 (2): 124–38.

Durán, C. R. 2006. 'Value Chains and Software Clusters in Mexico.' In *Upgrading to Compete Global Value Chains, Clusters, and SMEs in Latin America*, edited by C. Pietrobelli and R. Rabellotti. Inter-American Development Bank: Washington.

Fernández-Stark, K., P. Bamber., and G. Gereffi. 2011. *The Offshore Services Global Value Chain. Economic Upgrading and Workforce Development.* Durham, NC: Duke University Center on Globalization, Governance and Competitiveness.

Fuller, C. J., and N. Haripriya. 2007. Information Technology Professionals and the New-rich Middle Class in Chennai (Madras). *Mod Asian Stud* 41 (1): 121–50.

Gereffi, G. 2001. 'Beyond Producer Driven/Buyer Driven Dichotomy: The Evolution of Global Value Chain in the Internet Era.' *IDS Bull* 32 (3): 30–40.

———. 2005. 'The Global Economy: Organization, Governance, and Development', In *The Handbook of Economic Sociology*, 2nd ed., edited by Neil J. Smelser and Richard Swedberg. Princeton, NJ: Princeton University Press, pp. 160–82.

———. 2006. *The New Offshoring and Global Development of Jobs.* ILO Social Policy Lectures, Jamaica, Geneva: ILO.

———. 2014. 'Global Value Chains in a Post-Washington Consensus World.' *Rev Int Polit Econ* 21 (1): 9–37.

Gereffi, G., and K. Fernandez-Stark. 2011. Global Value Chain Analysis: A Primer. North Carolina, USA: Center on Globalization, Governance & Competitiveness (CGGC), Duke University.

Gereffi, G., and F. Mayer. 2006. 'Globalization and the Demand for Governance.' In *The New Offshoring and Global Development of Jobs.* ILO Social Policy Lectures, Jamaica, Geneva: ILO.

Gereffi, G., J. Humphrey, R. Kaplinsky, and T. J. Sturgeon. 2001. 'Introduction: Globalisation, Value Chains and Development.' *IDS Bull* 32 (3): 1–8.

Goger, A., A. Hull, S. Barrientos, G. Gereffi, and S. Godfrey. 2014. Capturing the Gains in Africa: Making the Most of Global Value Chain Participation. Center on Globalization, Governance & Competitiveness, *Social Science Research Institute,* 1–32.

Hanson, A. 2009. 'Legal Process Outsourcing to India: So Hot Right Now!' *SMU Law Rev* 62: 1889–914.

Heeks, R. 1996. *India's Software Industry: State Policy, Liberalization and Industrial Development.* New Delhi: Sage Publications.

Helfen, M., and M. Fichter. 2013. 'Building Transnational Union Networks Across Global Production Networks: Conceptualising a New Arena of Labour–Management Relations.' *Brit J Indus Relat.* doi: 10.1111/bjir.12016.

Helg, R., and L. Tajoli. 2005. 'Patterns of International Fragmentation of Production and the Relative Demand for Labour.' *The North American Journal of Economics and Finance* 16 (2): 233–54.

Illavarasan, P. V. 2008. 'Software Work in India: A Labour Process View.' In *In an Outpost of the Global Economy: Work and Workers in India's Information Technology Industry,* edited by C. Upadhaya and A. R. Vasavi. London: Routledge.

Krishnan, J. K. 2007. 'Outsourcing and the Globalizing Legal Profession.' *William and Mary Law Review* 48: 2189–2214.

Lakha, S. 1994. 'The New International Division of Labour and the Indian Computer Software Industry.' *Mod Asian Stud* 28 (2): 381–408.

Lee, J., and G. Gereffi. 2013. 'The Co-evolution of Concentration in Mobile Phone Global Value Chains and its Impact on Social Upgrading in Developing Countries.' *Capturing the Gains Working Paper No. 25.*

Lutgen-Sandvik, P. 2006. 'Take This Job and…: Quitting and Other Forms of Resistance to Workplace Bullying.' *Communication Monographs* 73: 406–33.

McMillin, D. 2006. 'Outsourcing Identities: Call Centres and Cultural Transformation in India.' *Econ Polit Weekly* 41 (3): 235–41.

Milberg, W., and D. Winkler. 2011. 'Economic and Social Upgrading in Global Production Networks: Problems of Theory and Measurement.' *Int Lab Rev* 150 (3–4): 341–65.

Mirchandani, K. 2004. 'Practices of Global Capital: Gaps, Cracks and Ironies in Transnational Call Centres in India.' *Global Netw* 4 (4): 355–73.

NASSCOM. 2012. *Strategic Review 2012.* New Delhi: NASSCOM.

———. 2013. 'The IT-BPM Sector in India.' *Strategic Review 2013.* New Delhi: NASSCOM.

Nath, P., and A. Hazra. 2002. 'Configurations of Indian Software Industry.' *Econ Polit Weekly* 37 (8): 737–42.

Neilson, J., B. Pritchard, and H. Y. Wai-chung. 2014. 'Global Value Chains and Global Production Networks in the Changing International Political Economy: An Introduction.' *Rev Int Polit Econ* 21 (1): 1–8.

Noronha, E., and P. D'Cruz. 2006. 'Organising Call Centre Agents: Emerging Issues.' *Econ Polit Weekly* 41 (21): 2115–21.

———. 2009a. *Employee Identity in Indian Call Centres: The Notion of Professionalism.* New Delhi: Sage/Response.

———. 2009b. 'Engaging the Professional: Organising Call Centre Agents in India.' *Indus Relat J* 40 (3): 215–34.

———. 2012. 'Indian Call Centres: Latent and Manifest Points of Conflict.' In *Containing Workplace Conflicts*, edited by P. Sinha. New Delhi: Bookline.

Noronha, E., P. D'Cruz, and S. Kuruvilla. 2016. 'The Globalization of Commodification: The Impact of Legal Process Outsourcing on Indian Lawyers.' *Journal of Contemporary Asia.* In press.

Parthasarathy, B. 2000. 'Globalization and Agglomeration in Newly Industrializing Countries: The State and the Information Technology Industry in Bangalore, India.' PhD thesis, University of California, Berkeley.

———. 2004. 'India's Silicon Valley or Silicon Valley's India? Socially Embedding the Computer Software Industry in Bangalore.' *Int J Urban Reg Res* 28: 664–85.

Parthasarathy, B., and Y. Aoyama. 2006. 'From Software Services to R&D Services: Local Entrepreneurship in the Software Industry in Bangalore, India.' *Environ Plan A* 38: 1269–85.

Penfold, C. 2009. 'Off-Shored Services Workers: Labour Law and Practice in India.' *Econ Lab Relat Rev* 19 (2): 91–106.

Poster, W. 2007. 'Who's on the Line? Indian Call Centre Agents Pose as Americans for US Outsourced Firms.' *Indus Relat* 46 (2): 271–304.

Posthuma, Anne, and Dev Nathan. 2010. 'Conclusion.' In *Labour in Global Production Networks*, edited by A. Posthuma, and D. Nathan. New Delhi: Oxford University Press.

Prasad, M. 1998. 'International Capital on "Silicon Plateau": Work and Control in India's Computer Industry.' *Soc Forces* 77 (2): 429–52.

Prasad, A., and P. Prasad. 1998. 'Everyday Struggle at the Workplace: The Nature and Implication of Routine Resistance in Contemporary Organization.' *Res Sociol Organ* 16: 225–57.

Rainnie, A., A. Herod, and S. McGrath-Champ. 2011. 'Review and Positions: Global Production Networks and Labour.' *Comp Change* 15 (2): 155–69.

Raj-Reichert, G. 2013. 'Safeguarding Labour in Distant Factories: Health and Safety Governance in an Electronics Global Production Network.' *Geoforum* 44: 23–31.

Raman, R., P. Budhwar, and G. Balasubramanian. 2007. 'People Management Issues in Indian KPOs.' *Employee Relat* 29 (6): 696–710.

Ramesh, B. 2004. 'Cybercoolies in BPOs.' *Econ Polit Weekly* 39 (5): 492–97.

Regan, M. C., and P. T. Heenan. 2010. 'Supply Chains and Porous Boundaries: The Disaggregation of Legal Services.' *Fordham Law Review* 78: 2137–91.

Robertson, C. B. 2011. 'Collaborative Model of Offshore Legal Outsourcing.' *Ariz State Law J* 43: 125–79.

Rossi, Arianna. 2011. 'Economic and Social Upgrading in Global Production Networks: The Case of the Garment Industry in Morocco.' DPhil dissertation. Brighton Institute of Development Studies, University of Sussex.

Rothboeck, S., M. Vijaybhaskar, and V. Gayatri. 2001. *Labor in the Indian Economy: The Case of the Indian Software Labor Market*. ILO: New Delhi.

Sahay, S., B. Nicholson, and S. Krishna. 2003. *Global IT Outsourcing*. New York, NY: Cambridge University Press.

Sako, M. 2010. 'Make-or-buy Decisions in Legal Services: A Strategic Perspective.' Available at, http://www.sbs.ox.ac.uk/centres/professionalservices/Documents /SAKO%20Make%20or%20buy%20in%20legal%20services%20June%20 2010%20ND%20WP.pdf.

Sarkar, S., B. S. Mehta, and Dev Nathan. 2013. 'How Social Upgrading Drives Economic Upgrading by Indian IT Majors: The Case of Telecom IT Services.' *Capturing the Gains Working Paper 27*, Capturing the Gains. Available at, www. capturingthegains.org.

Schultz, C. I. 2010. 'Legal Off Shoring: A Cost-Benefit Analysis.' *The Journal of Corporation Law* 35: 640–61.

Selwyn, B. 2013. 'Social Upgrading and Labour in Global Production Networks: A Critique and an Alternative Conception.' *Comp Change* 17 (1): 75–90.

Saxenian, A. 2002. 'Transnational Communities and the Evolution of Global Production Networks: The Cases of Taiwan, China, and India.' *Indus Innov, Special Issue on Global Production Networks* Fall (2002): 1–35.

Siegmann, K. A., J. Merk, and P. Knorringa. 2014. 'Voluntary Initiatives in Global Value Chains. Towards Labour-Led Social Upgrading?' *Civic Innovation Research Initiative Working Paper No. 4*: 1–24.

Singh, P., and A. Pandey. 2005. 'Women in Call Centres.' *Econ Polit Weekly* 40 (7): 684–88.

Staritz, Cornelia, and M. Morris. 2013. 'Local Embeddedness and Economic and Social Upgrading in Madagascar's Export Apparel Industry.' *Capturing the Gains Working Paper No. 21*, Capturing the Gains. Available at, www.capturingthe gains.org.

Taglioni, D., and D. Winkler. 2014. 'Making Global Value Chains Work for Development.' *Econ Manage (Prem) Network* 1: 1–10.

Taylor, P. 2010. 'The Missing Link: Analysing the Global Call Centre Value Chain.' Paper presented to the International Labour Process Conference, Rutgers State University of New Jersey, New Brunswick, 15–17 March.

Taylor, P., and P. Bain. 2006. *An Investigation into the Offshoring of Financial Services Business Processes*. Glasgow, UK: University of Strathclyde.

Thatchenkery, T., D. Kash, and R. Stough. 2004. 'Information Technology Services and Economic Development: The Indian Experience.' *Technol Forecast Soc* 71, 771–76.

Tisza, S. 2005. 'Trip Puts Human Face on Global Outsourcing.' Available at, http://www.cwaunion.org/news/entry/trip_puts_human_face_on_global_ outsourcing.

Upadhya, C. 2010. 'Taking the High Road? Labour in the Indian Software Outsourcing Industry.' In *Labour in Global Production Networks in India*, edited by Anne Posthuma and Dev Nathan, 300–320. New Delhi: Oxford University Press.

Veloso, F., A. Botelho, T. Tschang, and A. Amsden, 2003. 'Slicing the Knowledge-Based Economy in Brazil, China and India: A Tale of Three Software Industries.' MIT Report.

Wadhwa, V., Kim De Vitton, and Gary Gereffi. 2008. *How the Disciple Became the Guru: Is it Time for the U.S. to Learn Workforce Development from Former Disciple India?* Durham, N.C.: Duke University and the Kauffman Foundation.

Wills, J. 1998. 'Taking on the Cosmocorps? Experiments in Transnational Labour Organization.' *Econ Geogr* 74: 111–30.

Woffinden, K. 2007. 'Surfing the Next Wave of Outsourcing: The Ethics of Sending Domestic Legal Work to Foreign Countries under New York City Opinion.' *Brigham Young University Law Review* 483–529.

Xiang, B. 2007. *Global 'Body Shopping': An Indian Labour System in the Information Technology Industry.* Princeton: Princeton University Press.

19

What Do Workers Gain from Being in a GVC? ICT in India

Sandip Sarkar and Balwant S. Mehta

19.1   Introduction

The application of digital technology such as telecommunication and IT has driven the deeper segmentation and geographical dispersal of services in the supply chain. Globalization, telecom reforms and the emergence of a wide range of IT services have driven the rapid growth of global supply chains of ICT (Information and Communication Technology) services. ICT services include a wide range of activities, such as back office services, call centres, software and IT maintenance services and infrastructure management.

India has successfully integrated into ICT services value chains by developing export-oriented software industries (UNCTAD, 2012). Figure 19.1 shows that

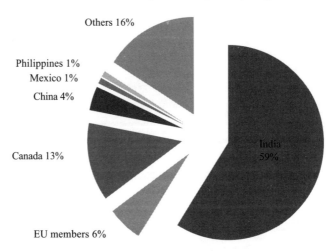

Figure 19.1   Share of global market for IT services off-shoring by destination, 2011
Source: Information Economy Report, 2012 (UNCTAD 2012).

India is the destination of choice for around 59 per cent of the global market for IT services off-shoring in 2011.

19.2   India's ICT sector

India's services sector has also emerged as the largest and fastest growing sector in the economy: it contributed around 57 per cent to the gross domestic product (GDP) in 2014. It is second fastest growing sector (at 9.0 per cent annually) after China (10.9 per cent) in the period 2001 to 2012 (Economic Survey, 2014). It has thus been argued that modern sectors such as information and communication technology (ICT) services have played a significant role in service sector growth in India (Eichengreen and Gupta, 2011; Nayyar, 2012).

The Indian ICT sector includes two large sub-sectors, namely telecommunication and information technology and information technology enabled services (ITES) sectors apart from two smaller component of ICT manufacturing and ICT trade. The telecommunication sub-sector within ICT is one of the largest recipients of foreign direct investment, having attracted 17.88 billion dollars in investment in this millennium (Ministry of Commerce, Government of India). The telecom sector is dominated by a few large corporate players (Reliance, Aditya Birla and Airtel), foreign mobile operators (Vodafone) and public sector companies (BSNL and MTNL). It is not part of the global value chain but it has strong global linkages.

The Indian IT-ITES industry has developed a better value-added model of software service delivery, which is now widely known as the onsite-offshore model. In recent years, large software industry companies have moved towards a global service delivery model in which India remains the headquarters but delivery services are located in India as well as other developing countries, and customer support offices near their clients in developed world. Through its explosive growth, the IT-ITES sector has increasingly been referred as the growth engine of the economy and is seen as providing a wide range of economic and social benefits. These include the creation of quality employment, a raise in income levels, the promotion of export and significant contributions to GDP. The availability of a large pool of qualified people at a comparatively cheaper cost as well as effective government policies[1] has made India a favoured outsourcing destination (NASSCOM, 2014). As a result, India continues to account for more than half of total global IT-ITES outsourcing.

---

[1] Reform in 1990s, opening of IT parks across the country; partial privatization of telecommunication; development of SEZs that help IT companies get tax benefits; a large number of resources readily available in the country, low operating costs, tax breaks and sops offered by the government.

Sandip Sarkar and Balwant S. Mehta

In this context, it would be useful to examine the contribution of the ICT sector to national income and employment generation; quality of employment created; educational (skill) levels of the workforce; and job profiles, which includes occupational profiles and workers' salaries depending on different skills/occupations. Further, the location of job creation is also discussed in an attempt to determine whether the industry continues to remain confined to a few metros.

Finally, as noted earlier there is a distinct difference in the value chain characteristics of the two major components of ICT sector, i.e., telecommunication and IT-ITES. We thus also examine to what extent there is a difference in nature of employment and the benefits that accrue to different layers of the workforce between the telecommunication sector, which is not part of GVCs, and the IT-ITES sector, which is dominated by GVC activities.

19.3   The contribution of the ICT sector to the national economy

There is no doubt that the ICT sector contributes significantly to economy: its share in GDP increased from 2 per cent in 2001 to 8 per cent in 2013, and its export constituted 20 per cent of total Indian exports in 2010–2011. It is the fastest growing sector in the economy (compound annual growth rate of 22.5 per cent from

Table 19.1   Distribution of ICT workers (in 000') by industry in 2011–2012

Industry	Rural		Urban		All areas	
	Number	Row percentage	Number	Row percentage	Number	Column percentage
Manufacturing	46.2	13.1	306.5	86.9	352.7	9.0
Trade	22.2	15.6	119.9	84.4	142.0	3.6
Telecommunications and IT-ITES services	437.6	12.8	2980.4	87.2	3418.0	87.4
Total	506.0	12.9	3406.7	87.1	3912.7	100.0

Source: Unit-level data of NSS 68th round of employment and unemployment schedule, 2011/2012.
Note: Row percentage shows percentage distribution across rural and urban and column percentage shows percentage distribution across sectors.

452

2004–2005 to 2011–2012) with a great deal of untapped potential. Revenues grew by 20.5 per cent annually from 10.2 billion USD in 2001 to 95.2 billion USD in 2013, with a larger share from exports, at 79.6 per cent (Cinni, 2014). It has contributed significantly towards direct employment generation: the sector was estimated to employ about 3.9 million people in 2011–2012, of which 13 per cent were women (Table 19.1). On the other hand, the sector also provides indirect employment opportunities to a further 10 million workers in associated industries like construction, catering, security services, retail and transport. Increased earnings and employment further drive the spending in services like food, entertainment, telecommunication and healthcare apart from contributing to the government's tax earnings (Cinni, 2014).

19.4   Database and methodology

There have been a few attempts made in the past to understand employment in the context of the ICT sector in India (Sarkar and Mehta, 2010; Jhoshi, 2004, 2010; Joseph and Abraham, 2005; Kumar, 2001; Chandrashekar, 2000; Babu, 2004; Mehta, 2010; Vijayabaskar et al., 2001). However, these studies examined the ICT sector overall, i.e., including manufacturing, trade, communication, IT and ITES. This paper attempts to explore employment patterns specifically in the services segment of the ICT sector in India. The definition of the ICT sector referred to in this paper is based on ISIC Rev.4 of the Organisation for Economic Cooperation Development (OECD) in 2012 (Annexure 1) and the new industrial classification of 2008. This new classification divides the ICT sector into three broad areas: manufacturing, trade and services.

Since this paper focuses on the services segment, we present a broad overview of employment in ICT sector (including manufacturing). Then we examine ICT services activities (communication, IT-ITES and trade) from sub-section entitled 'The Industrial Composition of Employment in ICT and non-ICT Service Sectors', and leave trade from the analysis from the section on 'Quality of Employment', as trade forms only a small part of the ICT service sector and it largely belongs to unorganized section of the economy. To compare ICT service with non-ICT service sector from section on 'quality of employment' we relied on one-digit industrial classification of old NIC (National Industrial Classification) of 1987. At this level of classification communications sector (part of ICT) falls under the broad industrial category of transport, storage and communications, while IT-ITES (part of ICT) belongs to industrial category of financial and business services. Therefore, comparison of ICT with non-ICT sector will be done between relatively similar sectors as they fall in similar aggregative classification.

Unit-level data from employment and unemployment schedule of national sample survey (NSS) for the years, 2011–2012 have been used for subsequent analysis. All analysis pertains to workers in the age group 15–59 years.

19.5 Employment structure

19.5.1 Employment profile of the ICT sector

In India, employment in the ICT sector made up about 1 per cent of total employment (428 million) in India in 2011–2012. Direct employment in the ICT sector was around 3.9 million in 2011–2012 (Table 19.1). This was urban-centric, with almost 87 per cent of employment occurring to urban areas, with 59 per cent of this located in the metros. Most ICT workers were involved in telecommunications and IT-ITES services (87.4 per cent) followed by manufacturing (9 per cent) and trade (3.6 per cent) in 2011/2012.

Among the three sub-sectors within the ICT sector, the service sub-sector was the most gender friendly, with a female employment share of around 14 per cent (Table 19.2). The service sub-sector was also relatively more urban-centric compared to the other two.

The statistics shown in Table 19.2 indicate that the ICT sector in India is largely service-led, hence further analysis in this paper will be confined to the service sub-sector.

Table 19.2 Distribution of ICT workers (in 000') by gender in 2011–2012

Industry	Male		Female	
	Number	Row percentage	Number	Row percentage
Manufacturing	313.4	88.9	39.3	11.1
Trade	131.0	92.3	11.0	7.7
Telecommunications and IT-ITES services	2951.1	86.3	466.9	13.7
Total	3395.5	86.8	517.2	13.2

Source: Unit-level data of NSS 68th round of employment and unemployment schedule, 2011/2012.
Note: Row percentage shows percentage distribution across male and female.

19.5.2 Industrial composition of employment in ICT and non-ICT service sectors

Industrial distribution statistics show that around 68 per cent of ICT service sector workers were involved in information technology and IT-enabled services (IT-ITES) industry while 29 per cent were involved in communication services (Table 19.3). In the IT-ITES segment, female employment was relatively higher, while the opposite is true in the case of communication services. The last column of Table 19.3 shows the share of employment of the ICT segment that belongs to the respective NIC

Table 19.3 Employment in ICT and non-ICT services by industry and gender (in %), 2011/2012

NIC 1987 code	Industry	ICT services			Non-ICT services			Share of ICT in Total employment
		Male	Female	All	Male	Female	All	
6	Trade, Hotel and restaurants (Trade in ICT products)	3.1	2.4	3.0	42.3	42.2	42.3	0.8
7	Transport, storage and communi-cation (Communi-cation)	31.0	18.5	29.0	34.9	9.4	32.8	10.0
8	Financial and, Business services etc. (IT-ITES)	65.9	79.2	68.0	22.8	48.4	25.0	30.8
	Total	100	100	100	100	100	100	11.3

Source: Unit-level data of NSS 68th round of employment and unemployment schedule, 2011/2012.

Note: 1. Description in parentheses indicates ICT industries and those outside the parentheses are non-ICT sectors.

2. NIC 1987 code refer to old National Industrial Classification of 1987 under which broad one digit codes existed.

one-digit level employment. ICT services have noticeable presence in two NIC one digit level codes of 7 and 8.

ICT services were a predominantly urban phenomenon, since 91.2 per cent of jobs were located in urban areas (Table 19.4). This is especially true of IT-ITES, the largest sub-sector of the ICT sector, which had a negligible presence in rural areas. However, trade and communication had some presence in rural areas. This reflects the urban-centric nature of jobs in IT-ITES services.

Table 19.4   Employment in ICT services by sector, 2011/2012

Industry	ICT services		
	Rural	**Urban**	**All areas**
Trade	22.4	77.6	100.0
Communication	17.0	83.0	100.0
IT-ITES	4.5	95.5	100.0
Total	8.8	91.2	100.0

Source: Unit-level data of NSS 68th round of employment and unemployment
    schedule, 2011/2012.

19.5.3   Education profiles of workers in ICT and non-ICT services

Around 72 per cent of workers in ICT services had a graduate-level or above education, as compared to just 35 per cent in the non-ICT sector, where the majority were educated up to secondary school or had lower qualifications (Figure 19.2)[2]. Similarly, the education levels of both female and male ICT workers were significantly higher than their counterparts in the non-ICT sector. Almost 81 per cent of female and 71 per cent of male workers had a graduate-level or above qualification compared to 40 per cent of female and only 34 per cent of male workers in the non-ICT sector. Interestingly, in both ICT and non-ICT sectors, female workers were better educated than male workers, i.e., the proportion of female graduates was higher than male graduates. However, in the non-ICT sector, one-fourth of female workers were educated only up to the primary level compared to one-fifth of males.

---

[2] The largest part of non-ICT services is trade that accounts for more than two-third of non-ICT sector workforce. More than two-third of workers in trade were educated up to secondary level (10th grade).

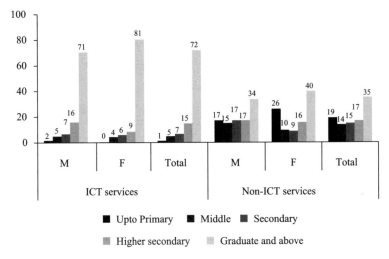

Figure 19.2   Educational composition of ICT and non-ICT services
workers (in %), 2011/2012

Source: Unit-level data of NSS 68th round of employment and unemployment
schedule, 2011/2012.
Note: M stands for male and F stands for females.

Further, the split between technical and non-technical qualifications, as shown
in Figure 19.3, that half of the workers surveyed in the ICT sector were technically
qualified, compared to just 9 per cent of workers in the non-ICT sector (Figure 19.3).

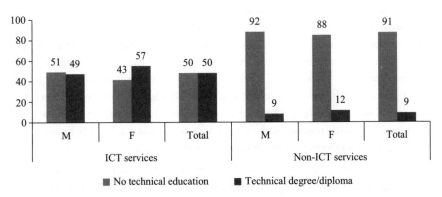

Figure 19.3   Technical educational composition of ICT services workers, 2011/2012

Source: Unit-level data of NSS 68th round of employment and unemployment schedule, 2011/2012.
Note: M stands for male and F stands for females.

The sub-sector with the highest number of workers with low technical qualifications was trade. The number of technically qualified female workers was higher compared to male workers in both ICT and non-ICT sectors. This reveals that the majority of highly qualified women were able to enter the services segment of economy.

19.5.4 Quality of employment

We have observed in the previous section that trade in the non-ICT sector had a workforce with low levels of education and technical qualifications, implying that the quality of employment available in trade is likely to be low. In addition, the trade sub-sector constituted less than 4 per cent of total ICT jobs. We thus exclude trade from further analysis in this chapter, in an attempt to put non-ICT and ICT services on a more equal footing for comparison. As a result, the non-ICT service sector will consist of transport, storage and financial and business services (excluding IT-ITES), while the ICT service sector will consist of telecommunications and IT-ITES services. The ICT and non-ICT service sectors together cover two broad industrial categories of transport, storage and communication and financial and business services.

We now examine quality of employment through employment status, employment by type of enterprise, nature of job contract, social security and unionization.

19.5.5 Status of employment

The status of employment indicates the quality of jobs, as regular (those who received salaries on regular basis) employment is considered to be of better quality compared to self-employment and casual (those who received salaries under periodic contract or on daily basis) employment due to the nature of the job, duration of contract and social security benefits. Casual work is purely temporary and does not offer any social security benefits (NSS report number 515, CSO, Government of India, 2006). The ICT service sector was dominated by regular employees (87 per cent) with casual workers forming just 2 per cent and the self-employed forming 11 per cent of the workforce (Figure 19.4). In contrast, regular employment was at 49 per cent in the non-ICT sector, while the self-employed made up 40 per cent and casual workers made up 11 per cent of the workforce. Female and male workers were predominantly regular workers in ICT sector whereas substantial presence of self-employed was found among male workers in non-ICT.

The distribution of regular workers in formal and informal employment shows that a significant higher proportion of ICT workers was in formal employment. Around 88 per cent of regular workers in the ICT sector were formally employed compared to 50 per cent in the non-ICT sector in 2011–2012 (Figure 19.5). The gender difference in the share of formal employment among regular workers within

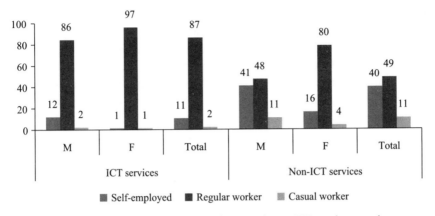

Figure 19.4 Employment status of ICT and non-ICT services workers, 2011/2012

Source: Unit-level data of NSS 68th round of employment and unemployment schedule, 2011/2012.

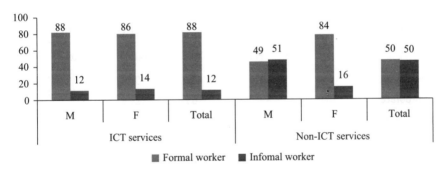

Figure 19.5 Formal and informal worker composition in ICT and non-ICT regular services workers, 2011/2012

Note: Formal worker includes all regular workers having any type of social security benefits.

the ICT sector was negligible, but in the non-ICT sector, female regular workers formed a much higher proportion of those in formal employment.

19.5.6 Regular employment by type of enterprise

The types of enterprises in each sector give some indication of the nature and quality of jobs available. Public sector (government and public enterprises) and corporate sector (public and private limited companies) jobs are considered to be of better quality compared to employment in the private (non-corporate those belonging to proprietorship and partnership enterprises) sector. In ICT services, workers were largely employed in corporate and then in the (non-corporate) private and public sectors, while in non-ICT services almost half of the workforce was in employed by the private sector followed by the public and corporate sectors (Table 19.5). The proportion of male workers in ICT services was relatively higher in the private and public sectors, while there were more female workers in the corporate sector in the ICT sector as well as in non-ICT services.

The division of ICT services into two segments, communication and IT-ITES services, is easily observable in the job distribution between corporate and public sectors. Corporate sector jobs completely dominated the IT-ITES segment, while the share of public sector jobs was much higher in the communications segment (Table 19.6). This is mainly due to the presence of two public enterprises, BSNL and MTNL, in the telecommunications sub-sector, alongside four large private operators—Airtel, Reliance, Tata and Idea.

Table 19.5 Employment by enterprise type of ICT and non-ICT regular services workers, 2011/2012

Enterprise type	ICT services			Non-ICT services		
	Male	Female	All	Male	Female	All
Public sector	11	7	10	28	37	28
Corporate	63	72	65	22	37	23
Private sector	26	21	25	51	27	49
Total	100	100	100	100	100	100

Source: Unit-level data of NSS 68th round of employment and unemployment schedule, 2011/2012.

Table 19.6 Employment by enterprise type of ICT regular services workers, 2011/2012

Enterprise type	Communication			IT-ITES		
	Male	Female	All	Male	Female	All
Public sector	27	27	27	3	3	3
Corporate	42	22	40	73	84	75
Private sector	31	51	33	24	14	22
Total	100	100	100	100	100	100

Source: Unit-level data of NSS 68th round of employment and unemployment schedule, 2011/2012.

19.5.7 Period of job contract and paid leave for regular workers

The higher number of public and corporate sector jobs does not necessarily mean that quality of jobs is concomitantly high. The nature of job contracts offered and the eligibility of workers for paid leave are two important aspects that indicate job quality. Analysing the nature of job contracts seems to indicate a dualistic pattern in the ICT sector: around half of the workers surveyed in the ICT sector had no written contract, with 63 per cent of workers in non-ICT services reporting the same (Table 19.7). A little more than one-third of ICT workers had contract duration of more than 3 years, which was relatively higher than non-ICT. In terms of a gender

Table 19.7 Distribution of period of contract of ICT and non-ICT regular services workers (in %), 2011/2012

Period of contract	ICT services			Non-ICT services		
	Male	Female	All	Male	Female	All
No job contract	46	50	47	64	51	63
Up to 1 year	10	12	10	4	2	4
1–3 yrs	7	4	6	3	7	4
3 yrs+	37	34	36	28	40	29
Total	100	100	100	100	100	100

Source: Unit-level data of NSS 68th round of employment and unemployment schedule, 2011/2012.

disparity, the proportion of male workers 'with any job contract' was higher in the ICT sector compared to the non-ICT sector. In the dynamic ICT sector, which boasts a high proportion of skilled workers and a high turnover rate, contract periods are not a major issue. However, contracts of shorter duration are not welcomed by the large proportion of workers who are involved in low-skill jobs in the ICT sector.

In the IT-ITES segment, 45 per cent of workers had no job contract, while 37 per cent had contracts of a 3-year or longer duration: 10 per cent up to 1 year and 8 per cent between 1 and 3 years (Table 19.8). The average contract duration was relatively lower in the communication segment, as the proportion of workers with no job contract or a contract that was of duration longer than 3 years was relatively higher (Table 19.8). Overall, these statistics raise the question of whether enterprises prefer a system of informal employment to permanent employment because temporary employees outperform permanent employees or because they cost less.

Table 19.8 Distribution of period of contract of ICT regular services workers (in %), 2011/2012

Period of contract	Communication			IT-ITES		
	Male	Female	All	Male	Female	All
No job contract	51	58	52	44	48	45
Up to 1 year	10	9	10	10	13	10
1–3 yrs	3	5	3	9	4	8
3 yrs+	36	27	35	37	35	37
Total	100	100	100	100	100	100

Source: Unit-level data of NSS 68th round of employment and unemployment schedule, 2011/2012.

The proportion of employees without a contract seems to be much lower in the ICT sector (as compared to the non-ICT sector) because this proportion includes maintenance and auxiliary service workers, such as cleaning staff, drivers, security staff, etc., who work in the sector. Within the ICT service sector, the comparatively higher proportion of employees without a contract in the communication segment is the result of the general practice of mobile operators like Airtel, who concentrate on core areas of marketing and finance and outsource all other work to several companies, such as outsourcing IT-related services and maintenance to IBM, and infrastructural maintenance to Indus Infrastructure Company (Mehta, 2014).

Eligibility for paid leave is another indicator of job quality in the labour market. ICT services companies were substantially more likely to offer paid leave than non-ICT services companies. A significantly higher proportion of female employees were eligible for paid leave compared to males in the non-ICT sector (Table 19.9),

Table 19.9 Proportion of ICT and non-ICT regular services workers eligible for paid leave (in %), 2011/2012

Sector	Gender		
	Male	Female	All
Non-ICT services	47	72	49
ICT services	76	74	76
Communications	66	50	64
IT-ITES	81	80	81

Source: Unit-level data of NSS 68th round of employment and unemployment schedule, 2011/2012.

although there was hardly any difference between the non-ICT and ICT sectors in terms of the eligibility of female employees for paid leave. Within the ICT sector, the availability of paid leave was relatively higher in the IT-ITES segment and it was virtually the same for both sexes; however, within the communication segment, only half of female employees were eligible for paid leave, compared to two-third of male employees.

19.5.8 Social security and unions/association of regular worker

The coverage of social security benefits and the presence of unions/associations are the other two indicators of quality employment. The prevalence of social security measures in the ICT services sector was significantly higher than in the non-ICT sector and much higher proportion of female in non-ICT had social security compared to male. In the ICT sector, gender difference was far less but it was in favour of female workers (Table 19.10).

Table 19.10   Eligibility for social security benefits of ICT and non-ICT regular services workers (in %), 2011/2012

Social security	ICT services			Non-ICT services		
	Male	Female	All	Male	Female	All
Not eligible	31	29	31	56	32	54
Any social security benefits	44	48	45	21	31	22
All benefits	25	23	24	23	37	24
Total	100	100	100	100	100	100

Source: Unit-level data of NSS 68th round of employment and unemployment schedule, 2011/2012.

In addition, within the ICT services sector, a relatively higher proportion of IT-ITES workers received some kind of social security benefit compared to workers in communication services (Table 19.11). Further, the gender-wise distribution shows that female employees in the IT-ITES segment received relatively higher social security benefits, while the opposite was true in the communications segment.

The likelihood of a union or association being present was substantially higher in the non-ICT segment than in ICT services, with a higher proportion of female employees were reporting about it in both segments (Table 19.12). Within ICT services, the communication sector had a higher presence of unions than the

Table 19.11 Eligibility for social security benefits among regular ICT services workers (in %), 2011/2012

Social security	Communications			IT-ITES		
	Male	Female	All	Male	Female	All
Not eligible	44	65	46	25	20	24
Any social security benefits	29	11	27	51	57	52
All benefits	27	24	27	23	23	23
Total	100	100	100	100	100	100

Source: Unit-level data of NSS 68th round of employment and unemployment schedule, 2011/2012.

Table 19.12 Presence of a union, as reported by regular workers, ICT and non-ICT services (in %), 2011/2012

Sector	Gender		
	Male	Female	All
Non-ICT services	43	45	43
ICT services	28	32	29
Communications	35	31	35
IT-ITES	25	33	27

Source: Unit-level data of NSS 68th round of employment and unemployment schedule, 2011/2012.

IT-ITES segment. The major reason behind this is the greater presence of public sector companies in the communication sector, in spite of larger presence of outsourcing job work. However, a higher proportion of female employees reported presence of union/association in their place of work in the IT-ITES sector.

Membership details are largely similar across both the ICT and non-ICT sectors, with the one significant difference being that the proportion of men who were members of a union or association was higher than the number of women – the reverse was true of the non-ICT sector. Further, within the ICT sector, it was observed that a higher number of male workers in the communication sector were members of a union or association compared to workers in the IT-ITES sector (Table 19.13).

Table 19.13 Proportion of ICT and non-ICT services regular workers as members of union/association (in %), 2011/2012

Sector	Gender		
	Male	Female	All
Non-ICT services	77	81	78
ICT services	78	75	78
Communications	88	73	87
IT-ITES	72	75	73

Source: Unit-level data of NSS 68th round of employment and unemployment schedule, 2011/2012.

19.5.9 Job profile of ICT service workers

The job profiles of ICT service workers have been examined on the basis of certain parameters, such as occupational profile, salary/earnings and the location of jobs. The analysis in this section is limited to the IT-ITES and communication segments of the ICT service industry.

For the first time, the 68th round of the National Sample Survey of 2011–2012 included the NCO-2004 classification of occupations that followed the ISCO-88 classification of occupations. The ISCO-88 classification allows skill level to be considered in the codification of occupations. This classification is used to identify the types of jobs/occupations of employees in the IT-ITES and communications segments of the ICT sector. These occupations are further combined and classified into broad categories on the basis of skill levels and hierarchy.

19.5.10 Occupational profile of regular worker

IT-ITES jobs

Occupations or job profiles in the IT-ITES services differ significantly on the basis of gender and skill type. The profile of mid-level technical professional involved in computing and other related professions (47.3 per cent) dominates, followed by top-level profiles, such as managers (19.4 per cent) and executives who work in sales and administrative positions (6.7 per cent) and clerks (4.7 per cent) (Table 19.14 for more details). Contrary to general perceptions, there was no significant gender disparity for IT-ITES services in technical or managerial positions, although 19 per cent of secretarial and clerical positions were filled by women, as opposed to 11 per cent filled by men. But in other occupations (not belonging to the top 10), which are largely low-skilled jobs, men had much a higher share compared to women.

Table 19.14 Employment in top 10 occupations of regular workers in IT-ITES services, 2011/2012

Occupation	Male	Female	All
Manager (204 + 121 + 122 + 123)	17.9	18.0	19.4
Technical professionals and technicians (213 + 312 + 311)	49.3	48.2	47.3
Business and administrative staff (241 + 232 + 112)	5.7	13.6	6.7
Clerical, secretarial, sales staff (411 + 412)	5.1	5.4	4.7
Sub-total of top 10 occupations	78.0	85.1	78.0
Rest occupations	22.0	14.9	22.0

Source: Unit-level data of NSS 68th round of employment and unemployment schedule, 2011/2012.
Note: 1. The top 10 occupations were aggregated into four groups.
   2. NCO codes are given in brackets, see detail in Annexure 2.1.

Communications jobs

Unlike in IT-ITES, where mid-level professionals dominate, in the communications sector it is mid- and low-level jobs that are most common: sales and desk associate jobs at the mid-level and low-skill jobs for drivers, mechanics, fitters, etc. The gender disparity in occupation profiles was also very stark (Table 19.15). At the top, there

Table 19.15 Employment in top 10 occupations of regular workers in communications services, 2011/2012

Occupation	Male	Female	All
Managers (122)	7.6	3.5	7.0
Professionals jobs (214 + 311 + 241)	16.5	17.8	16.9
Associate professional, desk and sales associates (522 + 422 + 419 + 341)	25.5	43.2	21.7
Other workers (724 + 421)	19.2	24.6	21.3
Sub-total top 10 occupations	68.7	78.1	67.0
Rest occupations	31.3	21.9	33.0

Source: Unit-level data of NSS 68th round of employment and unemployment schedule, 2011/2012.
Note: 1. The top 10 occupations were aggregated into four groups.
   2. NCO codes are given in brackets, see detail in Annexure 2.2.

were twice as many men as women in managerial jobs. Women's jobs were more concentrated at mid-level and relatively greater proportion of women also worked at the lowest level, possibly due to the greater presence of women in the hospitality industry (Annexure 2.2).

19.5.11 Salary/earnings of paid workers

The average daily earnings of workers in ICT services were significantly higher—almost three times more—than workers in non-ICT services (Table 19.16). This is because regular workers in the ICT sector earn almost double what non-ICT

Table 19.16 Average daily earning (in Rs.) in ICT and non-ICT service workers, 2011/2012

Employment status	ICT			Non-ICT		
	Male	Female	Persons	Male	Female	Persons
Regular	779	818	779	401	291	401
Casual	165	84	165	135	84	135
Total	759	808	759	248	158	248

Source: Unit-level data of NSS 68th round of employment and unemployment schedule, 2011/2012.

sector workers earn; also, the proportion of regular workers in the ICT sector is much higher. Overall, regular workers earned several times more than casual workers, but casual workers earned more or less similar salaries in both the ICT and non-ICT sectors. Further, while the industry in which they were employed did not make a substantial difference to wages, a gender disparity was observable: male casual workers earned 20 per cent more in the ICT sector compared to the non-ICT. Higher salaries for regular workers mean that there is a larger wage differential between regular and casual workers within the ICT sector. Also, in the same sector, casual female workers earned half as much as men, but in regular employment they earned somewhat more than men on average. In the non-ICT sector, women earned considerably less than men in regular employment and with this difference being relatively greater in casual employment. In consequence, the contrast in salaries was starker among women workers than among men.

In IT-ITES services, managers earned 3.5 times the salaries of business and administrative staff and 5 times the salaries of clerical and secretarial staff (Table 19.17). Male managers earned 25 per cent more than female managers, indicating that top management positions in IT and ITES are overwhelmingly

Table 19.17 Average daily earning (in Rs.) of regular IT-ITES workers across occupation

Occupation	Male	Female	Persons
Managers (204 + 121 + 122 + 123)	1555.2	1244.7	1502.3
Technical professional and technicians (213 + 312 + 311)	1009.2	1089.3	1024.2
Business and administrative staff (241 + 232 + 112)	393.3	494.5	419.0
Clerical, secretarial, sales staff (411 + 412)	291.4	282.6	289.4

Source: Unit-level data of NSS 68th round of employment and unemployment schedule, 2011/2012.
Note: NCO codes are given in brackets (see detail in Annexure 2.1).

occupied by men. A gap in average daily earnings between men and women was observed despite there being no gender difference in the share of jobs at managers' level in IT-ITES services. Such differences were not observable at other levels of employment: in fact, women in business and administrative positions earned 25 per cent more than their male counterparts.

The difference in average daily earnings across occupations was comparatively lower in the communications sector than in IT-ITES services (Table 19.18). Although the female average daily salary at the managerial level in the communications sector was relatively higher, it was lower at all other levels. One surprising observation is that the average daily earning at the lower level in the communications sector was lower than the same average for other low-skill jobs. This is an effect of the practice of outsourcing these types of jobs, which results in lower salaries.

Table 19.18 Average daily earning (in Rs.) of regular communications workers across occupation

Occupation	Male	Female	Persons
Managers (122)	886.1	928.6	946.8
Professionals jobs (214 + 311 + 241)	1012.6	814.8	986.7
Associate professional, desk and sales associates (522 + 422 + 419 + 341)	387.5	215.7	359.6
Other workers (724 + 421)	437.1	314.3	418.3

Source: Unit-level data of NSS 68th round of employment and unemployment schedule, 2011/2012.
Note: NCO codes are given in brackets, see detail in Annexure 2.2.

Managers in the IT-ITES sector earned more than one-and-a-half times the salaries of managers in the communications sector. In technical and professional roles, workers in IT-ITES earned somewhat more than their counterparts in the communications sector. In lower occupational categories, there was hardly any difference in salaries between the IT-ITES and communications sectors. IT-ITES enterprises generally form part of a global value chain (GVC) and communication is a modern sector with considerable FDI (foreign direct investment) and the presence of MNCs and large domestic corporate bodies. It can be inferred that the greater profit/rent that IT-ITES companies make from being in a GVC is shared with workers largely at the managerial level and to a lesser extent with professionals. Other regular workers and casual workers have gained little from being part of a GVC.

19.5.12   Location-wise distribution of regular jobs

The IT sector is concentrated in metros but has been gradually shifting to smaller cities and towns over the years. Around 65 per cent of employees in ICT services were employed in metros, of which 73 per cent were in the IT-ITES segment.

More than four-fifths of IT-ITES jobs are located in metros in the following states: Karnataka, Maharashtra, Tamil Nadu, Andhra Pradesh and Delhi (Table 19.20). The top three metros, i.e., Bangalore (Karnataka), Mumbai and Pune (Maharashtra) accounted for almost three-fifths of all metro jobs. The Indian IT-ITES industry is thus urban-centric, both in terms of delivery centres and human capital. IT-ITES jobs are also spreading to other metros but in much smaller magnitude.

Communication sector jobs are also urban-centric but they are more dispersed, with non-metro urban settlements accounting for two-thirds of all urban jobs (Table 19.19). Within the metros, communication jobs were concentrated in Maharashtra, Karnataka, West Bengal, Gujarat, Andhra Pradesh and Delhi (Table 19.21).

Table 19.19   Regular employment by metro/non-metro in urban area

Sector	Non-metro	Metro	All urban
IT-ITES	24.3 (50.7)	75.7 (84.9)	100.0 (73.0)
Communication	63.7 (49.3)	36.3 (15.1)	100.0 (27.0)
Total	34.9 (100.0)	65.1 (100.0)	100.0

Source: Unit-level data of NSS 68th round of employment and unemployment schedule, 2011/2012.
Note: Numbers in parentheses are column percentages.

Table 19.20 Regular IT-ITES jobs in metros

State	Number	In percentages
Karnataka	550,150	38.4
Maharashtra	336,814	23.5
Tamil Nadu	168,150	11.7
Andhra Pradesh	153,571	10.7
Delhi	101,608	7.1
Madhya Pradesh	35,949	2.5
Gujarat	35,713	2.5
West Bengal	24,599	1.7
Haryana	18,475	1.3
Uttar Pradesh	4,797	0.3
Punjab	3,678	0.3
Rajasthan	235	0.0
Total	1,433,740	100.0

Source: Unit-level data of NSS 68th round of employment and unemployment schedule, 2011/2012.

Table 19.21 Regular communications jobs in metros

State	Number	In percentages
Maharashtra	74,940	29.4
Karnataka	34,638	13.6
West Bengal	29,705	11.7
Gujarat	28,965	11.4
Andhra Pradesh	27,691	10.9
Delhi	20,660	8.1
Rajasthan	13,905	5.5
Uttar Pradesh	9,616	3.8
Tamil Nadu	4,943	1.9
Bihar	3,112	1.2
Punjab	2,289	0.9
Haryana	2,269	0.9
Madhya Pradesh	1,778	0.7
Total	254,509	100.0

Source: Unit-level data of NSS 68th round of employment and unemployment schedule, 2011/2012.

19.6 Conclusion

This chapter shows that the ICT sector not only contributes to employment, GDP and exports but also provides better quality employment compared to the non-ICT sector. The ICT sector also has a higher share of women employees. However, the employees in this sector are mainly concentrated in metros, among young and highly qualified people. The wages/salaries in the sector are relatively higher than other traditional sectors of the economy.

However, working in the ICT sector does not ensure better earnings for all categories of employees. Regular workers in the ICT sector earned much more than they would in the non-ICT sector, but casual workers earned almost the same salaries as casual workers in the non-ICT sector. Comparing the communication and IT-ITES sub-sectors within the ICT sector showed that workers in managerial positions earned substantially more in IT-ITES compared to communications. Professionals in IT-ITES earned somewhat more than their counterparts in the communications sector. The benefit of being part of a GVC (for IT-ITES) is largely shared by managers and to a smaller extent by professionals but not by those at other levels. However, these two levels of employment constituted two-thirds of all regular jobs in the IT-ITES sector compared to one-fourth in the communication sector.

Further, the development of IT-ITES is confined to tier-I cities like Bengaluru, Chennai, Hyderabad, Pune and NCR Delhi. It would be useful if the sector expanded to tier-II or III cities and employed a new pool of educated unemployed youth, as the sector has thus far not been able to employ a large number of educated youth from smaller towns and rural areas.

Social security measures exist in the ICT sector but the communications sector fared far better than IT-ITES. The communications sector also performed better on the criteria of unionization. On the other hand, the IT-ITES sector performed better on the criteria of job contracts, although this may be because a much larger proportion of the sector's workforce is made up of highly skilled employees who would not work without a contract. Employment conditions, particularly the low presence of an association or union and the high proportion of short-term contractual jobs (<3 years) raise concerns about the working conditions and quality of jobs in the sector. Overall, compared to communications, the IT-ITES sector does not show a clear advantage in terms of providing all-round benefits to its workforce despite being so integrated into global value chains.

There is an urgent need to create more employment opportunities for rural and disadvantaged communities through skill generation or upgrading existing skills through training or retraining. Extending social security benefits with more regular jobs would also improve working conditions.

References

Babu, P. Ramesh. 2004. 'Labour in Business Process Outsourcing: A Case Study of Call Centre Agents.' *Working Paper Number 051/2004*. Uttar Pradesh: National Labour Institute.

Brockman, Jane Drake. 2014. 'The Role of Services in Domestic and International Value Chains: An Initial Analysis of Trends in Services Value Added in the Indian Economy.' Presentation to Centre for WTO Studies Indian Institute for Foreign Trade, New Delhi, 22 August 2014, International Trade Centre.

Chandrasekhar C. P. 2000. 'ICT in a Developing Country Context: An Indian Case Study.' Available at, http://hdr.undp.org/sites/default/files/chandrasekhar-1.pdf.

Cinni, K. R. 2014. 'The Role of IT Industry in India's Economic Development.' Available at, http://www.lfymag.com/admin/issuepdf/25-27_Economic%20Development%20and%20IT_FFYJune14.pdf. Ministry of Finance, Government of India. 2011–2012. 'Economic Survey.'

Eichengreen, B., and P. Gupta. 2013. 'The Two Waves of Services Sector Growth.' *Oxford Economic Papers* 65 (1): 124–46.

Joseph, K. J., and V. Abraham. 2005. 'Moving Up or Lagging Behind? An Index of Technological Competence in India's ICT Sector.' In *ICTs and Indian Economic Development*, edited by A. Saith and M. Vijayabaskar. New Delhi: Sage Publications.

Joshi Seema. 2010. 'IT and ITES as an Engine of Growth: An Exploration into the Indian Experience.' *Working Paper Series No. E/294/2009*. University of Delhi: Institute of Economic Growth.

Joshi, S. 2004. 'Tertiary Sector Driven Growth in India: Impact on Employment and Poverty.' Economic and Political Weekly 39 (37): 879–924.

Kumar, N. 2001. 'Indian Software Industry Development: International and National Perspective.' *Economic and Political Weekly* 36 (45): 4278–290.

Mehta, Balwant Singh. 2011. 'Nature of Work, Quality of Employment and Working Conditions in ICT Sector: A Case of India.' Project Report. Singapore: SIRCA.

———. 2014. 'State Policy and Mobile Telephony in India.' Unpublished PhD thesis. New Delhi: JMI.

Nayyar, Gaurav. 2012. *The Service Sector in India's Development*. New Delhi: Cambridge University Press.

Government of India Ministry of Statistics & Programme Implementation. 2010. 'Report on 'Value Addition & Employment Generation in the ICT Sector in India.' New Delhi: National Statistical Organisation Central Statistics Office.

Sarkar, Sandip, and Balwant Singh Mehta. 2010. 'Labour Market Patterns and Trends in India's ICT Sector.' In *Labour in Global Production Network*, edited by Anne Posthuma and Dev Nathan. New Delhi: Oxford University Press.

UNCAD. 2012. 'Information Economy Report, 2012.' Available at, unctad.org/en/publications library/ier2012_en.pdf.

Vijayabaskar M., Sandra Rothboeck, and V. Gayathri 2001. 'Labour in the New Economy: Case of the Indian Software Industry.' *Indian Journal of Labour Economics* 44 (1): 39–54.

Annexure 1

ICT definition based on new classification ISIC rev.4 [OECD]

(1) ICT Manufacturing

2610 Manufacture of electronic components

2620 Manufacture of computers and peripheral equipment

2630 Manufacture of communication equipment

2640 Manufacture of consumer electronics

2680 Manufacture of magnetic and optical media

(2) ICT Trade

4651 Wholesale of computers, computer peripheral equipment and software

4652 Wholesale of electronic and telecommunications equipment and parts

(3) ICT Services

5820 Software publishing

61 Telecommunications

6110 Wired telecommunications activities

6120 Wireless telecommunications activities

6130 Satellite telecommunications activities

6190 Other telecommunications activities

62 Computer programming, consultancy and related activities

6201 Computer programming activities

6202 Computer consultancy and computer facilities management activities

6209 Other information technology and computer service activities

631 Data processing, hosting and related activities; web portals

6311 Data processing, hosting and related activities

6312 Web portals

951 Repair of computers and communication equipment

9511 Repair of computers and peripheral equipment

9512 Repair of communication equipment

Annexure 2.1   Detailed top 10 jobs in IT-ITES

Code	Occupation	No(in 000)	%
	Persons		
213	Computing Professionals	860.6	43.4
204	Architects, Engineers and Related Professionals	136.5	6.9
121	Directors and Chief Executives	105.1	5.3
122	Production and Operations Department Managers	103.5	5.2
241	Business Professionals	88.8	4.5
312	Computer Associate Professionals	76.7	3.9
411	Secretaries and Key Board-Operating Clerks	53.7	2.7
232	Secondary Education Teaching Professionals	43.3	2.2
123	Other Department Managers	40.2	2.0
412	Numerical Clerks	38.5	1.9
	Male		
213	Computing Professionals	693.6	43.0
204	Architects, Engineers and Related Professionals	110.2	6.8
122	Production and Operations Department Managers	90.2	5.6
121	Directors and Chief Executives	87.8	5.4
312	Computer Associate Professionals	65.8	4.1
241	Business Professionals	58.1	3.6
411	Secretaries and Key Board-Operating Clerks	47.6	3.0
311	Physical and Engineering Science Technicians	36.2	2.2
343	Administrative Associate Professionals	34.9	2.2
232	Secondary Education Teaching Professionals	34.3	2.1
	Female		
213	Computing Professionals	167.0	45.2
241	Business Professionals	30.7	8.3
204	Architects, Engineers and Related Professionals	26.3	7.1
412	Numerical Clerks	19.9	5.4
121	Directors and Chief Executives	17.3	4.7
122	Production and Operations Department Managers	13.3	3.6
312	Computer Associate Professionals	10.9	2.9
112	Administrative and Executive Officials	10.5	2.9
123	Other Department Managers	9.5	2.6
232	Secondary Education Teaching Professionals	9.0	2.4

Source: Unit-level data of 68th round of NSS.

Annexure 2.2   Detailed top 10 jobs in communication

Code	Occupation	No (in 000)	%
	Persons		
724	Electrical and Electronic Equipment Mechanics and Fitters	149.9	17.8
522	Shop Salespersons and Demonstrators	67.7	8.0
214	Architects, Engineers and Related Professionals	63.4	7.5
422	Client Information Clerks	45.9	5.4
419	Other Office Clerks	41.6	4.9
311	Physical and Engineering Science Technicians	35.8	4.2
241	Business Professionals	34.9	4.1
122	Production and Operations Department Managers	33.1	3.9
421	Cashiers, Tellers and Related Clerks	29.8	3.5
341	Finance and Sales Associate Professionals	27.8	3.3
	Male		
724	Electrical and Electronic Equipment Mechanics and Fitters	145.1	19.2
522	Shop Salespersons and Demonstrators	58.0	7.7
214	Architects, Engineers and Related Professionals	57.6	7.6
422	Client Information Clerks	45.4	6.0
311	Physical and Engineering Science Technicians	34.4	4.5
419	Other Office Clerks	33.9	4.5
122	Production and Operations Department Managers	33.1	4.4
241	Business Professionals	33.1	4.4
341	Finance and Sales Associate Professionals	27.8	3.7
421	Cashiers, Tellers and Related Clerks	27.7	3.7
	Female		
522	Shop Salespersons and Demonstrators	9.8	11.4
222	Health Professionals (except nursing)	8.8	10.2

(Contd)

Annexure 2.2 (Contd)

832	Motor Vehicle Drivers	7.8	9.1
419	Other Office Clerks	7.7	8.9
827	Food and Related Products Machine Operators	6.9	8.1
214	Architects, Engineers and Related Professionals	5.8	6.8
721	Metal Moulders, Welders, Sheet Metal Workers	5.4	6.3
724	Electrical and Electronic Equipment Mechanics and Fitters	4.8	5.5
343	Administrative Associate Professionals	4.0	4.7
741	Food Processing and Related Trades Workers	3.2	3.7

Source: Unit-level data of 68th round of NSS.

Conclusions

20

Governance Types and Employment Systems[1]

Dev Nathan

20.1 Introduction

In the Introduction, we held, modifying Gereffi et al. (2005), that knowledge, both in terms of complexity and codifiability, is the key in the out-sourcing of tasks. Alongside this, of course, is the fact that the costs of production are lower in developing countries for tasks where the capability to carry out those tasks exists. We also identified distributional issues (the distribution of rents within the chain) and business practices (the flexibility of orders), both working within the context of national institutional conditions, including that of the labour market, as other aspects of GVC relations that impact on employment relations. How do these knowledge-based GVC relationships, along with distributional factors, business practices and national institutional factors relate to the quality of employment? That is the question we will take up in this chapter, utilizing the case studies in this book, as well as some supplementary material. The attempt is to generalize from the case studies, particularly in linking governance types with employment systems.

The next two sections discuss the concepts of employment systems and governance types. This is followed by a summarization of the case studies in the book on the basis of governance types and employment systems. Section 20.4 discusses the connection between governance types and employment systems.

[1] This chapter has been developed from a study done for the ILO. My thanks to the ILO for granting permission to use the study material, and to Marva Corley-Couliba and Christian Viegelahn for their comments and questions. Thanks also to Stephanie Barrientos, Gerry Rodgers and particularly to Gary Gereffi for detailed comments. The points in this chapter have been discussed at various times with Sandip Sarkar. The usual caveats apply.

Dev Nathan

20.2 Employment systems

The case studies have revealed a number of aspects of employment relations – the security or otherwise of employment; the levels of remuneration, including whether they are around the minimum wage or living wage levels, or somewhat above that; types of incentive payments; and the type of supervision that is carried out, whether that of the strictly hierarchical method or some sort of quality circle (QC) approach.

In making a connection between governance types and employment, we need to go beyond a simple listing of employment practices, such as the security of employment, wages paid, and so on. Rather, we work on the premise that '… employment policies, procedures, and institutions … [have] to be conceived of as fitting into *systems* of interlocking and mutually reinforcing elements. The individual components of such systems cannot be understood in isolation or changed piecemeal' (Locke et al., 1997, p. xxiii, emphasis in original).

Consequently, different aspects of employment relations (contract type— direct or indirect; security of employment; wages and incentive payments; methods of supervision) are linked together to form employment systems. The first type of employment system we consider is that of the high-quality employment system (HQES). The core of the HQES is the link between security of employment, incentives and the delegation of some shop floor decision-making authority with process improvements initiated or suggested by workers. This leads to a high level of commitment, on the part of both employer and employee. While workers benefit through security and/or higher earnings, employers could benefit through productivity improvements.

In contrast to the HQES, there is the low-quality employment system (LQES) or 'sweated labour'. Security of employment is unlikely and workers are treated as replaceable or disposable (Wright, 2006). Wages are market-determined and generally cluster around the legal minimum wage.

While we started with a binary classification into high-quality and low-quality employment systems, it has become clear that it is necessary to distinguish between degrees of quality. For instance, there could also be a moderate quality employment system (MQES), which could be one of fixed-term employment, a system that is frequent in Germany. Such fixed-term employment has been discussed in Indian business and trade union circles as an alternative to the current low security employment system of indirectly contracted labour (Nathan et al., 2013). It has been initiated in the BMW factory in India and is being formulated as an alternative to existing indirect employment. In addition, an indefinite contract with, however, easy dismissal would turn a high security system into one of moderate security. In what follows the three employment systems of HQES, MQES and LQES and their aspects will be discussed below.

In any such system of classification of employment systems into a few types that can be used analytically, there could well be the elimination of some aspects of employment relations. But, it is argued here, following Locke et al. (1987), that there are connections between aspects of employment relations, such as security of employment, levels of wages, supervisory methods, incentive payments and the like, so that they form employment systems. But it should also be recognized that this is an approach that has been not been adequately theorized or explored in practice. This chapter is a step in this direction, but a lot more needs to be done in not just describing employment relations but also analysing employment systems.

The classification of employment systems developed here is somewhat similar to the simplification of governance systems in Gereffi et al. (2005) or even Gereffi's earlier differentiation between buyer-driven and supplier-driven supply chains (1995). There will also be definitely some opposition to such simplification, whether it be of governance or employment systems. But without such simplification and classification one merely ends with innumerable cases and no overall pattern or no overall theory. The attempt here is to formulate a theory of the relationship between GVC governance types and employment systems.

20.3   Governance types

Governance relations, in the first place, are the way in which tasks are divided and managed and re-integrated within a GVC. They are the way in which a functional integration of internationally dispersed production is carried out (Dicken, 2007). Of course, as stressed by Gereffi (1995) behind this disintegration and re-integration lies the power of the lead firms and their ability to dictate prices, quality standards, production location and related factors. Further, governance involves more than the division and integration of tasks within a GVC. It also involves the setting and achieving of norms in production, not just technical but also social norms (Gibbon et al., 2008; Gibbon and Sturgeon, 2014). In this chapter, these other aspects of GVC governance are not ignored; rather they are brought into the analysis in a secondary manner, as factors that modify the structures resulting from the interaction of knowledge and power structures in GVC relations.

Pre-GVC economic theory identified two forms of production governance—that of integration of production through the market and intra-firm integration through hierarchical decisions within a firm (Coase, 1988 (1937); Williamson, 1985). GVC analysis has introduced input supply relationships that lie in between market and hierarchical supply. Firms, or lead firms, enter into contractual supply relationships with other firms that, however, are not those of arms-length market transactions. GVC contractual relationships involve the setting of specifications and interactions of various types. These governance relations are characterized and classified into five types: markets, modular value chains, relational value chains, captive value chains, and hierarchy; with the Coase–Williamson governance relations at the two ends.

To recapitulate the main features of the governance types from Gereffi, Humphrey and Sturgeon (2005, p. 83–84):

1. Market linkages—this is the traditional arms-length relation of purchase and sale on the market, which is the staple of trade theories.
2. Captive value chains—where suppliers make products or services to lead firm specifications, but where there are many suppliers compared to the number of buyers, which makes the suppliers depend on large buyers to whom they are captive.
3. Modular value chains—where suppliers make products or supply services to the customer or lead firm's specifications, but where the ratio of suppliers or producers to buyers is not so large.
4. Relational value chains—where there are complex interactions between suppliers and lead firms, often resulting in mutual dependence and asset specificity.
5. Hierarchical linkages—where lead firms set up their own FDI units, in the manner of vertical integration; this is an intra-firm relationship.

As is discussed in more detail in the further sections, of the case studies in this book, fresh fruits, garments and tourism exhibit captive governance relations, while electronics, automobiles and call centres exhibit modular relations. One part of garments, i.e., lingerie, may be of modular rather than captive governance relations. IT software services alone exhibit relational governance. In many of the above, there are also instances of hierarchical governance, in cases where off-shore units are branches of the parent firm.

In the Table 20.1, hierarchical or intra-firm and market governance are listed at the end with a reason. They are the pre-GVC modes of analysing governance in production systems; while the first three (captive, modular and relational) are production governance systems introduced by GVC analysis.

Table 20.1 Case studies in this book and their governance type

No.	Governance type	Case studies
1.	Captive	Garments Fresh fruits Tourism
2.	Modular	Lingerie Electronics Automobiles Call centres
3.	Relational	IT software services
4.	Hierarchical	MNC branches
5.	Market	Raw materials (cotton; coltan)

20.4 Chapter findings

This section deals with the chapter findings with regard to employment systems in GVCs exhibiting different governance types.

20.4.1 Captive governance

We start with captive governance, where the complexity of production is relatively low: the complexity of production in garments and agro-foods, for instance, is low compared to electronics. The capability of developing those types of production is also more easily acquired, and thus there is more competition among suppliers in garments, agro-foods and tourism.

Employment systems in the three captive governance sectors can be summed up as follows:

- Garments—low-skill workers are employed; they have low security, high levels of supply through brokers, along with hyper-mobility of migrants; high levels of overtime work; wages are low, at around the national minimum; and supervision is in the Taylorist mode or by piece rate.
- Agro-foods—low-skill workers are employed, but there is an increasing skill level because of high standards required; low security of employment; wages at around the rural minimum; skilled workers tend to be paid more and at daily rather than piece rates.
- Tourism—the educational requirements are higher than in the above two sectors; but other than a core of regular employees, most workers are either on short-term contracts or self-employed; additionally, given the seasonal nature of work in most destinations, employment is on the whole insecure.

These aspects of employment systems in captive governance are set out in more detail below.

Garments

The knowledge required for the manufacture of garments is not very complex, though the level of complexity increases when moving from CMT, to full package supply, to being an intermediary. Nonetheless, the knowledge and information that go into the production of garments are easily codified. External supplier capability is correspondingly low but increases in moving up the value chain.

Profit rates are low and wages are generally at national minimum wage level. Orders are unstable, with seasonal variation that is exacerbated by the phenomenon of 'fast fashion'. Compliance requirements are also high, as garment sweatshops are a GVC segment that has attracted a very significant amount of media coverage. National institutional factors used to influence the use of child labour, but the impact of these is being reduced under compliance requirements and national developments.

Low prices and margins leave little room for supplier firms to invest in being flexible; rather, they manage flexibility in orders through a combination of increasing the number of casual workers employed, sub-contracting to smaller suppliers and demanding high levels of overtime. The proportion of insecure employment is high, and the high proportion of migrant workers makes it possible to combine high overtime with workers' interest in maximizing short-term earnings. What was described as the hyper-mobility of migrant workers (Carswell and de Neve, 2012) fits in with the employers' strategy of providing a high proportion of non-standard work. But some larger units (e.g., the Indian Shahi Exports, with 12 factories and 70,000 workers) manage flexibility through shuffling orders among various units with different wage levels in India, and even sub-contracting to Bangladesh.[2] Chinese garment units also sub-contract to Cambodia and Vietnam (Zhu and Pickles, 2014), though it is not clear if this is just in order to secure a cost advantage through lower wages or also to deal with flexibility.

Garment production is often on piece rates, with forced overtime when production schedules have to be met. With a low level of education needed for workers to enter into this segment of GVC production, wages are correspondingly low, i.e., at or just above the minimum wage. But under various pressures, including that of numerous strikes, minimum wages themselves have been raised, as in Bangladesh in the current decade, or in China because of tight labour markets.

---

[2] Author's field notes, 2014.

Agro-foods

Production for fresh fruit and other agro-food GVCs requires a greater degree of skill than traditional fruit production. Skill requirements have also led to a change in wage systems. While the main mechanism for improving productivity in agro-foods is piecework, where quality is important, as in pack houses, but it could also be so in field work, workers are paid a daily wage.

One would expect skilled workers to be those who are issued more standard, i.e., secure, contracts. In the Indian case, given the overall poor conditions of agricultural labour, workers do not have standard contracts including social security benefits and long-term contracts that industrial workers have, but skilled workers are paid retainers (advances) to return to their sites of employment. The payment of a retainer to secure the return of skilled workers is a practice even in the leather products GVC, which too is seasonal in nature (Damodaran, 2010).

The seasonal nature of work in agro-foods reduces employment security. Further, the skills and knowledge required in agro-food processing are generic, in the sense that they are not specific to a particular firm or farm. Consequently, employers in India (Chapter 5) find it possible to secure workers who have the necessary skills or educational background from the labour market and do not have to utilize secure employment practices or internal labour market systems to retain skilled workers.

Within an agro-food product, such as tea or coffee, there are different value chain segments, such as the cultivation of the plant, either in large-scale plantations or small-holder farms, processing, branding and marketing. In some cases, the various segments were integrated into single firms, as was the case with Tata Tea. But the separation of the commoditized production segment from the rent-capturing processing and marketing segment in Tata Tea, had an effect on employment quality in the plantations. This effect was reflected in an increase in the share of casual workers from 13 per cent in 1997 to 24 per cent in 2000 (ActionAid, 2005, 6, quoted in Neilson and Pritchard, 2009, p. 149).

Tourism

Many sections of tourism employees, such as tour guides, are required to have higher educational levels and training, than those employed in garments or agro-foods. However, except a few who are retained as regular employees, large numbers of employees are on short-term contracts or even piece-rated, i.e., paid per tour. In China, large numbers are not even paid, and therefore have to earn their living from commissions from shops and restaurants (Chapter 6). In addition, there are large numbers of other service providers, such as sellers of tourist souvenirs, providers of beach services who are self-employed or own-account workers (Chapter 8). There is some similarity with agro-foods in that there is a very large informal segment of self-employment. But this informal section is part of the tourism value chain and provides various kinds of services.

The differentiation in tourism employment is between those who work for foreign and those who work for domestic tourists. From hotels down to tour guides, there is a difference in the conditions of work and remuneration, with both being uniformly higher for those providing services to foreign tourists (Chapter 6). Those who provide services to foreign tourists tend to be paid better, while those who provide services to domestic tourists work on piece rates or commissions. The seasonal nature of much tourism employment adds to the insecurity of jobs, although the high volume would mean that some form of employment would be available. The oversupply of tourism services and the ease of entry reinforce the precarity of employment in tourism.

20.4.2 Modular governance

For modular governance, our examples are the electronics and automobiles sectors and call centres. Modular governance exists with turnkey production, i.e., where the supplier manufactures to given specifications, undertaking all the operations required, including procuring the various materials for production. It corresponds to what is called 'contract manufacturing' in the electronics sector and 'full package supply' in the garments sector. Because the complexity level of knowledge required is somewhat higher in assembly of electronics, or automobiles and call centre operations than in garment cut-make-trim (CMT), the capabilities to carry out the latter (CMT of garments) are more widely distributed than for the former. There are a few centres of electronics production in developing economies, mostly in East Asia though also in Brazil and India (Chapter 14). Garment production, on the other hand, is more widely located across Asia, Southern Africa and Central and South America.

While the garments sector as a whole is included under captive governance, there are products, such as lingerie, that are more complex than standard outerwear. The knowledge level required in these is at an intermediate level. There are few producers of lingerie, with the two main producers being Sri Lanka and Turkey. Lingerie production, because of the higher level of knowledge complexity required, can be included under modular rather than captive governance. Working conditions in garment manufacture in Sri Lanka are generally thought to be 'ethical' (Chapter 12), certainly in comparison to those in Bangladesh or Indian run-of-the-mill garment manufacture.

Employment systems in GVCs under modular governance can be summed up as follows:

- Electronics assembly requires a moderate level of knowledge; high levels of brokered employment, on repeated short-term contracts, giving a moderate security of employment, as it is difficult to take workers off the street and maintain quality; high levels of overtime or use of migrants for overtime; wages are above minimum wages; and supervision is very strongly Taylorist.
- Call centre work requires a moderate level of knowledge; employment is moderately secure, but there has been a high level of attrition related to the growth of the sector and shortage of persons with the required language skills; wages are higher than for individuals with similar educational levels in other industries; supervision is a modified form of office-Taylorism.
- Automobile assembly requires a moderate level of knowledge; high levels of brokered employment, which is changing to moderately secure fixed-term employment; wages are higher than minimum wages; and supervision is Taylorist.

The use of the term Taylorist in this section draws upon the distinction made by Piore and Sabel (1994) between supervision in mass and small-batch production. Supervision in the former was characterized as being hierarchical while in the latter, there was a greater decision-making autonomy at the shop-floor level and multi-skilling of the work group. In a sense, the Japanese system of quality circles tries to change the assembly line by mimicking the autonomy and multi-skilling of small-batch production.

Below the details of employment systems in the modular governance cases are set out.

Electronics

Electronics assembly requires knowledge that is of moderate complexity, but high codifiability. It also requires workers with a reasonable level of education, rather than merely literate workers as in garment manufacture or agro-processing. However, orders are volatile and this is reflected in the high level of temporary and agency workers, the low stability of employment in some countries and high levels of overtime in others.

National institutional structures, laws and rules have an impact on the ways in which GVC-supplier firms react to production flexibility. In Thailand, there are high numbers of agency and temporary workers (Holdcroft, 2012), but in Malaysia (Samel, 2012) and China (Chapter 14), there are high levels of overtime. In Malaysia, overtime is carried out by short-term migrant workers, who are keen to get in as much overtime as possible since they are intent on maximizing their short-term incomes and remittances.

Chinese factories have been legally required since March 2014 to limit the proportion of temporary workers to 10 per cent of the workforce. The flexibility they require is then secured through making regular workers work overtime. In March 2015, the All-China Workers' Federation pointed out that Foxconn makes its employees work for more than the legal 40 hours per week (GoodElectronics, 2015).

However, the necessity of having somewhat trained or experienced workers in order to maintain required quality standards means that temporary workers cannot be brought in off the street. 'When demand is very high it is difficult to suddenly hire 20 per cent more ...' (Chapter 14). Workers are regularly repeated on short-term contracts (ILO, 2014, p. 28). As a result of repeated short-term contracts, one may say that employment is moderately insecure, rather than highly insecure.

A connection between rates of return (or rents secured) and the ability to keep a check on overtime is seen in the case of electronics assembly. Chapter 14 showed that working conditions, including overtime, are generally better in OEM assemblers, such as Nokia, than in those of contract manufacturers, such as Foxconn. In terms of GVC governance structures, what this would mean is that labour conditions in MNC branches that are governed hierarchically tend to be better than labour conditions in independent supplier firms that are governed in a modular manner.

Supervisory and monitoring systems in electronics are of the Taylorist variety, with the speed of the assembly line setting the pace of work. The electronics GVCs' requirement for high quality with strict delivery deadlines creates a very stressful work environment. This leads to high levels of overtime work that has to be of high quality ('close attention every minute at a fast pace') and is also a major source of work stress (Chapter 15), reflected in the worker suicides at the Apple assembler, Foxconn.

Automobiles

The proportion of skilled workers in automobile assembly is not very different from that in electronics (Sarkar, Nathan and Mehta, 2014). Wages are generally above the minimum wage, and can go up to almost three times the minimum wage, making it around what is called a living wage.[3] In large units, skilled workers' wages are around US$ 350 per month (*ibid.*). There are, however, varied systems of employment, with large proportions of non-secure, broker-mediated employees (Chapter 17). Supervision is of the Taylorist variety. In India, outside of the assemblers and main component suppliers, there are many small and even household units, all linked as suppliers. Employment conditions in these small units are very insecure and wages remain around the minimum wage, with many violations.

---

[3] Chapter 4 on the Asia Floor Wage, sets out the concept of the living wage.

In terms of employment security, however, there has been a recent development in the automobile assemblers in India. After numerous strikes and other workers' struggles, the main employers have decided to abandon broker-mediated employment and replace it with direct, but fixed-term contracts (Sarkar, Nathan and Mehta, 2014). This would result in a shift to an intermediate level of employment security.

Call centres

In call centres, the business requirements are part of the service-level agreement (SLA). In turn, the SLA between the customer and the service provider becomes the basis for evaluation of employee performance (Chapter 18). In addition, there is continuous monitoring both by supervisors and managers. These are new forms of employment relations that can both control output and be used to intensify work. It has been argued that this leads to a Taylorist form of office work (Atkin, 1997; also Chapter 18), which can intensify work and degrade the quality of employment. Taylorism in application to call centre and other office work relates to hierarchical supervision with strict time and work specifications (such as response time, time spent on a call). As argued in Chapter 18, these call centre work standards are strictly defined by the contracting company, which operates like the lead firms or original equipment manufacturers (OEM) in the case of electronics or automobile manufacture.

Wages in call centres are much higher than the minimum wage (D'Cruz and Noronha, 2011; Chapter 18), with college graduates usually being employed in this sector. With the high rate of growth of the call centre industry in the first decade of this century, there was a shortage of English-language speaking candidates for employment. This led to high levels of attrition in call centres, as much as 50 per cent in a year, as employees could easily shift from one call centre to another. It was only with the stagnation of the market after the 2008 recession that some control over wage increases and over employees was established.

Contracts in call centres are of indefinite length, but the security of this type of contract is reduced by the allowance for termination with a notice period of 2–4 weeks, and the exemption of call centres from labour laws, which reduce the level of job security. At the same time, high rates of growth and the possibilities of job-hopping, mean that security is not an issue (Penfold, 2008).

20.4.3 Relational governance

IT software services

The one case of relational governance taken up in this book is that of the IT software services sector. The knowledge requirements are complex, involving the design, development and maintenance of IT software services. Such work involves a substantial amount of consultation between customer and supplier, which qualifies the governance relationship as being relational, with 'complex interactions between buyers and sellers that often create mutual dependence and high levels of asset specificity' (Gereffi et al., 2005, p. 84). However, as will be seen below, within IT software services too there are different levels of complexity, with Indian IT companies being concentrated in the middle to lower complexity sections.

Employment systems in IT software services, which are subject to relational governance, are substantially different from the other employment systems considered in this book and can be summarized as follows:

- IT software service work requires high level of knowledge; employment is secure, but moderated by the risk of 'bell curve' dismissal; earnings are higher than for employees of comparable qualifications in other sectors, along with high incentive payments; and supervision is through the project team method.
- High margins allow IT companies to maintain bench strength or a reserve workforce to manage sudden increases in staff requirements. More than in other GVCs that we have considered, staff cannot just be recruited here; they need in-house training before they can perform required tasks.

What the above shows is that there is an important connection between two factors—the ability to deploy workers from the company's own cadre when business requires a larger numbers of workers, and the rates of return on services supplied. When CMT suppliers or electronics assemblers receive returns of between 3 and 5 per cent, their capacity to keep extra workers in reserve is limited, if at all possible. But when suppliers secure a margin of 25 per cent or more[4], as in IT services, then they can afford to maintain a reserve of programmers.

IT service companies have evolved systems of work and payment that try to combine monitoring, incentives and commitment. The project team works together as a unit and thus fosters a commitment to the organization that is likely to be stronger than for programmers working on their own. This commitment is reinforced by an incentive system that relates to both team and individual performance (Ross School of Business, 2010). Infosys went so far as to give stock options to all employees at the time of its IPO, increasing the likely commitment of employees to the company.

---

[4] The margins of IT companies have been falling, because of both increasing competition and rising salaries. This has been much commented on in the Indian press.

However, the Indian IT industry has a systematic policy of removing the so-called poorest performers. Even when all employees surpass a required performance level, such as in a brilliantly performing team, there will always be a tail of poorer performers, based on the normal distribution or bell curve. This tail is removed and newcomers with the same skill sets are recruited. An official of the IT/ITES Technology Employees Centre (ITEC) pointed out, "IT employees would never have thought of 'bell curve' being so dangerous. Companies have been terminating employees with a 'C' rating, which stands for 'met expectations' ... the employees who get the lowest rating are terminated ... While employees are terminated for 'skill mismatch', companies like TCS go on recruiting new employees for the same skill", ITEC (quoted in John, 2015).

The replaceability of employees may work for run-of-the-mill programming tasks, but security of employment becomes crucial when moving to innovation. The current CEO of Infosys, one of the major Indian IT firms, has laid emphasis on innovation and automation, rather than continuing with the 'drudgery of repetitive tasks' (Vishal Sikka, quoted in Sharma, 2015). But would employees come up with cost cutting solutions and identify processes that could be automated if such innovations were likely to result in their jobs becoming obsolete? In manufacturing, for instance, what are called High Performance Work Systems are based on security of employment along with incentive payments for cost-reducing suggestions.

Even while writing this chapter, Infosys (along with Cisco world-wide) has abandoned the bell curve method of evaluating and replacing the bottom tail of workers (John, 2015). It is reported that Microsoft abandoned this practice in 2013, while Adobe and GE, which pioneered the bell curve method of assessment, abandoned it even earlier. 'From an employee's perspective it is the most hated process that you have. Even leaders are saying they are not getting what they want from the system', says Francine Katsoudas, chief human resources officer at Cisco (John, 2015).

The key question here is not that of the bell curve versus an alternative assessment system. Instead, it is this: what do you do with the assessment? If assessment were used to grade incentives then it might not damage employee morale, but if assessment were used to give 'pink slips', then it goes against the tenet of employment security, and is likely to damage employee morale.

The spread of knowledge and skill-intensive work is not confined to the IT sector. All sectors, whether agro-foods, garments and other labour-intensive sectors or auto components, have a higher knowledge requirement now than they did earlier. In auto components, there is a clear IT-ization of design and production processes (Nathan and Kalpana, 2007; Hirakawa et al., 2013). The simultaneous spread and separation of more knowledge-based processes from the routine tasks results in a continuing segmentation among the workforce, i.e., between those who are more skilled and even have cognitive and analytical skills and those who are operators or manual workers or programmers. Consequent upon this are also different employment systems, with Taylorist methods of control in routinized tasks and more worker-involved employment systems in knowledge-intensive work.

20.4.4 Market governance

Market governance is the traditional, hands-off relation. It can be carried out in standardized or commoditized products that are purchased on the market or off-the-shelf. Inputs purchased on the market are standardized. High codifiability makes it easy to purchase these standard inputs. Market governance often exists in the procurement of raw materials in value chains; when the skill requirements are minimal it can often lead to very exploitative conditions of forced labour.

Raw materials

Market governance often impacts the treatment of raw materials within a chain: margins are low and processing or manufacturing units prefer not to own raw material extracting units, since more value can be captured in the branding and marketing segments. For example, Tata Tea, mentioned earlier, gave up its ownership of tea plantations in favour of market-based purchase of tea from plantations that it earlier owned, establishing a market-based relationship with the plantations.

For both agricultural inputs, such as raw cotton, and minerals, the specifications are easily codified. In small-scale production, including artisanal mining, the knowledge required is low in complexity. These features allow for market governance of raw material production. The influence of local market conditions is high, promoting forms of forced labour. In coltan mining in the Congo (Nathan and Sarkar, 2011), financier-traders and armed gangs (including sections of the so-called national armies) control mining. They advance working expenses to the bonded workers, who get not more than a pittance, while the financier-traders sell the coltan to processors.

Of course, not all small-scale production of agricultural inputs or mining of raw minerals is carried out by bonded labour. Nonetheless, the dispersed nature of this production, whether in fields, small-scale mines or even households, lends itself to the prevalence of forms of forced labour, including bonded labour and child labour (Phillips and Mieres, 2014).

Employment systems in market governance of raw materials can be summarized as:

- When work is of low skill level, as in artisinal extraction, there may be no security of employment; low wages, generally below minimum wages, since there is a high level of debt bondage; supervision is often through use of force.

20.4.5 Hierarchical governance

Hierarchical governance occurs within firms, i.e., it is a matter of intra-firm transfers, as between MNC branches. Such MNC branches could exist in any type of production, but they are certainly likely to exist where there are intellectual property issues. For instance, MNC research institutes set up in China or India are owned by parent companies, who assume ownership of the technologies developed in these R&D branches. An important factor in hierarchical governance relationships is that profits of the MNC can accrue to its overseas branches carrying out off-shored tasks.

MNC branches

Two factors stand out in hierarchical governance: the first is that the profits the branches earn depend on intra-firm transfer pricing and could be higher than prices realized in market transactions. This would allow for better wage conditions in these branches than in locally owned units. This was observed in FDI-based garment units in Bangladesh, which generally had better conditions of employment, including wages and factory work conditions, than locally owned units (Ahmed and Nathan, Chapter 18). This was also the case at MNC branches as compared to non-branch assemblers of electronic products in China (Lee, Gereffi, and Lee, Chapter 18).

A second feature of MNC branches is the absence of large amounts of overtime. In electronics, it would seem that MNCs did not put the overtime burden of flexibility on their branches (Lee, Gereffi, and Lee, Chapter 18), but shifted this onto non-branch facilities.

Employment systems in hierarchical governance of MNC branches, carrying out production of varying skill levels, can be summarized as:

- More secure employment, lower overtime and higher wages than in comparable non-MNC units.

20.5 Governance types, knowledge and employment quality

In this chapter, we have identified a number of aspects of GVC relations that have an impact on the employment practices of GVC-supplier firms in developing countries. These aspects of GVC relations are knowledge requirements, the distribution of rents and flexibility of order systems. All of the above aspects of GVC relations, including distributional and business practices, work in the context of national institutional systems, the labour market and its regulation, or lack of it. Employment systems, in turn, are found to be related to governance systems in GVCs. We now examine possible patterns in the relations between governance types and employment systems.

The first type of employment system we consider is that of the high quality employment system (HQES). The core of the HQES is the link between security of employment, incentives and delegation of some shop-floor decision-making authority with process improvements initiated or suggested by workers. This leads to a high level of commitment, on the part of both employer and employee. While workers benefit through security and/or higher earnings, employers could benefit through productivity improvements.[5]

In contrast to the HQES, there is the non-standard employment system, alternatively called the low security employment system, low-quality employment system (LQES) or 'sweated labour.'[6] Security of employment is unlikely and workers are treated as replaceable or disposable (Wright, 2006). Wages are market-determined and generally cluster around the legal minimum wage.[7]

While we started with a binary classification into high-quality and low-quality employment systems, it has become clear that it would be necessary to distinguish degrees of quality. There could also be a moderate quality employment system (MQES), which could be one of fixed-term employment, a system that is frequent in Germany. As mentioned earlier, such fixed-term employment has been discussed in Indian business and trade union circles as an alternative to the current low-quality employment system of indirectly contracted labour (Nathan et al., 2013). It has been initiated in the BMW factory in India and is being formulated for existing contract labour. In addition an indefinite contract with, however, easy dismissal would turn a high-quality system into one of moderate quality.

A fourth type of employment system is that of forced employment, including both bonded and child labour. This is characterized by coercion both in being in employment (through economic or non-economic bondage) and during work (with

---

[5] See Ichinowski and Shaw (2003), for a review of the literature on the connection between employment relations and productivity in manufacturing. Also Atkin (1997); Arthur (1994); Macduffie (1995); Youndt et al. (1996); Applebaum et al. (2000).

[6] Dolado and Stucchi (2008) specifically analyse the adverse effect of temporary employee contracts on firm productivity in Spain.

[7] The terms and 'high-quality employment system', 'moderate quality employment system' and 'low-quality employment system', to my knowledge, have not been used in the literature. In the literature, there are 'high performance work system' and also 'high commitment work system' (Arthur, 1994; Macduffie, 1995; Atkin, 1997; Youndt et al., 1996; Applebaum et al., 2000; and Ichinowski and Shaw, 2003, for a survey of the literature). The latter term uses 'commitment' that could refer to commitment from both employer and employee. But 'high performance work system' refers not only to the nature of the employment relation, but also its likely or assumed effect on firm performance. In a way, this term assumes what needs to be established—that high-quality employment is associated with higher productivity.

unrestricted hours of work or physical and verbal abuse). Wages are very low, often just around the starvation level. Forced labour is not included in Table 20.2, in order to keep the discussion simple and concentrated on the main forms of employment relations in GVCs.

In Table 20.2, we combine firm or plant characteristics, in terms of the GVC segment and its knowledge base or governance type, with workers' characteristics, in terms of the quality of employment, here proxied by just one feature of employment, i.e., security of employment. But in extending this initial analysis, it would be useful to go beyond a single dimension of employment quality. There may be connections between security and, say, overall payments, but this need not always be so. There could be, as seems to be the case in IT services, a trade-off between the level of salaries and security. High salaries may be offset by low security and low salaries by high security. Consequently, in a more detailed analysis, it would be useful to use not just a uni-dimensional measure but a multi-dimensional measure. At present, however, since the object of this exercise is to derive a few readily analysable

Table 20.2 Governance types, knowledge and employment quality

		Employment quality (Q) as proxied by security		
		Low (1)	Moderate (2)	High (3)
Knowledge level (K) of out-sourced tasks	Low (1) captive governance	**Low knowledge; Low employment quality** **[A]**	Low Knowledge; Moderate Employment Quality [B]	Low knowledge; High employment quality [C]
	Moderate (2) modular governance	Moderate knowledge; low employment quality [D]	**Moderate knowledge: moderate employment quality** **[E]**	Moderate knowledge; High employment quality [F]
	High (3) relational governance	High knowledge; low employment quality [G]	High knowledge; moderate wmployment quality [H]	**High knowledge; high employment quality** **[I]**

categories we stick to the uni-dimensional measure of employment quality as being equal to employment security.

For both security or quality and knowledge base of the GVC segment, we consider three levels—high, moderate and low. The three knowledge levels also broadly correspond to the three governance types—low knowledge with captive governance; moderate knowledge with modular governance; and high knowledge with relational governance.[8] This gives us nine possibilities of the combinations of the two variables, knowledge and quality of employment, with three levels for each of the variables.

The above 3 × 3 matrix is a framework through which the links between governance and employment quality can be classified. But, we could apply a theory or hypothesis to this framework. The simplest one is that the level of employment quality is determined by or related to governance type of the GVC or the knowledge level of a task. This would give us the highlighted cells along the diagonal. Captive governance (garments, agro-foods and tourism) or low knowledge tasks lead to low-quality employment; modular governance (electronics, automobiles, and call centres) or moderate knowledge tasks lead to moderate quality employment; while relational governance (IT software services) or knowledge-intensive tasks lead to high-quality employment.[9] The segmentation of the labour market by employment quality is, in this analysis, related to the knowledge level of outsourced work and its governance relations.

The above is a technologically deterministic theory. Both governance and knowledge can be substituted by technology, and employment quality is then uniquely determined by technology—low-tech with low-quality employment, medium-tech with moderate quality employment, and high-tech with high-quality employment. On the basis of such a theory, the only way to improve employment quality would be to technologically, one might even say economically, upgrade.

However, the discussions in this book have shown that the relationships between governance types and employment systems are moderated by other GVC factors, such as the distribution of rents, and the flexibility of orders. They are also moderated by the context within which GVCs function, such as national employment regulatory institutions (including not only the state but

---

[8] We could also substitute low-tech, medium-tech and high-tech for the three knowledge levels.

[9] While there is no denying the importance of security of employment, the IT software employment system needs more analysis, since the nature of employment for a professional class, who could also work in high-earning self-employment or as consultants, could be different from that of other employees. Such employees may have job security within the industry, rather than in a particular firm.

also trade unions), and the state of the labour market. The state of the labour market includes not only matters like the overall or specific scarcity of workers but also additional social conditions, such as the gender relations within which workers exist.

How do these additional GVC factors, i.e., other than that of the knowledge level of the outsourced task, influence employment outcomes, in terms of quality of employment? When profits remain low and orders unstable, then the GVC relationship reinforces the poor quality of employment in low-knowledge tasks, as in garments and agro-foods. But redistribution of rents to supplier factories in a chain or stability of orders could together enable higher wages and more secure employment. However, there is nothing automatic about such a change, as has been emphasized in the literature on the connection between economic (i.e., firm) and social (i.e., worker) upgrading (Barrientos et al., 2011). As studies of Bangladesh (Ahmed and Nathan, Chapter 3) and Cambodia (Arnold, 2013) argue, workers' action is often needed to translate possible into actual improvements in employment conditions. A redistribution of rents and stable orders, along with the assertion of workers' power, could result in employment in garments' production becoming more secure and thus its quality move from A to B. If garment manufacture were carried out in an integrated firm, such as in an MNC branch, then the quality of employment could even move from A to C, i.e., become secure and involve some rent-sharing in wages.

National institutional factors also influence employment relations. For instance, China's Contract Labour Law (Tan et al., 2015) increased security of employment. China also has a regulation that restricts flexible labour to less than 10 per cent of the total workforce of an enterprise. There may well be breaches of these laws, but their very existence changes the context in which employment relations are decided upon. Similarly, the state of the labour market influences both security of employment and wages. At the national level in developing countries, the overall scarcity of labour can push up wages, as has happened in China (Chapter 9); local scarcity, increased by language problems, can lead employers to offer more secure employment, e.g., in Tamil Nadu, India (Nathan et al., 2013). Both labour regulations and the state of the labour market would strengthen the security of employment and move employment in both captive and modular governance towards the right in Table 20.1, i.e., in the direction of increasing employment security and quality.

Women's gender-based domestic responsibilities, on the other hand, negatively affect their participation in the labour market. The need to combine domestic responsibilities, especially child care, with paid work can lead women to chose insecure and low paid, but flexible work from home rather than more secure and better paid work in the factory (Pani and Singh, 2010). This would reduce the employment quality of women workers. On the other hand, as Tewari (Chapter 13) points out organizing women workers, enabling them to work in community locations close to home, along with eliminating brokers, could improve the quality of employment of piece-rated women workers in garments production.

Thus, GVC relations and institutional and labour force factors can influence in various ways the type of employment systems that prevail. These influences can be both positive and negative. In terms of Table 20.1, positive effects would move the employment relation in a right-ward or downward direction, while negative influences would move them in a left-ward or upward direction.

The organization of a GVC within a hierarchically governed but geographically dispersed MNC, could also affect employment systems. As we have seen in case studies of garment production in Bangladesh (Chapter 3), and electronics manufacturing in China and India (Chapter 14), wages are higher and there is less overtime in MNC branches than in outsourced units.

These systems of high-, moderate- and low-quality employments may well exist side-by-side within the same enterprise or firm. A firm may institute a high-quality system for its core functions and a low-quality system for non-core functions; or, as in a GVC, it may retain only core functions with a high-quality system, but outsource the non-core part of the overall production process. For instance, a garment unit that carries out full package supply, may have a high-quality employment system in its design centre, low-quality employment in its factory-based production lines, and forced labour, in the form of child labour, in home-based hand embroidery units.

Similarly, an IT software services firm may have high-quality employment with high incentive payments and work team-type work for its high-level software cadre, along with a moderate quality system for a large number of programmers who, though employed in indefinite contracts, face the insecurity of bell curve dismissal. In addition, there may also be low-quality employment for out-sourced services, such as transport, catering or housekeeping services.

One thing that GVC theory tells us is that it is not adequate to look just at products, but also at tasks or more complex processes (bundling together of a number of discrete tasks that make up, say, maintenance) that go into making a product. An additional point can be added—that it is necessary to distinguish between the knowledge levels of core and subordinate tasks in considering employment systems. Where ancillary tasks are out-sourced then they would be subject to the logic of out-sourcing, which is to pay labour its market price and this, in turn, would affect the quality of employment in that task. But when ancillary tasks are not out-sourced but carried out by employees of the same firm, then a share of the overall profits earned in that GVC segment could be shared or the overall system of employment relations of that firm may prevail in carrying out that ancillary task too. For instance, security or janitorial staff of an IT firm may earn a higher wage and have better quality employment, than would be the case were these provided as out-sourced tasks, as usually happens with transporting employees to and from work.

As mentioned above, we have left out of Table 20.1, forced employment systems, so as not to make its reading more complicated. Bonded and child labour are in hard to reach and dispersed production locations, such as fields or homes. These exist in various GVCs, whether in electronics, garments or even the automotive sector; un-free labour is usually involved either in the production of raw materials or in low productivity, labour-intensive tasks (Phillips and Mieres, 2014).

20.6 Conclusion

In concluding this chapter, it should be pointed out that the objective of the 3 × 3 matrix, based on parsimonious definitions of both GVC governance and the quality of employment, is to be able to formulate a theory of how GVC relations and employment systems are related. It is argued here that there is a broad relationship between the knowledge level of outsourced tasks and employment quality. Along with this, it has also been pointed out that other GVC factors (such as the distribution of rents or profits, and the flexibility of orders) have an impact on the quality of employment. In addition, national regulations and labour market conditions, including that of the gendered distribution of work, also affect employment quality in GVC segments.

This structure of relationships between the knowledge base of GVC production and the quality of employment systems is a first approximation, arrived at from, but going beyond, the case studies in this book. This relationship can be used to study employment systems in other GVC cases in order to see whether the pattern depicted here holds in a more general manner and identify the factors that modify that pattern.

References

Applebaum, Eileen, Thomas Bailey, Peter Berg, and Arne Kalleberg. 2000. *Manufacturing Advantage: Why High Performance Work Systems Pay Off*. Ithaca, NY: ILR Press.

Arnold, Dennis. 2014. 'Workers' Agency and Power relations in Cambodia's Garment Industry.' In *Towards Better Work: Understanding Labour in Global Value Chains*, edited by Arianna Rossi, Amy Luinstra and John Pickles. ILO and Palgrave Macmillan.

Arthur, J. B. 1994. 'Effects of Human Resource Systems on Manufacturing Performance and Turnover.' *Acad Manage J* 37 (3): 670–87.

Atkin, A. 1997. 'Hold the Production Line.' *People Manage* 3 (3): 22–27.

Barrientos, Stephanie, Gary Gereffi, and Arianna Rossi. 2011. 'Economic and Social Upgrading in Global Production Networks: A New Paradigm for A Changing World' *Int Labour Rev* 150 (3–4): 319–40.

Carswell, Grace and Geert de Neve. 2012. 'Labouring for Global Markets: Conceptualizing Labour Agency in GPNs.' *Geoforum.*

Coase, Ronald, 1988 (1937). 'The Nature of the Firm.' In *The Firm, The Market and the Law*, Chicago and London: The University of Chicago Press.

Damodaran, Sumangala. 2010. 'Labour in Leather GVCs.' In *Labour in Global Production Networks in India*, edited by Anne Posthuma and Dev Nathan. New Delhi: Oxford University Press.

D'Cruz, Premilla, and Ernesto Noronha. 2010. 'Employee Dilemmas in the Indian ITES-BPO Sector.' In *Offshoring and Working Conditions in Remote Work*, edited by Messenger, Jon and Naj Ghosheh. Geneva: ILO.

Dicken, Peter. 2007. *Global Shift: Mapping the Changing Contours of the World Economy.* 6th ed., London: Sage Publications.

Dolado, J. J., and R. Stucchi. 2008. 'Do Temporary Contracts Affect TFP? Evidence from Spanish Manufacturing Firms.' Discussion paper No. 3832, Institute for the Study of Labor, Bonn, Nov. 2008.

Gereffi, Gary, John Humphrey, and Timothy Sturgeon. 2005. 'The Governance of Global Value Chains.' *Rev Int Polit Econ* 12 (1): 78–104.

Gibbon, Peter, Jennifer Bair, and Stefano Ponte. 2008. 'Governing Global Value Chains: An Introduction.' *Econ Soc.* 37(3): 315–38.

Good Electronics Newsletter, 2015, 11-02-2015. Available at, https://bay174.mail.live.com/?tid=cm3hhGE86x5BG1HgAiZMFhFg2&fid=flinbox. Accessed February 13, 2015.

Hirakawa, Hitoshi, Kaushesh Lal, Shinkai Naoko, Norio Tokumane, eds. 2013. *Servitization, IT-ization and Innovation Models.* London: Routledge.

Holdcroft, Jenny, 2012. *The Triangular Trap: Unions Take Action Against Agency Labour.* Geneva: IndustriALL.

Ichinowski, C. and K. Shaw. 2003. 'Beyond Incentive Pay: Insiders' Estimates of the Value of Complementary Resource Management Practices.' *J Econ Persp* 17 (1): 155–80.

ILO. 2014. 'Ups and downs in the electronics industry: Fluctuating production and the use of temporary and other forms of employment.' Issues paper for discussion at the Global Dialogue Forum, Geneva 9–11, December, 2014.

ITEC. 2015. 'Stress on Making It Mandatory for IT Firms to Follow Labour Laws.' *ITEC Newsletters*, Issue 9, January. Available at, http://itecentre.co.in./node/232.

John, Sujit. 'Cisco Replaces Bell Curve Assessment with Feedback.' *The Times of India*, February 21.

Lakhani, T., S. Kuruvilla, and A. Avgar. 2013. 'From the Firm to the Network: Global Value Chains and Employment Relations Theory.' *Brit J Indus Relat* 51(3): 440–72.

Lan, Tu, John Pickles and Shengun Zhu, 2015. 'State Regulation, Economic Reform and Worker Rights: The Contingent Effects of China's Labour Contract Law.' *J Contemp Asia* 45 (2): 266–93.

Locke, Richard. 2013. *The Promise and Limits of Private Power: Promoting Labor Standards in a Global Economy.* Cambridge: Cambridge University Press.

Locke, Richard, Thomas Kochan and Michael Piore, 1999. *Employment Relations in a Changing World Economy.* Cambridge, MA: The MIT Press.

Macduffie, J. P. 1995. 'Human Resource Bundles and Manufacturing Performance: Organizational Logic and Flexible Production Systems in the World Auto Industry.' *Indus Labor Relat J* 48 (2): 197–221.

Nathan, Dev. 2013. 'Industrial Relations in a Global Production Network: What Can Be Done.' *Econ Polit Weekly* 48 (30): 29–33.

Nathan, Dev and Harishwar Dayal. 2014. *Better Practices on Contract Labour: Emerging Trends*, Planning Commission, CII and GIZ, (mimeo).

Nathan, Dev and V. Kalpana. 2007. 'Issues in the Analysis of Global Value Chains and Their Impact on Employment and Income in India.' *IILS Working Paper*, Available at, http://www.ilo.org/wcmsp5/groups/public/---dgreports/---inst/documents/publication/wcms_193512.pdf.

Nathan, Dev and Sandip Sarkar. 2010. 'Blood on Your Mobile?.' *Econ Polit Weekly.* 45 (43), Oct 23, 2010.

Neilson, Jeff and Bill Pritchard. 2009. *Value Chain Struggles: Institutions and Governance in the Plantation Districts of South India.* London: Wiley-Blackwell.

Penford, Carolyn. 2008. 'Off-shoring and Decent Work: Worlds Apart.' *Int J Comp Labour Law Indus Relat* 24 (4): 573–94.

Phillips, Nicola, and Fabiola Mieres. 2014. 'The Governance of Forced Labour in the Global Economy.' *Globalizations.* doi: 10.1080/14747731.2014.932507.

Ponte, Stefano and Timothy Sturgeon. 2014. 'Explaining Governance in Global Value Chains: A Modular Theory-Building Effort.' *Rev Int Polit Econ* 21 (1): 195–223.

Purcell, J. 1999. 'The Search for Best Practice and Best Fit in Human Resource Management: Chimera or cul-de-sac?' *Hum Res Manage J* 9 (3): 26–41.

Ross School of Business. 2010. *Tata Consultancy Services: Global Talent Leverage.* Case 1-428-835, Michigan, mimeo.

Samel, Hiram A. 2012. 'Upgrading Under Volatility in a Global Economy.' MIT Sloan School of Management. Available at, http://ssrn.com/abstract+2102643. Accessed on December 9, 2014.

Sarkar, Sandip, Dev Nathan, and Balwant Mehta. 2014. *Skills and Manufacturing in India: A Study of the Electronics and Automotive Sectors*, ILO and IHD, mimeo.

Sharma, Punit Itika. 2014. 'Sikka Suggests New 'Habits' to Infy Staff to Make 2015 a Year to Remember.' *Business Standard*, December 25.

Williamson, John. 1985. *The Economic Institutions of Capitalism: Firms, Markets and Relational Contracting*, New York: The Free Press.

Wright, Melissa. 2006. *Disposable Women and Other Myths of Global Capitalism*, New York: Routledge.

Youndt, M. A., S. A. Snell, J. W. Dean, and D. P. Lepak. 1996. 'Human Resource Management, Manufacturing Strategy and Firm Performance.' *Acad Manage J* 39 (4): 836–66.

Zhu, Shengjun, and John Pickles. 2014. 'Bring In, Go Up, Go West, Go Out: Regionalisation and De-localisation in China's Regional Production Networks.' *J Contemp Asia* 44 (1): 36–63.

21

The Double Movement of Labour in the Re-formation of GVCs

Meenu Tewari, Dev Nathan and Sandip Sarkar

21.1 Introduction

We began this book with a question about how employment relations are shaped and reshaped within a GVC world. We posed this question in the context of supplier firms in developing countries. That is, firms that produce intermediate products or carry out processes on contract for one or a few lead firms. Such firms, bound in contractual supply relationships within GVCs generally do not sell their product on the open market. As in other developing countries, such supplier firms have come to dominate the GVC landscape across Asia. What then are the implications for labour, working conditions and upward mobility for GVC-linked production within such 'supplier countries?' To address this question, we laid out a framework of GVC analysis in terms of 'vertical' relations between lead and supplier firms, and 'horizontal' relations between suppliers and labour. Vertical relations captured issues of distribution (i.e., of surplus across a value chain) as well as firms' business practices. Horizontal relations included wage determination and GVC interactions with national institutional contexts and norms.

Relations between lead firms and suppliers were in turn mapped on to and encapsulated within different forms of GVC governance. By governance we mean the management of relationships between lead firms and independent firms located at different nodes of the value chain, as well as the management of distribution and marketing. The intersection of these vertical and horizontal relationships, we argued, produced the differentiation and variation in outcomes experienced by different kinds of workers in different sectors, segments and geographies. These experiences are hardly static. The same vertical and horizontal intersections within GVCs and their juxtaposition with national institutions and norms have also helped transform the agency of work and workers themselves. Over time, these shifting interactions and the evolving agency of workers have also given rise to new spaces of protest, worker pushback, resistance and reform within GVCs, however, incremental or in-process they might be.

The individual case studies that form the core of this book illustrate this broad arc of change within GVCs with evidence drawn from Asia. They examine labour conditions in a variety of sectoral GVCs (agro-foods, garments, tourism, electronics, automobiles, call centres and IT software services) and in a number of Asian countries (Bangladesh, Cambodia, China, India, Indonesia, and Vietnam). The case studies employ a variety of conceptual lenses, ethnographic, political-economic and institutional, and examine a variety of supplier relations and governance types. Taken together, the findings present a portrait of two broad, seemingly opposing tendencies in labour relations within global GVCs and their Asian segments. The first is evidence of the variegated nature of labour relations within different kinds of GVCs, and how contingency, vulnerability and uncertainty are produced and re-produced within these chains, particularly among supplier firms anchored at the base of the value chain in developing economies across Asia. The second dynamic is of contestation of these vulnerabilities and of change and forward movement in labour conditions and employment relations within several GVC segments studied in this book.

What factors have led to these improvements, and why now? How can we, by way of conclusion, reconceptualize the coexistence of vulnerability and advance with respect to labour's place in value chains in supplier countries using the evidence that our cases identify?

In articulating a reconceptualization of labour relations within GVCs in Asia, we begin by summing up the evidence from the case studies. We then place these changes in the context of the trajectory of GVC evolution with respect to labour as a Polaniyan double movement, in the manner described in *The Great Transformation,* and also recently articulated and interrogated by other scholars such as Piore (2006; 2009) and Mayer and Pickles (2014). The first phase of the movement can be described as the early years of GVC emergence when institutions of the economy dominated over society and social relations, interpreted here as the period during which lead firms held unmitigated sway over global production relations. During this period, politically the Washington Consensus of market fundamentalism reigned supreme in matters of labour policy. Social analysis and industrial relations in the early period of GVC growth in the 1980s was a mirror image of the Washington Consensus. If neoliberal orthodoxy held that it was not desirable for states to intervene in labour markets, then the consensus within GVC observers was that the working classes had been so weakened by the global flow of footloose and mobile capital that workers, with their declining associative capacities (e.g., weakened unions), did not have the power to stage meaningful interventions on their own

(Castells, 1997; Burawoy, 2010). Even in countries where import-substitution industrialization led to long periods of dirigisme such as in China or India, and where working class organizations – at least in the large parastatals and public sector unions—did have some power in the pre-GVC, import substituting phase of the late 1960s and 1970s, the regulatory power of the state of organized labour was uneven and relatively disembodied from the start. This strength further unravelled with the neoliberal turn in the 1980s. In the other countries of Asia, the regulatory state played a mixed role: e.g., in South Korea and Taiwan, despite land reforms and liberal investments in public health and education, increases in real wages were consistently lower than increases in nominal wages and productivity till well after the region's industrial maturity (Amsden, 1989; 2001).[1]

This political economic and regulatory environment was mirrored in the evolution of global value chains and production networks in the 1980s. The first generation of GVC relations focused on the power of the industrial country-lead firms in driving buyer–supplier relations (Gereffi, 1994). But gradually this began to change as technology, market conditions and the agency of firms within GVCs evolved. The second generation of GVCs thus included modularity, the rise of full-package production and growing interdependence between lead firms and their large first-tier suppliers. Either as aggregators of orders (Li and Fung) or as co-generators of innovation and product development this phase of GVC evolution in the 2000s saw the rise of quite powerful intermediaries in value chains—nested between lead firms and lower-tier suppliers. The gains to labour, however, were limited. They came primarily from the rise of standards, systems of monitoring and the larger system of private governance that was driven not by workers themselves, but by firms under consumer pressure and media activism. With high profile cases of child labour and accounts of poor working conditions in lead firms' supplier factories reported in the press the reputational risks of public shaming began to push consumer facing firms to institute changes in labour conditions in their chains. These gains, many of which were top-down, did benefit labour, but unevenly (as we discuss in detail below).

However, real change in the conditions for labour began to percolate from the bottom-up in what can be called the third generation of value chain evolution.[2] In the face of growing analyses and consensus over the limits of lead-firm driven private voluntary governance, new centres of worker struggles have emerged in

---

[1] We thank John Pickles for drawing attention to the weakness of the regulatory state in early industrialization in most of Asia.

[2] We thank Charles Sabel for pointing out the three generations framework of global value chain evolution in earlier communications, as well as in his writing (2007).

new areas of worker concentration in the garments, electronics and automobile industries in Asia. The entrance of millions of women into the workforce and the sustained struggles of low-wage workers and informal workers have also contributed to shifting perceptions among workers of their own voice within the workplace and without. This has in many cases been accompanied a new rights-based political economy in some countries (e.g., MGNREGA in India). The agency of workers themselves is thus in the process of transformation and re-formation as reflected not only in changes in workplace conditions, but also in challenges to established gender relations, as several of our case studies illustrate (Chapters 7, 11, and 12) .

Thus, alongside examining the ways in which forms of upgrading of labour in GVCs have taken shape, as well as their successes and limitations, we also look at the manner in which participation in GVCs changes the framework of labour and broader relations outside the workplace, i.e., in society. Has there been an impact on gender relations within the household and within the communities of women workers? Thus, in this concluding chapter, we examine the interaction of labour and GVCs in terms of both the nature of employment relations and their interaction with broader social features of work, in particular, gender relations. At the end, we bring this trajectory back to the growing evidence today of a double movement in labour relations in GVCs, and how a re-formation of employment relations in GVCs may be underway in Asia. We ask what the current limits of these processes are and what may be done about them.

In detailing the analysis of this concluding chapter, we begin with the findings from the case studies in this book.

21.2 Findings of the book: Gains for labour amid contestation within GVCs

In Chapter 20, Nathan related employment systems of labour in GVCs in Asia to the governance types under which the tasks were being carried out. Three employment systems, low quality, intermediate quality and high quality, were distinguished and they were found to largely relate to captive, modular and relational governance types, respectively, which, in turn, relate to low, medium and high knowledge complexity of the tasks being performed in the GVC units. Most of the case studies in this book fall in the first two types of governance types and employment systems. In a sense, this is not a surprising statement—since most outsourcing has been of tasks that are relatively labour-intensive and of low to moderate knowledge complexity. Only in IT services do we find a high-quality employment system related to the high knowledge complexity of relational governance, where there is considerable interaction between customer and supplier in developing the services to be delivered.

The above statements need to be qualified by an important fact emphasized in recent GVC analyses as well as the task trade literature, that products of any type of complexity would embody within the tasks that are of differing knowledge complexities (Barrientos, Gereffi and Rossi, 2011; Autor et al., 2003; Acemoglu and Autor 2011). In fact, outsourcing of tasks in the production of a commodity is based on just such a distinction, with tasks of lower complexities generally being outsourced to regions with low factor costs. Correspondingly the production of a commodity, or even a GVC segment, may also contain within it employment systems of differing qualities. A low-knowledge product, such as garments or furniture, would embody high knowledge tasks, such as design or supply chain management, which require higher quality human capital and may be associated with higher quality employment systems. By contrast tasks such as basic assembly of products or cut-make-trim in the same sector—garments or furniture would likely be associated with low-quality employment systems, and different career ladders or prospects for mobility. In Chapter 20, Nathan also argued that the quality of employment, while mainly determined by the knowledge of the task being performed, can, however, be modified by national structural factors, such as the tightness of the labour market, or institutional factors, such as the strength of unions. It can also be modified by a redistribution of rents in favour of supplier firms.

In the light of the above, one of the more striking findings of the case studies is the extent to which gains have been possible for labour—or rather have been wrested—in the midst of contestation and unequal power within GVCs. These advances in the conditions of work, however, incomplete or tentative, are evident even in the supplier countries of Asia that this book reports on, and they are evident across various kinds of GVCs—captive, modular and relational. To illustrate, in the Bangladesh garment industry, even in the context of relatively captive GVC relations, minimum wages increased by 30 per cent in real terms in 2012 over 2000 (Chapter 3). With continued workers' unrest in 2013, there has been a further increase in garment workers' wages. After the Rana Plaza disaster, where more than 1,100 people lost their lives in a factory collapse, lead firms, brands and retailers committed considerable sums of money to invest in improving factory safety in the garment industry in Bangladesh. Discussions with those in the business community and newspaper reports suggest that there is evidence of improvements in factory safety on the ground in Bangladesh.

Similarly, in Chapter 2, we saw that garment workers in Cambodia and Vietnam have also seen an increase in wages, following the implementation of multi-stakeholder programmes such as better work and better enforcement of existing labour laws in these countries. Besides lead firms and governments, unions and labour advocates have played an important role in securing these gains. For example, labour activists and unions in many Asian countries (Bangladesh, Cambodia, China, India, Indonesia, Sri Lanka) have come together to formulate and push for a minimum living wage across Asia, called the Asia Floor Wage (AFW), that will blunt the effect of the regional race to the bottom wherein countries try to keep wages low to attract investment (Chapter 4). In the case of the agro-foods industry, we lacked the data to make temporal observations about wage increases over time, but some of the case studies reported strong increase in wages. In the case of the grape export production, for example, wages were generally higher than in other agricultural operations in the region. Indeed skilled workers in pack-houses did even better in getting retainers, thus overcoming the problem of seasonality in agricultural employment (Chapter 5).

In the tourism sector in China we found that despite the relatively weak bargaining position of local suppliers of various tourism-related services (largely due to over-supply), successful coordination between local governments and inter-enterprise collaboration and collective action among local suppliers enabled them to address the oversupply that was keeping firm earnings low. Over time this collaboration has played a major role in moving whole communities, as in Lijiang, China, out of poverty through their work in tourism (Chapter 7).

Chapter 9 by Lixia Mei and Jici Wang analyses the local effects of the phenomenon of labour shortage in the East coast of China, now the centre of world manufacturing. This shortage led to an increase in wages and, in turn, a movement of many firms, to the interior parts of China, where wages were lower and land also cheaper. While Richard Freeman (2005) had wondered how the labour movement would overcome the doubling of the world's labour force, in the largest country just about two decades of fast growth turned a labour surplus into a labour shortage. Wages went up even in labour-intensive sectors, such as furniture or footwear manufacture, leading to the Chinese policy of upgrading, regionalization and delocalization, briefly discussed in this chapter and elaborated in Zhu and Pickles (2014).

The cases of more modular governance covered in the book span across several sectors: high-quality garments in Sri Lanka, embellishment for the export market in Mewat, India, automobiles in India and electronics in China and call centres in India. The common thread that runs through them is that for different reasons and under different circumstances all the cases document some improvements in the conditions of work for workers in their respective GVC segments over time. These gains are still works in progress, but significant all the same. In Sri Lanka, women workers in the garment export sector have not only secured higher wages, but also a measure of respect as an important social force (Chapter 11). In Mewat's embroidery cluster a novel, layered form of collaboration between a government ministry, exporters, brands and worker-led NGOs helped provide stable jobs and fair wages to two communities of women in one of the most vulnerable, complex and invisible segments of the garment export trade—handwork and embroidery. This segment is not only hard to reach because of its location in the informal segment of the garment chain, but precisely that reason is usually mired in exploitative relationships. The gains were therefore striking (Chapter 13).

In the Indian automotive sector, the worker protest has forced lead firms to negotiate with unions to find ways to help reduce the sharp divide between permanent and contract (precarious) workers. Some of the large auto assemblers have begun, or at least announced their intention, to do away with the contract labour system in core production functions. This change occurred after the period covered in the study in Chapter 17 but was a result of strikes over the early years of this decade. In the electronics industry in China, wage increases and improvements in working conditions have occurred after numerous struggles at Foxconn and elsewhere (Chapter 15). In call centres in India earnings from employment are higher than for employment with comparable educational qualifications in other sectors outside IT (Chapter 19). With all their weakness and lack of career prospects, call centres have also become an important avenue for young women to challenge restrictive gender norms.

Examples of relational governance were analysed by only two chapters in the book—reflecting perhaps the paucity, still, of ties of greater reciprocity and more parity or at least mutual gains between suppliers and their global buyers within Asian GVCs. The two cases both came from the technical services and IT sectors in India, Chapters 18 and 19. Chapter 19 found that employees' earnings in the IT sector are substantially higher than for similarly educated employees in other (non-IT) service industries. There have also been increases in employees' earnings, partly as a result of growing demand and the resulting skill shortages. This has led to a seeming 'problem' of reduced competitiveness of the old model of IT service supply based on wage arbitrage (Sarkar, Mehta and Nathan, 2013), which has pushed subsets of the industry to higher value segments or automation associated with higher wages albeit a smaller labour pool. At the same time, in the lower skilled BPO segment, there is evidence of clear resistance by some workers–as well as their associations–against the Taylorist-style management systems that have dominated the majority of Indian call centres. There is also a growing opposition to what is identified (Chapter 20) as the bell curve system of firing that makes employment insecure. This resistance, in the context of tight labour supply and shifting market conditions has generated positive results for workers in these sectors.

In sum then, a majority of the case studies featured in this book show that across sectors (garments, agro-foods and tourism) and across various types of GVCs and governance forms (captive, modular and relational chains), there is evidence of some improvement in labour's conditions of work and of recent increases in wages. These improvements are often partial, uneven and incomplete; and the normative goals of safe, year-round, stable work at living wages with positive sum industrial relations is still a long way off. Still, there is evidence that subsets of workers have secured some gains in the course of participation in GVCs in Asia.

Given the often polarized rhetoric—and reality—around exploitation, exclusion and segmentation within GVCs that can keep wages low and workers and contractors trapped in dead-end jobs, why and how was labour able to secure improvements in its conditions of work in GVCs as the case studies in this book suggest? What broader conceptual lessons do our cases offer about the conditions under which workers can make gains within GVCs in Asia? It is to these questions that we turn next.

21.3 Structure, institutions and agency: Sources of labour reform within GVCs

In the Introduction to this book we highlighted that GVCs in Asia allow us to focus on labour relations within 'supplier countries,' where the predominant relationship of production was a contractual one. Most firms in Asia that participate in GVCs start out in lower segments of the value chain where they generally cannot sell their product on the open market but produce it on contract for buyers up the chain. We also distinguished between scenarios where the presence of many suppliers led to competition at the bottom and hence low margins and low profits, versus those did not. The question was how labour fares where most of the GVC participation in a country is of the contract or 'supplier' variety, particularly in labour-intensive segments where barriers to entry are low and price competition keeps wages down?

From a narrowly structuralist perspective one would expect only very limited scope for positive change in wages and worker well-being under these conditions. With suppliers in competitive markets there is not much scope for rents that could be shared with labour in the form of wage increases. The only structural change that could be identified as being beneficial to labour in these circumstances is that of increasing labour shortages (such as in China), stemming from an exhaustion of surplus labour in agriculture and its shift to industry (Lewis, 1954, Fang and Wang 2010; Nathan and Sarkar, 2014). Similar conditions can apply in upper tiers of the service sector with a turn toward more advanced services demanding higher skills (as was the case with IT professionals in India). In these national and sectoral cases, changes in structural market power (Wright, 2000 and Silver, 2003) could be identified as the factors behind increases in wages. One could add in the

Chinese case that workers' associational power, manifested through numerous strikes and other forms of struggle, had a role in turning market power into wage increases.

Our cases showed that while structural power can be translated into higher wages through workers also having associational power, there are other routes to wage increases besides the presence of active associational power, unlike the analysis of Selwyn (2007). These structural shifts are associated with conditions in the industry segment and product markets, and they can be passive or they can be deliberative. For example, in the passive category completely unorganized workers, such as IT employees, managed to get higher wages largely through exploiting supply shortages. A similar outcome was evident in the agro-food sector, where higher production standards in the export sector led to wages being higher in the grapes GVC relative to in domestic production, despite the absence of any form of union organization among GVC grape workers (Chapter 5). The higher quality standards of GVC production led to demand for higher quality labour and produced higher wages in export segments as compared to production for the domestic market. At the same time, some of the case studies suggested that structural drivers, such as labour shortages can also under certain conditions be conducive to more *deliberative* collective action that can lead to labour organizing itself and developing associational power. This was the case in the Chinese Tourism industry described in the book. (Chapters 6 and 7)

Where structural changes cannot account for the observed improvements in labour conditions, we need to map the institutional routes and processes through which contestation in GVCs is actively overcome—by labour, their advocates, firms and governments—to produce change. It is to these institutional shifts that we turn next.

21.4 First movement of labour relations in GVCs in an era of unmitigated lead-firm control

Following Mayer and Pickles (2014) and Piore (2008), we see elements of a Polanyian double movement playing out in GVC labour relations as they have evolved over the past 40 years. In the first phase, when GVCs first rose to prominence in the late 1970s, there was a relative disembedding of lead-firm driven GVCs and their globally dispersed production networks from institutions that traditionally governed labour practices, namely national governments, national tri-partite industrial relations and national unions. As production spilled out beyond national boundaries, lead firms had virtual sole, private control over labour processes and labour relations in their cross-border production chains.

In response to some of the excesses of this relatively unmitigated control by lead firms of suppliers and workers in their chains, and their price-driven labour practices, a pushback emerged in the mid-1990s. These excesses, dramatized by workplace tragedies ranging from the 1993 Kader Toy Factory fire in Thailand to the 2013 Rana Plaza factory collapse in Bangladesh, have given rise to counter-movements to improve conditions of work, with attempts at multiple levels to re-embed GVCs into the wider institutions that govern labour practices. During the early phase of the spread of GVCs in the post-OPEC 1970s, the condition of labour within GVC-based operations was influenced by two factors. On the one hand, the lead firms, chiefly in labour-intensive buyer-driven sectors such as garments, shoes and toys, sought to gain competitive advantage by cheapening the costs of production through shifting manufacturing to low-wage locations in East Asia. On the other hand, East Asian economies that had newly embarked on the path of industrialization sought employment to promote structural transformation through the Lewisian transfer of surplus labour from agriculture at a relatively constant real wage rates. Participating in labour-absorbing manufacturing activities was an attractive path to job creation and economic growth for many Asian economies.

The justification for this convergence on market ideology by buyers, suppliers and supplier country governments lay in what Polanyi called a shared notion of 'progress', '... an economic system consisting of markets and under the sole control of market prices ... appeared as the goal of all progress' (Polanyi, 1957, p. 249). An economic policy based on market-determined prices and wage rates is of course generally labelled as 'neoliberalism', but a better characterization of it would be market fundamentalism, or an economic policy based on not intervening in factor markets and allowing factor prices to be determined by the market. In line with this policy of market-determinism, public interventions in labour markets, such as the regulation of minimum wages, hours of work, benefits and so on were taken as obstructions in the initial formulation of the 'ease of doing business' criteria of multilateral institutions such as the World Bank (Mayer and Pickles, 2014; Dasgupta, 2014). This had evolved into the 'Washington Consensus phase of GVCs' by the mid-1990s.

The Washington Consensus period of GVCs can be characterized, following Gereffi and Mayer (2006), as a period marked by a deficit of global governance, in the sense of an absence of institutions—public or multilateral—to regulate lead-firm driven, private, GVC-style relationships between buyers, suppliers and labour. There were national institutions, stronger or weaker, that were supposed to regulate the national labour conditions and labour relations at least for national employers, if not MNCs and absentee global buyers. But the essence of a GVC world is that national employers, many of whom themselves supply to MNC-lead firms on contract, are not the sole or final arbiters of labour relations; such relations depended crucially and in many ways on the unregulated relationships between global lead firms and their suppliers.

Along with this unregulated relationship between lead firms and suppliers, the Washington Consensus phase of hard budget constraints, privatization of social welfare, and deregulation saw an erosion, even a dismantling, of the regulation of the relationship between national manufacturers and labour. The deregulation of labour markets in the context of surplus labour, further weakened labour's bargaining power within GVCs, producing a 'race to the bottom' where buyers drove hard cost-cutting bargains in exchange for orders and hence jobs.

In this period, when capital held unmitigated sway over social relations, social analysts were generally pessimistic about the possibilities of labour winning any gains in the struggle within GVCs (Castells, 1997; Burawoy, 2010). The mobility of capital, the dispersion of production, and competition among workers were all held to have strengthened capital and in the bargain weakened labour. The low or even non-existent rents of developing country suppliers and manufacturers did not seem to leave much scope for increasing wages. For example, Castells, in his analysis of the developing network society, virtually wrote off any possible role for labour: 'Torn by internationalization of finance and production, unable to adapt to the networking of firms and the individualization of work, and challenged by the engendering of employment, the labour movement fades away as a major source of social cohesion and workers representation' (1997, p. 354). Similarly, Burawoy expressed an 'uncompromising pessimism' against what he termed the Polyannish expectation of a Polanyi second movement arguing that the 'commodification of nature, money and labour… destroys the very ground upon which a "counter-movement" would be built' (2010, p. 312).

At the micro-institutional level studies of labour-intensive manufacturing in developing countries (mainly Asia and Latin America) highlighted the constraints faced by low-wage workers, especially as the labour force in developing markets became more feminised. The limited room to manoeuvre for women workers with family responsibilities, for example, and the low prices paid to suppliers, as well as buyers' and global brands' opposition to union organizing, were cited by many scholars as reasons for the structural weakness of the new class of women workers in developing countries (Elson and Pearson, 1981; Heyzer, 1986; Ong, 1987; Ghosh, 2001). In addition, women workers, as new entrants into the workforce, were often socially stigmatized, which itself made it difficult for them to organize (Gunawardana, 2007).

On the whole, market conditions in low-wage occupations in labour-surplus developing economies were not conducive to increases in wages and improvements in working conditions. What then happened to enable labour to move beyond market-based wage determination, even in low-skilled areas, such as cut-sew-trim and assembly work in garment production?

21.5 Build-up to the second movement of labour relations

In this section, we explore seven sources of change and transformation within the seemingly rigid and closed labour relations in the first movement of GVC production. These sources of change were shaped by agency, enforcement, as well as by shifting institutional norms and firm responses to a series of high profile labour tragedies within GVC production (child and unfree labour, fires, and factory collapses) that helped open up new spaces for change, however, uneven or incomplete they were.

21.5.1 Initial responses: Accountability and the rise of third-party monitoring and enforcement

In response to the growing media spotlight on a series of serious labour violations in supplier factories of GVCs, starting with the well-publicised case of Nike's suppliers in East Asia a number of social actors became involved in reforming GVCs in ways that yielded a somewhat better position for labour. Some actors were in the home countries of the GVC-lead firms, others were in the manufacturing countries, and yet others were in international agencies and government.

Consumers emerged as the first and strongest voice against poor labour conditions in supplier countries, expressed as brand boycotts and other forms of pressure on the reputation of consumer facing companies from whom they bought products such as footwear, garments, toys and so on. Even while consumers in industrial markets benefited from low prices of garments and other commodities produced through GVCs based on wage arbitrage between developed and developing economies, media reports of sweatshop conditions in offshore supplier factories created moral outrage among a subset of consumers, leading to the rise of ethical trade as well as credence goods (Humphrey and Schmitz, 2008). Campus-based student organizations joined trade unions in home countries to put pressure on image conscious brands to change labour practices in their overseas supplier factories (Quan, 2008). Through their consumption decisions consumers—or a subset of them—made clear that they cared about the conditions under which the products they purchased were made and could penalize brands by withholding demand. Indirectly, this outrage against brands that were seen as violating labour standards abroad perhaps drew on a deeper economic anxiety over deindustrialization and the job-loss that had resulted from the outsourcing of production to low-wage countries by these same brands. Nevertheless, the moral economies of consumption helped foster a link between consumers in rich countries and labour in developing countries (Evans, 2010).

This was not, as Robert Ross (2014) points out, the power of the atomized, individual consumer that was the cornerstone of Hayek's choice-theoretic analysis (1945). Rather, this pushback against global brands and companies was an expression of the power of the organized consumer, or the *political consumer* (Beck, 2002, p. 7, italics in original) who, through membership in a variety of associations (University Students Against Sweatshops (USAS) and civic organizations (consumer advocacy groups and labour organizations such as Worker Rights Consortium (WRC), later the brands-sponsored FLA and the Ethical Trade Initiative) not only concentrated the knowledge made available through various sources, but also utilized the power of social opinion, even before the advent of Internet-based social media, to influence the buying practices of image conscious brands (Beck, 2005).

Brands and lead firms' responses to sweatshop exposes in the media resulted in several specific actions by them: the first and most prominent was the adoption by most of the brands of company codes of conduct that were expected to govern their relationship with suppliers. These codes were voluntary, but to participate in their value chain suppliers were required to adhere to a set of production and labour standards and working conditions. The monitoring of compliance with company codes was eventually shifted to third-party actors that gave rise to a 80 billion dollar auditing industry (Miller et al., 2011, p. 10). Simultaneously consortia of companies in alliance with multilateral NGOs established ethical trade practices, branding and labelling—to signal compliance. Labelling was particularly used in the matter of child labour, which was initially the focus of many consumer campaigns. The rise of these voluntary codes of conduct resulted in a broader 'privatization of labour enforcement' driven by lead firms and other private, non-profit and multilateral actors, often outside the nation state (Applebaum, 2004; Locke, 2013).

With this new form of labour enforcement, the auditors or certifiers, and their sponsors, the brands and retailers, turned into the active agents in the process of monitoring labour standards (Ross, 2014). Workers and their unions, wherever they existed, were brought into the auditing process only to be interviewed about standards. They did not drive the process of setting, monitoring or securing implementation of standards.

21.5.2 Limits of private governance

As several recent studies have shown, there is a growing consensus that the privatization of labour enforcement of the 1990s and early 200s had limited beneficial results, and left large areas of labour violation quite untouched (Locke, 2013; Barrientos et al., 2010); Ahmed and Nathan on Bangladesh (Chapter 3); and the papers in Bair et al. (2014) are some examples of assessments of the effectiveness of the private labour enforcement process. The findings of these studies suggest that enforcement was most successful in the case of child labour, and somewhat successful in matters that could be easily checked, such as the provision of toilets and other such facilities on the shop floor. In other words, private compliance worked to some extent in areas where reputational risk directly threatened business—such as in the case of consumer facing lead firms coordinating their GVCs brands and retailers were much more exposed to risk of reputation than in more arm's-length markets.

Equally, at the suppliers' end, in cases such as child labour, what was important was the threat of losing business. This calculation was clear in the case of Bangladesh and India, where suppliers reported that it was the threat of losing business that forced them into compliance with 'big-ticket' company codes such as eliminating child labour from the shop floor (for Bangladesh, Chapter 3; for India, Carswell and de Neve 2012). But even in the matter of child labour, successful interventions combined private threats with support from government agencies (Departments of Labour and Child Welfare that monitored conditions and implemented projects), civil society groups (national and international NGOs that implemented projects), and international organizations (such as the ILO and UNICEF). The media also played an important role and was often instrumental in publicizing child labour abuse.

By contrast, however, company codes of conduct and voluntary compliance did poorly in matters that were less visible, such as forced overtime in response to tight turnaround times, or the non-provision of statutory benefits, such as a contributory Provident Fund (PF). Audits were less stringent and often neglected the lower levels of supply chains, such as home-based work. And, as the series of factory fires and collapses across Asia (from the 1997 Kader toy factory in Hong Kong to the 2013 Rana Plaza building collapse in Bangladesh) show, they failed to detect or bring to light glaring structural defects in wider supplier production systems.

The impacts and limitations of private compliance have been discussed in numerous case studies, including our book, but a recent compilation of data from audits conducted by the brands-sponsored Fair Labour Association (FLA) in more than 100 supplier units in the garment sector in Asia by Daniel Vaughan-Whitehead (2014), is illustrative. The study found that 48 per cent of companies inspected pursued dual record-keeping, one set of books shown to the auditors and the other remaining concealed; this was more prevalent in Bangladesh, China, Sri Lanka and Turkey. Two-thirds or 66 per cent of companies reported under-payment of wages; this problem was acute in India (82 per cent) and China (71 per cent). Minimum wages, which are most often well below any living wage (ILO, 2008), were not paid by 20 per cent of firms, more in India (45 per cent) but also in Vietnam and China. Insurance was not provided to workers by 43 per cent of firms. Some 32 per cent of companies did not provide paid holidays, but paid holidays were, in any case, not effective in this context, since the piece rate system meant that workers, bent on maximizing their earnings, often did not take the holidays. There were high levels of overtime, and the average working time per week was 71 hours. Workers, bent on maximizing earnings and thus remittances to families, preferred high levels of overtime, but were often exploited. In 52 per cent of companies, workers were not aware of how their wages were calculated.

Surprisingly, however, the study found a substantial presence of unions, or other forms of workers' representation among the audited factories. Some 42 per cent of units had unions, while another 35 per cent had workers' councils. Yet, despite the presence of worker representation, there was little evidence that workers and their organizations, where they existed, were involved in setting or monitoring standards in any significant way.

In sum, then, Vaughan-Whitehead (2014) shows there is a long way to go in terms of a widespread living wage and other aspects of decent work. As Locke put it, in a world of fast fashion and cut-throat price-competition, 'Suppliers are asked to invest in improving labour and environmental conditions but are pressured to (and rewarded for) producing ever-cheaper goods with shorter lead times', (Locke 2013, p. 35). Indeed, the pressure on suppliers to both reduce costs and invest in improving labour conditions without price supports—public or private—stands out as a central point of contention and contestation within several analyses of GVCs (e.g., Anner, Bair and Blasi, 2014). Nevertheless, reputational risk to non-compliant consumer-facing buyers did generate the first source of pushback against the power of lead firms in the emerging second movement of labour relations in GVCs.

21.5.3 Institutionalizing the 'market for labour standards'

Second source was the effort in the mid-2000s to harness these moral economies of consumption and institutionalize them through programs of 'better work'. In arguing that labour standards could improve under globalization, Elliott and Freeman (2003) maintained that there exists a 'market for labour standards', meaning that some customers could respond to information about better labour standards with a willingness to pay a higher price for the product. This willingness to pay a higher price could then be used as a form of pressure on the brands and retailers.

This link between reputation-conscious brands and better labour standards was turned into an international programme that brought together brands and suppliers in a labour standards programme. Organized by the ILO and funded by the International Finance Corporation (the World Bank's private sector finance wing), the Better Work (BW) programme started in Cambodia with providing an incentive to improve labour conditions by giving them preferential access to the US market. When the programme was extended to other countries with a so-called business case for improved standards by arguing that improving labour conditions would increase productivity. Initially, those suppliers that met threshold standards were given assured access to the US market. This approach was then generalized to brands and retailers who bought the labour standards' performance reports of supplier firms, on the assumption that these reports would reinforce their brand reputations. But whether or not brands benefit through premium prices or preferential access for products that meet minimum labour standards, they at least did not suffer the risk of consumer actions.

Chapter 2 assesses the extent to which efforts such as better work (BW) have helped improve labour conditions among suppliers. Starting in Cambodia, the programme has spread to Vietnam and Indonesia and now also Bangladesh in Asia, besides Nicaragua and Haiti in Central America and Lesotho in Africa, and Rossi concludes that there has been some improvement in labour standards as a result of BW interventions. Others have shown that suppliers working for reputation-conscious brands have better labour standards than suppliers working for less reputation-conscious brands and retailers (Oka, 2010). While there have definitely been some improvements in labour standards of suppliers within these programs there still are significant limits. In Cambodia, reports of mass fainting by workers in garment and shoe factories show that there is still some distance to go in moving from poverty-level wages to achieving relatively decent work (Arnold, 2014). Still, union activism did help stop forced overtime, even as low wages compel workers to continue to seek more work to support themselves and their families.

21.5.4 Cross-border alliances and the federation of unions

GVC-based investment in Asia began with a strong anti-union bias. Most Special Economic Zone (SEZ) enclaves did not allow workers the right to form organizations, though units outside SEZs did not have such restrictions. But ironically, the presence of new forms of union activity have grown in places where large numbers of workers demand or require worker intermediation to be able to deal with grievances of workers directly, or through workers' councils, and hence have been supported in various guises by large factories (Miller et al., 2011). But the nature of these unions and other workers' organizations can be quite varied, from state-led unions in China and Vietnam to national and local unions in many countries and even NGO-type pro-worker organizations in Bangladesh, or women's organizations, for that matter. There are also federations of unions in particular industries, most famously the International Textile, Garment and Leather Workers Federation (ITGLWF), which, along with the Metal Workers' and other Federations, is now part of the umbrella federation, IndustriAll.

The importance of new forms of union engagement with buyers and brands is illustrated by the role of the ITGLWF in entering into a multi-national agreement with the Spanish firm Inditex, the owner of the brand Zara, and the innovator of the 'fast fashion' system of changing product lines every few weeks, as against the earlier standard seasonal fashions.[3] Under this Global Framework Agreement (GFA) or International Framework Agreement (IFA) between Inditex and ITGLWF, Inditex agreed to the application of the ILOs core labour standards throughout the company's supply chain; the extension of the agreement to all workers, '... whether directly employed by Inditex or by its external manufacturers or suppliers'; and for the scope of this agreement to include workplaces not represented by the ITGLWF (IndustriAll, 2014).

At the renewal of the Inditex-IndustriAll GFA in July 2014, the GFA covered some 6,000 factories and 1 million workers worldwide (IndustriAll, 2014). The agreement applies to all categories of workers, whether those of contractors, sub-contractors, or home workers. The hiring of contractors and sub-contractors without prior approval of Inditex is forbidden and contractors are held responsible for employment conditions in sub-contractor organizations. But as IndustriAll admits, '... the task [of implementing and monitoring] is not easy due to the fragmentation of production and the high number of subcontractors who themselves subcontract production' (IndustriAll, 2014a, p. 9).

At the end of 2012, there were 88 functional GFAs (Helfen and Fichter, 2013). They represent a new possibility in the improvement of labour standards, an international agreement on labour standards between a GVC-lead firm and an international workers' federation. The limitation of this GFA, however, is that it remains a 'statement of intent' and is not a legal document that is justiciable: 'While [GFAs] aim to establish certain rules that regulate the corporation's labour practices at the global level, they are not collective bargaining agreements that can be enforced in national or international law' (Stevis and Boswell, 2007, p. 175). But they constitute, as Helfen and Fichter put it an 'arena', a political space that is 'still contested and emergent, and hence more applicable to processes of

---

[3] For an analysis of fast fashion and workers see Plank et al. (2014).

institutionalization' (2013, p. 55). Institutionalization of global labour relations could, at some point, lead to an International Labour Court, as suggested by Miller et al. (2011) and Nathan (2013).

Between global unions, as in G4S and DHL, and GFAs what is being carried out is the creation of a new transnational or even global sphere (Beck, 2005, p. 239), this time in the realm of labour relations. These organizations and agreements are still in their infancy. But they point to the stirrings of the global organization of labour in the process of re-creating itself as a countervailing power in globalization.

21.5.5 Development of workers' agency

Looking at and beyond our case studies, a picture emerges of the development of workers' agency in GVCs in developing countries. This development has been studied to a greater extent in the context of labour-intensive manufacturing industries, especially garments, but there are similar instances of organization among automobile workers in India (Jha and Chakravorty, Chapter 17) and electronics workers in China (Chan, Ngai and Selden, Chapter 15).

Pun Ngai (2005) and Chang (2012) show, for example, that the creation of a workforce in labour-intensive GVCs was simultaneously one of feminization as of the growing migration from rural to the free-trade zones on the urban border and the incorporation of these 'new' and 'hyphenated' workers into industrial identities. This process seeded agency. To start with, most of the workers in the labour-intensive, assembly GVCs of Asia were often were first-generation women migrants from rural areas. But 'initially women workers saw themselves as temporary workers. Gradually, over time, their self-perception shifted, giving them a new consciousness as workers' (Rosa, 1994). As workers, they identified with their own common interests. Over time, seeing themselves as no longer temporary, many developed a stake in investing time to secure an increase in wages and improvements in working conditions.

Ironically, FTZs often indirectly helped carve out collaborative spaces that aided labour. For example, in many free trade zones, dormitories were set up, whether by factories, local authorities or merely by workers in village houses. On the one hand, these highly monitored institutions were ways of controlling labour—e.g., determining how and when they would be bussed to work and when they could be brought back (Ngai, 2005). On the other hand, by putting many workers together, they also contributed to enabling informal relationships and social and class identification among them (Chang, 2012). Social experiences were also shared, including negative ones of women workers being derided as 'morally loose' (Gunawardana, 2007, p. 79; Lynch, 2007, p. 22). Their distinct lifestyles and consumption all contributed to the shared social experiences that have been pointed to as important for developing class interests (Thompson, 1984, p. 939).

These experiences have, in many cases, given rise to new institutions that directly or indirectly afforded greater agency to workers. Among women in Sri Lanka (Gunawardana, 2007) and India (Jenkins, 2013) gradually various kinds of 'pre-union' organizations emerged among factory workers, such as credit unions, or Self-Help Groups (SHGs), while in Sri Lanka and Bangladesh, women's organizations, and not unions, were often the first to link up with women workers. These were important hubs of communication around which discussion about social justice could develop (Jenkins, 2013). These efforts were supported by the ITGLWF, international NGOs and also governments.

The development of agency was stimulated not only by factories with large numbers of workers, but also the agglomerations of industries in some areas. Coastal China, with up to 100 million workers is the new heartland of world manufacturing, and has supply chain cities and regions for every type of product. Countries in Southeast Asia have large concentrations of labour, around Bangkok and along the coast in Thailand, Kuala Lumpur and Penang in Malaysia, Jakarta-Bogor in Indonesia, Metro Manila in the Philippines, and so on. India has its centres of millions of workers around the capital, Delhi; around Chennai in the South; the Pune-Mumbai belt in the West; all of which have emerged as new centres of worker resistance. As Shyam Sundar asks provocatively in his paper on industrial conflict in India, 'Who Said All Is Quiet on the Industrial Front?' (2015, p. 43). Bangladesh has two large areas of concentration of garment workers around the two cities of Dhaka and Chittagong, which together account for about 5 million workers. These include workers in all types of industries: labour-intensive units in low-tech industries, such as garments or leather products, mid-tech industries such as the automotive and machinery sectors, and high-tech electronics manufacturing.

In a way, the splitting up of production through GVCs has weakened, even destroyed the power of old centres of production (especially labour-intensive production) in the industrial West, but it has also created new centres of manufacturing power across Asia. In such areas of workers concentration, organizations, whether formal or informal, have spread from individual factories to encompass regions (Chapters 9 and 13).

IT software and BPO employees are also similarly concentrated in a few locations in India, i.e., Bengaluru, Chennai, Hyderabad and the Delhi National Capital Region (NCR), which also includes Gurgaon and NOIDA. IT employees do not see themselves as workers but as professionals. However, as discussed in Chapter 18, there are various forms of resistance to the Taylorist mode of work control. These are largely individual or in small groups and seem reminiscent of James Scott's *Weapons of the Weak*. However, the possibility of their developing into something more substantial and even organized cannot be ruled out.

21.5.6 Social upgrading: Looking beyond wages

Income alone does not qualify employment as decent work: work also needs to be more enjoyable and engaging for workers. If auto-assemblers can replace Fordist–Taylorist assembly lines that utilize low-skill workers performing repetitive jobs with Quality Control Circles (QCCs) that utilize multi-skilled workers with incentives for improvements, can the same be done for IT service sector and call centre jobs? There have been steps taken to create a better ambience at work in major Indian IT firms, but these mainly deal with the more creative aspects of work. The shift to better quality jobs, rather than an army of programmers and operators supervised in a service version of Taylorist management, is something that needs consideration. Given that these tasks are necessary and create large-scale employment, it would be useful to pay attention to improving the quality of these jobs. Studies of IT service employees point to two different kinds of issues. On the one hand, Sarkar and Mehta (2010) show that the earnings of employees in this sector have gone up and they earn a premium over similarly qualified employees in other sectors. The existence of such a premium continues to show up in their study of the 2011–2012 Indian labour force data (Chapter 19). On the other hand, Chapter 18 points out the stress of repetitive relatively dead-end work even in these high-tech service sectors. It remains to be seen how these more educated workers craft pathways of their own mobility.

21.5.7 GVCs and gender relations: Contestation and reconstitution

The early focus on the manner in which participation in GVCs affected gender issues has shifted in recent years to a discussion on the ways in which gender relations and practices themselves constitute the way in which GVCs are structured and function (Bair, 2010). However, while attention is paid to how gender relations frame women's work in GVCs, the issue of how work in GVCs enables a contestation of patriarchal gender relations has not been addressed sufficiently. Work is not just work, but also the creation of social relations of various types, including gender relations. While working in factories and offices, do women not also help to remake gender relations? Does participation in GVCs enable women to turn patriarchal relations into, as Castells asked, '... a contested domain, rather than a sphere of cultural reproduction' (1997, p. 2–3)?

The impact that women's work in GVCs has on gender relations depends in part on the nature of existing gender relations and initial conditions. This impact would be different in, say, China which went through a substantial reworking of Confucian gender relations during the Communist revolution. In such a situation, the GVC-based introduction of CMT or electronics assembly factories was not novel in initiating a new class of women into the world of factory work. What was novel in the Chinese situation was the mass migration of rural women to work in urban factories.

On the other hand, in Southeast and South Asia, it was the garment and electronics assembly factories that introduced women to working in the non-domestic sphere. The women entering these factories were often first-generation factory workers, or even carried out assembly operations at home. As a growing number of women became income earners, assumptions about their role in the household and financial dependence on other male members of the household had to be contested in order for women to continue in these new jobs. Gaining the ability to contest existing patriarchal gender relations is an important component of social upgrading for women.

At the basic level, the act of earning an income is a starting point of contestation. 'Garment employment and industrial upgrading in Sri Lanka have, literally, put more earnings in the hands of female workers and threatened previously existing patriarchal power in significant ways' (Goger, Chapter 11). Twenty-five per cent of women employed in the IT services sector are the chief wage earners for their families (NASSCOM and Mercer, 2009). Some feminist theories stress the importance of women's independent economic positions as important to improving their bargaining position within the household (e.g., Amartya Sen's analysis of household bargaining using the game theoretic model of cooperative conflict). This improvement in women's position is reflected in a number of ways. Simple matters, such as the freedom to choose their own clothes as mentioned by women in Bangladesh or independent consumption decisions (Kelkar et al., 2001). Independent income also allowed women to go beyond drudgery, even if their workloads increased. Women in the IT services sector in India mentioned that 'they were happy to be away from the everyday drudgery of home work for at least a few hours' (Kelkar et al., 2002).

Other aspects of work in GVCs, such as night shifts are ways in which GVC-work challenges existing gender norms. After demands by women in Chennai working in the leather GVCs, the Indian Factories Act was amended in 2005 in order to allow night work by women (Damodaran, 2010). This change in the law is surely a redoing of gender rules and not merely a recreation of existing rules. Working the night shift importantly requires being mobile in the night. This too is a challenge to existing norms of women's seclusion, leading to the mobility–morality narrative being recodified (Patel 2011, p. 48). For instance, in Bangladesh, the regular movement of women garment workers across public spaces challenges the earlier norm of *purdah* or women's seclusion (Hossain, 2012). To counter cultural stereotypes that stigmatized women working at night, or even working for an income at all, '... [Call centre] organizations put in considerable effort to convince society that women working at night occupy perfectly safe and decent work environments' (Chapter 18). In the garments industry in Sri Lanka too owners worked to change their 'their image ... [which was] a problem they needed to fix' (Chapter 11). But there is the continuing and challenging problem of ensuring women's safety as they traverse public spaces, particularly at night.

Whether in garments, call centres or even IT software services, women are largely confined to the lower rungs of the career ladder. In IT services, for instance, at the entry level, there is a fairly equal representation of women and men, but at higher levels, women form just around 20–25 per cent of the workforce (NASSCOM and Mercer, 2009). But even here it should be noted that the figure of 30 per cent of women in technical positions in the IT industry (NASSCOM and Mercer, 2009) is higher than in any other sector of industry. The high attrition of women in the IT sector is related to their continuing domestic duties. As Noronha and D'Cruz (Chapter 18) point out, this is related to life events such as marriage or pregnancy, or to domestic responsibilities, which make it harder for women to accept transfers (Kelkar et al., 2002). In the garments industry, Carswell and de Neve (2012) point out that women with children prefer to shift from higher-paid factory work to lower-paid home-based work, as the latter can be more easily be combined with childcare responsibilities. This, however, is the case in India, where there is a high-level of home-based work; in Bangladesh, where the extent of home-based work is very low, the proportion of married women workers in garment factories has gone up quite substantially, from 38 per cent in 1990 to 59 per cent in 2006 (Khatun et al., 2007). The differences between gendered trajectories in the two counties would be interesting to be explored in future research.

A standard argument by firms is that the 'high cost' of employing women, because of pregnancy and childbirth allowances, also makes it more expensive to train women than men, leading to the well-known phenomenon of lower numbers of women in technical positions. But a re-framing of the issue is underway as new unions such as the New Trade Union Initiative (NTUI) in India argue for a joint or public role in ensuring that women's child-bearing costs not jeopardize their role as workers. However, there is a debate over whether publicly financing such necessary expenditures, lets firms off the hook from contributing their fair share to the hiring and training women workers.[4]

---

[4] It is interesting to note that Ester Boserup had, a long time ago, pointed out that it would be possible to counter the firm-level argument of the high cost of employing women by shifting '... the financial

In conclusion, the relations between women and GVCs point to two opposing directions. Existing gender relations frame and restrict the manner of women's employment and career paths in factories and offices. At the same time, and we would say more importantly, women's work in factories and offices, promoted by the spread of GVC-related work in Asia, has also enabled women to, at least partially, rewrite some aspects of gender relations related to earning independent income, working at night and occupying public spaces. As a result, gender relations do not merely reproduce pre-existing cultural systems but have become an arena of fresh contestation and re-constitution.

21.6   Re-working of labour relations in a GVC world: Opportunity and institutional ambiguity

Earlier in this discussion, we pointed to the importance of the agency of different actors, workers in the main, but also the political consumer (Beck, 2002) in buying countries, international agencies and also lead and supplier firms. These are factors that are important at a political level to enable some kind of re-embedding of labour norms within GVCs. In bringing about these changes, however, there is also the need for some changes at the economic level. In the Introduction, we pointed to the concentration of rents in GVC-lead firms and the appropriation of mere competitive profits at the GVC-supplier levels. One way for changes in labour conditions to come about at the supplier level is via redistribution of some part of the surpluses or rents from lead firms to suppliers. A change in the international rent distribution within GVCs in favour of capital-plus-labour in developing countries enables an improvement in labour conditions. Some of this may be ad hoc, such as in the money committed to building improvements in the wake of the Rana Plaza disaster in Bangladesh.

Such redistribution, however, is not the only way improvements in labour conditions can come about. Two more possibilities exist. One is that within the supplier countries, labour may be successful in affecting the profit-wage distribution. This is more likely in a situation of labour shortage, such as in China, and not in situations of continuing surplus labour, as in the countries of South Asia. The other possibility at the local level is that suppliers respond to higher wages by increasing productivity, possibly through the adoption of labour-saving technologies, or even by shifting to lower cost locations. Both of these types of changes are visible in GVCs.

---

burden of these special benefits [for maternal leave, etc.] from the employer of the women who benefit from them, to all employers, independently of whether they employ women or men' (1970, p. 112).

Labour shortage in coastal China is provoking two types of responses from capital. One is the technological shift to higher productivity methods, replacing labour with capital. The other is the shift to locations with lower wages, such as Western China or even overseas to Vietnam and Bangladesh.

In ending this book, we then note that the second movement of labour not only reforms work in GVCs, though to a limited extent, but also prompts changes in the institutional, technological and geographic constitution of capital in supplier countries. As our case examples illustrate, over the past 40 years of GVC dominance in global trade, labour has gained new forms of agency and re-gained some associational power (international union alliances and so on). This, coupled with other mechanisms has led to some advances in wages setting, overtime, conditions of work and so on. However, as Webster asks, 'Is it possible to sustain engagement in the 'new rules' through associational power alone? Put differently, is associational power sustainable without institutional power?' (2013, p. 327). Who gets to be at the table? How are the rules enforced in accountable ways?

Some scholars have recently put forth the idea that to gain greater institutional accountability in rule setting around work, and effective enforcement it might be necessary to shifting the traditional tri-partite system industrial relations to a quadripartite one. The standard model of industrial relations involves bargaining between employers, workers and the state. The argument being made today is that in a GVC world, the key institutional drivers of these chains, namely, global brands and buyers must be on the table as well (Anner et al., 2013; Nathan 2013). If buyers are at the bargaining table, they will also be accountable for enforcement.

The post-Rana Plaza Accord points to the beginning of a shift in the approach to factory conditions in supplier countries. The Accord, entered into between the global union, IndustriAll, and 200 garment buyers, unlike earlier private codes, is legally binding. It can be the beginning of the development of new institutional structures in industrial relations in GVCs (Jenny Holdcroft, 2015).

In a move in this direction, IndustriAll has entered into an MOU with a number of brands to work for industry-level bargaining in a supplier country (ACT, 2015). The objective is to eliminate wage competition at the supplier-country level, or 'to take labour costs out of competition' (ACT, 2015) so as to support a movement towards a living wage. Taking labour costs out of competition, however, would require, at some point, action on a regional or even global level.

Bringing buyers into the industry-wide bargaining structure raises numerous legal questions. Buyers or lead firms are established in their own countries of origin (or possibly even in tax havens). Supplier countries might not be willing to allow such foreign entities to sit at the table in their sovereign industrial relations space;

lead firms too might be unwilling to let their representatives be part of supplier country industrial relations negotiations. But in their contracted buying the bigger firms usually set up local entities in supplier countries. They can thus be required to be part of a newly-formed quadripartite mechanism, bringing together lead firms (buyers), suppliers, national governments and workers.

Is there any precedent for such a quadripartite industrial relations structure? A recent paper on how sweatshops in America during the last century were tackled (Anner et al., 2013) throws light on the 'joint responsibility' approach that was established. The U.S. industry was divided into two groups of enterprises. One, called jobbers, undertook design. They contracted production to the manufacturers, who were the direct employers of workers. Once the jobber–manufacturer structure was set up, wages and working conditions in the manufacturers' factories declined. One would presume that as with today's lead firms, the jobbers captured the lion's share of the rent, while the numerous manufacturers (stitchers) got not much more than competitive profits.

The International Ladies Garment Workers Union (ILGWU) was successful in insisting that the jobbers who gave the orders to manufacturers and determined supply prices needed to be brought into the picture to deal with sweatshop conditions. They argued that 'jobbers and contractors were part of an "integrated process of production" and as such, were jointly liable for wages and working conditions in contracting shops' (Anner et al., 2013, p. 11). Related agreements were entered into between the jobbers, manufacturers and the unions. Of course, with a government that supported the improvement of work conditions, there was a substantial improvement.

Today's GVC is only the international extension of the outsourcing model followed by the jobbers—brands/buyers concentrate on the core competence of design and outsource stitching to the manufacturers. However, while there has been some acceptance of 'joint employers' at the national level, e.g., in the USA's Fair Labour Standards Act (FSLA) of 1938, or India's Contract Labour Act of 1970, such notions have not been extended to the international level (Miller et al., 2011), although the California Transparency in Supply Chains Act of 2012 is a step in this direction. The post-Rana Plaza Accord on Safety is also an important step in making lead firms legally accountable for financially contributing to improving safety conditions in garment factories in Bangladesh.

If the legal responsibility of lead firms for labour conditions in GVCs is accepted, then the existence of an institution through which such responsibility can be adjudicated is integral. Could this be an International Labour Court? The world now has an International Criminal Court (ICC). It also has a WTO forum for adjudicating trade disputes. Could there someday be an International Labour Court? If it were at all possible, it surely seems far away. But the increasing organization of the production of goods and services on GVC lines[5] makes it necessary to think of ways in which global brands and lead firms can be brought into a framework where they share accountability with suppliers and national governments for labour conditions in GVCs.

This is a big move, since it requires a second-order transformation: 'the Great Transformation of the state-centred order per se' (Beck, 2005, p. 3). The Bangladesh post-Rana Plaza Accord does have a legal framework and a dispute resolution mechanism. This could be the beginning of making firms involved in GVCs accountable in a global manner. Ending sweatshops will require a combination of national-level actions with global interventions and dispute resolution mechanisms that extend accountability beyond the national to the global sphere.

A little more than a hundred years ago the Triangle Shirtwaist Factory fire in New York in 1911 was the tipping point in ending sweatshop conditions in the US. If the Bangladesh Rana Plaza tragedy is to be a similar tipping point in ending sweatshop conditions in GVC production, then new institutions of an international governance framework including for dealing with institutional labour issues may be possible.

In closing, then we have argued that there are shifts underway within GVCs that portend the carving out of and defending of a space where workers have the capacity to exert greater agency over their well-being and growth in alliance with a variety of institutional partners, and in bargaining with buyers, brands and capital.

Through our analysis of the case studies presented in this book we argue that a second movement of labour relations may be emergent at the current juncture of interdependent global trade and production. At one level, this inchoate movement mirrors the global fragmentation of production in a GVC world, and is itself fragmented and segmented. As our case studies show, the gains to labour are deeply uneven—across sectors, types of value chains and spaces. Yet, at the same time, precisely because of the supra-national nature of GVCs, the larger institutional efforts on the part of advocates for labour to achieve improvements in the conditions of work are aimed at an institutional architecture that is just as transnational in nature. Or at least that is where the promise might lie—in nesting deeply local, varied and customized efforts by and on behalf of labour, within a wider more international institutional process of rule-setting and their accountable enforcement. Just as our case studies point to pan-Asian efforts such as the 'Asian'

---

[5] In discussing GVCs we should not forget the fact that services too are increasingly being organized in GVCs, with IT software services being the prime example of globalized service production.

living wage campaign, or more institutionalized programs such as Better Work that act locally, but seeks to diffuse good labour practices in countries all along the value chain, other examples include the growing federation of international unions. It will be worth watching how these incipient efforts can be complemented by the rise of flexible, malleable and adaptive institutions that can straddle the particular and local along with the universal; where commitments to basic labour standards, working conditions, and labour rights are enforced locally but are honoured across multiple sovereign jurisdictions.

References

Acemoglu, D., and David Autor. 2011. 'Skills, Tasks and Technologies: Implications for Employment and Earning.' *Handbook Labor Econ* 4: 1043–71.

ACT, 2015. *Factsheet*. www.industriALL-union.org, last accessed August 6, 2015.

Amsden, Alice H. 1989. *Asia's Next Giant. South Korea and Late Industrialization.* Oxford and New York: Oxford University Press.

———. 2001. *The Rise of the Rest: Challenges to the West from Late Industrializing Economies.* Oxford and New York: Oxford University Press.

Autor, David, Frank Levy and Richard Murnane. 2003. 'The Skill Content of Recent Technological Change: An Empirical Investigation.' *Quart J Econ* 118 (4): 1279.

Anner, Mark, Jennifer Bair, and Jeremy Blasi. 2014. 'Towards Joint Liability in Global Supply Chains: Addressing the Root Causes of Labor Violations in International Subcontracting Networks.' *Comp Labor Law Policy J* 35 (1):1–43.

Applebaum, Richard. 2004. 'Fighting Sweatshops: Problems of Enforcing Global Labour Standards.' In *Critical Globalization Studies*, edited by R. P. Applebaum and W. I. Robinson, pp. 369–78. New York: Routledge,

Arnold, Dennis. 2014. 'Workers' Agency and Power Relations in Cambodia.' In *Towards Better Work: Understanding Labour in Apparel Global Value Chains*, edited by Arianna Rossi, Amy Luinstra and John Pickles, pp. 212–231. Palgrave Macmillan.

Bair, Jennifer, Marsha A. Dickson, and Doug Miller. 2013. *Workers' Rights and Labor Compliance in Global Supply Chains*. New York and London: Routledge.

Barrientos, Stephanie, Gary Gereffi and Arianna Rossi. 2011. 'Social and Economic Upgrading in GVCs.' *Int Labour Rev.*

Barrientos, Stephanie, Kanchan Mathur, and Atul Sood. 2010. 'Decent Work in Global Production Networks: Challenges for Vulnerable Workers in the Indian Garments Sector.' In *Labour in Global Production Networks in India*, edited by Anne Posthuma and Dev Nathan. New Delhi: Oxford University Press.

Basu, Sreeradha. 2013. 'Women Workforce Productivity Impacted by 40 Per cent in Delhi-NCR after Delhi Gang-rape: Assocham.' *The Economic Times*, January 3.

Beck, Ulrich. 2005. *Power in the Global Age*. Cambridge: Polity Press.

Boserup, Ester. 1970. *Women's Role in Economic Development*. London: Allen and Unwin.

Burawoy, Michael. 2010. 'From Polanyi to Pollyanna: The False Optimism of Global Labor Studies.' *Global Labour J* 1 (2): 301–13.

Carswell, G., and G. de Neve. 2013. Labouring for Global Markets: Conceptualising Labour Agency in Global Production Networks. *Geoforum* 44: 62–79.

Castells, Manuel. 1997. *The Rise of the Network Society: Volume 1, The Information Age: Economy, Society and Culture*. Oxford: Blackwell.

Chang, Leslie. 2012. *Factory Girls: From Village to City in a Changing China*, New York: Spiegel and Grau.

Croll, Elizabeth. 200. *Changing Identities of Chinese Women: Rhetoric, Experience and Self-Perception*. London: Zed Press.

Damodaran, Sumangala. 2010. 'Upgradation or Flexible Casualization? Exploring the Dynamics of Global Value Chain Incorporation.' In *Labour in Global Production Networks in India*, edited by Anne Posthuma and Dev Nathan. New Delhi: Oxford University Press.

Dasgupta, Sukti. 2014. 'The "Employing Workers Index": A Critique and Review.' *Econ Polit Weekly* 49 (17): 97–103.

Elliott, Kimberley, and Richard Freeman. 2003. *Can Labor Standards Improve Under Globalisation?* Washington, D.C.: Institute for International Economics.

Elson, Diane, and Ruth Pearson. 1981. 'Nimble Fingers Make Cheap Workers: An Analysis of Women's Employment in Third World Manufacturing.' *Feminist Rev* 7 (Spring): 87–107.

Evans, Peter. 2010. 'Is It Labour's Turn to Globalize? Twenty-first Century Opportunities and Strategic Responses.' *Global Labour J* 1(3): 352–79.

———. 2010. 'National Labour Movements and Transnational Connections: Global Labour's Emerging Architecture Under Neoliberalism.' *Global Labour J* 1 (2): 258–82.

Fang, Cai, and M. Wang. 2010. 'Growth and Structural Changes in Employment in Transition China.' *J Develop Econ* 38: 71–81.

Fincher, Leta Hong. 2014. *Leftover Women: The Resurgence of Gender Inequality in China*. London: Zed Books.

Gaynair, Gillian. 2013. 'ICRW Survey.' Available at, crw.org/media/news//icrw-survey-95-percent-women-and-girls-consider-new-delhi-unsafe. Accessed on 24-11-2014.

Gereffi, Gary. 1994. 'The Organization of Buyer-Driven Global Commodity Chains: How US Retailers Shape Overseas Production Networks.' In *Commodity Chains and Global Capitalism*, edited by G. Gereffi and M. Korzeniewicz, pp. 95–122. Westport: Praeger.

Gereffi, Gary, and Frederick Mayer. 2006. 'Globalization and the Demand for Governance.' In *The New Offshoring of Jobs and Global Development, ILO Social Policy Lectures*, pp. 39–58. Geneva: International Institute for Labour Studies.

Ghosh, Jayati. 2001. 'Globalization, Export-Oriented Employment for Women and Social Policy: A Case Study of India.' Paper prepared for UNRISD Project on Globalization, Export-Oriented Employment for Women and Social Policy, Geneva, UNRISD (mimeo).

Gunawardana, Samantha. 2007. 'Struggle, Perseverance, and Organizing in Sri Lanka's Export Processing Zones.' In *Global Unions: Challenging Transnational Capital Through Cross-Border Campaigns*, edited by Kate Bronfenbrenner, pp. 78–98. Ithaca, Cornell University Press.

Hayek, F. A. 1945. *Individualism and Economic Order*. London: Routledge and Kegan Paul.

Helfen, Markus, and Michael Fichter. 2013. 'Building Transnational Union Networks Across Global Production Networks: Conceptualising a New Arena of Labour-Management Relations.' *Brit J Indus Relat* 51 (3): 553–76.

Heyzer, Noeleen, ed. 1986. *Working Women in South-East Asia: Development, Subordination and Emancipation*. Philadelphia: Open University Press.

Holdcroft, Jenny. 2015. 'Transforming Supply Chain Industrial Relations.' *Int J Labour Relat*. 7 (forthcoming).

Hossain, Naomi. 2012. *Exports, Equity and Empowerment: The Effects of Readymade Garments Manufacturing Employment on Gender Equity in Bangladesh*. World Development Report, 2012, Background Paper.

Humphrey, John, and Hubert Schmitz. 2008. 'Inter-firm Relationships in Global Value Chains: Trends in Chain Governance and Their Policy Implications.' *Int J Technol Learn, Innov Develop* 1 (3): 258–82.

IndustriAll. 2014. 'IndustriAll Renews Agreement with World's Largest Fashion Retailer.' Available at, http://www.industriall-union.org/issues/confronting-global-capital/global-framework-agreements. Accessed October 20, 2014.

———. 2014a. *Negotiating Security: Trade Union Bargaining Strategies Against Precarious Work*. www.industriall-union.org. Accessed October 20, 2014.

Jenkins, Jena. 2013. 'Organizing "Spaces of Hope": Union Formation by Indian Garment Workers.' *Brit J Indus Relat* 51 (3): 623–43.

Kelkar, Govind, Girija Shreshta, and N. Veena. 2002. 'Women's Agency and the IT Industry in India.' *Gend Technol Develop* 6 (1): 63–84.

Khatun, F., M. Rahman, D. Bhattacharya, and K. Golam Moazzem. 2008. *Gender and Trade Liberalization in Bangladesh: The Case of Readymade Garments*. Dhaka: CPD.

Locke, Richard. 2013. *The Promise and Limits of Private Power: Promoting Labor Standards in a Global Economy*. New York: Cambridge University Press.

Lewis, W. A. 1954. 'Economic Development with Unlimited Supplies of Labour.' *The Manchester School* 22 (2): 139–91.

Lynch, Caitrin. 2007. *Juke Girls, Good Girls: Gender and Politics in Sri Lanka's Global Garment Industry*. Ithaca, NY: ILR Press.

Mayer, Frederick, and John Pickles. 'Re-embedding the Market: Global Apparel Value Chains, Governance and Decent Work.' In *Towards Better Work: Understanding Labour in Apparel Global Value Chains*, edited by Arianna Rossi, Amy Luinstra and John Pickles. Palgrave Macmillan.

Miller, D., S. Tuner, and T. Grinter. 2011. 'A Critical Reflection on Neil Kearney's Nature Systems of Industrial Relations Perspective on the Governance of Outsourced Apparel Supply Chains.' *Capturing the Gains Working Paper*.

Munck, Ronaldo. 2010. 'Globalization and the Labour Movement: Challenges and Responses.' *Global Labour J* 1 (2): 218–32.

NASSCOM, and Mercer. 2009. *Gender Inclusivity in India: Building Empowered Organizations*. New Delhi: NASSCOM.

Nathan, Dev. 'Industrial Relations in a Global Production Framework.' *Econ Polit Weekly* 48 (30).

Nathan, Dev, and Sandip Sarkar. 2013. 'Global Inequality, Rising Powers and Labour Standards.' *Oxford Development Studies*, 2014.

Ngai, Pun, 2005. *Made in China: Women Factory Workers in A Global Workplace*, Durham: Duke University Press.

Oka, Chikako. 2010. 'Accounting for the Gaps in Labour Standard Compliances: The Role of Reputation-Conscious Buyers in the Cambodian Garment Industry.' *Eur J Develop Res* 22 (1): 59–78.

Ong, Aiwa. 1987. *Spirits of Resistance and Capitalist Discipline: Factory Women in Malaysia*. Albany: SUNY Press.

Patel, Reena. 2010. *Working the Night Shift: Women in India's Call Center Industry*. New Delhi: Orient Blackswan.

Piore, Michael. 2006. 'Economy vs. Community: Macroeconomic Policy & Decent Work.' Paper presented at the DESA Forum on Productive Employment and Decent Work, United Nations, New York, NY, May 8–9.

———. 2009. 'Second Thoughts: On Economics, Sociology, Neoliberalism, Polanyi's Double Movement and Intellectual Vacuums.' *Socio-Econ Rev* 7 (1): 161.

Plank, Leonhard, Arianna Rossi, and Cornelia Staritz. 2014. 'What Does "Fast Fashion" Mean for Workers?' In *Towards Better Work: Understanding Labour in Apparel Global Value Chains*, edited by Arianna Rossi, Amy Luinstra and John Pickles, pp. 127–47. Palgrave Macmillan.

Quan, Katie. 2008. 'Use of Global Value Chains by Labor Organizers.' *Comp Change* 12 (1): 89–104.

Rainnie A, A. Herod, and S. McGrath-Champ. 2011. 'Review and Positions: Global Production Networks and Labour.' *Comp Change* 15 (2): 155–69.

Roberts, Alan. 2014. 'The Bangladesh Accord Finds More than 80,000 Safety Hazards.' *The Guardian*, October 15.

Rosa, Kumudhini. 1994. 'The Conditions and Organizational Activities of Women in Free Trade Zones: Malaysia, Philippines and Sri Lanka.' In *Dignity and Daily Bread,* edited by Rowbotham and Mitter. London: Routledge.

Ross, Robert. 2014. 'Consumers and Producers: Agency, Power and Social Enfranchisement.' In *Workers' Rights and Labor Compliance in Global Supply Chains,* edited by Jennifer Bair, Marsha A. Dickson and Doug Miller, pp. 23–46. New York and London: Routledge.

Sabel, Charles, and Sanjay Reddy. 2007. 'Learning to Learn: Undoing the Gordian Knot of Development Today.' *Challenge* 50 (5): 73–92.

Sarkar, Sandip, and Balwant Singh Mehta. 2010. 'Global Production Networks and Decent Work: Recent Experience in India and Global Trends.' In *Labour in Global Production Networks in India,* edited by Anne Posthuma and Dev Nathan, pp. 321–47. New Delhi: Oxford University Press.

Sarkar, Sandip, Balwant Mehta, and Dev Nathan. 2013. 'How Social Upgrading Drives Economic Upgrading by Indian IT majors.' *Capturing the Gains, Working Paper No. 27.* Available at, www.capturingthegains.org. Accessed on July 25, 2015.

School of Global Studies. 2012a. 'Worker Welfare in Export Zones: Lessons from a Garment Cluster in South India.' Insights 03, University of Sussex, School of Global Studies, available at, http://www.sussex.ac.uk/global/. Accessed on March 10, 2014.

Selwyn, B. 2007. 'Labour Process and Workers' Bargaining Power in Export Grape Production, North-east Brazil.' *J Agrar Change* 7 (4): 526–53.

ShyamSundar, K. R. 2015. 'Industrial Conflict in India in the Post-Reform Period: Who Said All Is Quiet on the Industrial Front.' *Econ Polit Weekly* 50 (3): 43–53.

Silver, Beverley. 2003. *Forces of Labor: Workers' Movement and Globalization since 1870.* Cambridge: Cambridge University Press.

Silver, Beverley, and Lu Zhang. 2009. 'China as an Emerging Epicenter of World Labour Unrest.' In *China and the Transformation of Global Capitalism,* edited by Ho-Fung Hung. Baltimore: The Johns Hopkins University Press.

Staritz, Cornelia, and Jose Guilherme Reis, eds. 2013. *Global Value Chains, Economic Upgrading and Gender: Case Studies of the Horticulture, Tourism and Call Center Industries.* Washington: The World Bank.

Stevis, Dimitris, and Terry Boswell. 2007. 'International Framework Agreements: Opportunities and Challenges for Global Unionism.' In *Global Unions: Challenging Transnational Capital Through Cross-Border Campaigns,* edited by Kate Bronfenbrenner. ILR Press: Ithaca.

Thompson, E. P. 1984. *The Making of the English Working Class.* Harmondsworth: Penguin Books.

Vaughan-Whitehead, Daniel. 2014. 'How 'Fair' are Wage Practices along the Supply Chain?' In *Towards Better Work: Understanding Labour in Apparel Global Value Chains*, edited by Arianna Rossi, Amy Luinstra and John Pickles, pp. 58–102. Palgrave Macmillan.

Webster, Edward. 2013. Review of McCallum, Jamie, *Global Unions, Local Power: The New Spirit of Transnational Labour Organising*, Ithaca, NY: Cornell University Press/ILR Press. *Brit J Indus Relat* 51 (3): 326–28.

Wright, Erik Olin. 2000. 'Working-Class Power, Capitalist-Class Interests and Class Compromise.' *Am J Sociol* 105 (4): 957–1002.

Wright, Melissa. 2006. *Disposable Women and Other Myths of Global Capitalism*. New York and London: Routledge.

Notes on Contributors

Amit Chakraborty is a research student at the Centre for Economic Studies and Planning, Jawaharlal Nehru University, New Delhi.

Anannya Bhattacharjee is a trade unionist with the New Trade Union Initiative (NTUI) and one of the founders of the Asia Floor Wage Movement.

Annelies Goger is Research Associate at IMPAQ International, USA.

Arianna Rossi is Research and Policy Officer for the ILO/IFC Better Work Programme, based in Geneva, Switzerland. She manages the programme's research and impact evaluation activities.

Ashim Roy is a trade unionist with the New Trade Union Initiative (NTUI) and one of the founders of the Asia Floor Wage Movement.

Balwant Singh Mehta is working as Associate Fellow at the Institute for Human Development, New Delhi. He has worked extensively in the areas of information and communication technology for development, labour market and child well-being.

Dev Nathan is Visiting Professor at the Institute for Human Development, New Delhi and Visiting Research Fellow at the Center for Globalization, Governance and Competitiveness (CGGC), Duke University.

Ernesto Noronha is Professor of Organizational Behaviour at the Indian Institute of Management, Ahmedabad where he teaches research methodology, sociology of work and employment, and organizational dynamics.

Gary Gereffi is Professor of Sociology and Director of the Center on Globalization, Governance, and Competitiveness at Duke University. Gereffi has published many books and articles on globalization and development with a focus on global value chains.

Girish Nanda was a consultant with Strategic Asia, Indonesia while conducting the study of tourism in Indonesia. Nanda is currently an MBA student at the Wharton School, USA.

Govind Kelkar is Senior Advisor at Landesa, India. She works on various aspects of gender relations with a focus on India and China. Her recent publications include *Women, Land* and *Power in Asia* and *Aadhaar: Gender, Identity and Development*.

Jenny Chan is Lecturer in Sociology and China Studies at the School of Interdisciplinary Area Studies, University of Oxford.

Jici Wang is Professor of the College of Urban and Environmental Sciences, Peking University. Her academic work focuses on industrial clusters, regional innovation systems and entrepreneurship.

Joonkoo Lee is Assistant Professor of Organization Studies in the School of Business at Hanyang University, Seoul. His research interests include globalization and development, global value chains, political economy in Asia, and cultural and creative industries.

Kanchana N. Ruwanpura is Senior Lecturer in Development Geography at the University of Edinburgh. Her research interests include feminism, ethnicity, disaster politics and labour.

Keith Hargreaves is a consultant, working as Project Manager, Strategic Asia, London and Indonesia.

Lixia Mei is Associate Professor at the School of Business and Administration, Zhongnan University of Economics and Law, China. Her research interests include industrial clusters and regional development, labour social reproduction in global production networks, innovation management and social transformation.

Mark Selden is Senior Research Associate in the East Asia Program at Cornell University and Visiting Researcher at NYU. Selden is a coordinator of the Asia-Pacific Journal.

Meenu Tewari is Associate Professor of Economic Development at the University of North Carolina, Chapel Hill. Her research focuses on the political economy of development, industrialization, urbanization, institutional reform, skill formation and upgrading within regional and global production networks.

Nazneen Ahmed is Senior Research Fellow at the Bangladesh Institute of Development Studies (BIDS). Her research areas encompass international trade, regional integration, industry, macro-economy, labour issues, social compliance and social protection issues, value chain analysis and gender. She is a Director of Palli Sanchay Bank, Bangladesh.

Ngai Pun is Professor at the Department of Applied Social Sciences and Director of China Development and Research Network, Hong Kong Polytechnic University. She is author of *Made in China: Women Factory Workers in a Global Workplace* and her work has been translated into various languages.

Praveen Jha is Professor of Economics at Jawaharlal Nehru University, New Delhi, and Chairperson, Centre for Informal Economy and Labour Studies, Jawaharlal Nehru University. He is also Honorary Visiting Professor at Rhodes University, South Africa.

Premilla D'Cruz is Professor of Organizational Behaviour at the Indian Institute of Management, Ahmedabad where she teaches micro organizational behaviour and workplace creativity. Her research interests include workplace bullying, emotions at work, self and identity, organizational control, and ICTs and organizations.

Sandip Sarkar is Professor at the Institute for Human Development, New Delhi. His areas of research interest include industry, poverty, labour and employment and information and communication technology (ICT).

Sang-Hoon Lee is a graduate student of organization studies and human resource management at the School of Business, Hanyang University, Seoul.

Sukhpal Singh teaches at the Indian Institute of Management, Ahmedabad. He has been a visiting fellow at the IDS, Sussex, Chulalongkorn University, Bangkok, University of Manchester, and CBS, Copenhagen.

Sumangala Damodaran is an economist, she teaches at the School of Development Studies, Ambedkar University Delhi. Her research has been in the areas of industrial and labour studies.

Yang Fuquan is an anthropologist and Vice President of the Yunnan Academy of Social Sciences, Kunming, China. He has published extensively on the Naxi and other indigenous communities in Yunnan.

Yuko Hamada is an official of the International Organization for Migration, Regional Office, Tokyo.

Yu Xiaogang is Director of Green Watershed, an environmental NGO that advocates environmentally sustainable development. He received the Goldman Prize in 2006 and the Magsaysay Award in 2009 for his work on environmental justice in Yunnan and Southwest China.

Yu Yin is an independent researcher based in Kunming and Beijing, China.

Index

Index